OECD Factbook 2013

FOREWORD

This is the 8th edition of the *OECD Factbook*. The world has changed since the first publication in 2005 in ways that few people could have envisaged. In 2005 for example, economic growth was strong, unemployment levels low and the financial sector considered sound. This latest *OECD Factbook* pictures a very different situation. It presents the evolution of economic, environmental and social indicators over this remarkable period in recent history.

The *OECD Factbook* is the Organisation's most comprehensive statistical publication that provides a longer-term presentation of data, making it an essential tool in evaluating country trends. The *OECD Factbook* offers what are considered a core range of valuable statistics covering the main statistical themes allowing for quick and simple navigation. This is important in a society where more and more data are easily obtainable everywhere, a situation characterised by the new term "Big Data".

This latest *OECD Factbook* includes new indicators, in particular on the income and wealth of households. A new chapter on this topic draws a statistical picture of the economic conditions of households, depicting indicators such as income distribution, saving rates and household assets. These indicators have been developed in response to policy-makers' enhanced interest in the household sector – a part of our society that has significantly suffered from the economic downturn in many OECD countries.

This year's *OECD Factbook* special chapter deals with "Gender Equality". Gender is a core OECD work stream and gender statistics are essential in understanding the economic and social situation of women in our countries. The chapter presents for instance gender-specific data on employment, income, education and health. The indicators presented here draw on a much more extensive report on gender that was recently released by the OECD – *"Closing the Gender Gap: Act Now"*. One of the report's conclusions is that there are still many gaps in gender statistics and more needs to be done to improve measurement in this important area.

The *OECD Factbook* includes statistics for more than just the 34 OECD member countries. When available and considered internationally comparable, data are included for Key Partner and accession countries, namely: Brazil, India, Indonesia, the People's Republic of China, the Russian Federation and South Africa. Additionally, data for aggregates such as the OECD countries, European Union, the euro area and World are compiled and published where possible.

The *OECD Factbook* is written in a non-technical language, providing users with a one-stop resource of country-based data, helping them to assess a country's performance relative to others, and encouraging readers to explore more in-depth the vast array of OECD statistics and statistical publications. All *OECD Factbook* data are available online through StatLinks at the bottom of each table and chart, as well as through the data and metadata available through OECD.Stat, the corporate platform for data dissemination, which take the form of thematic databases and country statistical profiles.

I trust that all users, citizens, researchers, analysts and policy-makers will consider the *OECD Factbook* as an indispensible tool that provides the information they need in their work and general life.

Martine Durand
OECD Chief Statistician and Director of Statistics

ACKNOWLEDGEMENTS

This publication, including the new e-version and the online up-to-date OECD Factbook database, would not have been possible without the co-operation of statistical authorities from OECD member, accession and Key Partner countries. The OECD Factbook represents a wealth of OECD-wide statistical activities and reflects the work of statisticians throughout the Organisation and its agencies – the *International Energy Agency* (IEA), the *Nuclear Energy Agency* (NEA) and the *International Transport Forum*.

The OECD Statistics Directorate provided overall co-ordination – with David Brackfield as editor of the volume, Ingrid Herrbach having overall technical responsibility and Lihan Wei providing further technical support. The OECD Public Affairs and Communications Directorate provided editorial guidance – led by Eileen Capponi with further reading material co-ordinated by Damian Garnys. The special chapter was prepared by Sue Kendall-Bilicki. The Authoring and Collaborative Systems section of the OECD Executive Directorate, Information Technology and Network Division provided invaluable assistance with the preparation of this volume.

TABLE OF CONTENTS

READER'S GUIDE

Main Features:

- Tables and charts are preceded by short texts that explain how the statistics are defined (**Definition**) and that identify any problems there may be in comparing the performance of one country with another (**Comparability**). To avoid misunderstandings, the tables and charts must be read in conjunction with the texts that accompany them.

- Tables and charts are also available as Excel files.

- While media comment on statistics usually focuses on the short term – what has happened to employment, prices, GDP and so on in the last few months – the *OECD Factbook* takes a longer view; the text and charts mostly describe developments during at least the last ten years to 2011. This long-term perspective provides a good basis for comparing the successes and failures of policies in raising living standards and improving social conditions in countries.

- To facilitate cross-country comparisons, many indicators in the *OECD Factbook* have been standardised by relating them to each country's gross domestic product (GDP). In cases where GDP needs to be converted to a common currency, purchasing power parities (PPPs) have been used rather than exchange rates. When PPPs are used, differences in GDP levels across countries reflect only differences in the volume of goods and services, *i.e.* differences in price levels are eliminated.

Conventions

Unless otherwise specified:

- OECD refers to all 34 OECD countries unless otherwise stated in the Comparability section; the indicator is presented either as the weighted average of country values or an unweighted arithmetic average.

- For each country, the average value in different periods takes into account only the years for which data are available. The *average annual growth rate* of an indicator over a period of time is the geometric average of the growth rates of that indicator across the period (*i.e.* the annual compound growth rate).

- Each table and chart specifies the period covered. The mention, XXXX *or latest available year* (where XXXX is a year or a period) means that data for later years are not taken into account.

Signs, abbreviations and acronyms

..	Missing value, not applicable or not available	ITF	International Transport Forum
0	Less than half of the unit precision level of the observation	ITU	International Telecommunications Union
–	Absolute zero	NAFTA	North American Free Trade Agreement
USD	US dollars	UN	United Nations
DAC	Development Assistance Committee	UNCTAD	United Nations Conference on Trade and Development
ILO	International Labor Organisation	UNECE	United Nations Economic Commission for Europe
IMF	International Monetary Fund	UNODC	United Nations Office on Drugs and Crime
		WTO	World Trade Organisation

For most of the charts, the OECD Factbook uses ISO codes for countries

AUS	Australia	JPN	Japan	DAC	DAC total
AUT	Austria	KOR	Korea	EA17	Euro area
BEL	Belgium	LUX	Luxembourg	EU27	European Union
CAN	Canada	MEX	Mexico	G7M	Major seven
CHL	Chile	NLD	Netherlands	OECD	OECD area
CZE	Czech Republic	NZL	New Zealand	WLD	World
DNK	Denmark	NOR	Norway		
EST	Estonia	POL	Poland	BRA	Brazil
FIN	Finland	PRT	Portugal	CHN	China
FRA	France	SVK	Slovak Republic	IND	India
GRC	Greece	SVN	Slovenia	IDN	Indonesia
DEU	Germany	ESP	Spain	RUS	Russian Federation
HUN	Hungary	SWE	Sweden	ZAF	South Africa
ISL	Iceland	CHE	Switzerland		
IRL	Ireland	TUR	Turkey		
ISR	Israel	GBR	United Kingdom		
ITA	Italy	USA	United States		

StatLinks

This publication includes the unique OECD *StatLink* service, which enables users to download Excel versions of tables and charts. *StatLinks* are provided at the bottom of each table and chart. *StatLinks* behave like Internet addresses: simply type the *StatLink* into your Internet browser to obtain the corresponding data in Excel format.

For more information about OECD *StatLinks*, please visit: *www.oecd.org/statistics/statlink*.

Accessing OECD publications

- OECD publications cited in the *OECD Factbook* are available through OECD iLibrary (*www.oecd-ilibrary.org*), the OECD online library.
- All the OECD working papers can be downloaded from OECD iLibrary.
- All OECD databases mentioned can also be accessed through OECD iLibrary.
- In addition, print editions of all OECD books can be purchased via the OECD online bookshop (*www.oecd.org/bookshop*).

Glossary of Statistical Terms

The online *OECD Glossary of Statistical Terms* (available at *http://stats.oecd.org/glossary*) is the perfect companion for the *OECD Factbook*. It contains almost 7 000 definitions of statistical terms, acronyms and concepts in an easy to use format. These definitions are primarily drawn from existing international statistical guidelines and recommendations that have been prepared over the last few decades by organisations such as the United Nations, ILO, OECD, Eurostat, IMF and national statistical institutes.

POPULATION AND MIGRATION

TOTAL POPULATION

The size and growth of a country's population are both causes and effects of economic and social developments. The pace of population growth has slowed in all OECD countries.

Population projections, which give indications of likely changes in the future population size and structure, are a common demographic tool. They provide a basis for other statistical projections (*e.g.* service provision, employment) and as such, they are a very valuable tool for helping governments in their decision making.

Definition

Data refer to the resident population, that is, they are a measure of the population that usually lives in an area. For countries with overseas colonies, protectorates or other territorial possessions, their populations are generally excluded. Growth rates are the annual changes resulting from births, deaths and net migration during the year. Working age population is those aged 15 to 64.

Comparability

For most OECD countries, population data are based on regular, ten-yearly censuses, with estimates for intercensal years derived from administrative data. In several European countries, population estimates are based entirely on administrative records. Population data are fairly comparable.

For some countries the population figures shown here differ from those used for calculating GDP and other economic statistics on a per capita basis, although differences are normally small.

Population projections are taken from national sources where these are available, but for some countries they are based on United Nations or Eurostat projections; the projection for the world comes from the UN. All population projections require assumptions about future trends in life expectancy, fertility rates and migration. Often, a range of projections is produced using different assumptions about these future trends. The estimates shown here correspond to the median or central variant, that is; there is an estimated 50 percent chance the population could be lower, and a 50 percent chance it could be higher.

It should be noted that in the case of Mexico, the population according to the Population and Household Census taken in 2010 was 112.3 million compared with the previous estimate of 108.4 million presented in the table. The time series with the results of the *Population and Housing Census for Mexico* is underway by the Ministry of Interior. As soon as data is available, it will be updated in the digital version of the OECD Factbook, available at: *http://dx.doi.org/10.1787/factbook-data-en.*

Overview

In 2010, OECD countries accounted for 18% of the world's population of 6.9 billion. China accounted for 19% and India for 18%. Within the OECD, in 2010, the United States accounted for 25% of the OECD total, followed by Japan (10%), Mexico (9%), Germany (7%) and Turkey (6%).

In the three years to 2010, growth rates above the OECD population average (0.6% per year) were recorded in Israel, Mexico and Turkey (high birth rate countries) and in Australia, Canada, Chile, Luxembourg, Norway, Sweden, Switzerland, the United Kingdom and the United States (high net immigration). New Zealand and Ireland also recorded population growth rates above the OECD total which can be attributed to both a birth rate equal to the replacement fertility rate (a total fertility rate of 2.1 children per woman) and a positive net migration rate.

In Hungary and Germany, populations declined mostly due to low birth rates. Growth rates were also negative in Estonia while they were very low, although still positive, in Japan, Poland, Portugal and the Slovak Republic. The population of OECD countries is expected to grow by less than 0.2% per year until 2050.

Sources
- For OECD member countries: national sources, United Nations and Eurostat.
- For Brazil, China, India, Indonesia, the Russian Federation and South Africa: United Nations, *World Population Prospects: The 2010 Revision.*

Further information

Analytical publications
- OECD (2011), *Doing Better for Families*, OECD Publishing.
- OECD (2011), *The Future of Families to 2030*, OECD Publishing.

Statistical publications
- OECD (2011), *Society at a Glance: OECD Social Indicators*, OECD Publishing.

Methodological publications
- OECD (2011), *Labour Force Statistics*, OECD Publishing.

Online databases
- *OECD Employment and Labour Market Statistics.*
- *United Nations World Population Prospects.*

Websites
- OECD Family Database, *www.oecd.org/els/social/family/database.*

Population levels
Thousands

	2001	2002	2003	2004	2005	2006	2007	2008	2009	2010	2011	2020	2050
Australia	19 413	19 651	19 895	20 127	20 395	20 698	21 015	21 499	21 955	22 298	22 618	25 288	33 959
Austria	8 042	8 082	8 121	8 172	8 228	8 269	8 301	8 337	8 365	8 390	8 421	8 724	9 360
Belgium	10 287	10 333	10 376	10 421	10 479	10 548	10 626	10 710	10 796	10 896	..	11 758	13 139
Canada	31 019	31 354	31 640	31 941	32 245	32 576	32 930	33 316	33 720	34 109	..	36 344	41 896
Chile	15 572	15 746	15 919	16 093	16 267	16 433	16 598	16 763	16 929	17 094	17 248	18 549	20 205
Czech Republic	10 236	10 205	10 207	10 216	10 236	10 269	10 334	10 424	10 487	10 520	..	10 287	9 457
Denmark	5 359	5 376	5 391	5 405	5 419	5 437	5 461	5 494	5 523	5 548	..	5 582	5 621
Estonia	1 364	1 359	1 354	1 349	1 346	1 344	1 342	1 341	1 340	1 340	..	1 328	1 250
Finland	5 188	5 201	5 213	5 228	5 246	5 266	5 289	5 313	5 339	5 363	5 388	5 636	6 090
France	59 476	59 894	60 304	60 734	61 182	61 597	61 965	62 300	62 628	62 959	63 294	66 098	72 341
Germany	82 350	82 488	82 534	82 516	82 469	82 376	82 266	82 110	81 902	81 777	..	79 914	69 412
Greece	10 950	10 988	11 024	11 062	11 104	11 148	11 193	11 237	11 283	11 308	..	11 426	10 605
Hungary	10 188	10 159	10 130	10 107	10 087	10 071	10 056	10 038	10 023	10 000	..	9 856	8 718
Iceland	285	288	289	293	296	304	311	319	319	318	319	345	420
Ireland	3 866	3 932	3 997	4 070	4 160	4 260	4 357	4 426	4 459	4 474	..	4 774	5 482
Israel	6 439	6 570	6 690	6 809	6 930	7 054	7 180	7 309	7 486	7 624	..	9 022	..
Italy	56 977	57 157	57 605	58 175	58 607	58 942	59 375	59 832	60 193	60 483	..	59 001	55 710
Japan	127 291	127 435	127 619	127 687	127 768	127 770	127 771	127 692	127 510	128 057	127 799	124 100	97 076
Korea	47 357	47 622	47 859	48 039	48 138	48 372	48 598	48 949	49 182	49 410	49 779	51 436	48 121
Luxembourg	442	446	452	458	465	473	480	489	498	507	..	523	644
Mexico	99 716	100 909	102 000	103 002	103 947	104 874	105 791	106 683	107 551	108 396	109 220	115 762	121 856
Netherlands	16 046	16 149	16 225	16 282	16 320	16 346	16 382	16 446	16 530	16 615	..	17 240	17 343
New Zealand	3 881	3 949	4 027	4 088	4 134	4 185	4 228	4 269	4 316	4 368	4 405	4 565	5 046
Norway	4 514	4 538	4 565	4 592	4 623	4 661	4 709	4 768	4 829	4 889	4 953	5 061	5 854
Poland	38 251	38 232	38 195	38 180	38 161	38 132	38 116	38 116	38 153	38 187	..	37 830	34 543
Portugal	10 293	10 368	10 441	10 502	10 549	10 584	10 608	10 622	10 632	10 637	..	10 832	10 674
Slovak Republic	5 379	5 379	5 380	5 382	5 387	5 391	5 397	5 407	5 419	5 430	..	5 417	4 880
Slovenia	1 992	1 995	1 996	1 997	2 000	2 007	2 010	2 021	2 040	2 049	..	2 066	1 994
Spain	40 720	41 314	42 005	42 692	43 398	44 116	44 879	45 556	45 909	46 071	..	45 568	42 703
Sweden	8 896	8 925	8 958	8 994	9 030	9 081	9 148	9 220	9 299	9 378	9 449	9 976	10 726
Switzerland	7 227	7 285	7 339	7 390	7 437	7 484	7 551	7 648	7 744	7 822	..	8 379	8 981
Turkey	65 133	66 008	66 873	67 723	68 566	69 395	70 215	71 079	71 897	72 698	..	80 257	96 496
United Kingdom	59 108	59 326	59 566	59 031	59 408	59 751	60 137	60 540	60 927	61 344	61 761	66 754	76 959
United States	284 969	287 625	290 108	292 805	295 517	298 380	301 231	304 094	306 772	309 330	311 592	341 387	439 010
EU 27	484 216	485 641	487 722	489 966	492 173	494 251	496 489	498 686	500 395	501 792	503 279	514 913	523 804
OECD	1 158 225	1 166 286	1 174 295	1 181 563	1 189 545	1 197 595	1 205 851	1 214 366	1 221 954	1 229 690	1 231 746	1 291 087	1 393 722
Brazil	173 808	176 304	178 741	181 106	183 383	185 564	187 642	189 613	191 481	193 253	194 933	207 143	215 288
China	1 277 904	1 285 934	1 293 397	1 300 552	1 307 594	1 314 581	1 321 482	1 328 276	1 334 909	1 341 335	1 348 010	1 387 792	1 295 604
India	1 071 374	1 088 694	1 105 886	1 122 991	1 140 043	1 157 039	1 173 972	1 190 864	1 207 740	1 224 614	1 241 948	1 386 909	1 692 008
Indonesia	216 204	219 026	221 839	224 607	227 303	229 919	232 462	234 951	237 415	239 871	242 206	262 570	293 456
Russian Federation	146 162	145 520	144 881	144 307	143 843	143 510	143 295	143 163	143 064	142 958	142 823	141 022	126 188
South Africa	45 390	46 015	46 631	47 227	47 793	48 331	48 842	49 319	49 752	50 133	50 385	52 573	56 757
World	6 200 003	6 276 722	6 353 196	6 429 758	6 506 649	6 583 959	6 661 638	6 739 611	6 817 737	6 895 889	6 975 114	7 656 528	9 306 128

StatLink http://dx.doi.org/10.1787/888932705843

World population
Millions, 2010

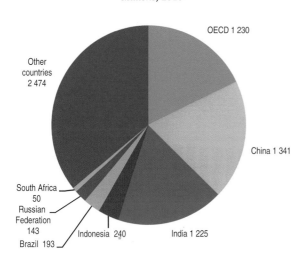

OECD 1 230
Other countries 2 474
China 1 341
India 1 225
Indonesia 240
Brazil 193
Russian Federation 143
South Africa 50

StatLink http://dx.doi.org/10.1787/888932705862

OECD population
Millions, 2010

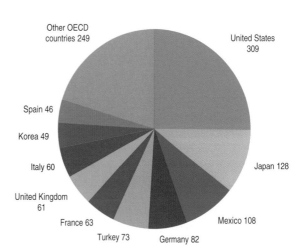

Other OECD countries 249
United States 309
Japan 128
Mexico 108
Germany 82
Turkey 73
France 63
United Kingdom 61
Italy 60
Korea 49
Spain 46

StatLink http://dx.doi.org/10.1787/888932705900

Population growth rates
Annual growth in percentage

	1999	2000	2001	2002	2003	2004	2005	2006	2007	2008	2009	2010	2011
Australia	1.15	1.20	1.36	1.23	1.24	1.17	1.33	1.49	1.53	2.30	2.12	1.56	1.44
Austria	0.19	0.24	0.38	0.49	0.49	0.62	0.68	0.50	0.39	0.44	0.34	0.29	0.37
Belgium	0.23	0.24	0.34	0.45	0.42	0.43	0.55	0.66	0.74	0.79	0.81	0.92	..
Canada	0.82	0.94	1.09	1.08	0.91	0.95	0.95	1.03	1.09	1.17	1.21	1.15	..
Chile	1.34	1.32	1.13	1.12	1.10	1.09	1.08	1.02	1.01	1.00	0.99	0.98	0.90
Czech Republic	-0.10	-0.11	-0.35	-0.31	0.02	0.08	0.19	0.33	0.63	0.87	0.60	0.31	..
Denmark	0.33	0.33	0.36	0.32	0.27	0.26	0.28	0.33	0.44	0.59	0.54	0.45	..
Estonia	-0.76	-0.45	-0.40	-0.40	-0.37	-0.32	-0.24	-0.19	-0.14	-0.07	-0.03	-0.01	..
Finland	0.23	0.21	0.23	0.24	0.24	0.29	0.34	0.38	0.43	0.47	0.48	0.46	0.46
France	0.48	0.66	0.70	0.70	0.68	0.71	0.74	0.68	0.60	0.54	0.53	0.53	0.53
Germany	0.06	0.14	0.17	0.17	0.06	-0.02	-0.06	-0.11	-0.13	-0.19	-0.25	-0.15	..
Greece	0.44	0.32	0.30	0.34	0.33	0.35	0.38	0.40	0.40	0.40	0.41	0.22	..
Hungary	-0.28	-0.26	-0.23	-0.28	-0.29	-0.22	-0.20	-0.16	-0.15	-0.17	-0.15	-0.23	..
Iceland	1.24	1.43	1.39	0.88	0.60	1.15	1.12	2.86	2.32	2.56	-0.03	-0.39	0.32
Ireland	1.13	1.34	1.60	1.70	1.64	1.85	2.20	2.41	2.27	1.58	0.75	0.35	..
Israel	2.59	2.68	2.38	2.03	1.82	1.78	1.78	1.78	1.79	1.79	2.42	1.84	..
Italy	0.02	0.05	0.06	0.32	0.78	0.99	0.74	0.57	0.74	0.77	0.60	0.48	..
Japan	0.16	0.19	0.29	0.11	0.14	0.05	0.06	0.00	0.00	-0.06	-0.14	0.43	-0.20
Korea	0.71	0.84	0.74	0.56	0.50	0.38	0.21	0.49	0.47	0.72	0.48	0.46	0.75
Luxembourg	1.36	1.35	1.20	1.05	1.22	1.43	1.54	1.61	1.56	1.80	1.87	1.84	..
Mexico	1.38	1.36	1.30	1.20	1.08	0.98	0.92	0.89	0.87	0.84	0.81	0.79	0.76
Netherlands	0.67	0.72	0.76	0.64	0.47	0.35	0.23	0.16	0.22	0.39	0.52	0.51	..
New Zealand	0.53	0.59	0.59	1.75	1.99	1.50	1.14	1.23	1.04	0.96	1.10	1.20	0.85
Norway	0.69	0.65	0.51	0.54	0.59	0.59	0.68	0.81	1.04	1.25	1.27	1.25	1.30
Poland	-0.03	-0.04	-0.01	-0.05	-0.10	-0.04	-0.05	-0.08	-0.04	0.00	0.10	0.09	..
Portugal	0.42	0.53	0.66	0.73	0.70	0.58	0.45	0.33	0.23	0.13	0.09	0.05	..
Slovak Republic	0.10	-0.14	-0.18	0.00	0.01	0.05	0.08	0.08	0.11	0.17	0.22	0.21	..
Slovenia	0.07	0.30	0.16	0.12	0.06	0.06	0.17	0.32	0.17	0.55	0.91	0.44	..
Spain	0.52	0.84	1.14	1.46	1.67	1.64	1.65	1.66	1.73	1.51	0.77	0.35	..
Sweden	0.08	0.16	0.27	0.33	0.37	0.39	0.40	0.56	0.74	0.78	0.86	0.86	0.76
Switzerland	0.48	0.56	0.59	0.80	0.74	0.69	0.64	0.63	0.90	1.28	1.26	1.01	..
Turkey	1.44	1.40	1.37	1.34	1.31	1.27	1.24	1.21	1.18	1.23	1.15	1.11	..
United Kingdom	0.33	0.36	0.37	0.37	0.41	-0.90	0.64	0.58	0.65	0.67	0.64	0.68	0.68
United States	1.15	1.12	0.99	0.93	0.86	0.93	0.93	0.97	0.96	0.95	0.88	0.83	0.73
EU 27	0.19	0.23	0.19	0.29	0.43	0.46	0.45	0.42	0.45	0.44	0.34	0.28	0.30
OECD	0.69	0.73	0.72	0.70	0.69	0.62	0.68	0.68	0.69	0.71	0.62	0.63	0.17
Brazil	1.50	1.50	1.48	1.44	1.38	1.32	1.26	1.19	1.12	1.05	0.99	0.93	0.87
China	0.84	0.77	0.69	0.63	0.58	0.55	0.54	0.53	0.52	0.51	0.50	0.48	0.50
India	1.75	1.70	1.66	1.62	1.58	1.55	1.52	1.49	1.46	1.44	1.42	1.40	1.42
Indonesia	1.33	1.32	1.32	1.31	1.28	1.25	1.20	1.15	1.11	1.07	1.05	1.03	0.97
Russian Federation	-0.31	-0.36	-0.41	-0.44	-0.44	-0.40	-0.32	-0.23	-0.15	-0.09	-0.07	-0.07	-0.09
South Africa	1.43	1.41	1.41	1.38	1.34	1.28	1.20	1.13	1.06	0.98	0.88	0.77	0.50
World	1.32	1.29	1.26	1.24	1.22	1.21	1.20	1.19	1.18	1.17	1.16	1.15	1.15

StatLink http://dx.doi.org/10.1787/888932705881

Population growth rates
Average annual growth in percentage

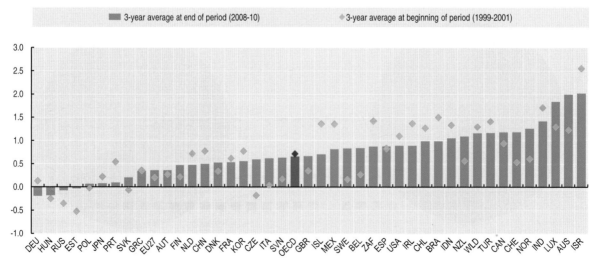

StatLink http://dx.doi.org/10.1787/888932705938

Working age population
As a percentage of total population

	1999	2000	2001	2002	2003	2004	2005	2006	2007	2008	2009	2010	2011
Australia	66.8	66.9	66.9	67.0	67.2	67.3	67.3	67.4	67.5	67.6	67.7	67.6	67.4
Austria	67.6	67.8	67.7	67.9	68.1	68.1	67.8	67.6	67.5	67.5	67.5	67.6	67.7
Belgium	65.7	65.6	65.6	65.6	65.6	65.6	65.6	65.8	66.0	66.1	66.0	65.9	..
Canada	68.1	68.3	68.5	68.7	68.8	69.0	69.2	69.4	69.5	69.5	69.4	69.4	..
Chile	64.8	65.0	65.5	65.9	66.3	66.7	67.1	67.5	67.8	68.1	68.4	68.7	68.7
Czech Republic	69.4	69.8	70.1	70.4	70.7	70.9	71.1	71.2	71.2	71.1	70.8	70.3	..
Denmark	66.8	66.7	66.5	66.4	66.3	66.2	66.1	66.1	66.0	65.9	65.7	65.4	..
Estonia	66.6	66.9	67.2	67.4	67.7	67.9	68.1	68.1	68.0	67.9	67.9	67.7	..
Finland	66.9	66.9	66.9	66.9	66.8	66.7	66.7	66.6	66.5	66.6	66.5	66.2	65.7
France	65.1	65.1	65.0	65.0	65.0	65.1	65.1	65.1	65.1	65.0	64.9	64.8	..
Germany	67.8	67.5	67.2	67.0	66.7	66.4	66.9	66.6	66.3	66.2	66.1	66.0	..
Greece	67.9	68.0	68.0	67.9	67.8	67.6	67.3	67.1	67.1	67.0	67.1	..	..
Hungary	68.0	68.2	68.3	68.5	68.6	68.7	68.8	68.8	68.8	68.8	68.7	68.7	..
Iceland	65.1	65.1	65.3	65.3	65.5	65.8	66.2	66.9	67.4	67.8	67.4	66.9	66.7
Ireland	66.6	67.0	67.3	67.8	67.9	68.0	68.3	68.7	68.8	68.5	67.9	67.2	..
Israel	61.5	61.6	61.7	61.8	61.7	61.7	61.7	61.8	61.8	61.9	62.3	62.2	..
Italy	68.0	67.8	67.6	67.5	67.5	66.7	66.5	66.3	66.1	66.0	65.9	65.9	..
Japan	68.5	68.1	67.7	67.3	66.9	66.6	66.1	65.5	65.0	64.5	63.9	63.8	63.6
Korea	71.7	71.7	71.6	71.6	71.6	71.7	71.7	71.9	72.1	72.3	72.6	72.8	73.0
Luxembourg	66.8	67.0	67.2	67.1	67.1	67.3	67.3	67.5	67.6	67.9	68.1	68.3	..
Mexico	60.9	61.2	61.6	62.0	62.5	63.0	63.5	64.0	64.5	65.0	65.5	63.6	..
Netherlands	67.9	67.8	67.8	67.7	67.7	67.6	67.5	67.4	67.4	67.3	67.2	67.0	..
New Zealand	65.5	65.5	65.5	65.8	66.1	66.3	66.4	66.5	66.5	66.6	66.5	66.5	66.4
Norway	64.7	64.8	65.0	65.1	65.3	65.5	65.6	65.9	66.1	66.3	66.3	66.2	66.1
Poland	68.0	68.3	68.8	69.2	69.6	70.0	70.3	70.6	70.9	71.2	71.3	71.3	..
Portugal	67.7	67.7	67.6	67.5	67.5	67.4	67.3	67.3	67.3	67.2	67.0	66.8	..
Slovak Republic	68.5	69.1	69.6	70.1	70.6	71.1	71.5	71.8	72.1	72.3	72.4	72.3	..
Slovenia	69.7	70.1	70.3	70.2	70.4	70.5	70.1	70.1	70.1	70.0	69.4	69.4	..
Spain	68.4	68.4	68.5	68.5	68.6	68.7	68.8	68.8	68.8	68.7	68.4	68.0	..
Sweden	64.2	64.3	64.7	64.7	64.9	65.1	65.3	65.5	65.7	65.6	65.4	65.1	64.7
Switzerland	67.3	67.3	67.5	67.6	67.8	67.9	68.0	68.0	68.1	68.1	68.1	68.0	..
Turkey	63.4	63.8	64.2	64.6	65.1	65.4	65.7	66.0	66.2	66.5	66.8	67.1	..
United Kingdom	65.0	65.2	65.4	65.5	65.7	66.1	66.3	66.6	66.7	66.3	66.5	66.4	66.2
United States	66.0	66.2	66.4	66.6	66.7	66.9	67.1	67.3	67.3	67.2	67.2	67.1	67.1
EU 27	..	68.5	68.4	68.2	68.2	68.2	68.3	67.4	67.4	67.3	67.2	67.1	66.9
OECD	66.4	66.4	66.5	66.6	66.7	66.7	66.8	66.9	66.9	66.9	66.9	..	..
Brazil	..	..	..	..	..	..	..	..	..	..	..	..	..
China	..	..	..	..	..	..	..	..	..	..	..	..	..
India	..	..	..	..	..	..	..	..	..	..	..	..	..
Indonesia	..	..	..	..	..	..	..	..	..	..	..	..	..
Russian Federation	..	..	..	..	..	..	..	..	..	..	..	..	..
South Africa	..	..	..	..	..	..	..	..	..	..	..	..	..
World	..	..	..	..	..	..	..	..	..	..	..	..	..

StatLink http://dx.doi.org/10.1787/888932705919

Working age population
As a percentage of total population

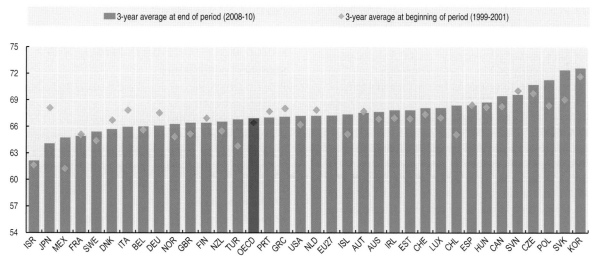

■ 3-year average at end of period (2008-10)   ◆ 3-year average at beginning of period (1999-2001)

StatLink http://dx.doi.org/10.1787/888932705957

FERTILITY

Together with mortality and migration, fertility is an element of population growth, which reflects both the causes and effects of economic and social developments.

Definition

The total fertility rate in a specific year is the total number of children that would be born to each woman if she were to live to the end of her child-bearing years and give birth to children in agreement with the prevailing age-specific fertility rates.

Comparability

The total fertility rate is generally computed by summing up the age-specific fertility rates defined over a five-year interval. Assuming there are no migration flows and that mortality rates remain unchanged, a total fertility rate of 2.1 children per woman generates broad stability of the population: it is also referred to as the "replacement fertility rate" as it ensures replacement of the woman and her partner with another 0.1 children per woman to counteract infant mortality.

Data are collected every year from national statistical institutes. 2010 refers to 2009 for Canada and Chile and 1970 refers to 1980 for Brazil, Estonia and Israel.

Trends in total fertility rates
Number of children born to women aged 15 to 49

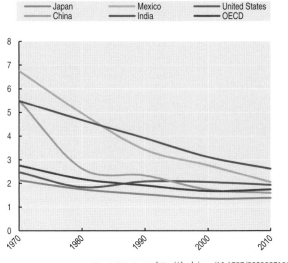

StatLink ⟲ http://dx.doi.org/10.1787/888932710156

Overview

Total fertility rates in OECD countries have declined dramatically over the past few decades, falling on average from 2.7 in 1970 to 1.7 children per woman of childbearing age in the 2000s. In all OECD countries, fertility rates declined for young women and increased at older ages. A modest recovery in total fertility rates started in the early 2000s, to an average level of 1.7 in 2010. The total fertility rate is below its replacement level of 2.1 in most OECD countries except Israel, Iceland and New Zealand, and in India, South Africa and Indonesia.

The last few years have seen various trends emerge in fertility rates. A drop in fertility rates has occurred, for example in Australia, New Zealand, Spain and the United States, while rates have continued to rise in Iceland, Israel, Sweden, and Switzerland. The increase in fertility stopped in many other countries. The effect of the economic downturn is as yet unknown, but persistent economic uncertainties can impact downward the number of children women may have over their reproductive life.

Sources

- For OECD member countries and Brazil, Russia and South Africa: National statistical offices.
- For China, India and Indonesia: World Bank *World Development indicators*.
- Fertility rates: OECD (2011), *Society at a Glance: OECD Social Indicators*, OECD Publishing.

Further information

Analytical publications
- OECD (2011), *Doing Better for Families*, OECD Publishing.

Statistical publications
- OECD (2011), *Society at a Glance: OECD Social Indicators*, OECD Publishing.

Methodological publications
- d'Addio, A.C. and M.M. d'Ercole (2005), "Trends and Determinants of Fertility Rates: The Role of Policies", *OECD Social Employment and Migration Working Papers*, No. 27.

Online databases
- United Nations World Population Prospects.

Websites
- OECD Family Database, *www.oecd.org/els/social/family/ database*.
- World Bank – World Development Indicators, *http://data.worldbank.org/indicator*.

Total fertility rates

Number of children born to women aged 15 to 49

	1970	1980	1990	2000	2002	2003	2004	2005	2006	2007	2008	2009	2010
Australia	2.86	1.89	1.90	1.76	1.76	1.75	1.76	1.79	1.82	1.92	1.96	1.90	1.89
Austria	2.29	1.65	1.46	1.36	1.39	1.38	1.42	1.41	1.41	1.38	1.41	1.39	1.44
Belgium	2.25	1.68	1.62	1.67	1.65	1.67	1.72	1.76	1.80	1.82	1.85	1.86	1.87
Canada	2.33	1.68	1.71	1.49	1.50	1.53	1.53	1.54	1.59	1.66	1.68	1.67	..
Chile	3.95	2.72	2.59	2.05	1.94	1.89	1.85	1.84	1.83	1.88	1.92	1.94	..
Czech Republic	1.91	2.10	1.89	1.14	1.17	1.18	1.23	1.28	1.33	1.44	1.50	1.49	1.49
Denmark	1.95	1.55	1.67	1.77	1.72	1.76	1.78	1.80	1.85	1.85	1.89	1.84	1.88
Estonia	..	2.02	2.05	1.39	1.37	1.37	1.47	1.50	1.55	1.63	1.65	1.62	1.63
Finland	1.83	1.63	1.79	1.73	1.72	1.76	1.80	1.80	1.84	1.83	1.85	1.86	1.87
France	2.48	1.95	1.78	1.87	1.86	1.87	1.90	1.92	1.98	1.96	1.99	1.99	1.99
Germany	2.03	1.56	1.45	1.38	1.34	1.34	1.36	1.34	1.33	1.37	1.38	1.36	1.39
Greece	2.40	2.23	1.40	1.26	1.27	1.28	1.30	1.33	1.40	1.41	1.51	1.52	1.51
Hungary	1.97	1.92	1.84	1.33	1.31	1.28	1.28	1.32	1.35	1.32	1.35	1.33	1.26
Iceland	2.81	2.48	2.31	2.08	1.93	1.99	2.03	2.05	2.07	2.09	2.14	2.22	2.20
Ireland	3.87	3.23	2.12	1.90	1.98	1.98	1.95	1.88	1.90	2.03	2.10	2.07	2.07
Israel	..	3.14	3.02	2.95	2.89	2.95	2.90	2.84	2.88	2.90	2.96	2.96	3.03
Italy	2.43	1.68	1.36	1.26	1.27	1.29	1.33	1.32	1.35	1.37	1.42	1.41	1.41
Japan	2.13	1.75	1.54	1.36	1.32	1.29	1.29	1.26	1.32	1.34	1.37	1.37	1.39
Korea	4.53	2.82	1.57	1.47	1.17	1.18	1.15	1.08	1.12	1.25	1.19	1.15	1.23
Luxembourg	1.98	1.50	1.62	1.78	1.63	1.62	1.66	1.62	1.64	1.61	1.60	1.59	1.63
Mexico	6.77	4.97	3.43	2.77	2.46	2.34	2.25	2.20	2.17	2.13	2.10	2.08	2.05
Netherlands	2.57	1.60	1.62	1.72	1.73	1.75	1.73	1.71	1.72	1.72	1.77	1.79	1.80
New Zealand	3.17	2.03	2.18	1.98	1.89	1.93	1.98	1.97	2.01	2.17	2.18	2.12	2.15
Norway	2.50	1.72	1.93	1.85	1.75	1.80	1.83	1.84	1.90	1.90	1.96	1.98	1.95
Poland	2.20	2.28	1.99	1.37	1.25	1.22	1.23	1.24	1.27	1.31	1.39	1.40	1.38
Portugal	2.83	2.18	1.56	1.56	1.47	1.44	1.40	1.41	1.36	1.33	1.37	1.32	1.37
Slovak Republic	2.40	2.31	2.09	1.29	1.19	1.20	1.24	1.25	1.24	1.25	1.32	1.41	1.40
Slovenia	2.21	2.11	1.46	1.26	1.21	1.20	1.25	1.26	1.31	1.31	1.53	1.53	1.57
Spain	2.90	2.22	1.36	1.23	1.26	1.31	1.32	1.34	1.38	1.39	1.46	1.39	1.38
Sweden	1.94	1.68	2.14	1.55	1.65	1.72	1.75	1.77	1.85	1.88	1.91	1.94	1.98
Switzerland	2.10	1.55	1.59	1.50	1.39	1.39	1.42	1.42	1.44	1.46	1.48	1.50	1.54
Turkey	5.00	4.63	3.07	2.27	2.17	2.09	2.11	2.12	2.12	2.15	2.15	2.07	2.03
United Kingdom	2.43	1.90	1.83	1.64	1.64	1.71	1.77	1.79	1.84	1.90	1.96	1.94	1.98
United States	2.48	1.84	2.08	2.06	2.01	2.04	2.05	2.05	2.10	2.12	2.08	2.00	1.93
EU 27	2.42	1.99	1.79	1.48	1.44	1.46	1.48	1.48	1.51	1.53	1.59	1.59	1.58
OECD	2.76	2.18	1.91	1.68	1.63	1.63	1.65	1.65	1.68	1.71	1.75	1.74	1.74
Brazil	..	4.06	2.79	2.39	2.27	2.20	2.13	2.06	1.99	1.95	1.89	1.94	..
China	5.51	2.63	2.34	1.74	1.71	1.69	1.68	1.67	1.66	1.64	1.63	1.61	1.60
India	5.49	4.68	3.92	3.12	2.99	2.93	2.88	2.83	2.79	2.74	2.70	2.66	2.63
Indonesia	5.47	4.43	3.12	2.45	2.39	2.35	2.32	2.28	2.25	2.21	2.18	2.15	2.12
Russian Federation	1.97	1.90	1.89	1.20	1.29	1.32	1.34	1.29	1.30	1.41	1.49	1.54	..
South Africa	5.65	4.56	3.32	2.90	2.86	2.81	2.75	2.69	2.64	2.58	2.52	2.47	2.41

StatLink ⌐ᵐˢ᠘ http://dx.doi.org/10.1787/888932705976

Total fertility rates

Number of children born to women aged 15 to 49

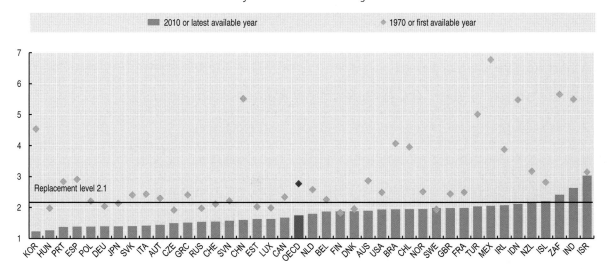

StatLink ⌐ᵐˢ᠘ http://dx.doi.org/10.1787/888932705995

DEPENDENT POPULATION

Demographic trends in OECD countries have implied a sharp increase in the share of the dependent population (*i.e.* the sum of the elderly and youth population) in the total population, and this increase is expected to continue in the future. These trends have a number of implications for government and private spending on pensions, healthcare and education and, more generally, for economic growth and welfare.

Overview

The share of dependent population reflects the combined effect of fertility rates, life expectancy and migration. In 2010, countries with a share of dependent population more than 1.3 percentage points above the OECD total (33% on average) were Israel, Japan, France, Sweden and Italy. Korea at 27% has the lowest recorded share of dependent population in the OECD and is closely followed by the Slovak Republic, Poland, the Czech Republic and Slovenia. There is a wide variation among the emerging countries, with this share ranging between 36% in India and 28% in the Russian Federation and China.

By 2050, the share of dependent population is projected to increase in all OECD countries, while declining only in the non-member economies of India and South Africa. The share of the dependent population is projected to be above 45% in Japan, Korea, Spain and Italy by 2050.

The youth population accounted for around 18% of the OECD total (on average) in 2010 with a steady decline since the 1970s. This fall is projected to continue as a result of lower fertility rates. By 2050 Japan and Korea are projected to have youth populations of 9% of the total, while only the United States (19%), Iceland (18%) and Estonia (18%) have projected youth populations close to the current OECD total.

In 2010, the share of the elderly in the total population ranged between less than 7% in South Africa, India, Indonesia and Mexico, to above 18% in Greece, Germany, Italy and Japan (the OECD average was 15%). By 2050, this share is projected to be below 11% in South Africa, and to exceed one third of the total population in Greece, Italy, Spain, Korea and Japan. A number of countries are projected to have large increases in their elderly population between 2010 and 2050. For example, the Slovak Republic, Spain, and Korea all see projected growth in the share of the elderly in the total population in excess of 17 percentage points. However, some countries see smaller projected increases between 2010 and 2050. For example, Sweden, South Africa, Estonia and the United States all see projected growth to be less than 8 percentage points for this period.

Definition

The total population is defined as the resident population, *i.e.* all persons, regardless of citizenship, who have a permanent place of residence in the country.

The elderly population refers to people aged 65 and over and the youth population to people aged less than 15. The share of dependent population is calculated as the sum of the elderly and youth population expressed as a ratio of the total population.

Comparability

Population projections by age and gender are taken from national sources where these are available; for other countries they are based on Eurostat and UN projections.

All population projections require assumptions about future trends in life expectancy, fertility rates and migration, and these assumptions may differ across countries. Often, a range of projections is produced. The estimates shown here correspond to the median or central variant of these projections.

Sources
- OECD (2011), *Labour Force Statistics*, OECD Publishing.
- Eurostat, United Nations, national sources and OECD estimates.

Further information

Analytical publications
- Burniaux, J., R. Duval and F. Jaumotte (2004), "Coping with Ageing", *OECD Economics Department Working Papers*, No. 371.
- OECD (2012), *OECD Employment Outlook*, OECD Publishing.
- OECD (2011), *OECD Pensions at a Glance*, OECD Publishing.
- OECD (2007), *Ageing and the Public Service: Human Resource Challenges*, OECD Publishing.
- OECD (2006), *Ageing and Employment Policies*, OECD Publishing.
- OECD (2003), *Ageing, Housing and Urban Development*, OECD Publishing.
- OECD (2001), *Ageing and Transport Mobility Needs and Safety Issues*, OECD Publishing.
- Oliveira Martins J., *et al.* (2005), "The Impact of Ageing on Demand, Factor Markets and Growth", *OECD Economics Department Working Papers*, No. 420.

Methodological publications
- OECD (2005), *Main Economic Indicators – Sources and Methods: Labour and Wage Statistics*, OECD Publishing.

Online databases
- *OECD Employment and Labour Market Statistics.*

Share of the dependent population
As a percentage of total population

	Youth population (under the age of 15)						Elderly population (age 65 and over)					
	2000	2010	2020	2030	2040	2050	2000	2010	2020	2030	2040	2050
Australia	20.7	18.9	18.4	17.6	16.9	16.7	12.4	13.5	16.8	19.7	21.3	22.2
Austria	17.0	14.8	14.3	14.2	13.5	13.3	15.4	17.6	19.6	24.0	27.2	28.3
Belgium	17.6	16.9	17.6	17.2	16.6	16.8	16.8	17.2	19.2	22.3	24.1	24.5
Canada	19.2	16.5	15.3	14.7	13.8	13.6	12.6	14.1	18.2	23.1	25.0	26.3
Chile	27.8	22.3	20.2	18.7	17.3	16.6	7.2	9.0	11.9	16.5	19.8	21.6
Czech Republic	16.4	14.3	13.7	12.7	12.2	12.4	13.8	15.4	20.1	22.7	26.5	31.2
Denmark	18.5	18.0	16.9	17.2	17.3	16.8	14.8	16.6	20.0	22.6	24.5	23.8
Estonia	18.0	15.2	18.1	17.2	16.0	17.8	15.1	17.0	18.3	20.4	21.8	23.8
Finland	18.2	16.6	16.6	16.1	15.5	15.6	14.9	17.3	22.9	26.1	26.9	27.6
France	18.9	18.4	17.9	17.1	16.7	16.7	16.1	16.9	20.6	23.6	25.8	26.2
Germany	15.6	13.4	12.5	12.4	11.5	11.3	16.4	20.6	23.3	28.8	32.1	33.1
Greece	15.3	14.4	14.0	12.6	12.1	12.3	16.6	19.1	21.3	24.8	29.4	32.5
Hungary	16.8	14.7	15.1	14.4	13.7	13.9	15.1	16.7	20.1	21.5	23.9	26.9
Iceland	23.3	20.9	20.4	19.0	17.8	17.5	11.6	12.1	15.2	19.2	21.5	23.4
Ireland	21.8	21.6	19.7	16.8	16.1	16.0	11.2	11.5	14.9	18.5	22.4	26.3
Israel	28.6	28.0	27.4	27.0	..	..	9.8	9.9	12.0	13.1	..	..
Italy	14.3	14.0	13.1	12.1	12.4	12.7	18.3	20.3	23.3	27.3	32.2	33.6
Japan	14.6	13.2	11.7	10.3	10.0	9.7	17.4	23.0	29.1	31.6	36.1	38.8
Korea	21.1	16.1	13.2	12.6	11.2	9.9	7.2	11.0	15.7	24.3	32.3	37.4
Luxembourg	18.9	17.7	17.0	17.3	16.9	16.6	14.1	13.9	16.6	20.0	22.3	22.1
Mexico	34.1	28.1	23.2	20.8	18.5	16.8	4.7	5.9	8.1	11.8	16.7	21.2
Netherlands	18.6	17.5	16.2	16.1	15.8	15.4	13.6	15.4	19.9	24.3	27.0	26.9
New Zealand	22.8	20.5	18.1	16.9	16.3	15.6	11.8	13.0	17.1	21.9	25.2	26.2
Norway	20.0	18.8	17.5	17.5	16.9	16.4	15.2	15.0	18.0	20.6	22.9	23.2
Poland	19.5	15.1	15.6	13.7	12.1	12.5	12.2	13.5	18.4	22.3	25.1	30.3
Portugal	16.1	15.2	13.7	12.4	12.2	12.1	16.2	18.0	20.8	24.4	28.6	32.0
Slovak Republic	19.5	15.3	14.6	13.4	12.6	13.2	11.4	12.3	17.3	21.6	25.0	30.1
Slovenia	15.9	14.1	14.7	13.9	13.5	14.7	14.0	16.5	20.5	24.7	27.6	30.0
Spain	14.8	15.0	14.1	11.6	11.3	11.4	16.8	17.0	20.0	25.1	31.6	35.7
Sweden	18.4	16.6	17.6	16.9	16.0	16.3	17.3	18.3	20.8	22.7	23.9	23.8
Switzerland	17.4	14.6	14.4	14.0	13.2	13.1	15.3	17.5	20.5	24.7	27.4	28.3
Turkey	29.4	25.8	22.9	..	..	..	6.8	7.7	9.5	..	..	..
United Kingdom	19.0	17.7	17.8	16.9	16.3	16.3	15.8	16.0	19.0	21.9	23.7	24.1
United States	21.4	19.8	20.0	19.5	19.3	19.3	12.4	13.1	16.1	19.3	20.0	20.2
EU 27	17.1	15.6	15.5	14.6	14.2	14.3	15.7	17.4	20.3	23.8	27.0	28.7
OECD	20.5	18.4	17.5	..	..	..	13.1	14.7	17.9	..	..	..
Brazil	29.8	25.6	20.1	17.0	14.9	13.1	5.4	6.8	9.2	13.3	17.5	22.7
China	25.5	19.5	16.7	14.6	13.6	13.5	7.0	8.2	12.0	16.5	23.3	25.6
India	34.7	30.6	27.1	23.8	21.1	19.0	4.2	4.9	6.3	8.3	10.5	13.5
Indonesia	30.7	27.0	23.5	20.1	17.9	16.5	4.6	5.6	7.0	10.5	14.9	19.2
Russian Federation	18.2	15.0	17.3	15.8	15.4	16.9	12.4	12.8	15.2	19.1	20.1	23.1
South Africa	33.7	30.1	27.6	25.2	23.1	21.1	3.7	4.6	6.2	7.8	8.5	10.1

StatLink http://dx.doi.org/10.1787/888932706014

Share of the dependent population
As a percentage of total population

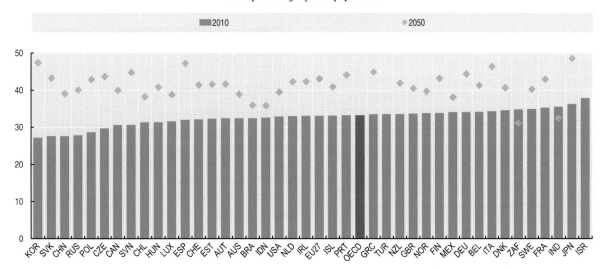

StatLink http://dx.doi.org/10.1787/888932706033

POPULATION BY REGION

Population is unevenly distributed among regions within countries. Differences in climatic and environmental conditions discourage human settlement in some areas and favour concentration of the population around a few urban centres. This pattern is reinforced by higher economic opportunities and wider availability of services stemming from urbanisation itself.

Definition

The number of inhabitants of a given region, *i.e.* its total population, can be measured as either its average annual population or as the population at a specific date during the year considered. The average population during a calendar year is generally calculated as the arithmetic mean of the population on 1 January of two consecutive years, although some countries estimate it on a date close to 1 July.

Comparability

The main problem with economic analysis at the sub-national level is the unit of analysis, *i.e.* the region. The word "region" can mean very different things both within and among countries, with significant differences in area and population.

The population across OECD regions ranges from about 400 inhabitants in Balance ACT (Australia) to 37 million in California (the United States).

Overview

In 2010, 10% of regions accounted for approximately 40% of the total population in OECD countries. The concentration of population was highest in Australia, Canada, Chile and Iceland, where differences in climatic and environmental conditions discourage human settlement in some areas.

Two-thirds of the OECD population live in urban areas, but the urban experience is very different according to country. Of the 21 million Canadians living in urban areas, half of them reside in large metropolitan areas. For the 21 million urban population in Poland, only 25% live in large metropolitan areas, while half of them reside in medium-sized or small urban areas.

In 2010, almost half of the total OECD population (48%) lived in predominantly urban regions, which accounted for around 6% of the total area.

Predominantly rural regions accounted for one-fourth of total population and 80% of land area. In Ireland, Finland, Norway and Slovenia the share of national population in rural regions was twice as high as the OECD average.

To address this issue, the OECD has classified regions within each member country to facilitate comparability at the same territorial level. The classification is based on two territorial levels: the higher level (TL2) consists of 362 large regions and the lower level (TL3) consists of 1 794 small regions. These two levels are used as a framework for implementing regional policies in most countries. In Brazil, China, India, the Russian Federation and South Africa only TL2 large regions have been identified. This classification (which, for European Union countries, is largely consistent with the Eurostat NUTS classification) facilitates comparability of regions at the same territorial level.

All the regional data shown here refer to small regions with the exception of Brazil, China, India, the Russian Federation and South Africa.

In addition, the OECD has established a regional typology to take into account geographical differences and enable meaningful comparisons between regions belonging to the same type. Regions have been classified as predominantly rural, intermediate and predominantly urban on the basis of the percentage of population living in local rural units.

The metropolitan database identifies more than 1 000 urban areas (with a population of 50 000 or more) in 28 OECD countries. Urban areas are defined on the basis of population density and commuting patterns to better reflect the economic function of cities in addition to their administrative boundaries. Urban areas in OECD countries are classified as large metropolitan areas if they have a population of 1.5 million or more, metropolitan areas if their population is between 500 000 and 1.5 million, medium-size urban areas with a population between 200 000 and 500 000 and small urban areas with a population between 50 000 and 200 000.

Sources
• OECD (2011), *OECD Regions at a Glance*, OECD Publishing.

Further information

Analytical publications
• OECD (2011), *OECD Regional Outlook 2011*, OECD Publishing.
• OECD (2012), *OECD Territorial Reviews*, OECD Publishing.

Statistical publications
• OECD (2011), *Labour Force Statistics*, OECD Publishing.

Online databases
• *OECD Regional Database*.

Websites
• Regional Development, *www.oecd.org/gov/ regionaldevelopment*.
• Regional Statistics and Indicators, *www.oecd.org/gov/ regional/statisticsindicators*.

Share of national population in the ten per cent of regions with the largest population

Percentage

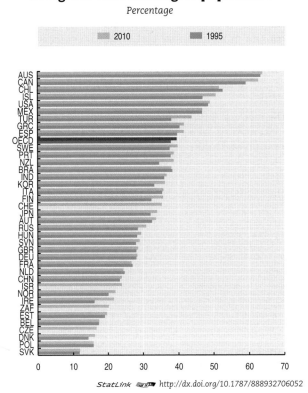

StatLink http://dx.doi.org/10.1787/888932706052

Distribution of the national population into urban, intermediate and rural regions

Percentage, 2010

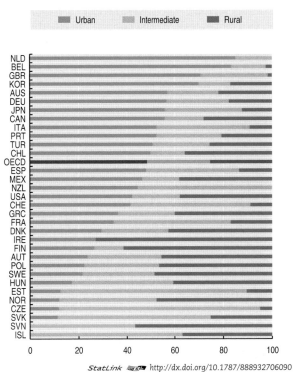

StatLink http://dx.doi.org/10.1787/888932706090

Percentage of urban population by city size

Percentage, 2008

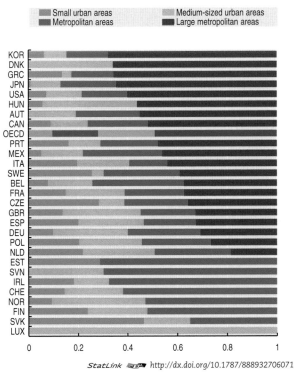

StatLink http://dx.doi.org/10.1787/888932706071

Distribution of the national area into urban, intermediate and rural regions

Percentage, 2010

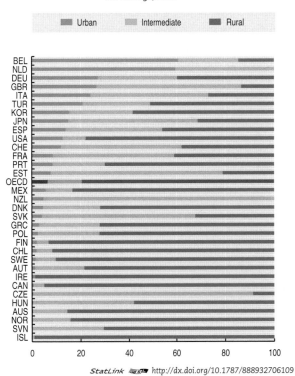

StatLink http://dx.doi.org/10.1787/888932706109

ELDERLY POPULATION BY REGION

In all OECD countries, populations aged 65 years and over have dramatically increased over the last 30 years, both in size and as a percentage of total population. Elderly people, it turns out, tend to be concentrated in few areas within each country, which means that a small number of regions will have to face a number of specific social and economic challenges raised by ageing population.

Definition

The elderly population is the number of inhabitants of a given region aged 65 or older. The population can be either the average annual population or the population at a specific date during the year considered. The average population during a calendar year is generally calculated as the arithmetic mean of the population on 1 January of two consecutive years.

The elderly dependency rate is defined as the ratio between the elderly population and the working age (15-64 years) population.

Overview

In most OECD countries the population is ageing. Due to higher life expectancy and low fertility rates, the elderly population (those aged 65 years and over), accounts for almost 15% of OECD population in 2010, up from just over 12% 15 years earlier. The proportion of elderly population is remarkably lower in the emerging economies (India, South Africa, Brazil and China) and Mexico, Turkey and Chile.

The elderly population in OECD countries has increased more than twice faster than the total population between 1995 and 2010. The rate of ageing between different parts of a country can be quite different, as an increase in the geographic concentration of the elderly may arise from inward migration of the elderly or by ageing "in place" because the younger generations have moved out of the regions.

The ratio of the elderly to the working age population, the elderly dependency rate, is steadily growing in OECD countries. The elderly dependency rate gives an indication of the balance between the retired and the economically active population. In 2010 this ratio was 22% in OECD countries, with substantial differences between countries (36% in Japan versus 8% in Mexico). Differences among regions within the same countries were also large. The higher the regional elderly dependency rate, the higher the challenges faced by regions in generating wealth and sufficient resources to provide for the needs of the population. Concerns may arise on the financial self-sufficiency of these regions to generate taxes to pay for these services.

Comparability

As for the other regional statistics, the comparability of elderly population data is affected by differences in the definition of the regions and the different geography of rural and urban communities, both within and among countries.

All the regional data shown here refer to small regions with the exception of Brazil, China, India, the Russian Federation and South Africa.

Sources

• OECD (2011), *OECD Regions at a Glance*, OECD Publishing.

Further information

Analytical publications

• OECD (2011), *OECD Regional Outlook 2011*, OECD Publishing.
• Oliveira Martins J., *et al.* (2005), "The Impact of Ageing on Demand, Factor Markets and Growth", *OECD Economics Department Working Papers*, No. 420.

Online databases

• *OECD Regional Database*.

Websites

• Regional Development, *www.oecd.org/gov/ regionaldevelopment*.
• Regional Statistics and Indicators, *www.oecd.org/gov/ regional/statisticsindicators*.

Elderly population

As a percentage of total population

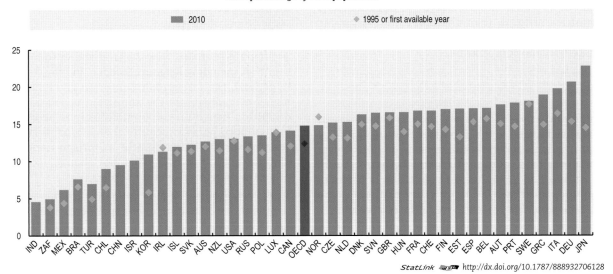

■ 2010   ◆ 1995 or first available year

StatLink ⟨≋⟩ http://dx.doi.org/10.1787/888932706128

Regional elderly population

Average annual growth in percentage, 1995-2010

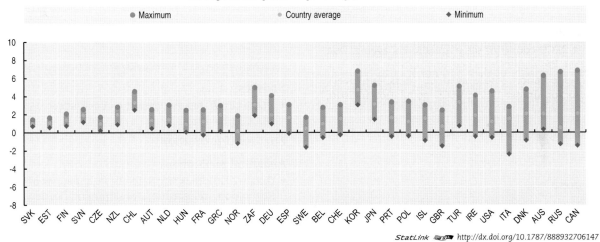

● Maximum   ● Country average   ◆ Minimum

StatLink ⟨≋⟩ http://dx.doi.org/10.1787/888932706147

Elderly dependency rate in urban and rural regions

Percentage, 2010

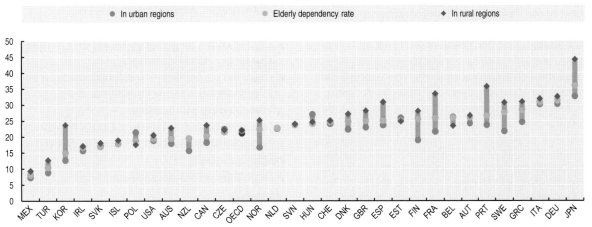

● In urban regions   ● Elderly dependency rate   ◆ In rural regions

StatLink ⟨≋⟩ http://dx.doi.org/10.1787/888932706166

IMMIGRANT AND FOREIGN POPULATION

As a result of migration flows of varying destinations and size, countries differ in their share of immigrants and foreign population. The exact definition of these shares is key for international comparisons.

Definition

Nationality and place of birth are the two criteria most commonly used to define the "immigrant" population. The foreign-born population covers all persons who have ever migrated from their country of birth to their current country of residence. The foreign population consists of persons who still have the nationality of their home country. It may include persons born in the host country.

Comparability

The difference across countries between the size of the foreign-born population and that of the foreign population depends on the rules governing the acquisition of citizenship in each country. In some countries, children born in the country automatically acquire the citizenship of their country of birth (jus soli, the right of soil) while in other countries, they retain the nationality of their parents (jus sanguinis, the right of blood). In some others, they retain the nationality of their parents at birth but receive that of the host country at their majority. Differences in the ease with which immigrants may acquire the citizenship of the host country explain part of the gap between the two series. For example, residency requirements vary from as little as three years in Canada to as much as ten years in some other countries.

The naturalisation rate is high in settlement countries such as Australia, Canada, New Zealand and in some European countries including Belgium, Sweden and the Netherlands. In general, the foreign-born criterion gives substantially higher percentages for the immigrant population than the definition based on nationality. This is because many foreign-born persons acquire the nationality of the host country and no longer appear as foreign nationals. The place of birth, however, does not change, except when there are changes in country borders.

Most of the data for this indicator are taken from the contributions of national correspondents who are part of the OECD Expert Group on International Migration.

The foreign-born population data shown here include persons born abroad as nationals of their current country of residence. The prevalence of such persons among the foreign-born can be significant in some countries, in particular France and Portugal who received large inflows of repatriates from former colonies.

Overview

The share of the foreign-born population in the total population is especially high in Luxembourg, Australia, Switzerland, Israel, New Zealand and Canada where it ranges from 21% to 42%. In a number of other European countries as well (namely, Belgium, Spain, Ireland, Germany, Estonia, Austria and Sweden), the share is higher than in the United States (13.1%). It has increased in the past decade in all countries for which data are available with the exception of the two most recent members of the OECD, namely Estonia and Israel.

The proportion of foreign-born in the population as a whole roughly doubled over the decade in Spain, Ireland and Norway. Other countries, such as Finland, South Africa and Chile report a low share of foreign-born in the total population but have seen a spectacular increase in recent years. By contrast, the foreign population tends to increase more slowly, because inflows of foreign nationals tend to be counterbalanced by persons acquiring the nationality of the host country.

Sources
- OECD (2012), *International Migration Outlook*, OECD Publishing.

Further information

Analytical publications
- OECD (2011), Tackling the Policy Challenges of Migration, Regulation, Integration, Development, *Development Centre Studies*, OECD Publishing.
- OECD (2008), *A Profile of Immigrant Populations in the 21st Century: Data from OECD Countries*, OECD Publishing.
- Widmaier, S. and J-C. Dumont (2011), "Are Recent Immigrants Different? A New Profile of Immigrants in the OECD based on DIOC 2005/06", *OECD Social, Employment and Migration Working Papers*, No. 126.

Statistical publications
- OECD (2012), *Connecting with Emigrants, A Global Profile of Diasporas*, OECD Publishing.
- OECD (2012), *Settling In: OECD Indicators of Immigrant Integration 2012*, OECD Publishing.

Methodological publications
- Lemaître, G. and C. Thoreau, (2006), *Estimating the foreign-born population on a current basis*, OECD, Paris.

Online databases
- OECD International Migration Statistics.

Websites
- Database on Immigrants in OECD Countries (DIOC), *www.oecd.org/els/migration/dioc*.

Foreign-born and foreign populations

	As a percentage of total population								As a percentage of all foreign-born
	Foreign-born population				Foreign population				Foreign-born nationals
	1995	2000	2005	2010	1995	2000	2005	2010	2010 or latest available year
Australia	23.0	23.0	24.2	26.8	..	..	..	..	..
Austria	..	10.4	14.5	16.7	8.5	8.8	9.7	10.4	41.9
Belgium	9.7	10.3	12.1	14.4	9.0	8.4	8.6	9.2	44.6
Canada	17.2	18.1	19.5	21.3	..	..	..	..	..
Chile	0.9	1.2	1.4	1.9	..	..	..	..	..
Czech Republic	..	1.2	1.5	2.9	..	..	..	1.1	63.1
Denmark	4.8	5.8	6.5	9.6	4.2	4.8	5.0	5.4	46.7
Estonia	..	18.4	17.5	16.6	..	..	..	17.6	35.7
Finland	2.1	2.6	3.4	3.7	1.3	1.8	2.2	2.1	47.2
France	..	10.1	11.0	12.6	..	..	..	5.9	53.4
Germany	11.5	12.5	12.6	16.4	8.8	8.9	8.8	9.0	55.1
Greece	..	..	..	8.7	..	2.9	5.2	7.0	22.1
Hungary	2.7	2.9	3.3	1.9	1.4	1.1	1.5	0.6	69.6
Iceland	..	..	..	7.9	..	..	..	3.7	54.7
Ireland	..	8.7	12.6	15.5	2.7	3.3	6.3	11.2	29.9
Israel	..	32.2	29.1	31.2	..	..	..	..	..
Italy	..	..	..	8.8	1.7	2.4	4.6	6.5	26.9
Japan	..	..	..	..	1.1	1.3	1.6	1.7	..
Korea	..	..	..	..	0.2	0.4	1.1	2.0	..
Luxembourg	30.9	33.2	35.0	42.4	33.4	37.3	39.6	41.8	13.2
Mexico	0.5	0.5	0.6	0.9	..	..	..	..	..
Netherlands	9.1	10.1	10.6	11.2	4.7	4.2	4.2	3.6	70.5
New Zealand	..	17.2	20.3	23.2	..	..	..	..	..
Norway	5.5	6.8	8.2	10.0	3.8	4.0	4.8	5.6	49.0
Poland	..	..	..	0.9	..	..	..	0.1	87.1
Portugal	5.2	5.1	6.3	7.3	1.7	2.1	4.1	3.5	53.9
Slovak Republic	..	..	4.6	0.7	0.4	0.5	0.5	0.2	74.4
Slovenia	..	..	..	9.1	..	..	..	1.3	85.5
Spain	..	4.9	11.1	14.9	..	..	..	12.3	18.3
Sweden	10.6	11.3	12.5	16.8	6.0	5.4	5.3	5.6	67.7
Switzerland	21.4	21.9	23.8	27.8	18.9	19.3	20.3	21.6	32.1
Turkey	..	1.9	..	3.8	..	..	..	..	..
United Kingdom	6.9	7.9	9.4	12.9	3.4	4.0	5.2	7.4	41.9
United States	10.1	11.5	13.3	13.1	6.1	6.5	7.5	7.1	54.0
EU 27	..	..	..	..	..	..	..	..	..
OECD	..	..	..	..	..	..	..	..	..
Brazil	0.4	0.4	0.4	0.4	..	..	..	..	..
China	0.0	0.0	0.0	0.1	..	..	..	..	..
India	0.7	0.6	0.5	0.4	..	..	..	..	..
Indonesia	0.1	0.1	0.1	0.1	..	..	..	..	..
Russian Federation	7.9	8.1	8.4	8.7	..	8.2	..	..	..
South Africa	2.7	2.3	2.6	3.7	..	1.0	..	..	57.1

StatLink http://dx.doi.org/10.1787/888932706185

Foreign-born population
As a percentage of total population

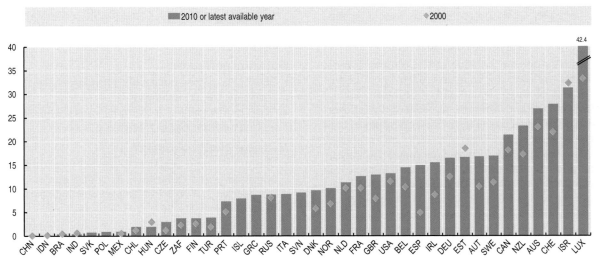

StatLink http://dx.doi.org/10.1787/888932706204

TRENDS IN MIGRATION

Permanent immigrant inflows are presented by category of entry which is a key determinant of immigrant outcomes. They cover regulated movements of foreigners as well as free movement migration.

Definition

Permanent immigrant inflows cover regulated movements of foreigners considered to be settling in the country from the perspective of the destination country. In countries such as Australia, Canada, New Zealand and the United States, this consists of immigrants who receive the right of "permanent" residence. In other countries, it generally refers to immigrants who are granted a residence permit which is indefinitely renewable, although the renewability is sometimes subject to conditions, such as the holding of a job. Excluded are international students, trainees, persons on exchange programmes, seasonal or contract workers, service providers, installers, artists entering the country to perform or persons engaging in sporting events, etc. Permits for persons in this latter group may be renewable as well, but not indefinitely.

Overview

Overall, in 2010, permanent immigrant inflows continued to decline for the third consecutive year. However, the decline was modest (minus 3%) and levels are still higher than their pre-crisis level. Furthermore, the trend in the absolute figures was largely attributable to the large decline in inflows for the United States (minus 8%).

In Ireland which has been hard hit by the crisis, the decline was particularly severe and inflow levels dropped to below a fifth of their pre-crisis level. Declines also continued to be significant in the Czech Republic, Japan, in Southern Europe as well as in the Russian Federation. In all other countries, it would appear that the decline has come to an end.

There is considerable variation in the composition of immigrant inflows. In countries such as Austria, Switzerland, Norway, Ireland and, to a lesser extent, the Netherlands and Germany, the bulk of the inflows consist of free movements from other countries of the enlarged European Union. On the other hand, regulated labour migration predominates in Korea, Mexico and Italy. The composition is mixed in some EU countries (such as Belgium, Denmark, Spain, Portugal) where labour migration is above the OECD average and where free movements represents at least 40% of the total inflows. In the United States, and to a lesser extent in France, Japan and Sweden, inflows of family members constitute the main component of permanent inflows.

The year of reference for these statistics is often the year when the permit was granted rather than the year of entry. Some persons admitted on a temporary basis are sometimes allowed to change to a permanent status. In the statistics presented here, they are counted in the year the change of status occurred.

Migrants are defined as "free movement" when they have some kind of basic rights, usually accorded through international agreements, to enter and leave a country that result in few restrictions being placed on their movements or durations of stay, such as citizens of EU states within the EU. Their movements are not always formally recorded and have sometimes had to be estimated.

Comparability

This standardisation according to the concept of "permanent immigrant inflows" represents a considerable improvement compared with compilations of national statistics, whose coverage can vary by a factor of one to three. However, the extent to which changes in status are identified and the coverage of "permanent" free movement may vary somewhat across countries. Overall, the standardisation is applied to 23 OECD countries as well as to the Russian Federation.

Sources
- OECD (2012), *International Migration Outlook*, OECD Publishing.

Further information

Analytical publications
- Widmaier, S. and J-C. Dumont (2011), "Are Recent Immigrants Different? A New Profile of Immigrants in the OECD based on DIOC 2005/06", *OECD Social, Employment and Migration Working Papers*, No. 126.

Statistical publications
- OECD (2012), *Connecting with Emigrants, A Global Profile of Diasporas*, OECD Publishing.
- OECD (2012), *Settling In: OECD Indicators of Immigrant Integration 2012*, OECD Publishing.

Methodological publications
- Dumont, J.C. and Lemaître G. (2005), "Counting Immigrants and Expatriates in OECD Countries: A New Perspective", *OECD Social, Employment and Migration Working Papers*, No. 25.
- Lemaitre G. (2005), "The Comparability of International Migration Statistics: Problems and Prospects", *OECD Statistic Brief*, No. 9.

Online databases
- *OECD International Migration Statistics.*

Permanent inflows by category of entry

Percentage of total permanent inflows, 2010

	Work	Free movements	Accompanying family of workers	Family	Humanitarian	Other
Australia	22.3	11.7	29.6	28.4	7.0	1.0
Austria	1.4	63.7	0.9	23.2	10.3	0.5
Belgium	18.3	39.6	-	36.2	5.9	..
Canada	27.3	..	39.3	21.5	11.9	0.0
Chile	..	..	..	..	..	..
Czech Republic	..	..	..	..	..	..
Denmark	19.6	50.9	5.9	12.3	5.1	6.2
Estonia	..	..	..	..	..	..
Finland	5.8	39.0	-	34.3	17.4	3.6
France	11.9	30.3	-	42.9	5.4	9.6
Germany	9.0	59.9	-	24.7	5.3	1.1
Greece	..	..	..	..	..	..
Hungary	..	..	..	..	..	..
Iceland	..	..	..	..	..	..
Ireland	16.3	71.8	4.0	7.0	0.9	..
Israel	..	..	..	..	..	..
Italy	40.5	28.2	1.2	27.4	1.3	1.5
Japan	34.6	..	-	39.3	0.7	25.4
Korea	68.1	..	-	19.9	0.0	9.9
Luxembourg	..	..	..	..	..	..
Mexico	54.4	..	-	33.9	0.8	10.9
Netherlands	10.9	56.9	-	21.7	10.5	..
New Zealand	25.4	8.7	31.7	28.3	5.9	..
Norway	5.1	67.4	-	18.0	9.5	..
Poland	..	..	..	..	..	..
Portugal	21.9	36.3	-	35.3	0.1	6.3
Slovak Republic	..	..	..	..	..	..
Slovenia	..	..	..	..	..	..
Spain	29.9	49.9	-	18.7	0.2	1.2
Sweden	5.7	35.9	-	39.6	18.7	..
Switzerland	2.1	71.4	-	18.8	5.8	2.0
Turkey	..	..	..	..	..	..
United Kingdom	33.1	17.4	14.6	11.8	1.2	21.9
United States	6.4	..	7.8	66.3	13.1	6.4
EU 27	..	..	..	..	..	..
OECD	..	..	..	..	..	..
Brazil	..	..	..	..	..	..
China	..	..	..	..	..	..
India	..	..	..	..	..	..
Indonesia	..	..	..	..	..	..
Russian Federation	25.5	..	-	52.3	0.6	21.6
South Africa	..	..	..	..	..	..

StatLink http://dx.doi.org/10.1787/888932706223

Permanent inflows by category of entry

Percentage of total permanent inflows, 2010

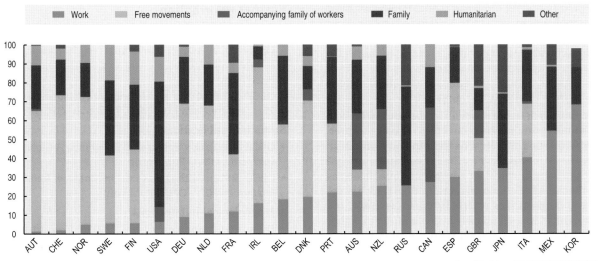

StatLink http://dx.doi.org/10.1787/888932706242

MIGRATION AND EMPLOYMENT

Changes in the percent of persons employed differ between immigrants and native-born. In particular, changes in the size of the working-age population affect more strongly the foreign-born than the natives for whom such changes are hardly noticeable from one year to another. In most OECD countries, employment rates for immigrants are lower than those for native-born persons. However, the situation is more diverse if one disaggregates employment rates by educational attainment.

Definition

The employment rate is calculated as the share of employed persons in the total population (active and inactive persons aged 15-64) of that same age. In accordance with ILO definitions, employed persons are those who worked at least one hour or who had a job but were absent from work during the reference week. The classification of educational attainment shown is based on the *International Standard Classification of Education* (ISCED) categories. Generally speaking, "low" corresponds to less than upper secondary education; "intermediate" to upper secondary education; and "high" to tertiary education. Tertiary education includes programmes of high-level vocational education whose graduates feed into technical or semi-professional occupations.

Comparability

Data for the European countries are from the European Union Labour Force Survey. Data for other countries are mostly taken from national labour force surveys. Even if employment levels can at times be affected by changes in survey design and by survey implementation problems (*e.g.* non-response), data on employment rates are generally consistent over time.

However, comparability of education levels between immigrants and the native-born population and across countries is only approximate. The educational qualifications of other countries may not fit exactly into national educational categories because the duration of study or the programme content for what appear to be equivalent qualifications may not be the same. Likewise, the reduction of the ISCED classification into three categories may result in some loss of information regarding the duration of study, the programme orientation, etc. For example, high educational qualifications can include programmes of durations varying from two years (in the case of short, university-level technical programmes) to seven years or more (in the case of PhDs).

Data for Brazil, Indonesia and the Russian Federation refer to the year 2000.

Overview

Labour market outcomes of immigrants and natives vary significantly across OECD countries, and differences by educational attainment are even larger. In all OECD countries, the employment rate increases with education level. While people with tertiary education find work more easily and are less exposed to unemployment, access to tertiary education does not necessarily guarantee equal employment rates for immigrants and native-born persons. In all OECD countries, employment rates are higher for native-born persons with high educational qualifications than for their foreign-born counterparts.

The situation is more diverse for persons with low educational attainment. In the United States, Luxembourg and to a lesser extent in some southern European countries such as Greece and Italy, foreign-born immigrants with low educational qualifications have much higher employment rates than their native-born counterparts. The reverse is true in Denmark, the Netherlands, Poland and New Zealand. The higher employment rate of foreign-born persons with low educational attainment in some countries may reflect the persistent demand for workers in low-skilled jobs which are hardly taken up by the in-coming cohorts of native-born workers.

Sources

- OECD (2012), *International Migration Outlook*, OECD Publishing.

Further information

Analytical publications

- OECD (2012), *Jobs for Immigrants (Vol. 3), Labour Market Integration in Austria, Norway and Switzerland*, OECD Publishing.
- OECD (2008), *A Profile of Immigrant Populations in the 21st Century: Data from OECD Countries*, OECD Publishing.

Statistical publications

- OECD (2012), *Connecting with Emigrants, A Global Profile of Diasporas*, OECD Publishing.
- OECD (2012), *Settling In: OECD Indicators of Immigrant Integration 2012*, OECD Publishing.

Methodological publications

- Dumont, J.C. and Lemaître G. (2005), "Counting Immigrants and Expatriates in OECD Countries: A New Perspective", *OECD Social, Employment and Migration Working Papers*, No. 25.

Online databases

- *OECD International Migration Statistics*.

Employment rates of native- and foreign-born population by educational attainment
As a percentage of total population

| | 2007 | | | | | | 2011 | | | | | |
| | Native-born | | | Foreign-born | | | Native-born | | | Foreign-born | | |
	Low	High	Total	Low	High	Total	Low	High	Total	Low	High	Total
Australia	..	..	..	..	..	..	57.6	86.1	74.2	53.2	78.6	68.7
Austria	32.9	77.9	58.5	47.7	67.9	57.6	48.6	88.2	73.3	53.7	76.0	66.7
Belgium	27.0	77.1	50.4	27.0	68.7	43.2	39.0	83.9	..	36.4	70.8	52.6
Canada	..	..	..	..	..	..	47.3	82.9	72.8	44.4	75.6	68.8
Chile	..	..	..	..	..	..	..	..	..	..	..	..
Czech Republic	17.2	75.7	55.7	24.2	74.9	52.1	20.9	81.1	65.7	34.3	79.2	67.8
Denmark	52.0	82.0	63.9	50.9	73.4	57.7	58.9	86.6	74.7	48.4	76.0	61.7
Estonia	29.5	82.5	59.7	20.1	69.2	48.3	31.0	80.8	65.3	29.3	69.6	63.9
Finland	29.1	76.3	57.0	39.2	71.6	59.9	41.0	84.8	69.4	44.9	69.2	61.1
France	30.8	75.4	52.7	35.3	64.0	46.4	44.2	81.7	64.8	48.5	70.7	57.4
Germany	29.8	74.1	55.9	..	..	..	43.2	89.3	73.8	53.4	77.3	66.5
Greece	31.1	76.7	47.9	62.2	67.5	63.6	43.7	74.8	55.2	58.4	60.5	58.4
Hungary	20.5	74.0	46.7	27.9	69.9	50.9	25.6	78.4	55.7	34.6	78.2	62.1
Iceland	74.1	90.3	80.7	78.3	87.5	82.1	68.8	89.5	78.7	70.0	82.5	76.3
Ireland	38.3	82.3	59.2	45.6	78.8	70.0	35.1	81.3	59.2	37.9	73.5	59.3
Israel	28.1	83.9	57.6	35.7	79.4	62.8	27.6	83.1	59.1	39.8	78.8	65.7
Italy	29.6	72.1	44.8	55.7	71.6	62.5	42.1	77.5	56.3	54.9	71.5	61.5
Japan	..	..	..	..	..	..	..	..	..	..	..	..
Korea	..	..	..	..	..	..	..	..	..	..	..	..
Luxembourg	26.5	72.0	47.2	55.3	80.1	63.9	32.3	84.9	59.5	58.6	83.0	70.3
Mexico	..	..	..	..	..	..	..	..	..	..	..	..
Netherlands	45.9	79.5	64.8	45.6	70.9	58.1	61.5	88.2	76.6	51.1	76.2	63.6
New Zealand	62.0	84.9	76.8	55.3	79.3	70.5	56.3	84.4	73.5	50.4	81.1	70.2
Norway	51.4	86.3	71.1	52.2	82.4	68.1	58.2	90.6	76.0	55.7	82.0	70.2
Poland	17.9	76.3	48.9	4.2	44.9	14.1	23.5	82.4	59.7	15.2	72.2	55.3
Portugal	53.4	78.5	56.9	63.2	82.7	68.6	59.5	81.0	63.8	61.1	80.3	68.7
Slovak Republic	9.9	76.8	52.3	18.2	68.4	50.7	14.9	76.9	59.5	26.3	66.8	59.7
Slovenia	31.4	79.5	56.9	44.6	65.2	56.4	33.3	86.0	64.7	46.6	78.5	61.9
Spain	38.5	78.6	51.5	60.3	72.5	66.2	47.5	78.1	58.4	46.2	66.9	54.4
Sweden	44.8	82.5	68.4	40.8	73.4	57.6	48.7	89.7	76.6	43.9	75.2	62.6
Switzerland	39.3	83.9	65.7	54.4	74.6	63.7	60.2	91.3	81.0	66.2	82.4	75.5
Turkey	..	..	..	..	..	..	38.1	70.5	43.1	33.9	64.2	49.7
United Kingdom	51.7	88.4	59.2	46.2	81.1	59.2	53.4	84.3	70.0	48.7	76.1	66.5
United States	35.1	83.8	69.5	61.4	79.7	71.1	25.3	80.1	64.0	55.3	76.4	66.6
EU 27	..	..	..	..	..	..	..	..	..	..	..	..
OECD	..	..	..	..	..	..	..	..	..	..	..	..
Brazil	49.3	80.8	54.0	29.7	70.9	44.0	..	..	..	..	..	..
China	..	..	..	..	..	..	..	..	..	..	..	..
India	..	..	..	..	..	..	..	..	..	..	..	..
Indonesia	66.4	78.8	66.1	35.8	77.8	57.4	..	..	..	..	..	..
Russian Federation	30.1	79.1	57.9	32.4	76.4	60.7	..	..	..	..	..	..
South Africa	27.8	79.9	36.3	60.8	75.3	63.7	..	..	..	..	..	..

StatLink ᴍᴱˢ⟋ http://dx.doi.org/10.1787/888932706261

Gap in employment rate between native- and foreign-born population by educational attainment
Percentage points, 2011 or latest available year

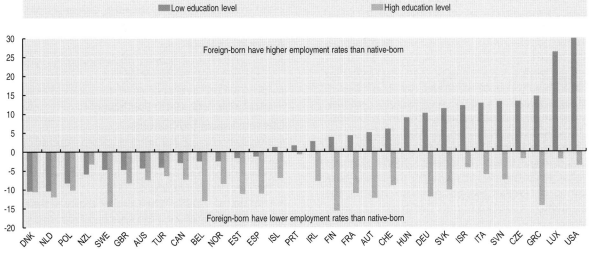

StatLink ᴍᴱˢ⟋ http://dx.doi.org/10.1787/888932706280

MIGRATION AND UNEMPLOYMENT

Immigrant workers are more affected by unemployment than native-born workers in traditional European immigration countries. Conversely, in some settlement countries (Australia, New Zealand) as well as in Israel, Hungary, Turkey and the United States, the unemployment rate depends less on the place of birth. Some groups, such as young immigrants, women or older immigrants have greater difficulties in finding jobs.

Definition

The unemployment rate is the share of the unemployed in the total labour force (the sum of employed and unemployed persons). In accordance with the ILO standards, unemployed persons consist of those persons who report that they are without work during the reference week, that they are available for work and that they have taken active steps to find work during the four weeks preceding the interview.

Comparability

Data for the European countries are from the European Union Labour Force Survey. Data for the United States from the Current Population Survey; those for other countries are taken from the national labour force surveys. Even if unemployment levels can at times be affected by changes in the survey design and by survey implementation problems (e.g. non-response), data on unemployment rates are generally consistent over time.

Overview

Immigrants have been hard hit, and almost immediately, by the economic downturn in most OECD countries. This is mainly explained by their greater presence in sectors that have been strongly affected by the crisis (e.g. construction, manufacturing, retail trade and financial sectors) as well as by their greater likelihood of being in precarious or informal jobs. However, differences exist across OECD countries and between migrant groups.

The ongoing economic downturn has seen unemployment rates increase, both for foreign- and native-born persons, in most OECD countries. However, immigrants in most European OECD countries were more affected by unemployment than the native population. In Spain, Greece and Estonia, immigrant unemployment increased by 20, 14 and 11 percentage points between 2007 and 2011 whereas that of the native-born increased by 12, 9 and 8 percentage points. In 2011, in Belgium, Estonia, Finland, France, Ireland, Portugal, the Slovak Republic and Sweden, the unemployment rate of immigrants was above 15%. It was close to 22% and 32% in Greece and Spain, respectively. The unemployment rate was more than twice the level observed for the native-born population in Norway, Sweden, Belgium, Austria, the Netherlands, Switzerland and Denmark. In some settlement countries (Australia, Canada, New Zealand) and in the United States, the unemployment rate does not vary much by birth status.

Sources
- OECD (2012), *International Migration Outlook*, OECD Publishing.

Further information

Analytical publications
- OECD (2012), *Jobs for Immigrants (Vol. 3), Labour Market Integration in Austria, Norway and Switzerland*, OECD Publishing.
- OECD (2008), *A Profile of Immigrant Populations in the 21st Century: Data from OECD Countries*, OECD Publishing.
- OECD (2008), *Jobs for Immigrants (Vol. 2): Labour Market Integration in France, Belgium, the Netherlands and Portugal*, OECD Publishing.
- OECD (2007), *Jobs for Immigrants (Vol. 1): Labour Market Integration in Australia, Denmark, Germany and Sweden*, OECD Publishing.

Statistical publications
- OECD (2012), *Connecting with Emigrants, A Global Profile of Diasporas*, OECD Publishing.
- OECD (2012), *Settling In: OECD Indicators of Immigrant Integration 2012*, OECD Publishing.

Methodological publications
- Dumont, J.C. and Lemaître G. (2005), "Counting Immigrants and Expatriates in OECD Countries: A New Perspective", *OECD Social, Employment and Migration Working Papers*, No. 25.
- Lemaitre G. (2005), "The Comparability of International Migration Statistics: Problems and Prospects", *OECD Statistic Brief*, No. 9.

Online databases
- *OECD International Migration Statistics.*

Unemployment rates of native- and foreign-born population

As a percentage of total population

| | Women | | | | Men | | | | Total | | | |
| | Native-born | | Foreign-born | | Native-born | | Foreign-born | | Native-born | | Foreign-born | |
	2007	2011	2007	2011	2007	2011	2007	2011	2007	2011	2007	2011
Australia	4.3	5.2	5.5	6.0	4.0	5.2	4.6	4.6	4.3	5.2	4.9	5.2
Austria	4.1	8.3	9.7	3.5	3.0	3.3	6.2	8.0	3.5	3.4	9.0	8.2
Belgium	7.5	14.6	17.1	6.0	5.5	5.7	9.9	15.5	..	5.8	16.3	15.1
Canada	..	6.4	..	9.5	..	7.8	..	8.4	..	7.2	..	8.9
Chile	..	..	..	..	..	..	..	..	..	..	..	..
Czech Republic	6.7	10.9	10.9	7.9	4.1	5.9	5.1	6.1	5.2	6.8	9.0	8.0
Denmark	3.8	15.1	7.8	6.5	3.0	7.2	6.0	13.8	3.4	6.9	8.1	14.5
Estonia	3.8	18.1	4.4	11.2	5.2	13.1	4.3	15.6	4.5	12.1	5.5	16.9
Finland	6.9	14.2	15.6	6.9	6.3	8.2	10.1	16.0	6.6	7.6	14.3	15.2
France	7.8	16.3	15.0	8.9	6.7	8.1	7.9	14.2	7.2	8.5	13.8	15.1
Germany	7.8	9.2	..	5.1	7.4	5.6	..	9.7	7.6	5.4	..	9.5
Greece	12.6	23.2	14.1	21.4	5.2	14.4	4.2	21.5	8.2	17.4	8.6	22.2
Hungary	7.7	10.1	6.1	11.0	7.2	11.1	1.6	8.9	7.4	11.0	4.3	9.5
Iceland	2.1	10.4	3.6	5.8	2.2	7.6	2.1	11.7	2.2	6.7	3.0	11.1
Ireland	3.9	14.1	5.8	10.0	4.5	17.5	5.3	19.8	4.2	14.1	6.0	17.3
Israel	8.6	6.2	6.8	4.5	7.1	5.8	6.3	5.6	7.8	6.0	6.5	5.0
Italy	7.5	14.1	11.4	8.9	4.8	7.4	4.4	9.7	5.9	8.0	7.9	11.7
Japan	..	..	..	..	..	..	..	..	..	..	..	..
Korea	..	..	..	..	..	..	..	..	..	..	..	..
Luxembourg	4.4	8.4	5.1	4.0	2.9	3.0	3.1	4.7	3.6	3.4	4.6	6.3
Mexico	..	..	..	..	..	..	..	..	..	..	..	..
Netherlands	3.1	8.5	7.4	3.8	2.4	3.8	4.3	9.7	2.7	3.8	6.6	9.2
New Zealand	3.9	5.1	5.3	6.4	3.6	5.0	3.6	5.6	3.8	5.4	4.4	6.2
Norway	2.2	7.0	4.7	2.5	2.2	2.9	4.9	8.3	2.2	2.7	5.6	7.7
Poland	10.3	14.5	8.0	10.5	9.0	9.1	2.0	9.9	9.6	9.8	8.4	12.1
Portugal	9.4	15.9	12.0	13.3	6.5	12.7	6.0	18.0	7.8	13.0	9.6	16.9
Slovak Republic	12.7	20.8	5.6	13.6	9.9	13.6	5.0	11.1	11.2	13.6	6.7	15.3
Slovenia	5.7	14.0	7.7	7.8	4.0	8.2	2.5	9.7	4.7	8.0	5.6	11.5
Spain	10.2	30.1	13.8	20.3	5.7	18.8	8.3	32.9	7.6	19.5	11.7	31.5
Sweden	5.5	15.9	12.5	5.9	5.0	6.1	8.1	16.0	5.2	6.0	12.0	16.0
Switzerland	3.1	7.5	8.7	3.3	2.0	2.8	4.5	6.2	2.5	3.1	7.0	6.8
Turkey	..	10.5	..	13.6	..	8.6	..	10.3	..	9.2	..	9.1
United Kingdom	4.5	9.7	8.2	7.0	5.4	8.8	4.9	9.1	5.0	8.0	7.3	9.4
United States	3.0	5.5	2.4	2.4	4.2	8.1	4.1	8.6	3.6	6.8	3.3	7.5
EU 27	..	..	..	..	..	..	..	..	..	..	..	..
OECD	..	..	..	..	..	..	..	..	..	..	..	..
Brazil	..	..	..	..	..	..	..	..	..	..	..	..
China	..	..	..	..	..	..	..	..	..	..	..	..
India	..	..	..	..	..	..	..	..	..	..	..	..
Indonesia	..	..	..	..	..	..	..	..	..	..	..	..
Russian Federation	..	..	..	..	..	..	..	..	..	..	..	..
South Africa	31.4	..	25.0	..	25.3	..	11.3	..	28.5	..	16.6	..

StatLink ⫸ http://dx.doi.org/10.1787/888932706299

Foreign-born unemployment rate relative to native-born unemployment rate

Ratio, 2011 or latest available year

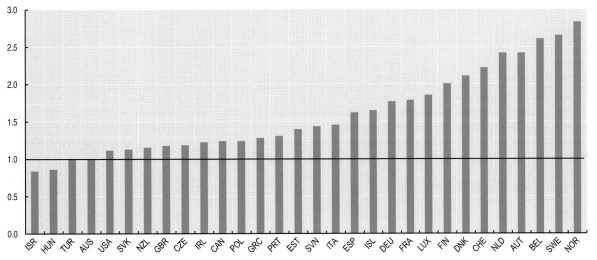

StatLink ⫸ http://dx.doi.org/10.1787/888932706318

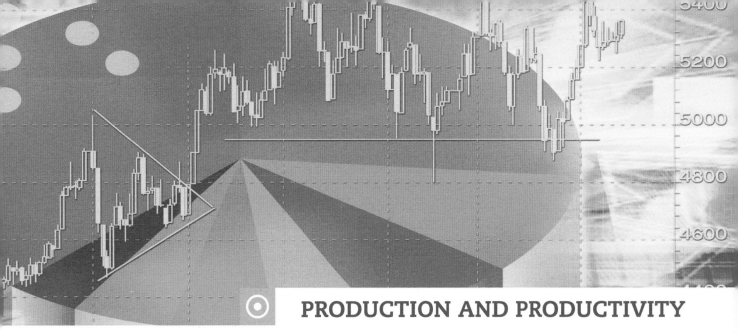

PRODUCTION AND PRODUCTIVITY

SIZE OF GDP

Gross Domestic Product (GDP) is the standard measure of the value of final goods and services produced by a country during a period minus the value of imports. While GDP is the single most important indicator to capture economic activity, it should not be looked upon as an all encompassing measure for societies' well-being, as it does not include several aspects of people's material living standards let alone other aspects of people's quality of life.

GDP per capita is a core indicator of economic performance and commonly used as a broad measure of average living standards or economic well-being; despite some recognised shortcomings.

Definition

What does gross domestic product mean? "Gross" signifies that no deduction has been made for the depreciation of machinery, buildings and other capital products used in production. "Domestic" means that it relates to the output produced on the economic territory of the country. The products refer to final goods and services, that is, those that are purchased, imputed or otherwise, as: the final consumption of households, non-profit institutions serving households and government; fixed capital formation; and exports (minus imports).

Comparability

All countries compile data according to the 1993 SNA "System of National Accounts, 1993" with the exception of Australia where data are compiled according to the new 2008 SNA. It's important to note however that differences between the 2008 SNA and the 1993 SNA do not have a significant impact of the comparability of the indicators presented here and this implies that data are highly comparable across countries.

For some countries, the latest year has been estimated by the Secretariat. Historical data have also been estimated for those countries that revise their methodologies but only supply revised data for some years.

For GDP per capita some care is needed in interpretation, for example Luxembourg and, to a lesser extent, Switzerland have a relatively large number of frontier workers. Such workers contribute to GDP but are excluded from the population figures.

Overview

Per capita GDP for the OECD as a whole was USD 33 971 in 2010. Five OECD countries had per capita GDP considerably in excess of USD 40 000 in 2010 – Luxembourg, Norway, the United States, Switzerland, and to a lesser extent the Netherlands. Four OECD countries had a per capita GDP just above USD 40 000 in 2010: Australia, Austria, Denmark and Ireland with 13 countries having per capita GDP below USD 30 000: Turkey, Chile and Mexico being at the bottom of the distribution.

While in 2000 per capita GDP for the United States was 44% higher than the OECD average, this has decreased to 37% in 2010. Japanese GDP per capita dropped to just below the OECD average in 2010, whereas it was just above the OECD average in 2000.

The largest decreases in per capita GDP relative to the OECD average between 2000 and 2010 were observed for Israel, Iceland and Italy. On the other hand, the largest increases of relative GDP per capita for this ten year time period are shown for Luxembourg, the Slovak Republic, Norway and Estonia. Also, the countries at the bottom of the distribution (Chile, Mexico and Turkey) showed increases in their relative position of GDP per capita to the OECD average.

Sources

- OECD (2012), *National Accounts of OECD Countries*, OECD Publishing.
- For Brazil and India: International Monetary Fund (IMF) (2009), *World Economic Outlook*, IMF, Washington DC.

Further information

Analytical publications

- OECD (2012), *OECD Economic Outlook*, OECD Publishing.
- OECD (2012), *OECD Economic Surveys*, OECD Publishing.
- OECD (2011), *Towards Green Growth*, OECD Publishing.
- OECD (2003), *The Sources of Economic Growth in OECD Countries*, OECD Publishing.

Statistical publications

- OECD (2011), *National Accounts at a Glance*, OECD Publishing.

Methodological publications

- OECD (2000), *System of National Accounts, 1993 – Glossary*, OECD Publishing.
- United Nations, OECD, IMF and Eurostat (eds.) (2010), *System of National Accounts 2008*, United Nations, Geneva.

Online databases

- *OECD National Accounts Statistics*.
- *OECD Economic Outlook: Statistics and Projections*.

Websites

- OECD Economic Outlook – Sources and Methods, *www.oecd.org/eco/sources-and-methods*.

GDP per capita

US dollars, current prices and PPPs

	1999	2000	2001	2002	2003	2004	2005	2006	2007	2008	2009	2010	2011
Australia	26 816	27 968	29 077	30 314	31 875	33 306	34 882	36 814	38 744	38 964	39 904	40 790	..
Austria	27 186	28 909	29 025	30 463	31 319	32 856	33 637	36 586	38 073	39 785	39 026	40 065	42 132
Belgium	25 366	27 669	28 524	30 054	30 292	31 190	32 204	34 254	35 667	37 033	36 744	37 728	38 711
Canada	27 138	28 485	29 332	29 911	31 267	32 837	35 106	36 863	38 350	38 985	37 842	39 050	40 440
Chile	9 088	9 572	10 004	10 272	10 784	11 736	12 690	13 734	14 628	15 328	15 201	16 156	17 312
Czech Republic	14 782	15 549	16 833	17 578	18 768	20 081	21 268	23 268	25 457	25 872	25 617	25 258	26 054
Denmark	26 926	28 831	29 432	30 756	30 430	32 290	33 196	36 048	37 723	39 841	38 303	40 190	40 929
Estonia	8 752	9 865	10 691	11 967	13 371	14 753	16 531	19 146	21 583	22 155	19 791	20 393	21 938
Finland	23 613	25 674	26 531	27 531	27 616	29 863	30 708	33 140	36 167	38 080	35 655	36 307	37 642
France	23 612	25 249	26 611	27 676	27 283	28 185	29 554	31 426	33 144	34 167	33 676	34 256	35 133
Germany	24 994	25 768	26 707	27 446	28 354	29 684	31 117	33 552	35 559	37 115	36 052	37 430	39 187
Greece	16 877	18 249	19 744	21 401	22 497	23 861	24 348	26 803	27 709	29 569	29 384	28 444	26 934
Hungary	11 059	11 884	13 394	14 669	15 344	16 188	16 975	18 299	18 933	20 432	20 157	20 556	21 547
Iceland	28 632	28 849	30 438	31 084	30 776	33 731	34 992	35 831	37 171	39 521	36 666	35 593	36 084
Ireland	26 176	28 932	30 776	33 274	34 768	36 796	38 896	42 522	45 418	42 575	39 754	40 478	..
Israel	21 333	23 487	23 400	23 468	22 195	23 497	23 256	23 872	25 449	25 481	25 479	26 531	..
Italy	24 345	25 758	27 276	26 942	27 271	27 528	28 280	30 399	32 056	33 372	32 250	31 911	32 939
Japan	24 600	25 958	26 567	27 233	27 966	29 327	30 443	31 796	33 370	33 592	32 119	33 785	..
Korea	15 601	17 197	18 151	19 656	20 180	21 624	22 783	24 247	26 102	26 689	26 931	28 797	30 254
Luxembourg	49 072	53 662	53 923	57 559	60 728	64 998	68 372	78 573	84 559	89 156	82 981	86 269	89 801
Mexico	9 259	10 042	10 134	10 396	10 882	11 529	12 461	13 741	14 486	15 267	14 343	15 195	..
Netherlands	26 933	29 414	30 783	31 943	31 705	33 197	35 111	38 088	40 736	42 929	41 094	42 196	42 847
New Zealand	20 165	21 036	22 017	22 775	23 433	24 498	25 219	27 020	28 600	29 077	29 386	29 711	..
Norway	29 800	36 137	37 085	37 052	38 262	42 479	47 640	53 846	55 874	61 332	54 713	57 259	61 870
Poland	9 996	10 570	10 948	11 563	11 986	13 010	13 786	15 077	16 759	18 024	18 926	19 908	..
Portugal	16 744	17 797	18 507	19 146	19 456	19 854	21 369	22 967	24 201	24 939	24 938	25 444	25 352
Slovak Republic	10 407	10 983	12 069	12 966	13 599	14 654	16 175	18 383	20 876	23 214	22 583	23 264	24 018
Slovenia	16 707	17 554	18 438	19 759	20 516	22 268	23 472	25 444	27 218	29 065	27 153	26 941	27 402
Spain	19 824	21 314	22 578	24 068	24 755	25 956	27 392	30 406	32 233	33 130	32 150	31 904	32 501
Sweden	25 976	27 957	28 226	29 278	30 420	32 494	32 701	35 703	38 478	39 613	37 339	39 346	41 348
Switzerland	30 626	32 403	33 062	34 354	34 245	35 593	36 648	40 537	44 362	47 552	46 343	48 657	..
Turkey	8 171	9 172	8 612	8 667	8 791	10 162	11 391	12 895	13 894	15 025	14 443	15 604	..
United Kingdom	24 253	26 072	27 568	28 884	29 845	31 766	32 732	34 999	35 736	35 882	34 487	35 687	35 441
United States	33 298	35 050	35 866	36 755	38 128	40 197	42 414	44 522	46 227	46 647	45 087	46 588	..
EU 27	20 607	21 912	23 045	23 968	24 521	25 707	26 868	29 070	30 770	31 976	31 142	31 784	32 721
OECD	23 002	24 404	25 185	25 958	26 715	28 135	29 573	31 517	33 087	33 882	32 860	33 971	..
Brazil	6 861	7 204	7 354	7 560	7 698	8 231	8 603	9 166	9 900	10 528	10 453	11 239	..
China	2 163	2 378	2 615	2 881	3 217	3 614	4 102	4 749	5 554	6 189	6 786	7 519	..
India	1 447	1 518	1 585	1 657	1 779	1 942	2 153	2 402	2 677	2 862	3 039	3 339	..
Indonesia	2 243	2 441	2 552	2 674	2 825	3 005	3 207	3 449	3 727	3 987	4 155	4 394	..
Russian Federation	5 895	6 798	7 336	8 010	9 231	10 228	11 826	14 923	16 729	20 268	18 892	19 833	..
South Africa	6 322	6 640	6 897	7 184	7 478	8 000	8 654	9 336	10 049	10 453	10 238	10 498	..

StatLink http://dx.doi.org/10.1787/888932706356

GDP per capita

US dollars, current prices and PPPs, 2011

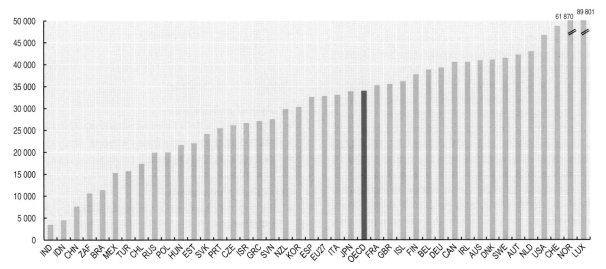

StatLink http://dx.doi.org/10.1787/888932706375

EVOLUTION OF GDP

Changes in the size of economies are usually measured by changes in the volume (often referred to as real) levels of GDP. Real reflects the fact that changes in GDP due to inflation are removed. This provides a measure of changes in the volume of production of an economy.

Definition

Converting nominal values of GDP to real values requires a set of detailed price indices, implicitly or directly collected. When applied to the nominal value of transactions, the corresponding volume changes can be captured. Since the 1993 *System of National Accounts* it has been recommended that weights should be representative of the periods for which growth rates are calculated. This means that new weights should be introduced every year, giving rise to chain-linked (volume) indices.

Comparability

All countries compile data according to the 1993 SNA "System of National Accounts, 1993" with the exception of Australia where data are compiled according to the new 2008 SNA. It's important to note however that differences between the 2008 SNA and the 1993 SNA do not have a significant impact of the comparability of the indicators presented here and this implies that data are highly comparable across countries. However, there is generally some variability in how countries calculate their volume

estimates of GDP, particularly in respect of services produced by government such as health and education.

With the exception of Mexico, all OECD countries derive their annual estimates of real GDP using annually chain-linked volume indices (that is the weights are updated every year). Mexico, like many non-OECD countries, revise their weights less frequently.

Real GDP growth
Annual growth in percentage

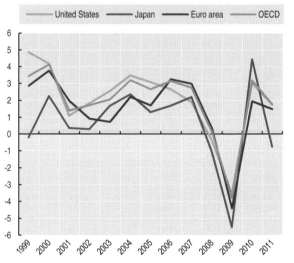

StatLink http://dx.doi.org/10.1787/888932706432

Sources
- OECD (2012), *National Accounts of OECD Countries*, OECD Publishing.
- For non-member countries: national sources.

Further information

Analytical publications
- OECD (2012), *OECD Economic Outlook*, OECD Publishing.
- OECD (2012), *Economic Policy Reforms*, OECD Publishing.
- OECD (2012), *OECD Journal: Economic Studies*, OECD Publishing.

Statistical publications
- OECD (2011), *National Accounts at a Glance*, OECD Publishing.

Online databases
- *OECD National Accounts Statistics*.
- *OECD Economic Outlook: Statistics and Projections*.

Websites
- OECD Economic Outlook – Sources and Methods, *www.oecd.org/eco/sources-and-methods*.

Real GDP growth

Annual growth in percentage

	1999	2000	2001	2002	2003	2004	2005	2006	2007	2008	2009	2010	2011
Australia	3.8	1.9	3.9	3.2	4.1	3.2	3.0	3.8	3.8	1.4	2.3	2.1	1.8
Austria	3.5	3.7	0.9	1.7	0.9	2.6	2.4	3.7	3.7	1.4	-3.8	2.1	2.7
Belgium	3.5	3.7	0.8	1.4	0.8	3.3	1.8	2.7	2.9	1.0	-2.8	2.2	1.9
Canada	5.5	5.2	1.8	2.9	1.9	3.1	3.0	2.8	2.2	0.7	-2.8	3.2	2.5
Chile	-0.7	4.5	3.3	2.2	4.0	7.0	6.2	5.7	5.2	3.3	-1.0	6.1	6.0
Czech Republic	1.7	4.2	3.1	2.1	3.8	4.7	6.8	7.0	5.7	3.1	-4.7	2.7	1.7
Denmark	2.6	3.5	0.7	0.5	0.4	2.3	2.4	3.4	1.6	-0.8	-5.8	1.3	0.8
Estonia	-0.3	9.7	6.3	6.6	7.8	6.3	8.9	10.1	7.5	-3.7	-14.3	2.3	7.6
Finland	3.9	5.3	2.3	1.8	2.0	4.1	2.9	4.4	5.3	0.3	-8.5	3.3	2.7
France	3.3	3.7	1.8	0.9	0.9	2.5	1.8	2.5	2.3	-0.1	-3.1	1.7	1.7
Germany	1.9	3.1	1.5	0.0	-0.4	1.2	0.7	3.7	3.3	1.1	-5.1	3.7	3.0
Greece	3.4	4.5	4.2	3.4	5.9	4.4	2.3	5.5	3.0	-0.2	-3.2	-3.5	-6.9
Hungary	3.2	4.2	3.7	4.5	3.9	4.8	4.0	3.9	0.1	0.9	-6.8	1.3	1.6
Iceland	4.1	4.3	3.9	0.1	2.4	7.8	7.2	4.7	6.0	1.3	-6.8	-4.0	3.1
Ireland	9.9	9.3	4.8	5.9	4.2	4.5	5.3	5.3	5.2	-3.0	-7.0	-0.4	0.7
Israel	3.4	9.3	-0.2	-0.6	1.5	4.8	4.9	5.6	5.5	4.0	0.8	4.8	4.8
Italy	1.5	3.7	1.9	0.5	0.0	1.7	0.9	2.2	1.7	-1.2	-5.5	1.8	0.4
Japan	-0.2	2.3	0.4	0.3	1.7	2.4	1.3	1.7	2.2	-1.0	-5.5	4.4	-0.7
Korea	10.7	8.8	4.0	7.2	2.8	4.6	4.0	5.2	5.1	2.3	0.3	6.3	3.6
Luxembourg	8.4	8.4	2.5	4.1	1.5	4.4	5.4	5.0	6.6	0.8	-5.3	2.7	1.6
Mexico	3.8	6.6	0.0	0.8	1.4	4.1	3.3	5.1	3.4	1.2	-6.3	5.6	3.9
Netherlands	4.7	3.9	1.9	0.1	0.3	2.2	2.0	3.4	3.9	1.8	-3.5	1.7	1.2
New Zealand	5.2	2.5	3.5	4.9	3.9	3.6	3.2	2.2	2.9	-1.1	0.8	1.2	0.3
Norway	2.0	3.3	2.0	1.5	1.0	4.0	2.6	2.5	2.7	0.0	-1.7	0.7	1.4
Poland	4.5	4.3	1.2	1.4	3.9	5.3	3.6	6.2	6.8	5.1	1.6	3.9	4.3
Portugal	4.1	3.9	2.0	0.8	-0.9	1.6	0.8	1.4	2.4	0.0	-2.9	1.4	-1.6
Slovak Republic	0.0	1.4	3.5	4.6	4.8	5.1	6.7	8.3	10.5	5.8	-4.9	4.2	3.3
Slovenia	5.3	4.3	2.9	3.8	2.9	4.4	4.0	5.8	6.9	3.6	-8.0	1.4	-0.2
Spain	4.7	5.0	3.7	2.7	3.1	3.3	3.6	4.1	3.5	0.9	-3.7	-0.1	0.7
Sweden	4.7	4.5	1.3	2.5	2.3	4.2	3.2	4.3	3.3	-0.6	-5.0	6.2	3.9
Switzerland	1.4	3.7	1.2	0.2	0.0	2.4	2.7	3.8	3.8	2.2	-1.9	3.0	2.1
Turkey	-3.4	6.8	-5.7	6.2	5.3	9.4	8.4	6.9	4.7	0.7	-4.8	9.2	8.5
United Kingdom	3.2	4.2	2.9	2.4	3.8	2.9	2.8	2.6	3.6	-1.0	-4.0	1.8	0.8
United States	4.9	4.2	1.1	1.8	2.6	3.5	3.1	2.7	1.9	-0.4	-3.5	3.0	1.7
Euro area	2.9	3.8	2.0	0.9	0.7	2.2	1.7	3.3	3.0	0.4	-4.4	2.0	1.5
EU 27	3.0	3.9	2.2	1.3	1.4	2.5	2.0	3.3	3.2	0.3	-4.4	2.1	1.5
OECD	3.4	4.1	1.4	1.7	2.1	3.2	2.7	3.2	2.8	0.1	-3.8	3.2	1.8
Brazil	0.3	4.3	1.3	2.7	1.1	5.7	3.2	4.0	6.1	5.2	-0.6	7.5	..
China	7.6	8.4	8.3	9.1	10.0	10.1	11.3	12.7	14.2	9.6	9.2	10.3	..
India	3.3	4.4	3.9	4.6	6.9	8.1	9.2	9.7	9.9	6.2	6.8	10.4	..
Indonesia	0.8	5.4	3.6	4.5	4.8	5.0	5.7	5.5	6.3	6.0	4.6	6.1	..
Russian Federation	6.4	10.0	5.1	4.7	7.3	7.2	6.4	8.2	8.5	5.2	-7.8	4.3	4.3
South Africa	2.4	4.2	2.7	3.7	2.9	4.6	5.3	5.6	5.6	3.6	-1.7	2.8	..

StatLink http://dx.doi.org/10.1787/888932706394

Real GDP growth

Average annual growth in percentage

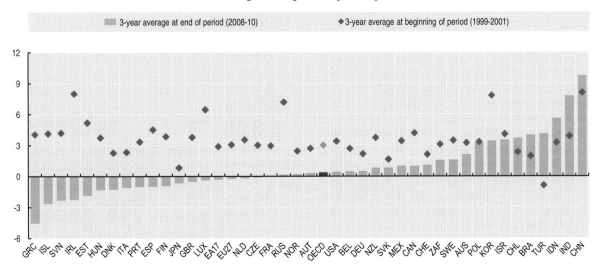

StatLink http://dx.doi.org/10.1787/888932706413

GDP BY REGION

Disparities in economic performance across OECD countries are often smaller than those prevailing among regions of the same country. Further, these regional disparities have persisted over time, even when economic disparities among countries were falling.

Definition

Regional inequalities in economic performance are here measured by regional GDP per capita or GDP per worker. The GDP of a country or a region is measured according to the definitions of the *1993 System of National Accounts*.

The Gini index is a measure of inequality among all regions of a given country. The index takes on values between 0 and 1, with zero interpreted as no disparity. It assigns equal weight to each region regardless of its size; therefore differences in the values of the index among countries may be partially due to differences in the average size of regions in each country.

While in the study of income inequality individuals are the obvious unit of analysis, there is no such straightforward parallel in regional economics. The size of regions varies significantly both within and between countries so that the degree of geographic concentration and territorial disparity depends on the very definition of a region. Typically, as the size of a region increases, territorial differences tend to be averaged out and disparities to decrease.

Comparability

As for the other regional statistics, comparability is affected by differences in the meaning of the word "region". The word "region" can mean very different things both within and among countries, with significant differences in terms of area and population. To address this issue, the OECD has classified regions within each member country based on two levels: territorial level 2 (TL2, large regions) and territorial level 3 (TL3, small regions). All the data shown here refer to small regions with the exception of Australia, Brazil, Canada, Chile, China, India, Mexico, the Russian Federation, South Africa, Turkey and the United States.

"2009 or latest available year" refers to 2009 in all countries except Chile (2007), Norway (2007), Sweden (2007) and Turkey (2008). "1995-2009 or latest available period" refers to data from 1995 to 2009 in all countries except Estonia (1996-2009), Norway (1997-2007), Poland (1999-2009), Turkey (2004-08), China (2004-08), India (2000-08), the Russian Federation (2005-08) and Sweden (1995-2007).

Overview

Regional disparities in productivity within countries are often substantial. Large differences are found in Chile, Turkey, the United Kingdom and France.

Typically a small number of regions account for a large part of national GDP growth. On average, 42% of OECD growth was accounted for by just 10% of regions over the period 1995-2009. At country level, the regional contribution to growth was very concentrated in Hungary, Greece, Sweden, Finland, Japan, Spain and the United Kingdom, and the Russian Federation among the non-OECD countries. In the above mentioned countries 10% of regions with the highest GDP increase were responsible for more than half of the national growth in 1995-2009.

The Gini index is a measure of inequality which assigns equal weight to each region of a country regardless of its size, while the number of people living in regions with low GDP per capita (under the national median), provide an indication of the different economic implications of disparities within a country. For example, while regional disparities as measured by the Gini index in GDP per capita are of the same magnitude in the Slovak Republic, Chile, Turkey and Estonia, the percentage of national population living in regions with low GDP per capita varies from almost 54% in the Slovak Republic to 23% in Estonia.

Sources
- *OECD Regional Database*.
- OECD (2011), *OECD Regions at a Glance*, OECD Publishing.

Further information

Analytical publications
- OECD (2012), *OECD Latin American Economic Outlook*, OECD Publishing.
- OECD (2012), *Promoting Growth in All Regions*, OECD Publishing.
- OECD (2012), *Southeast Asian Economic Outlook*, OECD Publishing.
- OECD (2011), *OECD Territorial Reviews*, OECD Publishing.
- OECD (2011), *Regional Outlook 2011*, OECD Publishing.
- OECD (2009), *How Regions Grow: Trends and Analysis*, OECD Publishing.
- OECD (2009), *Regions Matter: Economic Recovery, Innovation and Sustainable Growth*, OECD Publishing.

Online databases
- *OECD Regional Database*.

Websites
- Regional Statistics and Indicators, *www.oecd.org/gov/regional/statisticsindicators*.

Range in regional GDP per capita

As a percentage of national GDP per capita, 2009 or latest available year

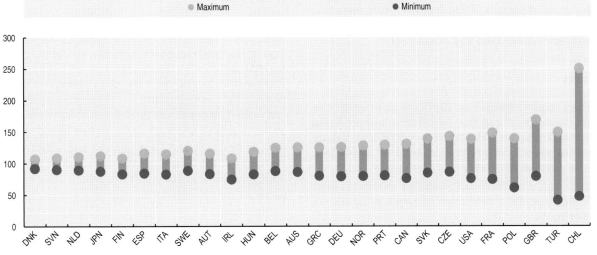

StatLink ⟨msl⟩ http://dx.doi.org/10.1787/888932706451

Share of GDP increase of each country due to the 10% of most dynamic regions

Percentage, 1995-2009 or latest available period

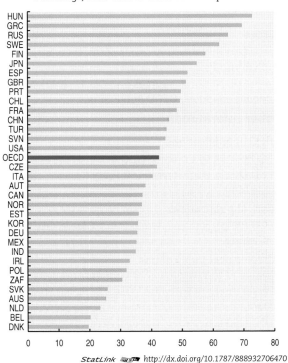

StatLink ⟨msl⟩ http://dx.doi.org/10.1787/888932706470

Gini index of regional GDP per capita and share of the population in regions with low GDP per capita

2009 or latest available year

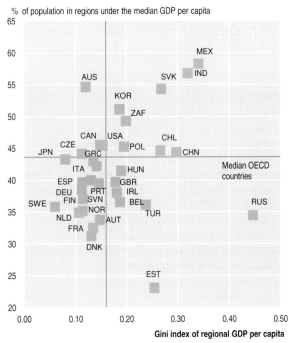

StatLink ⟨msl⟩ http://dx.doi.org/10.1787/888932706489

INVESTMENT RATES

Investment, or to be more precise, gross fixed capital formation, is an important determinant of future economic growth and an essential variable in economic analyses, such as analyses of demand and productivity.

Definition

Gross fixed capital formation (GFCF) is defined in the national accounts as acquisition less disposals of produced fixed assets. The relevant assets relate to products that are intended for use in the production of other goods and services for a period of more than a year.

Acquisition includes both purchases of assets (new or second-hand) and the construction of assets by producers for their own use.

The term produced assets signifies that only those assets that come into existence as a result of a production process recognised in the national accounts are included. The national accounts also record transactions in non-produced assets such as land, oil and mineral reserves for example; which are recorded as (acquisitions less disposals of) non-produced assets in the capital account and the balance sheet.

Acquisition prices of capital goods include transport and installation charges, as well as all specific taxes associated with purchase.

Comparability

When the *System of National Accounts (SNA)* was revised in 1993, the scope of GFCF was widened to include mineral exploration and computer software, as well as literary and artistic originals. Comparability of these items has improved in recent years but the coverage of the various items differs across countries. This applies particularly in the case of own-account production of software.

The scope of assets has been widened in the 2008 SNA to include Research and Development and military weapons systems but the figures contained here do not reflect these additions (except for Australia which follows the *2008 System of National Accounts*).

Overview

Investment over the period 2008-10 fell on average by 4.2% per year for the OECD as a whole, largely reflecting the retrenchment in investment that occurred at the height of the recent crisis, with investment volumes falling by more than 12% in 2009. Australia was the only country in the OECD to record investment growth (3%) in 2009. Ireland, Iceland and Greece all recorded annual average falls in investment of around 20% in the period 2008-10. As a consequence, the levels of investments in 2010 were less than half of the 2007 levels in these countries.

In 2011, investment growth rates were highest in Estonia (26.8%), Turkey (18.3%), Chile (17.6%) and Iceland (13.4%), as a consequence of which Estonia and Iceland managed to regain some of the dramatic drop in investment in the previous three year period. On the other hand, investment contracted by more than 10% in Portugal and Slovenia in 2011, and by more 20% in Greece. In the latter country, the investment level in 2011 is little more than half of the 2007 level.

Sources
- OECD (2012), *National Accounts of OECD Countries*, OECD Publishing.
- For Brazil: National sources and OECD (2011), *Main Economic Indicators*, OECD Publishing.

Further information

Analytical publications
- OECD (2012), *OECD Economic Outlook*, OECD Publishing.
- OECD (2012), *OECD Investment Policy Reviews*, OECD Publishing.

Statistical publications
- OECD (2011), *National Accounts at a Glance*, OECD Publishing.

Methodological publications
- Ahmad, N. (2004), "Towards More Harmonised Estimates of Investment in Software", *OECD Economic Studies*, No. 37, 2003/2.
- OECD (2000), *System of National Accounts, 1993 – Glossary*, OECD Publishing.
- United Nations, OECD, International Monetary Fund and Eurostat (eds.) (2010), *System of National Accounts 2008*, United Nations, Geneva.

Websites
- OECD Economic Outlook – Sources and Methods, *www.oecd.org/eco/sources-and-methods*.

Gross fixed capital formation

Annual growth in percentage

	1999	2000	2001	2002	2003	2004	2005	2006	2007	2008	2009	2010	2011
Australia	8.2	-7.9	9.0	12.7	9.0	6.9	9.3	5.1	9.6	1.4	2.3	4.1	..
Austria	1.2	5.2	-1.0	-4.0	4.8	0.6	0.6	0.5	3.6	0.7	-7.8	0.8	7.3
Belgium	2.6	5.1	1.0	-4.5	0.1	7.8	6.4	2.5	6.3	1.9	-7.9	-0.8	5.2
Canada	7.3	4.7	4.0	1.6	6.2	7.8	9.3	7.1	3.5	2.0	-13.0	10.0	..
Chile	-18.2	8.9	4.3	1.5	5.7	11.4	23.5	4.3	10.8	17.9	-12.1	14.3	17.6
Czech Republic	-2.1	6.5	4.5	3.8	0.6	3.0	6.0	5.8	13.2	4.1	-11.5	0.1	-1.2
Denmark	-0.1	7.6	-1.4	0.1	-0.2	3.9	4.7	14.3	0.4	-4.2	-13.4	-3.8	0.2
Estonia	-15.5	16.7	13.1	24.2	16.7	6.0	15.2	23.0	9.3	-15.1	-37.9	-9.1	26.8
Finland	3.3	6.4	2.9	-3.7	3.0	4.9	3.6	1.9	10.7	-0.6	-13.2	1.9	6.8
France	8.5	6.8	2.2	-1.9	2.2	3.4	4.4	4.0	6.3	0.3	-10.6	1.2	3.5
Germany	4.5	2.6	-3.3	-6.1	-1.2	-0.2	0.8	8.2	4.7	1.7	-11.4	5.5	6.4
Greece	11.0	8.0	4.8	9.5	11.8	0.4	-6.3	20.4	5.4	-6.7	-15.2	-15.0	-20.7
Hungary	7.4	6.0	1.9	7.4	1.5	7.2	4.5	-2.7	3.8	2.9	-11.0	-9.7	-5.5
Iceland	-4.1	11.8	-4.3	-14.0	11.1	28.7	34.4	24.4	-12.2	-20.0	-51.6	-8.1	13.4
Ireland	13.4	6.2	0.2	2.5	6.5	9.5	14.7	4.4	2.3	-10.1	-28.8	-25.1	..
Israel	0.4	3.4	-3.4	-6.7	-4.1	0.0	3.5	13.1	14.6	4.2	-4.1	13.6	..
Italy	4.0	6.4	2.7	3.4	-1.3	2.0	1.3	3.4	1.8	-3.7	-11.7	2.1	-1.9
Japan	-0.6	0.7	-2.1	-4.9	0.2	0.4	0.8	1.5	0.3	-4.1	-10.6	-0.2	..
Korea	8.7	12.3	0.3	7.1	4.4	2.1	1.9	3.4	4.2	-1.9	-1.0	5.8	-1.1
Luxembourg	22.0	-4.7	8.8	5.5	6.3	2.7	2.5	3.8	17.9	3.2	-13.0	3.0	7.7
Mexico	7.7	11.4	-5.6	-0.6	0.4	8.0	7.5	9.9	6.9	5.5	-11.8	6.4	..
Netherlands	8.7	0.6	0.2	-4.5	-1.5	-1.6	3.7	7.5	5.5	4.5	-10.2	-4.4	5.8
New Zealand	10.6	0.4	6.8	7.8	12.9	7.6	5.2	-2.3	4.7	-5.2	-12.0	2.2	..
Norway	-5.4	-3.5	-1.1	-1.1	0.8	11.1	13.5	9.8	11.4	0.2	-7.5	-5.2	6.4
Poland	6.6	2.7	-9.7	-6.3	-0.1	6.4	6.5	14.9	17.6	9.6	-1.2	-0.4	8.1
Portugal	6.0	3.9	0.6	-3.2	-7.1	0.0	-0.5	-1.3	2.6	-0.3	-8.6	-4.1	-11.4
Slovak Republic	-15.7	-9.6	12.9	0.2	-2.7	4.8	17.5	9.3	9.1	1.0	-19.7	12.4	5.7
Slovenia	14.7	2.6	1.3	0.3	7.6	5.0	3.0	10.4	13.3	7.8	-23.3	-8.3	-10.7
Spain	10.4	6.6	4.8	3.4	5.9	5.1	7.1	7.1	4.5	-4.7	-16.6	-6.3	..
Sweden	8.7	5.7	0.5	-1.3	1.6	5.7	8.1	9.2	8.9	1.4	-15.5	7.7	6.2
Switzerland	2.3	4.7	-3.3	-1.0	-2.0	4.2	4.1	5.3	5.4	0.7	-8.0	4.8	..
Turkey	-16.2	17.5	-30.0	14.7	14.2	28.4	17.4	13.3	3.1	-6.2	-19.0	30.5	18.3
United Kingdom	2.8	2.6	2.7	3.6	1.1	5.1	2.4	6.4	8.1	-4.8	-13.4	3.1	-1.2
United States	9.1	6.9	-1.1	-3.0	3.2	6.2	5.3	2.3	-1.6	-5.8	-16.0	1.8	..
Euro area	6.0	4.7	0.7	-1.5	1.1	2.2	3.2	5.7	4.7	-1.1	-12.4	0.0	1.4
EU 27	5.4	4.5	0.8	-0.7	1.1	3.0	3.5	6.4	5.9	-0.9	-12.7	0.2	1.4
OECD	5.2	5.2	-0.9	-1.0	2.4	4.6	4.6	4.6	2.8	-2.5	-12.3	2.5	..
Brazil	..	..	..	..	..	..	..	..	..	..	..	..	..
China	..	..	..	..	..	..	..	..	..	..	..	..	..
India	..	..	..	..	..	..	..	..	..	..	..	..	..
Indonesia	-18.2	16.7	6.5	4.7	0.6	14.7	10.9	2.6	9.3	11.9	3.3	8.5	..
Russian Federation	8.1	16.6	10.9	3.1	13.9	12.0	10.2	17.9	21.1	9.7	-14.7	6.4	8.4
South Africa	-7.6	3.9	2.8	3.5	10.2	12.9	11.0	12.1	14.0	14.1	-2.2	-3.7	..

StatLink http://dx.doi.org/10.1787/888932706508

Gross fixed capital formation

Average annual growth in percentage

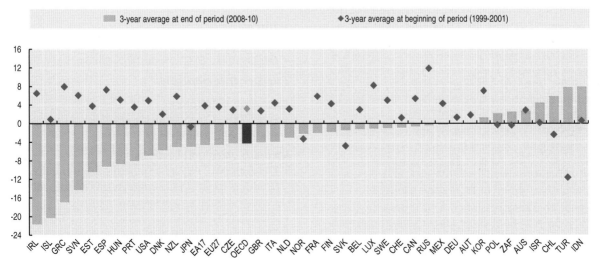

StatLink http://dx.doi.org/10.1787/888932706527

LABOUR PRODUCTIVITY LEVELS

Productivity is a measure of the efficiency with which available resources are used in production. Labour productivity, together with use of labour resources, is one of the main determinants of living standards.

Definition

Labour productivity is measured as GDP per hour worked. GDP data at current prices are from the *OECD Annual National Accounts*. For international comparisons and to obtain a volume or "real" measure of GDP, data are converted to a common currency using the OECD Purchasing Power Parities (PPPs) for the year 2011. Hours worked data are derived from two sources, the *OECD Annual National Accounts* and the *OECD Employment Outlook*.

The indicator hereafter shows labour productivity and income levels in each country with respect to the labour productivity and income levels of the United States. Differences in GDP per capita levels with respect to the United States can be decomposed into differences in labour productivity levels and differences in the extent of labour utilisation, measured as the number of hours worked per capita.

Overview

In 2011, Norway and Luxembourg had the highest levels of labour productivity, followed by Ireland. Norway's level of productivity (GDP per hour worked) was roughly five times that of Mexico's. Countries with low labour productivity levels in 2011, such as Mexico and Chile, often record the highest average working time (well above 2 000 hours annually) among the countries presented.

In the same year, differences in per capita GDP with respect to the United States varied a lot across countries. Much of the differences observed in GDP per capita reflect differences in labour productivity, with gaps relative to the United States ranging between 65 percentage points or more in Chile and Mexico, to 15 percentage points or less in Austria, Ireland, the Netherlands and several European countries. In 2011, like in 2010, Norway and Luxembourg maintained substantial positive gaps in GDP per capita and in GDP per hour worked relative to the United States.

Cross-country differences in labour utilisation reflect high unemployment and low participation rates of the working age population, on the one hand, and lower working hours among employed people, on the other hand. Labour utilisation cross-country differences relative to the United States were significantly smaller than in the case of GDP per capita and per hour worked. In Belgium, France and Ireland, lower labour utilisation accounted for 92%, 88% and 159%, respectively, of the gap in GDP per capita relative to the US (*i.e.* for Belgium 18 points out of the 19 points gap in GDP per capita; for France, 23 points out of 27; for Ireland 21 points out of 13). In 2011, the contribution of lower labour utilisation in Turkey was about 34%.

Among the countries presented, 17 (the majority being non-EU countries) had higher labour utilisation levels than that of the United States, therefore contributing to narrow their gap in GDP per capita. This was notably the case of Australia, Canada, Iceland, Japan, Korea, Mexico, New Zealand, the Russian Federation and Switzerland.

Comparability

Comparisons of productivity and income levels across countries first require comparable data on output. All OECD countries have implemented the *1993 System of National Accounts*, except Australia that has already implemented the 2008 SNA. Second, in a number of countries, employment data are derived from labour force surveys that may not be entirely consistent with national account concepts; this reduces the comparability of labour utilisation across countries. Third, the measure of labour inputs also requires hours worked data, which are derived either from labour force surveys or from business surveys. Several OECD countries estimate hours worked from a combination of these sources or integrate these sources in a system of labour accounts, which is comparable to the national accounts. Cross-country comparability of hours worked remains limited, generating a margin of uncertainty in estimates of productivity levels.

Sources
- OECD (2012), *OECD National Accounts Statistics* (database).
- OECD (2012), *OECD Productivity Statistics* (database).

Further information

Analytical publications
- OECD (2011), *OECD Reviews of Labour Market and Social Policies*, OECD Publishing.

Methodological publications
- OECD (2004), "Clocking In (and Out): Several Facets of Working Time", *OECD Employment Outlook: 2004 Edition*, OECD Publishing. See also Annex I.A1.
- OECD (2001), *Measuring Productivity – OECD Manual: Measurement of Aggregate and Industry-level Productivity Growth*, OECD Publishing.

Websites
- OECD Compendium of Productivity Indicators, *www.oecd.org/statistics/productivity/compendium*.
- OECD Productivity, *www.oecd.org/statistics/productivity*.

GDP per hour worked

US dollars, current prices and PPPs, 2011

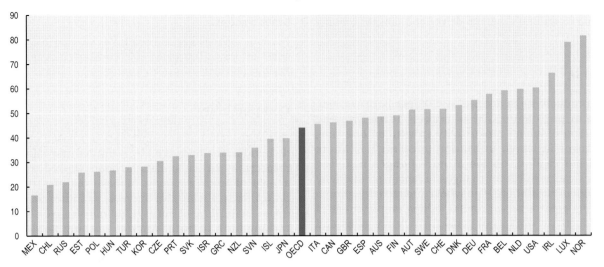

StatLink http://dx.doi.org/10.1787/888932706546

Levels of GDP per capita and labour productivity

Percentage point differences with respect to the United States, 2011

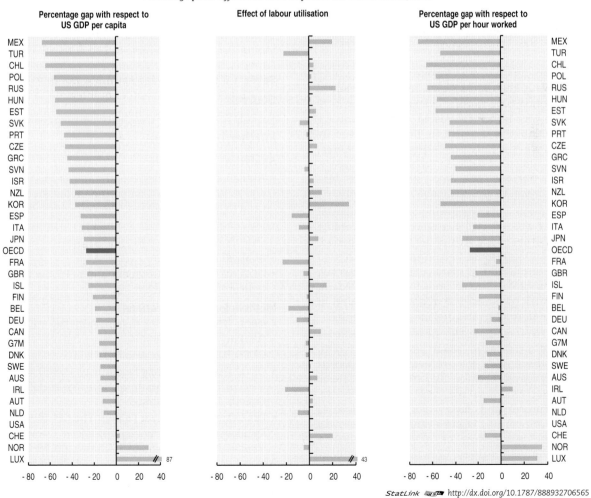

StatLink http://dx.doi.org/10.1787/888932706565

LABOUR PRODUCTIVITY GROWTH

Labour productivity growth is a key dimension of economic performance and an essential driver of changes in living standards.

Definition

Labour productivity is defined as GDP per hour worked. Growth in per capita GDP is broken down into the contribution of labour productivity growth, on one side, and changes in labour utilisation (measured as hours worked per capita), on the other. Changes in living standards can result from changes in labour productivity and in labour utilisation. High labour productivity growth can reflect greater use of capital, falling employment of low-productivity workers or general efficiency gains and innovation.

The indicators shown here are based on measures of GDP and population coming from the *OECD Annual National Accounts*. Actual hours worked are derived from either the *OECD Annual National Accounts* or the *OECD Employment Outlook*. Hours worked reflect regular hours worked by full-time and part-time workers, paid and unpaid overtime, hours worked in additional jobs, and time not worked because of public holidays, annual paid leaves, strikes and labour disputes, bad weather, economic conditions and other reasons.

For zone aggregates, GDP estimates have been converted to constant US dollars using 2005 constant Purchasing Power Parities (PPPs).

Comparability

Although national accounts data are based on common definitions, methods used by countries may differ in some respects. In particular, data on hours worked are based on a range of primary sources. In most countries, the data are drawn from labour force surveys, but other countries rely upon establishment surveys, administrative sources or a combination of both. Annual working hours for non-European countries are provided by national statistics offices. In general, these data are most suited for comparing changes rather than levels of hours worked across countries.

The estimates shown here are not adjusted for differences in the business cycle; cyclically adjusted estimates might show different patterns.

Overview

Over the period 2009 to 2011, average growth in GDP per capita was rather contrasted across countries. Highest growth was recorded in Turkey, followed by Chile, Estonia, the Russian Federation and Korea, whilst the greatest decrease occurred in Greece. Growth in income over the same period was essentially driven by growth in labour productivity.

The economic downturn following the global financial crisis of 2007 was reflected in most countries recording negative GDP per capita growth in the 2007-09 period. In some cases like Estonia, Iceland and Ireland, this led to a significant decline in labour utilisation. However, from 2009 to 2011, Estonia and, to a lesser extent, Iceland have shown evidence of a strong rebound in their labour utilisation rates; Ireland still lags behind.

Between 2009 and 2011, nearly all countries experienced increases in labour productivity growth. In some countries, the turnaround in labour productivity growth between 2007-09 and 2009-11 was high, notably this was the case for Luxembourg, Slovenia, Finland and Turkey. For other countries however, comparing labour productivity growth between the two periods of 2007-09 and 2009-11 revealed a different pattern. Growth in GDP per hour worked decreased in Australia, Iceland, Greece and New Zealand, whilst it saw a moderate upturn in Canada, Ireland, Spain and the United States.

Sources
- OECD (2012), *OECD Productivity Statistics* (database).

Further information

Analytical publications
- Ahmad, N., F. Lequiller, P. Marianna, D. Pilat, P. Schreyer and A. Wölfl (2003), "Comparing Labour Productivity Growth in the OECD Area: The Role of Measurement", *OECD Science, Technology and Industry Working Papers*, No. 2003/14.

Statistical publications
- OECD (2012), OECD Compendium of Productivity Indicators, OECD Publishing.

Methodological publications
- OECD (2004), "Clocking In (and Out): Several Facets of Working Time", *OECD Employment Outlook: 2004 Edition*, OECD Publishing. See also Annex I.A1.
- OECD (2001), *Measuring Productivity – OECD Manual: Measurement of Aggregate and Industry-level Productivity Growth*, OECD Publishing.
- Pilat, D. and P. Schreyer (2004), "The OECD Productivity Database – An Overview", *International Productivity Monitor*, No. 8, Spring, CSLS, Ottawa, pp. 59-65.

Websites
- OECD Compendium of Productivity Indicators, *www.oecd.org/statistics/productivity/compendium*.
- OECD Productivity, *www.oecd.org/statistics/productivity*.

Contribution of labour productivity and labour utilisation to GDP per capita

Percentage change, annual rate

	GDP per capita			GDP per hour worked			Labour utilisation		
	2001-07	2007-09	2009-11	2001-07	2007-09	2009-11	2001-07	2007-09	2009-11
Australia	2.0	-0.2	0.7	1.0	1.1	-0.1	1.0	-1.3	0.8
Austria	1.9	-1.6	2.3	2.0	0.0	1.7	-0.1	-1.6	0.6
Belgium	1.6	-1.7	1.2	1.5	-1.4	0.1	0.1	-0.3	1.1
Canada	1.6	-2.2	1.7	1.0	0.2	0.8	0.6	-2.4	0.9
Chile	3.9	0.1	5.0	3.1	1.3	2.8	0.8	-1.2	2.2
Czech Republic	4.8	-1.7	1.9	4.5	-0.6	2.6	0.4	-1.1	-0.7
Denmark	1.4	-3.9	0.6	1.2	-2.2	2.2	0.2	-1.7	-1.6
Estonia	8.2	-9.1	4.9	5.8	0.0	1.5	2.4	-9.0	3.4
Finland	3.1	-4.6	2.8	2.5	-3.1	2.9	0.5	-1.6	-0.1
France	1.1	-2.2	1.1	1.5	-0.8	1.4	-0.4	-1.4	-0.2
Germany	1.4	-1.8	3.4	1.6	-1.3	1.4	-0.2	-0.5	2.0
Greece	3.7	-2.1	-5.3	3.1	-0.9	-1.8	0.6	-1.2	-3.5
Hungary	3.7	-2.9	1.7	3.8	-0.6	0.8	0.0	-2.3	0.8
Iceland	3.2	-4.1	-0.5	3.4	2.1	-1.3	-0.2	-6.1	0.8
Ireland	2.9	-6.1	-0.1	2.5	2.6	3.1	0.4	-8.7	-3.2
Israel	1.7	0.5	3.0	1.5	0.0	1.7	0.2	0.6	1.3
Italy	0.5	-4.0	0.7	0.2	-1.4	1.2	0.3	-2.6	-0.6
Japan	1.5	-3.2	1.3	1.6	-0.3	1.7	-0.1	-2.9	-0.4
Korea	4.3	0.7	4.3	4.7	2.8	4.3	-0.4	-2.1	0.1
Luxembourg	3.1	-4.1	0.0	2.8	-7.5	0.5	0.2	3.5	-0.5
Mexico	2.0	-3.4	3.8	1.1	-2.9	1.3	0.8	-0.5	2.4
Netherlands	1.6	-1.3	0.9	1.8	-1.1	1.6	-0.1	-0.2	-0.7
New Zealand	2.0	-1.2	-0.3	1.2	0.9	-1.1	0.8	-2.0	0.8
Norway	1.6	-2.1	-0.2	1.0	-1.7	-0.1	0.7	-0.4	-0.1
Poland	4.6	3.3	4.0	3.3	2.0	3.9	1.3	1.3	0.2
Portugal	0.5	-1.6	-0.2	1.4	-0.2	2.5	-0.9	-1.4	-2.7
Slovak Republic	6.6	0.1	3.5	5.5	0.0	3.3	1.0	0.1	0.3
Slovenia	4.4	-2.9	0.3	4.0	-3.2	3.0	0.4	0.3	-2.7
Spain	1.7	-2.6	0.1	0.7	1.8	2.0	1.0	-4.4	-1.9
Sweden	2.8	-3.6	4.2	2.9	-2.0	2.2	0.0	-1.7	1.9
Switzerland	1.3	-1.1	2.0	1.1	-0.8	1.4	0.2	-0.3	0.5
Turkey	5.4	-3.2	7.4	7.7	-2.6	2.8	-2.3	-0.7	4.6
United Kingdom	2.3	-3.4	0.6	2.3	-1.5	1.9	0.1	-1.9	-1.2
United States	1.6	-2.8	1.5	2.0	1.4	1.9	-0.4	-4.2	-0.4
EU 27	..	..	..	..	..	..	..	..	..
OECD	1.9	-2.5	1.8	1.9	-0.2	1.4	0.0	-2.3	0.4
Brazil	..	..	..	..	..	..	..	..	..
China	..	..	..	..	..	..	..	..	..
India	..	..	..	..	..	..	..	..	..
Indonesia	..	..	..	..	..	..	..	..	..
Russian Federation	7.5	-1.4	4.8	5.4	0.1	4.1	2.1	-1.5	0.7
South Africa	..	..	..	..	..	..	..	..	..

StatLink ᴹᔆᴸ http://dx.doi.org/10.1787/888932706584

Growth in GDP per hour worked

Average annual growth in percentage

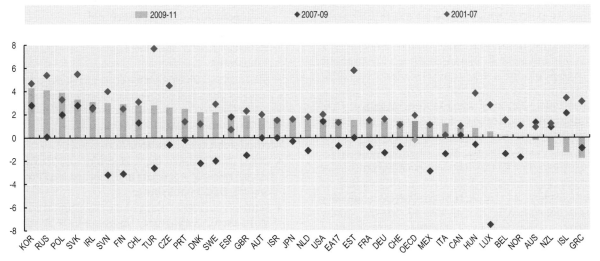

StatLink ᴹᔆᴸ http://dx.doi.org/10.1787/888932706603

PRODUCTIVITY AND GROWTH ACCOUNTING

Economic growth can be increased either by raising the labour and capital inputs used in production, or by greater overall efficiency in how these inputs are used together, *i.e.* higher multi-factor productivity (MFP). Growth accounting involves breaking down GDP growth into the contribution of labour inputs, capital inputs and MFP growth.

Definition

Growth accounting explains output growth by the rates of change of labour and capital inputs and by MFP growth, computed as a residual. In these calculations, the contribution of labour (capital) to GDP growth is measured as the speed with which labour (capital) input grows, multiplied by the share of labour (capital) in total costs.

In the tables and graphs, the contribution of capital to GDP growth is broken down into Information and Communication Technologies (ICT) capital (which includes hardware, communication and software) and non-ICT capital (transport equipment and non-residential construction; products of agriculture, metal products and machinery other than hardware and communication equipment; and other products of non-residential gross fixed capital formation).

Comparability

The appropriate measure for capital input in the growth accounting framework is the flow of productive services that can be drawn from the cumulative stock of past investments in capital assets. These services are estimated by the OECD using the rate of change of the "productive capital stock". This measure takes into account wear and tear and retirements, *i.e.*, reductions in the productive capacity of the fixed assets. The price of capital services for each type of asset is measured as their rental price. In principle, the latter could be directly observed if markets existed for capital services. In practice, however, rental prices have to be imputed for most assets, using the implicit rent that capital goods' owners "pay" themselves (or "user costs of capital"). There are differences in how countries deal with quality adjustment with possible consequences for the international comparability of price and volume measures of ICT investment. The OECD uses a set of "harmonised" deflators assuming that the ratios between ICT and non-ICT asset prices evolve in a similar manner across countries, using the United States as the benchmark.

Note: 1985-2007 for Denmark, the Netherlands and the United Kingdom, 1985-2008 for Australia and Japan, 1985-2009 for France and Sweden, 1991-2010 for Germany, 1995-2010 for Switzerland, 1995-2007 for Austria.

Overview

From 1985 to 2010, GDP growth in most OECD countries was for a large part driven by growth in capital and MFP. In many countries, growth in capital input accounted for around one third of GDP growth from 1985 to 2010. ICT capital services represented between 0.2 and 0.6 percentage points of growth in GDP, with largest contribution in Sweden, Denmark, the United Kingdom, Australia and the United States, and smallest in Ireland and Finland. Growth in labour input was important for a few countries over 1985-2010, notably Australia, Spain, and Canada, while Japan, Finland and Germany experienced negative GDP contributions from labour inputs. Over the same period, MFP growth was a significant source of GDP growth in Korea, Ireland and Finland, while MFP growth was very weak in Italy, Canada and Spain.

Averages for the period 1985-2010 mask volatility in growth drivers over time, though. For instance, the contribution of ICT capital slowed in the 2000s compared to the 1990s in all countries for which data are available, and MFP growth also slowed in most countries, with the Austria, Belgium, Japan, the Netherlands, Sweden, and the United States being noticeable exceptions.

Sources
- OECD (2012), *OECD Productivity Statistics* (database).

Further information

Analytical publications
- OECD (2011), *OECD Science, Technology and Industry Scoreboard 2011*, OECD Publishing.
- OECD (2011), *Public Servants as Partners for Growth, Toward a Stronger, Leaner and More Equitable Workforce*, OECD Publishing.
- OECD (2004), *Understanding Economic Growth: A Macro-level, Industry-level, and Firm-level Perspective*, OECD Publishing.
- OECD (2003), *The Sources of Economic Growth in OECD Countries*, OECD Publishing.

Methodological publications
- OECD (2001), *Measuring Productivity – OECD Manual: Measurement of Aggregate and Industry-level Productivity Growth*, OECD Publishing.
- Schreyer, P. (2004), "Capital Stocks, Capital Services and Multi-factor Productivity Measures", *OECD Economic Studies*, Vol. 2003/2.

Websites
- OECD Compendium of Productivity Indicators, *www.oecd.org/statistics/productivity/compendium*.
- OECD Productivity, *www.oecd.org/statistics/productivity*.

Contributions to GDP growth

Average annual growth in percentage, 1985-2010 (or closest comparable year)

	Labour input	ICT capital				Non-ICT capital	Multi-factor productivity	GDP growth
		IT equipment	Telecommunication equipment	Software	Total			
Australia	1.35	0.30	0.09	0.14	0.53	0.57	0.87	3.33
Austria	0.58	0.19	0.04	0.10	0.33	0.25	1.43	2.59
Belgium	..	..	..	..	..	..	..	..
Canada	1.04	0.21	0.07	0.13	0.42	0.65	0.35	2.44
Chile	..	..	..	..	..	..	..	..
Czech Republic	..	..	..	..	..	..	..	..
Denmark	0.24	0.35	0.02	0.19	0.56	0.43	0.74	1.99
Estonia	..	..	..	..	..	..	..	..
Finland	-0.17	0.07	0.04	0.13	0.24	0.33	1.67	2.06
France	0.19	0.11	0.05	0.16	0.32	0.38	0.97	1.85
Germany	-0.20	0.15	0.05	0.07	0.27	0.27	0.89	1.22
Greece	..	..	..	..	..	..	..	..
Hungary	..	..	..	..	..	..	..	..
Iceland	..	..	..	..	..	..	..	..
Ireland	0.87	0.12	0.05	0.06	0.23	0.62	2.72	4.43
Israel	..	..	..	..	..	..	..	..
Italy	0.24	0.01	0.18	0.09	0.28	0.50	0.36	1.38
Japan	-0.32	0.22	0.05	0.13	0.40	0.48	1.36	1.91
Korea	0.60	0.11	0.11	0.15	0.37	1.30	3.83	6.07
Luxembourg	..	..	..	..	..	..	..	..
Mexico	..	..	..	..	..	..	..	..
Netherlands	1.00	0.23	0.07	0.14	0.44	0.39	0.95	2.78
New Zealand	0.78	0.19	0.14	0.14	0.48	0.40	0.67	2.32
Norway	..	..	..	..	..	..	..	..
Poland	..	..	..	..	..	..	..	..
Portugal	..	..	..	..	..	..	..	..
Slovak Republic	..	..	..	..	..	..	..	..
Slovenia	..	..	..	..	..	..	..	..
Spain	1.20	0.16	0.11	0.12	0.39	0.82	0.36	2.78
Sweden	0.19	0.28	0.04	0.24	0.56	0.37	0.86	1.98
Switzerland	0.56	0.15	0.08	0.15	0.38	0.34	0.48	1.76
Turkey	..	..	..	..	..	..	..	..
United Kingdom	0.47	0.29	0.07	0.20	0.56	0.40	1.51	2.95
United States	0.67	0.25	0.10	0.19	0.53	0.32	1.06	2.58
EU 27	..	..	..	..	..	..	..	..
OECD	..	..	..	..	..	..	..	..
Brazil	..	..	..	..	..	..	..	..
China	..	..	..	..	..	..	..	..
India	..	..	..	..	..	..	..	..
Indonesia	..	..	..	..	..	..	..	..
Russian Federation	..	..	..	..	..	..	..	..
South Africa	..	..	..	..	..	..	..	..

StatLink http://dx.doi.org/10.1787/888932706622

Contributions to GDP growth

Average annual growth in percentage, 1985-2010 (or closest comparable year)

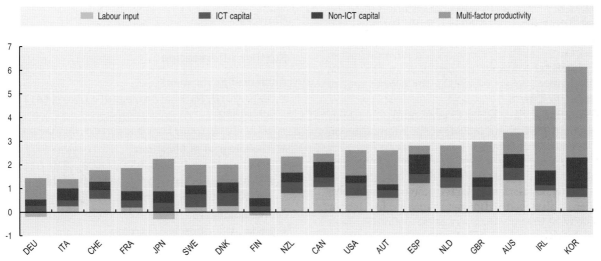

StatLink http://dx.doi.org/10.1787/888932706641

UNIT LABOUR COSTS

Unit labour costs (ULC) is the most commonly used indicator of competitiveness of the productive system of a country. Unit labour costs reflect the combined evolution of total labour costs per unit of labour input and of labour productivity, and can be an indicator of producer inflationary pressures.

Definition

Unit labour costs measure the average cost of labour per unit of output produced. They are calculated as the ratio of total labour costs to real output. Equivalently, they may be expressed as the ratio of total labour costs per hour worked to output per hour worked. Alternatively if information on total hours worked are not available, proxies such as employees and counterpart labour compensation data (compensation of employees) or the numbers of persons employed may be used. It can be shown therefore that labour productivity estimates are produced as a by-product of calculating unit labour costs. Data are presented as annual growth rates in unit labour costs for the economy as a whole.

Overview

Unit labour costs in the total economy increased at an annual average rate of 2.0% for the OECD area as a whole over the past decade. G7 countries and most of the early members of the Euro area have been able to increase their competitiveness vis-à-vis the OECD average, as reflected in lower growth in ULCs relative to other countries. The opposite is notably true for countries with relatively lower competitiveness such as Turkey, Mexico, and South Africa, as well as Estonia, Iceland, Hungary and Norway. Within Europe, some adjustment in competitiveness has occurred since the recent financial crisis in Ireland, Spain, Portugal and Greece, with temporary declines in ULCs witnessed in France and Italy. In Germany, improvements in competitiveness during the first half of the 2000s shows signs of being reversed in the second half of 2000s.

Comparing the data for ULC with those for labour productivity growth can provide some information on the sources for changes in competitiveness. For instance, over the past ten years, some countries, notably those countries with relatively low growth in ULCs, such as Germany, Israel, Korea, Poland and Sweden, displayed stronger growth in labour productivity than in ULCs. In these countries, high productivity growth coincided with wage moderation. In contrast, most of those countries for which one can observe a relative deterioration in competitiveness displayed weak growth in labour productivity.

Comparability

These indicators are compiled according to a common methodological framework so as to ensure comparability across countries. The primary data source is the OECD *Annual National Accounts*, where available, and where data are compiled on a similar basis across countries according to the 1993 *System of National Accounts*.

The use of different labour input measures (hours worked or number of employees depending on data availability) may reduce comparability across countries and time.

Unit labour costs, total economy
Average annual growth in percentage

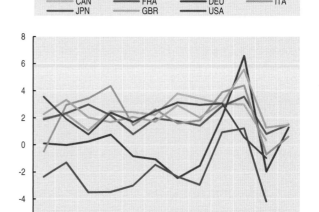

StatLink ⌐⌐⌐ http://dx.doi.org/10.1787/888932706698

Sources
- OECD (2012), *Main Economic Indicators*, OECD Publishing.

Further information

Analytical publications
- OECD (2011), *National Accounts at a Glance*, OECD Publishing.
- OECD (2012), *OECD Economic Surveys*, OECD Publishing.

Methodological publications
- McKenzie, R. and D. Brackfield (2008), "The OECD System of Unit Labour Cost and Related Indicators", *OECD Statistics Working Papers*, No. 2008/04.

Online databases
- *Labour, Main Economic Indicators*.

Websites
- OECD Compendium of Productivity Indicators, *www.oecd.org/statistics/productivity/compendium*.
- OECD Productivity, *www.oecd.org/statistics/productivity*.

Unit labour costs, total economy

Annual growth in percentage

	1999	2000	2001	2002	2003	2004	2005	2006	2007	2008	2009	2010	2011
Australia	3.0	2.1	1.3	3.2	2.0	3.9	3.4	4.6	4.5	2.5	0.2	5.6	..
Austria	0.3	-0.1	0.6	0.2	1.2	-0.8	0.5	0.7	0.6	3.1	5.3	-0.6	0.7
Belgium	1.6	0.6	3.7	2.4	0.9	-0.1	1.4	2.0	2.2	3.8	4.0	-0.1	2.3
Canada	-0.4	2.0	2.3	1.1	2.5	2.4	2.2	3.8	3.4	3.0	3.0	0.4	..
Chile	..	..	..	..	..	..	..	..	..	..	..	..	..
Czech Republic	1.6	2.7	5.5	5.9	4.1	2.5	-1.4	-0.4	2.2	2.7	2.7	-1.2	0.3
Denmark	1.6	0.2	4.2	3.7	2.2	1.1	2.8	2.3	4.5	5.3	5.4	-0.6	0.5
Estonia	3.5	2.5	3.7	4.5	4.4	5.9	3.5	9.7	17.5	13.0	2.1	-5.9	1.2
Finland	0.5	0.0	3.5	1.2	1.6	0.0	2.3	0.5	-0.2	6.7	9.7	-1.5	2.4
France	0.8	1.9	2.3	3.0	2.2	0.8	2.0	1.8	1.4	2.9	3.6	0.8	1.5
Germany	0.9	0.1	0.0	0.2	0.8	-0.8	-1.1	-2.5	-1.5	2.1	6.6	-2.0	1.3
Greece	4.2	1.5	-0.1	9.2	1.2	1.3	3.5	-1.9	3.9	6.5	6.2	-1.0	-4.1
Hungary	6.2	11.4	11.1	8.6	5.9	4.2	2.5	2.0	6.4	4.5	3.0	-3.8	3.5
Iceland	6.3	4.5	6.4	7.8	1.4	2.1	4.6	10.5	7.9	5.6	0.8	..	..
Ireland	1.3	5.0	5.1	1.3	5.0	3.8	7.1	4.3	4.0	6.3	-5.6	-7.2	..
Israel	6.6	0.8	3.9	1.1	-2.5	-2.4	1.1	4.0	0.7	2.1	0.3	..	..
Italy	1.4	-0.5	3.0	3.4	4.3	2.6	2.6	1.6	1.8	3.9	4.4	-0.7	0.6
Japan	-2.7	-2.4	-1.3	-3.5	-3.5	-3.0	-1.5	-2.3	-2.9	0.9	1.2	-4.2	..
Korea	-6.3	-0.2	5.5	1.2	5.3	1.1	2.4	0.2	0.7	2.2	0.7	-1.4	2.5
Luxembourg	1.0	3.4	5.7	2.3	1.5	1.6	1.9	0.8	1.4	6.2	8.5	1.5	..
Mexico	17.6	11.1	10.6	6.8	6.1	2.1	3.2	2.5	3.2	4.6	9.0	..	..
Netherlands	2.0	3.1	4.7	4.5	2.3	0.3	-0.3	0.7	1.6	2.3	4.7	-0.9	..
New Zealand	-2.5	0.3	3.1	2.0	3.2	4.7	4.5	4.5	4.3	6.6	2.1	..	..
Norway	4.3	2.0	4.3	3.5	2.0	0.9	3.3	6.9	8.3	9.2	4.4	3.5	4.6
Poland	3.9	5.4	3.2	-1.8	-2.8	-2.0	0.6	-0.7	2.6	7.8	1.9	1.2	..
Portugal	2.9	4.5	3.5	3.1	3.5	0.8	3.7	0.6	0.8	3.1	2.4	-1.5	..
Slovak Republic	4.2	11.0	0.9	4.3	8.0	3.4	4.4	0.5	0.8	3.7	7.1	-1.7	-0.4
Slovenia	5.2	6.9	8.4	5.4	4.3	3.5	1.6	0.8	2.5	6.5	8.7	0.0	0.3
Spain	2.0	2.7	3.0	3.0	3.1	2.6	3.6	3.1	3.9	4.7	1.0	-2.6	-1.9
Sweden	-1.2	4.5	5.3	0.6	0.4	-1.2	0.6	-0.7	4.1	2.6	4.9	-2.4	-1.3
Switzerland	1.2	1.0	4.7	2.1	0.4	-2.3	1.1	0.6	1.6	2.8	4.5	-2.0	..
Turkey	82.4	33.1	49.9	30.0	21.2	2.2	0.9	4.9	..	..	..	..	..
United Kingdom	2.8	2.3	3.3	2.0	1.7	2.1	1.7	2.9	2.0	3.1	5.6	1.3	1.5
United States	1.2	3.6	1.9	0.8	2.4	1.7	2.5	3.1	3.0	3.1	0.6	-1.0	..
EU 27	1.6	2.4	3.1	2.5	2.3	0.9	1.8	1.0	1.7	3.6	4.4	-0.7	0.7
OECD	3.1	2.8	3.2	1.7	2.1	0.8	1.6	1.7	1.7	3.1	2.6	-1.1	..
Brazil	..	..	..	..	..	..	..	..	..	..	..	..	..
China	..	..	..	..	..	..	..	..	..	..	..	..	..
India	..	..	..	..	..	..	..	..	..	..	..	..	..
Indonesia	..	..	..	..	..	..	..	..	..	..	..	..	..
Russian Federation	..	..	..	..	..	..	..	..	..	..	..	..	..
South Africa	..	..	..	3.5	5.3	5.3	5.4	6.5	4.9	6.0	9.3	8.7	..

StatLink http://dx.doi.org/10.1787/888932706660

Unit labour costs and labour productivity, total economy

Average annual growth in percentage, 2000-11 or latest available period

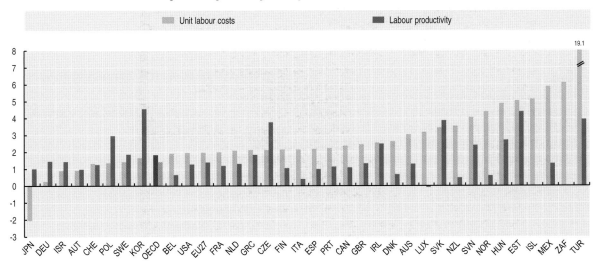

StatLink http://dx.doi.org/10.1787/888932706679

LABOUR COMPENSATION

Labour compensation per unit of labour input shows the average remuneration received by employed persons in the economy. This item is closely linked with the indicators unit labour costs, productivity and GDP per capita.

Definition

Labour compensation per unit of labour input is defined as total compensation of employed persons divided by total hours worked. For all countries, for which data on hours worked are not available, labour input is approximated using compensation of employees and number of employee data. Compensation of employed persons is the sum of gross wages and salaries and of employers' social security contributions. Data refer to the total economy.

The annual measures of labour compensation shown here provide one of the building blocks for international comparisons of competitiveness elaborated by the OECD.

Comparability

The primary data source for constructing the indicator of total compensation per unit of labour is the *OECD Annual National Accounts*, where data are compiled on a similar basis across countries according to the 1993 *System of National Accounts*. This assures a fairly good degree of comparability across countries despite differences in the ways in which countries may implement international guidelines in this field.

In order to derive the measure of total compensation of all employed persons, and not only of employees, an adjustment is made for self-employment, assuming that labour compensation per hour worked is equivalent for self-employed and employees. The validity of this assumption will vary across different countries, economic activities and over time, potentially affecting the comparability of the estimates.

For Poland, there is a break in the hours worked data in 2000-01; from 2001, hours worked for Poland are fully consistent with the 1993 *System of National Accounts*.

Labour compensation per unit labour input, total economy
Annual growth in percentage

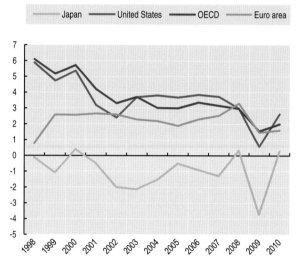

StatLink ⛵ http://dx.doi.org/10.1787/888932706755

Overview

Labour compensation per unit of labour input grew by 3.3% on average for the OECD area as a whole in the period from 2000 to 2010, and by 3.2% for EU27 (2000 to 2011). About three-quarters of all OECD countries recorded annual growth rates of less than 5%. In 2010 and, in part in 2011, following the financial and the Euro area crises, average remuneration fell in Estonia, Germany, Greece, Hungary, Ireland and Spain.

With the exception of Australia, Japan, Poland, Spain and the United Kingdom, the average growth in hourly labour compensation has trended downwards over the last ten years. On average across the OECD, annual growth of labour compensation per unit of labour input declined from 5.2% in 2001 to 2.0% in 2010, the decline being most marked in Hungary and Turkey.

Sources
• OECD (2012), *Main Economic Indicators*, OECD Publishing.

Further information

Analytical publications
• OECD (2011), *OECD Reviews of Labour Market and Social Policies*, OECD Publishing.

Statistical publications
• OECD (2012), *National Accounts at a Glance*, OECD Publishing.

Websites
• Main Economic Indicators, *www.oecd.org/std/mei*.
• OECD Compendium of Productivity Indicators, *www.oecd.org/statistics/productivity/compendium*.
• OECD Productivity, *www.oecd.org/statistics/productivity*.

Labour compensation per unit labour input, total economy
Annual growth in percentage

	1999	2000	2001	2002	2003	2004	2005	2006	2007	2008	2009	2010	2011
Australia	3.5	4.2	5.4	3.4	4.4	4.8	4.3	5.6	5.4	3.0	2.6	4.7	..
Austria	1.8	2.5	1.7	2.2	2.1	0.9	2.9	4.4	2.9	3.8	4.6	1.7	1.6
Belgium	3.5	2.1	3.7	3.8	1.9	1.6	1.7	3.6	3.4	3.6	1.2	1.4	3.1
Canada	2.6	5.4	3.2	2.4	3.1	2.9	4.8	5.0	3.5	2.7	3.2	2.0	..
Chile	..	..	..	..	..	..	..	..	..	..	..	..	..
Czech Republic	5.0	7.9	13.8	8.2	8.8	7.0	3.4	7.0	6.5	4.0	0.4	2.2	2.7
Denmark	2.9	3.0	3.7	4.5	3.9	3.1	3.3	3.0	4.3	3.1	3.7	2.6	1.5
Estonia	8.5	14.6	9.6	9.1	10.9	11.3	9.7	14.7	24.9	11.3	3.8	-1.1	-0.8
Finland	2.1	3.8	4.6	1.7	2.7	3.7	3.7	2.9	3.7	4.4	2.3	1.8	3.4
France	2.4	5.2	3.2	6.0	3.0	1.4	3.4	4.7	1.6	2.0	3.2	2.0	2.9
Germany	1.6	3.2	2.8	1.9	1.8	0.5	0.3	1.2	0.7	2.1	3.4	-0.2	2.8
Greece	4.1	5.5	3.3	11.8	6.8	4.9	4.9	2.2	5.8	5.3	6.8	-3.8	-4.7
Hungary	5.6	15.4	17.6	13.0	11.7	9.5	6.8	5.7	6.6	6.5	-0.5	-2.3	4.1
Iceland	..	..	..	..	..	..	..	..	..	..	..	..	..
Ireland	5.1	8.2	8.1	6.3	6.9	5.8	5.4	5.2	6.6	6.4	0.8	-3.1	..
Israel	6.6	5.5	4.4	0.0	-1.0	1.9	2.9	6.8	0.6	2.4	0.2	4.3	..
Italy	1.7	2.2	3.8	2.8	2.9	2.8	3.5	2.1	2.3	3.2	2.0	1.9	0.9
Japan	-1.1	0.4	-0.5	-2.0	-2.1	-1.5	-0.5	-0.9	-1.3	0.3	-3.7	0.3	..
Korea	1.2	3.3	8.1	7.4	10.0	5.6	6.9	4.3	6.6	7.0	2.2	5.4	9.0
Luxembourg	4.0	5.3	3.5	3.1	1.1	3.3	4.6	2.6	3.7	2.2	1.8	2.6	..
Mexico	16.7	19.7	12.1	3.0	9.6	3.8	1.9	5.5	5.6	4.4	8.2	..	..
Netherlands	4.2	5.1	5.3	5.3	3.8	3.7	1.7	2.5	3.2	2.7	2.9	1.4	..
New Zealand	-0.6	3.3	4.2	3.8	4.6	5.3	3.7	3.1	6.5	2.9	2.9	..	..
Norway	5.5	6.1	7.6	5.4	5.1	2.8	4.3	5.6	5.7	5.8	4.4	3.0	4.3
Poland	11.3	12.2	-14.7	2.9	1.7	1.8	1.9	1.9	4.9	9.3	4.3	4.7	..
Portugal	5.1	6.3	4.0	3.4	3.5	2.6	4.7	1.8	3.6	3.0	2.8	1.4	..
Slovak Republic	7.3	13.4	6.8	11.9	13.4	5.5	7.0	7.9	8.2	6.8	4.8	2.4	1.6
Slovenia	8.6	10.5	11.8	8.2	7.8	7.7	6.0	5.4	6.2	7.2	1.8	4.3	2.0
Spain	1.9	2.8	3.1	3.3	3.5	2.9	3.9	4.1	5.6	5.7	4.0	-0.3	-0.3
Sweden	0.8	8.6	5.8	4.5	4.3	2.4	3.4	2.2	4.4	0.9	2.1	0.7	0.7
Switzerland	..	..	..	..	..	..	..	..	..	..	..	..	..
Turkey	74.8	44.9	43.6	37.8	27.9	20.7	7.1	10.8	..	..	..	..	..
United Kingdom	4.7	5.4	4.8	3.5	4.5	3.7	3.4	4.4	5.1	1.9	3.0	3.8	2.0
United States	4.7	5.4	3.2	2.4	3.7	3.8	3.7	3.8	3.7	3.0	0.6	2.6	..
EU 27	3.1	4.6	3.4	4.0	3.8	2.7	3.3	3.5	3.5	3.4	3.1	1.4	1.8
OECD	5.2	5.7	4.2	3.3	3.7	3.0	3.0	3.4	3.2	3.0	1.5	2.0	..
Brazil	..	..	..	..	..	..	..	..	..	..	..	..	..
China	..	..	..	..	..	..	..	..	..	..	..	..	..
India	..	..	..	..	..	..	..	..	..	..	..	..	..
Indonesia	..	..	..	..	..	..	..	..	..	..	..	..	..
Russian Federation	..	..	..	..	..	..	..	..	..	..	..	..	..
South Africa	..	..	..	..	..	..	..	..	..	..	..	..	..

StatLink ⟪⟫ http://dx.doi.org/10.1787/888932706717

Labour compensation per unit labour input, total economy
Average annual growth in percentage, 2000-11 or latest available period

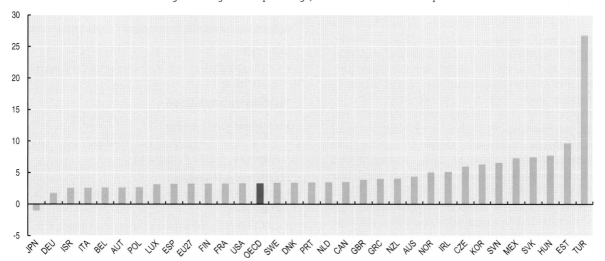

StatLink ⟪⟫ http://dx.doi.org/10.1787/888932706736

VALUE ADDED BY ACTIVITY

Value added reflects the contribution of labour and capital to production. The sum of value added in the economy equals GDP, so value added is also a measure of output and frequently used in productivity and structural analysis.

One of the major advantages of value added is that it avoids problems inherent in the measurement of gross output - gross in the sense that it counts the output of all production units including those that produce intermediate inputs for other units. Countries with fragmented production networks therefore will have, all other things equal, higher output than those with more consolidated networks, complicating international comparisons. This is also a temporal problem as production networks can become more or less consolidated (through outsourcing for example) within a country from one year to another.

Definition

Value added at basic prices can be simply defined as the difference between gross output (at basic prices) and intermediate consumption (at purchasers prices) and can be decomposed into the following components: Compensation of employees; Gross operating surplus; Mixed income; and Other taxes on production less Subsidies on production.

Overview

The share of agriculture in total value added within the OECD fell by approximately 0.5% between 2000 and 2011 continuing its long term decline. In only four countries (Turkey, Hungary, Iceland and New Zealand) agriculture accounts for more than 5% of total value added. The share of industry in total value added has also continued its decline in recent decades. However, among the countries for which data are available, especially the Czech Republic, Estonia, Hungary, Iceland, Korea and Poland and the Slovak Republic experienced rises over the period. The share of industry also fell in non-member countries but remains at considerably higher levels than in most OECD countries, with the share for China and Indonesia remaining close to 40%. Norway, where mining and quarrying are large contributors to activity, come closest to these rates in the OECD.

Conversely the share of financial intermediation, real estate, renting and business activities increased over the period 2000-11. The share of these activities nowadays ranges from a low of just over 15% in the Slovak Republic to close to 50% in Luxembourg. Also the share of other service activities, among which health and education, show an upward trend in most countries.

The 1993 System of National Accounts recommends the basic price valuation for value added but it can also be measured on different price bases such as producers prices and at factor cost.

Comparability

All countries compile data according to the 1993 SNA with the exception of Australia where data are compiled according to the new 2008 SNA. It's important to note however that differences between the 2008 SNA and the 1993 SNA do not have a significant impact of the comparability of the indicators presented here and this implies that data are highly comparable across countries.

However, not all countries produce value added on the basis of basic prices. Japan uses approximately market prices. New Zealand uses producer prices, and Iceland and the United States use factor costs.

The tables and figures showing breakdowns by activity are based on the ISIC Rev. 4 industrial classification system except for Canada, Israel, Japan, Luxembourg, Mexico, New Zealand, Turkey, the United States, India, Indonesia, the Russian Federation and South Africa which are based on ISIC Rev.3. Countries generally collect information using their own industrial classification systems. The conversion from a national classification system to ISIC may create some comparability issues. For example, for Japan, Hotels (which form approximately 2.8-3.0% of value added) are included in Other services not wholesale, retail, etc. That said, for most countries the activities presented here are generally comparable.

Sources

- OECD (2012), *National Accounts of OECD Countries*, OECD Publishing.

Further information

Analytical publications

- OECD (2002), *Measuring the Non-Observed Economy: A Handbook*, OECD Publishing.

Statistical publications

- OECD (2012), *Quarterly National Accounts*, OECD Publishing.
- OECD (2011), *National Accounts at a Glance*, OECD Publishing.

Online databases

- *STAN: OECD Structural Analysis Statistics.*

Websites

- OECD National Accounts, *www.oecd.org/std/ nationalaccounts.*

Value added by activity

As a percentage of total value added

	Agriculture, hunting, forestry, fishing		Industry, including energy		Construction		Trade, transport; accommodation, restaurants; communication		Financial and insurance; real estate; business services		Other service activities	
	2000	2011 or latest available year	2000	2011 or latest available year	2000	2011 or latest available year	2000	2011 or latest available year	2000	2011 or latest available year	2000	2011 or latest available year
Australia	3.8	2.8	20.6	20.1	5.6	7.7	22.5	20.2	28.1	30.4	19.4	18.8
Austria	1.9	1.6	23.7	22.5	7.7	6.8	26.2	25.4	20.7	23.5	19.8	20.1
Belgium	1.3	0.6	21.9	17.1	5.2	5.8	23.1	24.4	26.6	27.8	21.8	24.3
Canada	2.3	..	28.2	..	5.0	..	20.3	..	25.0	..	19.2	..
Chile	..	3.4	..	31.0	..	8.1	..	16.9	..	18.8	..	21.8
Czech Republic	3.6	2.1	30.9	31.1	6.6	6.7	27.1	23.8	15.0	18.5	16.8	17.9
Denmark	2.5	1.4	21.1	17.5	5.5	4.8	24.4	23.6	21.1	25.0	25.4	27.8
Estonia	4.8	3.6	21.6	23.9	5.9	6.3	29.4	26.5	21.6	22.1	16.7	17.6
Finland	3.5	2.9	28.0	20.9	6.3	6.8	21.9	22.3	19.6	22.7	20.6	24.4
France	2.5	1.8	17.8	12.6	5.0	6.2	23.1	23.4	27.5	30.1	24.1	26.0
Germany	1.1	1.0	25.2	25.7	5.3	4.4	20.3	19.1	26.2	27.4	21.9	22.5
Greece	..	3.1	..	13.5	..	4.5	..	31.4	..	23.5	..	24.0
Hungary	5.9	5.4	27.1	28.7	5.3	3.8	21.5	22.0	19.2	20.5	21.0	19.5
Iceland	8.5	7.8	17.2	18.8	9.3	4.5	24.8	20.0	18.5	24.5	21.8	24.6
Ireland	3.4	1.7	33.8	28.1	7.0	2.8	19.0	18.6	20.4	26.1	16.4	22.7
Israel	1.7	2.1	19.2	16.5	5.8	4.9	18.2	16.8	30.5	36.5	24.6	23.3
Italy	2.8	2.0	22.6	18.6	5.1	6.0	26.1	25.0	24.4	27.8	18.9	20.6
Japan	1.5	1.2	24.3	21.9	7.0	5.6	20.7	23.9	15.9	16.9	30.7	30.6
Korea	4.6	2.7	31.6	33.8	6.9	5.9	21.6	18.8	19.3	19.3	15.9	19.5
Luxembourg	0.7	0.3	12.6	7.8	5.7	5.6	21.8	19.8	43.8	49.7	15.4	16.9
Mexico	4.2	3.5	29.4	27.7	6.4	6.6	29.8	28.6	19.0	19.7	12.7	13.8
Netherlands	2.5	1.7	19.1	18.7	5.7	5.5	26.1	23.8	25.6	25.7	21.0	24.6
New Zealand	8.5	..	19.9	..	4.4	..	21.8	..	27.8	..	17.6	..
Norway	2.1	1.5	37.7	36.4	4.0	5.9	21.0	16.0	15.3	18.6	20.0	21.6
Poland	4.9	3.6	23.3	25.5	7.8	7.9	29.2	29.8	18.0	16.4	16.8	16.8
Portugal	3.6	2.1	20.3	17.0	8.2	6.3	26.7	28.5	19.2	22.2	22.0	23.8
Slovak Republic	4.5	3.2	28.9	32.5	7.2	9.4	26.3	22.7	16.6	15.4	16.6	16.8
Slovenia	3.4	2.5	28.1	24.5	6.7	5.2	22.6	25.0	19.8	21.9	19.4	20.9
Spain	4.2	2.6	20.8	16.9	10.3	11.5	28.1	28.4	16.9	19.2	19.6	21.4
Sweden	2.0	1.7	24.2	20.5	4.3	5.6	22.2	23.6	22.5	22.2	24.7	26.2
Switzerland	1.3	0.8	21.2	20.7	5.2	5.4	25.7	27.3	21.3	20.1	25.1	25.7
Turkey	10.8	9.2	24.6	22.6	5.4	5.0	29.1	30.9	19.5	20.2	10.6	12.1
United Kingdom	1.0	0.6	20.3	14.9	6.5	6.9	27.0	24.4	24.7	29.8	20.5	23.4
United States	1.2	1.2	18.4	16.2	5.0	3.7	20.0	18.2	31.7	33.5	23.7	27.1
Euro area	2.4	1.7	22.1	19.3	5.9	6.2	23.7	23.4	24.6	26.5	21.3	22.9
EU 27	2.3	1.7	22.0	19.3	6.0	6.3	24.4	23.8	24.2	26.1	21.2	22.8
OECD	..	..	..	..	..	..	..	..	..	..	..	..
Brazil	..	..	..	..	..	..	..	..	..	..	..	..
China	15.1	10.1	40.4	40.0	5.6	6.8	16.6	15.8	8.3	10.7	14.1	16.6
India	..	17.6	..	19.1	..	8.1	..	16.2	..	16.8	..	22.2
Indonesia	15.6	15.3	40.4	36.8	5.5	10.3	20.8	20.2	8.3	7.2	9.3	10.2
Russian Federation	6.4	4.3	31.1	30.5	6.6	6.5	33.1	28.9	4.6	15.9	18.3	14.0
South Africa	3.3	2.4	29.3	26.1	2.5	4.5	24.3	22.7	18.6	21.2	22.0	23.1

StatLink ⛓ http://dx.doi.org/10.1787/888932706774

Value added in industry, including energy

As a percentage of total value added

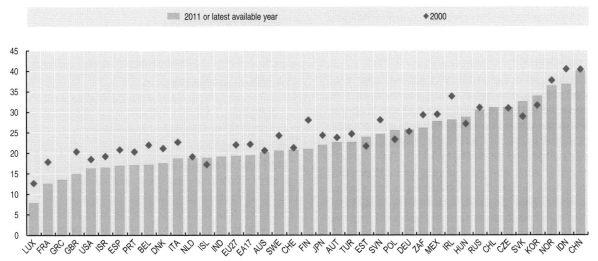

StatLink ⛓ http://dx.doi.org/10.1787/888932706793

REAL VALUE ADDED BY ACTIVITY

Like its nominal counterpart, real value added can be derived as the difference between real output and real intermediate consumption, an approach known as double-deflation.

One of the major advantages of value added is that it avoids problems inherent in the measurement of gross output - gross in the sense that it counts the output of all production units including those that produce intermediate inputs for other units. Countries with fragmented production networks therefore will have, all other things equal, higher output than those with more consolidated networks, complicating international comparisons. Production networks have become increasingly globalised in recent years, further affecting temporal and cross-country comparability. Value added avoids these problems by measuring the value that a resident unit adds to that of the units that supply its inputs.

Definition

The growth rates shown here refer to volume estimates of gross value added. Value added at basic prices can be simply defined as the difference between gross output (at basic prices) and intermediate consumption (at purchasers prices) and can be decomposed into the following components: Compensation of employees; Gross operating surplus; Mixed income; and Other taxes on production less Subsidies on production.

The 1993 System of National Accounts recommends the basic price valuation for value added but it can also be measured on different price bases such as producers prices and at factor cost.

Comparability

All countries compile data according to the 1993 SNA with the exception of Australia where data are compiled according to the new 2008 SNA. It's important to note however that differences between 2008 SNA and the 1993 SNA do not have a significant impact of the comparability of the indicators presented here and this implies that data are highly comparable across countries.

However, not all countries produce value added on the basis of basic prices. Japan uses approximately market prices. New Zealand uses producer prices, and Iceland and the United States use factor costs.

The tables and figures showing breakdowns by activity are based on the ISIC Rev. 4 industrial classification system except for Canada, Israel, Japan, Luxembourg, Mexico, New Zealand, Turkey, the United States, India, Indonesia, the Russian Federation and South Africa which are based on ISIC Rev.3. Countries generally collect information using their own industrial classification systems. The conversion from a national classification system to ISIC may create some comparability issues. For example, for Japan, Hotels (which form approximately 2.8-3.0% of value added) are included in Other services not wholesale, retail, etc. That said, for most countries the activities presented here are generally comparable.

Overview

The table shows how the various economic activities fared in 2011, as the recent crisis still continues to have an impact on the economic circumstances. Hardest hit in 2010 was construction, mainly because of lower investment levels.

In the construction sector for 2011 (or the latest year available), falls in the growth rate greater than 10% were recorded in Greece, Iceland, Ireland and Slovenia. On the other hand, in Chile, Estonia, Poland and Turkey, construction increased by more than 10%. China's construction increased by 13.5%.

Industry (including energy) generally showed positive growth figures, the exceptions being especially Greece (minus 9.1%), New Zealand (minus 4.4%) and Israel (minus 4.1%). Growth in services was generally positive across the OECD countries, although Greece, Iceland, Ireland, Portugal and the Slovak Republic saw service activities going down.

Sources
- OECD (2012), *National Accounts of OECD Countries*, OECD Publishing.

Further information

Analytical publications
- OECD (2012), *OECD Economic Outlook*, OECD Publishing.

Statistical publications
- OECD (2012), *Quarterly National Accounts*, OECD Publishing.
- OECD (2011), *National Accounts at a Glance*, OECD Publishing.

Methodological publications
- OECD (2000), *System of National Accounts, 1993 – Glossary*, OECD Publishing.
- United Nations, OECD, International Monetary Fund and Eurostat (eds.) (2010), *System of National Accounts 2008*, United Nations, Geneva.

Online databases
- *STAN: OECD Structural Analysis Statistics.*

Real value added by activity

Annual growth in percentage

	Agriculture, hunting, forestry, fishing		Industry, including energy		Construction		Trade, transport; accommodation, restaurants; communication		Financial and insurance; real estate; business services		Other service activities	
	2000	2011 or latest available year	2000	2011 or latest available year	2000	2011 or latest available year	2000	2011 or latest available year	2000	2011 or latest available year	2000	2011 or latest available year
Australia	3.8	9.1	3.5	-0.1	-14.4	6.3	2.5	1.5	4.5	3.3	3.2	1.5
Austria	-3.6	15.3	6.0	8.2	0.6	3.5	3.1	1.0	7.5	2.1	-0.3	0.6
Belgium	5.0	7.9	4.9	2.4	5.5	4.8	1.2	2.7	4.2	1.4	3.4	1.4
Canada	-1.8	1.9	8.4	5.9	5.2	7.8	6.0	3.9	5.2	2.2	2.6	2.1
Chile	..	11.8	..	0.8	..	11.1	..	10.2	..	8.5	..	4.5
Czech Republic	1.4	6.5	10.8	5.1	-8.7	-7.2	5.0	-1.6	2.1	2.0	0.7	2.3
Denmark	7.9	0.5	3.4	-1.3	1.0	2.9	7.6	3.1	5.7	1.8	1.5	-0.8
Estonia	16.9	2.6	18.4	17.3	24.9	17.7	7.4	6.9	7.6	-0.2	1.6	2.7
Finland	8.0	3.2	12.6	0.9	0.4	4.6	5.7	3.3	2.9	2.8	1.8	0.8
France	-1.7	3.9	3.6	0.5	5.4	0.0	4.0	2.8	5.9	2.4	0.1	1.0
Germany	-3.1	-9.2	6.3	6.2	-2.3	4.6	4.3	2.8	2.9	2.1	1.9	0.6
Greece	..	2.5	..	-9.1	..	-17.9	..	-8.0	..	-2.9	..	-5.8
Hungary	-9.6	27.2	5.5	5.7	14.2	-7.8	3.0	0.5	4.7	-2.8	4.6	0.3
Iceland	-2.1	-8.1	1.4	-1.8	14.2	-14.7	9.1	-3.9	10.2	0.6	1.5	-3.2
Ireland	..	0.9	..	11.0	..	-30.1	..	-3.4	..	0.0	..	-5.0
Israel	6.6	9.5	13.7	-4.1	-1.3	-0.9	6.8	-2.1	17.0	2.3	1.4	2.9
Italy	-2.3	-0.5	3.2	1.2	4.7	-3.5	6.1	1.1	4.9	1.2	1.5	0.0
Japan	2.1	-7.4	4.7	17.3	-3.5	-0.9	-0.9	1.7	4.1	1.2	2.1	0.5
Korea	1.1	-2.0	16.6	6.7	-4.4	-4.6	13.0	4.6	4.2	1.7	2.0	1.7
Luxembourg	-13.0	-1.7	7.9	6.3	1.9	3.6	8.1	4.7	11.0	-0.7	0.8	1.9
Mexico	0.4	3.9	6.4	7.6	4.2	0.0	11.1	9.3	5.5	3.5	2.9	1.4
Netherlands	1.8	1.7	5.6	0.5	3.5	4.8	7.0	2.4	2.0	0.4	1.7	1.5
New Zealand	2.7	0.1	2.4	-4.4	-6.5	-7.9	5.0	-2.3	2.2	3.5	3.3	1.7
Norway	-2.7	-0.9	4.0	-1.3	-0.4	3.9	3.9	2.8	6.4	2.4	0.9	2.1
Poland	..	-0.3	..	6.3	..	11.8	..	4.0	..	1.2	..	1.0
Portugal	-4.7	2.8	3.4	0.0	6.0	-9.2	6.1	-1.2	1.8	-0.6	3.8	-1.2
Slovak Republic	..	-20.2	..	12.8	..	2.1	..	-1.7	..	1.5	..	-1.6
Slovenia	1.3	-2.3	9.0	2.8	-1.0	-20.3	4.7	0.7	3.7	0.8	2.4	1.2
Spain	..	0.6	..	1.9	..	-3.8	..	1.4	..	1.2	..	0.5
Sweden	2.6	1.1	8.1	5.2	1.4	8.8	5.2	5.7	6.2	4.8	1.6	1.6
Switzerland	7.8	-3.0	0.8	4.6	-0.1	6.9	6.0	5.6	5.1	0.0	2.1	1.4
Turkey	7.1	5.3	6.6	9.2	4.9	11.2	9.8	10.9	4.2	7.7	1.6	4.1
United Kingdom	..	..	2.1	-0.8	1.1	3.1	6.2	0.6	6.2	1.5	3.2	1.3
United States	12.9	-3.6	2.6	8.3	3.3	-3.3	6.5	6.0	6.1	1.2	1.2	1.6
Euro area	..	1.7	..	3.4	..	-1.0	..	1.7	..	1.4	..	0.5
EU 27	..	2.7	..	3.1	..	0.1	..	1.7	..	1.4	..	0.6
OECD	..	..	..	..	..	..	..	..	..	..	..	..
Brazil	..	..	..	..	..	..	..	..	..	..	..	..
China	2.4	4.3	9.8	12.1	5.7	13.5	9.0	12.3	6.8	8.5	13.0	7.9
India	..	0.5	..	8.3	..	7.0	..	6.7	..	9.1	..	13.1
Indonesia	1.9	2.9	5.9	4.3	5.6	7.0	6.6	10.3	4.6	5.7	2.3	6.0
Russian Federation	..	15.7	..	3.7	..	4.7	..	4.2	..	3.6	..	1.7
South Africa	4.7	0.9	4.9	4.9	5.6	1.5	8.1	2.5	3.2	1.9	0.6	2.3

StatLink http://dx.doi.org/10.1787/888932706812

Real value added in industry, including energy

Annual growth in percentage

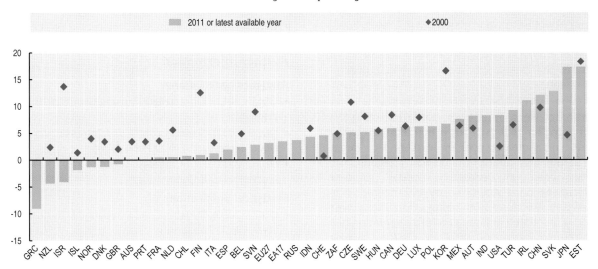

StatLink http://dx.doi.org/10.1787/888932706831

SMALL AND MEDIUM-SIZED ENTERPRISES

Small firms, and especially recent start-ups, can be very dynamic and innovative. A few very high-performance new and small firms can make an important contribution to employment creation and economic growth. Although the majority of small firms have more modest economic impacts individually, taken together they make an important contribution.

Definition

An enterprise is a legal entity possessing the right to conduct business on its own; for example to enter into contracts, own property, incur liabilities and establish bank accounts. It may consist of one or more establishments situated in a geographically separate area.

Employees include all persons covered by a contractual arrangement, working in the enterprise and receiving compensation for their work. They include salaried managers, students who have a formal commitment whereby they contribute to the unit's process of production in return for remuneration and/or education services, and employees engaged under a contract designed to encourage the recruitment of unemployed persons. They also include persons on sick leave, paid leave or vacation, while excluding working proprietors, active business partners, unpaid family workers and home-workers, irrespective of whether or not they are on the payroll.

Number of persons employed is defined as the total number of persons who worked in or for the concerned unit during the reference year. Total employment excludes directors of incorporated enterprises and members of shareholders' committees who are paid solely for their attendance at meetings, labour force made available to the concerned unit by other units and charged for, persons carrying out repair and maintenance work in the unit on the behalf of other units, and home-workers. It also excludes persons on indefinite leave, military leave or those whose only remuneration from the enterprise is by way of a pension.

Comparability

An area where considerable differences do arise concerns the coverage of data on enterprises/establishments. In many countries, this information is based on business registers, economic censuses or surveys that may have a size cut-off. All countries have thresholds of one sort or another, often depending on tax legislation and legal provisions reducing administrative burdens on small enterprises. For Ireland, only enterprises with three or more persons employed are reflected, while the data for Japan and Korea do not include establishments with fewer than 4 and 5 persons employed respectively.

Data refer to 2008 in the case of the Czech Republic, Denmark, the Netherlands, the Slovak Republic, the United Kingdom and Turkey; to 2007 for Greece and Norway; and to 2005 for Iceland. Employment data for Switzerland refer to the total number of persons employed rather than to the number of employees.

Overview

The contribution of small enterprises to employment varies considerably across countries. In most economies, the share of enterprises with less than 20 persons employed exceeds 70% of the total, ranging between 69% in Ireland and above 95% in Greece. Small enterprises account for a smaller share of the total number of employees, ranging between around 9% in the United States and the Czech Republic to around 35% in Greece.

Some larger economies are characterised by a lower proportion of small enterprises, partly reflecting the greater scope for growth in larger markets (due to the existence of a greater pool of workers and larger demand) but also due to a statistical phenomenon, namely, when an enterprise opens a new establishment in the same country within which it is registered, it will move from being a small to a large enterprise. In other words, an enterprise operating in a small country often will grow by creating a new establishment abroad rather than expanding in the internal market.

Sources

- OECD (2011), *OECD Studies on SMEs and Entrepreneurship*, OECD Publishing.
- OECD (2010), *Structural and Demographic Business Statistics* (database).

Further information

Analytical publications

- OECD (2012), *Entrepreneurship at a Glance 2012*, OECD Publishing.
- OECD (2012), *Financing SMEs and Entrepreneurs 2012, An OECD Scoreboard*, OECD Publishing.
- OECD (2011), *Financing High-Growth Firms, The Role of Angel Investors*, OECD Publishing.

Statistical publications

- OECD (2010), *Structural and Demographic Business Statistics 2009*, OECD Publishing.

Methodological publications

- OECD and Eurostat (2008), *Eurostat-OECD Manual on Business Demography Statistics*, OECD Publishing.

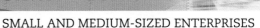

Number of employees and number of enterprises in manufacturing

Breakdown by size-class of enterprise, 2009 or latest available year

| | Number of persons employed | | | | | | | | | |
| | As a percentage of total number of employees in manufacturing | | | | | As a percentage of total number of enterprises in manufacturing | | | | |
	Less than 10	10-19	20-49	50-249	250 or more	Less than 10	10-19	20-49	50-249	250 or more
Australia	..	..	..	..	..	..	..	..	..	..
Austria	6.9	6.8	11.1	27.3	48.0	71.9	12.1	8.5	5.8	1.8
Belgium	7.5	7.0	13.1	..	..	82.4	7.4	5.9	..	..
Canada	..	..	..	..	..	..	..	..	..	..
Chile	..	..	..	..	..	..	..	..	..	..
Czech Republic	5.9	5.5	10.5	29.8	48.3	90.6	3.5	3.0	2.3	0.6
Denmark	5.6	6.4	14.0	27.7	46.3	70.8	10.7	10.6	6.5	1.4
Estonia	10.1	8.3	16.5	39.6	25.6	69.2	11.2	10.7	7.7	1.1
Finland	7.8	6.2	10.8	23.3	51.9	82.0	7.5	5.8	3.7	1.0
France	12.1	7.2	11.9	22.9	45.9	84.1	6.9	5.2	3.0	0.8
Germany	4.3	7.2	8.1	25.7	54.7	60.5	19.4	8.9	8.9	2.2
Greece	30.4	4.9	12.1	25.6	27.1	96.5	1.2	1.3	0.8	0.2
Hungary	10.4	7.0	11.6	27.1	43.8	85.4	6.2	4.6	3.1	0.7
Iceland	..	..	..	..	..	80.2	8.7	6.7	3.8	0.7
Ireland	5.8	6.8	12.3	30.3	44.9	49.6	20.3	15.8	11.3	3.0
Israel	10.2	7.6	13.0	29.5	39.7	70.8	12.1	9.4	6.5	1.2
Italy	15.6	15.1	17.7	24.8	26.8	81.9	10.6	5.1	2.1	0.3
Japan	8.4	10.2	16.9	31.0	33.5	46.2	23.8	18.1	10.2	1.8
Korea	0.2	16.1	23.5	31.5	28.8	1.1	51.3	32.6	13.6	1.4
Luxembourg	4.1	..	..	..	..	64.1	12.8	11.0	9.2	3.0
Mexico	0.2	..	..	16.8	80.2	1.0	..	..	2.1	95.5
Netherlands	8.8	9.1	16.3	31.6	34.2	77.8	9.2	7.7	4.4	0.9
New Zealand	13.1	10.5	15.2	24.4	36.8	69.4	15.1	9.8	4.8	0.9
Norway	9.3	8.2	14.6	28.2	39.6	79.6	8.6	6.9	4.1	0.9
Poland	10.2	4.0	10.2	31.0	44.5	87.5	3.6	4.4	3.6	0.9
Portugal	19.1	12.4	19.7	30.2	18.6	81.8	8.7	6.1	3.0	0.3
Slovak Republic	3.5	7.5	7.5	26.5	55.1	42.1	30.2	10.6	13.0	4.1
Slovenia	10.2	6.3	10.0	30.3	43.2	87.1	5.4	3.7	3.1	0.7
Spain	15.5	11.9	19.2	24.4	29.0	81.1	9.2	6.6	2.6	0.5
Sweden	9.2	6.8	10.9	24.0	49.1	87.2	5.5	4.0	2.6	0.7
Switzerland	8.8	9.0	13.2	29.6	39.4	56.3	19.0	13.6	9.1	2.1
Turkey	..	..	14.4	26.2	35.8	..	..	3.5	2.0	0.4
United Kingdom	10.5	7.0	12.0	26.8	43.6	74.7	10.7	8.1	5.3	1.3
United States	4.7	4.8	..	..	..	60.2	15.4	..	..	..
EU 27	..	..	..	..	..	81.0	8.9	5.9	3.6	0.8
OECD	..	..	..	..	..	..	..	..	..	..
Brazil	..	..	..	..	..	..	..	..	..	..
China	..	..	..	..	..	..	..	..	..	..
India	..	..	..	..	..	..	..	..	..	..
Indonesia	..	..	..	..	..	..	..	..	..	..
Russian Federation	..	..	..	..	..	..	..	..	..	..
South Africa	..	..	..	..	..	..	..	..	..	..

StatLink http://dx.doi.org/10.1787/888932706850

Manufacturing enterprises with less than twenty persons employed: number of employees and number of enterprises

As a percentage of total number of employees or total number of enterprises, 2009 or latest available year

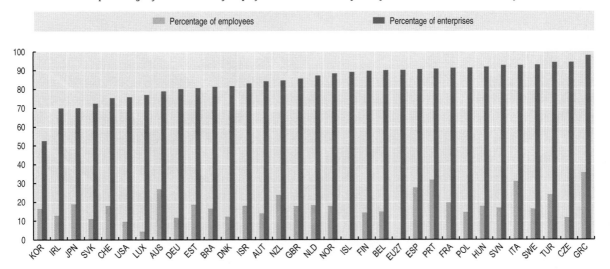

StatLink http://dx.doi.org/10.1787/888932706869

HOUSEHOLD INCOME AND WEALTH

INCOME AND SAVINGS
NATIONAL INCOME PER CAPITA
HOUSEHOLD DISPOSABLE INCOME
HOUSEHOLD SAVINGS

INCOME INEQUALITY AND POVERTY
INCOME INEQUALITY
POVERTY RATES AND GAPS

HOUSEHOLD WEALTH
HOUSEHOLD FINANCIAL ASSETS
HOUSEHOLD DEBT
NON-FINANCIAL ASSETS BY HOUSEHOLDS

NATIONAL INCOME PER CAPITA

While per capita gross domestic product is the indicator most commonly used to compare income levels, two other measures are preferred, at least in theory, by many analysts. These are per capita Gross National Income (GNI) and Net National Income (NNI). Whereas GDP refers to the income generated by production activities on the economic territory of the country, GNI measures the income generated by the residents of a country, whether earned on the domestic territory or abroad.

Definition

GNI is defined as GDP plus receipts from abroad less payments to abroad of wages and salaries and of property income plus net taxes and subsidies receivable from abroad. NNI is equal to GNI net of depreciation.

Wages and salaries from abroad are those that are earned by residents who essentially live and consume inside the economic territory but work abroad (this happens in border areas on a regular basis) or for persons that live and work abroad for only short periods (seasonal workers) and whose centre of economic interest remains in their home country. Guest-workers and other migrant workers who live abroad for twelve months or more are considered to be resident in the country where they are working. Such persons may send part of their earnings to relatives at home, but these remittances are treated as transfers between resident and non-resident households and are recorded in national disposable income but not national income.

Property income from/to abroad includes interest and dividends. It also includes all or part of the retained earnings of foreign enterprises owned fully or in part by residents (and *vice versa*). In this respect, it is important to note that retained earnings of foreign enterprises owned by residents do not actually return to the residents concerned. Nevertheless, the retained earnings are recorded as a receipt.

Comparability

All countries compile data according to the 1993 SNA "System of National Accounts, 1993" with the exception of Australia where data are compiled according to the new 2008 SNA. It's important to note however that differences between the 2008 SNA and the 1993 SNA do not have a significant impact of the comparability of the indicators presented here and this implies that data are highly comparable across countries.

However, there are practical difficulties in the measurement both of international flows of wages and salaries and property income and of depreciation. It is for that reason that GDP per capita is the most widely used indicator of income or welfare, even though, GNI is theoretically superior.

Sources
- OECD (2012), *National Accounts of OECD Countries*, OECD Publishing.

Further information

Analytical publications
- OECD (2012), *OECD Economic Outlook*, OECD Publishing.
- OECD (2011), *Perspectives on Global Development*, OECD Publishing.
- OECD (2003), *The Sources of Economic Growth in OECD Countries*, OECD Publishing.

Statistical publications
- OECD (2011), *National Accounts at a Glance*, OECD Publishing.

Methodological publications
- OECD (2000), *System of National Accounts, 1993 – Glossary*, OECD Publishing.
- United Nations, OECD, International Monetary Fund and Eurostat (eds.) (2010), *System of National Accounts 2008*, United Nations, Geneva.

Online databases
- *OECD National Accounts Statistics*.
- *OECD Economic Outlook: Statistics and Projections*.

Websites
- OECD Economic Outlook – Sources and Methods, *www.oecd.org/eco/sources-and-methods*.

Overview

Ranking countries according to GNI per capita, shows that on average GNI per capita is usually around 15-19% higher than NNI per capita. The country rankings are not greatly affected by the choice of income measure. The only countries that would be more than one place lower in the ranking if NNI per capita were used instead of GNI are Belgium, Hungary and Japan; the only countries that would be more than one place higher in the ranking if NNI per capita were used are Canada, Israel, Korea and the Russian Federation.

GNI per capita does not differ significantly from GDP per capita. Usually, the differences are (significantly) smaller than USD 2 000. There are, however, four exceptions. For Luxembourg, GNI per capita in 2010, although still highest in the OECD, is nearly USD 25 000 lower than GDP per capita. In Iceland and Ireland, GNI is USD 6 000-7 000 lower. On the other hand, GNI in Switzerland is higher than GDP per capita by approximately USD 3 000.

Gross national income per capita
US dollars, current prices and PPPs

	1999	2000	2001	2002	2003	2004	2005	2006	2007	2008	2009	2010	2011
Australia	26 053	27 197	28 299	29 470	30 973	32 074	33 527	35 169	37 098	37 531	38 429	39 136	..
Austria	26 705	28 421	28 408	30 086	31 016	32 611	33 310	36 193	37 614	39 692	38 651	39 972	41 988
Belgium	25 859	28 301	28 981	30 461	30 753	31 534	32 415	34 547	36 025	37 564	36 512	38 396	39 374
Canada	26 220	27 743	28 502	29 162	30 530	32 167	34 448	36 501	37 860	38 493	37 256	38 372	..
Chile	8 863	9 259	9 693	9 888	10 159	10 809	11 629	12 104	13 034	14 226	14 221	15 058	16 336
Czech Republic	14 543	15 281	16 362	16 926	18 115	19 129	20 372	22 072	23 640	24 659	23 901	23 557	24 285
Denmark	26 699	28 221	29 017	30 393	30 243	32 438	33 659	36 721	38 129	40 472	38 918	41 128	42 237
Estonia	8 632	9 542	10 255	11 475	12 678	14 044	15 902	18 145	20 151	20 970	19 224	19 376	20 825
Finland	23 307	25 478	26 494	27 577	27 407	30 088	30 849	33 454	36 183	38 244	36 224	36 847	37 846
France	23 994	25 608	26 972	27 862	27 554	28 554	30 017	31 988	33 722	34 769	34 298	34 910	35 796
Germany	24 694	25 496	26 405	27 077	28 114	29 939	31 469	34 235	36 171	37 590	36 816	38 124	39 944
Greece	17 025	18 320	19 894	21 485	22 392	23 721	23 994	26 219	26 928	28 604	28 668	27 668	26 077
Hungary	10 433	11 294	12 720	13 906	14 630	15 341	16 058	17 312	17 611	19 112	19 265	19 555	..
Iceland	28 071	28 051	29 482	31 033	30 294	32 362	33 731	33 740	35 338	31 011	29 504	29 365	30 759
Ireland	22 574	24 973	26 063	27 656	29 764	31 562	33 553	37 286	39 365	36 897	33 070	33 552	..
Israel	20 347	21 923	22 351	22 518	21 309	22 746	23 012	23 745	25 414	24 962	24 813	25 764	..
Italy	24 225	25 562	27 093	26 759	27 082	27 432	28 288	30 491	32 039	33 008	32 101	31 751	32 720
Japan	24 940	26 339	27 008	27 671	28 429	29 874	31 150	32 700	34 489	34 699	32 980	34 645	..
Korea	15 407	17 109	18 109	19 668	20 197	21 688	22 762	24 284	26 150	26 888	27 051	28 834	30 336
Luxembourg	44 091	46 759	47 898	47 736	47 079	56 788	58 720	59 764	68 022	67 210	55 760	61 346	..
Mexico	9 027	9 807	9 925	10 214	10 690	11 370	12 243	13 469	14 219	15 030	14 101	14 982	..
Netherlands	27 226	30 049	31 015	32 235	32 066	34 086	35 281	39 112	41 412	42 017	40 064	41 838	43 277
New Zealand	18 954	19 812	20 869	21 618	22 299	23 106	23 570	25 159	26 474	27 012	28 170	..	..
Norway	29 550	35 649	37 118	37 166	38 501	42 560	47 967	53 884	55 698	61 049	55 026	57 945	62 954
Poland	9 940	10 532	10 922	11 524	11 869	12 641	13 516	14 693	16 160	17 660	18 270	19 239	..
Portugal	16 579	17 429	18 035	18 840	19 268	19 642	21 052	22 274	23 433	24 048	23 922	24 616	24 431
Slovak Republic	10 348	10 922	12 066	12 918	12 924	14 065	15 717	17 816	20 224	22 728	22 227	22 945	23 564
Slovenia	16 761	17 565	18 477	19 649	20 358	22 011	23 273	25 142	26 639	28 248	26 601	26 544	26 950
Spain	19 638	21 135	22 214	23 705	24 468	25 611	27 003	29 896	31 481	32 243	31 431	31 437	31 736
Sweden	25 739	27 722	28 021	29 163	30 795	32 488	32 936	36 161	39 355	40 995	38 042	40 136	42 253
Switzerland	32 540	34 737	34 515	35 425	36 724	38 042	40 027	43 850	44 724	44 368	47 385	51 537	..
Turkey	..	..	..	..	..	..	..	..	..	..	..	..	..
United Kingdom	24 145	26 024	27 732	29 318	30 258	32 226	33 281	35 215	36 234	36 665	34 971	35 844	35 885
United States	33 652	35 658	36 410	37 002	38 307	40 583	43 063	45 575	46 675	47 209	45 331	47 195	..
Euro area	23 101	24 427	25 608	26 382	26 863	28 091	29 380	31 828	33 557	34 547	33 810	34 381	35 387
EU 27	20 510	21 817	22 938	23 855	24 449	25 753	26 933	29 164	30 801	31 943	31 124	31 772	32 752
OECD	23 023	24 497	25 253	25 953	26 715	28 234	29 762	31 828	33 217	34 012	32 905	..	..
Brazil	..	..	..	..	..	..	..	..	..	..	..	..	..
China	..	..	..	..	..	3 608	4 121	4 773	5 589	6 210	..	..	..
India	..	..	..	..	..	..	..	..	..	..	..	..	..
Indonesia	..	2 280	2 458	2 594	2 712	2 861	3 051	3 301	3 571	3 844	4 014	4 221	..
Russian Federation	5 661	6 622	7 234	7 857	8 951	10 007	11 531	14 482	16 335	19 673	18 278	..	..
South Africa	6 254	6 545	6 716	7 028	7 276	7 820	8 429	9 079	9 599	10 065	10 006	10 322	10 743

StatLink http://dx.doi.org/10.1787/888932706888

Gross and net national income per capita
US dollars, current prices and PPPs, 2011 or latest available year

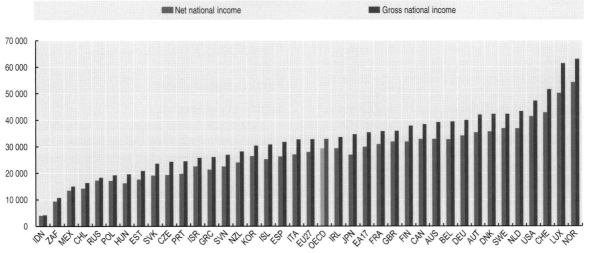

■ Net national income   ■ Gross national income

StatLink http://dx.doi.org/10.1787/888932706907

HOUSEHOLD DISPOSABLE INCOME

Disposable income, as a concept, is closer to the concept of income generally understood in economics, than either national income or GDP. At the total economy level it differs from national income in that additional income items are included, mainly other current transfers such as remittances. For countries where these additional items form significant sources of income the importance of focusing on disposable income in formulating policy is clear. Another important difference between national income and disposable income concerns the allocation of income across sectors. At this level significant differences arise, reflecting the reallocation of national income. Disposable income can be seen as the maximum amount that a unit can afford to spend on consumption goods or services without having to reduce its financial or non-financial assets or by increasing its liabilities.

Definition

Household disposable income is the sum of household final consumption expenditure and savings (minus the change in net equity of households in pension funds). It also corresponds to the sum of wages and salaries, mixed income, net property income, net current transfers and social benefits other than social transfers in kind, less taxes on income and wealth and social security contributions paid by employees, the self-employed and the unemployed.

The indicator for the household sector includes the disposable income of non-profit institutions serving households (NPISH).

Comparability

All countries compile data according to the 1993 SNA "System of National Accounts, 1993" with the exception of Australia where data are compiled according to the new 2008 SNA. It's important to note however that differences between the 2008 SNA and the 1993 SNA do not have a significant impact of the comparability of the indicators presented here and this implies that data are highly comparable across countries.

Real household disposable income
Annual growth in percentage

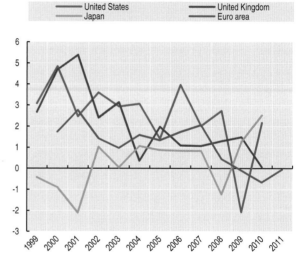

StatLink ⟨⟨⟨ http://dx.doi.org/10.1787/888932706964

Overview

In average over the period 2008-10, household disposable income in real terms increased for all OECD countries with some notable exceptions. In Greece, Hungary and Estonia, household disposable income fell by 9-13% in the three year period. Of the 28 OECD countries where information is available, decreases in disposable income were also recorded in Italy, Mexico, Portugal, the Netherlands and Austria. All other countries saw increases in real household disposable income in the period 2008-10. Chile, New Zealand, Norway and the Slovak Republic showed increases of over 10% for this three year period.

Across OECD countries, comparisons of growth of real household disposable income over the three years to 2010 compared to growth in the three years to 2001 show a rather consistent picture, with most countries showing slower growth. An exception is Japan, where moderate growth rates in the recent period compare to an average fall in the three years up to 2001.

Sources
- OECD (2012), *National Accounts of OECD Countries*, OECD Publishing.
- OECD (2011), *National Accounts at a Glance*, OECD Publishing.

Further information

Statistical publications
- OECD (2012), *Taxing Wages*, OECD Publishing.
- OECD (2011), *OECD Pensions at a Glance*, OECD Publishing.
- OECD (2011), *Society at a Glance: OECD Social Indicators*, OECD Publishing.

Methodological publications
- OECD (2007), *Understanding National Accounts*, OECD Publishing.
- United Nations, OECD, International Monetary Fund and Eurostat (eds.) (2010), *System of National Accounts 2008*, United Nations, Geneva.

Online databases
- OECD Social Expenditure Statistics.

Real household disposable income

Annual growth in percentage

	1999	2000	2001	2002	2003	2004	2005	2006	2007	2008	2009	2010	2011
Australia	3.4	3.3	3.5	1.1	4.3	4.0	4.5	5.5	2.7	6.9	..	..	..
Austria	4.0	1.8	-0.5	1.5	1.8	2.6	2.8	2.7	2.6	0.7	-1.5	-0.2	..
Belgium	2.5	1.8	3.1	-0.2	-0.2	-0.2	0.1	2.7	2.2	2.1	2.8	-1.3	-1.1
Canada	2.9	4.8	2.8	1.8	2.1	3.8	2.5	5.7	3.8	4.2	1.1	3.5	..
Chile	-0.9	3.5	3.2	2.2	3.4	7.8	7.7	7.0	7.1	4.9	7.4	5.9	..
Czech Republic	2.0	2.0	2.3	3.0	4.0	1.8	5.1	5.6	3.8	2.1	1.3	0.2	..
Denmark	-3.8	0.5	3.7	2.0	2.4	2.7	2.2	1.8	0.1	-0.2	0.2	3.8	1.1
Estonia	-1.9	11.2	5.9	7.0	7.3	2.0	11.0	10.8	11.8	0.4	-6.7	-2.7	..
Finland	4.5	0.6	3.2	2.2	6.0	4.8	1.0	2.7	3.6	2.4	1.9	2.5	0.0
France	2.7	3.1	3.1	3.5	0.5	2.1	1.1	2.4	3.0	0.2	1.2	0.9	0.6
Germany	1.8	0.9	1.7	0.0	0.7	0.6	0.4	1.2	0.0	1.0	-0.7	0.9	..
Greece	..	..	4.1	2.6	4.7	3.1	1.9	2.9	9.4	-4.5	1.7	-10.3	..
Hungary	1.5	1.2	5.2	6.4	5.5	4.0	3.6	1.7	-3.0	-1.8	-4.3	-4.0	..
Iceland	..	..	..	..	..	..	..	..	..	..	..	..	..
Ireland	..	..	..	..	0.3	5.8	7.8	4.3	6.9	5.0	-2.0	-2.2	..
Israel	..	..	..	..	..	..	..	..	..	..	..	..	..
Italy	1.5	0.1	3.0	1.2	0.5	0.9	0.6	0.9	1.0	-1.4	-3.0	-0.9	..
Japan	-0.4	-0.9	-2.1	1.0	0.0	1.1	0.9	0.8	0.8	-1.2	1.3	2.5	..
Korea	2.8	0.4	0.9	3.4	4.9	4.7	2.3	2.6	2.7	1.3	1.6	4.1	0.9
Luxembourg	..	..	..	..	..	..	..	..	4.0	4.2	1.4	..	..
Mexico	..	..	..	..	..	4.0	4.6	5.5	3.4	1.0	-7.7	4.1	..
Netherlands	2.1	2.2	5.6	-0.6	-2.5	0.6	-0.3	0.5	2.6	-0.3	-1.1	-0.1	-0.2
New Zealand	7.8	-4.1	3.7	-0.5	8.4	5.8	2.4	2.1	..	..	..	..	..
Norway	2.5	3.8	0.0	8.0	4.6	3.3	7.8	-6.4	6.3	3.9	3.9	3.5	4.2
Poland	3.5	1.7	4.1	-1.0	1.2	1.7	1.5	4.5	4.6	4.0	4.8	2.7	..
Portugal	6.6	3.6	1.6	1.0	0.3	1.7	0.7	-0.4	1.9	1.6	1.8	1.3	-4.6
Slovak Republic	-1.3	2.0	3.0	5.1	-0.7	3.9	6.2	3.4	9.1	5.0	2.2	3.2	..
Slovenia	3.5	4.5	4.6	3.2	0.6	3.9	4.1	3.2	4.5	2.7	-0.4	0.3	..
Spain	..	..	3.1	3.0	3.7	2.7	3.8	3.0	3.2	3.0	2.2	-4.6	..
Sweden	2.9	5.1	6.5	3.1	0.9	1.3	1.9	3.6	5.5	2.3	2.2	1.2	3.0
Switzerland	3.0	2.7	2.9	-1.3	-0.8	2.3	2.2	3.7	4.1	0.1	1.5	1.8	..
Turkey	..	..	..	..	..	..	..	..	..	..	..	..	..
United Kingdom	2.7	4.7	5.4	2.4	3.2	0.4	2.0	1.1	1.1	1.3	1.5	0.5	..
United States	3.1	4.8	2.5	3.6	2.9	3.1	1.4	4.0	2.0	2.7	-2.1	2.2	..
Euro area	..	1.7	2.8	1.4	1.0	1.6	1.3	1.7	2.1	0.4	-0.1	-0.6	-0.1
EU 27	..	2.2	3.5	1.6	1.6	1.5	1.6	1.8	2.1	1.1	0.5	-0.4	-0.1
OECD	..	..	..	..	..	..	..	..	..	..	..	..	..
Brazil	..	..	..	..	..	..	..	..	..	..	..	..	..
China	..	..	..	..	..	..	..	..	..	..	..	..	..
India	..	..	..	..	..	..	..	..	..	..	..	..	..
Indonesia	..	..	..	..	..	..	..	..	..	..	..	..	..
Russian Federation	..	..	..	..	7.7	9.4	11.9	13.6	14.1	8.0	-1.4	..	..
South Africa	2.0	3.7	2.8	3.5	4.0	5.8	5.0	6.9	5.2	0.3	1.8	5.8	..

StatLink http://dx.doi.org/10.1787/888932706926

Real household disposable income

Average annual growth in percentage

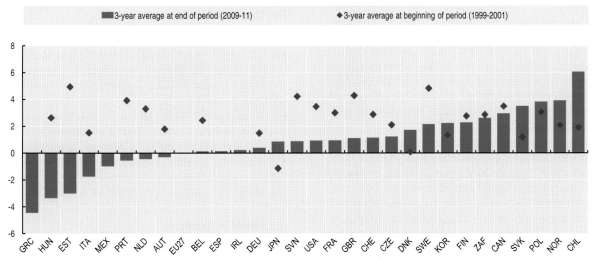

StatLink http://dx.doi.org/10.1787/888932706945

HOUSEHOLD SAVINGS

Household saving is the main domestic source of funds to finance capital investment, which is a major impetus for long-term economic growth. Household saving rates vary considerably between countries because of institutional, demographic and socio-economic differences. For example, government provisions for old-age pensions and the demographic age structure of the population will all influence the rate at which populations save (older persons tend to run down their financial assets during their retirement to the detriment of saving). Equally the availability and price of credit, as well as attitudes towards debt, may also influence choices made by individuals regarding whether to spend or save.

Definition

Household saving is estimated by subtracting household consumption expenditure from household disposable income plus the change in net equity of households in pension funds.

Household disposable income consists essentially of income from employment and from the operation of unincorporated enterprises, plus receipts of interest, dividends and social benefits minus payments of current taxes, interest and social contributions. Note that enterprise income includes imputed rents "paid" by owner-occupiers of dwellings.

Household consumption expenditure consists mainly of cash outlays for consumer goods and services but it also includes the imputed expenditures that owner occupiers pay, as occupiers, to themselves as owners of their dwellings and the production of goods for own-final use such as agricultural products - the values of which are also included in income.

The household saving rate is calculated as the ratio of household saving to household disposable income.

Comparability

All countries compile data according to the 1993 SNA "System of National Accounts, 1993" with the exception of Australia where data are compiled according to the new 2008 SNA. It's important to note however that differences between the 2008 SNA and the 1993 SNA do not have a significant impact of the comparability of the indicators presented here and this implies that data are highly comparable across countries.

Saving rates may be measured on either a net or a gross basis. Net saving rates are measured after deducting consumption of fixed capital (in respect of assets used in unincorporated enterprises and in respect of owner-occupied dwellings), from saving and from the disposable income of households, so that both saving and disposable income are shown on a net basis.

Overview

Household saving rates differ significantly across countries. In 2011 or the most recent available year (2010 in most cases), saving rates of above 10% were recorded in France, Germany, Slovenia, Switzerland and the Russian Federation. Savings rates were slightly negative in Denmark (minus 0.2%), whereas Greece reported a negative savings rate of 11.1% in 2010. Of the 27 countries where data is available for 2010, more than two thirds saw decreases in their savings rate compared to 2009.

Considering the years covered in the graph, household saving rates in Japan decreased markedly in 2001, with a much more moderate decrease in the following years. Saving rates have also decreased in Canada, although to a much lesser extent. Rates have remained broadly stable in Germany and France, at rather high levels of 10-12% and 11-13%, respectively. The United States saw a rather stable development of its household saving rate in the period 1999-2007; after that year, the household saving rate started to pick up and is now above 5%.

Sources

- OECD (2012), *National Accounts of OECD Countries*, OECD Publishing.

Further information

Analytical publications

- Fournier, J. and I. Koske (2010), "A Simple Model of the Relationship between Productivity, Saving and the Current Account", *OECD Economics Department Working Papers*, No. 816.
- Hüfner, F. and I. Koske (2010), "Explaining Household Saving Rates in G7 Countries: Implications for Germany", *OECD Economics Department Working Papers*, No. 754.
- de Laiglesia, J. and C. Morrison (2008), "Household Structures and Savings: Evidence from Household Surveys", *OECD Development Centre Working Papers*, No. 267.

Statistical publications

- OECD (2011), *National Accounts at a Glance*, OECD Publishing.

Websites

- OECD Economic Outlook – Sources and Methods, *www.oecd.org/eco/sources-and-methods*.

Household net saving rates

As a percentage of household disposable income

	1999	2000	2001	2002	2003	2004	2005	2006	2007	2008	2009	2010	2011
Australia	2.8	2.6	2.6	0.2	-0.9	-1.5	0.4	1.3	0.5	4.5	8.9	9.2	..
Austria	10.0	9.4	7.6	8.0	8.8	9.2	9.7	10.4	11.7	11.5	10.7	8.3	..
Belgium	13.2	12.5	13.8	13.1	12.3	10.7	9.9	10.7	11.4	11.5	13.3	10.1	8.8
Canada	4.1	4.8	5.3	3.5	2.7	3.2	2.2	3.6	2.9	4.0	4.7	4.9	..
Chile	6.8	6.1	6.6	6.4	6.1	6.8	6.7	7.3	7.3	6.0	10.9	8.1	..
Czech Republic	4.7	5.8	5.2	5.2	4.1	2.9	4.8	6.1	5.7	4.8	6.1	5.7	..
Denmark	-5.6	-4.0	2.1	2.1	2.4	-1.3	-4.2	-2.3	-4.0	-3.7	-0.4	-0.2	-0.2
Estonia	-5.4	-3.0	-4.0	-6.4	-7.1	-12.8	-10.8	-13.1	-8.2	-2.6	5.7	3.7	..
Finland	2.4	0.5	0.3	0.4	1.4	2.7	0.9	-1.1	-0.9	-0.3	4.2	3.3	..
France	11.3	11.0	11.7	13.0	11.9	12.2	11.1	11.2	11.7	11.7	12.6	12.1	12.3
Germany	9.6	9.4	9.5	10.1	10.4	10.6	10.7	10.8	11.0	11.7	11.1	11.3	..
Greece	..	-4.5	-5.5	-7.6	-6.2	-6.9	-1.7	-3.1	2.2	-6.5	-3.4	-11.1	..
Hungary	7.8	6.2	6.7	5.3	2.9	5.4	6.7	7.2	3.3	2.7	4.5	2.5	..
Iceland	..	..	..	..	..	..	..	..	..	..	..	..	..
Ireland	..	..	..	0.4	-0.6	0.9	1.7	-0.9	-0.1	5.5	10.1	8.9	..
Israel	..	..	..	..	..	..	..	..	..	..	..	..	..
Italy	10.0	7.9	10.0	10.8	10.3	10.5	10.2	9.5	8.9	8.5	6.9	5.1	..
Japan	10.2	8.8	3.8	3.3	2.7	2.3	1.6	1.3	1.1	0.5	2.3	2.3	..
Korea	16.1	9.3	5.2	0.4	5.2	9.2	7.2	5.2	2.9	2.9	4.6	4.3	3.1
Luxembourg	..	..	..	..	..	..	..	3.8	4.3	5.0	6.4	..	..
Mexico	..	..	..	..	11.4	10.1	10.1	10.1	9.6	8.9	8.9	8.4	..
Netherlands	9.0	6.9	9.7	8.7	7.6	7.4	6.4	6.1	6.9	5.9	5.6	3.4	5.0
New Zealand	1.0	-4.6	-3.6	-9.1	-6.9	-5.6	-7.6	-8.0	..	..	..	..	..
Norway	4.7	4.3	3.1	8.2	8.8	6.9	9.6	-0.5	0.8	3.4	6.6	6.1	8.0
Poland	10.5	10.0	11.9	8.3	7.7	5.5	5.9	6.1	4.6	-0.3	6.8	6.4	..
Portugal	3.9	3.8	3.8	3.3	3.6	2.8	2.7	0.4	-0.7	-0.8	3.2	2.4	1.8
Slovak Republic	6.2	6.0	3.8	3.3	1.1	0.3	1.1	0.1	2.2	1.1	..	..	..
Slovenia	4.5	7.8	9.8	10.5	8.2	9.5	11.2	11.7	10.3	9.4	9.1	10.0	..
Spain	..	6.1	5.9	5.8	6.7	5.2	4.8	3.9	4.0	7.5	13.0	7.7	..
Sweden	1.6	3.1	7.3	7.1	5.9	4.7	4.0	4.9	7.2	8.9	11.2	8.5	..
Switzerland	10.6	10.6	11.2	9.9	8.6	8.0	8.8	10.7	12.5	11.7	11.4	11.3	..
Turkey	..	..	..	..	..	..	..	..	..	..	..	..	..
United Kingdom	0.9	0.1	1.6	-0.1	0.3	-1.7	-1.5	-2.5	-3.1	-1.8	3.1	2.7	..
United States	3.2	3.0	2.8	3.7	3.8	3.5	1.7	2.7	2.4	5.5	5.3	5.5	..
Euro area	9.2	8.2	8.9	9.4	9.2	9.2	8.6	8.2	8.6	8.7	9.7	8.2	7.9
EU 27	7.2	6.3	7.3	7.1	6.9	6.3	6.0	5.6	5.5	5.9	8.1	6.7	6.1
OECD	..	..	..	..	..	..	..	..	..	..	..	..	..
Brazil	..	..	..	..	..	..	..	..	..	..	..	..	..
China	..	..	..	..	..	..	..	..	..	..	..	..	..
India	..	..	..	..	..	..	..	..	..	..	..	..	..
Indonesia	..	..	..	..	..	..	..	..	..	..	..	..	..
Russian Federation	..	..	..	..	..	..	11.0	12.4	12.1	10.1	13.6	..	..
South Africa	1.2	1.0	0.4	0.7	0.6	0.4	0.1	-0.8	-1.2	-1.1	-0.7	-0.3	-0.1

StatLink ⧉ http://dx.doi.org/10.1787/888932706983

Household net saving rates

As a percentage of household disposable income

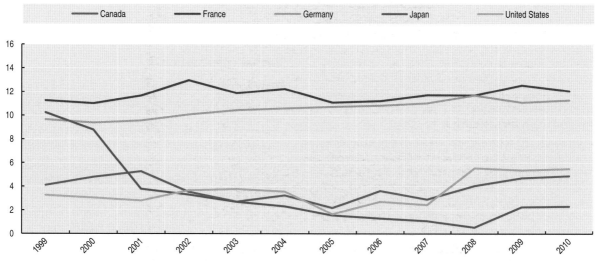

StatLink ⧉ http://dx.doi.org/10.1787/888932707002

INCOME INEQUALITY

Income inequalities are one of the most visible manifestations of differences in living standards within each country. High income inequalities typically imply a waste of human resources, in the form of a large share of the population out of work or trapped in low-paid and low-skilled jobs.

Definition

Income is defined as household disposable income in a particular year. It consists of earnings, self-employment and capital income and public cash transfers; income taxes and social security contributions paid by households are deducted. The income of the household is attributed to each of its members, with an adjustment to reflect differences in needs for households of different sizes (i.e. the needs of a household composed of four people are assumed to be twice as large as those of a person living alone).

Income inequality among individuals is measured here by four indicators. The Gini coefficient is based on the comparison of cumulative proportions of the population against cumulative proportions of income they receive, and it ranges between 0 in the case of perfect equality and 1 in the case of perfect inequality. The P90/P10 ratio is the ratio of the upper bound value of the ninth decile (i.e. the 10% of people with highest income) to that of the first decile; the P90/P50 ratio is the ratio of the upper bound value of the ninth decile to the median income; and the P50/P10 ratio is the ratio of median income to the upper bound value of the first decile.

Comparability

Data used here were provided by national experts applying common methodologies and standardised definitions. In many cases, experts have made several adjustments to their source data to conform to standardised definitions. While this approach improves comparability, full standardisation cannot be achieved. Also, small differences between periods and across countries are usually not significant.

Results refer to different years. "Late-2000s" data refer to the income in 2008 in all countries except Japan (2006); Denmark, Hungary and Turkey (2007); and Chile (2009). "Mid-1990s" data refer to the income earned between 1993 and 1996. "Mid-1980s" data refer to the income earned between 1983 and 1987 in all countries for which data are available except Greece (1988); Portugal (1990); and the Czech Republic (1992). "Mid-1980s" data refer to the western Lander of Germany. "Late-2000s" data for Austria, Belgium, Ireland, Portugal and Spain are based on EU-SILC and are not deemed to be fully comparable with those for earlier years.

For non-OECD countries, 2008/9 Gini coefficients are not strictly comparable with OECD countries as they are based on per capita incomes except India and Indonesia for which per capita consumption was used.

Overview

There is considerable variation in income inequality across OECD countries. Inequality as measured by the Gini coefficient is lowest in Slovenia, Denmark and Norway and highest in Chile, Mexico and Turkey. It is above-average in Israel, Portugal and the United States, and below-average in the remaining Nordic and many Continental European countries. The Gini coefficient for the most unequal country (Chile) is double the value of the most equal country (Slovenia). Overall, the different measures of income inequalities provide similar ranking across countries.

From the mid-1980s to the late-2000s, inequality rose in 15 out of 19 countries for which longer-run data are available. The increase was strongest in Finland, New Zealand and Sweden. Declines occurred in France, Greece, and Turkey. Income inequality generally rose faster from the mid-1980s to the mid-1990s than in the following period.

With measurement-related differences in mind, non-OECD countries have higher levels of income inequality than OECD countries, particularly in Brazil and South Africa.

Sources

- OECD (2011), *Divided We Stand: Why Inequality Keeps Rising*, OECD Publishing.

Further information

Analytical publications

- OECD (2011), *How's Life? Measuring Well-being*, OECD Publishing.
- OECD (2011), *Society at a Glance: OECD Social Indicators*, OECD Publishing.
- OECD (2010), *Tackling Inequalities in Brazil, China, India and South Africa: The Role of Labour Market and Social Policies*, OECD Publishing.
- OECD (2008), *Growing Unequal?: Income Distribution and Poverty in OECD Countries*, OECD Publishing.

Websites

- OECD Income Distribution and Poverty, *www.oecd.org/els/social/inequality*.
- OECD Social and Welfare Statistics, *www.oecd.org/social/statistics*.

Income inequality

Different summary measures, level and rank from low to high inequality, late 2000s

	Gini coefficient		Interdecile ratio P90/P10		Interdecile ratio P90/P50		Interdecile ratio P50/P10	
	Level	Rank	Level	Rank	Level	Rank	Level	Rank
Australia	0.34	26	4.5	24	2.0	23	2.1	20
Austria	0.26	9	3.2	9	1.8	9	1.8	8
Belgium	0.26	6	3.3	11	1.7	6	1.9	16
Canada	0.32	23	4.2	21	1.9	19	2.1	19
Chile	0.49	34	8.5	33	3.2	34	2.7	33
Czech Republic	0.26	4	2.9	2	1.7	7	1.7	2
Denmark	0.25	2	2.8	1	1.6	1	1.7	4
Estonia	0.32	21	4.3	22	2.0	26	2.3	25
Finland	0.26	8	3.2	7	1.7	5	1.9	10
France	0.29	12	3.4	14	1.9	17	1.8	7
Germany	0.30	15	3.5	15	1.8	14	1.9	14
Greece	0.31	18	4.0	19	2.0	21	2.2	21
Hungary	0.27	10	3.1	6	1.7	8	1.8	6
Iceland	0.30	16	3.2	10	1.8	11	1.7	3
Ireland	0.29	13	3.7	17	1.9	16	2.2	22
Israel	0.37	30	6.2	32	2.3	30	2.7	32
Italy	0.34	27	4.3	23	2.0	27	2.1	18
Japan	0.33	24	5.0	29	2.0	24	2.4	29
Korea	0.31	19	4.8	27	1.9	18	2.4	28
Luxembourg	0.29	11	3.4	13	1.8	12	1.9	9
Mexico	0.48	33	9.7	34	3.0	33	2.9	34
Netherlands	0.29	14	3.3	12	1.8	13	1.9	12
New Zealand	0.33	25	4.2	20	2.1	28	2.1	17
Norway	0.25	3	3.0	3	1.6	2	1.8	5
Poland	0.31	20	4.0	18	2.0	22	2.4	27
Portugal	0.35	29	4.9	28	2.3	31	2.2	24
Slovak Republic	0.26	5	3.1	5	1.8	10	1.9	13
Slovenia	0.24	1	3.0	4	1.6	3	1.9	11
Spain	0.32	22	4.6	25	2.0	20	2.3	26
Sweden	0.26	7	3.2	8	1.7	4	1.7	1
Switzerland	0.30	17	3.7	16	1.9	15	1.9	15
Turkey	0.41	32	6.2	31	2.5	32	2.7	30
United Kingdom	0.34	28	4.6	26	2.0	25	2.2	23
United States	0.38	31	5.9	30	2.2	29	2.7	31
EU 27	..	..	..	..	..	..	..	..
OECD	0.31	..	4.3	..	2.0	..	2.1	..
Brazil	0.55	..	..	..	..	..	..	..
China	0.41	..	..	..	..	..	..	..
India	0.38	..	..	..	..	..	..	..
Indonesia	0.37	..	..	..	..	..	..	..
Russian Federation	0.42	..	..	..	..	..	..	..
South Africa	0.70	..	..	..	..	..	..	..

StatLink ᵐˢ᷉ http://dx.doi.org/10.1787/888932707021

Trends in income inequality

Percentage point changes in the Gini coefficient

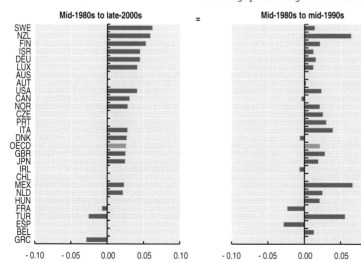

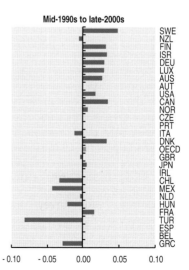

StatLink ᵐˢ᷉ http://dx.doi.org/10.1787/888932707040

POVERTY RATES AND GAPS

Avoiding economic hardship is a primary objective of social policy. As perceptions of "a decent standard of living" vary across countries and over time, no commonly agreed measure of "absolute" poverty across OECD countries exists. A starting point for measuring poverty is therefore to look at "relative" poverty, whose measure is based on the income that is most typical in each country in each year.

Definition

Relative income poverty is measured here by the poverty rate and the poverty gap. The poverty rate is the ratio of the number of people whose income falls below the poverty line and the total population; the poverty line is here taken as half the median household income. However, two countries with the same poverty rates may differ in terms of the relative income-level of the poor. To measure this dimension, the poverty gap, *i.e.* the percentage by which the mean income of the poor falls below the poverty line, is also presented.

Income is defined as household disposable income in a particular year. It consists of earnings, self-employment and capital income and public cash transfers; income taxes and social security contributions paid by households are deducted. The income of the household is attributed to each of its members, with an adjustment to reflect differences in needs for households of different sizes (*i.e.* the needs of a household composed of four people are assumed to be twice as large as those of a person living alone).

Overview

Across OECD countries, the average poverty rate was about 11% in the late-2000s. There is considerable diversity across countries: poverty rates are 20% or more in Israel and Mexico, but below 7% in the Czech Republic, Denmark, Hungary and Iceland. On average, in OECD countries, the mean income of poor people is 27% below the poverty line (poverty gap), with larger gaps in Korea, Mexico, Spain and the United States and lower ones in Belgium, Luxembourg, Finland and the Netherlands. In general, countries with higher poverty rates also have higher poverty gaps but this is not universal; for example Norway combines low poverty rates and high poverty gaps, while the opposite occurs in Estonia.

From the mid-1980s to the late-2000s, poverty rates rose in 16 out of 19 countries for which longer-run data are available, resulting in an overall increase of 2 percentage points for the OECD as a whole. The largest rise was experienced by Israel, and the largest decline was registered in Greece.

Comparability

Data used here were provided by national experts applying common methodologies and standardised definitions. In many cases, experts have made several adjustments to their source data to conform to standardised definitions. While this approach improves comparability, full standardisation cannot be achieved.

Measurement problems are especially severe at the bottom end of the income scale. As large proportions of the population are clustered around the poverty line used here, small changes in their income can lead to large swings in poverty measures. Small differences between periods and across countries are usually not significant.

"Late-2000s" data refer to the income in 2008 in all countries except Japan (2006); Denmark, Hungary and Turkey (2007); and Chile (2009). "Mid-1990s" data refer to the income earned between 1993 and 1996. "Mid-1980s" data refer to the income earned between 1983 and 1987 in all countries for which data are available except Greece (1988); Portugal (1990); and the Czech Republic (1992). "Mid-1980s" data refer to the western Lander of Germany. "Late-2000s" data for Austria, Belgium, Ireland, Portugal and Spain are based on EU-SILC and are not deemed to be fully comparable with earlier years.

Sources

- OECD (2011), *Divided We Stand: Why Inequality Keeps Rising*, OECD Publishing.

Further information

Analytical publications

- OECD (2011), *How's Life? Measuring Well-being*, OECD Publishing.
- OECD (2011), *Society at a Glance: OECD Social Indicators*, OECD Publishing.
- OECD (2008), *Growing Unequal?: Income Distribution and Poverty in OECD Countries*, OECD Publishing.
- Atkinson, A.B., and A. Brandolini (2004), "*Global World Income Inequality: Absolute, Relative or Intermediate?*", paper presented at the 28th General Conference of the International Association for Research in Income and Wealth, Cork, 22-28 August.
- Förster, M. (1994), "Measurement of Low Incomes and Poverty in a Perspective of International Comparisons", *OECD Labour Market and Social Policy Occasional Papers*, No. 14.

Websites

- OECD Social and Welfare Statistics, *www.oecd.org/social/statistics*.
- OECD Income Distribution and Poverty, *www.oecd.org/els/social/inequality*.

Poverty rates and poverty gaps
Late-2000s

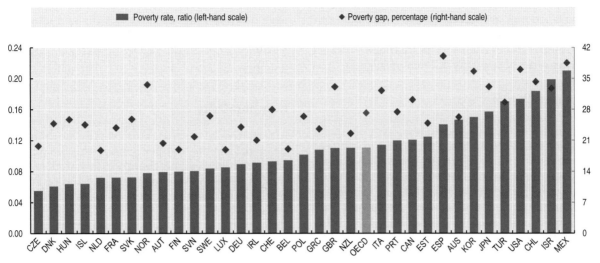

StatLink ᵐˢᴸ http://dx.doi.org/10.1787/888932707059

Trends in poverty rates
Percentage point changes in income poverty rate at 50% median level

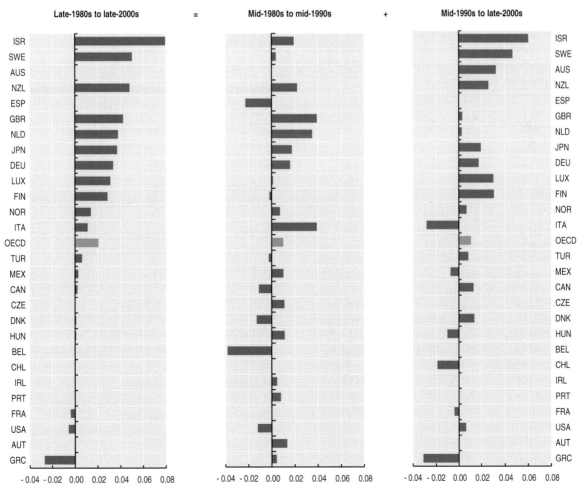

StatLink ᵐˢᴸ http://dx.doi.org/10.1787/888932707078

HOUSEHOLD FINANCIAL ASSETS

Along with income, wealth is the central measure of households' economic resources. Households hold both non-financial and financial wealth. The structure of financial assets affects households financial risks as different types of securities carry different risk levels.

Definition

This set of indicators shows the share of each financial asset category according to the *1993 System of National Accounts* (currency and deposits; securities other than shares, except financial derivatives; shares and other equity, except mutual fund shares; mutual fund shares; net equity of households in life insurance reserves; and, net equity of households in pension funds) in the total

financial assets of the households and NPISHs sector. It excludes financial derivatives, loans and other accounts receivable.

The financial assets are classified according to their liquidity.

Comparability

International comparability may be hampered by differences in the way pension systems are organised and operated in the various countries. In countries with highly funded pension systems, more pension reserves will be recognised and recorded as part of the assets of households.

It should be noted that any changes in the stocks of financial assets over a period are the result of two components: net acquisitions of financial assets and changes in valuations (holding gains and losses depending on the performance of financial markets), of which those for quoted shares are the most relevant.

In the graph, 2011 data are shown for Belgium, Canada, Chile, Denmark, Greece, Korea, the Netherlands, Norway, Portugal, Slovenia, Spain, the United Kingdom and the United States.

Overview

The comparison of the structure of households' stocks of financial assets between 2007 and 2010 gives some insight into the impact of recent economic developments on the restructuring of their portfolio towards financial instruments better adapted to the new environment, *i.e.* more liquid and less risky. The increase in the share of currency and deposits in almost all OECD countries is noticeable, with a significant rise in Greece (from 52% in 2007 to 77% in 2010). Also the share of life insurance and pension funds assets increased in a large number of OECD countries. On the other hand, shares became less popular in most OECD countries, the largest fall being observed in Greece (from 28% to 8%), followed by Spain (31% to 24%), Poland (31% to 20%), and Slovenia (28% to 21%).

Considerable differences in national preferences for financial instruments can be observed across the OECD. Currency and deposits, the most liquid of the asset categories and also considered the one with the least risk, represents more than 50% in six OECD countries (the Czech Republic, Greece, Japan, Luxembourg, the Slovak Republic and Slovenia) in 2010. The proportion of securities held by households is low in most OECD countries in 2010 with the exception of Mexico (37% in 2009) and Italy (20%). Furthermore, despite the financial crisis, shares remained a predominant portfolio asset held by households in for example Estonia (67%), Mexico (39% in 2009) and the United States (32%). Household reserves in life insurance and pension funds represented more than half of the stock of total financial assets in Chile (60%), the Netherlands (59%), Australia (59%) and the United Kingdom (52%), whereas they remained at a very low level in Greece (3%) and Estonia (5%).

Sources
- OECD (2012),"Financial Balance Sheets", *OECD National Accounts Statistics* (database).

Further information

Analytical publications
- OECD (2012), *OECD Economic Outlook*, OECD Publishing.
- Ynesta, I. (2009), "Households' wealth composition across OECD countries and financial risks borne by households", *OECD Journal: Financial Market Trends*, Vol. 2008/2.

Statistical publications
- OECD (2012), *National Accounts of OECD Countries, Financial Accounts*, OECD Publishing.
- OECD (2012), *National Accounts of OECD Countries, Financial Balance Sheets*, OECD Publishing.
- OECD (2011), *National Accounts at a Glance*, OECD Publishing.

Methodological publications
- Lequiller, F. and D. Blades (2007), *Understanding National Accounts*, OECD Publishing.
- OECD et al. (2009), *System of National Accounts*, United Nations, New York.

Online databases
- *OECD National Accounts Statistics.*

Websites
- Financial statistics, *www.oecd.org/std/financialstatistics.*

Financial assets of households by type of assets

As a percentage of total financial assets

	Currency and deposits		Securities other than shares		Shares and other equity		Mutual funds shares		Life insurance reserves		Pension funds	
	2007	2010	2007	2010	2007	2010	2007	2010	2007	2010	2007	2010
Australia	19.0	25.4	0.7	0.2	17.1	10.8	0.0	0.0	2.6	2.3	55.6	56.3
Austria	44.4	45.1	8.3	9.1	16.3	15.9	10.8	9.3	13.3	13.4	3.1	3.3
Belgium	29.0	31.7	8.3	8.8	22.1	20.9	16.6	11.7	19.4	22.2	1.2	1.4
Canada	19.4	22.8	2.5	2.1	..	..	..	..	..	..	..	..
Chile	12.2	11.4	1.1	0.7	23.9	21.2	4.4	5.2	11.1	11.9	47.1	48.4
Czech Republic	54.5	56.5	0.3	0.8	22.4	21.4	7.7	5.1	6.4	6.9	5.2	5.9
Denmark	20.4	19.2	4.8	3.7	23.4	22.3	7.4	6.8	22.6	24.9	17.8	20.0
Estonia	17.4	21.8	2.0	0.1	67.2	66.8	1.1	0.4	2.4	1.5	4.0	3.9
Finland	31.6	34.4	1.9	3.1	34.6	34.1	10.0	7.8	7.4	6.3	8.7	8.7
France	28.5	29.0	1.7	1.6	21.1	18.2	8.7	7.5	27.8	29.8	3.8	4.3
Germany	36.3	40.1	6.7	5.5	13.2	9.2	10.5	9.4	..	..	..	..
Greece	52.2	77.3	9.4	7.5	28.0	7.5	5.2	1.4	2.1	2.4	0.3	0.8
Hungary	35.3	34.8	4.9	5.5	26.3	27.1	9.8	8.1	6.0	5.7	11.5	13.7
Iceland	..	..	..	..	..	..	..	..	..	..	..	..
Ireland	37.6	40.5	0.0	0.1	20.8	17.7	0.0	0.0	17.0	18.6	23.1	21.6
Israel	20.9	20.0	13.8	11.8	26.1	18.3	0.0	7.0	7.9	9.7	26.6	28.6
Italy	27.4	30.6	19.8	19.8	24.8	21.3	8.6	6.6	9.7	11.5	5.5	5.9
Japan	51.2	54.0	4.3	3.9	8.8	7.0	4.1	3.5	14.4	14.1	13.0	13.0
Korea	42.5	45.1	12.7	9.7	20.9	19.7	0.5	0.3	18.0	18.9	2.0	2.0
Luxembourg	55.5	51.6	10.0	14.5	12.1	12.9	12.8	10.2	6.7	8.1	2.4	1.8
Mexico	14.3	..	32.1	..	44.6	..	5.6	..	1.9	..	0.9	..
Netherlands	21.3	23.1	3.0	2.5	11.4	9.7	3.3	3.1	10.3	11.1	47.6	48.2
New Zealand	..	..	..	..	..	..	..	..	..	..	..	..
Norway	31.2	32.4	1.3	0.7	11.1	9.2	5.5	5.2	6.0	6.4	28.0	29.8
Poland	33.6	43.2	0.8	0.6	30.8	20.3	10.6	6.5	6.0	6.0	14.1	19.1
Portugal	34.5	37.4	5.2	5.7	25.4	23.4	7.3	4.1	10.7	12.5	6.1	5.7
Slovak Republic	58.5	60.6	1.7	3.2	4.4	3.8	7.6	2.3	4.2	4.8	13.5	16.6
Slovenia	45.9	53.7	1.2	1.2	27.5	21.2	9.2	6.2	4.5	5.5	2.2	3.0
Spain	38.3	48.3	2.6	2.6	31.3	23.5	10.8	7.1	6.2	7.2	5.9	6.2
Sweden	18.0	18.2	3.1	2.1	28.2	28.7	10.2	7.9	13.8	13.8	19.4	24.0
Switzerland	26.5	29.9	8.7	7.4	12.7	11.0	11.3	9.3	5.3	5.1	32.5	33.9
Turkey	..	..	..	..	..	..	..	..	..	..	..	..
United Kingdom	27.1	28.0	0.8	0.9	10.7	11.5	4.1	3.1	53.2	52.2	0.0	0.0
United States	11.7	13.5	9.3	10.6	36.0	32.1	11.5	11.6	2.1	2.3	26.0	26.6
EU 27	..	..	..	..	..	..	..	..	..	..	..	..
OECD	..	..	..	..	..	..	..	..	..	..	..	..
Brazil	..	..	..	..	..	..	..	..	..	..	..	..
China	..	..	..	..	..	..	..	..	..	..	..	..
India	..	..	..	..	..	..	..	..	..	..	..	..
Indonesia	..	..	..	..	..	..	..	..	..	..	..	..
Russian Federation	..	..	..	..	..	..	..	..	..	..	..	..
South Africa	..	..	..	..	..	..	..	..	..	..	..	..

StatLink http://dx.doi.org/10.1787/888932707097

Financial assets of households by type of assets

As a percentage of their total financial assets, 2010 or latest available year

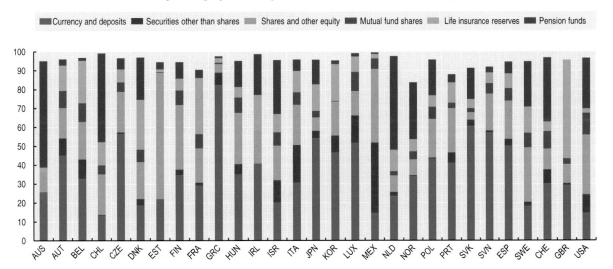

Legend: Currency and deposits ■ Securities other than shares ■ Shares and other equity ■ Mutual fund shares ■ Life insurance reserves ■ Pension funds

StatLink http://dx.doi.org/10.1787/888932707116

HOUSEHOLD DEBT

This household leverage ratio measures the indebtedness of households in relation with their income, that is their spending and saving capacity. High leverage ratios are often interpreted as a sign of financial vulnerability though not only debt and liabilities but also assets should be considered in such an assessment. High indebtedness levels generally increase the financing costs of the borrower, deteriorate balance sheet positions and may restrict access to new financing.

The household debt-to-GDI ratio shows the debt of households and non-profit institutions serving households (NPISHs), as a percentage of their Gross Disposable Income (GDI).

Definition

Debt is a commonly used concept, defined as a specific subset of liabilities identified according to the types of financial instruments included or excluded. Generally, debt is defined as all liabilities that require payment or payments of interest or principal by the debtor to the creditor at a date or dates in the future.

Consequently, all debt instruments are liabilities, but some liabilities such as shares, equity and financial derivatives are not considered as debt. Debt is thus obtained as the sum of the following liability categories (according to the *1993 System of National Accounts*), whenever available/applicable in the financial balance sheet of the households and NPISHs sector: currency and deposits; securities other than shares, except financial derivatives; loans; insurance technical reserves; and other accounts payable. For the households sector, liabilities predominantly consist of loans, and more particularly mortgage loans for the purchase of houses.

According to the 1993 SNA, most debt instruments are valued at market prices.

Comparability

As a number of OECD countries are not able to provide a breakdown between households and NPISHs, household debt refers to the aggregated sector "Households and NPISHs" to ensure the highest level of comparability between countries.

Overview

Households remain highly indebted in a large number of OECD economies. In 2010, the ratio of household debt to gross disposable income (GDI) is far higher than the average of OECD countries, in Denmark, the Netherlands, Ireland and Norway. Mexico has the lowest debt ratio at 9.4% in 2009.

The level of household debt rose in most OECD countries over the period 2007-10. As a percentage of GDI, the Netherlands and Greece recorded the largest increases during this period (respectively around 35 and 21 percentage points). Hungary, Poland and the Slovak Republic showed increases of 18 percentage points. A net fall was observed in the United Kingdom (minus 15 percentage points) and the United States (minus 14 percentage points), and to a (far) lesser extent in Germany, Norway, Spain and Japan.

According to the most recent figures, long-term loans, mainly consisting of mortgage loans, remain the largest component of household debt, contributing more than 80% of the total household debt in twenty OECD countries and even more than 90% in eleven countries. The highest level was recorded in Luxembourg (96% in 2010) and the lowest ratios were observed in the Slovak Republic (61%), and Italy (70%). In the Netherlands, the contribution of long-term loans to the total household debt, while decreasing since 2007, is still above 92%. The same tendency can be observed since 2008 in two other countries (Estonia and the United States at around 90% and 73% respectively).

Sources
- OECD (2012), *National Accounts of OECD Countries*, OECD Publishing.

Further information

Analytical publications
- OECD (2012), *Economic Policy Reforms*, OECD Publishing.
- OECD (2012), *OECD Economic Outlook*, OECD Publishing.
- OECD (2012), *OECD Economic Surveys*, OECD Publishing.
- Sebastian Schich and Jung-Hyun Ahn (2007), "Housing Markets and Household Debt: Short-term and Long-term Risks", *Financial Market Trends*, Vol. 2007/1.

Statistical publications
- OECD (2012), *Quarterly National Accounts*, OECD Publishing.
- OECD (2011), *National Accounts at a Glance*, OECD Publishing.

Methodological publications
- OECD (2000), *System of National Accounts, 1993 - Glossary*, OECD Publishing.
- United Nations, OECD, International Monetary Fund and Eurostat (eds.) (2010), *System of National Accounts 2008*, United Nations, Geneva.

Online databases
- *OECD National Accounts Statistics*.

Household debt

Debt of households and non-profit institutions serving households, as a percentage of gross disposable income

	1999	2000	2001	2002	2003	2004	2005	2006	2007	2008	2009	2010	2011
Australia	103.7	108.4	114.3	126.3	138.0	150.0	156.3	160.6	170.9	167.3	..	..	..
Austria	71.9	73.8	75.6	77.5	77.0	80.3	85.2	86.5	86.1	87.5	88.8	91.4	..
Belgium	67.3	65.2	61.3	62.8	65.8	68.9	73.6	76.8	80.0	82.0	82.7	86.9	..
Canada	110.9	109.8	111.1	113.9	117.3	120.9	125.9	128.6	134.1	137.9	144.5	146.5	..
Chile	..	..	..	..	..	..	..	..	..	..	..	..	..
Czech Republic	19.3	20.0	20.7	25.5	27.5	32.6	37.8	42.2	51.4	56.5	60.0	60.5	..
Denmark	..	..	..	..	238.5	251.8	267.0	284.1	308.3	314.9	322.1	309.5	..
Estonia	16.1	20.2	23.8	30.7	39.3	51.5	67.6	89.6	99.3	100.8	105.2	102.0	..
Finland	61.8	64.6	64.8	69.7	74.0	82.0	91.8	101.1	105.7	108.1	108.4	110.2	..
France	68.1	66.0	66.1	67.5	70.5	72.6	78.6	82.9	86.8	86.5	90.3	93.6	..
Germany	107.6	109.0	106.7	106.7	105.5	104.0	101.5	99.2	96.1	92.8	93.3	91.1	..
Greece	..	..	..	..	..	..	57.7	65.7	69.5	77.3	77.6	90.9	..
Hungary	12.7	15.2	18.2	24.2	33.1	38.4	44.0	50.0	57.6	70.2	70.7	75.5	..
Iceland	..	..	..	..	..	..	..	..	..	..	..	..	..
Ireland	..	..	..	115.0	135.6	154.5	181.2	197.5	209.9	208.8	221.0	217.8	..
Israel	..	..	..	..	..	..	..	..	..	..	..	..	..
Italy	49.0	52.8	54.6	57.1	60.2	63.9	68.4	73.1	77.4	78.2	83.3	85.9	..
Japan	..	..	130.4	129.6	128.2	127.7	128.2	127.7	124.3	122.9	123.2	121.3	..
Korea	..	..	..	125.0	120.5	116.4	123.2	131.3	139.0	142.6	146.9	150.8	156.3
Luxembourg	..	..	..	..	..	..	..	118.5	126.2	126.7	132.2	..	..
Mexico	..	..	..	..	7.3	7.4	8.4	10.4	11.4	9.4	9.4	..	..
Netherlands	153.5	163.7	166.1	178.2	197.4	208.8	226.4	238.5	242.4	253.5	270.3	277.3	..
New Zealand	..	..	..	..	..	..	..	..	..	..	..	..	..
Norway	130.8	135.1	146.5	147.0	150.3	159.5	164.0	191.3	199.9	198.1	196.1	196.3	200.0
Poland	10.4	11.5	17.1	21.7	19.1	20.6	23.7	29.7	37.5	49.2	51.3	55.5	..
Portugal	97.6	106.4	110.7	112.9	118.5	123.7	128.8	136.9	143.3	142.0	145.6	142.9	139.5
Slovak Republic	14.1	20.1	21.0	25.9	29.5	28.7	37.9	51.0	58.4	64.4	73.6	75.9	..
Slovenia	..	..	30.4	30.7	32.4	32.8	36.9	41.1	47.0	48.4	51.3	53.7	..
Spain	..	81.5	84.5	91.0	99.0	109.2	120.9	134.0	139.5	135.0	132.1	136.3	..
Sweden	102.0	105.5	115.7	117.0	124.3	133.1	143.0	150.4	154.3	155.8	160.9	168.4	..
Switzerland	177.4	173.9	172.3	178.8	189.9	189.6	193.2	192.8	188.2	186.5	190.5	..	..
Turkey	..	..	..	..	..	..	..	..	..	..	..	..	..
United Kingdom	108.5	111.7	115.7	127.3	138.1	151.3	153.9	166.2	172.2	169.0	162.0	157.0	..
United States	99.2	100.5	104.2	109.0	116.5	123.0	129.9	134.0	136.4	127.8	128.5	122.5	..
EU 27	..	..	..	..	..	..	..	..	..	..	..	..	..
OECD	..	..	..	..	..	..	..	..	..	..	..	..	..
Brazil	..	..	..	..	..	..	..	..	..	..	..	..	..
China	..	..	..	..	..	..	..	..	..	..	..	..	..
India	..	..	..	..	..	..	..	..	..	..	..	..	..
Indonesia	..	..	..	..	..	..	..	..	..	..	..	..	..
Russian Federation	..	..	..	..	..	..	..	..	..	..	..	..	..
South Africa	..	..	..	..	..	..	..	..	..	..	..	..	..

StatLink http://dx.doi.org/10.1787/888932707135

Households and NPISHs debt

As a percentage of gross disposable income

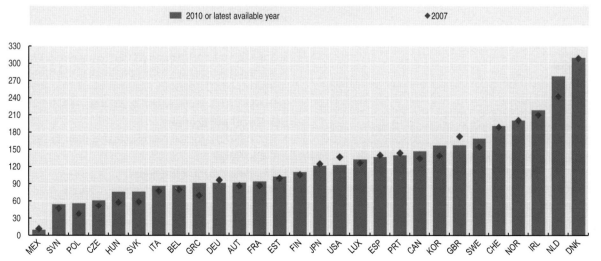

StatLink http://dx.doi.org/10.1787/888932707154

NON-FINANCIAL ASSETS BY HOUSEHOLDS

Non-financial assets held by households reflect the assets owned by unincorporated household enterprises and dwellings owned by households, with the latter component forming by far the bulk of non-financial assets held by households. They form an important part of overall wealth and can provide an important additional source of revenue; either through their sale or refinancing, or as income via rentals of residential property for example. Estimates of non-financial assets held by households also play an important role in economic analyses, such as studies of asset bubbles, and analyses of living standards.

Definition

Non-financial assets held by households include, in theory, both produced and non-produced nonfinancial assets and therefore include: dwellings, other buildings and structures, and land improvements; machinery and equipment including livestock; and even intellectual property products, such as software and literary originals, and non-produced assets such as land and taxi-licenses. In practice dwellings form by far the most significant component.

Except for dwellings, only those assets owned by household unincorporated enterprises, and used in production, are included as non-financial assets. For example a car used by a household purely for household transport is not a non-financial asset whereas a car used by a self-employed taxi driver is.

Non-financial assets are valued at the market prices of the time of the balance sheet, and are recorded net of depreciation.

Comparability

Information on non-financial assets held by households typically relies on household based surveys. As a consequence, the quality of this information, except for that pertaining to dwellings and land, is generally of lower quality than it is for similar information collected on incorporated businesses.

Moreover, in practice, countries use a variety of methods to differentiate between the value of dwellings and the land on which the dwellings sit, meaning that comparisons of these subcomponents across countries are challenging. Some countries include the value of land under dwellings within the figures for dwellings. This matters not only for international comparability but also because dwellings, as produced assets depreciate whereas (most) land, as a non-produced asset, does not. A particular challenge arises from capturing quality change and quality differences in the housing stock and valuing it accordingly.

The caveats above, pertaining to the distinction between land and dwellings, mean that users should be particularly careful in using the figures in making international comparisons. The OECD is working with national statistics institutes so that future versions of these data reflect a greater degree of international comparability.

Data are assets net of depreciation for all countries except for the Slovak Republic and Poland (gross recording).

Sources
- OECD (2012), *National Accounts of OECD Countries*, OECD Publishing.

Further information

Analytical publications
- Babeau, A. and T. Sbano (2003), "Household Wealth in the National Accounts of Europe, the United States and Japan", *OECD Statistics Working Papers*, No. 2003/02.
- OECD (2012), *Economic Policy Reforms*, OECD Publishing.

Statistical publications
- OECD (2011), *National Accounts at a Glance*, OECD Publishing.

Methodological publications
- OECD (2000), *System of National Accounts, 1993 – Glossary*, OECD Publishing.
- United Nations, OECD, International Monetary Fund and Eurostat (eds.) (2010), *System of National Accounts 2008*, United Nations, Geneva.

Online databases
- *OECD National Accounts Statistics*.

Websites
- National accounts, *www.oecd.org/std/nationalaccounts*.

Overview

Prior to the recent financial crisis, dwellings per capita values rose almost continually, with few exceptions, in all OECD countries. The United Kingdom saw the strongest growth over this period (1996-2007) with values trebling. Growth was also strong in many other countries such as Australia, Finland, France, the Netherlands, the Slovak Republic, Sweden and the United States, with values doubling over the period. In 2008 however at the height of the recent crisis the average value fell by 11% in the United Kingdom and by 3% in the United States. For the United States the contraction continued into 2009, with values falling again by 3% before stabilising in 2010. The average growth in most other countries also slowed over this period, with growth turning negative in Japan in 2009 and Finland in both 2009 and 2010.

Non-financial assets of households

US dollars at current PPPs, per capita

	Dwellings				Land				Other			
	2007	2008	2009	2010	2007	2008	2009	2010	2007	2008	2009	2010
Australia	42 469	42 256	43 965	43 696	86 849	77 480	95 181	85 326	16 737	16 212	16 815	16 215
Austria	43 418	46 184	47 975	49 222	..	..	..	..	..	..	..	..
Belgium	39 981	44 275	46 032	47 023	..	..	..	..	..	..	..	..
Canada	34 690	35 239	36 494	37 598	30 072	30 908	32 804	33 502	1 587	1 693	1 675	1 599
Chile	..	..	..	..	..	..	..	..	..	..	..	..
Czech Republic	21 972	22 773	23 882	23 879	2 652	2 926	2 963	2 824	4 816	4 594	4 673	4 807
Denmark	53 465	58 300	60 880	61 702	..	..	..	..	..	..	..	..
Estonia	23 687	24 183	24 295	..	..	..	..	..	..	..	..	..
Finland	35 627	38 965	38 652	37 502	..	..	..	..	..	..	..	..
France	51 547	54 244	55 840	57 690	63 944	60 795	57 289	66 769	7 339	7 445	7 487	7 516
Germany	47 581	51 491	54 091	54 907	..	..	..	..	..	..	..	..
Greece	..	..	..	..	..	..	..	..	..	..	..	..
Hungary	20 308	22 169	23 544	..	..	..	..	..	..	..	..	..
Iceland	..	..	..	..	..	..	..	..	..	..	..	..
Ireland	..	..	..	..	..	..	..	..	..	..	..	..
Israel	25 758	..	..	..	..	..	..	..	..	..	..	..
Italy	39 513	42 644	43 559	..	..	..	..	..	..	..	..	..
Japan	20 295	21 141	20 606	..	54 363	54 263	52 911	..	4 816	4 842	4 648	..
Korea	..	..	..	..	..	..	..	..	..	..	..	..
Luxembourg	63 298	69 178	72 122	73 688	..	..	..	..	..	..	..	..
Mexico	..	..	..	..	..	..	..	..	..	..	..	..
Netherlands	48 245	51 652	53 819	54 836	55 232	58 541	54 139	51 925	..	..	..	..
New Zealand	..	..	..	..	..	..	..	..	..	..	..	..
Norway	..	..	..	..	..	..	..	..	..	..	..	..
Poland	6 529	7 496	7 728	..	..	..	..	..	..	..	..	..
Portugal	..	..	..	..	..	..	..	..	..	..	..	..
Slovak Republic	26 157	28 778	31 047	31 198	..	..	..	..	..	..	..	..
Slovenia	32 187	33 829	34 158	35 007	..	..	..	..	..	..	..	..
Spain	..	..	..	..	..	..	..	..	..	..	..	..
Sweden	23 861	26 147	26 372	..	..	..	..	..	..	..	..	..
Switzerland	..	..	..	..	..	..	..	..	..	..	..	..
Turkey	..	..	..	..	..	..	..	..	..	..	..	..
United Kingdom	103 646	92 311	94 676	98 417	..	..	..	..	..	..	..	..
United States	54 288	52 833	51 328	51 099	..	..	..	..	..	..	..	..
EU 27	..	..	..	..	..	..	..	..	..	..	..	..
OECD	..	..	..	..	..	..	..	..	..	..	..	..
Brazil	..	..	..	..	..	..	..	..	..	..	..	..
China	..	..	..	..	..	..	..	..	..	..	..	..
India	..	..	..	..	..	..	..	..	..	..	..	..
Indonesia	..	..	..	..	..	..	..	..	..	..	..	..
Russian Federation	..	..	..	..	..	..	..	..	..	..	..	..
South Africa	..	..	..	..	..	..	..	..	..	..	..	..

StatLink http://dx.doi.org/10.1787/888932707173

Non-financial assets of households per capita: dwellings

US dollars at current PPPs

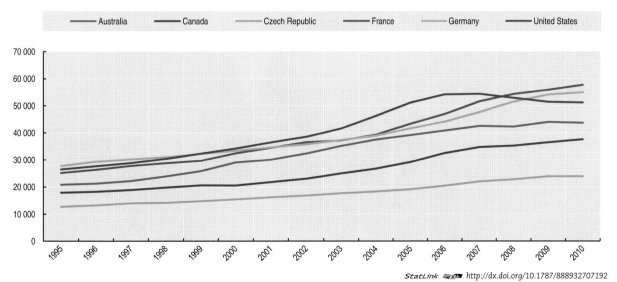

StatLink http://dx.doi.org/10.1787/888932707192

GLOBALISATION

TRADE
SHARE OF INTERNATIONAL TRADE IN GDP
INTERNATIONAL TRADE IN GOODS
INTERNATIONAL TRADE IN SERVICES
TRADING PARTNERS

FDI AND BALANCE OF PAYMENTS
FOREIGN DIRECT INVESTMENT
BALANCE OF PAYMENTS

SHARE OF INTERNATIONAL TRADE IN GDP

In today's increasingly globalised world, exports and imports are key aggregates in the analysis of a country's economic situation. Whenever an economy slows down or accelerates, all other economies are potentially affected.

Definition

Exports of goods and services consist of sales, barter or gifts or grants, of goods and services (included in the production boundary of GDP) from residents to non-residents. Equally, imports reflect the same transactions from non-residents to residents.

Not all goods need to physically enter a country's border to be recorded as an export or import. Transportation equipment, goods produced by residents in international waters sold directly to non-residents, and food consumed in ships or planes are but a few examples of transactions which may be recorded as exports or imports without physically crossing borders.

Equally not all goods that enter a country's borders are necessarily imports or exports. Transportation equipment, goods sent abroad for minor processing (or which enter and leave a country in their original state and ownership) are examples of goods that cross borders but are not recorded as imports or exports.

Comparability

Goods (merchandise trade) reflect the bulk of import and exports, and these are generally well covered and afford good comparability across countries; although discrepancies between total imports and exports of traded goods at the global level reveal that measurement in practice is not trivial. Growth in trade through the Internet has increased measurement difficulties.

The comparability of trade in services is greater affected by practical measurement issues however; even if the conceptual approach, as it is for goods, is the same for all OECD countries.

Until recently, exports and imports of services mainly consisted of transport services (sea, air) and insurance. But increases in outsourcing, merchanting, processing services and transactions in intellectual property, such as software and artistic originals, have increased the difficulties inherent in the measurement of trade in services.

Overview

Before the recent economic crisis international trade in goods and services, both for imports and exports, showed a steady increase throughout the OECD area, with the OECD total increasing (on average) by between 4 and 5 percentage points for both measures between 2004 and 2008, with imports slightly outpacing exports. In 2009 however, in the midst of the recent crisis, the ratio for both imports and exports in GDP fell markedly, wiping out nearly all of the increases recorded after 2004. The GDP ratio for exports in 2009 at 24.9%, was significantly below the one for 2008 (28.0%). This pattern was mirrored by the import-to-GDP ratio for the OECD total, which decreased on average from 29.6% in 2008 to 25.2% in 2009. In 2010, the shares of both imports and exports regained more than half of their previous losses. These increases continued in 2011, for almost all countries for which data are available. A majority of these countries has now shares of imports and exports that are larger than the pre-crisis levels.

Looking at the balance of exports and imports, Luxembourg, Norway, Switzerland and Ireland show large and consistent surpluses of more than 10% of GDP, whereas the Netherlands, Sweden and Germany have surpluses of more than 5%. On the other hand, South-European countries (especially Greece and Portugal), Mexico, the United Kingdom and the United States have persistent deficits on their trade with the rest of the world.

Sources
- OECD (2012), *National Accounts of OECD Countries*, OECD Publishing.

Further information

Analytical publications
- OECD (2012), *Policy Priorities for International Trade and Jobs*, OECD Publishing.
- OECD (2011), *Globalisation, Comparative Advantage and the Changing Dynamics of Trade*, OECD Publishing.

Statistical publications
- OECD (2012), *International Trade by Commodity Statistics*, OECD Publishing.
- OECD (2012), *Statistics on International Trade in Services*, OECD Publishing.
- OECD (2011), *National Accounts at a Glance*, OECD Publishing.

Methodological publications
- OECD, *et al.* (2002), *Manual on Statistics of International Trade in Services*, United Nations.

Websites
- OECD International Trade and Balance of Payments Statistics, *www.oecd.org/std/its*

International trade in goods and services

As a percentage of GDP

	Imports						Exports					
	2006	2007	2008	2009	2010	2011	2006	2007	2008	2009	2010	2011
Australia	21.1	22.0	22.1	20.0	19.7	..	20.0	19.9	22.7	19.6	21.2	..
Austria	51.3	53.2	53.5	45.6	49.9	54.0	56.4	58.9	59.3	50.1	54.1	57.3
Belgium	77.0	78.7	84.1	70.1	77.6	83.1	80.8	82.5	84.9	72.8	79.9	84.3
Canada	33.6	33.0	33.6	30.4	31.3	..	36.1	35.0	35.1	28.7	29.4	..
Chile	29.6	31.9	39.5	29.5	31.9	34.7	43.9	45.2	41.5	37.0	38.1	38.1
Czech Republic	64.0	65.6	62.1	55.7	64.7	70.7	67.0	68.2	64.4	59.7	67.9	74.9
Denmark	48.9	49.9	51.6	43.8	45.1	48.4	52.1	52.2	54.7	47.6	50.3	53.8
Estonia	82.9	76.3	75.1	58.9	72.5	87.8	72.7	67.1	70.8	64.7	79.4	92.7
Finland	40.8	40.7	43.1	35.7	39.0	41.4	45.5	45.8	46.8	37.3	40.3	40.7
France	28.1	28.4	29.1	25.2	27.7	29.8	27.0	26.9	26.9	23.4	25.6	27.0
Germany	39.9	40.2	41.9	37.5	41.4	45.1	45.5	47.2	48.2	42.4	47.0	50.2
Greece	33.7	37.0	38.6	30.5	30.4	31.5	22.9	23.5	24.1	19.2	21.5	24.0
Hungary	78.7	80.4	81.2	72.7	80.0	85.1	77.7	81.3	81.7	77.6	86.5	92.5
Iceland	50.5	45.3	47.1	44.3	46.1	50.2	32.2	34.6	44.4	52.7	56.1	58.4
Ireland	69.3	71.3	74.4	75.4	82.0	..	78.9	80.2	83.4	90.9	101.1	..
Israel	42.5	43.9	41.6	32.3	34.9	..	42.7	42.4	40.3	34.7	36.9	..
Italy	28.4	29.1	29.3	24.3	28.5	30.2	27.6	28.9	28.5	23.7	26.6	28.8
Japan	14.9	16.1	17.5	12.3	14.0	..	16.2	17.7	17.7	12.7	15.2	..
Korea	38.3	40.4	54.2	46.0	49.7	54.1	39.7	41.9	53.0	49.7	52.3	56.2
Luxembourg	139.1	143.6	142.6	129.8	133.8	135.2	169.9	175.9	174.7	161.0	165.0	164.7
Mexico	29.3	29.6	30.4	29.2	31.6	..	28.1	28.0	28.1	27.7	30.4	..
Netherlands	65.1	66.0	68.0	61.6	70.1	74.1	72.8	74.2	76.3	68.6	78.2	83.0
New Zealand	30.0	29.2	32.1	26.5	26.8	..	28.6	28.3	30.8	27.9	28.3	..
Norway	28.2	30.5	29.5	28.0	28.8	28.3	45.4	44.1	46.8	39.4	41.1	42.1
Poland	42.2	43.6	43.9	39.4	43.5	45.9	40.4	40.8	39.9	39.4	42.2	44.8
Portugal	39.6	40.2	42.5	35.4	38.2	39.3	30.9	32.2	32.4	28.0	31.0	35.5
Slovak Republic	88.5	88.0	85.9	71.7	82.6	86.5	84.5	86.9	83.5	70.9	81.2	89.1
Slovenia	67.1	71.3	70.4	57.0	64.9	71.3	66.5	69.6	67.1	58.4	65.4	72.3
Spain	32.7	33.6	32.3	25.8	29.4	31.1	26.3	26.9	26.5	23.9	27.2	30.3
Sweden	43.0	44.4	46.8	41.5	43.5	43.9	51.1	51.9	53.5	48.0	49.7	50.1
Switzerland	42.8	44.4	43.2	39.3	40.5	..	50.8	54.4	54.3	50.4	51.7	..
Turkey	27.6	27.5	28.3	24.4	26.8	32.7	22.7	22.3	23.9	23.3	21.2	23.8
United Kingdom	31.7	29.6	32.1	30.3	32.7	34.1	29.1	26.9	29.8	28.8	30.5	32.5
United States	16.8	17.0	18.0	14.2	16.3	..	11.0	11.9	13.0	11.4	12.7	..
Euro area	39.2	40.1	41.1	35.4	39.6	42.4	40.4	41.5	42.0	36.7	40.9	43.8
EU 27	39.1	39.5	41.1	35.8	39.8	42.4	39.5	40.1	41.3	36.8	40.6	43.5
OECD	27.5	28.0	29.6	25.2	27.9	..	25.9	26.8	28.0	24.9	27.2	..
Brazil	..	..	..	..	..	..	..	..	..	..	..	..
China	31.4	29.6	27.3	22.3	25.6	26.0	39.1	38.4	35.0	26.7	29.4	28.6
India	..	..	..	..	..	..	..	..	..	..	..	..
Indonesia	25.6	25.4	28.8	21.4	23.0	..	31.0	29.4	29.8	24.2	24.6	..
Russian Federation	21.0	21.5	22.1	20.5	21.7	22.3	33.7	30.2	31.3	27.9	30.0	31.1
South Africa	32.5	34.2	38.6	28.3	27.5	..	30.0	31.5	35.6	27.4	27.3	..

StatLink http://dx.doi.org/10.1787/888932707211

International imports and exports in goods and services

As percentage of GDP, 2011 or latest available year

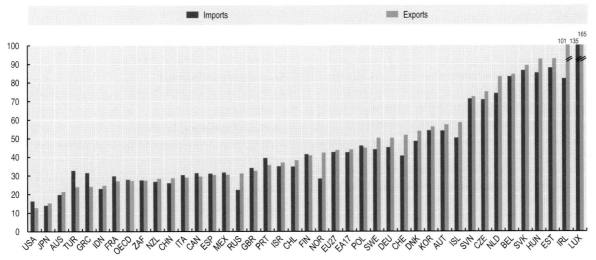

StatLink http://dx.doi.org/10.1787/888932707230

INTERNATIONAL TRADE IN GOODS

Since its creation, the OECD has sought to promote international trade, considering it an effective way of enhancing economic growth and raising living standards. Member countries benefit from increased trade as do OECD's trade partners in the rest of the world.

Definition

According to United Nations guidelines, international merchandise trade statistics record all goods which add to, or subtract from, the stock of material resources of a country by entering (as imports) or leaving (as exports) its economic territory. Goods being transported through a country or temporarily admitted or withdrawn (except for goods for inward or outward processing) are not included in merchandise trade statistics.

Comparability

All OECD countries use the United Nations guidelines so far as their data sources allow. There are some, generally minor, differences across countries in the coverage of certain types of transactions such as postal trade, imports and exports of military equipment under defence agreements, sea products traded by domestic vessels on the high seas and goods entering or leaving bonded customs areas.

Exports are usually valued free on board (f.o.b.), with the exception of the United States which values exports free alongside ship (f.a.s.), which is lower than f.o.b. by the cost of loading the goods on board. Imports are valued by most countries at cost, insurance and freight (c.i.f.) i.e. the cost of the goods plus the costs of insurance and freight to bring the goods to the borders of the importing country. Canada, however, reports imports at f.o.b. values.

The introduction by the European Union of the single market in 1993 resulted in some loss of accuracy for intra-EU trade because custom documents were no longer available to record all imports and exports. Note that while the OECD data mostly follow the UN recommendations, trade statistics reported by Eurostat follow Community definitions, and are not strictly comparable with those reported here.

The OECD aggregate includes all 34 member economies only from 1999.

Overview

For all countries shown in the table, merchandise trade has grown steadily during the period under consideration. However between 2008 and 2009, the impact of the global financial crisis on merchandise trade is manifest. The impact of the crisis on imports was in relative terms more moderate for China, Switzerland, India and Australia as imports fell by less than 15%. It was more severe for the Russian Federation and Iceland as imports of these countries contracted by more than 35%. Exports were also affected by the crisis between 2008 and 2009 as they collapsed for instance by more than 35% in Finland and the Russian Federation but fell by less than 15% in India, Ireland, Korea, Switzerland and Indonesia.

The deficit of the merchandise trade balance has grown in several OECD countries over the period presented in the table. It was, for instance, the case for the United States, France, the United Kingdom and Turkey. However, China and the Russian Federation have continued running a merchandise trade surplus.

Of note, is the sharp deterioration in the Japanese merchandise trade balance in 2011, which moved to its first annual deficit in 30 years, most likely due to the aftermath of the earthquake tand tsunami.

Sources
- OECD (2012), *International Trade by Commodity Statistics*, OECD Publishing.
- United Nations (2012), *United Nations Commodity Trade Statistics* (database).

Further information

Analytical publications
- OECD (2011), *Globalisation, Comparative Advantage and the Changing Dynamics of Trade*, OECD Publishing.
- OECD (2006), *Aid for Trade: Making it Effective, The Development Dimension*, OECD Publishing.
- OECD (2006), *Trade Based Money Laundering*, OECD Publishing.
- OECD (2005), *Trade and Structural Adjustment: Embracing Globalisation*, OECD Publishing.

Statistical publications
- OECD (2012), *Monthly Statistics of International Trade*, OECD Publishing.

Methodological publications
- OECD (2012), *International Trade by Commodity Statistics*, OECD Publishing.
- United Nations (2004), *International Merchandise Trade Statistics: Compilers Manual*, United Nations.

Online databases
- *International Trade by Commodity Statistics*.
- *Monthly Statistics of International Trade*.

Websites
- OECD International Trade and Balance of Payments Statistics, *www.oecd.org/std/its*.

International trade in goods
Billion US dollars

	Trade balance				Imports				Exports			
	2000	2005	2010	2011	2000	2005	2010	2011	2000	2005	2010	2011
Australia	-4.0	-12.8	18.6	11.3	67.8	118.9	193.3	234.3	63.8	106.0	211.8	245.6
Austria	-5.2	-2.2	-5.7	..	67.4	120.0	150.6	..	62.3	117.7	144.9	..
Belgium	13.5	13.8	21.0	12.7	171.7	320.2	390.1	465.2	185.2	334.0	411.1	477.9
Canada	37.6	46.1	-5.5	-0.2	240.0	314.4	392.1	450.4	277.6	360.6	386.6	450.1
Chile	1.6	10.4	13.1	6.5	16.6	29.5	56.2	74.9	18.2	39.9	69.4	81.4
Czech Republic	-3.2	1.7	6.5	11.6	32.2	76.5	125.7	150.5	29.1	78.2	132.1	162.1
Denmark	5.2	8.3	12.3	13.0	44.4	75.0	84.5	88.5	49.6	83.3	96.8	101.5
Estonia	-1.2	-2.8	-0.4	-0.6	5.1	11.0	13.2	18.8	3.8	8.2	12.8	18.2
Finland	11.7	6.8	1.4	-5.1	34.1	58.5	68.8	83.9	45.8	65.2	70.1	78.8
France	-8.5	-41.6	-87.5	-119.3	304.0	476.0	599.2	700.9	295.6	434.4	511.7	581.5
Germany	54.8	197.3	204.3	221.9	495.4	779.8	1 066.8	1 260.3	550.2	977.1	1 271.1	1 482.2
Greece	-18.8	-37.4	-41.8	-29.1	29.8	54.9	63.3	60.8	11.0	17.5	21.6	31.7
Hungary	-4.0	-3.6	7.3	9.5	32.1	65.9	87.4	101.5	28.1	62.3	94.7	111.1
Iceland	-0.7	-1.9	0.7	0.5	2.6	5.0	3.9	4.8	1.9	3.1	4.6	5.3
Ireland	25.6	39.7	57.8	62.3	50.7	70.3	60.5	67.1	76.3	110.0	118.3	129.3
Israel	-4.3	-2.3	-0.8	-5.7	35.7	45.0	59.2	73.5	31.4	42.8	58.4	67.8
Italy	1.9	-11.9	-39.9	-34.3	238.1	384.8	486.6	557.5	239.9	373.0	446.8	523.2
Japan	99.6	79.1	75.7	-31.3	379.7	515.9	694.1	854.6	479.2	594.9	769.8	823.3
Korea	11.8	23.2	41.2	30.8	160.5	261.2	425.2	524.4	172.3	284.4	466.4	555.2
Luxembourg	-2.8	-4.9	-6.5	-8.9	10.6	17.6	20.4	25.3	7.9	12.7	13.9	16.3
Mexico	-5.8	-7.6	-3.2	-1.3	171.1	221.8	301.5	350.8	165.3	214.2	298.3	349.6
Netherlands	5.4	36.9	52.7	..	174.7	283.2	440.0	..	180.1	320.1	492.6	..
New Zealand	-0.6	-4.5	0.8	1.5	13.9	26.2	30.2	36.1	13.3	21.7	30.9	37.6
Norway	25.5	48.3	54.1	68.5	34.4	55.5	77.3	90.8	59.9	103.8	131.4	159.4
Poland	-17.2	-12.2	-17.1	-19.7	48.8	101.5	174.1	203.0	31.6	89.4	157.1	183.3
Portugal	-15.6	-23.1	-26.5	-21.4	39.9	61.2	75.2	80.3	24.4	38.1	48.8	58.9
Slovak Republic	-0.9	-2.4	-0.4	1.8	12.7	34.2	64.4	76.7	11.8	31.9	64.0	78.5
Slovenia	-1.4	-1.7	-2.2	-2.3	10.1	19.6	26.4	30.8	8.7	17.9	24.2	28.5
Spain	-39.5	-96.8	-70.6	..	152.9	289.6	318.2	..	113.3	192.8	247.6	..
Sweden	14.2	18.9	9.7	11.2	73.1	111.4	148.4	176.0	87.4	130.3	158.1	187.2
Switzerland	-2.0	4.4	19.3	27.2	82.5	126.6	176.3	207.3	80.5	130.9	195.6	234.4
Turkey	-26.7	-43.3	-71.6	-105.9	54.5	116.8	185.5	240.8	27.8	73.5	114.0	134.9
United Kingdom	-56.6	-131.4	-156.6	-162.3	339.4	515.8	562.4	634.4	282.9	384.4	405.8	472.1
United States	-477.7	-828.0	-689.4	-782.9	1 258.1	1 732.3	1 966.5	2 262.6	780.3	904.3	1 277.1	1 479.7
EU 27	..	-157.8	-204.7	..	..	1 465.1	1 990.5	..	..	1 307.3	1 785.8	..
OECD	-398.0	-737.1	-629.1	..	4 861.6	7 493.9	9 587.4	..	4 463.6	6 756.8	8 958.3	..
Brazil	-0.7	44.9	16.9	29.8	55.9	73.6	180.5	226.2	55.1	118.5	197.4	256.0
China	24.1	102.0	181.8	155.0	225.1	660.0	1 396.0	1 743.4	249.2	762.0	1 577.8	1 898.4
India	-10.6	-40.5	-129.6	..	52.9	140.9	350.0	..	42.4	100.4	220.4	..
Indonesia	28.6	28.0	22.1	26.1	33.5	57.7	135.7	177.4	62.1	85.7	157.8	203.5
Russian Federation	69.2	142.7	151.4	193.3	33.9	98.7	248.7	284.7	103.1	241.5	400.1	478.0
South Africa	-0.5	-8.0	-8.7	-6.8	26.8	55.0	80.1	99.7	26.3	47.0	71.5	93.0

StatLink http://dx.doi.org/10.1787/888932707268

Evolution of the merchandise trade balance
Annual growth rate in percentage

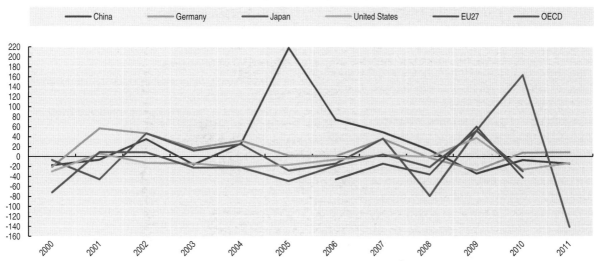

StatLink http://dx.doi.org/10.1787/888932707287

INTERNATIONAL TRADE IN SERVICES

International trade in services is growing in importance both among OECD countries and with the rest of the world. Traditional services – transport, insurance on merchandise trade, and travel – account for about half of international trade in services, but trade in newer types of services, particularly those that can be conducted via the Internet, is growing rapidly.

Definition

International trade in services is defined according to the International Monetary Fund (IMF) *Balance of Payments Manual*. Services include transport (both freight and passengers), travel (mainly expenditure on goods and services by tourists and business travellers), communications services (postal, telephone, satellite, etc.), construction services, insurance and financial services, computer and information services, royalties and license fees, other business services (merchanting, operational leasing, technical and professional services, etc.), cultural and recreational services (rents for films, fees for actors and other performers, but excluding purchases of films, recorded music, books, etc.) and government services not included in the list above.

Comparability

In 1993 the fifth *Balance of Payments Manual* was issued and countries began implementation. All OECD countries now report international trade in services broadly according to

the BPM5 framework. Data for Australia are issued according to the new BPM6 standard. By end 2014, most OECD countries will have made the transition from BPM5 to BPM6.

Services trade balance: exports of services minus imports of services
As a percentage of GDP

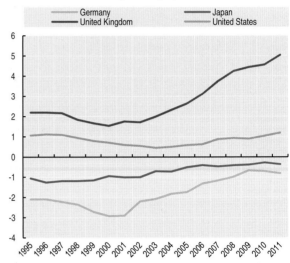

StatLink http://dx.doi.org/10.1787/888932707344

Sources

- OECD (2012), *Main Economic Indicators*, OECD Publishing.
- OECD (2012), *OECD Statistics on International Trade in Services*, OECD Publishing.

Further information

Analytical publications

- OECD (2012), *Strategic Transport Infrastructure Needs to 2030*, OECD Publishing.

Statistical publications

- OECD (2012), *International Trade by Commodity Statistics*, OECD Publishing.
- OECD (2012), *Statistics on International Trade in Services*, OECD Publishing.

Methodological publications

- International Monetary Fund (IMF) (2009), *Balance of Payments and International Investment Position Manual*, 6th edition, IMF, Washington DC.
- OECD, *et al.* (2010), *Manual on Statistics of International Trade in Services*, United Nations.

Websites

- International trade and balance of payments statistics, *www.oecd.org/std/trade-services*.
- Services Trade Restrictiveness Index, *www.oecd.org/trade/stri*.

Overview

Between 2008 and 2011, the United States have by far the largest services surplus, followed by the United Kingdom, Switzerland and Spain.

In 2011, services exports were highest in the United States, the United Kingdom, Germany and France. Over the same period, the United States is the largest importer of services, whereas Germany and France have overtaken the United Kingdom.

As a percentage of GDP, averaged over the 3 years ending 2011, only 4 member countries, namely Luxembourg, Estonia, Switzerland and Greece have recorded trade in services surpluses of more than 5% of GDP. Ireland, Canada, the Slovak Republic and Mexico experienced deficits over 1% of GDP for this period.

It should be noted that the total services trade deficit for Ireland fell from an average of 11.7% of GDP in period 2000-02 to an average of 3.2% of GDP in period 2009-11 as Irish services exports expanded faster than imports, in particular due to dynamic computer services.

International trade in services
Billion US dollars

	Trade balance				Imports				Exports			
	2000	2008	2010	2011	2000	2008	2010	2011	2000	2008	2010	2011
Australia	0.5	-4.0	-3.5	-9.2	19.3	47.9	51.1	60.9	19.8	44.0	47.6	51.7
Austria	6.5	20.8	17.4	19.5	16.5	42.8	37.0	42.4	23.0	63.4	54.5	61.8
Belgium	2.1	5.0	8.2	4.7	32.3	83.0	82.4	89.8	34.3	88.1	90.6	94.5
Canada	-3.9	-20.2	-22.1	-24.9	44.1	88.1	91.3	100.5	40.2	67.9	69.2	75.6
Chile	..	-1.2	-1.8	-2.4	4.8	11.9	12.6	14.8	4.1	10.7	10.8	12.4
Czech Republic	1.4	4.3	3.9	3.8	5.4	17.4	17.0	19.4	6.9	21.8	20.9	23.1
Denmark	2.4	10.1	8.6	8.6	22.1	62.3	51.9	57.1	24.5	72.4	60.5	65.7
Estonia	0.6	1.9	1.8	1.7	0.9	3.3	2.8	3.7	1.5	5.3	4.6	5.4
Finland	-1.7	1.0	0.3	0.4	9.4	30.7	26.6	26.7	7.7	31.7	26.9	27.1
France	17.2	24.1	21.0	33.7	65.7	141.0	171.2	191.0	82.8	165.1	192.2	224.7
Germany	-55.0	-37.4	-24.2	-31.6	138.2	292.8	267.7	296.5	83.2	255.4	243.5	265.0
Greece	8.2	25.1	17.5	20.4	11.5	24.8	20.2	19.4	19.6	49.8	37.7	39.8
Hungary	0.8	2.3	3.9	4.5	4.8	18.0	15.5	17.2	5.6	20.2	19.4	21.8
Iceland	-0.1	-0.3	0.3	0.3	1.2	2.4	2.2	2.6	1.0	2.1	2.5	2.9
Ireland	-13.0	-11.2	-8.8	-2.5	31.4	110.6	107.2	115.8	18.4	99.3	98.4	113.3
Israel	3.7	4.1	6.6	6.6	12.1	19.8	18.1	20.2	15.7	23.9	24.8	26.8
Italy	1.1	-12.6	-12.0	-9.1	55.4	127.8	110.8	116.1	56.5	115.2	98.8	107.0
Japan	-45.8	-20.7	-16.1	-22.1	115.0	169.4	157.4	167.5	69.2	148.7	141.3	145.4
Korea	-2.0	-5.7	-8.6	-4.4	33.6	96.4	95.9	99.4	31.5	90.6	87.3	95.0
Luxembourg	6.8	29.2	30.0	32.0	13.2	39.0	36.7	41.1	20.0	68.0	66.7	73.1
Mexico	-3.6	-7.1	-10.1	-14.2	17.1	24.7	25.3	29.5	13.4	17.6	15.2	15.3
Netherlands	-2.1	13.0	10.5	13.5	51.4	92.2	85.2	94.0	49.3	105.2	95.7	107.5
New Zealand	-0.1	-0.5	-0.3	-0.8	4.5	9.7	9.3	10.9	4.4	9.3	9.0	10.1
Norway	2.7	0.3	-3.2	..	15.0	44.5	42.9	..	17.8	44.8	39.7	..
Poland	1.4	5.0	3.1	6.1	9.0	30.5	29.6	31.0	10.4	35.5	32.7	37.0
Portugal	2.0	9.7	8.9	10.8	7.0	16.5	14.4	15.9	9.1	26.1	23.3	26.7
Slovak Republic	0.4	-0.7	-1.0	-0.5	1.8	9.2	6.8	7.1	2.2	8.5	5.8	6.6
Slovenia	0.5	2.1	1.7	2.0	1.7	5.2	4.4	4.7	2.2	7.2	6.1	6.7
Spain	19.4	37.7	36.4	47.6	33.2	105.4	88.0	94.6	52.6	142.8	124.3	142.2
Sweden	-1.5	16.6	17.8	20.4	24.6	53.8	47.7	55.2	23.1	70.2	65.3	75.6
Switzerland	17.9	46.3	48.8	56.0	12.8	30.8	34.7	40.7	30.7	77.1	83.4	96.5
Turkey	11.4	17.7	15.5	18.3	8.1	17.8	19.3	20.7	19.5	33.1	34.7	39.0
United Kingdom	22.6	111.8	103.5	122.4	101.9	215.1	177.9	188.0	124.7	324.9	281.4	310.3
United States	69.0	131.8	150.4	178.5	219.0	403.4	403.2	427.4	288.0	535.2	553.6	606.0
EU 27	..	..	..	..	..	..	..	..	..	..	..	..
OECD	67.1	396.1	405.2	..	1 143.6	2 492.4	2 363.8	..	1 210.2	2 889.5	2 769.2	..
Brazil	-7.2	-16.7	-30.8	-37.9	16.7	47.1	62.6	76.3	9.5	30.5	31.8	38.4
China	-5.6	-11.8	..	..	36.0	158.9	..	..	30.4	147.1	..	..
India	-2.5	19.5	6.9	..	19.2	88.0	116.7	..	16.7	107.5	123.6	..
Indonesia	-10.4	-13.0	-9.3	-11.8	15.6	28.2	26.1	32.4	5.2	15.2	16.8	20.5
Russian Federation	-6.7	-24.3	-28.7	-35.9	16.2	75.5	73.7	90.0	9.6	51.2	45.0	54.0
South Africa	-0.8	-4.2	-4.5	-4.8	5.8	17.0	18.5	19.7	5.0	12.8	14.0	14.8

StatLink http://dx.doi.org/10.1787/888932707306

Services trade balance: exports of services minus imports of services
As a percentage of GDP

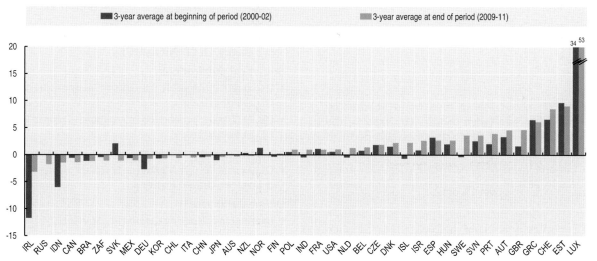

StatLink http://dx.doi.org/10.1787/888932707325

TRADING PARTNERS

The pattern of OECD merchandise trade – where imports come from and where exports go to – has undergone significant shifts over the last decade. These shifts have occurred in response to changes in the distribution of global income and to globalisation – in particular, the outsourcing of manufacturing from OECD countries to the rest of the world.

Definition

The data shown here refer to total imports and exports declared by all 34 member economies of the OECD. It shows merchandise trade both within the OECD area and with selected countries of the rest of the world.

According to United Nations guidelines, international merchandise trade statistics record all goods which add to, or subtract from, the stock of material resources of a country by entering (as imports) or leaving (as exports) its economic territory. Goods being transported through a country or temporarily admitted or withdrawn (except for goods for inward or outward processing) are not included in merchandise trade statistics.

Comparability

OECD countries follow common definitions and procedures in compiling their merchandise trade statistics. These statistics are therefore comparable and of good quality. The removal of customs frontiers following the creation of a common market in Europe required EU countries to adopt a system of recording trade flows through sample surveys of exporters and importers. This led to a fall in the reliability of merchandise trade statistics for trade between the EU countries.

Overview

Since 2000, there has been a steady decline in the share of OECD imports and exports coming from other OECD countries. In 2000, imports from OECD countries accounted for about 74% of total world imports; by 2010, this share had fallen to 62%. For exports, the share directed to other OECD countries also declined from 79% in 2000 to 68% in 2010.

OECD imports from non-OECD countries have risen from 26% to 38% of the total over the same period, while exports to these countries have increased from 21% to 32%. A large change occurred in trade between OECD countries and China. In 2000, China supplied only 5% of total OECD imports but by 2010 this share had risen to 12%. China's importance as a destination for OECD exports has increased less sharply, rising from 2% in 2000 to 6% in 2010.

Partner countries and regions of OECD merchandise trade

As a percentage of total world merchandise trade

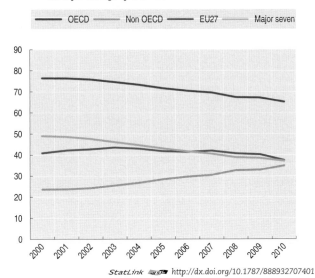

StatLink ᴍᴏᴘ http://dx.doi.org/10.1787/888932707401

Sources
- OECD (2012), *International Trade by Commodity Statistics*, OECD Publishing.

Further information

Analytical publications
- OECD (2010), *Smart Rules for Fair Trade: 50 Years of Export Credits*, OECD Publishing.
- OECD (2006), *Aid for Trade: Making it Effective*, The Development Dimension, OECD Publishing.
- OECD (2005), *Trade and Structural Adjustment: Embracing Globalisation*, OECD Publishing.
- OECD and World Trade Organisation (2011), *Aid for Trade at a Glance*, OECD Publishing.

Statistical publications
- OECD (2012), *Monthly Statistics of International Trade*, OECD Publishing.
- OECD (2012), *Statistics on International Trade in Services*, OECD Publishing.

Methodological publications
- OECD, et al. (2010), *Manual on Statistics of International Trade in Services*, United Nations.

Online databases
- *International Trade by Commodity Statistics.*
- *Monthly Statistics of International Trade.*
- *STAN Bilateral Trade Database.*

Websites
- OECD International Trade and Balance of Payments Statistics, *www.oecd.org/std/its*.

Partner countries and regions of OECD merchandise trade

	Imports of OECD area As a percentage of total OECD merchandise imports				Exports of OECD area As a percentage of total OECD merchandise exports				Total merchandise trade (Imports+Exports) of OECD area As a percentage of total OECD merchandise trade			
	2000	2005	2009	2010	2000	2005	2009	2010	2000	2005	2009	2010
Australia	0.9	1.1	1.4	1.5	1.0	1.0	1.1	1.1	1.0	1.0	1.3	1.3
Austria	1.0	1.1	1.2	1.1	1.3	1.3	1.3	1.2	1.1	1.2	1.2	1.2
Belgium	2.5	2.7	2.5	2.3	2.9	3.1	3.0	2.7	2.7	2.9	2.7	2.5
Canada	5.1	4.2	3.1	3.2	4.4	3.5	3.0	3.0	4.8	3.9	3.1	3.1
Chile	0.3	0.4	0.5	0.5	0.2	0.2	0.3	0.4	0.3	0.3	0.4	0.4
Czech Republic	0.5	0.7	1.0	1.0	0.6	0.8	1.0	1.0	0.6	0.8	1.0	1.0
Denmark	0.8	0.8	0.8	0.7	0.8	0.8	0.8	0.7	0.8	0.8	0.8	0.7
Estonia	0.1	0.1	0.1	0.1	0.1	0.1	0.1	0.1	0.1	0.1	0.1	0.1
Finland	0.8	0.7	0.6	0.5	0.7	0.8	0.6	0.6	0.7	0.7	0.6	0.6
France	4.9	4.5	4.3	3.8	5.6	5.5	5.3	4.8	5.3	5.0	4.8	4.3
Germany	9.1	10.0	9.6	8.9	8.6	8.4	8.2	7.8	8.8	9.2	8.9	8.4
Greece	0.1	0.1	0.1	0.1	0.5	0.5	0.6	0.4	0.3	0.3	0.4	0.3
Hungary	0.5	0.6	0.7	0.6	0.6	0.7	0.7	0.6	0.5	0.6	0.7	0.6
Iceland	0.0	0.0	0.0	0.0	0.0	0.1	0.0	0.0	0.0	0.0	0.0	0.0
Ireland	1.4	1.6	1.5	1.3	1.0	0.9	0.6	0.5	1.2	1.3	1.0	0.9
Israel	0.5	0.4	0.4	0.4	0.6	0.5	0.4	0.4	0.5	0.4	0.4	0.4
Italy	3.6	3.5	3.3	3.0	3.7	3.8	3.5	3.3	3.6	3.6	3.4	3.1
Japan	6.8	5.6	4.7	4.9	4.4	3.7	3.2	3.4	5.7	4.7	4.0	4.2
Korea	2.5	2.8	2.8	3.0	2.0	2.1	2.2	2.4	2.2	2.4	2.5	2.7
Luxembourg	0.1	0.2	0.2	0.1	0.2	0.3	0.2	0.2	0.2	0.2	0.2	0.2
Mexico	3.0	2.5	2.3	2.5	2.8	2.1	2.0	2.1	2.9	2.3	2.2	2.3
Netherlands	3.5	3.4	3.4	3.3	4.0	4.0	4.2	4.1	3.7	3.7	3.8	3.7
New Zealand	0.2	0.2	0.2	0.2	0.2	0.2	0.2	0.2	0.2	0.2	0.2	0.2
Norway	1.1	1.1	1.1	1.0	0.6	0.6	0.7	0.6	0.8	0.9	0.9	0.8
Poland	0.5	0.8	1.1	1.1	0.9	1.1	1.5	1.5	0.7	0.9	1.3	1.3
Portugal	0.4	0.4	0.4	0.3	0.7	0.7	0.7	0.6	0.6	0.6	0.5	0.5
Slovak Republic	0.2	0.3	0.5	0.5	0.2	0.4	0.5	0.5	0.2	0.3	0.5	0.5
Slovenia	0.1	0.1	0.2	0.2	0.2	0.2	0.2	0.2	0.2	0.2	0.2	0.2
Spain	1.8	2.0	1.9	1.8	2.7	3.1	2.5	2.3	2.3	2.5	2.2	2.0
Sweden	1.5	1.4	1.2	1.1	1.3	1.3	1.1	1.1	1.4	1.3	1.1	1.1
Switzerland	1.5	1.5	1.7	1.7	1.7	1.6	1.8	1.7	1.6	1.6	1.7	1.7
Turkey	0.4	0.7	0.7	0.6	0.8	1.0	1.0	1.1	0.6	0.8	0.8	0.9
United Kingdom	12.8	8.8	8.4	8.2	18.3	15.6	12.5	12.7	15.5	12.1	10.4	10.4
United States	4.8	3.8	3.1	2.9	5.9	5.3	4.8	4.5	5.3	4.5	3.9	3.7
EU 27	38.8	39.5	38.1	35.3	43.0	44.1	42.3	39.7	40.8	41.7	40.2	37.5
OECD	73.7	68.1	64.7	62.4	79.2	75.3	69.6	67.9	76.4	71.6	67.1	65.1
Brazil	0.8	1.1	1.2	1.3	0.8	0.7	1.0	1.2	0.8	0.9	1.1	1.3
China	5.3	9.4	11.6	12.2	2.1	3.9	5.4	6.2	3.8	6.7	8.5	9.2
India	0.6	0.8	1.0	1.1	0.5	0.8	1.4	1.5	0.6	0.8	1.2	1.3
Indonesia	1.0	0.9	1.0	1.1	0.5	0.5	0.6	0.7	0.8	0.7	0.8	0.9
Russian Federation	1.6	2.1	2.3	2.5	0.6	1.3	1.4	1.6	1.1	1.7	1.8	2.0
South Africa	0.5	0.5	0.5	0.6	0.4	0.5	0.5	0.5	0.4	0.5	0.5	0.6

StatLink ⬛⬛ http://dx.doi.org/10.1787/888932707363

Partner countries and regions of OECD merchandise trade

As a percentage of total world merchandise trade

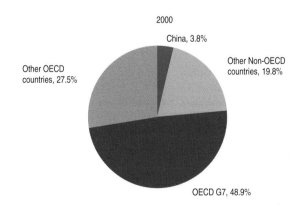

2000

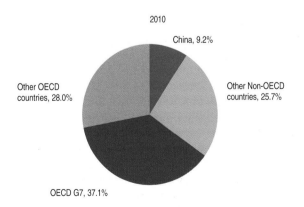

2010

StatLink ⬛⬛ http://dx.doi.org/10.1787/888932707382

FOREIGN DIRECT INVESTMENT

Foreign direct investment (FDI) is a key element in international economic integration. FDI creates direct, stable and long-lasting links between economies. It encourages the transfer of technology and know-how between countries, and allows the host economy to promote its products more widely in international markets. FDI is also an additional source of funding for investment and, under the right policy environment, it can be an important vehicle for development.

Definition

FDI is defined as cross-border investment by a resident entity in one economy with the objective of obtaining a lasting interest in an enterprise resident in another economy. The lasting interest implies the existence of a long-term relationship between the direct investor and the enterprise and a significant degree of influence by the direct investor on the management of the enterprise. Ownership of at least 10% of the voting power, representing the influence by the investor, is the basic criterion used.

Inward stocks at a given point in time refer to all direct investments by non-residents in the reporting economy; outward stocks are the investments of the reporting economy abroad. Corresponding flows relate to investment during a period of time. Negative flows generally indicate disinvestments or the impact of substantial reimbursements of inter-company loans.

The FDI index gauges the restrictiveness of a country's FDI rules through four types of restrictions: foreign equity limitations; screening or approval mechanisms; restriction on key foreign employment; operational restrictions.

The OECD FDI regulatory restrictiveness indexes presented here demonstrate that the services sector tend to have higher FDI restrictions across countries, followed by primary sectors. The manufacturing sector remains the most open economic sector.

Comparability

In recent years the comparability of FDI statistics has improved significantly but asymmetries remain between inward and outward FDI.

Overview

FDI activity slowed down in 2011 following a brief period of recovery in 2010. FDI outflows world-wide increased in 2011 by 12% to USD 1 558 billion as opposed to 24% increase in 2010 and remained well below the historically high level in 2007 (USD 2 170 billion). OECD investors accounted for around 83% of global FDI outflows (USD 1 293 billion), representing a 20% increase from 2010. The top three investing countries were the United States (USD 419 billion), Japan (USD 114 billion) and the United Kingdom (USD 107 billion) which made a spectacular recovery from very low levels of investments observed since 2009. Investors from the European Union (EU) as a whole accounted for 36% of global outflows in 2011, at USD 557 billion maintaining its steady share since 2009 but well below investments in 2008 when EU accounted for 51% of world outflows.

OECD countries hosted only 56% (USD 826 billion) of global FDI inflows (as compared to 87% of inflows in 2000). The United States by itself received 28% (USD 234 billion) of the OECD total, slightly above the combined inflows to Belgium, the United Kingdom, France and Germany (USD 225 billion in aggregate or USD 89 billion, USD 54 billion, USD 41 billion and USD 40 billion, respectively). OECD investors have continued diversifying the destination of their investments, with around 36% of their investments hosted outside the OECD area.

Sources

- OECD (2012), *OECD International Direct Investment Statistics* (database).
- Foreign Direct Investment Statistics – OECD Data, Analysis and Forecasts, *www.oecd.org/investment/statistics*.

Further information

Analytical publications

- OECD (2012), *Annual Report on the OECD Guidelines for Multinational Enterprises*, OECD Publishing.
- OECD (2012), *OECD Investment Policy Reviews*, OECD Publishing.
- OECD (2009), *OECD Investment Policy Perspectives*, OECD Publishing.

Statistical publications

- OECD (2010), *Measuring Globalisation: OECD Economic Globalisation Indicators*, OECD Publishing.

Methodological publications

- Kalinova, B., A. Palerm and S. Thomsen (2010), "OECD's FDI Restrictiveness Index: 2010 Update", *OECD Working Papers on International Investment*, No. 2010/03.
- OECD (2008), *OECD Benchmark Definition of Foreign Direct Investment*, Fourth edition, OECD Publishing.
- OECD (2005), *Measuring Globalisation: OECD Handbook on Economic Globalisation Indicators*, OECD Publishing.

Websites

- OECD International Investment, *www.oecd.org/daf/ investment*.

Outward and inward FDI stocks
Million US dollars

	Outward direct investment stocks						Inward direct investment stocks					
	1990	1995	2000	2009	2010	2011	1990	1995	2000	2009	2010	2011
Australia	37 491	60 484	95 978	343 908	414 298	382 197	80 333	111 310	118 858	428 611	515 981	554 987
Austria	4 747	11 832	24 820	163 233	170 363	195 756	11 098	21 363	31 165	172 598	167 958	164 704
Belgium	40 636	80 690	179 773	891 802	901 924	970 371	58 388	112 960	181 650	946 549	899 252	998 836
Canada	84 813	118 106	237 647	593 580	616 134	670 417	112 850	123 182	212 723	523 247	561 111	595 002
Chile	..	..	11 154	41 339	49 838	55 602	..	..	45 753	121 395	139 538	144 729
Czech Republic	..	345	738	14 805	14 923	15 470	..	7 350	21 647	125 829	128 505	125 245
Denmark	..	..	73 117	213 099	219 900	242 243	..	..	73 585	154 052	138 747	145 719
Estonia	..	..	256	6 410	5 698	4 740	..	..	2 611	16 222	16 474	16 726
Finland	11 227	14 993	52 109	129 195	137 042	138 703	5 132	8 465	24 272	84 668	85 588	82 864
France	110 121	204 430	445 087	1 492 563	1 536 081	1 581 384	84 931	191 433	259 773	985 236	948 442	953 182
Germany	130 760	233 107	486 750	1 346 227	1 405 807	1 406 650	74 067	104 367	462 564	944 747	910 381	902 187
Greece	..	..	5 852	39 457	42 623	42 936	..	..	14 113	42 101	35 025	28 079
Hungary	..	278	1 279	19 244	19 954	23 756	569	11 304	22 856	99 091	90 783	84 447
Iceland	75	179	663	10 180	11 887	11 302	147	129	497	8 622	11 784	12 541
Ireland	..	..	27 925	289 333	348 733	313 746	..	..	127 088	247 466	247 094	251 660
Israel	..	758	9 091	57 371	68 973	71 870	365	5 741	22 367	55 797	60 237	66 554
Italy	60 195	106 319	180 274	486 424	487 610	512 175	60 009	65 347	121 169	364 456	331 960	332 647
Japan	201 440	238 452	278 441	740 965	831 110	962 790	9 850	33 508	50 322	200 151	214 890	225 785
Korea	..	..	..	120 440	143 160	160 640	..	..	..	121 100	134 230	135 730
Luxembourg	..	..	..	192 381	194 257	194 469	..	..	..	150 594	138 172	142 089
Mexico	..	..	..	81 216	104 302	112 088	22 424	41 130	97 170	277 898	330 161	302 309
Netherlands	105 085	172 348	305 458	956 506	961 526	978 994	68 699	115 756	243 730	660 507	593 101	582 216
New Zealand	3 320	7 676	6 065	14 737	16 101	18 979	8 065	25 728	28 070	64 801	67 706	74 299
Norway	10 889	22 521	22 937	168 871	185 827	..	12 404	19 836	25 282	148 315	154 558	..
Poland	..	539	1 018	29 304	39 029	50 044	109	7 843	34 233	185 182	201 003	197 538
Portugal	..	..	19 793	68 477	66 732	68 048	..	18 973	32 043	114 718	111 685	109 028
Slovak Republic	..	139	373	3 152	3 334	4 209	..	1 297	4 761	52 541	50 283	51 290
Slovenia	..	727	870	9 055	8 175	7 802	..	2 617	3 278	15 186	14 466	15 107
Spain	15 652	31 037	129 192	625 849	651 314	640 276	65 916	110 291	156 347	632 296	640 799	634 497
Sweden	50 720	73 143	123 260	353 376	368 785	358 886	12 636	31 089	93 998	332 108	349 777	338 484
Switzerland	66 087	142 481	232 176	826 780	934 126	991 966	34 245	57 064	86 810	492 346	559 333	583 455
Turkey	..	..	3 668	22 250	22 509	26 398	..	..	19 209	143 724	185 806	138 752
United Kingdom	236 118	330 665	923 366	1 579 715	1 626 819	1 731 065	233 305	226 626	463 134	1 104 273	1 162 649	1 198 850
United States	616 655	885 506	1 531 607	4 029 457	4 306 843	4 681 569	505 346	680 066	1 421 017	2 398 208	2 597 707	2 908 791
Euro area	..	..	..	6 713 441	6 934 737	7 068 109	..	..	..	5 457 875	5 224 897	5 281 510
EU 27	..	..	..	8 928 974	9 230 199	9 495 659	..	..	..	7 605 056	7 438 191	7 515 827
OECD	1 786 030	2 736 756	5 410 736	15 960 699	16 915 737		1 460 888	1 861 984	4 502 095	12 414 636	12 795 187	
Brazil	..	..	..	164 523	188 637	202 586	..	..	..	400 808	674 764	669 670
China	..	..	..	245 800	310 800	364 200	..	..	..	1 314 800	1 476 400	1 804 200
India	..	..	2 609	80 943	96 431	111 267	..	..	20 278	171 437	204 715	201 743
Indonesia	..	..	0	33	1 731		..	..	..	108 795	154 158	..
Russian Federation	..	2 420	20 141	302 542	366 301	362 101	..	345	32 204	378 837	490 560	457 474
South Africa	15 010	23 301	32 325	72 583	89 453	..	9 198	15 014	43 451	117 434	153 133	..

StatLink http://dx.doi.org/10.1787/888932707420

FDI stocks
As a percentage of GDP, 2011 or latest available year

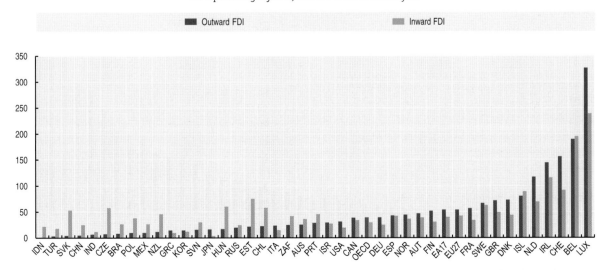

StatLink http://dx.doi.org/10.1787/888932707439

Outflows and inflows of foreign direct investment
Million US dollars

	Outflows of foreign direct investment						Inflows of foreign direct investment					
	2006	2007	2008	2009	2010	2011	2006	2007	2008	2009	2010	2011
Australia	25 411	16 855	33 469	16 693	27 279	16 197	31 070	45 530	47 008	26 554	33 969	67 471
Austria	13 678	39 034	29 395	10 007	7 732	30 479	7 936	31 159	6 845	9 304	4 265	14 141
Belgium	50 713	80 141	220 595	9 207	55 710	70 772	58 926	93 448	193 575	61 748	81 197	89 222
Canada	44 404	57 719	79 752	41 728	38 583	49 566	59 765	114 642	57 147	21 438	23 412	40 929
Chile	2 171	2 573	8 041	8 061	8 743	8 847	7 298	12 534	15 150	12 874	15 095	14 324
Czech Republic	1 469	1 621	4 322	950	1 168	1 155	5 465	10 446	6 449	2 929	6 147	5 417
Denmark	8 438	20 624	13 264	6 320	3 471	23 677	2 715	11 815	1 827	3 942	-7 404	14 806
Estonia	1 107	1 746	1 112	1 549	142	-1 460	1 797	2 725	1 729	1 839	1 600	257
Finland	4 808	7 202	9 279	4 917	10 472	5 333	7 656	12 455	-1 142	398	6 733	-47
France	110 734	164 341	154 747	107 142	76 878	90 228	71 888	96 240	64 060	24 216	30 634	40 982
Germany	118 767	170 650	72 617	75 395	109 328	54 418	55 657	80 223	8 093	24 158	46 863	40 439
Greece	4 047	5 247	2 413	2 055	978	1 790	5 358	2 112	4 490	2 435	373	1 825
Hungary	3 877	3 622	2 230	1 987	1 308	4 541	7 021	5 447	6 313	2 051	2 276	4 709
Iceland	5 555	10 181	-4 206	2 291	-2 357	-29	3 858	6 822	917	86	246	1 013
Ireland	15 332	21 150	18 912	26 617	22 350	-4 294	-5 545	24 712	-16 421	25 717	42 807	11 478
Israel	15 462	8 604	7 210	1 695	9 088	3 080	15 296	8 798	10 877	4 438	5 510	11 374
Italy	42 089	90 795	66 870	21 277	32 657	47 253	39 259	40 209	-10 814	20 078	9 179	29 086
Japan	50 243	73 545	127 981	74 698	56 276	114 300	-6 503	22 548	24 417	11 938	-1 251	-1 758
Korea	11 175	19 720	20 251	17 197	23 278	20 355	3 586	1 784	3 311	2 249	1 094	4 661
Luxembourg	7 183	73 364	11 737	7 213	15 124	11 751	31 803	-28 265	11 195	22 478	9 211	17 546
Mexico	5 758	8 256	1 157	7 019	13 570	8 946	20 119	31 492	27 140	16 119	20 709	19 554
Netherlands	71 214	55 618	68 202	28 182	55 220	31 896	13 984	119 406	4 540	36 044	-8 967	17 145
New Zealand	182	3 702	-239	-308	591	2 798	4 689	3 440	4 984	-1 293	636	3 591
Norway	21 321	13 595	17 298	30 688	23 085	20 020	6 413	5 803	12 254	14 570	17 518	3 573
Poland	8 864	5 410	4 413	4 701	5 488	5 870	19 599	23 582	14 833	12 936	8 861	15 165
Portugal	7 143	5 494	2 736	817	-7 494	12 650	10 914	3 063	4 656	2 707	2 646	10 353
Slovak Republic	512	600	529	432	328	491	4 700	3 583	4 685	-50	526	2 145
Slovenia	862	1 865	1 465	260	-212	112	644	1 515	1 944	-653	359	1 000
Spain	104 306	137 078	74 573	13 072	38 343	37 290	30 819	64 277	76 843	10 406	40 764	29 504
Sweden	26 613	38 811	31 298	25 910	17 969	26 896	28 908	27 740	37 120	10 024	-1 348	12 111
Switzerland	75 863	51 036	45 312	27 845	64 793	69 545	43 740	32 446	15 137	28 696	20 385	-196
Turkey	924	2 106	2 549	1 554	1 464	2 464	20 185	22 047	19 504	8 409	9 038	15 878
United Kingdom	82 808	325 473	182 437	39 325	39 489	107 076	156 218	200 068	88 678	76 375	50 587	53 944
United States	244 922	414 039	329 080	289 450	327 877	419 332	243 151	221 166	310 091	150 443	205 831	233 988
Euro area	553 411	855 577	738 200	308 638	418 323	386 918	339 469	550 093	356 525	245 128	269 999	306 340
EU 27	686 543	1 252 669	977 776	387 804	487 525	556 613	582 075	855 856	538 685	361 775	334 791	419 796
OECD	1 187 954	1 931 815	1 640 800	905 945	1 078 720	1 293 347	1 008 391	1 355 010	1 057 433	645 847	679 498	825 630
Brazil	28 202	7 067	20 457	-10 084	11 589	-1 029	18 822	34 585	45 058	25 949	48 506	66 661
China	21 200	17 000	53 500	43 900	60 100	43 000	124 100	160 100	175 100	114 200	185 000	228 600
India	14 344	17 281	19 257	15 928	14 789	12 416	20 336	25 483	43 407	35 597	25 882	34 247
Indonesia	2 726	4 675	5 900	2 249	2 664	7 771	4 914	6 929	9 318	4 878	13 771	18 906
Russian Federation	23 151	45 916	55 594	43 666	52 523	67 283	29 701	55 073	75 002	36 500	43 288	52 878
South Africa	6 063	2 966	-3 134	1 151	-76	-635	-527	5 695	9 007	5 696	1 228	5 807

StatLink http://dx.doi.org/10.1787/888932707458

FDI flows
Billion US dollars, 2011

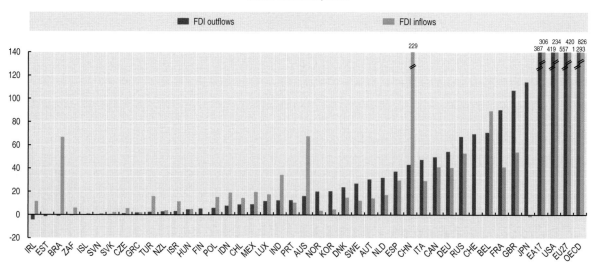

StatLink http://dx.doi.org/10.1787/888932707477

FDI Regulatory Restrictiveness Index
2011

	Total FDI Index	Primary sector	Manufacturing	Electricity	Distribution	Transport	Media	Communications	Financial services	Business services
Australia	0.128	0.078	0.075	0.075	0.075	0.267	0.200	0.400	0.133	0.078
Austria	0.106	0.150	0.000	1.000	0.000	0.182	0.000	0.000	0.002	0.322
Belgium	0.040	0.035	0.023	0.023	0.023	0.114	0.023	0.023	0.024	0.248
Canada	0.166	0.188	0.100	0.100	0.100	0.267	0.700	0.625	0.067	0.100
Chile	0.068	0.150	0.000	0.000	0.000	0.413	0.413	0.000	0.017	0.013
Czech Republic	0.055	0.025	0.000	0.000	0.000	0.075	0.000	0.000	0.010	0.000
Denmark	0.072	0.056	0.000	0.000	0.000	0.083	0.000	0.000	0.002	0.363
Estonia	0.022	0.000	0.000	0.000	0.000	0.150	0.000	0.000	0.002	0.000
Finland	0.019	0.015	0.009	0.084	0.009	0.092	0.009	0.009	0.011	0.046
France	0.045	0.155	0.000	0.000	0.000	0.150	0.048	0.000	0.054	0.003
Germany	0.023	0.069	0.000	0.000	0.000	0.200	0.025	0.000	0.005	0.000
Greece	0.039	0.079	0.000	0.000	0.000	0.150	0.113	0.000	0.020	0.056
Hungary	0.049	0.000	0.000	0.000	0.000	0.167	0.000	0.000	0.005	0.000
Iceland	0.231	0.463	0.112	1.000	0.112	0.295	0.112	0.112	0.119	0.112
Ireland	0.043	0.135	0.000	0.000	0.000	0.125	0.000	0.000	0.009	0.000
Israel	0.118	0.060	0.020	0.770	0.020	0.403	0.264	0.396	0.037	0.020
Italy	0.050	0.130	0.000	0.000	0.000	0.150	0.363	0.000	0.018	0.000
Japan	0.265	1.000	0.077	0.000	0.000	0.667	0.200	0.480	0.000	0.000
Korea	0.143	0.250	0.000	0.417	0.000	0.508	0.563	0.500	0.050	0.000
Luxembourg	0.004	0.000	0.000	0.000	0.000	0.075	0.000	0.000	0.002	0.000
Mexico	0.225	0.394	0.103	0.100	0.175	0.528	0.663	0.350	0.133	0.100
Netherlands	0.015	0.062	0.000	0.000	0.000	0.083	0.000	0.000	0.002	0.000
New Zealand	0.240	0.325	0.200	0.200	0.200	0.283	0.200	0.400	0.233	0.200
Norway	0.080	0.156	0.000	0.000	0.000	0.350	0.125	0.000	0.033	0.313
Poland	0.072	0.050	0.000	0.000	0.000	0.092	0.298	0.075	0.003	0.000
Portugal	0.007	0.006	0.000	0.000	0.000	0.083	0.000	0.000	0.017	0.000
Slovak Republic	0.049	0.000	0.000	0.000	0.000	0.075	0.000	0.000	0.002	0.000
Slovenia	0.007	0.000	0.000	0.000	0.000	0.150	0.000	0.000	0.002	0.000
Spain	0.021	0.011	0.000	0.000	0.000	0.075	0.225	0.000	0.002	0.113
Sweden	0.059	0.138	0.000	0.000	0.000	0.292	0.200	0.200	0.002	0.051
Switzerland	0.083	0.000	0.000	0.500	0.000	0.250	0.467	0.000	0.067	0.000
Turkey	0.077	0.013	0.000	0.000	0.000	0.383	0.125	0.000	0.000	0.125
United Kingdom	0.061	0.160	0.023	0.023	0.023	0.114	0.248	0.023	0.024	0.023
United States	0.089	0.181	0.000	0.197	0.000	0.550	0.250	0.110	0.042	0.000
EU 27	..	..	..	..	..	..	..	..	..	..
OECD	0.081	0.133	0.022	0.132	0.022	0.231	0.171	0.109	0.034	0.067
Brazil	0.086	0.188	0.025	0.025	0.025	0.275	0.488	0.025	0.025	0.025
China	0.409	0.454	0.193	0.463	0.238	0.633	1.000	0.750	0.525	0.350
India	0.300	0.405	0.053	0.050	0.431	0.263	0.463	0.425	0.313	0.563
Indonesia	0.311	0.286	0.070	0.110	0.435	0.423	1.000	0.410	0.206	0.579
Russian Federation	0.180	0.150	0.092	0.030	0.050	0.350	0.117	0.100	0.515	0.175
South Africa	0.054	0.010	0.010	0.010	0.010	0.193	0.298	0.010	0.043	0.260

StatLink http://dx.doi.org/10.1787/888932707496

FDI regulatory restrictiveness index
2011

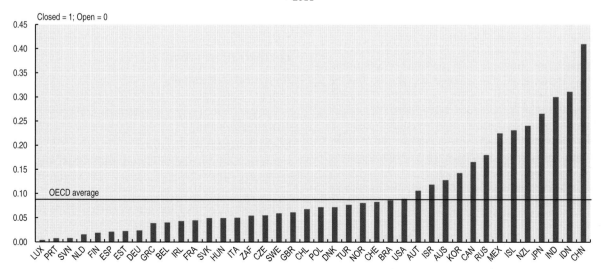

StatLink http://dx.doi.org/10.1787/888932707515

BALANCE OF PAYMENTS

The current account balance is the difference between current receipts from abroad and current payments to abroad. When the current account is positive, the country can use the surplus to repay foreign debts, to acquire foreign assets or to lend to the rest of the world. When the current account balance is negative, the deficit will be financed by borrowing from abroad or by liquidating foreign assets acquired in earlier periods.

Definition

Current account transactions consist of exports and imports of goods; exports and imports of services such as travel, international freight and passenger transport, insurance and financial services; income flows consisting of wages and salaries, dividends, interest and other investment income (i.e. property income in *System of National Accounts*); and current transfers such as government transfers (i.e. international cooperation), worker's remittances and other transfers such as gifts, inheritances and prizes won from lotteries.

Investment income includes retained earnings (i.e. profits not distributed as dividends to the direct investor) of foreign subsidiaries. In general, earnings of direct investment enterprises are treated as if they were remitted abroad to the direct investor, with the part that is actually retained in the country where the direct investment enterprises are located shown as direct investment income-reinvested earnings (debit) in the current account and (with the opposite sign) as inward direct investment in the financial account.

Comparability

The data are taken from balance of payments statistics compiled according to the International Monetary Fund (IMF) *Balance of Payments Manual* (BPM5). Data for Australia and for Chile are already updated and presented according to the new BPM6 standard. By end 2014, most OECD countries will have made the transition from BPM5 to BPM6. The IMF closely monitors balance of payments statistics reported by its member countries through regular meetings of balance of payments compilers. As a result, there is relatively good comparability across countries.

Because all earnings of direct investment enterprises are treated as though they are remitted to the direct investor even though a large part may in practice be retained by the direct investment enterprise in the countries where they are located, the existence of direct investment enterprises in an economy will tend to reduce its current account balance.

It should also be noted that portfolio income plays a role of growing importance for current account balances.

Overview

Current account balances as a percentage of GDP have been negative throughout the period since 1990 in Australia, Mexico, New Zealand, Spain, the United Kingdom and the United States; this is partly due to the way in which earnings of direct investment enterprises are treated. The portfolio investment balance, as well as the balance on goods, had a significant impact on trends in current account balances up to the recent crisis that affected the world economy. Countries which have recorded current account surpluses throughout the crisis period include Germany, Israel, Japan, Luxembourg, the Netherlands, Norway, Slovenia and Switzerland.

Since 1990, current account balances have generally moved from deficit to surplus in Austria, Germany and Korea.

Current account balances, as a percentage of GDP and averaged over the three years to 2011, recorded deficits of 5% of GDP or more in Iceland, Greece, Portugal and Turkey. Surpluses in excess of 5% were recorded by Denmark, Switzerland, Germany, Luxembourg, the Netherlands, Slovenia and Sweden.

Sources
• OECD (2012), *Main Economic Indicators*, OECD Publishing.

Further information

Analytical publications
• OECD (2008), *Export Credit Financing Systems in OECD Member Countries and Non-Member Economies*, OECD Publishing.

Methodological publications
• International Monetary Fund (IMF) (2009), *Balance of Payments and International Investment Position Manual*, 6th edition, IMF, Washington DC.
• OECD et al. (2010), *Manual on Statistics of International Trade in Services*, United Nations.

Online databases
• *Main Economic Indicators*.
• *OECD Economic Outlook: Statistics and Projections*.

Websites
• OECD Economic Outlook – Sources and Methods, *www.oecd.org/eco/sources-and-methods*.

Current account balance

As a percentage of GDP

	1999	2000	2001	2002	2003	2004	2005	2006	2007	2008	2009	2010	2011
Australia	-5.2	-3.9	-2.0	-3.6	-5.3	-6.1	-5.7	-5.3	-6.2	-4.4	-4.2	-2.9	-2.3
Austria	-1.7	-0.7	-0.8	2.7	1.7	2.2	2.2	2.8	3.5	4.9	2.7	3.0	1.9
Belgium	5.1	4.0	3.4	4.3	3.5	3.2	2.1	2.0	1.7	-1.6	-1.7	1.3	-1.1
Canada	0.3	2.7	2.3	1.7	1.2	2.3	1.9	1.4	0.8	0.3	-3.0	-3.1	-2.8
Chile	..	..	..	..	-4.8	10.4	5.7	18.1	16.6	-13.8	7.6	5.8	-5.2
Czech Republic	-2.2	-4.5	-5.1	-5.2	-5.8	-4.9	-0.9	-1.9	-4.2	-2.0	-2.5	-3.7	-2.7
Denmark	1.9	1.6	2.5	2.8	3.4	2.2	4.3	3.0	1.3	2.6	3.5	5.5	6.5
Estonia	-4.4	-5.4	-5.2	-10.6	-11.2	-11.3	-10.0	-15.3	-16.0	-9.2	3.4	2.9	1.9
Finland	5.2	7.7	8.4	8.5	4.8	6.0	3.5	4.1	4.1	2.6	1.8	1.3	-1.3
France	3.2	1.4	1.8	1.2	0.8	0.5	-0.5	-0.6	-1.0	-1.7	-1.3	-1.6	-2.0
Germany	-1.3	-1.8	0.0	2.0	1.9	4.6	5.0	6.2	7.5	6.2	5.9	5.9	5.7
Greece	..	-7.8	-7.2	-6.5	-6.6	-5.8	-7.5	-11.3	-14.3	-14.7	-11.0	-10.0	-9.8
Hungary	-7.8	-8.6	-6.1	-6.9	-8.0	-8.6	-7.5	-7.4	-7.2	-7.3	-0.2	1.2	1.3
Iceland	-6.8	-10.1	-4.6	1.5	-4.8	-9.9	-16.2	-23.9	-16.2	-24.5	-11.7	-8.1	-6.9
Ireland	0.7	0.1	-0.6	-1.0	0.0	-0.5	-3.5	-3.5	-5.3	-5.7	-2.3	1.1	1.1
Israel	-1.4	-3.0	-1.5	-1.0	0.6	1.4	3.2	5.1	2.4	1.4	3.7	3.9	0.5
Italy	0.7	-0.5	-0.1	-0.8	-1.3	-0.9	-1.6	-2.6	-2.4	-2.9	-2.0	-3.5	-3.2
Japan	2.6	2.5	2.1	2.8	3.2	3.7	3.7	3.9	4.8	3.3	2.9	3.7	2.0
Korea	5.3	2.8	1.7	1.3	2.4	4.5	2.2	1.5	2.1	0.5	3.9	2.9	2.4
Luxembourg	8.7	13.4	8.8	10.2	8.3	12.2	11.5	10.3	10.2	5.5	7.0	7.9	7.7
Mexico	-2.7	-2.9	-2.6	-2.0	-1.0	-0.7	-0.7	-0.5	-0.9	-1.5	-0.6	-0.3	-0.8
Netherlands	4.1	2.0	2.6	2.6	5.6	7.8	7.5	9.3	6.7	4.2	4.1	7.1	8.5
New Zealand	-6.1	-4.6	-2.2	-3.6	-3.9	-5.7	-7.9	-8.3	-8.1	-8.8	-2.6	-3.4	-4.2
Norway	5.4	14.9	16.1	12.6	12.3	12.6	16.2	17.1	13.9	17.3	11.7	12.4	..
Poland	..	-6.0	-3.1	-2.8	-2.5	-5.3	-2.4	-3.8	-6.2	-6.5	-4.0	-4.6	-4.3
Portugal	-8.7	-10.5	-10.3	-8.2	-6.4	-8.2	-10.5	-10.8	-9.9	-12.6	-10.7	-10.0	-6.7
Slovak Republic	-4.7	-3.2	-8.1	-7.8	-6.3	-7.8	-8.1	-7.8	-5.0	-5.9	-2.9	-2.6	-0.2
Slovenia	3.9	5.1	8.6	10.2	7.9	6.9	9.2	10.2	10.5	8.9	11.0	10.9	13.8
Spain	-2.9	-4.0	-3.9	-3.3	-3.5	-5.2	-7.3	-8.9	-10.0	-9.6	-4.8	-4.5	-3.5
Sweden	4.0	3.7	3.7	3.8	7.0	6.5	6.8	8.4	9.3	8.8	7.1	6.9	7.0
Switzerland	10.6	11.7	8.0	8.5	12.9	13.0	13.6	14.4	8.7	1.7	10.6	14.5	14.3
Turkey	-0.4	-3.7	2.0	-0.3	-2.5	-3.7	-4.6	-6.1	-5.9	-5.5	-2.1	-6.3	-9.8
United Kingdom	-2.7	-2.9	-2.3	-2.1	-1.7	-2.1	-2.1	-2.9	-2.3	-1.0	-1.3	-2.5	-1.9
United States	-3.2	-4.2	-3.9	-4.3	-4.7	-5.3	-5.9	-6.0	-5.1	-4.7	-2.7	-3.0	-3.1
EU 27	..	..	..	..	..	..	..	..	..	..	..	..	..
OECD	-0.7	-1.3	-1.1	-1.1	-1.0	-0.9	-1.4	-1.5	-1.3	-1.5	-0.4	-0.4	-0.6
Brazil	-4.3	-3.8	-4.2	-1.3	0.7	1.7	1.6	1.2	0.2	-1.7	-1.4	-2.2	..
China	..	..	..	..	0.7	0.9	1.9	2.5	3.1	3.2	2.1	..	..
India	-0.7	-1.0	0.3	1.4	1.5	0.2	-1.2	-1.0	-0.6	-2.5	-1.9	-3.2	..
Indonesia	3.7	4.9	4.3	4.0	3.4	0.6	0.1	3.0	2.4	0.0	1.9	0.7	0.3
Russian Federation	..	..	..	..	8.4	10.0	11.1	9.7	6.0	6.2	3.8	4.8	5.3
South Africa	-0.5	-0.1	0.3	0.8	-1.0	-3.0	-3.4	-5.3	-7.0	-7.2	-4.1	-2.9	..

StatLink ᵐˢᵇ http://dx.doi.org/10.1787/888932707534

Current account balance

As a percentage of GDP

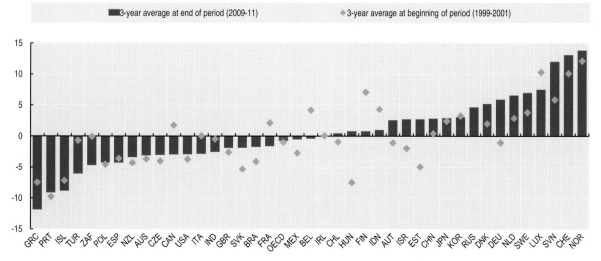

■ 3-year average at end of period (2009-11)   ◆ 3-year average at beginning of period (1999-2001)

StatLink ᵐˢᵇ http://dx.doi.org/10.1787/888932707553

```
            ...•  -
   300,000•  +
85,679,200•  -
43,628,500•  -
36,286,400•  +
34,432,741,064•  ◊

34,432,741,064•  *

220,061,246•  +
   242,765•  +
54,975,316•  -
3,458,295,462•  +
9,423,290,000•  -
627,646,320•  -
242,347,296•  +
   312,759•  +
...184,652,108•  ◊
```

PRICES

INFLATION (CPI)

Consumer price indices have a long history in official statistics. They measure the erosion of living standards through price inflation and are probably one of the best known economic statistics used by the media and general public.

Definition

Consumer price indices (CPI) measure the change in the prices of a basket of goods and services that are typically purchased by specific groups of households. The CPI shown in these tables cover virtually all households except for "institutional" households – people in prisons and

military barracks, for example – and, in some countries, households in the highest income group.

The CPI for all items excluding food and energy provides a measure of underlying inflation, which is less affected by short-term effects. The index for food covers food and non-alcoholic beverages but excludes purchases in restaurants. The index for energy covers all forms of energy, including fuels for motor vehicles, heating and other household uses.

Comparability

There are a number of differences in the ways that these indices are calculated. The most important ones concern the treatment of dwelling costs, the adjustments made for changes in the quality of goods and services, the frequency with which the basket weights are updated, and the index formulae used. In particular, country methodologies for the treatment of owner-occupied housing vary significantly. The European Harmonised Indices of Consumer Prices (HICP) exclude owner-occupied housing as do national CPIs for Belgium, Chile, Estonia, France, Greece, Italy, Luxembourg, Poland, Portugal, Slovenia, Spain, Turkey, the United Kingdom and most of the countries outside the OECD area. For the United Kingdom, the national CPI is the same as the HICP. The European Union and euro area CPI refer to the HICP published by Eurostat and cover the 27 and 17 countries respectively for the entire period of the time series.

Overview

The annual average inflation rate from 2009-11 has been below 4.5% in all OECD countries except Iceland and Turkey. The CPI for the OECD total dropped from 3.5% in the 3-year average from 2000-02 to 1.8% in the 3-year average from 2009-11. Over the entire period from 2000 to 2011, Japan experienced negative inflation (deflation) while Hungary, Mexico, Turkey, Iceland, the Slovak Republic and Slovenia all experienced periods or years of substantial inflation during this period.

Annual inflation has been higher for countries outside the OECD area presented here in the table, in particular the Russian Federation has only in the last few years recorded inflation rates comparable to other non-member countries.

During the years presented in the table (2000, 2010 and 2011), the main driver of total inflation has been energy prices, which have risen faster than the total consumer price index. Consumer prices for energy have been, however, volatile during the whole period (2000-2011) and have recorded large swings, with spikes in 2000, 2005, and 2011 and sharp decreases in 2002 and 2009. Food prices have risen by less than total consumer prices in 2000 and 2010 but for the most recent period, 2011, they have risen faster. When excluding these more volatile items, the underlying consumer price index (i.e. all items excluding food and energy) points to a progressive decline in inflation rates from 2000 to 2010 followed by a slight increase in 2011.

A noticeable long-term trend highlighted in the table has been the convergence of inflation rates for OECD countries over the last decade or so. This is most clearly seen when looking at the two OECD countries that recorded the lowest (Japan) and highest (Turkey) annual inflation rates in both 2000 and 2011: minus 0.7% versus 54.9% and minus 0.3% versus 6.5% respectively.

Sources
• OECD (2012), *Main Economic Indicators*, OECD Publishing.

Further information

Analytical publications
• Brook, A.M. *et al.* (2004), "Oil Price Developments: Drivers, Economic Consequences and Policy Responses", *OECD Economics Department Working Papers*, No. 412.
• OECD (2012), *OECD Economic Outlook*, OECD Publishing.

Methodological publications
• International Labour Office (ILO) *et al.* (2004), *Consumer Price Index Manual: Theory and Practice*, ILO, Geneva.
• OECD (2012), *Main Economic Indicators*, OECD Publishing.
• OECD (2002), "Comparative Methodological Analysis: Consumer and Producer Price Indices", *Main Economic Indicators, Volume 2002, Supplement 2*, OECD Publishing.

Websites
• OECD Main Economic Indicators, *www.oecd.org/std/mei*.

Inflation (CPI)

Annual growth in percentage

	All items			All items non-food, non-energy			Food			Energy		
	2000	2010	2011	2000	2010	2011	2000	2010	2011	2000	2010	2011
Australia	4.5	2.8	3.4	4.3	2.7	2.3	0.5	1.2	5.6	17.2	8.1	11.0
Austria	2.3	1.8	3.3	1.7	1.4	2.3	0.6	0.5	4.3	10.7	7.6	10.9
Belgium	2.5	2.2	3.5	1.5	1.3	1.7	0.9	1.5	2.4	14.3	9.4	16.8
Canada	2.7	1.8	2.9	1.7	1.3	1.4	1.1	0.9	4.2	16.2	6.6	12.3
Chile	3.8	1.4	3.3	3.1	0.5	1.3	1.1	2.2	6.7	22.0	7.1	12.7
Czech Republic	3.9	1.5	1.9	3.5	1.1	0.3	1.1	1.5	4.6	14.2	3.8	6.9
Denmark	2.9	2.3	2.8	2.1	1.9	1.8	2.5	0.4	4.0	11.8	9.0	8.8
Estonia	4.0	3.0	5.0	3.9	0.8	2.3	2.4	3.0	9.7	8.0	12.3	8.2
Finland	3.0	1.2	3.4	2.6	1.2	2.0	1.1	-3.4	6.3	12.6	10.6	14.6
France	1.7	1.5	2.1	0.5	0.9	0.9	2.2	0.8	2.0	12.2	9.6	12.1
Germany	1.4	1.1	2.3	0.8	0.7	1.2	-0.7	1.4	2.9	13.8	4.0	10.0
Greece	3.2	4.7	3.3	2.3	3.3	1.2	1.9	0.1	3.1	17.3	28.8	16.2
Hungary	9.8	4.9	3.9	8.4	3.7	1.0	9.2	2.8	7.2	17.3	10.8	9.0
Iceland	5.1	5.4	4.0	4.7	4.7	2.6	4.1	4.2	3.8	11.9	15.5	17.1
Ireland	5.6	-0.9	2.6	5.6	-1.2	2.0	3.1	-4.6	1.2	13.6	9.6	12.0
Israel	1.1	2.7	3.5	0.4	2.6	3.0	2.3	2.5	3.3	9.5	3.9	8.6
Italy	2.5	1.5	2.8	2.1	1.6	2.0	1.6	0.2	2.5	11.6	3.5	11.3
Japan	-0.7	-0.7	-0.3	-0.5	-1.2	-0.9	-2.3	-0.3	-0.5	3.0	2.7	5.9
Korea	2.3	2.9	4.0	1.8	1.8	2.6	0.9	6.4	8.1	9.6	6.5	9.9
Luxembourg	3.2	2.3	3.4	2.2	1.6	2.3	2.0	0.8	2.6	19.8	9.8	12.7
Mexico	9.5	4.2	3.4	10.4	4.2	3.0	5.4	3.4	4.4	16.8	5.4	5.5
Netherlands	2.3	1.3	2.3	1.9	1.7	1.7	0.2	-0.1	2.2	14.9	-0.3	8.5
New Zealand	2.6	2.3	4.0	2.4	1.9	2.7	1.1	1.0	5.2	11.0	7.0	11.4
Norway	3.1	2.4	1.3	2.5	0.9	2.7	1.9	0.2	-0.1	11.3	15.5	1.6
Poland	9.9	2.6	4.2	9.3	1.6	2.3	9.7	2.8	5.2	13.4	5.8	8.9
Portugal	2.9	1.4	3.7	2.8	0.6	2.4	2.1	-0.2	2.1	5.7	8.9	12.5
Slovak Republic	12.0	1.0	3.9	11.5	2.1	3.2	5.2	1.6	6.1	41.8	-0.2	9.2
Slovenia	8.9	1.8	1.8	7.3	0.2	0.0	-13.8	1.0	4.4	25.2	13.2	8.4
Spain	3.4	1.8	3.2	2.9	0.6	1.3	2.1	-0.8	2.1	13.3	12.5	15.7
Sweden	0.9	1.2	3.0	-0.3	-0.4	2.4	0.0	1.4	1.3	7.2	6.8	6.1
Switzerland	1.6	0.7	0.2	1.2	0.2	0.1	1.6	-1.1	-3.3	18.0	9.2	7.0
Turkey	54.9	8.6	6.5	58.0	7.2	5.9	46.6	10.6	6.2	56.4	10.5	9.9
United Kingdom	0.8	3.3	4.5	0.1	2.9	3.2	-0.5	3.4	5.5	7.1	6.1	12.2
United States	3.4	1.6	3.2	2.4	1.0	1.7	2.2	0.3	4.8	16.9	9.5	15.4
EU 27	3.5	2.1	3.1	1.2	1.3	1.7	3.9	1.1	3.4	12.7	7.2	11.4
OECD	4.0	1.9	2.9	3.5	1.3	1.7	2.4	1.2	3.8	14.6	7.8	12.1
Brazil	7.0	5.0	6.6	..	..	..	5.1	6.1	8.8	..	..	..
China	0.4	3.3	5.4	..	..	..	-2.6	7.2	11.8	..	..	..
India	4.0	12.0	8.9	..	..	..	..	..	..	..	..	..
Indonesia	3.7	5.1	5.4	..	..	..	-4.8	9.4	8.5	..	..	..
Russian Federation	20.8	6.9	8.4	..	..	..	17.8	7.0	10.3	..	..	..
South Africa	5.3	4.1	5.0	..	4.0	3.5	7.8	1.2	7.1	..	15.4	18.9

StatLink http://dx.doi.org/10.1787/888932707572

CPI: all items

Average annual growth in percentage

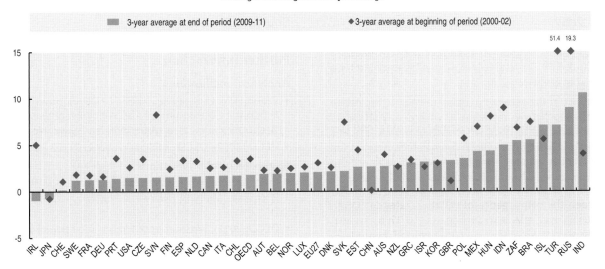

StatLink http://dx.doi.org/10.1787/888932707591

PRODUCER PRICE INDICES

A variety of price indices may be used to measure inflation in an economy. These include consumer price indices (CPI), price indices relating to specific goods and/or services, GDP deflators and producer price indices (PPI). Whereas CPIs are designed to measure changes over time in average retail prices of a fixed basket of goods and services taken as representing the consumption habits of households, PPIs aim to provide measures of average movements of prices received by the producers of various commodities. They are often seen as advanced indicators of price changes throughout the economy, including changes in the prices of consumer goods and services.

Definition

Producer price indices measure the rate of change in prices of products sold as they leave the producer. They exclude any taxes, transport and trade margins that the purchaser may have to pay. Manufacturing covers the production of semi-processed goods and other intermediate goods as well as final products such as consumer goods and capital equipment. The indexes shown here are weighted averages of monthly price changes in the manufacturing sector.

Comparability

The precise ways in which PPIs are defined and constructed depend on their intended use. In this context, national practices may differ and these differences may affect cross-country comparability. This is especially the case for aspects such as the weighting and aggregation systems, the treatment of quality differences, the sampling and collection of individual prices, the frequency with

which the weights are updated, and in the index formulae used. Differences may also arise concerning the scope of the manufacturing sector and the statistical unit used for measurement. In some countries, for example, indices may reflect price changes in the output of the manufacturing sector as opposed to manufactured products.

While the PPI series for most countries refer to domestic sales of manufacturing goods, those for Australia, Canada, Chile, New Zealand and the United States include prices applied for foreign sales (i.e. "total market").

PPI: domestic manufacturing
Average annual growth in percentage

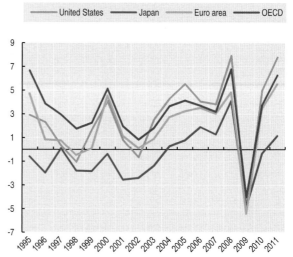

StatLink ⟶ http://dx.doi.org/10.1787/888932707648

Sources
- OECD (2012), *Main Economic Indicators*, OECD Publishing.

Further information

Analytical publications
- Brook, A.M. *et al.* (2004), "Oil Price Developments: Drivers, Economic Consequences and Policy Responses", *OECD Economics Department Working Papers*, No. 412.
- OECD (2012), *OECD Economic Outlook*, OECD Publishing.

Methodological publications
- International Monetary Fund (IMF) *et al.* (2004), *Producer Price Index Manual: Theory and Practice*, IMF, Washington, DC.
- OECD (2011), *Producer price Indices - Comparative Methodological Analysis*, OECD, Paris.

Online databases
- *Main Economic Indicators: Producer prices.*

Websites
- OECD Main Economic Indicators, *www.oecd.org/std/mei.*

PPI: domestic manufacturing

Annual growth in percentage

	1999	2000	2001	2002	2003	2004	2005	2006	2007	2008	2009	2010	2011
Australia	0.7	7.1	3.1	0.2	0.5	4.0	6.0	7.9	2.3	8.3	-5.4	1.9	3.4
Austria	..	3.4	0.0	-1.4	0.3	2.2	3.7	1.8	3.4	3.4	-2.2	4.4	5.0
Belgium	0.0	9.8	-1.0	0.1	0.9	4.2	6.0	5.5	3.6	5.7	-4.9	6.3	6.8
Canada	1.8	4.3	1.0	0.1	-1.2	3.2	1.6	2.3	1.5	4.3	-3.5	1.0	4.6
Chile	..	..	..	..	..	..	2.9	5.0	6.0	15.9	-3.3	5.5	4.6
Czech Republic	0.1	5.7	2.4	-1.3	-0.4	5.7	2.0	1.8	3.5	3.1	-5.5	1.5	5.7
Denmark	0.3	4.0	2.9	1.0	1.0	1.0	3.1	3.4	4.8	5.7	-1.2	3.2	4.6
Estonia	..	..	..	-1.0	-0.6	3.4	2.3	4.8	10.1	7.6	-3.9	2.1	5.7
Finland	-0.8	5.7	-1.5	-2.0	-1.4	0.4	4.7	5.6	4.5	8.1	-7.5	6.5	7.6
France	-0.1	4.0	1.3	-0.6	0.8	2.8	3.0	3.3	3.0	5.3	-7.3	3.3	5.9
Germany	-0.3	3.1	1.3	0.2	0.6	1.7	2.4	2.3	2.3	3.1	-3.4	2.5	4.4
Greece	2.4	5.9	3.4	2.1	2.1	3.8	6.4	7.9	3.5	9.7	-7.2	6.9	8.6
Hungary	6.9	16.1	9.4	2.0	3.7	7.3	4.3	5.7	4.3	8.6	-0.1	5.6	8.6
Iceland	..	..	..	..	..	..	..	17.5	1.8	31.0	11.3	11.8	9.2
Ireland	1.5	7.5	2.4	2.1	0.8	0.4	1.9	3.4	2.2	5.9	-3.6	1.6	4.6
Israel	7.1	3.6	-0.1	3.9	4.3	5.4	6.2	5.7	3.5	9.6	-6.3	4.0	7.7
Italy	0.2	4.0	1.1	0.8	1.4	3.3	3.1	4.0	3.3	5.0	-5.6	3.6	5.4
Japan	-1.8	-0.4	-2.6	-2.4	-1.4	0.3	0.8	1.9	1.3	4.1	-4.8	-0.3	1.1
Korea	-3.3	2.9	-2.1	-1.5	1.8	7.5	6.8	0.2	0.8	11.9	-1.6	4.3	7.7
Luxembourg	-2.3	6.4	2.5	0.9	3.3	14.8	0.0	9.0	7.6	12.9	-19.2	8.3	7.7
Mexico	15.1	8.9	4.1	3.2	6.6	8.6	4.5	6.0	5.0	8.6	5.4	4.7	6.5
Netherlands	0.3	9.1	1.9	-0.6	1.3	3.6	4.6	4.2	5.2	7.3	-8.1	6.4	9.2
New Zealand	1.3	8.5	5.5	0.0	-1.7	2.8	5.6	6.5	4.0	14.9	-4.8	4.3	5.7
Norway	3.0	5.0	1.9	-0.4	1.4	3.1	3.5	3.0	4.4	7.8	0.3	3.2	6.5
Poland	..	7.4	0.5	-1.7	0.8	8.0	1.4	1.9	3.6	3.4	-2.6	2.9	8.5
Portugal	3.6	15.0	2.7	0.4	0.4	2.9	3.2	4.2	2.5	5.2	-5.6	3.5	5.7
Slovak Republic	3.9	8.6	3.8	2.5	-0.1	2.5	1.3	1.5	0.2	2.0	-5.9	0.1	4.0
Slovenia	2.7	8.4	9.9	4.9	2.9	4.2	3.3	2.4	4.4	5.2	-2.0	2.1	4.1
Spain	0.9	5.7	1.7	0.6	1.4	3.7	4.7	5.0	3.4	6.0	-5.5	3.5	5.9
Sweden	0.4	3.9	3.1	0.6	-0.9	1.8	4.0	3.9	3.3	3.9	1.0	0.3	1.3
Switzerland	..	..	..	..	..	2.0	2.0	2.7	2.8	4.4	-2.8	0.5	0.1
Turkey	57.2	56.1	66.7	48.3	23.8	11.0	9.6	9.3	5.6	11.8	-0.6	6.0	13.3
United Kingdom	-0.2	1.9	-0.6	-0.3	1.1	2.2	4.0	3.1	3.0	9.5	-1.5	5.5	7.9
United States	1.7	4.1	0.8	-0.7	2.5	4.3	5.5	4.0	3.8	7.9	-4.9	5.0	7.8
Euro area	0.1	4.5	1.1	0.1	0.9	2.7	3.2	3.5	3.0	4.8	-5.4	3.4	5.5
EU 27	0.1	4.3	1.1	0.1	1.0	3.0	3.4	3.5	3.2	5.2	-3.8	3.0	5.9
OECD	2.3	5.1	2.0	0.8	1.8	3.7	4.1	3.7	3.2	6.8	-4.0	3.7	6.3
Brazil	..	..	..	..	..	..	..	..	..	..	..	..	..
China	..	..	..	..	..	..	..	..	..	..	..	..	..
India	..	..	..	..	..	..	..	..	..	..	..	..	..
Indonesia	..	..	..	..	..	..	..	..	..	..	..	..	..
Russian Federation	69.3	38.6	13.4	8.0	16.0	19.4	13.8	11.1	13.2	21.1	-5.1	11.5	14.0
South Africa	5.3	7.6	7.1	13.3	4.6	2.0	3.7	6.4	9.8	15.2	0.7	1.9	5.7

StatLink http://dx.doi.org/10.1787/888932707610

PPI: domestic manufacturing

Average annual growth in percentage

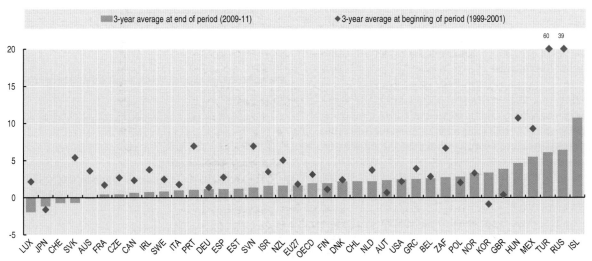

StatLink http://dx.doi.org/10.1787/888932707629

LONG-TERM INTEREST RATES

Long-term interest rates are one of the determinants of business investment. Low long-term interest rates encourage investment in new equipment and high interest rates discourage it. Investment is, in turn, a major source of economic growth.

Definition

Long-term interest rates as measured here refer to government bonds with a residual maturity of about ten years. They are not the interest rates at which the loans were issued, but the interest rates implied by the prices at which these government bonds are traded on financial markets. For example if a bond was initially bought at a price of 100 with an interest rate of 9%, but it is now trading at a price 90, the interest rate shown here will be 10% ([9/90] × 100).

The long-term interest rates shown are, where possible, averages of daily rates. In all cases, they refer to bonds whose capital repayment is guaranteed by governments.

Overview

From the mid-1990s until the mid-2000s long-term interest rates fell steadily in most OECD countries, and for many countries these long-term interest rates reached a low point in 2005. However, the financial bubble and resulting financial crisis saw long-term interest rates rise and peak between 2007 and 2009 for a large number of countries. For just over half the of the OECD countries, long-term interest rates in 2011 are now below the low recorded in 2005. However, those OECD countries experiencing ongoing financial difficulties, namely Greece, Ireland, Italy, Portugal and Spain have seen their long-term rates at levels in the last few years in excess of the levels seen over a decade ago in these countries.

There is a divergence in long-term interest rates appearing in 2011 between European and non-European countries, and in particular those countries in the euro zone. While long-term interest rates for the major non-European countries have remained steady or fallen in recent years, this is not the case for a number of European countries and particularly those in the euro area which have seen their long-term interest rates rise.

Japan and Switzerland remain the OECD countries with the lowest long-term interest rates, and both countries have seen their rates fall over the last four to five years with Japan recording a long-term interest rate of 1.10% in 2011 and Switzerland not far above at 1.47%.

Long-term interest rates are mainly determined by three factors: the price that lenders charge for postponing consumption; the risk that the borrower may not repay the capital; and the fall in the real value of the capital that the lender expects to occur because of inflation during the lifetime of the loan. The interest rates shown here refer to government borrowing and the risk factor is assumed to be very low. To an important extent the interest rates in this table are driven by expected inflation rates.

Comparability

Comparability of these data is considered to be high. There may be differences, however, in the size of these government bonds outstanding, and in the extent to which these rates are representatives of financial conditions in various countries.

Evolution of long-term interest rates
Percentage

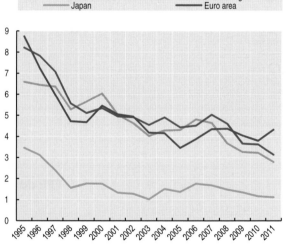

 StatLink http://dx.doi.org/10.1787/888932707705

Sources
- OECD (2012), *Main Economic Indicators*, OECD Publishing.

Further information

Analytical publications
- OECD (2012), *OECD Economic Outlook*, OECD Publishing.
- OECD (2012), *OECD Journal: Financial Market Trends*, OECD Publishing.

Methodological publications
- OECD (1998), *Main Economic Indicators – Sources and Methods: Interest Rates and Share Price Indices*, OECD Publishing.

Websites
- Main Economic Indicators, *www.oecd.org/std/mei*.

Long-term interest rates
Percentage

	1999	2000	2001	2002	2003	2004	2005	2006	2007	2008	2009	2010	2011
Australia	6.01	6.31	5.62	5.84	5.37	5.59	5.34	5.59	5.99	5.82	5.04	5.37	4.88
Austria	4.68	5.56	5.08	4.97	4.15	4.15	3.39	3.80	4.30	4.36	3.94	3.23	3.32
Belgium	4.71	5.57	5.06	4.89	4.15	4.06	3.37	3.81	4.33	4.40	3.82	3.35	4.18
Canada	5.54	5.93	5.48	5.30	4.80	4.58	4.07	4.21	4.27	3.60	3.23	3.24	2.79
Chile	..	..	..	..	..	..	6.05	6.16	6.09	7.07	5.71	6.27	6.03
Czech Republic	..	..	6.31	4.88	4.12	4.82	3.54	3.80	4.30	4.63	4.84	3.88	3.71
Denmark	4.92	5.66	5.09	5.06	4.31	4.30	3.40	3.81	4.29	4.28	3.59	2.93	2.73
Estonia	..	..	..	..	..	..	..	..	..	..	..	..	..
Finland	4.72	5.48	5.04	4.98	4.14	4.11	3.35	3.78	4.29	4.29	3.74	3.01	3.01
France	4.61	5.39	4.94	4.86	4.13	4.10	3.41	3.80	4.30	4.23	3.65	3.12	3.32
Germany	4.50	5.27	4.80	4.78	4.07	4.04	3.35	3.76	4.22	3.98	3.22	2.74	2.61
Greece	6.31	6.11	5.30	5.12	4.27	4.26	3.59	4.07	4.50	4.80	5.17	9.09	15.75
Hungary	..	8.55	7.95	7.09	6.77	8.29	6.60	7.12	6.74	8.24	9.12	7.28	7.64
Iceland	8.47	11.20	10.36	7.96	6.65	7.49	8.64	8.83	9.42	11.07	8.26	6.09	5.98
Ireland	4.77	5.48	5.02	4.99	4.13	4.06	3.32	3.79	4.33	4.55	5.23	5.99	9.58
Israel	5.20	5.48	..	5.35	..	7.56	6.36	6.31	5.55	5.92	5.06	4.68	4.98
Italy	4.73	5.58	5.19	5.03	4.30	4.26	3.56	4.05	4.49	4.68	4.31	4.04	5.42
Japan	1.75	1.74	1.32	1.26	1.00	1.49	1.35	1.74	1.67	1.47	1.33	1.15	1.10
Korea	..	..	6.86	6.59	5.05	4.73	4.95	5.15	5.35	5.57	5.17	4.77	4.20
Luxembourg	4.67	5.52	4.86	4.68	3.32	2.84	2.41	3.30	..	..	..	..	2.92
Mexico	24.13	16.94	..	10.13	8.98	9.54	9.42	8.39	7.77	..	..	..	..
Netherlands	4.63	5.40	4.96	4.89	4.12	4.10	3.37	3.78	4.29	4.23	3.69	2.99	2.99
New Zealand	6.41	6.85	6.39	6.53	5.87	6.07	5.88	5.78	6.26	6.08	5.46	5.60	4.94
Norway	5.50	6.22	6.24	6.38	5.05	4.37	3.75	4.08	4.77	4.46	4.00	3.53	3.14
Poland	..	..	10.68	7.36	5.78	6.90	5.22	5.23	5.48	6.07	6.12	5.78	5.96
Portugal	4.78	5.60	5.16	5.01	4.18	4.14	3.44	3.91	4.42	4.52	4.21	5.40	10.24
Slovak Republic	..	..	8.04	6.94	4.99	5.03	3.52	4.41	4.49	4.72	4.71	3.87	4.42
Slovenia	..	..	..	..	6.40	4.68	3.81	3.85	4.53	4.61	4.38	3.83	4.97
Spain	4.73	5.53	5.12	4.96	4.13	4.10	3.39	3.78	4.31	4.36	3.97	4.25	5.44
Sweden	4.98	5.37	5.11	5.30	4.64	4.43	3.38	3.70	4.17	3.89	3.25	2.89	2.61
Switzerland	3.04	3.93	3.38	3.20	2.66	2.74	2.10	2.52	2.93	2.90	2.20	1.63	1.47
Turkey	..	..	..	..	..	..	..	..	..	..	..	..	..
United Kingdom	5.09	5.33	4.93	4.90	4.53	4.88	4.41	4.50	5.01	4.59	3.65	3.61	3.12
United States	5.64	6.03	5.02	4.61	4.02	4.27	4.29	4.79	4.63	3.67	3.26	3.21	2.79
Euro area	4.66	5.44	5.03	4.92	4.16	4.14	3.44	3.86	4.33	4.36	4.03	3.79	4.31
Brazil	..	..	..	..	..	..	..	..	..	..	..	..	..
China	..	..	..	..	..	..	..	..	..	..	..	..	..
India	..	..	..	..	..	..	..	..	..	..	..	..	..
Indonesia	..	..	..	..	..	..	..	..	..	..	..	..	..
Russian Federation	87.38	35.16	19.38	15.82	9.12	8.29	8.11	6.98	6.72	7.52	9.87	7.83	8.06
South Africa	14.90	13.79	11.41	11.50	9.62	9.53	8.07	7.94	7.99	9.10	8.70	8.62	8.52

StatLink ᵐˢˡ http://dx.doi.org/10.1787/888932707667

Long-term interest rates
Percentage

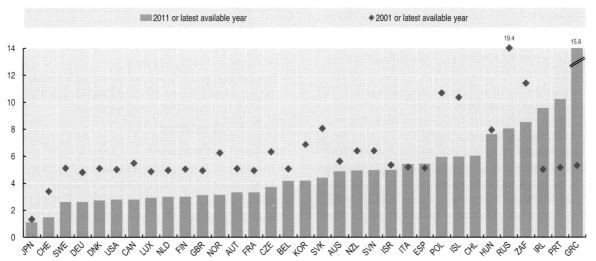

StatLink ᵐˢˡ http://dx.doi.org/10.1787/888932707686

RATES OF CONVERSION

To compare a single country's real GDP over a period of years, it is necessary to remove movements that are due to price changes. In the same way, in order to compare the real GDPs of a group of countries at a single point in time, it is necessary to remove any differences in their GDPs that are due to differences in their price levels. Price indices are used to remove the effects of price changes in a single country over time; purchasing power parities (PPPs) are used to remove the effects of the different levels of prices within a group of countries at a point in time.

Market exchange rates are sometimes used to convert GDP in different currencies to a common currency. However, comparisons of GDP based on exchange rates do not reflect the real volumes of goods and services in the GDP of the countries being compared. For many of the low-income countries, for example, the differences between GDP converted using market exchange rates and GDP converted using PPPs are considerable. In general, the use of market exchange rates understates the real GDP of low-income countries and overstates the real GDP of high-income countries.

Definition

PPPs are currency converters that equalise price levels between countries. The PPPs shown here have been calculated by comparing the prices in OECD countries of a common basket of about 2 500 goods and services. Countries are not required to price all the items in the common basket because some of the items may be hard to find in certain countries. However, the common basket has been drawn up in such a way that each country can find prices for a wide range of the goods and services that are representative of their markets.

The goods and services to be priced cover all those that enter into final expenditure: household consumption, government services, capital formation and net exports. Prices for the different items are weighted by their shares in total final expenditure to obtain the PPPs for GDP shown here.

Comparative price level indices are the ratios of PPPs to market exchange rates. At the level of GDP they provide a measure of the differences in the general price levels of countries.

Comparability

The PPPs shown here for the OECD and the Russian Federation have been calculated jointly by the OECD and Eurostat using standard procedures. In consultation with their member countries, OECD and Eurostat keep their methodology under review and improvements are made regularly. PPPs for non-OECD countries, with the exception of the Russian Federation, are calculated within the framework of the International Comparison Programme (ICP). There are six regions in the ICP programme of which five – Africa, Asia-Pacific, the Commonwealth of Independent States (CIS), Latin America & Caribbean and Western Asia – are ICP regions overseen by the Global Office at the World Bank.

Overview

Over the period 1999-2011, there were significant differences between changes in PPPs and changes in market exchange rates; even when the two indicators moved in the same direction, changes differed in their magnitude.

For Turkey, the Russian Federation and Poland the difference between GDP estimates for 2011 based on either PPPs or market exchange rate is over 60%. For India, the difference is around 190%.

Price level indices are PPPs estimates for 2011 divided by market exchange rates for the same year, with the OECD set equal to 100. In general, there is a positive correlation between GDP levels and the price level. Australia Denmark, Norway and Switzerland, four OECD countries with high per capita income, also recorded the highest price levels in 2011, exceeding the OECD level by 35% or more, while India had price levels of around 40% of the OECD average. Changes in price level indices should be however interpreted with caution as they are highly dependent on changes in exchange rates.

Sources
- OECD (2012), "PPP benchmark results 2008", OECD National Accounts Statistics(database).
- For Brazil, China, Indonesia and South Africa: International Monetary Fund (IMF) (2011), World Economic Outlook Database, IMF, Washington DC.

Further information

Analytical publications
- Bournot, S., F. Koechlin and P. Schreyer (2011), "2008 benchmark PPPs: Measurement and Uses", OECD Statistics Brief, No. 17.

Online databases
- OECD (2012), OECD National Accounts Statistics (database).

Statistical publications
- OECD (2011), National Accounts at a Glance, OECD Publishing.

Websites
- OECD Prices and Purchasing Power Parities (PPP), www.oecd.org/std/ppp.

Purchasing power parities
National currency units per US dollar

	1999	2000	2001	2002	2003	2004	2005	2006	2007	2008	2009	2010	2011
Australia	1.30	1.31	1.33	1.34	1.35	1.37	1.39	1.41	1.43	1.48	1.46	1.53	1.56
Austria	0.917	0.900	0.918	0.896	0.885	0.874	0.886	0.856	0.867	0.852	0.846	0.852	0.848
Belgium	0.921	0.891	0.886	0.865	0.879	0.897	0.900	0.883	0.886	0.874	0.860	0.864	0.867
Canada	1.19	1.23	1.22	1.23	1.23	1.23	1.21	1.21	1.21	1.23	1.20	1.22	1.23
Chile	277	284	288	296	307	321	334	363	372	365	376	400	402
Czech Republic	14.1	14.2	14.2	14.3	14.0	14.3	14.3	14.0	13.9	14.3	13.9	14.2	13.9
Denmark	8.47	8.41	8.47	8.30	8.54	8.40	8.59	8.32	8.23	8.01	7.89	7.87	7.82
Estonia	0.44	0.46	0.48	0.48	0.48	0.49	0.50	0.52	0.55	0.55	0.52	0.52	0.54
Finland	1.00	0.99	1.01	1.00	1.01	0.98	0.98	0.95	0.94	0.92	0.91	0.92	0.93
France	0.960	0.939	0.919	0.905	0.938	0.940	0.923	0.903	0.893	0.882	0.868	0.872	0.872
Germany	0.975	0.967	0.956	0.942	0.918	0.897	0.867	0.837	0.830	0.812	0.804	0.809	0.802
Greece	0.681	0.678	0.671	0.660	0.689	0.696	0.714	0.699	0.718	0.701	0.699	0.707	0.706
Hungary	101.1	107.9	110.7	114.9	120.6	126.3	128.6	128.5	131.3	129.4	126.8	130.1	130.7
Iceland	79.7	84.3	89.0	91.3	94.5	94.2	99.1	107.2	113.0	117.4	127.8	135.5	141.6
Ireland	0.930	0.962	0.993	1.004	1.014	1.006	1.010	0.984	0.958	0.952	0.904	0.861	0.839
Israel	3.50	3.44	3.42	3.46	3.63	3.53	3.72	3.83	3.74	3.87	4.02	4.02	4.02
Italy	0.818	0.817	0.808	0.845	0.854	0.873	0.867	0.833	0.817	0.789	0.783	0.805	0.790
Japan	162	155	149	144	140	140	134	130	125	120	117	115	111	107
Korea	755	746	758	770	794	796	789	775	769	786	804	825	821
Luxembourg	0.941	0.940	0.949	0.934	0.942	0.923	0.953	0.914	0.924	0.906	0.906	0.922	0.920
Mexico	5.63	6.10	6.31	6.55	6.82	7.22	7.13	7.19	7.38	7.47	7.71	7.93	8.19
Netherlands	0.907	0.892	0.907	0.902	0.927	0.909	0.896	0.868	0.857	0.842	0.841	0.839	0.842
New Zealand	1.43	1.44	1.47	1.47	1.50	1.51	1.54	1.49	1.50	1.49	1.48	1.51	1.53
Norway	9.33	9.13	9.18	9.11	9.12	8.99	8.90	8.69	8.77	8.75	8.92	9.01	8.88
Poland	1.74	1.84	1.86	1.83	1.84	1.86	1.87	1.84	1.84	1.86	1.86	1.86	1.87
Portugal	0.697	0.700	0.706	0.708	0.706	0.716	0.684	0.662	0.660	0.649	0.635	0.638	0.633
Slovak Republic	0.501	0.526	0.522	0.528	0.555	0.573	0.566	0.555	0.545	0.533	0.513	0.520	0.528
Slovenia	0.511	0.532	0.565	0.588	0.615	0.611	0.612	0.608	0.629	0.634	0.637	0.642	0.634
Spain	0.733	0.734	0.740	0.733	0.753	0.759	0.765	0.736	0.728	0.720	0.710	0.715	0.716
Sweden	9.29	9.13	9.35	9.35	9.34	9.11	9.38	9.08	8.88	8.77	8.94	9.03	8.95
Switzerland	1.87	1.85	1.84	1.77	1.78	1.75	1.74	1.66	1.60	1.55	1.53	1.52	1.46
Turkey	0.202	0.283	0.428	0.613	0.774	0.812	0.831	0.847	0.864	0.890	0.917	0.967	1.005
United Kingdom	0.653	0.636	0.627	0.628	0.641	0.633	0.636	0.627	0.645	0.651	0.654	0.659	0.678
United States	1.00	1.00	1.00	1.00	1.00	1.00	1.00	1.00	1.00	1.00	1.00	1.00	1.00
Brazil	0.92	0.96	1.02	1.11	1.23	1.30	1.36	1.39	1.43	1.52	1.59	1.69	..
China	3.30	3.29	3.29	3.25	3.27	3.40	3.45	3.47	3.62	3.82	3.76	3.95	..
India	13.3	13.6	13.8	14.0	14.2	14.5	14.7	14.9	15.3	16.2	16.9	18.4	..
Indonesia	2 612	2 775	3 102	3 233	3 338	3 531	3 934	4 347	4 698	5 432	5 829	6 237	..
Russian Federation	5.54	7.31	8.32	9.27	9.87	11.55	12.74	12.64	13.97	14.34	14.48	15.96	18.10
South Africa	2.93	3.12	3.28	3.58	3.70	3.81	3.87	4.00	4.19	4.47	4.75	4.99	..

StatLink http://dx.doi.org/10.1787/888932707724

Changes in exchange rates and purchasing power parities
Average annual growth in percentage, 2000-11

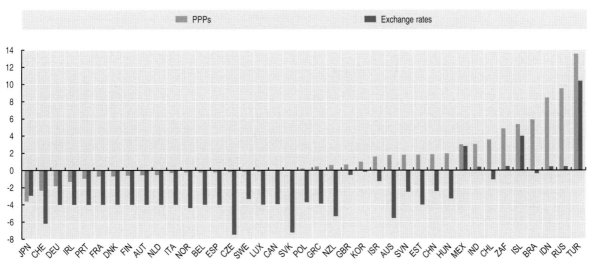

StatLink http://dx.doi.org/10.1787/888932707743

Exchange rates
National currency units per US dollar

	1999	2000	2001	2002	2003	2004	2005	2006	2007	2008	2009	2010	2011
Australia	1.5500	1.7248	1.9334	1.8406	1.5419	1.3598	1.3095	1.3280	1.1951	1.1922	1.2822	1.0902	0.9695
Austria	0.93863	1.08540	1.11751	1.06255	0.88603	0.80537	0.80412	0.79714	0.73064	0.68268	0.71984	0.75505	0.71936
Belgium	0.93863	1.08540	1.11751	1.06255	0.88603	0.80537	0.80412	0.79714	0.73064	0.68268	0.71984	0.75505	0.71936
Canada	1.4857	1.4851	1.5488	1.5693	1.4011	1.3010	1.2118	1.1344	1.0741	1.0670	1.1431	1.0302	0.9895
Chile	508.78	539.59	634.94	688.94	691.40	609.53	559.77	530.28	522.46	522.46	560.86	510.25	483.67
Czech Republic	34.569	38.598	38.035	32.739	28.209	25.700	23.957	22.596	20.294	17.072	19.063	19.098	17.696
Denmark	6.9762	8.0831	8.3228	7.8947	6.5877	5.9911	5.9969	5.9468	5.4437	5.0981	5.3609	5.6241	5.3687
Estonia	0.938	1.084	1.117	1.062	0.886	0.805	0.804	0.797	0.731	0.683	0.719	0.755	0.719
Finland	0.93863	1.08540	1.11751	1.06255	0.88603	0.80537	0.80412	0.79714	0.73064	0.68268	0.71984	0.75505	0.71936
France	0.93863	1.08540	1.11751	1.06255	0.88603	0.80537	0.80412	0.79714	0.73064	0.68268	0.71984	0.75505	0.71936
Germany	0.93863	1.08540	1.11751	1.06255	0.88603	0.80537	0.80412	0.79714	0.73064	0.68268	0.71984	0.75505	0.71936
Greece	0.89698	1.07234	1.11751	1.06255	0.88603	0.80537	0.80412	0.79714	0.73064	0.68268	0.71984	0.75505	0.71936
Hungary	237.15	282.18	286.49	257.89	224.31	202.75	199.58	210.39	183.63	172.11	202.34	207.94	201.06
Iceland	72.335	78.616	97.425	91.662	76.709	70.192	62.982	70.180	64.055	87.948	123.638	122.242	115.954
Ireland	0.93863	1.08540	1.11751	1.06255	0.88603	0.80537	0.80412	0.79714	0.73064	0.68268	0.71984	0.75505	0.71936
Israel	4.1397	4.0773	4.2057	4.7378	4.5541	4.4820	4.4877	4.4558	4.1081	3.5880	3.9323	3.7390	3.5781
Italy	0.93863	1.08540	1.11751	1.06255	0.88603	0.80537	0.80412	0.79714	0.73064	0.68268	0.71984	0.75505	0.71936
Japan	113.91	107.77	121.53	125.39	115.93	108.19	110.22	116.30	117.75	103.36	93.57	87.78	79.81
Korea	1 188.8	1 131.0	1 291.0	1 251.1	1 191.6	1 145.3	1 024.1	954.8	929.3	1 102.1	1 276.9	1 156.1	1 108.3
Luxembourg	0.93863	1.08540	1.11751	1.06255	0.88603	0.80537	0.80412	0.79714	0.73064	0.68268	0.71984	0.75505	0.71936
Mexico	9.560	9.456	9.342	9.656	10.789	11.286	10.898	10.899	10.928	11.130	13.514	12.636	12.423
Netherlands	0.93863	1.08540	1.11751	1.06255	0.88603	0.80537	0.80412	0.79714	0.73064	0.68268	0.71984	0.75505	0.71936
New Zealand	1.8896	2.2012	2.3788	2.1622	1.7221	1.5087	1.4203	1.5421	1.3607	1.4227	1.6002	1.3874	1.2659
Norway	7.7992	8.8018	8.9917	7.9838	7.0802	6.7408	6.4425	6.4133	5.8617	5.6400	6.2883	6.0442	5.6046
Poland	3.9671	4.3461	4.0939	4.0800	3.8891	3.6576	3.2355	3.1032	2.7680	2.4092	3.1201	3.0153	2.9629
Portugal	0.93863	1.08540	1.11751	1.06255	0.88603	0.80537	0.80412	0.79714	0.73064	0.68268	0.71984	0.75505	0.71936
Slovak Republic	1.3730	1.5281	1.6051	1.5046	1.2206	1.0707	1.0296	0.9858	0.8197	0.7091	0.7198	0.7550	0.7194
Slovenia	0.75851	0.92913	1.01297	1.00254	0.86427	0.80279	0.80414	0.79715	0.73064	0.68268	0.71984	0.75505	0.71936
Spain	0.93863	1.08540	1.11751	1.06255	0.88603	0.80537	0.80412	0.79714	0.73064	0.68268	0.71984	0.75505	0.71936
Sweden	8.2624	9.1622	10.3291	9.7371	8.0863	7.3489	7.4731	7.3783	6.7588	6.5911	7.6538	7.2075	6.4935
Switzerland	1.5022	1.6888	1.6876	1.5586	1.3467	1.2435	1.2452	1.2538	1.2004	1.0831	1.0881	1.0429	0.8880
Turkey	0.4188	0.6252	1.2256	1.5072	1.5009	1.4255	1.3436	1.4285	1.3029	1.3015	1.5500	1.5029	1.6750
United Kingdom	0.61806	0.66093	0.69466	0.66722	0.61247	0.54618	0.55000	0.54349	0.49977	0.54397	0.64192	0.64718	0.62414
United States	1.000	1.000	1.000	1.000	1.000	1.000	1.000	1.000	1.000	1.000	1.000	1.000	1.000
Euro Area	0.9386	1.0854	1.1175	1.0626	0.8860	0.8054	0.8041	0.7971	0.7306	0.6827	0.7198	0.7550	0.7194
Brazil	1.8139	1.8294	2.3496	2.9204	3.0775	2.9251	2.4344	2.1753	1.9471	1.8338	1.9994	1.7592	..
China	8.2783	8.2785	8.2771	8.2770	8.2770	8.2768	8.1943	7.9734	7.6075	6.9487	6.8314	6.7703	6.4615
India	43.055	44.942	47.186	48.610	46.583	45.316	44.100	45.307	41.349	43.505	48.405	45.726	46.670
Indonesia	7 855.15	8 421.78	10 260.90	9 311.19	8 577.13	8 938.85	9 704.74	9 159.32	9 141.00	9 698.96	10 389.90	9 090.43	8 770.43
Russian Federation	24.620	28.129	29.169	31.349	30.692	28.814	28.284	27.191	25.581	24.853	31.740	30.368	29.382
South Africa	6.1095	6.9398	8.6092	10.5407	7.5648	6.4597	6.3593	6.7716	7.0454	8.2612	8.4737	7.3212	7.2611

StatLink http://dx.doi.org/10.1787/888932707762

Differences in GDP when converted to US dollars using exchange rates and PPPs
PPP-based GDP minus exchange rate-based GDP as per cent of exchange rate-based GDP, 2011

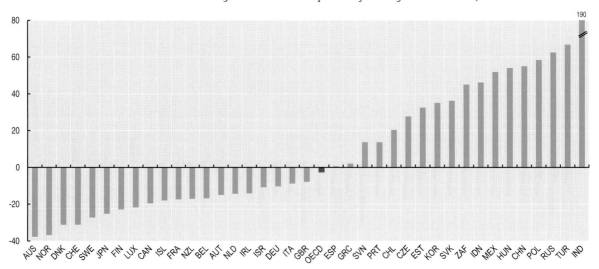

StatLink http://dx.doi.org/10.1787/888932707781

Indices of price levels

OECD=100

	1999	2000	2001	2002	2003	2004	2005	2006	2007	2008	2009	2010	2011
Australia	85	81	77	81	90	99	104	106	115	117	112	137	152
Austria	100	89	92	94	103	107	109	108	115	118	116	110	111
Belgium	100	88	89	91	102	109	110	111	117	121	117	111	113
Canada	82	89	88	87	90	93	99	107	109	109	103	115	117
Chile	56	56	51	48	46	52	59	69	69	66	66	76	78
Czech Republic	42	39	42	49	51	55	59	62	66	79	72	72	74
Denmark	124	111	114	117	133	138	141	140	146	148	145	136	137
Estonia	48	45	48	50	56	59	61	65	73	76	71	68	71
Finland	109	98	102	105	117	119	120	119	124	127	124	118	122
France	104	93	92	95	109	115	113	113	118	122	119	112	114
Germany	106	95	96	99	106	109	106	105	110	112	110	104	105
Greece	77	68	67	69	80	85	87	88	95	97	95	91	92
Hungary	43	41	43	50	55	61	63	61	69	71	62	61	61
Iceland	112	115	102	111	127	132	155	153	170	126	102	108	115
Ireland	101	95	100	105	118	123	124	124	127	131	124	111	110
Israel	86	90	91	81	82	77	82	86	88	102	100	105	106
Italy	89	80	81	89	99	106	106	105	108	109	107	104	103
Japan	145	154	138	128	124	122	116	107	99	107	121	123	126
Korea	65	71	66	68	69	68	76	81	80	67	62	69	70
Luxembourg	102	93	95	98	109	112	117	115	122	125	124	119	121
Mexico	60	69	76	76	65	63	64	66	65	63	56	61	62
Netherlands	98	88	91	94	108	111	110	109	113	116	115	108	110
New Zealand	77	70	69	76	89	98	106	97	107	99	91	106	114
Norway	122	111	115	127	132	131	136	136	144	146	140	145	149
Poland	45	45	51	50	49	50	57	59	64	73	59	60	60
Portugal	76	69	71	74	82	87	84	83	87	90	87	82	83
Slovak Republic	37	37	36	39	47	52	54	56	64	71	70	67	69
Slovenia	69	61	63	65	73	75	75	76	83	88	87	83	83
Spain	80	72	74	77	87	92	94	92	96	99	97	92	94
Sweden	115	107	102	107	119	122	124	123	127	126	115	122	130
Switzerland	127	117	122	126	136	138	138	132	129	135	139	141	154
Turkey	49	48	39	45	53	56	61	59	64	64	58	63	57
United Kingdom	108	103	101	105	108	114	114	115	125	113	100	99	102
United States	102	107	112	111	103	98	98	100	97	94	98	97	94
EU 27	94	86	86	90	98	103	102	102	107	108	103	99	100
OECD	100	100	100	100	100	100	100	100	100	100	100	100	100
Brazil	52	56	49	42	41	44	55	64	71	78	79	95	102
China	41	43	44	44	41	40	41	44	46	52	54	57	61
India	32	32	33	32	31	31	33	33	36	35	34	38	39
Indonesia	30	35	34	39	40	39	40	48	50	53	55	67	71
Russian Federation	23	28	32	33	33	39	44	47	53	54	45	51	58
South Africa	49	48	43	38	50	58	60	59	58	51	55	67	69

StatLink 🔗 http://dx.doi.org/10.1787/888932707800

Indices of price levels

OECD=100, 2011

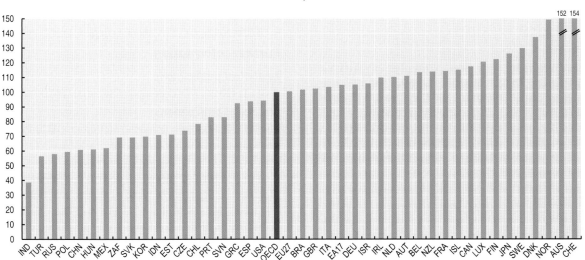

StatLink 🔗 http://dx.doi.org/10.1787/888932707819

REAL EFFECTIVE EXCHANGE RATES

Effective exchange rates are a summary measure of the changes in the exchange rates of a country *vis-à-vis* its trading partners. This section shows one indicator of real effective exchange rates, namely changes in consumer good prices of a given country relative to those of its competitors. This indicator provides a broad interpretation of a country's price competitiveness. This competitiveness is, in turn, a major determinant of the success of different countries in raising productivity, fostering innovation and improving living standards.

There are several ways of looking at exchange rates as a measure of price competitiveness. One indicator is the nominal effective exchange rate; other things being equal, a nominal depreciation of any country's currency leads, in the short run, to a decrease in the relative price of its products internationally. Potential competitiveness gains derived from nominal exchange rate depreciations however, can be eroded by local inflation.

Real effective exchange rates try to eliminate this factor by correcting effective nominal exchange rates for differences in inflation rates. In the index at hand, these are measured as consumer price changes. While consumer price indexes are readily available, this raises another issue, namely the assumption that the relative price of domestic tradable goods as compared with foreign tradables evolves in parallel to the relative consumer prices. In an attempt to remove these differences, relative production costs can be used; these are generally measured by trade weighted relative unit labour costs in the manufacturing sector.

Definition

Nominal effective exchange rate indices are calculated by comparing, for each country, the change in its own exchange rate against the US dollar to a weighted average of changes in its competitors' exchange rates, also against the US dollar. Changes in the competitor exchange rates are weighted using a matrix measuring the importance of bilateral trade flows in the current year.

The indicator of real effective exchange rates shown here, relative consumer price indices, takes into account not only changes in market exchange rates but also variations in relative prices using, consumer prices.

The change in a country's relative consumer prices between two years is obtained by comparing the change in the country's consumer price index converted into US dollars at market exchange rates to a weighted average of changes in its competitors' consumer price indices, also expressed in US dollars. The weighted average of competitors' prices is based on a matrix for the current year expressing the importance of bilateral trade.

A rise in the index represents a deterioration in that country's competitiveness. Real exchange rates are a major short-run determinant of any country's capacity to compete. Note that the index only shows changes in the international competitiveness of each country over time. Differences between countries in the levels of the indices have no significance.

Comparability

The index shown here is constructed using a common procedure that assures a high degree of comparability both across countries and over time.

Sources

• OECD (2012), *OECD Economic Outlook*, OECD Publishing.

Further information

Analytical publications

• OECD (2012), *OECD Economic Surveys*, OECD Publishing.

Statistical publications

• OECD (2012), *Main Economic Indicators*, OECD Publishing.

Methodological publications

• Durand, M., C. Madaschi and F. Terribile (1998), "Trends in OECD Countries' International Competitiveness", *OECD Economics Department Working Papers*, No. 195.

• Durand, M., J. Simon and C. Webb (1992), "OECD's Indicators of International Trade and Competitiveness", *OECD Economics Department Working Papers*, No. 120.

Online databases

• *OECD Economic Outlook: Statistics and Projections.*

Websites

• OECD Economic Outlook – Sources and Methods, *www.oecd.org/eco/sources-and-methods.*

Overview

The last ten years have seen a number of patterns emerge among OECD countries. Germany and France have seen little variation in their real effective exchange rates and are now only just above values recorded 10 years ago. After a rise in real effective exchange rates in the first half of the decade, both have seen declines (an increase in competitiveness) in the last few years.

The United States and the United Kingdom have both seen their international competitiveness increase significantly in the last ten years, and in particular the United Kingdom since 2007. The same cannot be said for other countries, for example Italy that has seen its international competitiveness deteriorate since 2001. Finally, Japan which from 2000 to 2007 saw a large improvement in its international competitiveness is now back at the same levels as 10 years ago.

Real effective exchange rates

Based on consumer price indices, 2005 = 100

	1999	2000	2001	2002	2003	2004	2005	2006	2007	2008	2009	2010	2011
Australia	81.5	77.7	74.7	79.1	89.5	97.0	100.0	99.9	105.9	103.8	100.6	114.9	123.2
Austria	98.4	95.9	96.1	96.6	99.5	100.5	100.0	99.4	99.8	100.0	100.6	98.2	98.6
Belgium	94.8	91.1	92.0	93.5	98.0	99.8	100.0	99.7	100.5	103.4	103.4	100.4	101.3
Canada	83.1	83.6	81.1	80.4	89.4	94.2	100.0	105.6	109.6	107.3	101.9	111.8	114.3
Chile	105.5	104.1	95.7	94.7	88.6	94.7	100.0	104.0	102.1	103.7	100.0	106.4	107.7
Czech Republic	78.9	80.4	85.9	95.5	93.5	94.3	100.0	105.5	108.3	123.9	118.9	120.9	123.2
Denmark	95.6	92.1	93.5	95.4	100.3	101.0	100.0	99.7	100.2	101.8	104.9	101.2	100.4
Estonia	90.7	88.5	91.2	93.7	97.0	99.3	100.0	101.7	106.4	113.9	116.3	112.4	113.6
Finland	100.3	96.0	97.3	98.5	102.7	102.6	100.0	99.0	100.3	102.1	103.0	97.1	96.7
France	97.8	93.3	93.2	94.7	99.4	101.0	100.0	99.6	99.9	100.7	100.8	97.5	96.8
Germany	100.9	94.8	94.8	95.8	100.5	101.9	100.0	99.4	100.5	100.4	101.2	96.2	95.5
Greece	94.2	88.0	89.0	91.7	97.3	99.6	100.0	100.9	102.6	104.8	106.1	105.5	106.2
Hungary	74.2	75.1	81.3	89.7	91.9	98.0	100.0	95.4	106.3	109.0	102.4	104.1	103.8
Iceland	82.7	85.9	76.3	81.6	85.8	88.1	100.0	93.7	97.5	76.4	62.0	66.0	66.8
Ireland	83.7	80.6	83.7	88.4	97.6	100.0	100.0	101.8	106.9	112.7	108.8	101.4	101.3
Israel	120.9	128.6	127.6	115.6	109.4	102.5	100.0	99.7	100.6	112.5	109.5	114.9	116.3
Italy	94.3	90.6	91.9	94.0	99.4	101.0	100.0	100.0	100.5	101.4	102.4	98.4	98.3
Japan	115.7	122.5	109.6	103.0	104.4	106.0	100.0	90.5	82.9	89.4	100.0	100.7	102.2
Korea	80.2	86.4	81.7	86.2	87.5	89.0	100.0	107.8	107.1	86.8	76.0	82.4	82.4
Luxembourg	95.5	93.5	94.1	95.4	98.9	100.2	100.0	100.9	102.3	103.1	102.9	101.4	101.9
Mexico	96.7	105.1	112.1	112.5	100.4	96.4	100.0	100.0	99.1	97.4	85.4	92.4	92.5
Netherlands	91.9	86.9	89.5	93.1	99.7	101.3	100.0	99.0	99.8	100.2	101.2	96.4	95.8
New Zealand	78.9	71.6	70.7	77.5	88.3	94.6	100.0	93.2	99.7	93.1	86.7	93.7	97.0
Norway	92.1	91.0	94.5	102.0	100.5	96.0	100.0	99.9	99.7	99.7	98.1	102.7	102.9
Poland	85.4	94.0	106.2	101.5	90.2	89.4	100.0	102.2	105.7	115.4	97.6	103.7	102.0
Portugal	93.6	91.7	94.0	96.2	99.9	100.7	100.0	100.6	101.2	101.2	100.3	97.7	98.4
Slovak Republic	69.7	76.9	77.9	78.9	89.1	97.6	100.0	105.4	116.2	125.8	135.2	129.5	130.6
Slovenia	97.3	94.1	93.9	96.3	100.9	101.4	100.0	99.8	101.6	104.2	106.0	102.1	101.1
Spain	90.1	88.1	90.1	92.5	97.2	99.3	100.0	101.5	103.0	105.1	105.1	102.2	102.6
Sweden	105.7	104.2	95.6	98.2	104.0	104.2	100.0	99.6	100.5	98.2	88.8	95.0	100.5
Switzerland	99.1	96.2	98.5	102.3	102.7	101.8	100.0	97.4	93.2	97.1	101.1	105.8	115.9
Turkey	82.8	92.4	75.4	82.3	86.9	89.9	100.0	99.6	108.1	109.7	102.5	113.3	100.1
United Kingdom	103.8	104.4	101.8	102.3	97.9	101.6	100.0	100.6	102.1	89.0	80.4	81.3	81.8
United States	102.3	105.6	111.6	112.0	105.7	101.4	100.0	99.3	95.1	91.5	95.3	91.1	86.8
Brazil	..	..	..	..	..	..	..	..	..	..	..	..	..
China	..	..	..	..	..	..	..	..	..	..	..	..	..
India	..	..	..	..	..	..	..	..	..	..	..	..	..
Indonesia	..	..	..	..	..	..	..	..	..	..	..	..	..
Russian Federation	..	..	..	..	..	..	..	..	..	..	..	..	..
South Africa	..	..	..	..	..	..	..	..	..	..	..	..	..

StatLink ⫘ http://dx.doi.org/10.1787/888932707838

Real effective exchange rates based on consumer price indices

1995 = 100

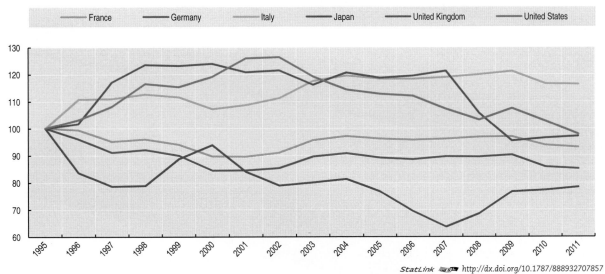

StatLink ⫘ http://dx.doi.org/10.1787/888932707857

ENERGY AND TRANSPORTATION

ENERGY SUPPLY

An analysis of energy problems requires a comprehensive presentation of basic supply and demand data for all fuels in a manner which allows the easy comparison of the contribution that each fuel makes to the economy and their interrelationships through the conversion of one fuel into another.

Definition

The table refers to total primary energy supply (TPES). TPES equals production plus imports minus exports minus international bunkers plus or minus stock changes. The International Energy Agency (IEA) energy balance methodology is based on the calorific content of the energy commodities and a common unit of account. The unit of account adopted is the tonne of oil equivalent (toe) which is defined as 10^7 kilocalories (41.868 gigajoules). This quantity of energy is, within a few per cent, equal to the net heat content of one tonne of crude oil. The difference between the "net" and the "gross" calorific value for each fuel is the latent heat of vaporisation of the water produced during combustion of the fuel. For coal and oil, net calorific value is about 5% less than gross, for most forms of natural and manufactured gas the difference is 9-10%, while for electricity there is no difference. The IEA balances are calculated using the physical energy content method to calculate the primary energy equivalent.

Comparability

Data quality is not homogeneous for all countries and regions. In some countries, data are based on secondary sources, and where incomplete or unavailable, the IEA has made estimates. In general, data are likely to be more accurate for production and trade than for international bunkers or stock changes. Moreover, statistics for biofuels and waste are less accurate than those for traditional commercial energy data.

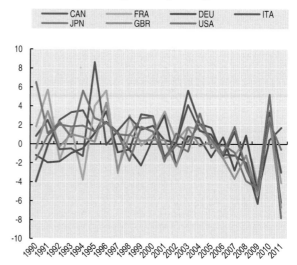

Total primary energy supply
Annual growth in percentage

StatLink ⟶ http://dx.doi.org/10.1787/888932707914

Overview

Between 1971 and 2010, the world's total primary energy supply increased by 130%, reaching 12 717 Mtoe (million tonnes of oil equivalent). This equates to a compound growth rate of 2.2% per annum. By comparison, world population grew by 1.5% and gross domestic product by 3.3% per annum in real terms over the same period.

Energy supply growth was fairly constant over the period, except in 1974-75 and in the early 1980s as a consequence of the first two oil shocks, and in the early 1990s following the dissolution of the Soviet Union. With the economic crisis in 2008, world energy supply declined by 1% in 2009. However, growth rebounded in 2010, increasing by 5%.

The share of OECD in world primary energy supply decreased from 61% in 1971 to 43% in 2010. Strong economic development in Asia led to a large increase in the share of non-OECD Asia (including China) in world energy supply, from 13% to 31% over the same period. By contrast, the combined share of non-OECD Europe and Eurasia (which includes the Former Soviet Union) decreased significantly in the late 1980s.

Sources

- IEA (2012), *Energy Balances of Non-OECD Countries*, IEA, Paris.
- IEA (2012), *Energy Balances of OECD Countries*, IEA, Paris.

Further information

Analytical publications

- IEA (2012), *Electricity and a Climate-Constrained World, Data and Analyses*, IEA, Paris.
- IEA (2012), *Energy Policies of IEA Countries*, series, IEA, Paris.
- IEA (2012), *Energy Technology Perspectives*, IEA, Paris.
- IEA (2012), *World Energy Outlook*, IEA, Paris.
- IEA (2011), *IEA Scoreboard 2011: Implementing Energy Efficiency Policy: Progress and challenges in IEA member countries*, IEA, Paris.

Online databases

- IEA World Energy Statistics and Balances.

Websites

- International Energy Agency, *www.iea.org*.

Total primary energy supply

Million tonnes of oil equivalent (Mtoe)

	1971	1990	2001	2002	2003	2004	2005	2006	2007	2008	2009	2010	2011
Australia	51.6	86.2	105.8	109.5	110.9	111.0	114.2	116.0	119.8	124.2	126.0	124.7	119.8
Austria	18.8	24.8	30.2	30.4	32.2	32.7	33.8	33.8	33.4	33.5	31.8	33.8	32.6
Belgium	39.7	48.3	58.4	56.4	59.2	58.9	58.7	58.1	57.0	58.6	57.1	60.9	55.9
Canada	141.4	208.5	247.9	248.2	262.0	267.6	272.2	268.3	271.7	264.7	250.7	251.8	256.1
Chile	8.7	14.0	24.7	25.6	25.8	27.5	28.4	29.5	30.6	30.3	29.5	30.9	32.4
Czech Republic	45.4	49.6	42.1	42.5	44.4	45.5	44.9	45.9	45.8	44.9	42.1	44.1	42.9
Denmark	18.5	17.4	19.2	19.0	20.1	19.4	18.9	20.3	19.8	19.2	18.4	19.3	17.5
Estonia	..	9.9	4.9	4.7	5.2	5.3	5.2	5.0	5.6	5.4	4.7	5.6	5.5
Finland	18.2	28.4	33.1	34.8	36.7	37.1	34.3	37.3	36.8	35.3	33.2	36.4	34.3
France	158.6	223.9	260.3	261.1	265.8	269.7	270.6	266.7	263.5	264.8	253.5	262.3	251.4
Germany	305.0	351.1	346.7	338.6	341.3	343.2	338.3	340.7	331.2	334.1	317.1	327.4	307.2
Greece	8.7	21.4	28.0	28.3	29.1	29.7	30.2	30.2	30.2	30.4	29.4	27.6	26.5
Hungary	19.0	28.8	25.6	25.6	26.1	26.2	27.6	27.3	26.7	26.5	24.9	25.7	25.1
Iceland	0.9	2.1	3.2	3.3	3.3	3.4	3.5	4.2	4.8	5.4	5.4	5.4	5.7
Ireland	6.7	10.0	14.5	14.6	14.4	14.6	14.5	14.8	15.1	15.0	14.4	14.4	13.5
Israel	5.7	11.5	19.2	18.8	19.7	19.3	18.5	20.4	20.7	22.9	21.5	22.9	24.3
Italy	105.4	146.6	172.1	172.4	179.4	182.0	183.9	181.8	179.6	176.0	164.9	170.2	165.1
Japan	267.5	439.3	510.8	510.4	506.2	522.5	520.5	519.8	515.2	495.4	472.1	496.8	458.1
Korea	17.0	93.1	191.0	198.7	202.7	208.3	210.2	213.6	222.1	226.9	229.2	250.0	257.6
Luxembourg	4.1	3.4	3.5	3.6	3.8	4.3	4.4	4.3	4.2	4.2	4.0	4.2	4.2
Mexico	43.0	122.5	146.1	150.7	153.6	159.1	170.2	171.4	175.9	181.1	174.6	178.1	187.0
Netherlands	50.9	65.7	75.6	75.7	78.0	79.1	78.8	76.8	79.3	79.6	78.2	83.4	77.5
New Zealand	6.9	12.9	17.1	17.1	16.8	17.4	16.8	17.0	17.1	17.4	17.5	18.2	18.0
Norway	13.3	21.0	26.8	24.9	27.0	26.4	26.8	27.1	27.5	29.8	28.2	32.5	29.9
Poland	86.1	103.1	89.7	88.9	91.1	91.4	92.4	97.2	96.8	97.9	94.0	101.5	102.6
Portugal	6.3	16.7	24.8	25.8	25.1	25.8	26.5	24.7	25.3	24.4	24.2	23.5	23.1
Slovak Republic	14.3	21.3	18.6	18.7	18.6	18.4	18.8	18.6	17.8	18.3	16.7	17.8	16.9
Slovenia	..	5.7	6.7	6.8	6.9	7.1	7.3	7.3	7.3	7.7	7.1	7.2	7.2
Spain	42.6	90.1	125.0	128.9	133.2	139.1	141.9	141.7	143.8	139.0	127.5	127.7	125.9
Sweden	36.0	47.2	50.5	51.8	50.6	52.6	51.6	50.2	50.1	49.6	45.4	51.3	49.4
Switzerland	16.4	24.3	26.6	25.9	26.0	26.1	25.9	27.1	25.8	26.8	27.0	26.2	25.5
Turkey	19.5	52.8	70.4	74.2	77.8	80.9	84.4	93.0	100.0	98.5	97.7	105.1	114.2
United Kingdom	208.7	205.9	223.8	218.5	222.2	221.9	222.4	219.0	211.0	208.4	197.1	202.5	189.0
United States	1 587.5	1 915.0	2 230.8	2 256.0	2 261.2	2 307.8	2 318.9	2 296.7	2 337.0	2 277.0	2 165.0	2 216.3	2 202.7
EU 27	..	1 636.1	1 725.0	1 720.0	1 759.4	1 778.2	1 779.7	1 778.7	1 757.7	1 749.5	1 653.9	1 714.3	..
OECD	3 372.3	4 522.5	5 273.8	5 310.4	5 377.0	5 481.1	5 515.1	5 506.0	5 548.8	5 473.2	5 229.7	5 405.9	5 305.0
Brazil	69.8	140.2	190.7	195.7	198.9	209.9	215.2	222.7	235.4	248.3	240.3	265.6	..
China	390.5	872.1	1 202.1	1 266.1	1 440.3	1 623.1	1 750.2	1 912.0	2 014.8	2 086.1	2 249.3	2 417.1	..
India	156.5	316.7	464.5	477.5	489.5	519.1	539.3	566.8	598.8	626.1	675.2	692.7	..
Indonesia	35.1	98.6	159.4	165.2	165.2	177.1	180.5	185.4	184.7	186.9	198.5	207.8	..
Russian Federation	..	879.2	626.0	623.1	645.3	647.4	651.7	670.7	672.6	688.5	646.9	701.5	..
South Africa	45.4	91.0	112.4	109.9	117.4	128.7	128.2	127.2	137.3	147.7	144.3	136.9	..
World	5 526.5	8 781.0	10 172.8	10 365.4	10 745.8	11 226.8	11 510.4	11 812.7	12 093.5	12 237.2	12 135.5	12 717.2	..

StatLink http://dx.doi.org/10.1787/888932707876

Total primary energy supply by region

Million tonnes of oil equivalent (Mtoe)

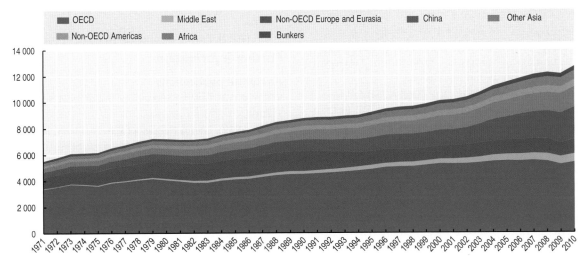

StatLink http://dx.doi.org/10.1787/888932707895

ENERGY INTENSITY

A common way to measure and compare the energy intensity of different countries, and how this changes over time, is to look at the ratio of energy supply to GDP. It should be noted that energy intensity is only a poor proxy of energy efficiency, as the latter depends on numerous elements (such as climate, output composition, outsourcing of goods produced by energy-intensive industries, etc.) that are not considered by the simple measure of energy supply to GDP shown here.

Definition

The table shows total primary energy supply (TPES) per thousand US dollars of GDP. The ratios are calculated by dividing each country's annual TPES by each country's annual GDP expressed in constant 2005 prices and converted to US dollars using purchasing power parities (PPPs) for the year 2005.

TPES consists of primary energy production adjusted for net trade, bunkers and stock changes. Production of secondary energy (*e.g.* oil/coal products, electricity from fossil fuels, etc.) is not included since the "energy equivalent" of the primary fuels used to create the secondary products or electric power has already been counted. TPES is expressed in tonnes of oil equivalent.

Comparability

Care should be taken when comparing energy intensities between countries and over time since different national circumstances (*e.g.* density of population, country size, average temperatures and economic structure) will affect the ratios. A decrease in the TPES/GDP ratio may reflect a restructuring of the economy and the transfer of energy-intensive industries such as iron and steel out of the country. The harmful effects of such outsourcing may increase the global damage to the environment if the producers abroad use less energy efficient techniques. Data for non-OECD Americas include the Caribbean islands.

Overview

Sharp improvements in the efficiency of key end uses, shifts to electricity, and some changes in manufacturing output and consumer behaviour have occurred in many OECD countries since 1971. As a consequence, energy supply per unit of GDP fell significantly, particularly in the 1979-1990 period.

Contributing to the trend were higher fuel prices, long-term technological progress, government energy efficiency programmes and regulations.

The ratio of energy supply to GDP (TPES/GDP) fell less than the ratio of energy consumption to GDP (total final consumption/GDP), because of increased use of electricity. The main reason for this divergence is that losses in electricity generation outweighed intensity improvements achieved in end uses such as household appliances.

Among OECD countries, the ratio of energy consumption to GDP varies considerably. Apart from energy prices, winter weather is a key element in these variations, as are raw materials processing techniques, the distance goods must be shipped, the size of dwellings, the use of private rather than public transport and other lifestyle factors.

Sources
- IEA (2012), *Energy Balances of Non-OECD Countries*, IEA, Paris.
- IEA (2012), *Energy Balances of OECD Countries*, IEA, Paris.

Further information

Analytical publications
- IEA (2012), *Cutting Energy Use in the Buildings Sector*, IEA, Paris.
- IEA (2012), *Energy Policies of IEA Countries*, IEA, Paris.
- IEA (2012), *Energy Technology Perspectives*, IEA, Paris.
- IEA (2011), *IEA Scoreboard 2011: Implementing Energy Efficiency Policy: Progress and challenges in IEA member countries*, IEA, Paris.
- IEA (2011), *World Energy Outlook*, IEA, Paris.
- IEA (2009), *Implementing Energy Efficiency: are IEA Countries on Track?*, IEA, Paris.

Online databases
- IEA World Energy Statistics and Balances.

Websites
- International Energy Agency, *www.iea.org*.

Total primary energy supply per unit of GDP

Tonnes of oil equivalent (toe) per thousand 2005 US dollars of GDP calculated using PPPs

	1971	1990	2001	2002	2003	2004	2005	2006	2007	2008	2009	2010	2011
Australia	0.21	0.20	0.17	0.17	0.16	0.16	0.16	0.16	0.15	0.16	0.16	0.15	0.14
Austria	0.16	0.13	0.12	0.12	0.12	0.12	0.12	0.12	0.11	0.11	0.11	0.11	0.11
Belgium	0.26	0.19	0.19	0.18	0.18	0.18	0.17	0.17	0.16	0.16	0.16	0.17	0.15
Canada	0.36	0.28	0.24	0.24	0.25	0.24	0.24	0.23	0.23	0.22	0.22	0.21	0.21
Chile	0.18	0.16	0.15	0.15	0.15	0.15	0.14	0.14	0.14	0.13	0.13	0.13	0.13
Czech Republic	0.38	0.29	0.23	0.23	0.23	0.22	0.21	0.20	0.19	0.18	0.17	0.18	0.17
Denmark	0.21	0.13	0.11	0.11	0.12	0.11	0.11	0.11	0.10	0.10	0.10	0.11	0.10
Estonia	..	0.61	0.29	0.26	0.27	0.26	0.23	0.21	0.21	0.21	0.22	0.25	0.23
Finland	0.30	0.25	0.23	0.24	0.24	0.24	0.21	0.22	0.21	0.20	0.20	0.22	0.20
France	0.19	0.16	0.15	0.15	0.15	0.15	0.15	0.14	0.14	0.14	0.13	0.14	0.13
Germany	0.24	0.17	0.14	0.13	0.14	0.13	0.13	0.13	0.12	0.12	0.12	0.12	0.11
Greece	0.08	0.12	0.12	0.12	0.12	0.11	0.11	0.11	0.10	0.10	0.10	0.10	0.10
Hungary	0.24	0.21	0.18	0.17	0.17	0.16	0.16	0.15	0.15	0.15	0.15	0.15	0.15
Iceland	0.30	0.32	0.37	0.38	0.37	0.35	0.34	0.38	0.42	0.46	0.50	0.52	0.53
Ireland	0.22	0.15	0.11	0.10	0.10	0.10	0.09	0.09	0.08	0.09	0.09	0.09	0.08
Israel	0.15	0.14	0.13	0.13	0.13	0.12	0.11	0.12	0.11	0.12	0.11	0.12	0.12
Italy	0.14	0.11	0.11	0.11	0.11	0.11	0.11	0.11	0.10	0.10	0.10	0.10	0.10
Japan	0.19	0.14	0.14	0.14	0.14	0.14	0.13	0.13	0.13	0.12	0.13	0.13	0.12
Korea	0.20	0.20	0.21	0.20	0.20	0.20	0.19	0.19	0.18	0.18	0.18	0.19	0.19
Luxembourg	0.51	0.21	0.13	0.13	0.13	0.14	0.14	0.13	0.12	0.12	0.12	0.12	0.12
Mexico	0.11	0.15	0.12	0.13	0.13	0.13	0.13	0.13	0.13	0.13	0.13	0.13	0.13
Netherlands	0.21	0.17	0.14	0.14	0.14	0.14	0.14	0.13	0.13	0.13	0.13	0.14	0.12
New Zealand	0.15	0.20	0.19	0.18	0.17	0.17	0.16	0.16	0.16	0.16	0.16	0.16	0.16
Norway	0.19	0.15	0.13	0.12	0.13	0.12	0.12	0.12	0.12	0.13	0.12	0.14	0.13
Poland	0.37	0.33	0.20	0.19	0.19	0.18	0.18	0.17	0.16	0.16	0.15	0.15	0.15
Portugal	0.08	0.10	0.11	0.12	0.11	0.12	0.12	0.11	0.11	0.10	0.11	0.10	0.10
Slovak Republic	0.33	0.34	0.26	0.25	0.24	0.22	0.22	0.20	0.17	0.17	0.16	0.16	0.15
Slovenia	..	0.17	0.17	0.16	0.16	0.16	0.16	0.15	0.14	0.14	0.14	0.14	0.14
Spain	0.10	0.12	0.12	0.12	0.12	0.12	0.12	0.11	0.11	0.11	0.10	0.10	0.10
Sweden	0.26	0.22	0.19	0.19	0.18	0.18	0.17	0.16	0.16	0.16	0.15	0.16	0.15
Switzerland	0.10	0.11	0.11	0.10	0.10	0.10	0.10	0.10	0.09	0.09	0.09	0.09	0.09
Turkey	0.11	0.12	0.12	0.12	0.12	0.11	0.11	0.11	0.11	0.11	0.12	0.12	0.12
United Kingdom	0.25	0.16	0.13	0.12	0.12	0.11	0.11	0.11	0.10	0.10	0.10	0.10	0.09
United States	0.36	0.24	0.20	0.20	0.19	0.19	0.18	0.18	0.18	0.17	0.17	0.17	0.17
EU 27	..	0.17	0.14	0.14	0.14	0.14	0.13	0.13	0.12	0.12	0.12	0.12	..
OECD	0.26	0.19	0.16	0.16	0.16	0.16	0.16	0.15	0.15	0.15	0.15	0.15	0.14
Brazil	0.15	0.13	0.14	0.14	0.14	0.14	0.14	0.14	0.13	0.14	0.13	0.14	..
China	1.30	0.70	0.33	0.32	0.33	0.34	0.33	0.32	0.29	0.28	0.27	0.26	..
India	0.34	0.30	0.25	0.24	0.23	0.23	0.21	0.21	0.20	0.20	0.20	0.18	..
Indonesia	0.35	0.27	0.27	0.27	0.26	0.27	0.26	0.25	0.23	0.22	0.23	0.22	..
Russian Federation	..	0.47	0.47	0.45	0.43	0.41	0.38	0.37	0.34	0.33	0.33	0.35	..
South Africa	0.25	0.32	0.33	0.31	0.32	0.33	0.32	0.30	0.30	0.32	0.31	0.29	..
World	0.29	0.24	0.21	0.21	0.21	0.20	0.20	0.20	0.19	0.19	0.19	0.19	..

StatLink http://dx.doi.org/10.1787/888932707933

Total primary energy supply per unit of GDP

Tonnes of oil equivalent (toe) per thousand 2005 US dollars of GDP calculated using PPPs

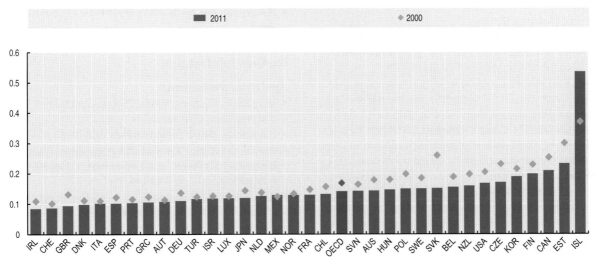

StatLink http://dx.doi.org/10.1787/888932707952

ELECTRICITY GENERATION

The amount of electricity generated by a country, and the breakdown of that production by type of fuel, reflects the natural resources, imported energy, national policies on security of energy supply, population size, electrification rate as well as the stage of development and rate of growth of the economy in each country.

Definition

The table shows data on electricity generation from fossil fuels, nuclear, hydro (excluding pumped storage), geothermal, solar, biofuels, etc. It includes electricity produced in electricity-only plants and in combined heat and power plants. Both main activity producer and autoproducer plants are included, where data are available. Main activity producers generate electricity for sale to third parties as their primary activity. Autoproducers generate electricity wholly or partly for their own use as an activity which supports their primary activity. Both types of plants may be privately or publicly owned.

Electricity generation is measured in terawatt hours, which expresses the generation of 1 terawatt (10^{12} watts) of electricity for one hour.

Overview

World electricity generation rose at an average annual rate of 3.7% from 1971 to 2010, greater than the 2.2% growth in total primary energy supply. This increase was largely due to more electrical appliances, the development of electrical heating in countries and of rural electrification programmes in developing countries.

The share of electricity production from fossil fuels has gradually fallen, from just under 75% in 1971 to 67% in 2010. This decrease was due to a progressive move away from oil, which fell from 20.9% to 4.6%.

Oil for world electricity generation has been displaced in particular by dramatic growth in nuclear electricity generation, which rose from 2.1% in 1971 to 17.7% in 1996. However, the share of nuclear has been falling steadily since then and represented 12.9% in 2010. Global nuclear power will likely be even lower in 2011 following the tsunami in Japan and the resulting Fukushima nuclear power plant accident.

Due to large development programmes in several OECD countries, the share of new and renewable energies, such as solar, wind, geothermal, biofuels and waste increased. However, these energy forms remain of limited importance: in 2010, they accounted for only 3.7% of total electricity production for the world as a whole.

Comparability

Some countries have trouble reporting electricity generation from autoproducer plants. In some non-member countries it is also difficult to obtain information on electricity generated by biofuels and waste.

World electricity generation by source of energy

As a percentage of world electricity generation

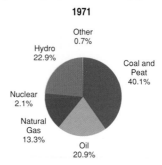

1971

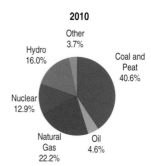

2010

StatLink ⓘ http://dx.doi.org/10.1787/888932708028

Sources

- IEA (2012), *Energy Balances of Non-OECD Countries*, IEA, Paris.
- IEA (2012), *Energy Balances of OECD Countries*, IEA, Paris.

Further information

Analytical publications

- IEA (2012), *Electricity and a Climate-Constrained World, Data and Analyses*, IEA, Paris.
- IEA (2012), *World Energy Outlook*, IEA, Paris.
- Cooke, D. (2011), "Empowering Customer Choice in Electricity Markets", *IEA Energy Papers*, No. 2011/13, OECD Publishing.
- IEA (2011), *IEA Scoreboard 2011: Implementing Energy Efficiency Policy: Progress and challenges in IEA member countries*, IEA, Paris.

Online databases

- *IEA Electricity Information Statistics.*
- *IEA World Energy Statistics and Balances.*

Websites

- International Energy Agency, *www.iea.org.*

Electricity generation

Terawatt hours (TWh)

	1971	1990	2001	2002	2003	2004	2005	2006	2007	2008	2009	2010	2011
Australia	53.0	154.3	224.3	227.4	226.2	236.3	228.3	232.5	242.9	243.1	244.4	241.5	238.5
Austria	28.2	49.3	61.1	60.7	58.1	61.9	64.1	62.1	62.6	64.5	66.3	67.9	62.2
Belgium	33.2	70.3	78.6	80.9	83.6	84.4	85.7	84.3	87.5	83.6	89.8	93.8	88.2
Canada	221.8	482.0	589.8	601.2	589.5	599.9	626.0	613.4	638.9	640.9	613.9	607.8	635.8
Chile	8.5	18.4	42.5	43.7	46.8	51.2	52.5	55.3	58.5	59.7	60.7	60.4	65.6
Czech Republic	36.4	62.3	74.2	76.0	82.8	83.8	81.9	83.7	87.8	83.2	81.7	85.3	86.9
Denmark	18.6	26.0	37.7	39.3	46.2	40.4	36.2	45.6	39.3	36.6	36.4	38.8	34.9
Estonia	..	17.4	8.5	8.6	10.2	10.3	10.2	9.7	12.2	10.6	8.8	13.0	12.9
Finland	21.7	54.4	74.5	74.9	84.3	85.8	70.6	82.3	81.2	77.4	72.1	80.7	73.5
France	155.8	417.2	545.7	553.9	561.8	569.1	571.5	569.3	564.1	569.3	530.9	564.3	557.4
Germany	327.2	547.7	581.9	582.0	601.5	608.5	613.4	629.4	629.5	631.2	584.3	622.1	608.3
Greece	11.6	34.8	53.1	53.9	57.9	58.8	59.4	60.2	62.7	62.9	61.1	57.4	53.2
Hungary	15.0	28.4	36.4	36.2	34.1	33.7	35.8	35.9	40.0	40.0	35.9	37.4	36.2
Iceland	1.6	4.5	8.0	8.4	8.5	8.6	8.7	9.9	12.0	16.5	16.8	17.1	17.2
Ireland	6.3	14.2	24.6	24.8	24.9	25.2	25.6	27.1	27.8	29.9	28.0	28.4	27.4
Israel	7.6	20.9	44.0	45.5	47.0	47.3	48.6	50.6	53.8	57.0	55.0	58.6	59.6
Italy	123.9	213.1	271.9	277.5	286.3	295.8	296.8	307.7	308.2	313.5	288.3	298.8	298.5
Japan	382.9	835.5	1 030.3	1 049.0	1 038.4	1 068.3	1 089.9	1 094.8	1 125.5	1 075.5	1 043.4	1 110.8	1 049.6
Korea	10.5	105.4	309.1	329.8	343.2	366.6	387.9	402.3	425.9	443.9	451.7	496.7	515.5
Luxembourg	1.3	0.6	0.9	2.8	2.8	3.4	3.3	3.5	3.2	2.7	3.2	3.2	2.6
Mexico	31.0	115.8	211.9	215.9	213.7	232.6	243.8	249.5	257.2	261.9	261.0	271.0	271.8
Netherlands	44.9	71.9	93.7	95.9	96.8	102.4	100.2	98.4	105.2	107.6	113.5	118.1	112.7
New Zealand	15.5	32.3	39.6	40.6	40.8	42.5	43.0	43.6	43.8	43.8	43.5	44.8	44.5
Norway	63.5	121.6	121.3	130.2	106.7	110.1	137.2	121.2	136.1	142.2	131.0	124.1	126.9
Poland	69.5	134.4	143.7	142.5	150.0	152.6	155.4	160.8	158.8	154.7	151.1	157.1	162.6
Portugal	7.9	28.4	46.2	45.7	46.5	44.8	46.2	48.6	46.9	45.5	49.5	53.7	51.8
Slovak Republic	10.9	25.5	31.9	32.2	31.0	30.5	31.4	31.3	27.9	28.8	25.9	27.5	25.7
Slovenia	..	12.4	14.5	14.6	13.8	15.3	15.1	15.1	15.0	16.4	16.4	16.2	15.9
Spain	61.6	151.2	233.2	241.6	257.9	277.2	288.9	295.5	301.8	311.1	291.8	299.9	289.7
Sweden	66.5	146.0	161.6	146.7	135.4	151.7	158.4	143.3	148.8	149.9	136.6	148.5	152.9
Switzerland	31.2	55.0	71.1	65.5	65.4	63.9	57.8	62.1	66.4	67.0	66.7	66.1	62.5
Turkey	9.8	57.5	122.7	129.4	140.6	150.7	162.0	176.3	191.6	198.4	194.8	211.2	228.4
United Kingdom	255.8	317.8	382.4	384.6	395.5	391.3	395.4	393.4	392.9	384.6	373.1	378.0	362.4
United States	1 703.4	3 202.8	3 838.8	4 026.4	4 054.6	4 148.1	4 268.9	4 275.0	4 323.9	4 343.0	4 165.4	4 354.4	4 320.9
EU 27	..	2 567.8	3 077.7	3 099.4	3 187.9	3 254.7	3 274.9	3 319.2	3 333.6	3 339.6	3 172.3	3 315.4	..
OECD	3 836.9	7 629.3	9 609.6	9 888.3	9 982.9	10 253.0	10 500.2	10 573.6	10 780.0	10 796.1	10 392.8	10 854.4	10 752.8
Brazil	51.6	222.8	328.5	345.7	364.3	387.5	403.0	419.3	445.1	462.9	466.0	515.7	..
China	138.4	621.2	1 481.6	1 654.9	1 911.7	2 204.7	2 502.5	2 869.8	3 287.5	3 482.0	3 742.1	4 208.3	..
India	66.4	289.4	579.9	597.3	634.0	666.6	698.2	753.3	813.9	841.7	906.8	959.9	..
Indonesia	1.8	32.7	101.3	108.2	114.5	120.2	127.4	133.1	142.2	149.4	156.8	169.8	..
Russian Federation	..	1 082.2	889.3	889.3	914.3	929.9	951.2	993.9	1 013.4	1 038.4	990.0	1 036.1	..
South Africa	54.6	165.4	208.2	218.6	231.2	240.9	242.1	250.9	260.5	255.5	246.8	256.6	..
World	5 245.0	11 819.0	15 528.4	16 136.2	16 707.9	17 498.6	18 250.4	18 949.7	19 809.9	20 201.4	20 133.5	21 431.5	..

StatLink ᗷᖨᔑ http://dx.doi.org/10.1787/888932707990

World electricity generation by source of energy

Terawatt hours (TWh)

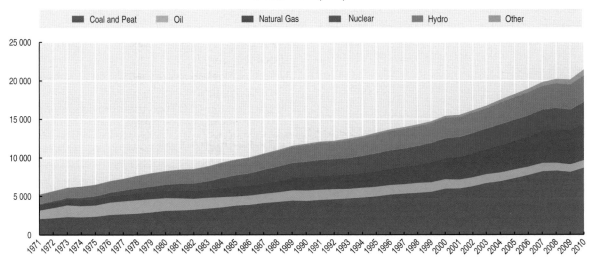

StatLink ᗷᖨᔑ http://dx.doi.org/10.1787/888932708009

NUCLEAR ENERGY

In 2010 nuclear energy provided nearly 22% of total electricity supply in OECD countries (and 14% of the world's electricity). However, the use of nuclear energy varies widely. In all, 18 of the 34 OECD countries use nuclear energy at present, with eight generating one-third or more of their power from this source in 2010. Collectively, OECD countries produce about 83% of the world's nuclear energy. The remainder is produced in 12 non-OECD economies.

Overview

Nuclear energy expanded rapidly in the 1970s and 1980s, but in the last 20 years only small numbers of new nuclear power plants have entered operation. The role of nuclear energy in reducing greenhouse gas emissions and in increasing energy diversification and security of supply has been increasingly recognised over the last few years, leading to renewed interest in building new nuclear plants in several countries. However, the accident at the Fukushima Daiichi nuclear power plant in Japan following a major earthquake and tsunami in March 2011 has led some countries to review their nuclear programmes. Nuclear capacity may thus grow more slowly than had been expected, at least over the next few years.

Much of the future growth in nuclear capacity is expected to be in non-OECD countries. China in particular has begun a rapid expansion of nuclear capacity, starting construction of 10 additional units during 2010. India and the Russian Federation also have several new plants under construction. Among OECD countries, Finland, France, Japan, Korea, the Slovak Republic and the United States all presently have one or more nuclear plants under construction, while Poland and Turkey are actively planning their first nuclear units.

The analysis in the International Energy Agency's Energy *Technology Perspectives 2012*, indicates that, as part of a scenario to limit global temperature rise to two degrees, nuclear generating capacity could rise from 370 GW at present to around 1 100 GW by 2050, supplying almost 20% of global electricity. This would be a major contribution to cutting the emissions of greenhouse gases from the electricity supply sector. However, uncertainties remain concerning the successful construction and operation of the next generation of nuclear plants, public and political acceptance of nuclear energy in the wake of the Fukushima Daiichi accident, and the extent to which other low-carbon energy sources are successfully developed.

Definition

Shown is nuclear electricity generation in terawatt hours (TWh) and the percentage share of nuclear in total electricity generation.

The table also provides information on the number of nuclear power plants in operation and under construction as of 1 June 2012.

Comparability

Some generation data are provisional and may be subject to revision. Generation data for Japan are for the fiscal year.

Nuclear electricity generation
Terawatt hours, 2010

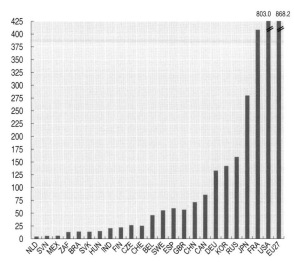

StatLink ⛓ http://dx.doi.org/10.1787/888932708085

Sources

- Nuclear Energy Agency (NEA) (2012), *Nuclear Energy Data*, OECD Publishing.
- Data for non-OECD countries provided by the *International Atomic Energy Agency* (IAEA).

Further information

Analytical publications

- International Energy Agency (IEA) (2012), *Energy Technology Perspectives*, IEA, Paris.
- NEA (2012), The Role of Nuclear Energy in a Low Carbon Future, *Nuclear Development*, OECD Publishing.
- NEA, International Atomic Energy Agency (IAEA) (2012), *Uranium 2011: Resources, Production and Demand*, OECD Publishing.

Websites

- Nuclear Energy Agency, *www.oecd-nea.org*.

Nuclear electricity generation and nuclear plants

	2010		Number as at 1 June 2012	
	Terawatt hours	As a percentage of total electricity generation	Plants connected to the grid	Plants under construction
Australia	-	-	-	-
Austria	-	-	-	-
Belgium	45.7	50.0	7	-
Canada	85.3	15.0	17	-
Chile	-	-	-	-
Czech Republic	26.4	33.2	6	-
Denmark	-	-	-	-
Estonia	-	-	-	-
Finland	21.9	28.4	4	1
France	407.9	74.1	58	1
Germany	133.0	24.5	9	-
Greece	-	-	-	-
Hungary	14.8	42.8	4	-
Iceland	-	-	-	-
Ireland	-	-	-	-
Israel	-	-	-	-
Italy	-	-	-	-
Japan	279.3	29.2	50	2
Korea	142.0	32.2	23	3
Luxembourg	-	-	-	-
Mexico	5.6	2.6	2	-
Netherlands	4.0	3.2	1	-
New Zealand	-	-	-	-
Norway	-	-	-	-
Poland	-	-	-	-
Portugal	-	-	-	-
Slovak Republic	13.5	52.9	4	2
Slovenia	5.4	37.5	1	-
Spain	59.2	20.1	8	-
Sweden	59.2	38.2	10	-
Switzerland	25.2	38.0	5	-
Turkey	-	-	-	-
United Kingdom	56.4	15.7	16	-
United States	803.0	20.3	104	1
EU 27	868.2	27.4	132	4
OECD	2 183.7	21.8	329	11
Brazil	13.9	3.1	2	1
China	71.0	1.8	16	26
India	20.5	2.9	20	7
Indonesia	-	-	-	-
Russian Federation	159.4	17.1	33	11
South Africa	12.9	5.2	2	-
World	2 630.0	13.5	435	62

StatLink ⌐⌐⌐ http://dx.doi.org/10.1787/888932708047

Nuclear electricity generation

As a percentage of total electricity generation, 2010

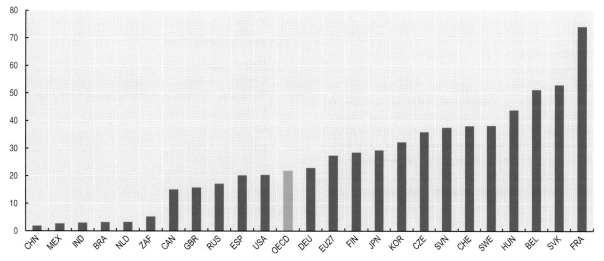

StatLink ⌐⌐⌐ http://dx.doi.org/10.1787/888932708066

RENEWABLE ENERGY

More and more governments are recognising the importance of promoting sustainable development and combating climate change when setting out their energy policies. Higher energy use has contributed to higher greenhouse gas emissions and higher concentration of these gases in the atmosphere. One way to reduce greenhouse gas emissions is to replace energy from fossil fuels by energy from renewables.

Definition

The table refers to the contribution of renewables to total primary energy supply (TPES) in OECD countries. Renewables include the primary energy equivalent of hydro (excluding pumped storage), geothermal, solar, wind, tide and wave. It also includes energy derived from solid biofuels, biogasoline, biodiesels, other liquid biofuels, biogases, and the renewable fraction of municipal waste. Biofuels are defined as fuels derived directly or indirectly from biomass (material obtained from living or recently living organisms). Included here are wood, vegetal waste (including wood waste and crops used for energy production), ethanol, animal materials/wastes and sulphite lyes. Municipal waste comprises wastes produced by the residential, commercial and public service sectors that are collected by local authorities for disposal in a central location for the production of heat and/or power.

Overview

In OECD countries, total renewables supply grew by 2.5% per annum between 1971 and 2011 as compared to 1.1% per annum for total primary energy supply. Annual growth for hydro (1.2%) was lower than for other renewables such as geothermal (5.3%) and biofuels and waste (2.7%). Due to a very low base in 1971, solar and wind experienced the most rapid growth in OECD member countries, especially where government policies have stimulated expansion of these energy sources.

For the OECD as a whole, the contribution of renewables to energy supply increased from 4.8% in 1971 to 8.2% in 2011. The contribution of renewables varied greatly by country. On the high end, renewables represented 84% of energy supply in Iceland, and 40% in both New Zealand and Norway. On the low end, renewables contributed 3% or less of the energy supply for Japan, Korea and Luxembourg.

In general, the contribution of renewables to the energy supply in non-OECD countries is higher than in OECD countries. In 2010, renewables contributed 44% to the energy supply of Brazil, 35% in Indonesia, 26% in India, 12% in China, 11% in South Africa and 3% in the Russian Federation.

Comparability

Biofuels and waste data are often based on small sample surveys or other incomplete information. Thus, the data give only a broad impression of developments and are not strictly comparable between countries. In some cases, complete categories of vegetal fuel are omitted due to lack of information.

Contribution of renewables to energy supply

As a percentage of total primary energy supply, 2011

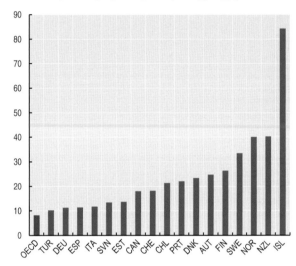

StatLink ⬛ http://dx.doi.org/10.1787/888932708142

Sources

- IEA (2012), *Energy Balances of Non-OECD Countries*, IEA, Paris.
- IEA (2012), *Energy Balances of OECD Countries*, IEA, Paris.

Further information

Analytical publications

- IEA (2012), *Medium-Term Renewable Energy Market Report 2012, Market Trends and Projections to 2017*, IEA, Paris.
- IEA (2012), Solar Heating and Cooling, *IEA Technology Roadmaps*, IEA, Paris.
- IEA (2011), *Deploying Renewables, Best and Future Policy Practice*, IEA, Paris.
- IEA (2011), *Harnessing Variable Renewables: A Guide To The Balancing Challenge*, IEA, Paris.

Statistical publications

- IEA (2012), *Renewables Information*, IEA, Paris.

Online databases

- IEA World Energy Statistics and Balances.

Websites

- International Energy Agency, *www.iea.org*.

Contribution of renewables to energy supply

As a percentage of total primary energy supply

	1971	1990	2001	2002	2003	2004	2005	2006	2007	2008	2009	2010	2011
Australia	8.8	5.9	6.1	6.2	5.9	5.8	5.6	5.7	5.7	5.7	5.5	5.5	6.1
Austria	11.0	20.3	22.1	21.3	18.7	19.7	21.0	22.1	24.1	25.3	27.9	26.8	24.8
Belgium	0.0	1.0	1.2	1.3	1.5	1.6	2.0	2.3	2.7	3.1	3.8	4.2	4.8
Canada	15.3	16.1	15.9	16.9	15.6	15.6	15.9	15.7	16.2	16.8	17.6	17.1	18.0
Chile	20.8	27.8	26.4	26.2	24.8	24.2	25.1	25.3	23.5	24.4	26.1	22.0	21.4
Czech Republic	0.2	1.8	3.5	3.7	3.4	3.8	4.0	4.2	4.7	4.9	5.8	6.3	7.2
Denmark	1.8	6.2	10.3	11.2	12.1	13.8	15.1	14.3	16.3	16.9	18.0	20.3	23.4
Estonia	..	1.9	11.0	11.7	11.2	11.4	11.4	10.5	10.7	11.9	15.2	15.3	13.7
Finland	27.3	19.3	22.6	22.3	21.3	23.4	23.6	23.3	23.5	25.8	24.0	25.3	26.4
France	8.6	6.8	6.4	5.8	5.9	5.9	5.8	5.9	6.3	7.1	7.5	8.0	7.3
Germany	1.2	1.5	2.8	3.2	3.8	4.4	4.9	5.8	7.9	8.0	8.7	9.9	11.3
Greece	7.8	5.1	4.7	4.9	5.3	5.3	5.4	5.9	5.7	5.6	6.4	7.7	7.2
Hungary	2.9	2.6	3.4	3.4	3.5	3.6	4.3	4.5	5.1	6.0	7.4	7.6	7.8
Iceland	46.7	67.0	75.6	75.0	75.2	74.8	75.9	78.4	81.6	81.3	81.8	82.5	84.3
Ireland	0.6	1.7	1.6	1.8	1.7	1.9	2.5	2.8	3.2	3.8	4.6	4.6	5.9
Israel	0.0	3.1	3.3	3.6	3.5	3.8	4.0	3.7	3.7	4.7	5.0	5.0	4.6
Italy	5.6	4.4	6.0	5.8	6.0	6.6	6.3	6.9	6.7	7.7	9.7	10.6	11.7
Japan	2.7	3.5	3.1	3.2	3.4	3.3	3.2	3.4	3.2	3.3	3.4	3.3	3.4
Korea	0.6	1.1	0.4	0.4	0.5	0.5	0.5	0.6	0.6	0.6	0.7	0.7	0.7
Luxembourg	0.0	0.6	1.1	1.1	1.0	1.2	1.6	1.8	3.1	3.1	3.0	3.1	3.1
Mexico	16.8	12.2	10.9	10.2	10.2	10.4	10.4	10.0	10.0	10.1	9.6	9.8	9.3
Netherlands	0.0	1.1	1.8	1.9	1.8	2.1	2.7	3.0	3.0	3.5	4.0	3.8	4.3
New Zealand	32.0	32.8	28.0	29.8	29.7	31.3	31.6	32.0	32.2	32.9	35.8	39.0	40.3
Norway	40.9	54.3	42.9	49.5	38.2	40.0	48.5	42.6	46.5	44.9	43.1	36.1	40.1
Poland	1.4	1.5	4.5	4.7	4.6	4.7	4.8	4.8	5.0	5.7	6.7	7.2	7.8
Portugal	19.6	19.6	16.2	13.7	16.9	14.7	13.1	17.1	17.7	17.7	19.9	23.3	22.1
Slovak Republic	2.3	1.5	4.1	4.0	3.5	4.0	4.3	4.5	5.4	5.4	7.2	7.8	7.4
Slovenia	..	9.1	11.6	10.5	10.3	11.5	10.6	10.5	10.1	11.0	14.2	14.8	13.4
Spain	6.5	6.9	6.5	5.5	6.9	6.4	5.9	6.5	7.0	7.6	9.7	11.8	11.4
Sweden	20.4	24.4	28.2	25.3	24.5	25.0	28.8	28.7	30.5	31.5	34.8	34.0	33.5
Switzerland	15.5	15.0	18.4	16.8	16.8	16.5	16.0	15.5	17.8	17.8	17.8	19.0	18.2
Turkey	31.0	18.3	13.3	13.5	12.9	13.3	12.0	11.1	9.6	9.5	10.2	11.1	10.2
United Kingdom	0.1	0.5	1.0	1.2	1.2	1.5	1.8	1.9	2.2	2.6	3.2	3.4	4.1
United States	3.7	5.0	4.0	4.0	4.3	4.4	4.5	4.8	4.7	5.1	5.4	5.6	6.1
EU 27	..	4.3	5.8	5.7	5.9	6.3	6.5	6.9	7.6	8.2	9.2	10.1	..
OECD	4.8	5.9	5.7	5.7	5.9	6.0	6.2	6.4	6.6	7.0	7.5	7.8	8.2
Brazil	56.4	46.8	37.3	39.3	41.9	42.3	42.9	43.3	44.4	44.4	45.8	43.9	..
China	40.2	24.2	19.2	18.3	16.1	14.6	13.8	12.9	12.6	12.6	12.0	11.6	..
India	62.8	44.1	33.9	33.2	32.9	31.7	31.2	30.3	29.2	28.2	26.5	26.3	..
Indonesia	75.3	46.6	38.3	37.3	37.5	35.4	34.7	34.4	35.0	36.1	35.0	34.5	..
Russian Federation	..	3.0	3.0	2.8	2.7	2.9	2.9	2.8	2.9	2.6	2.8	2.5	..
South Africa	10.4	11.5	11.6	12.1	11.3	10.5	10.7	11.0	10.2	9.6	9.9	10.7	..
World	13.1	12.7	12.7	12.7	12.5	12.4	12.4	12.4	12.5	12.7	13.1	13.0	..

StatLink http://dx.doi.org/10.1787/888932708104

OECD renewable energy supply

Million tonnes of oil equivalent (Mtoe)

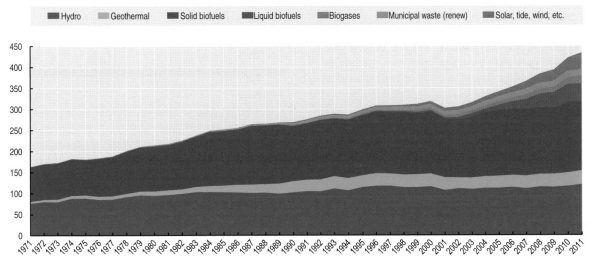

■ Hydro ■ Geothermal ■ Solid biofuels ■ Liquid biofuels ■ Biogases ■ Municipal waste (renew) ■ Solar, tide, wind, etc.

StatLink http://dx.doi.org/10.1787/888932708123

OIL PRODUCTION

The Middle East and North Africa are exceptionally well-endowed with energy resources, holding about 65% of the world's proven conventional oil reserves at the end of 2010. Current oil production is relatively low in comparison to these reserves and further development of them will be critical to meeting global energy needs in the coming decades. Unconventional oil (*e.g.* oil shale and sands, liquid supplies based on coal and biomass, and liquids arising for the chemical processing of natural gas) is also expected to play an increasing role in meeting world demand.

Definition

Crude oil production refers to the quantities of oil extracted from the ground after the removal of inert matter or impurities. It includes crude oil, natural gas liquids (NGLs) and additives. Crude oil is a mineral oil consisting of a mixture of hydrocarbons of natural origin, being yellow to black in colour, of variable density and viscosity. NGLs are the liquid or liquefied hydrocarbons produced in the manufacture, purification and stabilisation of natural gas. Additives are non-hydrocarbon substances added to or blended with a product to modify its properties, for example, to improve its combustion characteristics (*e.g.* MTBE and tetraethyl lead).

Refinery production refers to the output of secondary oil products from an oil refinery.

Overview

World crude oil production increased by 61% over the 40 years from 1971 to 2011. In 2011, production reached 4 011 million tonnes or about 88 million barrels per day. Growth was not constant over the period as production declined in the aftermath of two oil shocks in the early and late 1970s.

In 2011, the Middle East region's share of oil production was 32% of the world total. However, both the level of production and its share in the world total varied significantly over the period, from 38% of the world total in 1974 to 19% in 1985. Increased production in the 1980s and 1990s put the OECD on par with the Middle East during that period, but by 2011, the share of OECD oil production had fallen to 21%.

Refinery production of secondary oil products changed significantly between 1971 and 2010. The share of fuel oil in the refinery mix fell from 34% in 1971 to 14% in 2010 whereas the share of middle distillates increased from 25% to 34%.

Comparability

In general, data on oil production are of high quality. In some instances, information has been based on secondary sources or estimated by the International Energy Agency.

Share of refinery production by product

As a percentage of refinery production

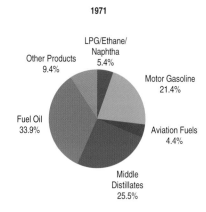

1971

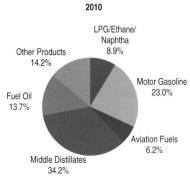

2010

StatLink ⟨ms⟩ http://dx.doi.org/10.1787/888932708199

Sources
- IEA (2012), *Energy Balances of Non-OECD Countries*, IEA, Paris.
- IEA (2012), *Energy Balances of OECD Countries*, IEA, Paris.
- IEA (2012), *Oil Information*, IEA, Paris.

Further information

Analytical publications
- IEA (2012), *Energy Policies of IEA Countries*, series, IEA, Paris.
- IEA (2012), *Medium-Term Oil Market Report*, IEA, Paris.

Online databases
- *IEA World Energy Statistics and Balances*.

Websites
- International Energy Agency, *www.iea.org*.

Production of crude oil

Million tonnes

	1971	1990	2001	2002	2003	2004	2005	2006	2007	2008	2009	2010	2011
Australia	14.3	27.5	33.1	31.3	29.1	26.2	24.1	22.0	24.5	22.6	23.7	22.5	19.4
Austria	2.6	1.2	1.0	1.0	1.0	1.1	1.0	1.0	1.0	1.0	1.0	1.0	1.0
Belgium	-	-	..	-	-	-	-	-	-	-	-	-	-
Canada	70.6	91.6	126.6	132.9	140.4	145.4	143.5	151.3	158.0	153.8	152.6	161.2	168.9
Chile	1.7	1.1	0.4	0.4	0.4	0.4	0.3	0.3	0.5	0.5	0.6	0.6	0.5
Czech Republic	-	0.2	0.4	0.4	0.5	0.6	0.6	0.4	0.4	0.3	0.3	0.3	0.3
Denmark	-	6.0	16.9	18.1	18.1	19.3	18.5	16.8	15.2	14.0	12.9	12.2	11.2
Estonia	-	-	..	-	-	-	-	-	-	-	-	-	-
Finland	-	-	0.1	0.1	0.1	0.1	0.1	0.2	-	-	0.1	0.1	0.1
France	2.5	3.5	1.6	1.5	1.6	1.6	1.4	1.2	1.4	1.5	1.2	1.2	1.2
Germany	7.6	5.3	4.3	4.6	4.8	4.9	5.2	5.2	5.2	4.9	4.5	3.8	3.9
Greece	-	0.8	0.2	0.2	0.1	0.1	0.1	0.1	0.1	0.1	0.1	0.1	0.1
Hungary	2.0	2.3	1.5	1.6	1.6	1.6	1.4	1.3	1.2	1.2	1.2	1.1	0.9
Iceland	-	-	..	-	-	-	-	-	-	-	-	-	-
Ireland	-	-	..	-	-	-	-	-	-	-	-	-	-
Israel	5.7	-	0.0	-	-	-	-	-	-	-	-	-	-
Italy	1.3	4.7	4.2	5.8	5.9	5.7	6.4	6.3	6.6	6.0	5.2	5.9	5.8
Japan	0.8	0.5	0.6	0.6	0.6	0.7	0.7	0.7	0.7	0.7	0.7	0.7	0.6
Korea	-	-	0.6	0.5	0.5	0.4	0.5	0.6	0.6	0.5	0.7	0.7	0.7
Luxembourg	-	-	..	-	-	-	-	-	-	-	-	-	-
Mexico	25.4	151.1	175.5	178.3	189.3	191.4	187.6	183.2	172.5	156.9	146.0	144.7	143.8
Netherlands	1.7	4.0	2.3	3.1	3.1	2.9	2.3	2.0	2.9	2.5	2.2	1.8	1.8
New Zealand	-	1.9	1.8	1.6	1.3	1.1	1.1	1.0	2.0	2.8	2.7	2.6	2.2
Norway	0.3	82.1	162.6	157.8	153.7	144.0	133.0	123.8	119.5	114.6	108.3	99.6	93.3
Poland	0.4	0.2	0.8	0.8	0.8	0.9	0.9	0.8	0.7	0.8	0.7	0.7	0.7
Portugal	-	-	..	-	-	-	-	-	-	-	-	-	-
Slovak Republic	0.2	0.1	0.1	0.1	-	-	-	-	-	-	-	-	-
Slovenia	-	-	..	-	-	-	-	-	-	-	-	-	-
Spain	0.1	1.1	0.3	0.3	0.3	0.3	0.2	0.1	0.1	0.1	0.1	0.1	0.1
Sweden	-	-	..	-	-	-	-	-	-	-	-	-	-
Switzerland	-	-	..	-	-	-	-	-	-	-	-	-	-
Turkey	3.5	3.7	2.5	2.4	2.4	2.3	2.3	2.2	2.1	2.2	2.4	2.5	2.4
United Kingdom	0.2	91.6	116.8	116.1	106.2	95.5	84.7	76.6	76.6	71.7	68.2	63.0	52.0
United States	527.7	413.3	349.9	348.1	338.4	325.9	310.0	304.4	304.0	299.4	321.7	332.4	345.8
EU 27	..	129.0	157.3	161.5	151.7	140.7	129.0	118.1	116.6	109.1	102.3	95.6	83.5
OECD	668.6	893.8	1 004.1	1 007.6	1 000.3	972.4	925.8	901.5	896.0	858.3	857.1	858.8	856.8
Brazil	8.5	32.7	67.1	75.4	77.9	77.1	85.1	90.3	92.2	95.5	102.1	107.5	110.1
China	39.4	138.3	164.1	167.1	169.7	175.9	181.4	184.9	186.4	190.6	189.6	203.2	203.2
India	7.3	34.6	36.2	37.4	37.7	38.3	36.3	38.1	37.9	37.5	37.7	41.9	43.2
Indonesia	44.1	73.2	66.6	61.9	56.7	53.5	52.4	49.3	46.7	48.3	47.3	47.5	45.7
Russian Federation	..	523.7	345.8	377.2	418.6	456.3	466.4	475.8	487.7	486.2	491.2	504.1	510.2
South Africa	-	-	0.8	1.0	0.7	1.7	0.9	0.8	0.2	0.1	0.1	0.1	0.1
World	2 488.7	3 169.3	..	3 592.1	3 736.4	3 909.9	3 965.0	3 982.5	3 958.1	3 994.0	3 901.2	3 974.0	4 010.9

StatLink http://dx.doi.org/10.1787/888932708161

Production of crude oil by region

Million tonnes

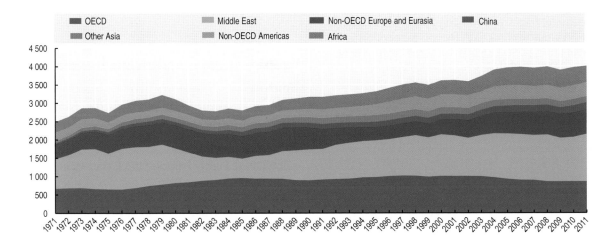

StatLink http://dx.doi.org/10.1787/888932708180

OIL PRICES

The price of crude oil, from which petroleum products such as gasoline are derived, is influenced by a number of factors beyond the traditional movements of supply and demand, notably geopolitics. Some of the lowest cost reserves are located in sensitive areas of the world. There is not one price for crude oil but many. World crude oil prices are established in relation to three market traded benchmarks (West Texas Intermediate [WTI], Brent, Dubai), and are quoted at premiums or discounts to these prices.

Overview

The 1973 Arab oil embargo had a major price impact as Arabian Light prices surged from USD 1.84/barrel in 1972 to USD 10.98 in 1974. The next spike after 1973 came in 1981, in the wake of the Iranian revolution, when prices rose to a high of nearly USD 40. Prices declined gradually after this crisis. They dropped considerably in 1986 when Saudi Arabia increased its oil production substantially. The first Gulf crisis in 1990 brought a new peak. In 1997, crude oil prices started to decline due to the impact of the Asian financial crisis.

Prices started to increase again in 1999 with OPEC target reductions and tightening stocks. A dip occurred in 2001 and 2002, but the expectation of war in Iraq raised prices to over USD 30 in the first quarter of 2003. Prices remained high in the latter part of 2003 and in 2004. Crude oil prices increased dramatically in late August 2005 after Hurricane Katrina hit the US coast of the Gulf of Mexico. Prices continued to increase throughout 2006 as the demand for oil in emerging economies, especially China, put pressure on the supply/demand balance, averaging 24 per cent higher than the previous year. In 2007, the increase continued with Dubai hitting USD 88.82/barrel at the beginning of November and WTI climbing to USD 96.50/barrel.

In early 2008, prices crossed the symbolic USD 100/barrel threshold and reached a new peak just under USD 150/barrel in July 2008; this brought the real price of oil in 2008 to an all time high. At the beginning of 2009, prices fell to USD 40/barrel as the impact of high prices and the onset of the global financial crisis sharply curbed oil demand. Later in the year, prices ranged between USD 70 and 80/barrel.

Crude oil prices increased steadily throughout 2010 and 2011 with the post-recession demand rebound, tightening stocks and low spare capacity. In 2012, prices continued to increase at the beginning of the year, averaging USD 122.40/barrel in March, before declining to under USD 100/barrel in June.

Definition

Crude oil import prices come from the Crude Oil Import Register. Information is collected according to type of crude and average prices are obtained by dividing value by volume as recorded by customs administrations for each tariff position. Values are recorded at the time of import and include cost, insurance and freight (c.i.f.) but exclude import duties.

The nominal crude oil spot price from 2003 to 2011 is for Dubai and from 1970 to 2002 for Arabian Light. These nominal spot prices are expressed in US dollars per barrel of oil. The real price was calculated using the deflator for GDP at market prices and rebased with base year 1970 = 100.

Comparability

Average crude oil import prices are affected by the quality of the crude oil that is imported into a country. High quality crude oils such as UK Forties, Norwegian Oseberg and Venezuelan Light are more expensive than lower quality crude oils such as Canadian Heavy and Venezuelan Extra Heavy. For a given country, the mix of crude oils imported each month will affect the average monthly price.

Sources
- IEA (2011), *Energy Prices and Taxes*, IEA, Paris.

Further information

Analytical publications
- IEA (2011), *Energy Policies of IEA Countries*, series, IEA, Paris.
- IEA (2011), *Medium-Term Oil and Gas Markets 2011*, IEA, Paris.
- IEA (2011), *Oil Market Report*, IEA, Paris.
- IEA (2011), *World Energy Outlook*, IEA, Paris.

Online databases
- IEA Energy Prices and Taxes Statistics.

Websites
- International Energy Agency, *www.iea.org*.

Crude oil import prices
US dollars per barrel, average unit value, c.i.f.

	1976	1990	2001	2002	2003	2004	2005	2006	2007	2008	2009	2010	2011
Australia	..	24.21	26.61	25.80	31.24	40.93	56.71	66.71	77.13	107.83	63.40	82.60	115.66
Austria	12.85	24.58	25.32	24.64	29.59	38.21	53.15	64.44	71.86	103.05	60.69	80.00	110.92
Belgium	12.64	21.11	24.20	24.35	27.72	35.35	50.06	61.06	70.35	96.01	61.77	79.65	110.50
Canada	..	24.15	24.87	24.97	29.53	38.13	52.37	64.33	70.04	101.41	60.29	79.14	110.80
Chile	..	..	..	..	..	..	..	..	..	..	..	..	..
Czech Republic	..	..	23.74	23.37	28.13	34.82	51.28	62.05	68.54	97.71	60.77	79.04	110.42
Denmark	12.98	23.18	24.82	24.88	29.68	38.78	54.40	66.92	74.94	96.48	62.87	80.40	112.77
Estonia	..	..	..	..	..	..	..	..	..	..	..	..	..
Finland	..	..	23.49	24.51	27.72	36.09	51.12	63.37	70.48	94.79	61.01	79.10	109.23
France	..	..	24.13	24.63	28.87	37.61	52.74	63.69	72.22	97.63	61.64	79.78	111.78
Germany	13.27	23.17	24.15	24.40	28.44	36.65	52.30	63.29	71.60	96.70	61.18	78.49	110.63
Greece	12.13	22.42	23.22	24.08	27.17	34.53	50.33	60.97	69.93	93.60	60.10	78.97	109.41
Hungary	..	..	..	..	..	..	..	..	..	..	..	..	..
Iceland	..	..	..	..	..	..	..	..	..	..	..	..	..
Ireland	..	25.55	25.31	25.52	29.66	39.24	55.24	66.38	74.16	100.39	62.61	80.95	113.92
Israel	..	..	..	..	..	..	..	..	..	..	..	..	..
Italy	12.41	23.23	23.87	24.34	28.58	36.60	51.33	62.50	70.20	96.67	60.69	79.29	110.23
Japan	12.59	22.64	25.01	24.96	29.26	36.59	51.57	64.03	70.09	100.98	61.29	79.43	109.30
Korea	..	..	24.87	24.12	28.80	36.15	50.19	62.82	70.01	98.11	61.12	78.72	108.63
Luxembourg	..	..	..	..	..	..	..	..	..	..	..	..	..
Mexico	..	..	..	..	..	..	..	..	..	..	..	..	..
Netherlands	13.06	21.83	23.48	23.99	27.67	35.02	50.00	61.47	68.74	97.89	60.54	78.55	109.19
New Zealand	..	21.97	26.14	25.89	31.00	41.71	56.07	67.36	73.84	105.80	65.85	80.62	112.38
Norway	..	18.46	23.43	24.46	30.41	39.20	53.08	58.83	70.16	80.22	69.08	81.06	111.18
Poland	..	..	..	..	..	..	..	..	..	94.02	60.83	77.89	109.58
Portugal	12.14	22.75	24.02	24.27	28.72	37.89	51.94	62.77	70.23	98.83	62.49	79.13	112.33
Slovak Republic	..	..	..	..	..	..	..	..	69.97	90.49	59.37	78.72	108.90
Slovenia	..	..	..	..	..	..	..	..	..	..	..	..	..
Spain	12.54	21.88	23.32	23.95	28.13	36.03	50.54	60.99	68.66	94.86	59.78	77.84	108.50
Sweden	13.22	23.02	24.03	23.86	28.60	36.47	51.78	62.50	70.13	95.09	60.58	79.00	110.67
Switzerland	13.87	24.23	25.04	25.34	30.26	38.73	55.81	66.76	74.92	101.03	63.27	80.92	112.51
Turkey	..	23.11	22.98	23.57	27.05	34.90	50.65	61.48	68.59	98.07	61.27	78.26	109.81
United Kingdom	12.57	22.92	24.45	24.58	29.13	37.75	53.79	65.00	73.80	99.34	62.39	80.60	113.49
United States	13.48	21.07	22.07	23.52	27.66	35.86	48.82	59.15	66.77	94.97	58.83	76.02	102.43
EU 27	..	..	..	..	..	..	..	..	..	..	..	..	..
OECD	..	..	..	..	..	..	..	..	..	..	..	..	..
Brazil	..	..	..	..	..	..	..	..	..	..	..	..	..
China	..	..	..	..	..	..	..	..	..	..	..	..	..
India	..	..	..	..	..	..	..	..	..	..	..	..	..
Indonesia	..	..	..	..	..	..	..	..	..	..	..	..	..
Russian Federation	..	..	..	..	..	..	..	..	..	..	..	..	..
South Africa	..	..	..	..	..	..	..	..	..	..	..	..	..

StatLink http://dx.doi.org/10.1787/888932708218

Crude oil spot prices
US dollars per barrel

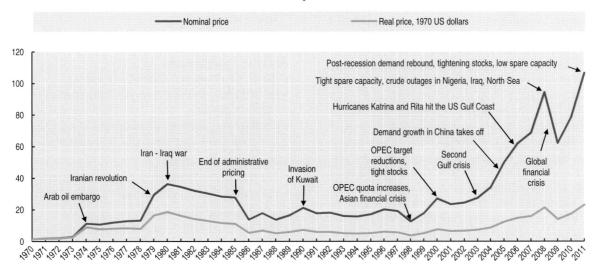

StatLink http://dx.doi.org/10.1787/888932708237

GOODS TRANSPORT

There is an increasing demand for data on the transport sector to assess its various impacts on the economy, the environment and societies. However comparability of transport data between countries is not always possible worldwide due to the lack of harmonised definitions and methods. The *Glossary for Transport Statistics* (4th edition) provides common definitions.

Definition

Goods transport data refer to the total movement of goods using inland transport modes (rail, road, inland waterways and pipelines) on a given network. Data are expressed in tonne-kilometres which represents the transport of one tonne over one kilometre. The distance to be taken into consideration is the distance actually run.

Comparability

Transport is classified as national if both loading and unloading take place in the same country. If one of them occurs in another country then the transport is considered as international. The statistics on international road transport, based on the nationality concept are different for statistics for other modes that are based on the territoriality concept.

Statistics based on the territoriality concept reflect the goods and the vehicles entering or leaving a country irrespective of the nationality of the transporting vehicle. Statistics based on the nationality concept only reflect the vehicles registered in the reporting country.

Inland goods transport
Billion tonne-kilometres

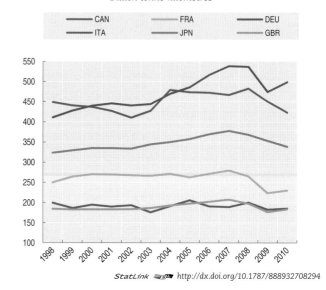

StatLink ⋙ http://dx.doi.org/10.1787/888932708294

Overview

Following the economic crisis and the collapse of world trade in 2009, most regions of the world embarked on the path of recovery in 2010. If global freight volume transported by sea and air rebounded strongly and reached a new high, for rail and road freight the recovery has been slower with volumes still below pre-crisis levels, reflecting domestic economic performance more than trade.

Rail freight transport was severely hit by the global economic crisis in 2009 and volumes still remain below pre-crisis levels. Rail tonne-kilometres increased overall 3% in 2010. In the European Union, rail freight volume increased by 10% to slightly less than 400 billion tonne-kilometres. This is still 7% below the level in 2008. In the Russian Federation and the United States, rail freight volumes increased by 8% and 6% respectively, nearly reaching their 2008 levels.

Road freight transport suffered in 2009 and recovery in road freight has been slow. Data for 2010 show an overall increase but volumes remain below their 2008 levels. The increase in activity, expressed in tonne-kilometres, was 4% in the EU in 2010 however there are marked differences between countries.

Sources

- International Transport Forum (ITF) (2012), *"Coastal Shipping"*, *International Transport Forum* (database).
- ITF (2012), *"Container Transport"*, *International Transport Forum* (database).
- ITF (2012), *"Inland Freight Transport"*, *International Transport Forum* (database).

Further information

Analytical publications

- ITF (2012), *Transport Outlook*, ITF, Paris.
- OECD (2012), *Strategic Transport Infrastructure Needs to 2030*, OECD Publishing.
- OECD (2011), *Environmental Impacts of International Shipping: The Role of Ports*, OECD Publishing.

Statistical publications

- ITF (2012), *Key Transport Statistics*, ITF, Paris.
- ITF (2012), *Trends in the Transport Sector*, OECD Publishing.

Methodological publications

- ITF, Statistical Office of the European Communities and United Nations Economic Commission (2010), *Illustrated Glossary for Transport Statistics, 4th Edition*, OECD Publishing.

Websites

- International Transport Forum, *www.internationaltransportforum.org*.

Inland goods transport
Billion tonne-kilometres

	1998	1999	2000	2001	2002	2003	2004	2005	2006	2007	2008	2009	2010
Australia	249.9	258.7	268.8	276.3	296.6	311.0	324.9	349.4	362.4	387.2	410.0	398.0	415.5
Austria	56.8	59.1	61.7	65.0	66.4	66.5	67.5	64.6	70.2	68.6	66.1	56.1	57.9
Belgium	57.5	62.3	67.6	69.5	70.5	67.7	65.6	62.1	62.1	60.7	57.0	49.2	49.5
Canada	449.1	440.7	437.1	427.3	410.4	427.4	479.5	473.9	472.6	467.2	483.1	450.6	423.3
Chile	..	..	..	..	..	..	..	..	..	..	..	..	..
Czech Republic	55.6	56.4	58.9	56.5	63.2	64.8	63.4	61.4	69.2	67.4	69.5	60.5	68.5
Denmark	16.1	16.6	17.7	17.5	18.1	18.2	17.9	18.2	18.3	18.2	16.8	15.6	16.3
Estonia	9.9	11.3	12.0	13.2	14.1	16.1	17.3	18.3	19.3	19.1	14.2	12.2	12.6
Finland	35.6	35.4	37.9	36.6	37.8	41.1	42.5	41.6	40.9	40.4	41.9	36.6	40.2
France	250.0	264.4	270.4	269.8	267.8	266.2	271.4	262.6	271.2	279.6	265.4	223.9	230.0
Germany	410.8	428.0	439.7	445.7	440.9	444.3	470.1	486.4	516.8	538.6	536.9	474.9	499.0
Greece	13.5	14.2	14.7	14.8	15.0	15.2	16.1	16.5	17.2	18.2	17.7	17.5	20.1
Hungary	26.3	25.2	25.2	32.4	31.5	33.0	36.7	41.9	48.4	53.9	53.5	50.1	50.5
Iceland	..	..	..	..	..	..	..	..	..	..	..	..	..
Ireland	8.7	10.8	12.8	12.9	14.9	16.3	17.7	18.5	17.9	19.3	17.4	12.1	11.0
Israel	..	..	..	..	..	..	..	..	..	..	..	..	..
Italy	199.6	186.4	194.9	190.0	193.9	176.4	191.2	205.8	191.1	189.2	200.5	183.1	185.9
Japan	323.6	329.7	335.3	335.3	334.2	344.7	350.1	357.8	369.7	378.1	368.7	353.3	339.0
Korea	..	..	..	..	..	..	..	..	..	..	..	..	..
Luxembourg	1.3	1.4	1.5	1.5	1.6	1.4	1.5	1.3	1.4	1.2	1.2	1.1	1.1
Mexico	226.0	245.2	242.4	238.5	244.5	249.3	254.2	276.4	283.1	299.6	301.9	280.8	299.1
Netherlands	79.7	84.1	83.2	82.9	84.1	82.3	89.4	88.0	87.8	90.7	90.3	79.2	87.8
New Zealand	11.3	16.1	17.2	17.9	18.6	19.5	20.5	20.7	20.8	21.5	21.8	..	..
Norway	18.7	18.6	18.3	18.9	18.9	19.2	21.7	22.7	22.8	22.9	24.1	22.8	23.3
Poland	150.0	146.0	150.6	147.2	150.0	160.3	188.7	196.4	216.9	238.6	248.8	258.9	297.1
Portugal	16.7	17.4	17.1	19.3	17.8	16.7	19.7	19.8	20.1	21.0	19.3	16.1	14.9
Slovak Republic	31.0	30.0	27.0	25.7	25.9	27.5	28.9	32.7	33.0	37.7	39.5	35.3	36.7
Slovenia	4.7	4.7	4.8	4.8	5.0	5.3	5.4	5.6	5.7	6.2	6.2	4.9	5.7
Spain	143.9	153.3	168.4	181.1	204.6	212.3	241.1	254.1	262.6	278.9	262.4	227.5	226.1
Sweden	50.6	51.3	51.4	49.5	51.0	51.6	53.5	56.4	57.7	59.6	60.9	52.5	56.2
Switzerland	22.6	23.2	25.0	25.7	25.6	26.0	27.2	27.8	29.2	29.3	29.9	27.6	28.1
Turkey	212.1	216.0	224.6	202.5	205.8	179.0	178.2	181.7	192.9	204.1	229.1	231.9	241.5
United Kingdom	184.5	182.9	183.4	183.3	183.9	186.4	192.9	197.8	202.0	207.5	197.6	176.7	183.8
United States	5 009.6	5 157.5	5 165.9	5 186.0	5 302.6	5 379.4	5 588.5	5 649.8	5 729.3	5 850.3	5 814.7	5 372.2	5 655.3
EU 27	1 907.8	1 934.1	1 991.4	2 017.2	2 072.1	2 094.0	2 239.2	2 314.6	2 399.2	2 491.7	2 457.4	2 185.8	2 303.3
OECD	8 336.1	8 557.1	8 646.3	8 749.2	8 917.9	9 034.2	9 455.1	9 621.1	9 832.2	10 091.0	10 083.2	9 183.0	9 577.7
Brazil	..	..	..	..	..	..	..	..	..	..	..	..	..
China	2 313.5	2 351.1	2 719.7	2 679.3	2 890.2	3 149.6	3 711.8	4 162.8	4 616.8	5 261.7	7 733.0	8 248.3	8 563.5
India	715.5	775.0	806.4	848.2	898.2	976.2	1 057.3	1 100.7	1 249.6	1 366.0	1 465.9	1 606.2	1 728.0
Indonesia	..	..	..	..	..	..	..	..	..	..	..	..	..
Russian Federation	1 904.9	2 120.1	2 341.9	2 473.5	2 657.9	2 925.4	3 192.4	3 295.2	3 390.1	3 523.1	3 509.1	3 220.9	3 387.6
South Africa	..	..	..	..	..	..	..	..	..	..	..	..	..

StatLink ᵐˢᴸ http://dx.doi.org/10.1787/888932708256

Inland goods transport
Average annual growth rate in percentage, 2000-10 or latest available period

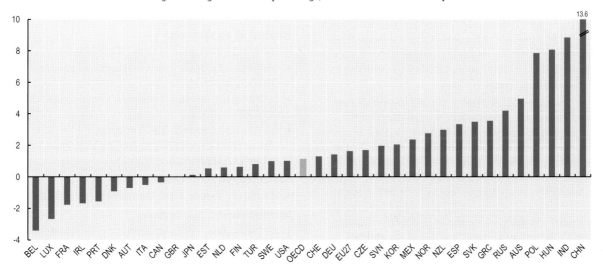

StatLink ᵐˢᴸ http://dx.doi.org/10.1787/888932708275

PASSENGER TRANSPORT

Although some studies have suggested a saturation of passenger travel by car in some developed countries, the demand for passenger mobility continues to increase worldwide. There is a need for good and comprehensive data on passenger mobility in order to develop sustainable passenger mobility systems. Comparability of transport data between countries is not always possible worldwide due to the lack of harmonised definitions and methods. The *Glossary for Transport Statistics* (4th edition) provides common definitions to all member states of the European Union, the International Transport Forum and the United Nations Economic Commission for Europe.

Overview

Rail passenger transport felt the full impact of the economic crisis later than other sectors. It was most visible in 2009 and continued to be felt in 2010. In the EU, passenger-kilometres stagnated in 2010 (0.2%) after falling 2% in 2009. Indeed, many European countries showed a decrease in their rail passenger traffic in 2010, notably in Austria (minus 10%), Poland (minus 4%) and Spain (minus 3%). A few countries resisted the otherwise downward trend; the United Kingdom (6%), Germany (2%) Switzerland (3%), Denmark (3%) and Finland (2%). Outside Europe, rail passenger-kilometres data for the Russian Federation show a drop of 8%. Preliminary data for China indicates rather flat growth (0.4%) however this still represents additional transport of three billion passenger-kilometres in 2010.

However, there continue to be marked differences between EU Member States. In France and Germany, passenger-kilometres have remained consistent at around their pre-crisis levels. Passenger transport by rail in the United Kingdom has experienced continuous growth in volumes while in contrast passenger traffic in Italy has continued to deteriorate since the economic crisis.

Data on passenger-kilometres travelled in private cars are less detailed and less up to date in many countries. Within the EU, the decline was on average 1.5% in the 13 countries where data are available for 2010. In the United States, passenger travel by car fell 3.8% in 2008, the largest drop since the economic crisis of the 1990s (passenger-kilometres by car fell 3.6% in 1991). Some studies have suggested a saturation of passenger travel by car in some developed countries and while the data available does not lend itself to a detailed analysis, it seems that some levelling off of car travel has taken place in some of the developed economies. How much these trends are due to the economic crisis or to oil price changes, amongst other potential factors, is as yet uncertain.

Definition

In the following table, passenger transport data refer to the total movement of passengers using rail or road (passenger cars, buses or coaches) transport modes. Data are expressed in passenger-kilometres which represents the transport of one passenger over one kilometre. The distance to be taken into consideration is the distance actually run.

Comparability

If passenger transport by rail or by regular buses and coaches can be estimated fairly easily, passengers transport by passenger car or by un-schedule coaches are much more difficult to track down. Some countries do not report passenger car transport at all, others carry out different types of surveys to estimate passenger travel on their territory. There is no common methodology for this and since no method provides a complete vision of passenger movements, data are not always comparable between countries.

Sources

- International Transport Forum (ITF) (2012), "*Inland passenger transport*", *International Transport Forum* (database).

Further information

Analytical publications

- ITF (2012), *Transport Outlook*, ITF, Paris.
- OECD (2012), *OECD Tourism Trends and Policies*, OECD Publishing.
- OECD (2012), *Strategic Transport Infrastructure Needs to 2030*, OECD Publishing.
- OECD and International Transport Forum (2010), *Improving Reliability on Surface Transport Networks*, OECD Publishing.

Statistical publications

- ITF (2012), *Trends in the Transport Sector*, OECD Publishing.

Methodological publications

- ITF, Statistical Office of the European Communities and United Nations Economic Commission (2010), *Illustrated Glossary for Transport Statistics, 4th Edition*, OECD Publishing.

Websites

- International Transport Forum, *www.internationaltransportforum.org*.

Inland passenger transport
Billion passenger-kilometres

	1998	1999	2000	2001	2002	2003	2004	2005	2006	2007	2008	2009	2010
Australia	259.2	264.9	270.2	268.5	274.4	281.1	293.2	294.0	293.3	296.5	297.4	297.5	296.1
Austria	8.0	8.0	8.2	8.2	8.3	8.2	8.3	8.5	9.3	9.6	10.8	10.7	10.3
Belgium	120.1	123.8	127.2	129.5	132.2	133.0	135.5	136.1	137.6	142.2	141.7	144.5	144.0
Canada	501.5	502.5	503.5	482.5	494.5	486.4	489.7	514.2	511.5	504.9	494.0	509.4	507.6
Chile	..	..	..	..	..	..	..	..	..	..	..	..	..
Czech Republic	75.5	78.0	80.6	81.4	81.6	83.3	82.7	83.9	86.1	88.0	88.6	88.3	81.0
Denmark	69.1	70.1	70.0	69.4	69.4	70.1	71.6	71.7	72.6	74.3	74.3	73.6	73.0
Estonia	2.5	2.5	2.9	2.9	2.8	2.8	2.9	3.2	3.4	3.2	3.0	2.6	2.5
Finland	64.5	65.9	66.8	68.0	69.3	70.6	71.9	72.9	73.5	75.1	75.0	75.7	76.2
France	771.1	794.4	799.8	828.6	838.2	843.3	846.9	840.2	842.4	852.5	852.0	856.3	863.1
Germany	968.3	990.2	975.7	997.1	1 001.9	996.5	1 009.1	998.9	1 008.2	1 011.0	1 017.3	1 030.4	1 029.1
Greece	39.5	41.9	42.1	42.9	43.6	43.6	44.3	44.3	44.1	44.5	43.8	44.5	44.3
Hungary	73.3	73.8	74.3	74.5	75.2	76.4	78.1	76.5	79.2	79.2	79.3	78.6	76.6
Iceland	3.9	4.1	4.3	4.5	4.6	4.7	4.9	5.1	5.5	5.7	5.6	5.6	5.6
Ireland	1.4	1.5	1.4	1.5	1.6	1.6	1.6	1.8	1.9	2.0	2.0	1.7	1.7
Israel	..	..	..	..	..	..	..	..	..	..	..	..	..
Italy	794.4	798.7	854.6	860.0	854.6	854.5	865.1	828.1	829.5	829.5	828.3	870.2	850.9
Japan	1 343.7	1 340.7	1 335.5	1 339.7	1 337.7	1 339.2	1 333.0	1 324.2	1 313.6	1 324.6	1 310.5	1 323.0	1 319.4
Korea	..	..	..	..	..	..	..	..	..	..	..	..	..
Luxembourg	0.3	0.3	0.3	0.3	0.3	0.3	0.3	0.3	0.3	0.3	0.3	0.3	0.3
Mexico	365.7	387.7	381.8	389.4	393.3	399.1	410.1	423.0	437.1	450.0	464.0	437.3	452.9
Netherlands	167.0	171.4	172.0	172.6	175.1	176.2	181.6	179.6	179.5	180.5	178.5	182.7	182.2
New Zealand	..	..	..	..	..	..	..	..	..	..	..	..	..
Norway	56.5	57.9	58.7	59.7	60.6	60.9	61.7	61.5	62.5	64.4	65.7	66.3	67.0
Poland	195.7	197.8	201.1	206.9	214.0	222.0	230.2	244.5	265.6	286.1	320.5	328.1	337.4
Portugal	91.8	97.5	98.0	98.9	99.5	100.1	101.4	101.3	101.1	101.7	101.0	103.2	102.8
Slovak Republic	31.2	32.3	35.2	35.1	35.9	35.3	34.4	35.7	35.9	35.9	35.3	33.4	33.7
Slovenia	23.5	24.8	24.5	24.9	25.4	25.6	26.0	26.3	26.9	28.4	28.9	29.8	29.6
Spain	339.8	361.0	350.4	357.3	383.8	392.3	404.0	412.6	412.4	424.3	427.4	430.6	414.9
Sweden	105.8	108.3	109.6	110.7	113.6	114.2	114.6	115.0	115.3	118.4	118.0	119.2	119.0
Switzerland	93.2	94.7	96.5	97.5	99.0	100.1	101.2	103.3	104.5	106.1	107.6	109.5	109.8
Turkey	192.3	181.4	191.5	173.8	168.5	170.2	179.5	187.2	192.9	214.7	211.2	217.8	232.4
United Kingdom	716.4	726.2	725.2	739.1	762.9	761.0	757.8	753.4	763.4	770.3	767.6	760.1	707.1
United States	4 212.8	4 285.1	4 362.7	4 364.7	4 459.5	4 492.3	4 573.3	4 590.9	4 538.8	5 855.6	5 664.2	5 007.5	5 008.7
EU 27	4 705.0	4 813.6	4 862.5	4 951.2	5 029.5	5 050.6	5 106.9	5 075.8	5 129.2	5 197.5	5 235.0	5 300.3	5 250.3
OECD	11 687.8	11 887.3	12 024.6	12 416.6	12 578.3	12 627.6	12 757.6	12 793.7	12 808.2	14 239.5	14 073.1	..	..
Brazil	..	..	..	..	..	..	..	..	..	..	..	..	..
China	971.6	1 033.5	1 119.0	1 197.4	1 277.5	1 248.4	1 446.1	1 535.4	1 675.3	1 872.3	2 025.5	2 139.0	2 138.1
India	2 129.1	2 262.3	2 532.5	2 904.0	3 329.7	3 611.4	4 045.0	4 867.3	4 969.9	5 115.2	5 174.1	5 339.7	5 294.4
Indonesia	..	..	..	..	..	..	..	..	..	..	..	..	..
Russian Federation	324.5	312.9	340.4	329.6	323.1	323.1	332.6	314.1	313.4	323.6	327.6	292.7	279.4
South Africa	..	..	..	..	..	..	..	..	..	..	..	..	..

StatLink http://dx.doi.org/10.1787/888932708313

Inland passenger transport
Average annual growth rate in percentage, 2000-10 or latest available period

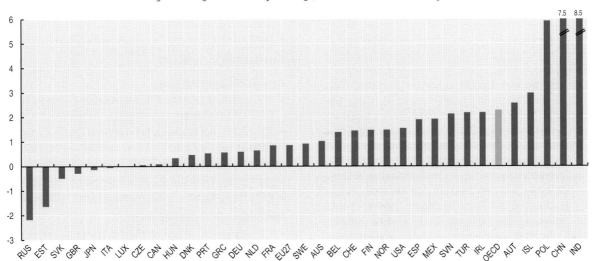

StatLink http://dx.doi.org/10.1787/888932708332

ROAD FATALITIES

The number of road motor vehicles is high amongst member countries of the International Transport Forum and reducing road accidents is a concern for all governments. Such concern becomes more challenging with increasing needs for more mobility.

Definition

A road motor vehicle is a road vehicle fitted with an engine whence it derives its sole means of propulsion, and which is normally used for carrying persons or goods or for drawing, on the road, vehicles used for the carriage of persons or goods. They include buses, coaches, trolley buses, goods road vehicles and passenger road motor vehicles. Although tramways (street-cars) are rail borne vehicles they are integrated into the urban road network and considered as road motor vehicles.

Road fatality means any person killed immediately or dying within 30 days as a result of a road injury accident. Suicides involving the use of a road motor vehicle are excluded.

Comparability

Road motor vehicles are attributed to the countries where they are registered while deaths are attributed to the countries in which they occur.

Fatalities per million inhabitants can be compared with other causes of death in a country (heart diseases, cancer, HIV, etc.) however when comparing countries road fatality risks, this indicator looses it relevance if countries do not have the same level of motorisation. Fatalities per vehicle-kilometre provides a better measure of fatality risk on road networks, but there is currently no harmonisation in the

methodology to calculate distances travelled, and not all countries collect this indicator.

The numbers of vehicles entering the existing stock is usually accurate, but information on the numbers of vehicles withdrawn from use is less certain. Shown here are the numbers of road fatalities per million inhabitants and the number of road fatalities per million inhabitants and per million vehicles.

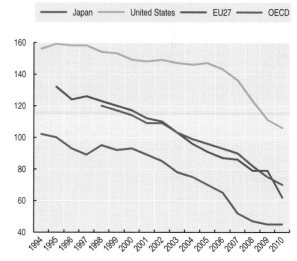

Road fatalities

Per million inhabitants

StatLink http://dx.doi.org/10.1787/888932708408

Overview

The first ten years of the 21st century saw record road safety performance in most countries of the International Transport Forum (ITF). Following two consecutive years of record improvements in 2008 and 2009, the number of people killed in crashes continued to fall in 2010 recording a drop of 6% in 2010 in ITF member countries (excluding China and India). In 2010 only 4 ITF countries reported an increase of people killed on the roads. These positive developments should not hide the economic costs and human tragedies behind the data. While high-income countries look back on a record decade in reducing road fatalities, 90% of global road deaths occur in low and middle income countries and estimates put annual world road fatalities above 1.3 million, with 50 million serious injuries.

Sources

- International Transport Forum (ITF) (2012), *Road Injury Accidents* (database).
- ITF (2012), *Quarterly Transport Statistics* (database).

Further information

Analytical publications

- ITF (2012), *IRTAD Road Safety Annual Report 2011*, OECD Publishing.
- ITF (2011), *Reporting on Serious Road Traffic Casualties*, ITF, Paris.

Statistical publications

- ITF (2012), *Trends in the Transport Sector*, OECD Publishing.
- ITF (2011), *Key Transport Statistics 2010*, ITF, Paris.

Methodological publications

- ITF, Statistical Office of the European Communities and United Nations Economic Commission (2010), *Illustrated Glossary for Transport Statistics 4th Edition*, OECD Publishing.

Websites

- International Transport Forum, *www.internationaltransportforum.org*.

Road fatalities

Per million inhabitants

	1998	1999	2000	2001	2002	2003	2004	2005	2006	2007	2008	2009	2010
Australia	94	93	95	90	87	82	79	81	78	77	68	70	61
Austria	121	135	122	119	118	114	108	94	89	83	81	76	66
Belgium	147	136	143	144	131	117	112	104	102	100	100	88	76
Canada	97	98	95	90	93	87	85	91	89	83	82	73	65
Chile	131	109	110	100	98	107	109	100	101	99	106	89	..
Czech Republic	132	141	145	130	140	142	136	126	104	118	103	86	76
Denmark	94	97	93	80	86	80	68	61	56	74	74	55	46
Estonia	200	206	169	149	146	164	121	126	126	146	98	75	58
Finland	78	83	76	83	80	73	72	72	64	72	65	53	51
France	143	136	129	130	121	96	87	88	77	75	69	69	64
Germany	95	95	91	85	83	80	71	65	62	60	55	51	44
Greece	207	201	193	178	159	145	151	150	149	141	138	130	111
Hungary	136	130	118	122	141	131	129	127	130	123	99	82	74
Iceland	98	75	113	84	101	80	79	64	104	48	38	54	25
Ireland	124	110	110	107	96	84	94	84	87	77	63	53	47
Israel	93	79	75	87	83	70	72	66	60	55	58	43	47
Italy	118	116	115	117	117	105	98	94	89	86	79	71	68
Japan	95	92	93	89	85	78	75	70	65	52	47	45	45
Korea	226	232	218	171	152	151	136	132	131	127	121	120	114
Luxembourg	134	133	172	159	140	118	109	101	78	90	72	98	63
Mexico	53	53	53	52	49	46	45	46	47	51	51	46	43
Netherlands	73	75	73	67	66	67	54	50	50	48	46	44	36
New Zealand	132	134	121	118	103	115	107	99	95	100	86	90	86
Norway	79	68	76	61	68	61	56	49	52	49	53	45	43
Poland	183	174	163	143	152	148	150	143	138	147	143	120	102
Portugal	213	200	186	161	165	148	124	118	104	81	83	69	88
Slovak Republic	160	125	120	116	116	121	113	111	113	122	112	71	65
Slovenia	156	168	157	140	134	121	137	129	130	145	105	84	68
Spain	150	144	143	135	129	128	115	89	94	85	68	60	54
Sweden	60	65	67	65	63	59	53	49	49	51	43	39	28
Switzerland	84	81	82	75	70	74	69	55	50	51	47	46	43
Turkey	76	69	58	45	62	56	62	62	62	68	57	58	56
United Kingdom	62	62	62	63	63	62	57	55	55	50	43	38	31
United States	154	153	149	148	149	147	146	147	143	136	123	111	106
EU 27	123	120	117	112	110	103	96	91	87	86	79	79	62
OECD	120	117	114	109	109	103	99	96	93	90	82	75	70
Brazil	..	..	..	..	..	..	..	..	..	..	..	..	..
China	..	..	..	..	..	..	82	76	68	62	55	51	50
India	77	81	80	80	82	84	91	98	106	115	101	104	110
Indonesia	..	..	..	..	..	..	..	..	..	..	..	..	..
Russian Federation	198	203	203	213	228	248	241	237	230	235	211	184	186
South Africa	216	247	196	253	270	268	274	301	325	312	287	..	..

StatLink http://dx.doi.org/10.1787/888932708370

Road fatalities

2010 or latest available year

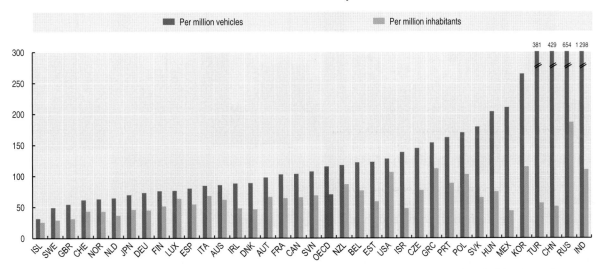

StatLink http://dx.doi.org/10.1787/888932708389

LABOUR

EMPLOYMENT RATES

Employment rates are a measure of the extent of utilisation of available labour resources. In the short term, these rates are sensitive to the economic cycle, but in the longer term they are significantly affected by government policies with regard to higher education and income support and by policies that facilitate employment of women and disadvantaged groups.

Definition

Employment rates are calculated as the ratio of the employed to the working age population. Employment is generally measured through household labour force surveys. According to the ILO Guidelines, employed persons are defined as those aged 15 or over who report that they have worked in gainful employment for at least one hour in the previous week or who had a job but were absent from work during the reference week. Those not in employment consist of persons who are classified as either unemployed or inactive, in the sense that they are not included in the labour force for reasons of experiencing difficulty to find a job, study, incapacity or the need to look after young children or elderly relatives or personal choice.

Overview

Employment rates for men are higher than those for women in all OECD countries with an average OECD difference of 16 percentage points. The employment gap dropped significantly since 2000 by about 5 percentage points in the OECD area due to an increase in women's employment rates while those of men declined since the onset of the crisis in late 2007 and in particular in countries hard hit by the crisis. The increase in employment rates for women was widespread before the crisis, exceeding 5 or more percentage points in 13 countries, in particular in Ireland, Greece and Spain.

Despite the recent increase, Turkey has by far the lowest women's employment rate, at 27.8%, with Iceland remaining the highest, at 77.3%. Chile has below OECD average employment rates for women despite increases (12 percentage points) over the last decade in excess of those recorded for men. By contrast, 9 countries have below OECD average employment rates for men and above OECD average employment rates for women, Among those countries, Portugal and the United States had above OECD average employment rates for men in 2000.

In the emerging economies, employment rates of men are markedly higher than those of women, by more than 23 percentage points in Brazil, 12 percentage points in South Africa and by more than 8 percentage points in the Russian Federation.

The working age population refers to persons aged 15 to 64.

Comparability

All OECD countries use the ILO Guidelines for measuring employment. Operational definitions used in national labour force surveys may vary slightly from country to country. Employment levels are also likely to be affected by changes in the survey design and the survey conduct. Despite these changes, the employment rates shown here are fairly consistent over time.

Employment rates: women
Share of women of working age in employment

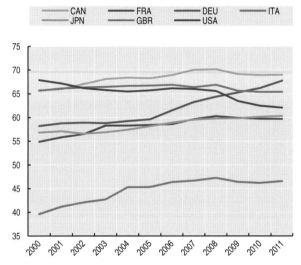

StatLink http://dx.doi.org/10.1787/888932708465

Sources

- OECD (2012), *OECD Employment Outlook*, OECD Publishing.

Further information

Analytical publications

- Jaumotte, F. (2003), "*Female Labour Force Participation*", *OECD Economics Department Working Papers*, No. 376.
- OECD (2011), *Divided We Stand: Why Inequality Keeps Rising*, OECD Publishing.
- OECD (2007), *Babies and Bosses – Reconciling Work and Family Life*, OECD Publishing.

Statistical publications

- OECD (2011), *Labour Force Statistics*, OECD Publishing.

Online databases

- *OECD Employment and Labour Market Statistics*.

Websites

- OECD Labour Statistics Database, *www.oecd.org/statistics/labour*.

Employment rates by gender

Share of persons of working age in employment

	Women				Men				Total			
	2000	2008	2010	2011	2000	2008	2010	2011	2000	2008	2010	2011
Australia	61.4	66.7	66.2	66.7	77.1	79.7	78.6	78.7	69.3	73.2	72.4	72.7
Austria	59.4	65.8	66.4	66.5	77.3	78.5	77.1	77.8	68.3	72.1	71.7	72.1
Belgium	51.9	56.2	56.5	56.7	69.8	68.6	67.4	67.1	60.9	62.4	62.0	61.9
Canada	65.6	70.1	68.8	68.9	76.2	77.2	74.2	75.0	70.9	73.6	71.5	72.0
Chile	35.1	42.1	46.7	49.1	71.9	72.6	72.1	73.6	53.3	57.3	59.3	61.3
Czech Republic	56.9	57.6	56.3	57.2	73.6	75.4	73.5	74.0	65.2	66.6	65.0	65.7
Denmark	72.1	74.1	71.1	70.4	80.7	81.6	75.6	75.9	76.4	77.9	73.3	73.1
Estonia	57.0	66.3	60.5	62.7	65.4	73.5	61.5	67.8	61.0	69.7	61.0	65.2
Finland	64.5	69.0	66.9	67.5	70.5	73.4	69.7	70.9	67.5	71.3	68.3	69.2
France	54.8	60.2	59.7	59.7	68.8	69.5	68.1	68.1	61.7	64.8	63.8	63.8
Germany	58.1	64.3	66.1	67.7	72.9	75.9	76.1	77.4	65.6	70.2	71.2	72.6
Greece	41.3	48.7	48.1	45.1	71.3	75.0	70.9	65.9	55.9	61.9	59.6	55.6
Hungary	49.6	50.6	50.6	50.6	62.7	63.0	60.4	61.2	56.0	56.7	55.4	55.8
Iceland	81.0	80.3	77.0	77.3	88.2	87.8	80.6	80.8	84.6	84.2	78.9	79.0
Ireland	53.8	60.5	56.4	56.0	76.1	75.7	64.5	63.3	65.0	68.1	60.4	59.6
Israel	50.9	55.6	56.9	57.5	61.4	64.1	63.4	64.3	56.1	59.8	60.2	60.9
Italy	39.6	47.2	46.1	46.5	68.2	70.3	67.7	67.5	53.9	58.7	56.9	56.9
Japan	56.7	59.7	60.1	60.3	80.9	81.6	80.0	80.2	68.9	70.7	70.1	70.3
Korea	50.0	53.2	52.6	53.1	73.1	74.4	73.9	74.5	61.5	63.8	63.3	63.9
Luxembourg	50.0	55.1	57.2	56.9	75.0	71.5	73.1	72.1	62.7	63.4	65.2	64.6
Mexico	39.6	44.1	43.8	43.4	82.8	80.7	78.5	77.8	60.1	61.3	60.3	59.8
Netherlands	62.7	69.3	69.4	69.9	81.2	82.4	80.0	79.8	72.1	75.9	74.7	74.9
New Zealand	63.2	68.7	66.7	67.2	77.9	80.9	78.2	78.2	70.4	74.7	72.3	72.6
Norway	74.0	75.4	73.3	73.4	81.7	80.6	77.4	77.2	77.9	78.1	75.4	75.3
Poland	48.9	52.4	53.0	53.1	61.2	66.3	65.6	66.3	55.0	59.2	59.3	59.7
Portugal	60.5	62.5	61.1	60.4	76.3	74.0	70.1	68.1	68.3	68.2	65.6	64.2
Slovak Republic	51.5	54.6	52.3	52.7	62.2	70.0	65.2	66.3	56.8	62.3	58.8	59.5
Slovenia	..	64.2	62.6	60.9	..	72.7	69.6	67.7	..	68.6	66.2	64.4
Spain	42.0	55.7	53.0	52.8	72.7	74.6	65.6	64.1	57.4	65.3	59.4	58.5
Sweden	72.2	73.2	70.3	71.9	76.3	78.3	75.0	76.3	74.3	75.8	72.7	74.1
Switzerland	69.4	73.5	72.5	73.2	87.3	85.4	84.6	85.3	78.4	79.5	78.6	79.3
Turkey	26.2	23.5	26.2	27.8	71.7	66.6	66.7	69.3	48.9	44.9	46.3	48.4
United Kingdom	65.6	66.8	65.3	65.3	78.9	78.6	75.3	75.5	72.2	72.7	70.3	70.4
United States	67.8	65.5	62.4	62.0	80.6	76.4	71.1	71.4	74.1	70.9	66.7	66.6
EU 27	..	..	..	..	..	..	..	..	..	..	..	..
OECD	55.0	57.6	56.6	56.7	76.1	75.6	72.7	73.0	65.4	66.5	64.6	64.8
Brazil	..	56.8	..	..	..	80.6	..	..	..	68.3	..	..
China	..	..	..	..	..	..	..	..	..	..	..	..
India	..	..	..	..	..	..	..	..	..	..	..	..
Indonesia	..	..	..	..	..	..	..	..	..	..	..	..
Russian Federation	58.9	64.8	63.5	63.8	67.2	73.0	71.6	72.2	62.9	68.7	67.4	67.8
South Africa	..	37.4	34.4	34.6	..	52.7	47.7	47.4	..	44.8	40.8	40.8

StatLink 🔢 http://dx.doi.org/10.1787/888932708427

Employment rates: total

Share of persons of working age in employment

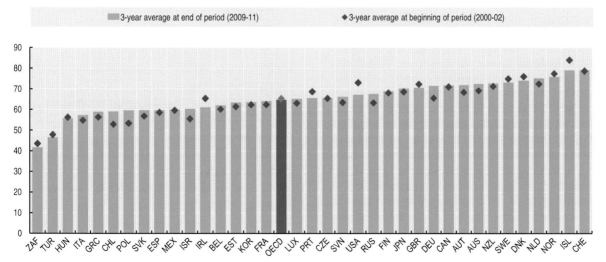

StatLink 🔢 http://dx.doi.org/10.1787/888932708446

EMPLOYMENT RATES BY AGE GROUP

Labour markets differ in how employment opportunities are allocated among people of different ages. Employment rates for people of different ages are significantly affected by government policies with regard to higher education, pensions and retirement age.

Definition

The employment rate for a given age group is measured as the number of employed people of a given age as a ratio of the total number of people in that same age group.

Employment is generally measured through national labour force surveys. In accordance with the ILO Guidelines, employed persons are those aged 15 or over who report that they have worked in gainful employment for at least one hour in the previous week or who had a job but were absent from work in the reference week. Those not in employment consist of persons who are classified as either unemployed or inactive, in the sense that they are not included in the labour force for reasons of experiencing difficulty to find a job, study, incapacity or the need to look after young children or elderly relatives or personal choice.

Employment rates are shown for three age groups: persons aged 15 to 24 are those just entering the labour market following education; persons aged 25 to 54 are those in their prime working lives; persons aged 55 to 64 are those who have passed the peak of their career and are approaching retirement.

Comparability

Employment levels are likely to be affected by changes in the survey design, the survey conduct and adjustments to the population controls based on census results and intercensal population estimates between censuses. Despite these changes, the employment rates shown here are fairly consistent over time.

Overview

Employment rates for people aged 25 to 54 are relatively similar between OECD countries, with rates in all countries except Turkey ranging between 68% and 87% in 2011. Cross-country differences are larger when looking at the youngest age group where, in 2011, employment rates ranged between less than 26% in nine countries – Greece, Hungary, Italy, the Slovak Republic, Luxembourg, Korea, Spain, the Czech Republic and Poland – and over 60% in just four countries – Australia, Switzerland, Iceland and the Netherlands. Employment rates for the oldest age group also vary considerably, between 70% or more in nine countries – Australia, Israel, Korea, Japan, Switzerland, Norway, Sweden, New Zealand and Iceland and less than 40% in eight countries – Slovenia, Turkey, Hungary, Poland, Italy, Belgium, Luxembourg and Greece. Eleven countries have prime-age rates below the OECD average – Chile, Greece, Hungary, Ireland, Italy, Israel, Korea, Mexico, Spain, Turkey, the United States, whereas Slovenia is 8 points above the average. In the emerging economies, employment rates for youth and older workers are above the OECD average only in Brazil, while those for people of prime working age exceed the OECD average by around 9 percentage points in the Russian Federation.

As a consequence of the ongoing jobs crisis, prime-age employment rates have fallen quite significantly in a few countries by 4 percentage points or more in Greece, Iceland, Ireland, Spain and the United States. The employment rates for older workers increased by 6 percentage points on average in the OECD area, even during the jobs crisis, with the largest increases recorded in New Zealand, the Netherlands, Germany, Australia, Belgium and Finland.

Sources

- OECD (2012), *OECD Employment Outlook*, OECD Publishing.
- For non-member countries: National sources.

Further information

Analytical publications

- Burniaux, J.M., R. Duval and F. Jaumotte (2004), "Coping with Ageing", *OECD Economics Department Working Papers*, No. 371.
- OECD (2012), *Better Skills, Better Jobs, Better Lives, A Strategic Approach to Skills Policies*, OECD Publishing.
- OECD (2010), *Off to a Good Start? Jobs for Youth*, OECD Publishing.
- OECD (2006), *Ageing and Employment Policies*, OECD Publishing.

Statistical publications

- OECD (2011), *Labour Force Statistics*, OECD Publishing.

Online databases

- *OECD Employment and Labour Market Statistics*.

Websites

- OECD Ageing and Employment Policies (supplementary material), *www.oecd.org/els/employment/olderworkers*.
- OECD Employment Policies, *www.oecd.org/els/employment*.
- OECD Jobs for Youth Project (supplementary material), *www.oecd.org/employment/youth*.
- OECD Labour Statistics, *www.oecd.org/std/labourstatistics*.

Employment rates by age group

As a percentage of population in that age group

	Persons 15-24 in employment				Persons 25-54 in employment				Persons 55-64 in employment			
	1990	2000	2005	2011	1990	2000	2005	2011	1990	2000	2005	2011
Australia	62.7	62.1	63.3	60.7	76.0	76.3	78.8	79.8	41.5	46.2	53.5	61.1
Austria	..	52.8	53.1	54.9	..	82.5	82.6	84.9	..	28.3	31.8	41.5
Belgium	30.4	30.3	27.5	26.0	71.7	77.9	78.3	79.3	21.4	25.0	31.8	38.7
Canada	61.3	56.2	57.7	55.4	78.1	79.9	81.3	81.0	46.2	48.1	54.7	58.7
Chile	..	26.4	25.4	31.7	..	65.0	67.5	74.2	..	47.5	51.0	59.7
Czech Republic	..	38.3	27.3	24.7	..	81.6	82.0	82.8	..	36.3	44.6	47.6
Denmark	65.0	67.1	62.3	57.5	84.0	84.3	84.5	82.3	53.6	54.6	59.5	59.5
Estonia	51.7	32.9	29.8	32.3	91.8	75.7	79.3	78.1	60.4	44.0	55.7	57.1
Finland	55.2	42.9	42.1	42.3	87.9	80.9	81.7	82.3	42.8	42.3	52.6	57.0
France	35.7	28.3	30.2	29.9	77.3	78.4	80.7	81.3	30.7	29.3	38.5	41.4
Germany	56.4	47.2	42.6	48.2	73.6	79.3	77.4	82.8	36.8	37.6	45.5	59.9
Greece	30.3	26.9	25.0	16.3	68.5	70.2	74.0	69.0	40.8	39.0	41.6	39.4
Hungary	..	32.5	21.8	18.3	..	73.0	73.7	73.1	..	21.9	33.0	35.8
Iceland	..	68.2	71.6	63.3	..	90.6	88.2	84.0	..	84.2	84.8	79.5
Ireland	41.4	49.4	47.9	28.1	60.0	75.5	77.8	69.8	38.6	45.2	51.6	50.8
Israel	23.6	28.2	26.6	26.6	66.5	70.4	70.6	74.8	48.5	46.6	52.4	61.2
Italy	29.8	27.8	25.5	19.4	68.2	68.0	72.2	71.1	32.6	27.7	31.4	37.9
Japan	42.2	42.7	40.9	39.1	79.6	78.6	79.0	80.2	62.9	62.8	63.9	65.1
Korea	32.5	29.4	29.9	23.1	73.2	72.2	73.4	74.4	61.9	57.8	58.7	62.1
Luxembourg	43.3	31.8	24.9	20.7	71.8	78.2	80.7	82.0	28.2	27.2	31.7	39.3
Mexico	..	48.9	43.7	42.0	..	67.4	68.8	69.5	..	51.7	52.6	53.4
Netherlands	54.5	66.5	61.7	63.6	71.2	81.0	81.5	84.2	29.7	37.6	44.8	56.1
New Zealand	59.1	54.2	56.4	49.9	76.3	78.3	81.6	80.4	41.8	56.9	69.5	73.7
Norway	53.4	58.1	52.9	51.4	82.2	85.3	83.2	84.7	61.5	67.1	67.6	69.6
Poland	..	24.5	20.9	24.9	..	70.9	69.5	77.2	..	28.4	29.1	36.9
Portugal	54.8	41.8	36.1	27.1	78.4	81.8	80.8	77.8	47.0	50.7	50.5	47.9
Slovak Republic	..	29.0	25.6	20.2	..	74.7	75.3	76.5	..	21.3	30.4	41.4
Slovenia	..	..	34.1	31.5	..	..	83.8	83.1	..	..	30.7	31.2
Spain	38.3	36.3	41.9	24.1	61.4	68.4	74.4	68.7	36.9	37.0	43.1	44.5
Sweden	66.1	46.7	43.3	40.4	91.6	83.8	83.9	86.0	69.5	65.1	69.6	72.5
Switzerland	..	65.1	59.9	62.9	..	85.4	85.1	86.4	..	63.3	65.1	69.5
Turkey	45.9	37.0	30.2	32.1	61.6	56.7	53.0	57.5	42.7	36.4	28.0	31.4
United Kingdom	70.1	61.5	58.7	50.1	79.1	80.2	81.1	80.1	49.2	50.4	56.7	56.8
United States	59.8	59.7	53.9	45.5	79.7	81.5	79.3	75.1	54.0	57.8	60.8	60.0
EU 27	..	..	..	..	..	..	..	..	..	..	..	..
OECD	49.1	45.5	42.7	39.5	75.8	75.9	75.8	75.4	47.7	47.6	51.7	54.4
Brazil	..	..	52.7	..	..	..	75.9	..	..	..	54.1	..
China	..	..	..	..	..	..	..	..	..	..	..	..
India	..	..	..	..	..	..	..	..	..	..	..	..
Indonesia	..	..	..	..	..	..	..	..	..	..	..	..
Russian Federation	..	34.3	32.5	35.8	..	79.6	82.6	84.6	..	34.6	44.3	43.8
South Africa	..	..	15.0	12.7	..	..	59.3	56.5	..	..	42.2	38.0

StatLink ⟶ http://dx.doi.org/10.1787/888932708484

Employment rates for age group 15-24

Persons in employment as a percentage of population in that age group

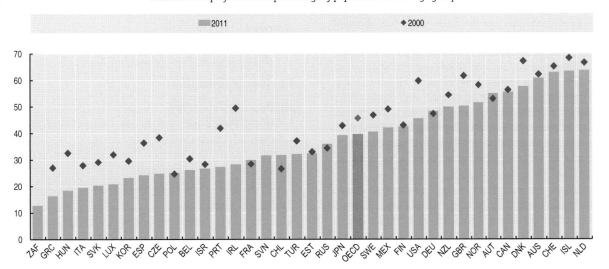

StatLink ⟶ http://dx.doi.org/10.1787/888932708503

PART-TIME EMPLOYMENT

Opportunities for part-time work are especially important for people who do not want to work full-time because of family circumstances, such as woman with young children and those caring for the elderly. Indeed, recent surveys in a large number of OECD countries show that most people who work part-time do so by choice. This suggests that countries with little part-time employment could foster increased employment by policies that promote the availability of part-time jobs.

Definition

Part-time employment refers to persons who usually work less than 30 hours per week in their main job. This definition has the advantage of being comparable across countries as national definitions of part-time employment vary greatly from one country to another. Part-time workers include both employees and the self-employed.

Overview

The incidence of part-time employment for the OECD area as a whole was 16.5% in 2011. But this incidence differed significantly across countries. In Ireland, the Netherlands and Switzerland over 25% of all those in employment were working part-time, while this share was under 10% in 7 OECD countries and below 5% in Hungary, the Slovak Republic and the Czech Republic. In the Russian Federation this rate is also low at 4.1%.

In recent years, part-time work has accounted for a substantial share of overall employment growth in many OECD countries. For the OECD as a whole, the incidence of part-time employment increased by close to 5 percentage points between 2000 and 2011, while overall employment rates declined since the onset of the jobs crisis in late 2007. Part-time employment rates grew by 5 percentage points or more in Austria, Korea and the Netherlands but also in Ireland and Spain, that were hard hit by the crisis. The largest increase in part-time employment rates occurred in Chile (12.5 percentage points) which benefited from an overall increase in employment rates over the 2000-11 period. In the Russian Federation and South Africa, part-time employment declined, by more than 1 percentage point in 2000-11.

The growth of part-time employment has been especially important for groups that are often under-represented in the labour force such as women – over 5 percentage points in Austria, Chile, Korea, Ireland, Italy, Spain and Turkey; youth – over 15 percentage points in Chile, Denmark, Ireland, Korea and Spain; and older workers – over 10 percentage points in Austria, Chile and Ireland.

Employment is generally measured through household labour force surveys. According to the ILO Guidelines, employed persons are those aged 15 or over who report that they have worked in gainful employment for at least one hour in the previous week or who had a job but were absent from work in the reference week. The rates shown here refer to the number of persons who usually work less than 30 hours per week as a percentage of the total number of those in employment.

Comparability

All OECD countries use the ILO Guidelines for measuring employment. Operational definitions used in national labour force surveys may, however, vary slightly across countries. Employment levels are also likely to be affected by changes in the survey design and the survey conduct. Despite these changes, the employment rates shown here are fairly consistent over time. Information on the number of hours usually worked is mostly collected in household labour force surveys. The part-time rates shown here are considered to be of good comparability.

Sources
- OECD (2012), *OECD Employment Outlook*, OECD Publishing.
- For non-member countries: National sources.

Further information

Analytical publications
- OECD (2007), *Babies and Bosses – Reconciling Work and Family Life*, series, OECD Publishing.
- OECD (2003), *The Sources of Economic Growth in OECD Countries*, OECD Publishing.
- OECD (1999), *The OECD Jobs Strategy*, OECD Publishing.

Statistical publications
- OECD (2011), *Labour Force Statistics*, OECD Publishing.

Online databases
- *OECD Employment and Labour Market Statistics*.

Websites
- OECD Employment Policies, *www.oecd.org/els/employment*.
- OECD Labour Statistics, *www.oecd.org/statistics/labour*.

Incidence of part-time employment

As a percentage of total employment

	1999	2000	2001	2002	2003	2004	2005	2006	2007	2008	2009	2010	2011
Australia	..	..	23.7	24.0	24.3	23.8	24.0	23.9	23.8	23.8	24.7	24.9	24.7
Austria	12.3	12.2	12.4	13.3	13.7	15.4	16.3	16.8	17.3	17.7	18.5	19.0	18.9
Belgium	19.9	19.0	17.0	17.6	18.3	18.5	18.5	18.7	18.1	18.3	18.2	18.3	18.8
Canada	18.4	18.1	18.1	18.8	19.0	18.6	18.4	18.2	18.3	18.5	19.3	19.4	19.9
Chile	4.6	4.7	5.6	5.2	5.7	6.6	7.2	7.7	8.0	9.1	10.5	17.4	17.2
Czech Republic	3.4	3.2	3.2	2.9	3.2	3.1	3.3	3.3	3.5	3.5	3.9	4.3	3.9
Denmark	15.3	16.1	14.7	15.5	16.2	17.0	17.3	17.9	17.3	17.8	18.8	19.2	19.2
Estonia	..	7.1	7.1	6.9	7.5	6.8	6.7	6.7	6.8	6.2	8.4	8.7	8.8
Finland	9.9	10.4	10.5	11.0	11.3	11.3	11.2	11.4	11.7	11.5	12.2	12.5	12.7
France	14.6	14.2	13.8	13.8	13.0	13.2	13.2	13.2	13.3	12.9	13.3	13.6	13.6
Germany	17.1	17.6	18.3	18.8	19.6	20.1	21.5	21.8	22.0	21.8	21.9	21.7	22.1
Greece	8.0	5.5	4.9	5.4	5.6	5.9	6.4	7.4	7.7	7.9	8.4	8.8	9.0
Hungary	3.2	2.9	2.5	2.6	3.2	3.3	3.2	2.7	2.8	3.1	3.6	3.6	4.7
Iceland	21.2	20.4	20.4	20.1	16.0	16.6	16.4	16.0	15.9	15.1	17.5	18.4	17.0
Ireland	17.9	18.1	17.9	18.4	18.9	18.9	19.3	19.3	19.8	20.8	23.7	24.8	25.7
Israel	14.8	14.6	15.3	15.5	15.3	15.2	15.1	15.2	14.8	14.7	14.8	14.0	13.7
Italy	11.8	12.2	12.2	11.6	11.7	14.7	14.6	15.0	15.2	15.9	15.8	16.3	16.7
Japan	..	..	..	17.7	18.2	18.1	18.3	18.0	18.9	19.6	20.3	20.2	20.6
Korea	7.7	7.0	7.3	7.6	7.7	8.4	9.0	8.8	8.9	9.3	9.9	10.7	13.5
Luxembourg	12.1	12.4	13.3	12.5	13.3	13.2	13.9	12.7	13.1	13.4	16.4	15.8	16.0
Mexico	13.7	13.5	13.7	13.5	13.4	15.1	16.8	17.0	17.6	17.6	17.9	18.9	18.3
Netherlands	30.4	32.1	33.0	33.9	34.5	35.0	35.6	35.4	35.9	36.1	36.7	37.1	37.2
New Zealand	23.0	22.2	22.3	22.5	22.2	21.9	21.6	21.2	22.0	22.2	22.5	21.9	22.0
Norway	20.7	20.2	20.1	20.6	21.0	21.1	20.8	21.1	20.4	20.3	20.4	20.1	20.0
Poland	14.0	12.8	11.6	11.7	11.5	12.0	11.7	10.8	10.1	9.3	8.7	8.7	8.3
Portugal	9.4	9.4	9.2	9.6	9.9	9.6	9.4	9.3	9.9	9.7	9.6	9.3	11.5
Slovak Republic	1.8	1.9	1.9	1.6	2.3	2.8	2.6	2.5	2.6	2.7	3.0	3.7	4.0
Slovenia	..	..	..	4.9	5.0	7.5	7.4	7.8	7.8	7.5	8.3	9.4	8.6
Spain	7.8	7.7	7.8	7.6	7.8	8.4	11.0	10.8	10.7	11.1	11.9	12.4	12.9
Sweden	14.5	14.0	13.9	13.8	14.1	14.4	13.5	13.4	14.4	14.4	14.6	14.0	13.8
Switzerland	24.8	24.4	24.8	24.8	25.1	24.9	25.1	25.5	25.4	25.9	26.5	26.1	25.9
Turkey	7.7	9.4	6.2	6.6	6.0	6.1	5.6	7.6	8.1	8.5	11.1	11.5	11.7
United Kingdom	22.9	23.0	22.7	23.2	23.5	23.6	23.0	23.2	22.9	23.0	23.9	24.6	24.6
United States	13.3	12.6	12.8	13.1	13.2	13.2	12.8	12.6	12.6	12.8	14.1	13.5	12.6
EU 27	..	..	..	..	..	..	..	..	..	..	..	..	..
OECD	12.0	11.9	12.0	14.4	14.6	15.0	15.2	15.2	15.4	15.6	16.4	16.6	16.5
Brazil	..	..	16.8	17.9	18.0	18.2	19.0	19.2	18.3	18.1	17.8	..	..
China	..	..	..	..	..	..	..	..	..	..	..	..	..
India	..	..	..	..	..	..	..	..	..	..	..	..	..
Indonesia	..	..	..	..	..	..	..	..	..	..	..	..	..
Russian Federation	8.2	7.4	5.2	3.8	5.3	5.5	5.6	5.3	5.1	5.0	4.8	4.3	4.1
South Africa	..	..	8.8	8.5	8.8	7.5	8.4	9.1	8.0	8.2	8.3	8.1	7.7

StatLink http://dx.doi.org/10.1787/888932708522

Incidence of part-time employment

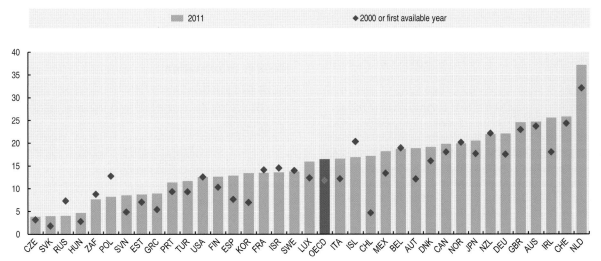

StatLink http://dx.doi.org/10.1787/888932708541

SELF-EMPLOYMENT

Self-employment may be seen either as a survival strategy for those who cannot find any other means of earning an income or as evidence of entrepreneurial spirit and a desire to be one's own boss. The self-employment rates shown here reflect these various motives.

Definition

Employment is generally measured through national labour force surveys. According to the ILO Guidelines, employed persons are defined as those aged 15 or over who report that they have worked in gainful employment for at least one hour in the previous week or who had a job but were absent from work in the reference week.

Self-employed persons include employers, own-account workers, members of producers' co-operatives, and unpaid family workers. People in the last of these groups do not have a formal contract to receive a fixed amount of income at regular intervals, but they share in the income generated by the enterprise; unpaid family workers are particularly important in farming and retail trade. Note that all persons who work in corporate enterprises, including company directors, are considered to be employees.

The rates shown here are the percentages of the self-employed in total employment.

Comparability

All OECD countries use ILO Guidelines for measuring employment. Operational definitions used in national labour force surveys may, however, vary slightly across countries. Only unincorporated self-employed are included in self-employed in Australia, Canada and the United States. Employment levels are also likely to be affected by changes in the survey design, questions sequencing and/or the ways in which surveys are conducted. Despite this, self-employment rates are likely to be fairly consistent over time.

Overview

In 2011, the share of self-employed workers in total employment ranged from under 8% in Luxembourg, Norway and the United States to well over 30% in Greece, Mexico and Turkey. In general, self-employment rates are highest in countries with low per capita income although Italy, with a self-employment rate of around 25%, is an exception. Ireland and Spain also combine high per capita incomes and high self-employment rates.

Over the period 2000-11, self-employment rates have fallen in most countries and by 1.6 percentage points in the OECD area. These falls have mostly occurred prior to the onset of the global financial crisis in late 2007. However the Czech Republic, the Netherlands, and the United Kingdom saw moderate increases and the Slovak Republic sharp increases, albeit from low levels. Conversely, and starting from a higher level, there have been sharp declines in self-employment rates in Chile, Greece, Italy, Korea, Poland, New Zealand, Mexico, Portugal and Spain.

Levels and changes in total self-employment rates conceal significant differences between men and women. In 2011, only Mexico, Switzerland and Turkey recorded self-employment rates for women higher than those rates for men. In the case of Turkey, almost half of all women with a paid job are self-employed, down from 78.4% recorded in 1990.

Sources

- OECD (2011), *Labour Force Statistics*, OECD Publishing.
- For non-member countries: National sources.

Further information

Analytical publications

- OECD (2012), *Entrepreneurship at a Glance*, OECD Publishing.
- OECD (2012), *OECD Employment Outlook*, OECD Publishing.
- OECD (2012), *Financing SMEs and Entrepreneurs 2012, An OECD Scoreboard*, OECD Publishing.
- OECD (2010), *OECD Studies on SMEs and Entrepreneurship*, OECD Publishing.
- OECD (2005), *OECD SME and Entrepreneurship Outlook 2005*, OECD Publishing.

Online databases

- *OECD Employment and Labour Market Statistics.*

Websites

- OECD Employment Policies, *www.oecd.org/els/employment*.
- OECD Centre for Entrepreneurship, SMEs and Local Development, *www.oecd.org/cfe*.

Self-employment rates

As a percentage of total employment by gender

	Women				Men				Total			
	2000	2008	2010	2011	2000	2008	2010	2011	2000	2008	2010	2011
Australia	10.4	8.9	8.9	..	16.1	13.9	13.9	..	13.6	11.6	11.6	..
Austria	12.2	11.5	11.3	11.3	13.9	15.7	16.0	15.9	13.1	13.8	13.8	13.8
Belgium	13.5	10.8	10.8	..	17.5	17.0	17.3	..	15.8	14.2	14.4	..
Canada	9.2	7.8	8.1	8.0	11.8	10.2	10.2	9.9	10.6	9.1	9.2	9.0
Chile	24.5	24.4	24.9	26.0	32.4	28.2	27.5	27.0	29.8	26.8	26.5	26.6
Czech Republic	10.2	10.6	12.2	12.9	19.1	20.3	22.0	22.0	15.2	16.2	17.8	18.1
Denmark	5.5	5.1	5.5	5.3	11.7	12.1	11.7	11.9	8.7	8.8	8.8	8.7
Estonia	6.4	4.9	5.3	..	11.6	10.6	11.5	..	9.1	7.7	8.3	..
Finland	9.2	8.6	9.0	8.8	17.8	16.8	17.7	17.7	13.7	12.8	13.5	13.4
France	7.3	6.8	6.8	..	11.0	11.1	11.5	..	9.3	9.0	9.2	..
Germany	7.9	8.9	8.4	..	13.4	14.1	14.4	..	11.0	11.7	11.6	..
Greece	38.9	30.9	31.0	31.7	43.7	37.8	38.6	39.5	42.0	35.1	35.5	36.3
Hungary	10.5	8.6	8.8	8.5	19.1	15.5	15.4	15.2	15.2	12.3	12.3	12.1
Iceland	11.0	7.3	8.4	..	24.0	17.0	16.4	..	18.0	12.6	12.6	..
Ireland	8.7	7.6	7.8	7.5	25.8	24.9	25.8	25.2	18.8	17.3	17.4	16.9
Israel	9.3	8.0	8.0	8.3	18.3	16.7	17.0	16.5	14.2	12.7	12.8	12.6
Italy	22.0	19.3	18.5	18.2	32.3	30.1	30.3	29.6	28.5	25.7	25.5	25.0
Japan	18.3	12.4	11.4	10.9	15.5	13.4	12.9	12.6	16.6	13.0	12.3	11.9
Korea	38.4	30.4	27.1	26.4	35.7	31.9	30.0	29.6	36.8	31.3	28.8	28.2
Luxembourg	6.9	4.7	..	..	7.7	6.7	..	..	7.4	5.8	5.8	5.7
Mexico	35.2	34.7	35.5	34.8	36.4	33.5	34.2	33.1	36.0	33.9	34.7	33.7
Netherlands	9.4	10.1	11.5	..	12.6	15.8	18.0	..	11.2	13.2	15.0	..
New Zealand	14.5	12.5	11.8	12.4	25.6	21.2	19.8	20.1	20.6	17.1	16.1	16.5
Norway	4.8	4.5	4.4	4.1	9.8	10.9	10.8	9.7	7.4	7.8	7.7	7.0
Poland	24.8	20.4	19.9	..	29.5	25.0	25.1	..	27.4	22.9	22.8	..
Portugal	24.4	22.4	20.1	17.0	27.4	25.6	25.3	25.0	26.0	24.1	22.9	21.3
Slovak Republic	4.6	7.8	9.4	9.7	10.8	18.4	21.3	20.8	8.0	13.8	16.0	15.9
Slovenia	13.0	11.3	14.0	13.4	18.6	16.5	20.0	19.7	16.1	14.1	17.3	16.8
Spain	16.6	13.3	12.4	12.3	22.2	20.9	20.5	20.1	20.2	17.7	16.9	16.6
Sweden	5.7	5.9	6.4	6.0	14.5	14.5	15.0	14.5	10.3	10.4	10.9	10.5
Switzerland	12.3	10.4	10.1	10.9	13.9	11.6	11.1	10.5	13.2	11.1	10.6	10.7
Turkey	64.7	46.8	49.3	48.4	46.5	36.1	35.1	34.2	51.4	39.0	39.1	38.3
United Kingdom	8.3	8.2	8.9	..	16.7	17.8	18.2	..	12.8	13.4	13.9	..
United States	6.1	5.6	5.6	..	8.6	8.3	8.3	..	7.4	7.0	7.0	..
EU 27	14.8	12.5	12.6	12.4	20.9	19.8	20.3	20.2	18.3	16.5	16.8	16.6
OECD	14.8	12.7	..	..	19.1	17.6	..	..	17.7	15.9	16.1	..
Brazil	..	31.6	..	..	..	35.3	..	..	..	33.7	..	..
China	..	..	..	..	..	..	..	..	..	..	..	..
India	..	..	..	..	..	..	..	..	..	..	..	..
Indonesia	..	..	..	..	..	..	..	..	..	..	..	..
Russian Federation	..	..	..	..	..	..	..	..	..	..	..	..
South Africa	..	..	..	..	..	..	..	..	..	..	..	..

StatLink http://dx.doi.org/10.1787/888932708560

Self-employment rates: total

As a percentage of total employment

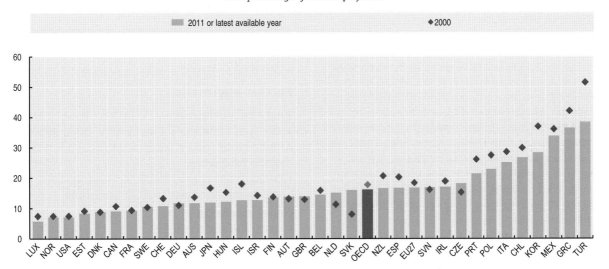

2011 or latest available year ◆ 2000

StatLink http://dx.doi.org/10.1787/888932708579

EMPLOYMENT BY REGION

Inequalities in economic performance across regions partly reflect the extent to which each region is able to utilise its available labour resources, and especially to increase job opportunities for under-represented groups.

Definition

Employed persons are all persons who during the reference week of the survey worked at least one hour for pay or profit, or were temporarily absent from such work. The employment rate is the number of employed persons as a percentage of the working age (15-64) population.

The employment rate for women is calculated as the ratio between women in employment and women of the working age (15-64) in the population.

Comparability

As for other regional statistics, comparability is affected by differences in the meaning of the word "region". This results in significant differences in terms of geographic area and population both within and among countries. To address this issue, the OECD has classified regions within each country based on two levels: territorial level 2 (TL2, large regions) and territorial level 3 (TL3, small regions). Labour market data for Canada refers to a different regional grouping, labelled non-official grids (NOG) comparable to TL3. For Brazil, China, India, the Russian Federation and South Africa only large regions have been defined so far.

Data on employment growth refer to period 1999-2010 for all countries except for Chile (1999-2009), Mexico (2000-10), Slovenia (2001-10), South Africa (1999-2009) and Switzerland (2001-10). Denmark and Turkey are excluded for lack of data on comparable years. Data on employment increase contributed by the top 10% of TL2 regions include only countries with average positive growth of employment over 1999-2010. Hungary and Japan are excluded.

Data on regional employment growth and female employment refer to large (TL2) regions for all countries.

Overview

Differences in employment opportunities within countries are often larger than across countries.

During 1999-2010 differences in regional employment growth rates across regions were above three percentage points in Mexico, the Russian Federation, Chile, South Africa and the United States.

A small number of regions drive employment creation at the national level. On average, 39% of overall employment creation in OECD countries between 1999 and 2010 was accounted for by just 10% of regions. The regional contribution to national employment creation was particularly concentrated in certain countries. In South Africa, the United States, the Russian Federation, Chile and Korea, more than half of employment growth was spurred by 10% of regions.

During the recent economic crisis, the regional concentration of employment creation has increased in 17 of the 31 countries, resulting in higher differences in employment among regions.

In around 26% of OECD regions, less than one out of two women was employed in 2010. Regional differences in employment for women were the largest in Turkey, Italy, Israel, Spain, the United States and Portugal.

Sources

- OECD (2011), OECD *Regions at a Glance*, OECD Publishing.

Further information

Analytical publications

- OECD (2011), *Regional Outlook 2011*, OECD Publishing.
- OECD (2009), *How Regions Grow: Trends and Analysis*, OECD Publishing.
- OECD (2009), *Regions Matter: Economic Recovery, Innovation and Sustainable Growth*, OECD Publishing.

Online databases

- *OECD Regional Database*.

Websites

- Regional Development, *www.oecd.org/gov/ regionaldevelopment*.
- Regional Statistics and Indicators, *www.oecd.org/gov/ regional/statisticsindicators*.

Differences in annual employment growth across regions
Percentage, 1999-2010 or latest available period

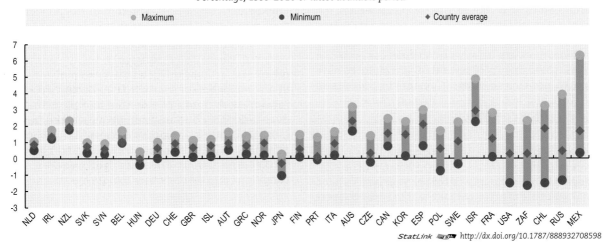

StatLink http://dx.doi.org/10.1787/888932708598

Share of national employment growth due to the 10% of most dynamic regions
Percentage

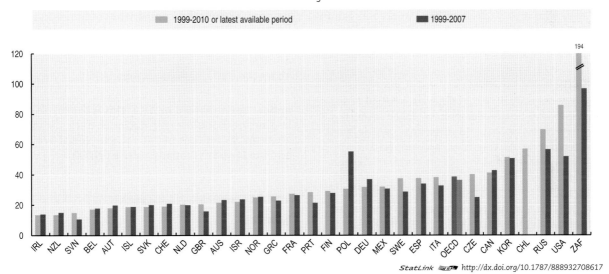

StatLink http://dx.doi.org/10.1787/888932708617

Regional differences in the employment rate of women
Percentage, 2010 or latest available year

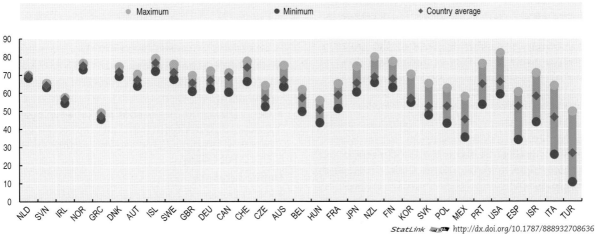

StatLink http://dx.doi.org/10.1787/888932708636

HOURS WORKED

Lower hours worked is one of the forms in which the benefits of productivity growth have been shared by people. Hours worked is also one of the ways that labour markets adjust most intensively during business cycles. In recent years, governments of several OECD countries have also pursued policies to make it easier for parents to reconcile work and family life, and some of these policies have tended to reduce working time.

Definition

The average number of hours worked per year is calculated as the total numbers of hours actually worked over the year divided by the average number of people in employment. The data cover employees and self-employed workers; they include both full-time and part-time employment.

Employment is generally measured through household labour force surveys. In accordance with the ILO Guidelines, employed persons are defined as those aged 15 years or over who report that they have worked in gainful employment for at least one hour in the previous week or were temporarily absent from work.

Estimates of the hours actually worked are based on national labour force surveys in many countries, while others use establishment surveys, administrative records or a combination of sources. Actual hours worked include regular work hours of full-time and part-time workers, over-time (paid and unpaid), hours worked in additional jobs, and time not worked because of public holidays, annual paid leave, illness, maternity and parental leave, strikes and labour disputes, bad weather, economic conditions and several other minor reasons.

Comparability

Data are based on a range of sources of varying reliability. Annual working hours reported for 30 out of 34 countries are provided by national statistical offices and are estimated using the best available sources. These national data are intended for comparisons of trends in productivity and labour inputs and are not fully suitable for inter-country comparisons of the level of hours worked because of differences in their sources and other uncertainties about their international comparability.

There has been a major revision to the Mexican data on annual hours worked in 2012. This is the result of a change in the methodology by national data providers – the Mexican Secretariat of Labour and Social Welfare (STPS) and the Mexican Statistics Office (INEGI).

Overview

In the large majority of OECD countries, average hours worked per employed person have fallen over the period from 2000 to 2011. However, this decline was rather small in most countries, as compared to the decline in earlier decades. Part of the observed decline in average hours worked between these two years reflect business cycle effects.

For the OECD as a whole, the average hours worked per employed person fell from 1 843 annual hours in 2000 to 1 775 in 2011; this is equivalent to a reduction of one and a half hours over a 40-hour work-week. Annual working hours fell in a majority of countries, increasing only in Belgium and Sweden, albeit only slightly. Reductions in annual hours worked over this period were most marked in Australia, Austria, Chile, the Czech Republic, Greece, Iceland, Ireland, Italy, Korea, Japan and Luxembourg, where they declined by over 80 hours or more or 5% or more, with Chile and Korea showing the largest decrease of 216 and 319 hours respectively. A decline of more than 50% in hours worked since the onset of the crisis occurred in Austria, Belgium, Denmark, Estonia, Ireland, Japan, Poland, Portugal, Turkey and the United Kingdom.

Although one should exercise caution when comparing levels across countries, actual hours worked are significantly above the OECD average, by 200 or more hours, in Mexico, Korea, Chile, Greece and Hungary and significantly below the OECD average, by 200 or less hours, in the Netherlands, Germany, Norway, France, Denmark and Ireland.

Sources

- OECD (2012), *OECD Employment Outlook*, OECD Publishing.

Further information

Analytical publications

- Durand, M., J. Martin and A. Saint-Martin (2004), "The 35 Hour Week: Portrait of a French Exception", *OECD Observer*, No. 244, September, OECD Publishing.
- Evans, J.M., D. Lippoldt and P. Marianna (2001), "*Trends in Working Hours in OECD Countries*",*OECD Labour Market and Social Policy Occasional Papers*, No. 45.

Methodological publications

- OECD (2009), *Productivity Measurement and Analysis*, OECD Publishing.
- OECD (2004), "Recent Labour Market Developments and Prospects: Clocking In (and Out): Several Facets of Working Time", *OECD Employment Outlook 2004*, OECD Publishing.

Online database

- *OECD Employment and Labour Market Statistics*.

Websites

- OECD Labour Statistics, *www.oecd.org/statistics/labour*.

Average hours actually worked

Hours per year per person in employment

	1999	2000	2001	2002	2003	2004	2005	2006	2007	2008	2009	2010	2011
Australia	1 779	1 776	1 737	1 731	1 735	1 733	1 725	1 715	1 711	1 716	1 685	1 687	1 693
Austria	1 733	1 727	1 714	1 710	1 705	1 714	1 696	1 673	1 667	1 648	1 608	1 599	1 600
Belgium	1 581	1 545	1 577	1 580	1 575	1 549	1 565	1 566	1 560	1 568	1 550	1 551	1 577
Canada	1 778	1 775	1 768	1 747	1 736	1 754	1 739	1 738	1 738	1 728	1 700	1 702	1 702
Chile	2 277	2 263	2 242	2 250	2 235	2 232	2 157	2 165	2 128	2 095	2 074	2 068	2 047
Czech Republic	1 899	1 904	1 827	1 825	1 815	1 827	1 827	1 808	1 793	1 800	1 764	1 795	1 774
Denmark	1 569	1 581	1 587	1 579	1 577	1 579	1 579	1 586	1 570	1 570	1 559	1 560	1 522
Estonia	..	1 987	1 978	1 983	1 985	1 996	2 010	2 001	1 999	1 969	1 831	1 879	1 924
Finland	1 764	1 751	1 733	1 726	1 719	1 723	1 716	1 709	1 706	1 688	1 672	1 684	1 684
France	1 560	1 523	1 514	1 476	1 473	1 501	1 495	1 473	1 485	1 492	1 472	1 478	1 476
Germany	1 491	1 471	1 453	1 441	1 436	1 436	1 431	1 424	1 422	1 422	1 383	1 408	1 413
Greece	2 117	2 130	2 131	2 118	2 112	2 092	2 095	2 066	2 038	2 051	1 995	2 017	2 032
Hungary	2 042	2 033	1 997	2 009	1 981	1 992	1 992	1 988	1 983	1 988	1 969	1 962	1 980
Iceland	1 873	1 885	1 847	1 812	1 811	1 827	1 818	1 807	1 783	1 787	1 706	1 691	1 732
Ireland	1 725	1 719	1 713	1 698	1 671	1 668	1 654	1 645	1 634	1 601	1 541	1 545	1 543
Israel	..	..	..	..	..	..	1 905	1 989	1 887	1 921	1 898	1 889	1 890
Italy	1 876	1 861	1 843	1 831	1 826	1 826	1 819	1 815	1 816	1 803	1 771	1 775	1 774
Japan	1 810	1 821	1 809	1 798	1 799	1 787	1 775	1 784	1 785	1 771	1 714	1 733	1 728
Korea	2 495	2 512	2 499	2 464	2 424	2 392	2 351	2 346	2 306	2 246	2 232	2 193	..
Luxembourg	1 690	1 683	1 667	1 656	1 651	1 607	1 590	1 601	1 537	1 577	1 622	1 636	1 601
Mexico	2 306	2 311	2 285	2 271	2 277	2 271	2 281	2 281	2 262	2 260	2 253	2 242	2 250
Netherlands	1 437	1 435	1 424	1 408	1 401	1 399	1 393	1 392	1 388	1 392	1 384	1 381	1 379
New Zealand	1 837	1 828	1 817	1 817	1 813	1 828	1 811	1 788	1 766	1 750	1 738	1 758	1 762
Norway	1 473	1 455	1 429	1 414	1 399	1 417	1 420	1 414	1 419	1 423	1 407	1 414	1 426
Poland	..	1 988	1 974	1 979	1 984	1 983	1 994	1 985	1 976	1 969	1 948	1 939	1 937
Portugal	1 838	1 791	1 795	1 793	1 768	1 790	1 778	1 784	1 754	1 772	1 746	1 742	1 711
Slovak Republic	1 816	1 816	1 801	1 754	1 698	1 742	1 769	1 774	1 791	1 793	1 780	1 807	1 793
Slovenia	..	1 710	1 696	1 720	1 724	1 737	1 697	1 667	1 655	1 670	1 670	1 676	1 662
Spain	1 732	1 731	1 736	1 734	1 719	1 704	1 686	1 673	1 658	1 663	1 669	1 674	1 690
Sweden	1 665	1 642	1 618	1 595	1 582	1 605	1 605	1 599	1 618	1 617	1 602	1 643	1 644
Switzerland	1 694	1 688	1 650	1 630	1 643	1 673	1 654	1 643	1 633	1 623	1 617	1 632	..
Turkey	1 925	1 937	1 942	1 943	1 943	1 918	1 936	1 944	1 911	1 900	1 881	1 877	1 877
United Kingdom	1 716	1 700	1 705	1 684	1 674	1 674	1 673	1 669	1 677	1 659	1 651	1 652	1 625
United States	1 847	1 836	1 814	1 810	1 800	1 802	1 799	1 800	1 798	1 792	1 767	1 778	1 787
EU 27	..	..	..	..	..	..	..	..	..	..	..	..	..
OECD	1 850	1 844	1 829	1 819	1 812	1 812	1 807	1 805	1 799	1 792	1 766	1 775	1 776
Brazil	..	..	..	..	..	..	..	..	..	..	..	..	..
China	..	..	..	..	..	..	..	..	..	..	..	..	..
India	..	..	..	..	..	..	..	..	..	..	..	..	..
Indonesia	..	..	..	..	..	..	..	..	..	..	..	..	..
Russian Federation	1 964	1 982	1 980	1 982	1 994	1 994	1 990	1 999	2 000	1 997	1 973	1 976	1 981
South Africa	..	..	..	..	..	..	..	..	..	..	..	..	..

StatLink http://dx.doi.org/10.1787/888932708655

Average hours actually worked

Hours per year per person in employment

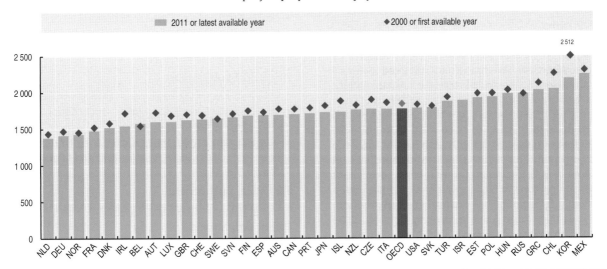

StatLink http://dx.doi.org/10.1787/888932708674

UNEMPLOYMENT RATES

The unemployment rate is one measure of the extent of labour market slack, as well as being an important indicator of economic and social well-being. Breakdowns of unemployment by gender show how women are faring compared to men.

Definition

Unemployed persons are defined as those who report that they are without work, that they are available for work and that they have taken active steps to find work in the last four weeks. The ILO Guidelines specify what actions count as active steps to find work; these include answering vacancy notices, visiting factories, construction sites and other places of work, and placing advertisements in the press as well as registering with labour offices.

The unemployment rate is defined as the number of unemployed persons as a percentage of the labour force, where the latter consists of the unemployed plus those in paid or self-employment.

Overview

When looking at total unemployment rates averaged over the three years ending 2011, countries can be divided into three groups: a low unemployment group with rates below 5% (Austria, Japan, Korea, Luxembourg, Norway, the Netherlands and Switzerland); a middle group with unemployment rates between 5% and 10%; and a high unemployment group with unemployment rates of 10% and above (Estonia, Greece, Hungary, Ireland, Portugal, Spain, the Slovak Republic and Turkey).

In most OECD countries, unemployment rates grew over the last three years, with marked increases in Estonia, Greece, Ireland and Spain.

The breakdown of unemployment by gender shows that, in line with the overall rate, the unemployment rates for both men and women increased sharply from 2007 to 2010. The unemployment rate for men, which had been lower than the rate for women, rose considerably faster and by 2009 was higher than the rate for women. This is first explained by the fact that job losses over the stage of the crisis were particularly severe in sectors which traditionally have been occupied by men – namely construction, manufacturing, mining and quarrying. Between 2009 and 2010, the rise in the overall OECD unemployment rates decelerated faster for men so that the men to women unemployment ratio began to decrease. In 2011, the OECD rate fell for the first time since the crisis began, and the rate for men had dropped back to a lower level than the rate for women.

The unemployment rates shown here differ from rates derived from registered unemployed at labour offices that are often published in individual countries. Data on registered unemployment have limited international comparability, as the rules for registering at labour offices vary from country to country.

When unemployment is high, some persons become discouraged and stop looking for work; they are then excluded from the labour force. This implies that the unemployment rate may fall, or stop rising, even though there has been no underlying improvement in the labour market.

Comparability

All OECD countries use the ILO Guidelines for measuring unemployment in their labour force surveys. The operational definitions used in national labour force surveys may, however, vary slightly across countries. Unemployment levels are also likely to be affected by changes in the survey design and the survey conduct. Despite these limits, the unemployment rates shown here are of good international comparability and fairly consistent over time.

Sources
- OECD (2012), *Main Economic Indicators*, OECD Publishing.
- For non-member countries: National sources.

Further information

Analytical publications
- OECD (2012), *OECD Employment Outlook*, OECD Publishing.
- OECD (2011), *Society at a Glance: OECD Social Indicators*, OECD Publishing.
- Venn, D. (2012), "Eligibility Criteria for Unemployment Benefits", *OECD Social, Employment and Migration Working Papers*, No. 131.

Statistical publications
- OECD (2011), *Labour Force Statistics*, OECD Publishing.

Online databases
- *OECD Employment and Labour Market Statistics.*

Websites
- OECD Employment Data, *www.oecd.org/els/employment/data.*
- OECD Employment Policies, *www.oecd.org/els/employment.*
- OECD Labour Statistics, *www.oecd.org/statistics/labour.*

Unemployment rates

As a percentage of labour force

	Women				Men				Total			
	2000	2008	2010	2011	2000	2008	2010	2011	2000	2008	2010	2011
Australia	6.1	4.6	5.4	5.3	6.5	4.0	5.1	4.9	6.3	4.2	5.2	5.1
Austria	4.3	4.1	4.2	4.3	3.1	3.6	4.6	4.0	3.6	3.8	4.4	4.1
Belgium	8.5	7.6	8.5	7.2	5.6	6.5	8.1	7.1	6.9	7.0	8.3	7.2
Canada	6.7	5.7	7.2	7.0	7.0	6.6	8.7	7.8	6.8	6.1	8.0	7.5
Chile	10.3	9.5	9.7	8.7	9.3	6.8	7.2	6.1	9.7	7.8	8.2	7.1
Czech Republic	10.3	5.6	8.4	7.9	7.3	3.5	6.4	5.8	8.7	4.4	7.3	6.7
Denmark	4.8	3.7	6.5	7.5	3.9	3.2	8.4	7.7	4.3	3.4	7.5	7.6
Estonia	12.7	5.2	14.3	11.8	14.7	5.8	19.5	13.1	13.7	5.5	16.9	12.5
Finland	10.6	6.7	7.6	7.1	9.1	6.1	9.1	8.4	9.8	6.4	8.4	7.8
France	10.8	8.4	10.2	10.3	7.5	7.3	9.4	9.2	9.0	7.8	9.8	9.7
Germany	8.4	7.7	6.6	5.7	7.8	7.4	7.5	6.2	8.0	7.5	7.1	5.9
Greece	17.1	11.4	16.2	21.4	7.4	5.1	9.9	15.0	11.2	7.7	12.6	17.7
Hungary	5.6	8.0	10.7	10.9	7.0	7.7	11.6	11.0	6.4	7.8	11.2	10.9
Iceland	..	2.6	6.7	6.2	..	3.3	8.3	7.9	..	3.0	7.6	7.1
Ireland	4.1	4.9	9.7	10.6	4.3	7.5	16.9	17.5	4.2	6.3	13.7	14.4
Israel	9.2	6.5	6.5	5.6	8.4	5.7	6.8	5.6	8.8	6.1	6.6	5.6
Italy	13.6	8.5	9.7	9.6	7.7	5.5	7.6	7.5	10.1	6.7	8.4	8.4
Japan	4.5	3.9	4.6	4.2	4.9	4.1	5.4	4.9	4.7	4.0	5.1	4.6
Korea	3.7	2.6	3.4	3.1	5.0	3.6	4.0	3.6	4.4	3.2	3.7	3.4
Luxembourg	2.9	5.9	5.5	6.2	1.8	4.1	3.8	3.9	2.2	4.9	4.6	4.9
Mexico	..	4.1	5.3	5.3	..	3.9	5.4	5.2	2.5	4.0	5.4	5.2
Netherlands	3.9	3.4	4.5	4.4	2.4	2.8	4.4	4.5	3.1	3.1	4.5	4.5
New Zealand	6.0	4.2	6.9	6.7	6.3	4.1	6.2	6.4	6.2	4.2	6.5	6.5
Norway	3.1	2.4	3.0	3.1	3.4	2.7	4.1	3.5	3.2	2.6	3.6	3.3
Poland	18.2	8.0	10.0	10.5	14.4	6.5	9.3	9.0	16.1	7.1	9.7	9.7
Portugal	5.0	9.0	12.1	13.2	3.2	6.6	10.0	12.7	4.0	7.7	11.0	12.9
Slovak Republic	18.7	11.0	14.7	13.7	19.1	8.4	14.3	13.6	18.9	9.6	14.5	13.6
Slovenia	7.0	4.8	7.1	8.2	6.5	4.0	7.4	8.2	6.7	4.4	7.3	8.2
Spain	17.0	13.0	20.5	22.2	8.2	10.1	19.7	21.2	11.7	11.3	20.1	21.6
Sweden	5.3	6.5	8.3	7.5	5.9	5.9	8.5	7.5	5.6	6.2	8.4	7.5
Switzerland	..	..	5.0	4.5	..	..	4.2	3.7	..	..	4.5	4.1
Turkey	..	10.0	11.4	10.1	..	9.6	10.4	8.3	..	9.7	10.7	8.8
United Kingdom	4.8	5.1	6.8	7.3	5.9	6.1	8.6	8.7	5.4	5.7	7.8	8.0
United States	4.1	5.4	8.6	8.5	3.9	6.1	10.5	9.4	4.0	5.8	9.6	9.0
EU 27	10.1	7.6	9.6	9.8	7.8	6.7	9.7	9.6	8.8	7.1	9.7	9.7
OECD	..	6.1	8.1	8.0	..	5.9	8.5	7.9	6.1	6.0	8.3	8.0
Brazil	..	..	..	..	..	..	..	..	12.7	7.9	6.8	6.0
China	..	..	..	..	..	..	..	..	..	..	..	..
India	..	..	..	..	..	..	..	..	..	..	..	..
Indonesia	..	9.5	..	..	..	7.7	..	..	6.1	8.4	7.3	6.7
Russian Federation	10.4	6.1	6.9	6.2	10.6	6.6	8.0	7.0	10.5	6.4	7.5	6.6
South Africa	26.5	26.3	27.5	27.9	20.4	20.0	22.8	22.4	23.3	22.9	24.9	24.9

StatLink http://dx.doi.org/10.1787/888932708693

Unemployment rates: total

As a percentage of labour force

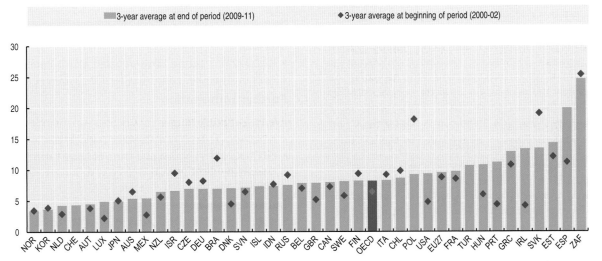

StatLink http://dx.doi.org/10.1787/888932708712

LONG-TERM UNEMPLOYMENT

Long-term unemployment is of particular concern to the people affected and to policy makers. Quite apart from the mental and material stress caused to the unemployed and their families, high rates of long-term unemployment indicate that labour markets are operating inefficiently.

Rates of long-term unemployment are generally lower in countries that have enjoyed high GDP growth rates in recent years. Lower rates of long-term unemployment may also occur at the onset of an economic downturn due to rising inflow of newly unemployed persons, as witnessed during the first years of the current jobs crisis. Subsequently, long-term unemployment may gradually begin to unfold in case of prolonged crisis as is currently the case in a number of OECD countries.

Definition

Long-term unemployment is defined as referring to people who have been unemployed for 12 months or more. The ratios calculated here show the proportion of these long-term unemployed among all unemployed, hereafter called long-term unemployment rates. Lower duration limits (*e.g.* six months or more) are sometimes considered in national statistics on the subject.

Overview

In 2011, about one-third of the unemployed were long-term unemployment in the OECD area with more than half of the countries recording around or above OECD average long-term unemployment rates. The rates varied from 10% or less in Korea, Mexico and New Zealand, to 50% or more in Estonia, Ireland, Italy and the Slovak Republic. In Germany, the share of long-term unemployed remains stubbornly high at 48% in 2011 despite a rising trend in employment rates since 2005.

Over the period 2000-11, long-term unemployment rates increased by close to 3 percentage points for the OECD as a whole. Country patterns differ depending on how deeply national labour markets were affected by the current crisis. Since 2000, sharp rises, of 5 percentage points or more, were recorded in 14 countries, exceeding 10 percentage points in Estonia, Ireland, Japan and Iceland, with a dramatic increase of 23 percentage points in the United States from just 6% in 2000. Falls of over 5 per cent occurred in just under one third of countries, with Slovenia and New Zealand recording the steepest fall of over 10 percentage points.

In the Russian Federation and South Africa, long-term unemployment declined markedly since 2000; by more than 9 percentage points. In South Africa however, more than 58% of unemployed people were still long-term unemployed in 2011.

Unemployment is defined in all OECD countries in accordance with the ILO Guidelines. Unemployment is usually measured by national labour force surveys and refer to persons who report that they have worked in gainful employment for less than one hour in the previous week, who are available for work and who have taken actions to seek employment in the previous four weeks. The ILO Guidelines specify the kinds of actions that count as seeking work.

Comparability

All OECD countries use the ILO Guidelines for measuring unemployment. Operational definitions used in national labour force surveys may vary slightly across countries. Unemployment levels may also be affected by changes in the survey design and the survey conduct. Despite these caveats the long-term unemployment rates shown here are fairly consistent over time.

In comparing rates of long-term unemployment, it is important to bear in mind differences in institutional arrangements between countries. Rates of long-term unemployment will generally be higher in countries where unemployment benefits are relatively generous and are available for long periods of unemployment. In countries where benefits are low and of limited duration, unemployed persons will more quickly lower their wage expectations or consider taking jobs that are in other ways less attractive than those which they formerly held.

Sources
- OECD (2011), *Labour Force Statistics*, OECD Publishing.
- For non-member countries: National sources.

Further information

Analytical publications
- OECD (2012), *OECD Employment Outlook*, OECD Publishing.
- OECD (2002), "The Ins and Outs of Long-term Unemployment", *OECD Employment Outlook 2002*, OECD Publishing.

Online databases
- *OECD Employment and Labour Market Statistics*.

Websites
- OECD Employment Outlook (supplementary material), *www.oecd.org/els/employmentoutlook*.
- OECD Employment Policies, *www.oecd.org/els/employment*.
- OECD Labour Statistics, *www.oecd.org/statistics/labour*.

Long-term unemployment

Persons unemployed for 12 months or more as a percentage of total unemployed

	1999	2000	2001	2002	2003	2004	2005	2006	2007	2008	2009	2010	2011
Australia	31.3	28.3	23.9	22.4	21.5	20.6	18.3	18.1	15.4	14.9	14.7	18.5	18.9
Austria	29.2	25.8	23.3	19.2	24.5	27.6	25.3	27.3	26.8	24.2	21.3	25.2	25.9
Belgium	60.5	56.3	51.7	48.8	45.4	49.0	51.7	51.2	50.4	47.6	44.2	48.8	48.3
Canada	11.7	11.3	9.5	9.6	10.0	9.5	9.6	8.7	7.4	7.1	7.8	12.0	13.5
Chile	..	..	..	..	..	..	..	..	..	..	..	..	..
Czech Republic	37.1	48.8	52.7	50.7	49.9	51.8	53.6	55.2	53.4	50.2	31.2	43.3	41.6
Denmark	20.5	20.0	22.2	19.1	20.4	21.5	23.4	20.8	16.1	13.5	9.5	20.2	24.4
Estonia	48.9	46.3	48.3	52.9	45.9	52.2	53.4	48.2	49.5	30.9	27.4	45.4	56.8
Finland	29.6	29.0	26.2	24.4	24.7	23.4	24.9	24.8	23.0	18.2	16.6	23.6	22.6
France	38.7	39.6	36.8	32.7	39.2	40.6	41.0	41.9	40.2	37.4	35.2	40.2	41.4
Germany	51.7	51.5	50.4	47.9	50.0	51.8	53.0	56.4	56.6	52.5	45.5	47.4	48.0
Greece	55.3	56.4	52.8	51.3	54.9	53.1	52.1	54.3	50.0	47.5	40.8	45.0	49.6
Hungary	49.4	48.9	46.5	44.8	42.2	45.1	46.1	46.1	47.5	47.6	42.6	50.6	49.1
Iceland	11.7	11.8	12.5	11.1	8.1	11.2	13.3	7.3	8.0	4.1	6.9	21.3	27.8
Ireland	55.3	..	33.1	30.1	32.8	34.9	33.4	31.6	29.5	27.1	29.2	49.3	59.4
Israel	11.3	12.0	11.8	13.5	18.0	24.2	25.3	27.3	24.9	22.7	20.3	22.4	20.2
Italy	61.4	61.3	63.4	59.6	58.1	49.2	49.9	49.6	47.3	45.7	44.4	48.5	51.9
Japan	22.4	25.5	26.6	30.8	33.5	33.7	33.3	33.0	32.0	33.3	28.5	37.6	39.4
Korea	3.8	2.3	2.3	2.5	0.6	1.1	0.8	1.1	0.6	2.7	0.5	0.3	0.4
Luxembourg	32.3	22.4	28.4	27.4	24.7	21.0	26.4	29.5	28.7	32.4	23.1	29.3	28.8
Mexico	1.5	1.2	1.0	0.9	0.9	1.1	2.3	2.5	2.7	1.7	1.9	2.4	2.0
Netherlands	43.5	..	..	26.5	27.8	34.2	40.2	43.0	39.4	34.4	24.8	27.6	33.6
New Zealand	21.1	19.8	17.2	14.8	13.6	11.7	9.7	7.8	6.1	4.4	6.3	9.0	9.0
Norway	7.1	5.3	5.5	6.4	6.4	9.2	9.5	14.5	8.8	6.0	7.7	9.5	11.6
Poland	34.8	37.9	43.1	48.4	49.7	47.9	52.2	50.4	45.9	29.0	25.2	25.5	31.6
Portugal	41.2	42.9	38.1	34.6	35.0	44.3	48.2	50.2	47.1	47.4	44.1	52.3	48.2
Slovak Republic	47.7	54.6	53.7	59.8	61.2	60.6	68.1	73.1	70.8	66.0	50.9	59.3	63.9
Slovenia	..	..	..	55.6	52.8	51.5	47.3	49.3	45.7	42.2	30.1	43.3	44.2
Spain	46.3	42.4	36.9	33.7	33.6	32.0	24.5	21.7	20.4	17.9	23.7	36.6	41.6
Sweden	30.1	26.4	22.3	20.9	17.8	18.9	..	..	13.0	12.4	12.8	16.6	17.2
Switzerland	39.6	29.0	29.9	21.8	26.1	33.5	39.0	39.1	40.8	34.3	30.1	33.1	38.8
Turkey	28.2	21.1	21.3	29.4	24.4	39.2	39.4	35.7	30.3	26.9	25.3	28.6	26.5
United Kingdom	29.6	28.0	27.8	21.7	21.5	20.6	21.0	22.3	23.7	24.1	24.5	32.6	33.4
United States	6.8	6.0	6.1	8.5	11.8	12.7	11.8	10.0	10.0	10.6	16.3	29.0	31.1
EU 27	..	..	..	..	..	..	..	..	..	..	..	..	..
OECD	31.2	30.8	29.1	29.0	30.1	31.3	32.0	31.4	28.6	25.0	23.7	31.6	33.6
Brazil	..	..	..	..	..	..	..	..	..	..	..	..	..
China	..	..	..	..	..	..	..	..	..	..	..	..	..
India	..	..	..	..	..	..	..	..	..	..	..	..	..
Indonesia	..	..	..	..	..	..	..	..	..	..	..	..	..
Russian Federation	47.0	46.2	39.2	38.9	37.3	38.7	38.5	41.7	40.6	35.2	28.7	29.9	32.8
South Africa	..	..	68.4	68.5	68.4	65.1	63.7	59.5	57.7	49.5	49.3	56.1	58.8

StatLink http://dx.doi.org/10.1787/888932708750

Long-term unemployment

Persons unemployed for 12 months or more as a percentage of total unemployed

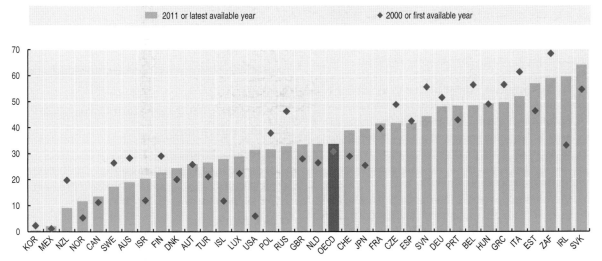

▪ 2011 or latest available year   ◆ 2000 or first available year

StatLink http://dx.doi.org/10.1787/888932708769

UNEMPLOYMENT BY REGION

The unemployment rate is an important indicator of economic and social well-being. Breakdowns by region show that large international differences hide even larger differences among regions within each country.

Definition

Unemployed persons are defined as those who are without work, who are available for work and have taken active steps to find work in the last four weeks. The unemployment rate is defined as the ratio between unemployed persons and the labour force, where the latter is composed of unemployed and employed persons.

The long-term unemployment rate is defined as the ratio of those unemployed for 12 months or more out of the total labour force. The youth unemployment rate is defined as the ratio between the unemployed persons aged between 15 and 24 and the labour force in the same age class.

The Gini index is a measure of inequality among all regions of a given country. The index takes on values between 0 and 1, with zero interpreted as no disparity. It assigns equal weight to each region regardless of its size; therefore differences in the values of the index among countries may be partially due to differences in the average size of regions.

Overview

Regional disparities in unemployment were already high before the economic crisis in countries such as Canada, Germany, Italy, Spain and the Slovak Republic. Overall the economic downturn has aggravated problems in the most fragile regions. The Gini index gives a measure of differences in unemployment rates among all regions in a country. According to this measure Belgium, Italy, the Slovak Republic and Iceland displayed the highest regional inequalities among OECD countries. Large regional differences were also found in China and the Russian Federation.

Youth unemployment, which is of particular concern in Italy, Spain, Belgium, France, the Slovak Republic, Greece and Ireland also displays large regional differences. In these countries, some regions record youth unemployment rates over 30%.

Among the unemployed, the long-term unemployed are of particular concern to policy makers both for their impact on social cohesion and because those individuals become increasingly unattractive to employers. The long-term unemployment rate shows large regional variations not only in dual economies such as Italy or Germany, but also in Spain, the Slovak Republic, Belgium, the Czech Republic and France.

While in the study of income inequality individuals are the obvious unit of analysis, there is no such straightforward parallel in regional economics. The size of regions varies significantly both within and between countries so that the degree of geographic concentration and territorial disparity depends on the very definition of a region. Typically, as the size of a region increases, territorial differences tend to be averaged out and disparities to decrease.

Comparability

As for the other regional statistics, the comparability of unemployment rates is affected by differences in the meaning of the word "region". This results in significant differences in terms of geographic area and population both within and among countries. To address this issue, the OECD has classified regions within each country based on two levels: territorial level 2 (TL2, large regions) and territorial level 3 (TL3, small regions). Labour market data for Canada refers to a different regional grouping, labelled non-official grids (NOG), which is comparable to the small regions. For Brazil, China, India, the Russian Federation and South Africa only large regions have been defined so far.

Data on unemployment, youth and long-term unemployment refer to large (TL2) regions.

Data on unemployment refer to period 2000-10 for all countries except Australia (2000-07), China (2000-08), Chile (2000-09), Switzerland (2001-10) and South Africa (2000-09).

Data on youth unemployment rate refer to 2010 for all countries except Australia (2007), Mexico (2007) and the United States (2008).

Data on long-term unemployment rate refer to 2010 for all countries except Australia (2007) and New Zealand (2009).

Sources
- OECD (2011), *OECD Regions at a Glance*, OECD Publishing.

Further information

Analytical publications
- OECD (2011), *Regional Outlook 2011*, OECD Publishing.
- OECD (2009), *Regions Matter: Economic Recovery, Innovation and Sustainable Growth*, OECD Publishing.

Online databases
- *OECD Regional Database*.

Websites
- Regional Development, *www.oecd.org/gov/ regionaldevelopment*.
- Regional Statistics and Indicators, *www.oecd.org/gov/ regional/statisticsindicators*.

Gini index of regional unemployment rates

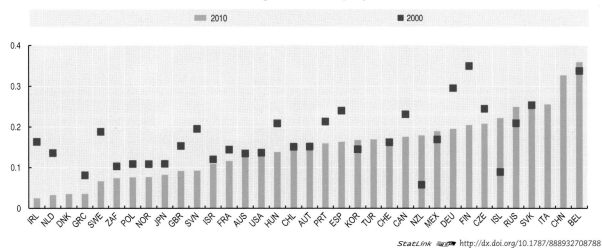

StatLink ᵐˢᵖ http://dx.doi.org/10.1787/888932708788

Regional variation of the youth unemployment rate

Percentage, 2010

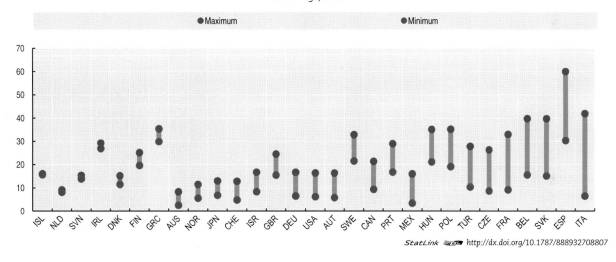

StatLink ᵐˢᵖ http://dx.doi.org/10.1787/888932708807

Regional variation in long-term unemployment rates

Percentage, 2010

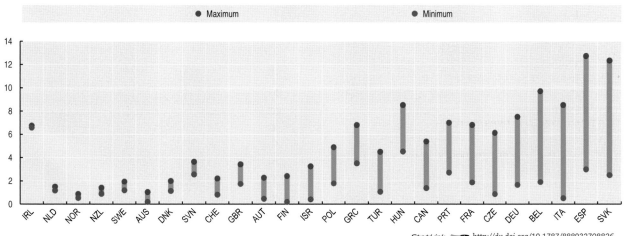

StatLink ᵐˢᵖ http://dx.doi.org/10.1787/888932708826

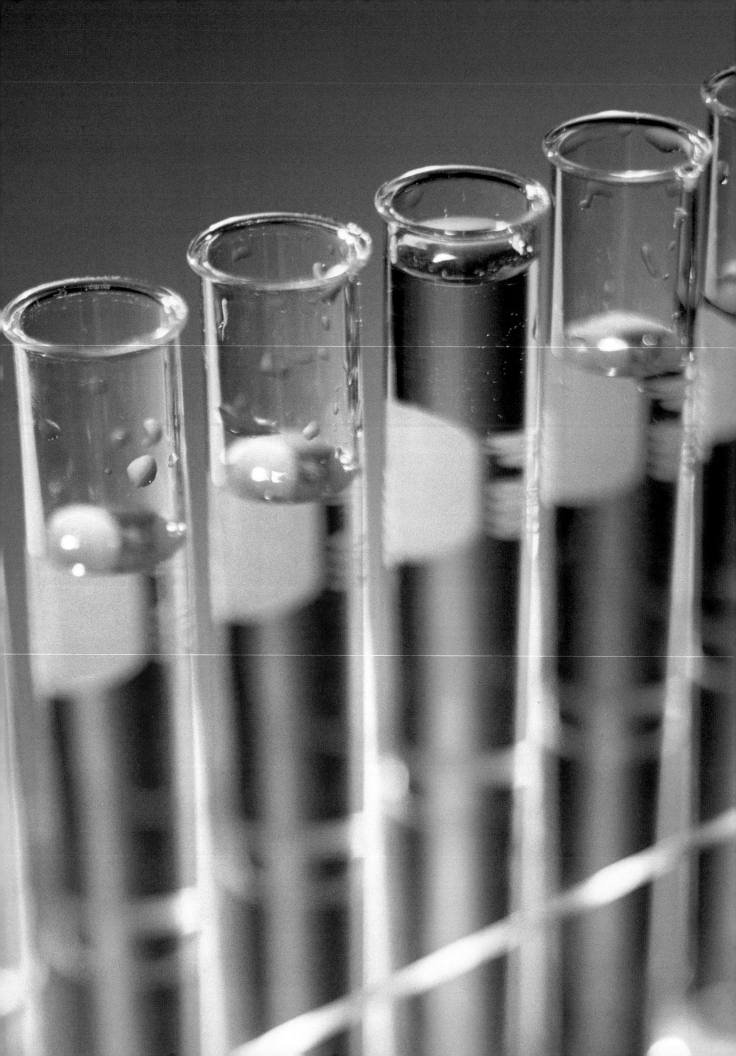

SCIENCE AND TECHNOLOGY

RESEARCH AND DEVELOPMENT

EXPENDITURE ON R&D

RESEARCHERS

PATENTS

BIOTECHNOLOGY

INFORMATION AND COMMUNICATIONS

SIZE OF THE ICT SECTOR

INVESTMENT IN ICT

EXPORTS OF ICT GOODS

COMPUTER, INTERNET AND TELECOMMUNICATION

EXPENDITURE ON R&D

Expenditure on research and development (R&D) is a key indicator of countries' innovative efforts.

Definition

Research and development (R&D) comprise creative work undertaken on a systematic basis in order to increase the stock of knowledge (including knowledge of man, culture and society) and the use of this knowledge to devise new applications. R&D covers three activities: basic research, applied research, and experimental development. Basic research is experimental or theoretical work undertaken primarily to acquire new knowledge of the underlying foundation of phenomena and observable facts, without any particular application or use in view. Applied research is also original investigation undertaken in order to acquire new knowledge; it is, however, directed primarily towards a specific practical aim or objective. Experimental development is systematic work, drawing on existing knowledge gained from research and/or practical experience, which is directed to producing new materials, products or devices, to installing new processes, systems and services, or to improving substantially those already produced or installed.

The main aggregate used for international comparisons is gross domestic expenditure on R&D (GERD). This consists of the total expenditure (current and capital) on R&D carried out by all resident companies, research institutes, university and government laboratories, etc. It includes R&D funded from abroad but excludes domestic funds for R&D performed outside the domestic economy. GERD is here expressed in constant 2005 dollars (adjusted for purchasing power parity) and as a share of GDP (R&D intensity).

Comparability

The R&D data shown here have been compiled according to the guidelines of the OECD *Frascati Manual*. Estimates of the resources allocated to R&D are affected by national characteristics such as the periodicity and coverage of national R&D surveys across institutional sectors and industries (and the inclusion of firms and organisations of different sizes); and the use of different sampling and estimation methods. R&D typically involves a few large performers, hence R&D surveys use various techniques to maintain up-to-date registers of known performers, while attempting to identify new or occasional performers.

Data for Israel exclude defence. Those for Korea, prior to 2007, exclude social sciences and the humanities. For the United States, R&D capital expenditures are excluded and depreciation charges of the business enterprises are included.

Overview

Among OECD countries, the United States is the main performer with 42% of the total OECD GERD in 2009, followed by Japan (15%) and Germany (9%). Since 1999, real R&D expenditure has been growing the fastest in Estonia, Korea, Portugal and Turkey, with average annual growth rates around 10%. Outside the OECD area, China's average annual real growth in R&D spending has been close to 20%, making it the world's second largest R&D performer and ahead of Japan since 2009.

In 2009, R&D amounted to 2.4% of GDP for the OECD as a whole. Denmark, Finland, Israel, Japan, Korea and Sweden were the only OECD countries whose R&D-to-GDP ratio exceeded 3%.

Over the last decade, R&D intensity grew in the EU (from 1.74% to 1.91%), in Japan (from 3.00% to 3.26%) and in the United States (from 2.71% to 2.90%). Estonia, Korea, Portugal and Turkey were the fastest growing OECD countries. In the same period (2000-10), R&D intensity in China almost doubled, increasing from 0.90% to 1.77%.

Sources
• OECD (2012), *Main Science and Technology Indicators*, OECD Publishing.

Further information

Analytical publications
• OECD (2012), *OECD Science, Technology and Industry Outlook*, OECD Publishing.
• OECD (2011), *OECD Science, Technology and Industry Scoreboard*, OECD Publishing.

Methodological publications
• OECD (2002), *Frascati Manual 2002: Proposed Standard Practice for Surveys on Research and Experimental Development*, The Measurement of Scientific and Technological Activities, OECD Publishing.

Online databases
• *OECD Science, Technology and R&D Statistics*

Websites
• OECD Science, Technology and Industry, *www.oecd.org/sti*.
• OECD Main Science and Technology Indicators, *www.oecd.org/sti/msti*.
• OECD Research and Development Statistics, *www.oecd.org/sti/rds*.
• OECD Measuring Science and Technology, *www.oecd.org/sti/measuring-scitech*.
• OECD Frascati Manual 2002 (supplementary material), *www.oecd.org/sti/frascatimanual*.

Gross domestic expenditure on R&D
Million US dollars – 2005 constant prices and PPPs

	1999	2000	2001	2002	2003	2004	2005	2006	2007	2008	2009	2010	2011
Australia	..	8 936	..	10 719	..	12 061	..	14 902	..	17 644	..	..	..
Austria	4 636	4 920	5 266	5 546	5 902	6 043	6 803	6 996	7 455	8 052	7 896	8 184	8 417
Belgium	5 810	6 125	6 497	6 165	6 018	6 149	6 171	6 440	6 750	7 081	7 090	7 109	..
Canada	17 032	19 063	21 215	21 352	21 687	22 709	23 090	23 336	23 356	22 796	22 416	21 708	21 448
Chile	..	..	..	..	..	..	..	..	712	889	..	..	..
Czech Republic	1 881	2 079	2 125	2 159	2 335	2 442	2 948	3 467	3 650	3 570	3 582	3 888	..
Denmark	3 554	..	4 063	4 289	4 421	4 363	4 419	4 608	4 875	5 342	5 408	5 471	..
Estonia	98	95	117	128	148	175	207	277	285	324	311	362	..
Finland	4 260	4 733	4 799	4 955	5 170	5 401	5 601	5 846	6 151	6 576	6 406	6 553	..
France	35 799	36 946	38 479	39 521	38 794	39 395	39 236	40 191	40 623	41 394	42 720	43 214	..
Germany	58 231	61 579	62 557	63 289	63 981	63 800	64 299	67 595	69 569	74 705	74 375	77 098	..
Greece	1 291	..	1 356	..	1 449	1 471	1 615	1 670	1 770	..	..	..	..
Hungary	915	1 124	1 348	1 516	1 474	1 447	1 616	1 788	1 751	1 803	1 955	1 967	..
Iceland	185	224	258	258	252	..	287	324	308	308	..	..	..
Ireland	1 360	1 413	1 449	1 543	1 706	1 878	2 009	2 119	2 297	2 528	2 858	2 844	..
Israel	4 700	6 228	6 628	6 607	6 296	6 610	7 146	7 684	8 714	8 937	8 422	8 719	..
Italy	15 474	16 411	17 376	18 110	17 766	17 920	17 999	19 095	20 204	20 527	20 337	20 606	..
Japan	106 715	110 017	113 086	114 930	117 927	120 301	128 695	134 844	139 916	138 684	126 872	128 581	..
Korea	17 574	20 213	22 641	23 586	25 067	28 305	30 618	34 712	38 923	41 685	44 311	49 394	..
Luxembourg	..	441	..	..	476	492	495	554	561	562	563	569	..
Mexico	4 334	4 011	4 239	4 727	4 769	5 014	5 346	5 266	5 215	..	..	..	..
Netherlands	10 220	10 385	10 572	10 290	10 533	10 823	10 904	11 157	11 134	11 071	11 016	11 379	..
New Zealand	831	..	1 006	..	1 144	..	1 189	..	1 304	..	1 427	..	..
Norway	2 687	..	3 009	3 082	3 208	3 175	3 316	3 503	3 832	4 023	4 048	4 024	..
Poland	2 989	2 912	2 850	2 595	2 606	2 831	2 982	3 107	3 384	3 790	4 304	4 876	..
Portugal	1 429	1 574	1 704	1 627	1 565	1 663	1 755	2 256	2 728	3 519	3 728	3 667	..
Slovak Republic	444	444	450	424	446	418	440	459	480	522	506	692	..
Slovenia	513	543	605	616	549	629	675	775	769	911	942	1 081	..
Spain	8 302	9 193	9 607	10 635	11 657	12 203	13 331	14 832	16 220	17 457	17 302	17 240	..
Sweden	8 864	..	10 814	..	10 443	10 233	10 510	11 346	10 809	11 686	10 804	10 835	..
Switzerland	..	6 308	..	..	..	7 525	..	..	..	8 728	..	..	..
Turkey	2 739	2 996	3 171	3 293	3 184	3 735	4 617	4 845	6 314	6 380	7 110	7 664	..
United Kingdom	29 856	31 056	31 594	32 399	32 759	32 524	34 081	35 331	37 219	37 018	36 731	35 615	..
United States	282 775	302 231	306 683	300 510	307 769	310 261	325 936	339 956	355 488	371 813	365 994	..	..
EU 27	197 094	208 068	215 363	219 609	221 669	223 960	229 931	242 058	251 118	262 891	262 780	267 201	..
OECD	650 059	690 857	712 638	715 336	730 083	743 415	779 529	818 588	857 502	888 551	873 833	..	..
Brazil	..	..	..	..	..	..	..	..	..	..	..	..	..
China	23 512	30 401	34 673	42 570	49 618	59 264	71 055	83 902	96 304	111 183	140 637	161 552	..
India	..	..	..	..	..	..	..	..	..	..	..	..	..
Indonesia	..	..	..	..	..	..	..	..	..	..	..	..	..
Russian Federation	11 419	13 242	15 602	17 308	19 139	18 364	18 121	19 689	22 230	21 891	24 185	23 394	..
South Africa	..	..	2 536	..	2 921	3 271	3 654	4 005	4 179	4 335	..	..	..

StatLink http://dx.doi.org/10.1787/888932708845

Gross domestic expenditure on R&D
As a percentage of GDP

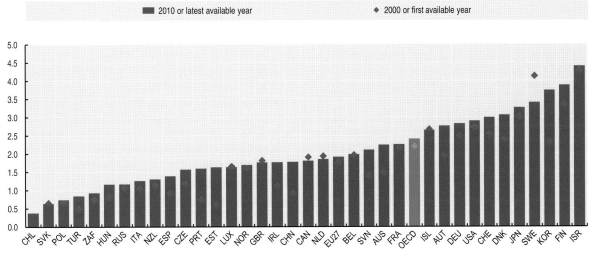

StatLink http://dx.doi.org/10.1787/888932708864

RESEARCHERS

Researchers are key actors in the research and development system. On average, in OECD countries, labour costs account for half of the R&D expenditure. Two-thirds of total R&D personnel are estimated to be researchers.

Definition

Researchers are professionals engaged in the conception and creation of new knowledge, products, processes, methods and systems, as well as those who are directly involved in the management of projects for such purposes. They include researchers working in both civil and military research in government, universities and research institutes as well as in the business sector.

Researchers are part of human resources devoted to R&D. Other categories of R&D personnel are technicians (and equivalent staff) who participate in R&D by performing scientific and technical tasks, and other supporting staff (skilled and unskilled craftsmen, secretarial and clerical staff participating in R&D projects).

The number of researchers is measured in full-time equivalents (i.e. a person working half-time on R&D is counted as 0.5 person-year) and expressed per thousand people employed in each country. The number of researchers includes staff engaged in R&D during the course of one year.

Comparability

The data on researchers have been compiled on the basis of the methodology of the OECD *Frascati Manual*. Comparability over time is affected to some extent by improvements in the coverage of national R&D surveys and by the efforts of countries to improve the international comparability of their data.

For the United States beginning in 2000, the total numbers of researchers are OECD estimates. Data for the United States exclude military personnel in the government sector since 1985. For China, from 2009 researcher data are collected according to the OECD *Frascati Manual* definition of researcher.

Overview

In the OECD area, around 4.2 million persons were employed as researchers in 2007. There were about 7.6 researchers per thousand of employed people, compared with 5.9 per thousand employed in 1995. This indicator has steadily increased over the last two decades.

The Nordic countries (Denmark, Finland, Iceland, Norway and Sweden) top the table for the numbers of researchers per thousand persons employed, with Finland the highest in the group, and the OECD, recording 17.0 researchers per thousand persons employed in 2010. Among the remaining OECD countries, rates are highest in Korea (11.1), Japan (10.4) and New Zealand (12.4 in 2009). Conversely, researchers per thousand of employed people are low (below 1.0) in Chile and Mexico. Other countries with low rates, below 5.0 researchers per thousand of employed people, include Italy, Poland and Turkey.

In 2007, in the OECD, about 2.7 million researchers were engaged in the business sector. It represents approximately two-thirds of the total although there are differences across countries: four out of five researchers work in the business sector in the United States, about three out of four in Japan and Korea, but less than one out of two in the EU. Chile, Mexico, Poland, the Slovak Republic and South Africa have a low intensity of business researchers (less than one per 1 000 employees in industry). In these countries, the business sector plays a much smaller role in the national R&D system than the higher education and government sectors.

Sources

- OECD (2012), Main Science and Technology Indicators, OECD Publishing.

Further information

Analytical publications

- OECD (2012), *OECD Science, Technology and Industry Outlook 2012*, OECD Publishing.
- OECD (2012), *OECD Science, Technology and Industry Working Papers*, OECD Publishing.
- OECD (2011), *OECD Science, Technology and Industry Scoreboard 2011*, OECD Publishing.
- OECD (2011), *Public Research Institutions, Mapping Sector Trends*, OECD Publishing.

Methodological publications

- OECD (2002), *Frascati Manual 2002: Proposed Standard Practice for Surveys on Research and Experimental Development*, The Measurement of Scientific and Technological Activities, OECD Publishing.

Online databases

- *OECD Science, Technology and R&D Statistics*

Websites

- OECD Main Science and Technology Indicators, *www.oecd.org/sti/msti*.
- OECD Research and Development Statistics, *www.oecd.org/sti/rds*.
- OECD Measuring Science and Technology, *www.oecd.org/sti/measuring-scitech*.

Researchers
Per thousand employed, full-time equivalent

	1998	1999	2000	2001	2002	2003	2004	2005	2006	2007	2008	2009	2010
Australia	7.3	..	7.3	..	7.8	..	8.3	..	8.5	..	8.5	..	..
Austria	5.1	..	..	..	6.3	..	6.7	7.3	7.3	7.8	8.4	8.5	8.7
Belgium	6.9	7.4	7.4	7.7	7.4	7.4	7.7	7.8	8.1	8.3	8.3	8.6	8.5
Canada	6.6	6.7	7.2	7.5	7.4	7.7	8.1	8.3	8.4	8.8	8.9	8.6	..
Chile	..	..	..	..	..	..	..	..	..	0.9	0.9	..	..
Czech Republic	2.5	2.7	2.8	3.0	3.0	3.2	3.3	4.8	5.2	5.3	5.6	5.5	5.6
Denmark	..	6.9	..	7.0	9.2	9.0	9.6	10.2	10.2	10.4	12.1	12.6	12.6
Estonia	4.9	5.2	4.7	4.6	5.2	5.1	5.7	5.5	5.4	5.6	6.1	7.3	7.2
Finland	13.9	14.5	15.2	15.9	16.5	17.8	17.4	16.6	16.6	15.7	16.2	16.6	17.0
France	6.7	6.8	7.1	7.2	7.5	7.7	8.1	8.1	8.3	8.6	8.8	9.1	..
Germany	6.3	6.6	6.6	6.7	6.8	6.9	6.9	7.0	7.2	7.3	7.5	7.9	8.1
Greece	..	3.5	..	3.4	..	3.5	..	4.3	4.2	4.4	..	..	..
Hungary	2.9	3.0	3.4	3.5	3.5	3.6	3.6	3.8	4.2	4.2	4.5	5.0	5.3
Iceland	9.6	10.3	..	11.7	..	12.2	..	13.4	14.2	12.5	12.9	17.0	..
Ireland	5.1	4.9	5.0	5.1	5.3	5.5	5.9	5.9	6.0	6.0	6.9	7.5	7.8
Israel	..	..	..	..	..	..	..	..	..	..	..	..	..
Italy	2.9	2.9	2.9	2.9	3.0	2.9	3.0	3.4	3.6	3.7	..	4.1	4.3
Japan	9.8	10.0	9.9	10.1	9.8	10.3	10.3	10.6	10.7	10.6	10.2	10.4	10.4
Korea	4.6	4.9	5.1	6.3	6.4	6.8	6.9	7.9	8.6	9.5	10.0	10.4	11.1
Luxembourg	..	..	6.2	..	..	6.7	6.8	7.2	6.4	6.6	6.6	6.8	7.1
Mexico	0.6	0.6	..	..	..	0.9	1.0	1.1	0.9	0.9	..	..	..
Netherlands	5.1	5.3	5.2	5.5	5.3	5.3	5.9	5.8	6.3	5.9	5.8	5.4	6.2
New Zealand	..	6.2	..	9.1	..	10.4	..	10.5	..	10.8	..	12.4	..
Norway	..	7.9	..	8.5	..	8.9	8.9	9.0	9.3	9.6	9.8	10.1	10.1
Poland	3.7	3.8	3.8	4.0	4.1	4.3	4.4	4.4	4.1	4.0	3.9	3.9	4.1
Portugal	3.0	3.2	3.3	3.5	3.7	4.0	4.0	4.1	4.8	5.5	7.8	8.8	9.3
Slovak Republic	4.8	4.5	4.9	4.7	4.5	4.7	5.2	5.2	5.5	5.7	5.6	6.1	7.1
Slovenia	4.9	5.0	4.8	4.9	5.0	4.1	4.4	5.7	6.3	6.5	7.1	7.7	8.1
Spain	4.0	3.9	4.7	4.7	4.8	5.2	5.5	5.7	5.8	5.9	6.4	7.0	7.2
Sweden	..	9.5	..	10.5	..	11.0	11.2	12.7	12.6	10.1	11.0	10.5	10.9
Switzerland	..	..	6.4	..	..	..	6.1	..	..	..	5.6	..	..
Turkey	1.0	1.0	1.2	1.2	1.2	1.7	1.7	2.0	2.1	2.4	2.5	2.7	2.9
United Kingdom	5.5	5.7	5.8	6.1	6.6	7.1	7.5	8.0	8.1	8.0	8.0	8.3	7.6
United States	..	9.3	9.3	9.5	9.7	10.2	9.8	9.6	9.6	9.5	..	..	..
EU 27	5.0	5.1	5.2	5.4	5.6	5.8	6.0	6.2	6.4	6.4	6.6	6.9	7.0
OECD	..	6.6	6.7	6.9	7.0	7.4	7.3	7.5	7.6	7.6	..	..	..
Brazil	..	..	..	..	..	..	..	..	..	..	..	..	..
China	0.7	0.7	1.0	1.0	1.1	1.2	1.2	1.5	1.6	1.9	2.1	1.5	1.6
India	..	..	..	..	..	..	..	..	..	..	..	..	..
Indonesia	..	..	..	..	..	..	..	..	..	..	..	..	..
Russian Federation	8.4	7.9	7.8	7.8	7.4	7.3	7.1	6.8	6.7	6.6	6.4	6.4	6.3
South Africa	..	..	..	1.3	..	1.2	1.5	1.4	1.5	1.5	1.4	..	..

StatLink http://dx.doi.org/10.1787/888932708883

Researchers
Per thousand employed, full-time equivalent

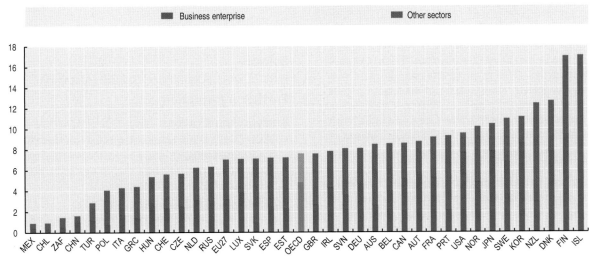

StatLink http://dx.doi.org/10.1787/888932708902

PATENTS

Patent-based indicators provide a measure of the output of a country's R&D, *i.e.* its inventions. The methodology used for counting patents can however influence the results, as simple counts of patents filed at a national patent office are affected by various kinds of limitations (such as weak international comparability) and highly heterogeneous patent values. To overcome these limits, the OECD has developed triadic patent families, which are designed to capture all important inventions and to be internationally comparable.

Definition

A patent family is defined as a set of patents registered in various countries (*i.e.* patent offices) to protect the same invention. Triadic patent families are a set of patents filed at three of these major patent offices: the European Patent Office (EPO), the Japan Patent Office (JPO) and the United States Patent and Trademark Office (USPTO).

Triadic patent family counts are attributed to the country of residence of the inventor and to the date when the patent was first registered.

Triadic patent families are expressed as numbers and per million inhabitants.

Overview

About 49 000 triadic patent families were filed in 2010, compared to over 45 000 registered in 2000. The United States accounts for 28.1% of patent families, a lower share compared to the one recorded in 2000 (30.5%). The share of triadic patent families originating from Europe has also tended to decrease, losing almost 1 percentage points between 2000 and 2010 (to 28.6% in 2010). The origin of patent families has shifted towards Asian countries. The most spectacular growth was observed by Korea, whose share of all triadic patent families increased from 1.6% in 2000 to 4.4% in 2010. Strong rises are also observed for China and India, with an average growth in the number of triadic patents of more than 28% and 15% a year respectively between 2000 and 2010.

When triadic patent families are expressed relative to the total population Japan, Switzerland, Sweden and Germany were the four most inventive countries in 2010, with the highest values recorded in Japan (118) and Switzerland (109). Ratios for Austria, Denmark, Finland, Israel, Korea, the Netherlands and the United States are also above the OECD average (39). Conversely, China has less than 0.7 patent families per million population.

Comparability

The concept of triadic patent families has been developed in order to improve the international comparability and quality of patent-based indicators. Indeed, only patents registered in the same set of countries are included in the family: home advantage and influence of geographical location are therefore eliminated. Furthermore, patents included in the triadic family are typically of higher economic value: patentees only take on the additional costs and delays of extending the protection of their invention to other countries if they deem it worthwhile.

Share of countries in triadic patent families
Percentage, 2010

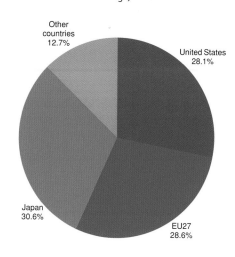

StatLink ⫘ http://dx.doi.org/10.1787/888932708959

Sources
- OECD (2011), *OECD Patent Statistics* (database).

Further information

Analytical publications
- OECD (2012), *OECD Science, Technology and Industry Outlook*, OECD Publishing.
- OECD (2011), *OECD Science, Technology and Industry Scoreboard*, OECD Publishing.

Methodological publications
- Dernis, H. and M. Khan (2004), "Triadic Patent Families Methodology", *OECD Science, Technology and Industry Working Papers*, No. 2004/2.
- OECD (2009), *OECD Patent Statistics Manual*, OECD Publishing.

Websites
- OECD Work on Patents, *www.oecd.org/sti/ipr-statistics*.

Triadic patent families
Number

	1998	1999	2000	2001	2002	2003	2004	2005	2006	2007	2008	2009	2010
Australia	301	295	373	276	350	342	367	342	332	318	304	287	284
Austria	270	259	275	257	322	339	384	429	428	411	389	406	407
Belgium	399	374	327	314	343	326	414	379	407	427	403	391	414
Canada	537	524	526	497	594	577	653	668	661	678	611	635	638
Chile	2	2	2	5	5	3	5	5	6	5	5	7	9
Czech Republic	16	10	9	12	14	15	15	15	16	21	22	21	20
Denmark	272	237	223	180	231	246	296	311	304	312	308	297	303
Estonia	2	1	1	2	1	3	1	2	5	5	6	8	8
Finland	454	453	350	303	275	301	339	344	367	364	349	346	353
France	2 289	2 348	2 140	1 960	2 217	2 268	2 412	2 402	2 431	2 477	2 476	2 431	2 447
Germany	6 163	6 016	5 804	5 653	5 502	5 446	5 635	5 779	5 960	5 942	5 741	5 625	5 685
Greece	12	6	6	7	8	13	9	15	14	15	12	12	9
Hungary	18	40	29	31	27	41	44	40	44	47	46	43	44
Iceland	6	7	11	3	9	4	2	4	4	4	4	5	4
Ireland	38	75	31	47	52	66	70	79	74	79	80	78	76
Israel	302	278	321	288	268	295	350	420	420	385	371	341	335
Italy	678	663	638	647	712	710	756	745	756	745	732	713	707
Japan	11 758	13 159	14 749	14 050	14 294	15 016	15 155	14 859	15 048	14 543	13 106	13 070	15 067
Korea	469	581	732	887	1 213	1 695	2 000	2 129	2 134	2 202	1 780	2 067	2 182
Luxembourg	22	22	20	26	10	20	23	18	22	17	21	17	17
Mexico	10	11	9	12	10	15	15	14	19	17	16	13	12
Netherlands	854	915	1 022	1 061	967	939	945	902	1 010	952	939	890	828
New Zealand	52	48	47	33	55	57	63	50	60	55	51	49	49
Norway	97	107	105	78	108	98	107	110	120	119	112	121	118
Poland	4	8	9	12	11	10	17	13	14	17	20	23	27
Portugal	5	5	3	6	6	7	6	12	17	32	30	27	25
Slovak Republic	3	3	2	2	3	5	1	2	3	3	3	3	4
Slovenia	12	4	9	6	14	13	12	18	13	14	16	15	13
Spain	127	126	145	153	164	156	218	220	207	221	227	233	242
Sweden	852	882	618	668	693	674	696	831	899	925	901	870	882
Switzerland	805	773	811	734	806	844	879	870	906	866	850	841	847
Turkey	7	3	4	10	8	9	13	13	14	21	21	26	35
United Kingdom	1 796	1 647	1 622	1 601	1 651	1 666	1 656	1 667	1 705	1 685	1 632	1 613	1 598
United States	14 515	14 574	13 794	13 605	14 471	14 803	15 185	15 352	15 857	15 033	14 096	13 862	13 837
EU 27	14 288	14 105	13 291	12 955	13 231	13 289	13 964	14 238	14 707	14 723	14 371	14 072	14 124
OECD	43 145	44 458	44 768	43 427	45 413	47 022	48 744	49 057	50 275	48 956	45 684	45 382	47 527
Brazil	29	27	29	45	42	43	49	52	49	68	67	60	60
China	49	60	71	100	155	219	228	312	365	467	507	709	875
India	32	39	54	83	126	133	115	130	147	150	162	179	201
Indonesia	3	1	4	2	3	2	0	1	4	1	2	2	3
Russian Federation	96	62	73	53	51	53	50	60	70	68	64	65	73
South Africa	37	28	36	17	27	32	30	35	39	32	31	27	26

StatLink http://dx.doi.org/10.1787/888932708921

Triadic patent families
Number per million inhabitants, 2010

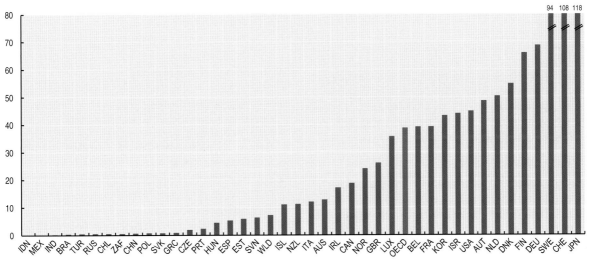

StatLink http://dx.doi.org/10.1787/888932708940

BIOTECHNOLOGY

Spending on biotechnology research and development (R&D) by the business enterprise sector within a country is a measure of this country's research focus on biotechnology.

Definition

The OECD developed both a single definition and a list-based definition of biotechnology. The single definition is deliberately broad. It covers all modern biotechnology but also many traditional or borderline activities. For this reason, the single definition should always be accompanied by the list-based definition.

The single definition is: The application of science and technology to living organisms, as well as parts, products and models thereof, to alter living or non-living materials for the production of knowledge, goods and services.

The (indicative, not exhaustive) list-based definition, which serves as an interpretative guideline to the single definition includes seven categories, and respondents are usually given a write-in option for new biotechnologies that do not fit any of the categories. A firm that reports activity in one or more categories is defined as a biotechnology firm. The categories are: DNA/RNA; proteins and other molecules; cell and tissue culture and engineering; process biotechnology techniques; gene and RNA vectors; bioinformatics; and, nanobiotechnology.

Comparability

Data availability and comparability depends on how each country collects biotechnology statistics.

A biotechnology firm is a firm engaged in biotechnology using at least one biotechnology technique to produce goods or services and/or to perform biotechnology R&D. Some firms may be large, with only a small share of total economic activity attributable to biotechnology.

Countries that collect biotechnology statistics through their R&D surveys may underestimate biotechnology activity by firms, as firms that use biotechnology but do not perform biotechnology R&D are excluded.

Although every effort has been made to maximise comparability across countries, caution must be used in comparing biotechnology activities among countries when the data are obtained from studies with very different methodologies.

Overview

The United States spends the most on biotechnology Business Enterprise R&D (BERD), PPP USD 22 030 million or approximately 7.8% of total US BERD. This accounts for almost 64% of total biotechnology BERD expenditures in the 26 countries for which data are available.

Biotechnology BERD as a share of total BERD is an indicator of country's research focus on biotechnology. On average, biotechnology BERD accounted for 5.7% of total BERD. Ireland spends the most as a percentage of BERD (15.1%). Belgium and Switzerland follow, both recording BERD spending of 12.6%.

Biotechnology R&D intensity (biotechnology R&D as a percentage of industry value added) is highest in Denmark (0.388%), followed by Switzerland (0.369%) and Belgium (0.258%).

Sources

- Key Biotechnology Indicators, *www.oecd.org/sti/ biotechnology/indicators*.

Further information

Analytical publications

- OECD (2012), *Knowledge Networks and Markets in the Life Sciences*, OECD Publishing.
- OECD (2011), *Future Prospects for Industrial Biotechnology*, OECD Publishing.
- OECD (2011), *OECD Science, Technology and Industry Scoreboard*, OECD Publishing.
- OECD (2009), *OECD Biotechnology Statistics 2009*, OECD Publishing.

Methodological publications

- OECD (2009), "*Guidelines for a Harmonised Statistical Approach to Biotechnology Research and Development in the Government and Higher Education Sectors*", OECD Working Party of National Experts on Science and Technology Indicators, unclassified document DSTI/EAS/STP/NESTI(2009)1/FINAL.
- OECD (2005), "*A Framework for Biotechnology Statistics*", OECD Working Party of National Experts on Science and Technology Indicators.
- OECD (2002), *Frascati Manual 2002: Proposed Standard Practice for Surveys on Research and Experimental Development*, The Measurement of Scientific and Technological Activities, OECD Publishing.

Websites

- OECD Key Biotechnology Indicators, *www.oecd.org/sti/ biotechnology/indicators*.

Biotechnology R&D expenditures in the business sector

2010 or latest available year

	Million US dollars, current prices and PPPs	As a percentage of total business enterprise R&D	As a percentage of industry value added
Australia	119.3	1.1	0.020
Austria	203.4	3.2	0.093
Belgium	574.0	12.6	0.258
Canada	944.5	7.2	0.109
Chile	..	..	..
Czech Republic	53.6	2.1	0.029
Denmark	463.7	11.0	0.388
Estonia	27.3	12.3	0.145
Finland	115.6	2.5	0.097
France	2 769.3	9.3	0.220
Germany	1 221.5	2.1	0.062
Greece	..	..	..
Hungary	..	..	..
Iceland	..	..	..
Ireland	301.6	15.1	0.244
Israel	..	..	..
Italy	572.4	4.5	0.049
Japan	1 230.1	1.2	0.043
Korea	1 082.7	2.7	0.114
Luxembourg	..	..	..
Mexico	..	..	..
Netherlands	420.2	6.9	0.095
New Zealand	..	..	..
Norway	158.6	6.5	0.085
Poland	19.6	1.3	0.004
Portugal	36.9	1.8	0.024
Slovak Republic	10.9	3.1	0.011
Slovenia	69.2	8.6	0.185
Spain	794.1	7.6	0.079
Sweden	411.3	4.9	0.194
Switzerland	922.3	12.6	0.369
Turkey	..	..	..
United Kingdom	..	..	..
United States	22 030.0	7.8	0.256
EU 27	..	..	..
OECD	..	..	..
Brazil	..	..	..
China	..	..	..
India	..	..	..
Indonesia	..	..	..
Russian Federation	91.8	0.5	0.005
South Africa	19.0	0.8	0.006

StatLink http://dx.doi.org/10.1787/888932708978

Total biotechnology R&D expenditures in the business sector

2010 or latest available year

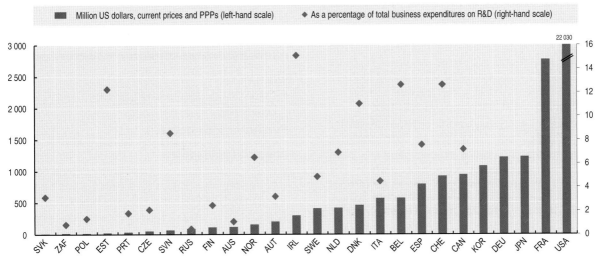

StatLink http://dx.doi.org/10.1787/888932708997

SIZE OF THE ICT SECTOR

Information and communication technologies (ICT) have been at the heart of economic changes for more than a decade and have proven resilient during the recent economic crisis. The ICT sector contributes to technological progress, output and productivity growth. The impacts of the ICT sector can be examined in several ways: directly, through its contribution to output, employment or productivity growth, or indirectly, as a source of technological change affecting other parts of the economy for instance.

Definition

In 1998, OECD member countries agreed on a definition of the ICT sector as a combination of manufacturing and services industries whose products capture, transmit or display data and information electronically. The industry-based definition of the ICT sector was based on Revision 3 of the *International Standard Industrial Classification (ISIC Rev. 3)*. This definition was slightly revised in 2002 according to the release of ISIC Rev. 3.1.

The principles underlying this definition were the following. For manufacturing industries, an ICT product must fulfil the function of information processing and communication, including transmission and display; or

must use electronic processing to detect, measure and/or record physical phenomena or to control a physical process. For services industries, ICT products must enable information processing and communication by electronic means.

In 2007, these principles were reviewed leading to a narrower definition. The production (goods and services) of an ICT industry must primarily fulfil or enable the function of information processing and communication by electronic means, including transmission and display. The revised definition is now based on ISIC Rev. 4.

As the ICT sector is an activity-based definition, a total business sector defined by activities may be preferable as a denominator, rather than a total business sector defined on an institutional basis. The business sector used here is defined as per the ISIC Rev. 3.1 activities 10 to 74, excluding 70.

Comparability

The existence of a widely accepted definition of the ICT sector is the first step towards making comparisons across time and countries possible. However, the implementation of the 2006-07 ICT sector definition is not feasible yet since not all OECD countries are using ISIC Rev. 4 in their national statistical systems. To assure comparability, the 2002 definition of the ICT sector has been used to measure the size of the sector.

Data provided by OECD countries have been combined with different data sources to estimate ICT aggregates compatible with national accounts totals. For this reason, statistics presented here may differ from data contained in national reports and in previous OECD publications. OECD shares are estimates based on available data.

Overview

The share of the ICT sector in the total business sector value added within the OECD has remained relatively stable over time, exhibiting a slight upward compound annual growth rate (CAGR) of 0.5% since 1995. In 2009, the share of value added attributed to the ICT sector was 8.3%, up from 7.7% in 1995. This upward trend indicates that output in the ICT sector is growing relative to the rest of the economy, highlighting the importance of the ICT sector overall. Data in the graph shows that in 2009, the ICT sector accounted for more than 10% of total business sector value added in Korea (13.2%), followed by Israel (13%), Ireland (11.4%) and with Finland, Sweden and Hungary (close to 11%).

The recent economic crisis has put pressure on the ICT labour market, but recovery in ICT services employment and ICT-skilled employment has been much faster than across the economy as a whole. The ICT sector contributes to a significant share of total employment, accounting for almost 15 million people in OECD countries in 2009, or almost 6% of total OECD business sector employment. Finland and Sweden represented the largest shares of ICT employment in total business employment at over 8%, shares that have increased markedly over time. The share of employment in the ICT sector declined in countries such as Austria, Ireland and the United States.

Sources

- OECD (2012), *OECD Internet Economy Outlook*, OECD Publishing.

Further information

Analytical publications

- OECD (2012), "ICT Skills and Employment: New Competences and Jobs for a Greener and Smarter Economy", *OECD Digital Economy Papers*, No. 198.
- OECD (2012), *OECD Science, Technology and Industry Outlook*, OECD Publishing.

Statistical publications

- OECD (2011), *OECD Guide to Measuring the Information Society 2011*, OECD Publishing.

Websites

- OECD Key ICT indicators, *www.oecd.org/sti/ictindicators*.

Share of ICT in value added and in employment

Percentage

	Share of ICT value added in business sector value added		Share of ICT employment in business sector employment	
	2009 or latest available year	Percentage point change 1995-2009	2009 or latest available year	Percentage point change 1995-2009
Australia	6.7	-0.8	4.7	0.0
Austria	5.9	-1.3	4.9	-0.3
Belgium	7.1	1.2	5.0	1.1
Canada	5.8	-1.1	5.6	0.1
Chile	..	..		
Czech Republic	9.2	3.7	5.9	3.0
Denmark	9.1	2.5	7.0	1.4
Estonia	8.4	2.1	2.6	..
Finland	10.9	2.2	9.4	1.7
France	7.4	0.3	6.5	0.3
Germany	7.1	0.0	5.3	0.5
Greece	6.0	1.3	3.3	2.3
Hungary	10.8	3.7	6.7	3.5
Iceland	5.2	1.0	..	..
Ireland	11.4	0.7	7.5	-0.2
Israel	13.0	..	..	..
Italy	6.2	1.3	5.5	1.4
Japan	8.9	1.3	6.2	0.4
Korea	13.2	1.9	6.1	0.8
Luxembourg	8.6	5.2	6.0	6.0
Mexico	5.3	1.4	..	..
Netherlands	8.9	1.3	6.6	1.5
New Zealand	..	..	..	..
Norway	8.3	2.1	6.2	1.8
Poland	5.7	..	..	..
Portugal	7.2	1.1	3.0	0.2
Slovak Republic	8.9	4.0	6.1	0.9
Slovenia	6.5	3.4	3.1	3.9
Spain	6.4	0.3	3.7	0.4
Sweden	10.9	1.9	8.7	0.8
Switzerland	3.7	2.0	4.0	4.2
Turkey	1.0	..	..	..
United Kingdom	9.6	0.5	6.2	0.8
United States	9.4	0.2	5.7	-0.5
EU 27	..	..	..	..
OECD	8.3	0.5	5.7	0.3
Brazil	..	..	..	..
China	..	..	..	..
India	..	..	..	..
Indonesia	..	..	..	..
Russian Federation	..	..	..	..
South Africa	..	..	..	..

StatLink ⟨⟩ http://dx.doi.org/10.1787/888932709016

Share of ICT in value added

As a percentage of business sector value added

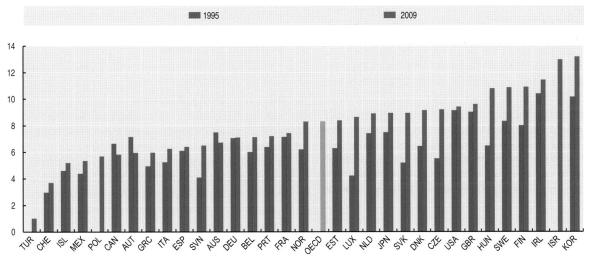

StatLink ⟨⟩ http://dx.doi.org/10.1787/888932709035

INVESTMENT IN ICT

Investment in information and communication technology (ICT) was the most dynamic component of investment in the late 1990s and early 2000s. This investment enabled new technologies to enter the production process, to expand and renew the capital stock, and to sustain economic growth.

Definition

Investment is defined in accordance with the 1993 *System of National Accounts*. ICT investment covers the acquisition of equipment and computer software that is used in production for more than one year. ICT has three components: information technology equipment (computers and related hardware); communications equipment; and software. Software includes acquisition of pre-packaged software, customised software and software developed in-house.

The investment shares presented here are percentages of each country's gross fixed capital formation, excluding residential construction.

Comparability

Data availability and measurement of ICT investment vary considerably across OECD countries, especially in terms of measurement of investment in software, deflators applied, breakdown by institutional sector and temporal coverage.

In the system of national accounts, expenditure on ICT is considered as investment only if the products can be physically isolated (*i.e.* ICT embodied in equipment is considered not as investment but as intermediate consumption). This may affect the comparability of ICT investment across countries depending on how they differentiate between intermediate consumption and investment in practice. In addition the form and nature of transactions, particularly those relating to software, can cause differences in recorded ICT investment. For example software purchased as a one-year license will be recorded as intermediate consumption but software purchased with a license for a longer period will be treated as investment. In addition measures of the individual components of ICT investment will differ depending on whether, for example, software is sold separately or bundled within other ICT products, such as hardware. However in practice these differences are not expected to significantly affect international comparability of total ICT investment.

Note that ICT components that are incorporated in other products, such as motor vehicles or machine tools, are included in the value of those other products and excluded from ICT investment as defined here.

Sources
- OECD (2012), *OECD Productivity Statistics* (database).

Further information

Analytical publications
- OECD (2012), *OECD Internet Economy Outlook*, OECD Publishing.
- OECD (2011), *OECD Communications Outlook*, OECD Publishing.
- OECD (2011), *OECD Information Technology Outlook*, OECD Publishing.
- OECD (2011), *OECD Science, Technology and Industry Scoreboard 2011*, OECD Publishing.
- OECD (2008), *Broadband Growth and Policies in OECD Countries*, OECD Publishing.

Statistical publications
- OECD (2012), *National Accounts of OECD Countries*, OECD Publishing.

Methodological publications
- Ahmad, N. (2003), "*Measuring Investment in Software*", OECD Science, Technology and Industry Working Papers, No. 2003/6.
- OECD (2010), *Handbook on Deriving Capital Measures of Intellectual Property Products*, OECD Publishing.
- OECD/Federal Statistical Office (2009), *Productivity Measurement and Analysis*, OECD Publishing.

Online databases
- STAN: OECD Structural Analysis Statistics.

Websites
- OECD work on patent statistics, *www.oecd.org/sti/ipr-statistics*.

Overview

ICT shares in total non-residential investment in 2010 (or the latest year available) differ significantly among OECD countries but were particularly high (at 20% or more of the total) in the United States, Sweden, Denmark, the United Kingdom and New Zealand, while they were only slightly above 10% in Italy and Korea.

Software has been the main component of ICT investment in many countries. Its share in non-residential investment in 2010 (or the latest year available) was highest in the United States, Sweden, Denmark, and the United Kingdom while it was below 6% in Italy and Austria. The share of IT equipment was highest in Denmark and in the United States, while it was lowest in Korea, France and Spain. The share of communication equipment in non-residential investment was higher than 5% in the United States, New Zealand and Switzerland and was below 2% in Denmark, Sweden and Japan.

Shares of ICT investment in non-residential gross fixed capital formation

As a percentage of total non-residential gross fixed capital formation, total economy

	1998	1999	2000	2001	2002	2003	2004	2005	2006	2007	2008	2009	2010
Australia	20.2	21.5	24.0	22.5	19.9	19.7	17.3	15.3	14.6	14.2	13.8	..	..
Austria	12.6	13.5	13.4	14.0	14.5	13.1	12.4	11.9	12.1	12.3	..	..	..
Belgium	..	..	..	..	..	..	..	..	..	..	..	..	..
Canada	18.8	19.9	20.6	20.2	19.2	18.8	18.5	17.6	16.8	16.7	15.9	17.5	17.0
Chile	..	..	..	..	..	..	..	..	..	..	..	..	..
Czech Republic	..	..	..	..	..	..	..	..	..	..	..	..	..
Denmark	19.5	21.6	19.9	19.2	22.0	22.1	23.7	24.8	24.5	24.6	..	..	..
Estonia	..	..	..	..	..	..	..	..	..	..	..	..	..
Finland	13.8	14.6	13.2	11.7	11.1	14.5	14.4	15.0	15.4	14.3	12.8	14.4	15.5
France	18.7	19.9	19.2	20.5	19.2	18.6	17.6	17.5	17.0	16.2	16.2	16.3	..
Germany	15.2	16.5	17.3	17.5	16.6	15.1	14.5	15.0	15.2	14.0	13.0	13.2	12.7
Greece	..	..	..	..	..	..	..	..	..	..	..	..	..
Hungary	..	..	..	..	..	..	..	..	..	..	..	..	..
Iceland	..	..	..	..	..	..	..	..	..	..	..	..	..
Ireland	11.6	11.0	11.0	11.2	9.3	9.1	9.0	7.5	9.0	8.9	7.5	11.3	12.4
Israel	..	..	..	..	..	..	..	..	..	..	..	..	..
Italy	14.2	13.9	14.6	13.6	12.3	11.6	11.5	11.7	10.9	10.7	10.4	10.9	11.0
Japan	12.0	13.0	15.0	15.1	14.8	14.8	14.6	14.3	13.5	13.4	13.5	..	..
Korea	12.8	15.8	18.0	17.0	15.7	13.2	11.9	12.2	12.4	12.1	11.7	11.4	10.7
Luxembourg	..	..	..	..	..	..	..	..	..	..	..	..	..
Mexico	..	..	..	..	..	..	..	..	..	..	..	..	..
Netherlands	18.9	19.1	19.9	19.9	19.1	20.0	21.3	22.0	22.3	19.5	..	..	..
New Zealand	24.4	23.3	26.1	22.3	21.1	21.8	21.7	21.6	22.3	22.4	22.9	21.6	21.2
Norway	..	..	..	..	..	..	..	..	..	..	..	..	..
Poland	..	..	..	..	..	..	..	..	..	..	..	..	..
Portugal	..	..	..	..	..	..	..	..	..	..	..	..	..
Slovak Republic	..	..	..	..	..	..	..	..	..	..	..	..	..
Slovenia	..	..	..	..	..	..	..	..	..	..	..	..	..
Spain	14.7	14.9	14.7	14.3	13.8	13.6	13.3	12.7	12.7	13.1	13.6	13.7	13.8
Sweden	27.8	28.8	30.3	27.9	26.2	24.9	24.8	25.1	24.4	23.0	21.9	24.7	..
Switzerland	16.5	17.5	17.2	17.8	18.9	18.3	19.0	18.4	17.9	17.7	17.9	18.8	18.5
Turkey	..	..	..	..	..	..	..	..	..	..	..	..	..
United Kingdom	25.6	27.2	30.0	28.0	26.5	24.5	25.0	24.6	24.7	23.8	..	..	..
United States	29.3	31.0	32.6	31.2	30.3	30.5	29.8	27.8	26.7	26.3	26.4	30.6	32.1
EU 27	..	..	..	..	..	..	..	..	..	..	..	..	..
OECD	..	..	..	..	..	..	..	..	..	..	..	..	..
Brazil	..	..	..	..	..	..	..	..	..	..	..	..	..
China	..	..	..	..	..	..	..	..	..	..	..	..	..
India	..	..	..	..	..	..	..	..	..	..	..	..	..
Indonesia	..	..	..	..	..	..	..	..	..	..	..	..	..
Russian Federation	..	..	..	..	..	..	..	..	..	..	..	..	..
South Africa	..	..	..	..	..	..	..	..	..	..	..	..	..

StatLink http://dx.doi.org/10.1787/888932709054

Shares of ICT investment in non-residential gross fixed capital formation

As a percentage of total non-residential gross fixed capital formation, total economy, 2010 or latest available year

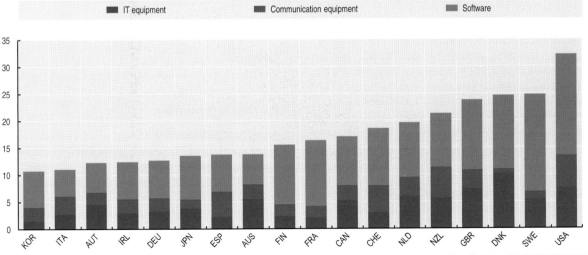

StatLink http://dx.doi.org/10.1787/888932709073

EXPORTS OF ICT GOODS

Information and communication (ICT) goods have been among the most dynamic components of international trade over the last decade.

Definition

Exports in ICT goods data are calculated using the World Customs Organisation's *Harmonised System* (HS).

A definition of ICT products (including ICT goods) was designed by the OECD to facilitate the construction of internationally comparable indicators on ICT consumption, investment, trade and production.

The first definition of ICT goods was established in 2003, based on a list of 6-digit items according to the HS 1996 and HS 2002. The second definition of ICT products was adopted in 2008, based on the then newly released second revision of the *Central Product Classification* (CPC rev. 2). The new definition includes ICT goods, ICT services and the first content and media product classification. The scope of the 2008 definition is narrower than the 2003 definition.

The 2008 definition is based on principles which emphasise the intended use or functionality of products. The guiding principles for the delineation of the ICT sector led to a definition of ICT goods as follows:

ICT goods must either be intended to fulfill the function of information processing and communication by electronic means, including transmission and display, or use electronic processing to detect, measure and/or record physical phenomena, or to control a physical process.

The result is an ICT goods definition which consists in the selection of 95 items from the HS 2007.

Comparability

It is difficult to compare values of the OECD ICT goods trade for 2007 and following years with those for earlier years owing to the new HS classification adopted in 2007, which differs radically from earlier revisions. The OECD developed a correspondence between the HS 1996, HS 2002 and the HS 2007 for ICT goods.

Adjustment efforts were required to quantify and correct the impact of Missing Trader Intra-Community (MTIC) VAT Fraud from the mid-2000s, which mainly affected the movements of ICT goods within the EU. Trade data for China are not corrected for re-exports.

Exports of ICT goods
Billion US dollars

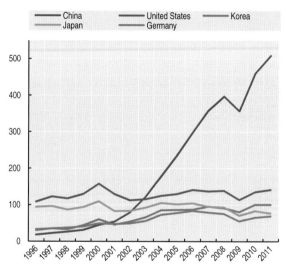

StatLink http://dx.doi.org/10.1787/888932709130

Sources

• OECD (2012), *International Trade by Commodity Statistics*, OECD Publishing.

Further information

Analytical publications

• OECD (2012), *OECD Science, Technology and Industry Working Papers*, OECD Publishing.

• OECD (2011), *OECD Communications Outlook*, OECD Publishing.

• OECD (2010), *OECD Information Technology Outlook*, OECD Publishing.

Methodological publications

• OECD (2011), *OECD Guide to Measuring the Information Society 2011*, OECD Publishing.

Websites

• OECD Key ICT indicators, *www.oecd.org/sti/ictindicators*.

Overview

The global financial crisis significantly disturbed trade worldwide, however recent figures on ICT goods exports shows significant signs of recovery. Exports of ICT goods by all OECD countries and the non-OECD countries listed reached about USD 1.25 trillion in 2011. During the global financial crisis, ICT goods experienced a similar situation to that of the dotcom bubble, following which ICTs recovered and grew strongly, for instance the exports of ICT goods grew 26% in the last two years.

The leading OECD exporters of ICT goods are the United States, Korea, Japan, Germany and the Netherlands. China is the world's largest player. In 2003, China overtook the United States in ICT goods exports. The OECD exporters mentioned above managed to develop their leading position in the export of communications equipment over the previous decade.

Exports of ICT goods

Million US dollars

	1999	2000	2001	2002	2003	2004	2005	2006	2007	2008	2009	2010	2011
Australia	1 562	1 727	1 619	1 372	1 571	1 713	1 781	1 788	1 918	2 076	1 646	1 992	2 043
Austria	3 176	3 941	4 006	4 533	5 002	5 908	6 467	6 710	7 315	7 469	5 272	5 720	..
Belgium	8 963	10 825	11 453	9 734	11 591	12 527	13 458	12 300	11 602	12 388	9 296	9 609	10 417
Canada	14 317	20 967	13 094	10 163	10 052	11 845	13 990	14 878	15 065	14 129	10 944	10 687	11 186
Chile	31	30	33	36	32	33	44	52	76	300	300	264	293
Czech Republic	752	1 334	2 582	4 148	5 207	7 907	8 668	12 330	16 806	20 614	16 305	19 835	24 593
Denmark	3 385	3 654	3 470	4 692	4 282	4 662	5 783	5 248	4 746	3 921	3 164	3 516	3 686
Estonia	408	967	853	579	820	1 126	1 405	1 310	730	743	494	1 006	2 074
Finland	8 499	10 781	8 526	8 944	10 026	10 412	13 238	13 243	13 994	14 421	6 745	4 463	3 875
France	29 015	31 939	26 310	23 629	23 277	26 864	27 331	31 584	26 140	25 342	19 762	22 584	24 814
Germany	39 677	48 717	46 634	48 601	55 200	72 250	77 168	82 809	78 319	74 643	54 743	64 652	68 219
Greece	280	466	347	338	389	511	490	629	562	667	496	542	638
Hungary	5 521	7 231	7 244	8 804	10 899	15 694	15 944	17 841	21 301	24 522	21 465	24 218	23 913
Iceland	1	2	2	2	3	2	3	5	7	9	3	3	4
Ireland	25 589	27 697	31 638	27 430	22 524	23 482	24 675	24 140	22 780	19 989	12 802	8 866	8 596
Israel	4 745	6 668	5 842	4 367	4 228	5 133	3 210	3 527	..	6 299	7 854	7 178	7 247
Italy	9 712	10 675	10 612	9 239	9 851	11 455	11 581	11 376	11 142	10 529	8 210	9 626	10 959
Japan	92 974	108 795	81 953	82 922	91 436	104 335	100 814	103 139	94 022	92 513	70 164	82 141	75 968
Korea	43 453	59 426	44 871	53 500	65 323	84 555	85 314	86 167	94 694	90 337	79 508	99 813	99 857
Luxembourg	707	889	1 179	945	720	859	998	840	757	526	402	399	452
Mexico	27 472	34 771	34 943	33 345	31 845	37 003	38 533	46 916	48 149	56 897	49 764	60 159	59 368
Netherlands	33 805	38 160	34 286	28 578	42 666	53 615	58 717	62 308	67 738	63 156	53 342	61 367	61 367
New Zealand	148	158	141	152	284	351	369	374	414	402	348	372	446
Norway	1 149	1 104	1 165	952	1 015	1 169	1 268	1 471	1 670	2 116	1 771	1 864	..
Poland	1 162	1 290	1 619	1 980	2 339	2 819	3 558	5 519	7 858	11 949	12 808	15 119	12 361
Portugal	1 472	1 492	1 701	1 711	2 364	2 545	2 972	3 673	4 041	3 843	1 758	1 941	2 254
Slovak Republic	354	388	487	492	852	1 698	2 991	5 267	8 454	11 823	11 574	12 245	12 633
Slovenia	130	169	204	220	251	275	229	291	384	618	520	528	556
Spain	5 367	5 355	5 270	5 000	6 523	7 014	7 197	7 347	6 688	6 820	4 883	5 395	..
Sweden	14 079	15 487	8 485	9 228	10 153	13 640	14 613	15 115	14 533	15 830	11 788	15 477	17 318
Switzerland	2 816	3 080	2 680	1 910	2 204	2 595	3 408	3 015	3 034	3 366	2 746	3 214	3 442
Turkey	840	1 024	1 056	1 603	1 988	2 933	3 227	3 178	2 884	2 407	2 033	2 094	2 236
United Kingdom	44 529	50 419	47 999	46 747	37 280	37 736	42 777	50 761	29 491	27 710	23 400	24 233	23 503
United States	128 678	156 670	128 513	111 448	114 860	124 097	128 943	140 314	136 219	138 001	113 157	134 549	140 568
EU 27	..	..	..	..	..	..	..	..	..	..	..	..	..
OECD	554 359	665 331	569 962	546 763	586 237	687 636	719 756	774 156	706 855	761 545	619 467	715 671	727 865
Brazil	1 243	2 232	2 329	2 178	2 106	2 013	3 701	3 969	2 975	3 139	2 320	1 985	1 792
China	30 522	44 135	53 221	78 243	121 365	177 742	234 086	297 653	357 974	396 424	356 301	459 522	508 012
India	501	714	858	781	957	1 082	1 113	1 344	..	..	6 099	4 404	4 404
Indonesia	3 069	7 573	6 095	6 301	5 687	6 527	6 944	6 138	6 025	6 517	6 921	7 862	7 845
Russian Federation	441	411	284	311	324	451	423	771	778	784	838	926	1 227
South Africa	432	417	442	390	462	578	587	745	846	805	677	695	763

StatLink http://dx.doi.org/10.1787/888932709092

Exports of ICT goods

Million US dollars, 2011

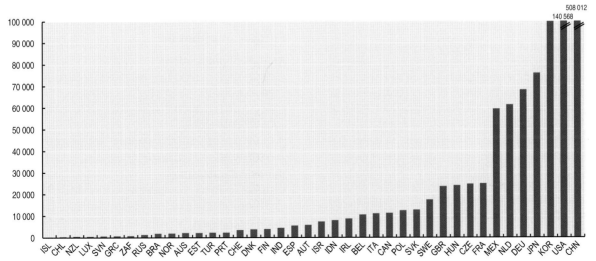

StatLink http://dx.doi.org/10.1787/888932709111

COMPUTER, INTERNET AND TELECOMMUNICATION

Communication access and computers are increasingly present in homes in OECD countries, both in countries that already have high penetration rates and in those where adoption has lagged.

Definition

Access to home computers is the number of households that reported having at least one personal computer in working order in their home.

Also presented are the percentage of households who reported that they had access to the Internet. In almost all cases this access is via a personal computer either using a dial-up, ADSL or cable broadband access.

Internet access with the Fixed (wired) broadband subscriptions per 100 inhabitants is based on the Fixed broadband subscriptions which include the total number of subscriptions to the following broadband technologies with download speeds greater than 256 kbit/s: DSL, Cable modem, fiber-to-the-home and other fixed technologies (such as broadband over power-line and leased lines).

Overview

Computer penetration rates are the highest in Iceland, the Netherlands, Luxembourg, Sweden, Norway and Denmark where over 90% of households had access to a home computer by 2011. Penetration rates in Chile and Mexico remain below 30%. Between 2000 and 2011, the share of households with access to a home computer increased by over 40 percentage points in France, Ireland, the United Kingdom, Austria and Spain.

The picture with regard to Internet access is similar. In Korea, the Netherlands, Iceland, Norway, Sweden, Luxembourg and Denmark, over 90% of all households had Internet access in 2011. In Turkey, Mexico and Chile less than 50% of all households had Internet access.

Fixed wired broadband subscriptions reached 314 million in the OECD area at the end of 2011, although growth slowed to 1.8% in the second half of the year. Year-on-year subscriptions rose by 4.1%. Greece, Poland and Chile experienced the highest growth (5%), to reach 21.8, 15.0 and 11.7 fixed wired broadband subscriptions respectively in 2011.

In 2011, Switzerland tops, for the first time, the OECD fixed broadband rankings, with 39.9 subscribers per 100 inhabitants, followed closely by the Netherlands (39.1) and Denmark (37.9). The OECD average is 25.6 subscribers per 100 inhabitants.

Comparability

The OECD has addressed issues of international comparability by developing a model survey on ICT used in households and by individuals. The model survey uses modules addressing different topics so that additional components can be added reflecting usage practices and policy interests.

Statistics on ICT use by households may run into problems of international comparability because of structural differences in the composition of households. On the other hand, statistics on ICT use by individuals may refer to people of different ages, and age is an important determinant of ICT use. Household- and person-based measures yield different figures in terms of levels and growth rates of ICT use and complicate international comparisons.

Fixed (wired) broadband subscriptions per 100 inhabitants data for OECD and non-OECD countries are collected according to agreed definitions and are highly comparable. The data shown for non-OECD countries were collected according to OECD definitions and provided by the International Telecommunication Union (ITU). The broadband definitions used by the ITU are harmonised with the OECD definitions. Data collected before 2009, Fixed wireless and Satellite subscriptions were included in the Fixed (wired) broadband data. From 2009 these two broadband technologies are excluded.

Sources
- Key ICT indicators, *www.oecd.org/sti/ICTindicators*.
- OECD Broadband Portal, *www.oecd.org/sti/ict/broadband*.

Further information

Analytical publications
- OECD (2012), *OECD Internet Economy Outlook*, OECD Publishing.
- OECD (2011), *OECD Communications Outlook*, OECD Publishing.
- OECD (2010), *OECD Information Technology Outlook*, OECD Publishing.

Statistical publications
- Eurostat (2012), *Eurostat community survey on ICT usage in households and by individuals*, Eurostat, Luxembourg.

Online databases
- International Telecommunication Union (ITU) (2012), *World Telecommunication/ICT Indicators Database*.

Websites
- OECD Science, Technology and Industry, *www.oecd.org/sti*.
- OECD Telecommunications and Internet Policy, *www.oecd.org/sti/telecom*.

Households with access to home computers, Internet and telephone

	Percentage of households with access to a home computer				Percentage of households with access to the Internet				Fixed (wired) broadband subscriptions per 100 inhabitants			
	2000	2005	2010	2011	2000	2005	2010	2011	2005	2007	2009	2011
Australia	53.0	70.0	82.6	..	32.0	60.0	78.9	..	13.2	22.8	23.1	24.6
Austria	34.0	63.1	76.2	78.1	19.0	46.7	72.9	75.4	14.1	19.3	22.5	25.5
Belgium	..	..	76.7	78.9	..	50.2	72.7	76.5	18.2	25.7	28.9	32.4
Canada	55.2	72.0	82.7	..	42.6	64.3	78.4	..	20.6	27.2	29.6	32.0
Chile	17.9	..	..	..	8.7	..	..	..	..	..	9.7	11.7
Czech Republic	..	30.0	64.1	69.9	..	19.1	60.5	66.6	4.5	14.6	12.9	15.7
Denmark	65.0	83.8	88.0	90.4	46.0	74.9	86.1	90.1	22.5	35.8	37.0	37.9
Estonia	..	43.0	69.2	71.4	..	38.7	67.8	70.8	..	..	22.5	24.8
Finland	47.0	64.0	82.0	85.1	30.0	54.1	80.5	84.2	22.3	30.7	28.7	29.6
France	27.0	..	76.5	78.2	11.9	..	73.6	75.9	15.1	24.6	30.7	35.9
Germany	47.3	69.9	85.7	86.9	16.4	61.6	82.5	83.3	12.9	23.7	30.5	33.3
Greece	..	32.6	53.4	57.2	..	21.7	46.4	50.2	1.4	9.7	17.0	21.8
Hungary	..	42.3	66.4	69.7	..	22.1	60.5	65.2	6.2	13.9	17.8	21.0
Iceland	..	89.3	93.1	94.7	..	84.4	92.0	92.6	25.8	32.2	32.8	34.6
Ireland	32.4	54.9	76.5	80.6	20.4	47.2	71.7	78.1	5.6	17.6	19.5	22.2
Israel	47.1	62.4	76.7	..	19.8	48.9	68.1	..	..	..	23.6	24.6
Italy	29.4	45.7	64.8	66.2	18.8	38.6	59.0	61.6	11.2	17.2	20.3	22.4
Japan	50.5	80.5	83.4	77.4	..	57.0	..	..	18.1	22.5	24.8	27.4
Korea	71.0	78.9	81.8	81.9	49.8	92.7	96.8	97.2	25.3	30.5	33.5	35.4
Luxembourg	..	74.5	90.2	91.7	..	64.6	90.3	90.6	14.4	27.3	29.2	32.6
Mexico	..	18.6	29.9	30.0	..	9.0	22.3	23.3	2.2	4.2	8.6	10.8
Netherlands	..	77.9	92.0	94.2	41.0	78.3	90.9	93.6	25.2	34.4	37.1	39.1
New Zealand	..	..	..	..	..	..	..	..	8.7	18.1	23.1	26.9
Norway	..	74.2	90.9	91.0	..	64.0	89.8	92.2	21.4	30.8	33.8	35.7
Poland	..	40.1	69.0	71.3	..	30.4	63.4	66.6	2.3	8.6	12.8	15.0
Portugal	27.0	42.5	59.5	63.7	8.0	31.5	53.7	58.0	11.0	14.3	17.7	21.1
Slovak Republic	..	46.7	72.2	75.4	..	23.0	67.5	70.8	2.3	7.7	11.6	13.7
Slovenia	..	61.0	70.5	74.4	..	48.2	68.1	72.6	..	..	22.0	24.2
Spain	30.4	54.6	68.7	71.5	..	35.5	59.1	63.9	11.4	17.9	21.2	24.5
Sweden	59.9	79.7	89.5	91.6	48.2	72.5	88.3	90.6	20.6	30.6	31.5	32.5
Switzerland	57.7	76.5	..	..	..	..	85.0	..	23.1	32.3	35.6	39.9
Turkey	..	12.2	44.2	..	6.9	7.7	41.6	..	2.1	5.9	9.0	10.4
United Kingdom	38.0	70.0	82.6	84.6	19.0	60.2	79.6	82.7	16.0	25.8	30.3	33.3
United States	51.0	..	77.0	..	41.5	..	71.1	..	15.8	23.4	25.5	27.7
EU 27	..	58.0	74.4	76.7	..	48.4	70.1	73.2	..	..	..	..
OECD	45.7	59.0	74.7	79.0	26.7	48.5	71.6	74.9	12.6	19.6	23.1	25.6
Brazil	..	18.5	34.9	45.4	..	13.6	27.1	37.8	2.3	4.6	11.9	10.8
China	..	25.0	35.4	38.0	..	11.0	23.7	30.9	5.6	6.5	8.4	..
India	..	2.0	6.1	6.9	..	1.6	4.2	6.0	0.6	1.1	1.3	1.5
Indonesia	..	3.7	10.8	12.0	..	1.0	4.6	7.0	0.8	0.7	0.7	..
Russian Federation	..	14.0	55.0	57.1	..	7.0	41.3	46.0	13.2	17.3	41.7	..
South Africa	..	13.0	18.3	19.5	..	3.0	10.1	9.8	..	..	..	..

StatLink http://dx.doi.org/10.1787/888932709149

Households with access to home computers
As a percentage of all households

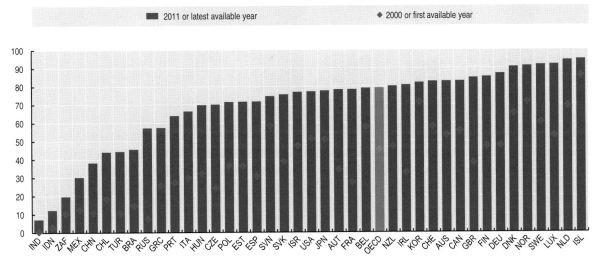

StatLink http://dx.doi.org/10.1787/888932709168

ENVIRONMENT

WATER AND NATURAL RESOURCES
WATER CONSUMPTION
FISHERIES

AIR AND LAND
EMISSIONS OF CARBON DIOXIDE
MUNICIPAL WASTE

WATER CONSUMPTION

Freshwater resources are of major environmental and economic importance. Their distribution varies widely among and within countries. In arid regions, freshwater resources may at times be limited to the extent that demand for water can be met only by going beyond sustainable use.

Freshwater abstractions, particularly for public water supplies, irrigation, industrial processes and cooling of electric power plants, exert a major pressure on water resources, with significant implications for their quantity and quality. Main concerns relate to the inefficient use of water and to its environmental and socio-economic consequences.

Definition

Water abstractions refer to freshwater taken from ground or surface water sources, either permanently or temporarily, and conveyed to the place of use. If the water is returned to a surface water source, abstraction of the same water by the downstream user is counted again in compiling total abstractions: this may lead to double counting.

Mine water and drainage water are included, whereas water used for hydroelectricity generation (which is considered an *in situ* use) is excluded.

Comparability

Definitions and estimation methods employed by countries to compile data on water abstractions and supply may vary considerably and change over time. In general, data availability and quality are best for water abstractions

for public supply, which represent about 15% of the total water abstracted in OECD countries. The OECD totals are OECD Secretariat's estimates based on linear interpolations to fill missing values. Data for the United Kingdom refers only to England and Wales.

Please note that breaks in time series exist for Estonia, France, Hungary, Luxembourg, Mexico, Turkey and the United Kingdom.

Water abstractions in OECD countries
1980 = 100

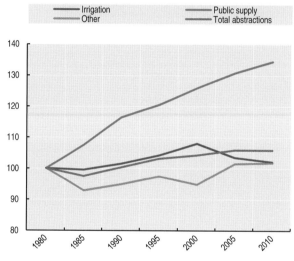

StatLink ⟶ http://dx.doi.org/10.1787/888932709225

Sources

- OECD (2013), *Environment at a Glance: OECD Environmental Indicators*, OECD Publishing.
- OECD (2012), *OECD Water Statistics*, OECD Environment Statistics (database).

Further information

Analytical publications

- OECD (2013), Water and Green Growth, *OECD Green Growth Studies*, OECD publishing.
- OECD (2012), *OECD Environmental Outlook*, OECD Publishing.
- OECD (2012), *OECD Studies on Water*, OECD Publishing.
- OECD (2012), *Water, OECD Insights*, OECD Publishing.
- OECD (2009), *Managing Water for All: An OECD Perspective on Pricing and Financing*, OECD Publishing.

Websites

- OECD Environmental Indicators, Modelling and Outlooks,*www.oecd.org/env/indicators*.
- The Water Challenge: OECD's Response, *www.oecd.org/water*.

Overview

Most OECD countries increased their total water abstractions over the 1960s and 1970s in response to higher demand by the agricultural and energy sectors. However, since the 1980s, some countries have succeeded in stabilising their total water abstractions through more efficient irrigation techniques, the decline of water-intensive industries (*e.g.* mining, steel), the increased use of cleaner production technologies and reduced losses in pipe networks. More recently, this stabilisation of water abstractions has partly reflected the consequences of droughts (with population growth continuing to drive increases in public supply).

At world level, it is estimated that, over the last century, the growth in water demand was more than double the rate of population growth, with agriculture being the largest user of water.

Water abstractions

	Water abstractions per capita m³per capita						Total abstractions Millions m³					
	1985	1990	1995	2000	2005	2010 or latest available year	1985	1990	1995	2000	2005	2010 or latest available year
Australia	920	..	1 330	1 130	920	640	14 600	..	24 070	21 700	18 770	14 100
Austria	470	490	430	..	..	..	3 580	3 810	3 450	..	..	..
Belgium	..	..	810	740	610	590	..	..	8 250	7 540	6 390	6 220
Canada	1 620	1 610	1 610	..	1 300	1 130	42 380	43 890	47 250	..	42 060	37 250
Chile	..	..	..	..	1 950	2 200	..	..	..	..	31 760	36 510
Czech Republic	360	350	270	190	190	190	3 680	3 620	2 740	1 920	1 950	1 950
Denmark	..	250	170	140	120	120	..	1 260	890	730	640	660
Estonia	..	2 050	1 240	1 070	970	1 380	..	3 220	1 780	1 470	1 300	1 840
Finland	820	470	510	450	320	..	4 000	2 350	2 590	2 350	1 680	..
France	630	660	710	550	550	530	34 890	37 690	40 670	32 720	33 870	33 440
Germany	680	760	530	470	430	390	41 220	47 870	42 920	38 770	35 560	32 300
Greece	550	780	730	910	870	850	5 500	7 860	7 790	9 920	9 650	9 470
Hungary	590	610	580	650	490	540	6 270	6 290	5 980	6 620	4 930	5 430
Iceland	460	660	620	580	560	..	110	170	170	160	170	..
Ireland	..	..	330	..	190	170	..	..	1 180	..	800	730
Israel	..	380	330	270	250	220	..	1 780	1 810	1 730	1 730	1 600
Italy	..	..	..	740	..	910	..	..	..	41 980	..	53 750
Japan	720	720	710	690	650	650	87 210	88 910	88 880	86 970	83 420	83 100
Korea	460	480	520	550	610	..	18 580	20 570	23 670	26 020	29 160	..
Luxembourg	180	150	140	140	..	90	70	60	60	60	..	50
Mexico	..	..	800	720	740	750	..	..	73 670	70 430	76 510	80 590
Netherlands	640	530	420	560	700	640	9 350	7 980	6 510	8 920	11 450	10 610
New Zealand	..	..	..	810	1 170	1 190	..	..	..	3 140	4 910	5 200
Norway	490	..	550	530	620	640	2 030	..	2 420	2 350	2 860	3 030
Poland	440	400	340	310	300	300	16 410	15 160	12 920	11 990	11 520	11 640
Portugal	..	730	1 080	860	860	..	..	7 290	10 850	8 810	9 150	9 150
Slovak Republic	400	400	260	220	170	140	2 060	2 120	1 390	1 170	910	790
Slovenia	..	..	..	450	460	470	..	..	..	900	920	950
Spain	1 200	950	850	910	820	710	46 250	36 900	33 290	36 690	35 660	32 470
Sweden	360	350	310	300	290	..	2 970	2 970	2 730	2 690	2 630	..
Switzerland	410	400	370	360	340	360	2 650	2 670	2 570	2 560	2 510	2 660
Turkey	390	510	560	680	650	560	19 400	28 070	33 480	43 650	44 320	40 560
United Kingdom	230	240	190	210	190	150	11 530	12 050	9 560	11 180	10 320	8 350
United States	1 960	1 880	1 770	1 690	1 630	..	467 340	468 620	470 510	476 800	482 390	..
EU 27	..	..	..	..	..	..						
OECD	1 000	980	940	910	890	850	1 000 200	1 022 510	1 033 260	1 038 460	1 051 740	1 043 880
Brazil	..	..	..	290	..	..	..	..	..	50 210	..	..
China	..	..	..	430	430	440	..	..	..	550 960	561 100	593 400
India	..	..	..	..	..	..	..	..	..	..	..	..
Indonesia	..	0	10	10	10	..	..	760	1 160	1 510	2 350	..
Russian Federation	820	740	620	550	520	490	117 270	110 400	91 920	80 780	74 370	69 920
South Africa	..	..	..	300	..	..	..	..	..	13 240		

StatLink http://dx.doi.org/10.1787/888932709187

Water abstractions
m³/capita, 2010 or latest available year

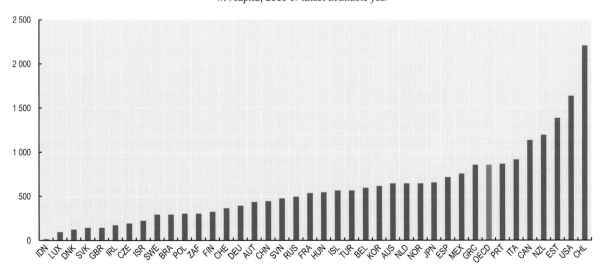

StatLink http://dx.doi.org/10.1787/888932709206

FISHERIES

Fisheries make an important contribution to sustainable incomes, employment opportunities and overall food protein intake. On the other hand, overfishing of some species in some areas is threatening stocks with depletion. In certain countries, including at least two OECD countries – Iceland and Japan – fish is the main source of animal protein intake.

Definition

The figures refer to the tonnage of landed catches of marine fish, and to cultivated fish and crustaceans taken from marine and inland waters and sea tanks. Landed catches of marine fish for each country cover landings in both foreign and domestic ports. The table distinguishes between marine capture fisheries and aquaculture because of their different production systems and growth rates.

Comparability

The time series presented are relatively comprehensive and consistent across the years, but some of the variation over time may reflect changes in national reporting systems. In one case, the data shown are estimated by the OECD Secretariat.

Fish landings in domestic and foreign ports

As a percentage of OECD total, 2009

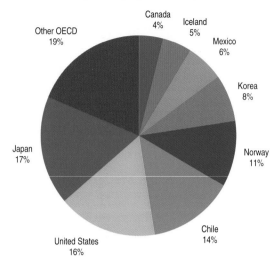

StatLink http://dx.doi.org/10.1787/888932709282

Overview

Marine capture fisheries landings in the OECD countries amounted to around 25 million tons in 2008, which is roughly 28% of the total world marine capture production. OECD catches have been trending downward since the late 1980s. This steady trend is due to changes in market demand and prices as well as from the need to rebuild stocks to maximum sustainable yield levels in order to achieve long-term sustainable use of marine resources.

Growth in aquaculture production in OECD countries has been relatively slow at around 3% per year. OECD countries produced around 10% of world aquaculture production in 2008 with the largest producers being Korea, Japan, Chile and Norway. Aquaculture is seen as playing a key role in future green growth, especially in many emerging economies, by virtue of its potential to contribute to increased food production while helping reduce pressure on fish resources.

Sources
- OECD (2012), *OECD Review of Fisheries: Policies and Summary Statistics*, OECD Publishing.

Further information

Analytical publications
- OECD (2012), *Rebuilding Fisheries, The Way Forward*, OECD Publishing.
- OECD (2011), *Fisheries and Aquaculture Certification*, OECD Publishing.
- OECD (2011), *The Economics of Adapting Fisheries to Climate Change*, OECD Publishing.
- OECD (2010), *Advancing the Aquaculture Agenda: Workshop Proceedings*, OECD Publishing.
- OECD (2010), *Globalisation in Fisheries and Aquaculture: Opportunities and Challenges*, OECD Publishing.
- OECD (2007), *Structural Change in Fisheries: Dealing with the Human Dimension*, OECD Publishing.
- OECD (2006), *Financial Support to Fisheries: Implications for Sustainable Development*, OECD Publishing.

Statistical publications
- OECD (2009), *Reducing Fishing Capacity: Best Practices for Decommissioning Schemes*, OECD Publishing.

Websites
- OECD Fisheries, *www.oecd.org/fisheries*.

Marine capture and aquaculture production
Thousand tonnes

	Fish landings in domestic and foreign ports						Aquaculture					
	2000	2005	2007	2008	2009	2010	2000	2005	2007	2008	2009	2010
Australia	185	236	182	172	..	..	37	47	64	70	..	..
Austria	..	..	..	..	..	..	..	..	..	..	..	..
Belgium	27	22	22	20	19	..	2	..	..	..	..	..
Canada	1 008	1 079	1 002	915	936	..	127	154	153	144	141	..
Chile	4 032	4 462	3 687	3 460	3 379	2 654	425	739	804	871	758	574
Czech Republic	..	..	..	..	..	..	19	20	20	20	20	20
Denmark	1 524	899	645	686	770	820	44	40	42	43	42	..
Estonia	101	90	97	100	..	..	..	..	1	1	..	..
Finland	92	77	117	111	116	..	15	14	13	13	14	..
France	682	606	474	452	446	..	267	238	..	238	236	..
Germany	194	247	262	243	211	210	45	46	45	44	39	41
Greece	93	92	95	87	83	..	88	110	155	115	118	..
Hungary	..	..	..	..	..	..	..	..	15	15	..	..
Iceland	1 930	1 411	1 419	1 305	1 151	..	4	8	5	5	6	..
Ireland	291	282	219	202	227	..	41	..	53	45	47	..
Israel	6	4	3	3	3	..	20	22	21	..	..	..
Italy	387	268	276	227	242	223	228	234	247	158	162	..
Japan	5 092	4 511	4 436	4 416	4 200	3 986	1 292	1 254	1 284	1 188	1 243	1 101
Korea	2 090	1 829	1 862	1 951	1 839	1 725	667	1 057	1 407	1 400	1 332	1 376
Luxembourg	..	..	..	..	..	..	..	..	..	..	..	..
Mexico	1 193	1 203	1 351	1 462	1 483	..	46	102	268	284	285	..
Netherlands	312	547	464	401	380	266	92	70	41	57	73	89
New Zealand	536	633	427	287	280	278	87	105	42	101	105	111
Norway	2 894	2 546	2 539	2 437	2 537	2 674	492	662	842	848	962	1 008
Poland	200	136	133	..	..	..	32	38	36	..	..	..
Portugal	172	172	197	195	191	201	8	7	7	8	8	8
Slovak Republic	..	..	..	..	..	..	..	1	1	1	1	..
Slovenia	2	1	1	1	1	1	..	..	..	..	..	..
Spain	1 002	717	752	802	728	924	312	273	285	253	268	..
Sweden	341	239	246	219	197	204	6	7	6	9	9	11
Switzerland	..	..	..	..	..	..	..	..	..	..	..	..
Turkey	461	523	589	443	..	..	79	118	140	152	..	..
United Kingdom	748	670	610	551	580	597	144	165	157	179	196	..
United States	4 245	4 463	4 294	3 890	..	..	373	358	373	351	..	..
EU 27	..	..	..	..	..	..	..	..	..	..	..	..
OECD	29 654	27 730	26 401	25 038	..	..	4 989	5 888	6 277	6 613	..	..
Brazil	..	..	..	..	..	..	..	..	..	..	..	..
China	..	..	..	..	..	..	..	..	..	..	..	..
India	..	..	..	..	..	..	..	..	..	..	..	..
Indonesia	..	..	..	..	..	..	..	..	..	..	..	..
Russian Federation	4 289	..	..	..	..	..	205	..	..	..	..	..
South Africa	..	..	..	..	..	..	..	..	..	..	..	..

StatLink http://dx.doi.org/10.1787/888932709244

Share of aquaculture in total fish capture and production
Percentage, average 2007-09

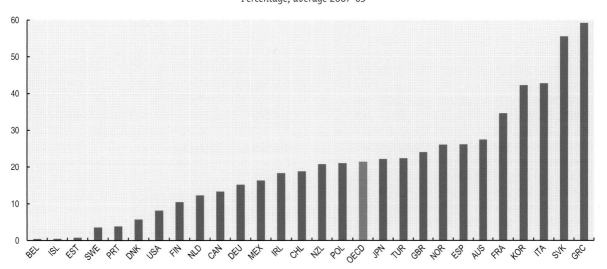

StatLink http://dx.doi.org/10.1787/888932709263

EMISSIONS OF CARBON DIOXIDE

Carbon dioxide (CO_2) makes up the largest share of greenhouse gases. The addition of man-made greenhouse gases to the atmosphere disturbs the earth's radiative balance (i.e. the balance between the solar energy that the earth absorbs and radiates back into space). This is leading to an increase in the earth's surface temperature and to related effects on climate, sea level and world agriculture.

Definition

The indicator refers to emissions of CO_2 from burning oil, coal and natural gas for energy use. Carbon dioxide also enters the atmosphere from burning wood and waste materials and from some industrial processes such as cement production. However, emissions of CO_2 from these other sources are a relatively small part of global emissions, and are not included in the statistics shown here. The *Revised 1996 IPCC Guidelines for National Greenhouse Gas Inventories* provide a fuller, technical definition of how CO_2 emissions have been estimated for this indicator.

Comparability

These emissions estimates are affected by the quality of the underlying energy data. For example, some countries, both OECD and non-OECD, have trouble reporting information on bunker fuels and incorrectly define bunkers as fuel used abroad by their own ships and planes. Since emissions from bunkers are excluded from the national totals, this affects the comparability of the estimates across countries. On the other hand, since these estimates have been made using the same method and emission factors for all countries, in general, the comparability across countries is quite good.

Overview

Global emissions of carbon dioxide have risen by 117%, or on average 2% per year, since 1971. In 1971, the current OECD countries were responsible for 67% of world CO_2 emissions. As a consequence of rapidly rising emissions in the developing world, the OECD contribution to the total fell to 41% in 2010. By far, the largest increases in non-OECD countries occurred in Asia, where China's emissions of CO_2 from fuel combustion have risen by 5.8% per annum between 1971 and 2010. The use of coal in China increased the levels of CO_2 emissions by 6.6 billion tonnes over the 39 years to 2010.

Two significant downturns in OECD CO_2 emissions occurred following the oil shocks of the mid-1970s and early 1980s. Emissions from the economies in transition declined over the last decade, helping to offset the OECD increases between 1990 and the present. However, this decline did not stabilise global emissions as emissions in developing countries continued to grow. With the economic crisis in 2008, world CO_2 emissions declined by 1.8% in 2009. However, the growth in CO_2 emissions rebounded in 2010 increasing by 4.9%.

Disaggregating the emissions estimates shows substantial variations within individual sectors. Between 1971 and 2010, the combined share of electricity and heat generation and transport shifted from one-half to two-thirds of the total. The share of fossil fuels in overall emissions changed slightly during the period. The weight of coal in global emissions has remained at approximately 40% since the early 1970s, while the share of natural gas increased from 15% in 1971 to 20% in 2010. The share of oil decreased from 48% to 36%. Fuel switching and the increasing use of non-fossil energy sources reduced the CO_2/total primary energy supply ratio by 6% over the past 39 years.

Sources

- International Energy Agency (IEA) (2011), *CO2 Emissions from Fuel Combustion*, IEA, Paris.

Further information

Analytical publications

- IEA (2012), *Electricity and a Climate-Constrained World: Data and Analyses*, OECD Publishing.
- IEA (2011), *Climate and Electricity Annual 2011: Data and Analyses*, IEA, Paris.
- IEA (2011), *IEA Scoreboard 2011: Implementing Energy Efficiency Policy: Progress and challenges in IEA member countries*, IEA, Paris.
- IEA (2011), *World Energy Outlook*, IEA, Paris.
- IEA (2010), *Energy Technology Perspectives*, IEA, Paris.

Statistical publications

- IEA (2012), *Energy Balances of Non-OECD Countries*, IEA, Paris.
- IEA (2012), *Energy Balances of OECD Countries*, IEA, Paris.

Methodological publications

- Intergovernmental Panel on Climate Change (IPCC) (1996), *Revised 1996 IPCC Guidelines for National Greenhouse Gas Inventories*, Institute for Global Environmental Strategies (IGES), Japan.

Online databases

- IEA CO2 Emissions from Fuel Combustion.

CO_2 emissions from fuel combustion

Million tonnes

	1971	1990	2000	2001	2002	2003	2004	2005	2006	2007	2008	2009	2010
Australia	144	260	339	351	359	361	371	369	374	384	386	384	383
Austria	49	56	62	66	67	73	74	75	72	70	71	64	69
Belgium	117	108	119	119	112	120	117	113	110	106	111	101	106
Canada	340	433	533	526	533	557	554	559	544	569	551	525	537
Chile	21	31	53	50	51	53	58	58	60	67	68	65	70
Czech Republic	151	155	122	121	117	121	122	120	121	122	117	110	114
Denmark	55	50	51	52	52	57	52	48	56	51	48	47	47
Estonia	..	36	15	15	15	17	17	17	16	19	18	15	18
Finland	40	54	55	60	63	71	67	55	67	65	57	55	63
France	432	352	377	384	376	385	385	388	380	373	370	351	358
Germany	979	950	825	843	831	840	841	809	821	796	800	747	762
Greece	25	70	87	90	90	94	93	95	94	98	94	90	84
Hungary	60	66	54	56	55	57	56	56	56	54	53	48	49
Iceland	1	2	2	2	2	2	2	2	2	2	2	2	2
Ireland	22	30	41	43	42	41	42	44	45	44	44	39	39
Israel	14	34	55	56	59	61	61	59	62	64	64	64	68
Italy	293	397	426	429	435	452	459	461	464	447	435	389	398
Japan	759	1 064	1 184	1 170	1 205	1 213	1 212	1 221	1 205	1 242	1 154	1 096	1 143
Korea	52	229	438	452	446	449	470	469	477	490	502	515	563
Luxembourg	15	10	8	9	9	10	11	11	11	11	11	10	11
Mexico	97	265	349	350	356	363	369	386	395	410	404	400	417
Netherlands	130	156	172	178	178	183	185	183	178	181	183	176	187
New Zealand	14	23	31	33	33	34	33	34	34	33	34	31	31
Norway	24	28	34	35	34	37	38	36	37	38	38	37	39
Poland	287	342	291	290	279	290	293	293	304	303	299	287	305
Portugal	14	39	59	59	63	58	60	63	56	56	53	53	48
Slovak Republic	39	57	37	38	38	38	37	38	37	37	36	33	35
Slovenia	..	13	14	15	15	15	15	16	16	16	17	15	15
Spain	120	205	284	286	302	310	327	339	332	344	317	282	268
Sweden	82	53	53	52	54	55	54	50	48	46	44	41	48
Switzerland	39	41	42	43	42	44	44	45	44	42	44	42	44
Turkey	41	127	201	182	192	202	207	216	240	265	264	256	266
United Kingdom	623	549	524	537	522	534	535	533	535	523	513	466	484
United States	4 291	4 869	5 698	5 678	5 605	5 680	5 764	5 772	5 685	5 763	5 587	5 185	5 369
EU 27	..	4 050	3 831	3 905	3 875	3 992	4 009	3 977	3 993	3 940	3 865	3 571	3 660
OECD	9 370	11 157	12 634	12 670	12 635	12 877	13 025	13 032	12 977	13 131	12 787	12 023	12 440
Brazil	91	194	304	309	309	303	321	322	328	342	362	338	388
China	824	2 256	3 317	3 403	3 608	4 180	5 005	5 560	6 082	6 471	6 656	6 962	7 428
India	200	582	972	984	1 015	1 041	1 117	1 165	1 256	1 362	1 439	1 564	1 626
Indonesia	25	146	273	291	297	325	331	336	354	369	365	381	411
Russian Federation	..	2 179	1 506	1 508	1 494	1 531	1 513	1 516	1 580	1 579	1 593	1 520	1 581
South Africa	157	254	297	282	293	319	336	329	330	355	387	369	347
World	14 089	20 973	23 767	23 993	24 354	25 483	26 802	27 654	28 530	29 462	29 620	29 095	30 523

StatLink http://dx.doi.org/10.1787/888932709301

World CO_2 emissions from fuel combustion, by region

Million tonnes

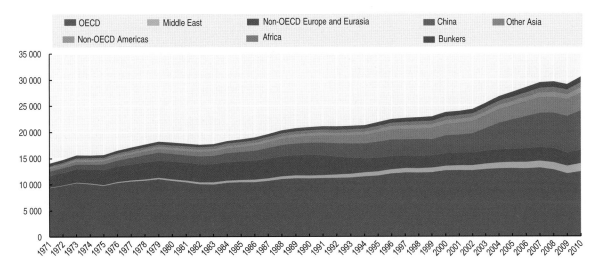

StatLink http://dx.doi.org/10.1787/888932709320

MUNICIPAL WASTE

The amount of municipal waste generated in a country is related to the rate of urbanisation, the types and patterns of consumption, household revenue and lifestyles. While municipal waste is only one part of total waste generated in each country, its management and treatment often absorbs more than one third of the public sector's financial efforts to abate and control pollution.

The main concerns raised by municipal waste are the potential impact from inappropriate waste management on human health and the environment (soil and water contamination, air quality, land use and landscape).

Definition

Municipal waste is waste collected and treated by or for municipalities. It covers waste from households, including bulky waste, similar waste from commerce and trade, office buildings, institutions and small businesses, yard and garden waste, street sweepings, the contents of litter containers, and market cleansing waste. The definition excludes waste from municipal sewage networks and treatment, as well as waste from construction and demolition activities.

The kilogrammes of municipal waste per capita produced each year – or "waste generation intensities" – provide one broad indicator of the potential environmental and health pressures from municipal waste. They should be complemented with information on waste management practices and costs, and on consumption levels and patterns.

Comparability

The definition of municipal waste and the surveying methods used to collect information vary from country to country and over time. Breaks in time series exist for: the Czech Republic, Denmark, Estonia, France, Germany, Hungary, Ireland, Italy, Korea, Luxembourg, Mexico, New Zealand, Norway, Poland, the Slovak Republic, Slovenia and Turkey.

The main problems in terms of data comparability relate to the coverage of waste from commerce and trade, and of separate waste collections carried out by private companies.

In some cases the reference year refers to the closest available year.

Data for New Zealand refer to the amount going to landfill only. Portugal includes Azores and Madeira Islands. Data for China do not cover waste produced in rural areas.

Time series data for the OECD total exclude Estonia, Israel and Slovenia.

Sources

- OECD (2013), *Environment at a Glance: OECD Environmental Indicators*, OECD Publishing.
- OECD (2012), *OECD Environmental Outlook*, OECD Publishing.
- OECD (2012), *OECD Waste Statistics*, OECD Environment Statistics

Further information

Analytical publications

- OECD (2013), *Greening Household Behaviour: Lessons from the Second Household Survey*, OECD Publishing.
- OECD (2008), *Conducting Sustainability Assessments*, OECD Sustainable Development Studies, OECD Publishing.
- OECD (2004), *Addressing the Economics of Waste*, OECD Publishing.
- Strange, T. and A. Bayley (2008), *Sustainable Development: Linking Economy, Society, Environment*, OECD Insights, OECD Publishing.

Methodological publications

- OECD (2009), *Guidance Manual for the Control of Transboundary Movements of Recoverable Wastes*, OECD Publishing.
- OECD (2007), *Guidance Manual on Environmentally Sound Management of Waste*, OECD Publishing.

Websites

- OECD Waste Prevention and Management, *www.oecd.org/env/waste*.

Overview

The quantity of municipal waste generated in the OECD area has risen strongly since 1980, and exceeded an estimated 650 million tonnes in 2010 (540 kg per capita).

In most countries for which data are available, increased affluence, associated with economic growth, and changes in consumption patterns tend to generate higher rates of waste per capita. Over the past twenty years, waste generation has however risen at a lower rate than private final consumption expenditure and GDP, with a slowdown in recent years.

The amount and composition of municipal waste going to final disposal depends on national waste management practices. Despite improvements in these practices, only a few countries have succeeded in reducing the quantity of solid waste to be disposed of.

Municipal waste generation

	Generation intensities kg per capita							Total amount generated Thousand tonnes
	1980	1985	1990	1995	2000	2005	2010 or latest available year	2010 or latest available year
Australia	700	..	690	..	690	..	..	..
Austria	..	..	420	430	530	560	580	4 840
Belgium	280	310	340	450	480	480	470	5 070
Canada	..	..	..	..	..	..	..	..
Chile	200	230	250	280	330	350	380	6 520
Czech Republic	..	..	..	300	330	290	320	3 330
Denmark	400	480	..	520	610	660	670	3 730
Estonia	..	..	..	370	460	440	310	420
Finland	..	..	..	410	500	480	470	2 520
France	..	..	450	480	510	530	530	34 540
Germany	..	..	790	620	640	560	580	47 690
Greece	260	300	300	300	410	440	460	5 180
Hungary	..	..	530	460	450	460	410	4 130
Iceland	..	..	..	430	460	520	550	180
Ireland	190	310	..	510	600	730	660	2 950
Israel	..	..	..	..	630	590	610	4 630
Italy	250	270	350	450	510	540	540	32 110
Japan	380	350	410	420	430	410	380	48 110
Korea	..	510	710	390	360	370	380	18 580
Luxembourg	350	360	580	580	650	680	680	340
Mexico	..	..	250	330	310	340	370	40 060
Netherlands	490	480	500	550	610	620	600	9 930
New Zealand	650	..	990	870	770	780	580	2 530
Norway	550	590	550	640	620	430	470	2 300
Poland	280	300	290	290	320	320	320	12 040
Portugal	200	230	300	390	440	450	510	5 460
Slovak Republic	..	360	300	300	320	270	320	1 720
Slovenia	..	..	..	600	510	420	420	860
Spain	..	..	..	510	660	590	540	24 660
Sweden	300	320	370	400	430	480	470	4 360
Switzerland	440	530	610	600	660	660	700	5 450
Turkey	270	360	360	460	480	460	390	28 210
United Kingdom	..	..	470	500	580	590	530	32 450
United States	610	630	760	740	780	770	720	220 410
EU 27	..	..	..	..	..	..	..	..
OECD	..	440	510	520	560	560	540	658 400
Brazil	..	..	..	..	330	320	270	51 430
China	..	..	210	280	260	280	250	157 340
India	..	..	..	..	20	..	..	..
Indonesia	..	..	..	..	..	..	40	..
Russian Federation	160	170	190	340	350	400	480	69 260
South Africa	..	..	..	..	..	..	..	..

StatLink http://dx.doi.org/10.1787/888932709358

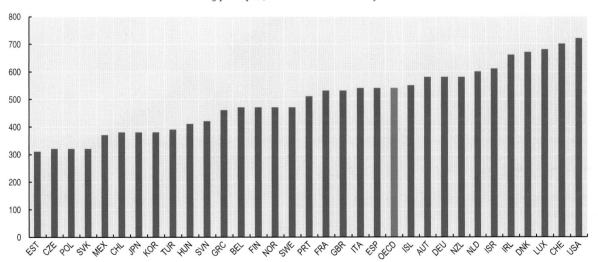

Municipal waste generation
kg per capita, 2010 or latest available year

StatLink http://dx.doi.org/10.1787/888932709377

EDUCATION

INTERNATIONAL STUDENT ASSESSMENT

How effective are school systems at providing young people with a solid foundation in the knowledge and skills that will equip them for life and learning beyond school? The OECD Programme for International Student Assessment (PISA) assesses student knowledge and skills at age 15, *i.e.* toward the end of compulsory education. The PISA 2009 survey focused on reading, but for the first time, also assessed the ability of students to read, understand and use digital texts.

Definition

The PISA survey covers reading, mathematics and science. In the 2009 round of PISA, one hour of testing time was devoted to reading, half an hour was devoted to mathematics and half an hour to science. Each student spent two hours on the assessment items. In 19 countries, students were given additional questions via computer to assess their capacity to read digital texts.

Reading literacy is the capacity to understand, use and reflect on written texts in order to achieve one's goals, develop one's knowledge and potential, and participate in society. Mathematical literacy is the capacity to identify and understand the role that mathematics plays in the world, make well-founded judgements, and use mathematics in ways that meet the needs of concerned and reflective citizens. Scientific literacy is the capacity to use scientific knowledge to identify questions, acquire new knowledge, explain scientific phenomena, and draw evidence-based conclusions about science-related issues.

The original PISA scales for reading (major domain in 2000 PISA survey), mathematics (major domain in 2003 PISA survey) and science (major domain in 2006 PISA survey) were set at 500 points for participating OECD countries as approximately two-third of students across OECD countries scored between 400 and 600. In 2009 PISA survey, with a slightly wider range of OECD countries, the average score changed for each domain: 493 points for reading, 496 for mathematics and 501 for science.

Comparability

Leading experts in countries participating in PISA advise on the scope and nature of the assessments, with final decisions taken by OECD governments. Substantial efforts and resources are devoted to achieving cultural and linguistic breadth and balance in the assessment materials. Stringent quality assurance mechanisms are applied in translation, sampling and data collection.

Over 520 000 15-year-old students in 75 participating countries or economies were assessed in PISA 2009. Because the results are based on probability samples, standard errors (S.E.) are normally shown in the tables.

Overview

The graph shows the difference between the OECD average score in reading (493 score points) and the mean scores of individual countries. As it did in PISA 2006, Korea tops all participating OECD countries in reading. The reading scores of the United States, Sweden, Germany, Ireland, France, Denmark, the United Kingdom, Hungary and Portugal are not significantly different from the OECD average. The graph also shows results for mathematics relative to the OECD average (496 score points). While most countries that do well in one subject also do well in the other, some countries show significant differences: Switzerland, for example, has better scores in mathematics than in reading.

The table presents scores by gender. As in PISA 2006, girls do significantly better in reading than boys in all countries, with an average gender gap of 39 score points. Conversely, boys outperform girls in mathematics by an average of 12 score points. On average, there is no gender gap in science performance, although in some countries, there are significant differences. For example, in the United States, boys perform significantly better in science than girls, while in Finland the opposite is true.

Sources

- OECD (2010), *PISA 2009 Results: What Students Know and Can Do: Student Performance in Reading, Mathematics and Science (Volume I)*, PISA, OECD Publishing.
- OECD (2007), *PISA 2006: Science Competencies for Tomorrow's World: Volume 1: Analysis*, PISA, OECD Publishing.

Further information

Analytical publications
- OECD (2010), *PISA 2009 Results* (series), OECD Publishing.
- OECD (2012), *Education at a Glance*, OECD Publishing.
- OECD (2012), *Highlights from Education at a Glance*, OECD Publishing.

Statistical publications
- OECD (2010), *PISA 2009 at a Glance*, OECD Publishing.

Methodological publications
- OECD (2009), *PISA 2009 Assessment Framework: Key Competencies in Reading, Mathematics and Science*, PISA, OECD Publishing.

Online databases
- OECD PISA Database.

Websites
- Programme for International Student Assessment (PISA), *www.pisa.oecd.org*.

Mean scores by gender in PISA

2009

	Reading scale				Mathematics scale				Science scale			
	Females		Males		Females		Males		Females		Males	
	Mean score	S.E.	Mean score	S.E.	Mean score	S.E.	Mean score	S.E.	Mean score	S.E.	Mean score	S.E.
Australia	533	2.6	496	2.9	509	2.8	519	3.0	528	2.8	527	3.1
Austria	490	4.0	449	3.8	486	4.0	506	3.4	490	4.4	498	4.2
Belgium	520	2.9	493	3.4	504	3.0	526	3.3	503	3.2	510	3.6
Canada	542	1.7	507	1.8	521	1.7	533	2.0	526	1.9	531	1.9
Chile	461	3.6	439	3.9	410	3.6	431	3.7	443	3.5	452	3.5
Czech Republic	504	3.0	456	3.7	490	3.0	495	3.9	503	3.2	498	4.0
Denmark	509	2.5	480	2.5	495	2.9	511	3.0	494	2.9	505	3.0
Estonia	524	2.8	480	2.9	508	2.9	516	2.9	528	3.1	527	3.1
Finland	563	2.4	508	2.6	539	2.5	542	2.5	562	2.6	546	2.7
France	515	3.4	475	4.3	489	3.4	505	3.8	497	3.5	500	4.6
Germany	518	2.9	478	3.6	505	3.3	520	3.6	518	3.3	523	3.7
Greece	506	3.5	459	5.5	459	3.3	473	5.4	475	3.7	465	5.1
Hungary	513	3.6	475	3.9	484	3.9	496	4.2	503	3.5	503	3.8
Iceland	522	1.9	478	2.1	505	1.9	508	2.0	495	2.0	496	2.1
Ireland	515	3.1	476	4.2	483	3.0	491	3.4	509	3.8	507	4.3
Israel	495	3.4	452	5.2	443	3.3	451	4.7	456	3.2	453	4.4
Italy	510	1.9	464	2.3	475	2.2	490	2.3	490	2.0	488	2.5
Japan	540	3.7	501	5.6	524	3.9	534	5.3	545	3.9	534	5.5
Korea	558	3.8	523	4.9	544	4.5	548	6.2	539	4.2	537	5.0
Luxembourg	492	1.5	453	1.9	479	1.3	499	2.0	480	1.6	487	2.0
Mexico	438	2.1	413	2.1	412	1.9	425	2.1	413	1.9	419	2.0
Netherlands	521	5.3	496	5.1	517	5.1	534	4.8	520	5.9	524	5.3
New Zealand	544	2.6	499	3.6	515	2.9	523	3.2	535	2.9	529	4.0
Norway	527	2.9	480	3.0	495	2.8	500	2.7	502	2.8	498	3.0
Poland	525	2.9	476	2.8	493	3.2	497	3.0	511	2.8	505	2.7
Portugal	508	2.9	470	3.5	481	3.1	493	3.3	495	3.0	491	3.4
Slovak Republic	503	2.8	452	3.5	495	3.4	498	3.7	491	3.2	490	4.0
Slovenia	511	1.4	456	1.6	501	1.7	502	1.8	519	1.6	505	1.7
Spain	496	2.2	467	2.2	474	2.5	493	2.3	485	2.3	492	2.5
Sweden	521	3.1	475	3.2	495	3.3	493	3.1	497	3.2	493	3.0
Switzerland	520	2.7	481	2.9	524	3.4	544	3.7	512	3.0	520	3.2
Turkey	486	4.1	443	3.7	440	5.6	451	4.6	460	4.5	448	3.8
United Kingdom	507	2.9	481	3.5	482	3.3	503	3.2	509	3.2	519	3.6
United States	513	3.8	488	4.2	477	3.8	497	4.0	495	3.7	509	4.2
EU 27	..	..	..	..	..	..	..	..	..	..	..	..
OECD	513	0.5	474	0.6	490	0.6	501	0.6	501	0.6	501	0.6
Brazil	425	2.8	397	2.9	379	2.6	394	2.4	404	2.6	407	2.6
China	..	..	..	..	..	..	..	..	..	..	..	..
India	..	..	..	..	..	..	..	..	..	..	..	..
Indonesia	420	3.9	383	3.8	372	4.0	371	4.1	387	4.0	378	4.2
Russian Federation	482	3.4	437	3.6	467	3.5	469	3.7	480	3.5	477	3.7
South Africa	..	..	..	..	..	..	..	..	..	..	..	..

StatLink http://dx.doi.org/10.1787/888932709396

Performance on the reading and mathematics scales in PISA 2009

Mean score

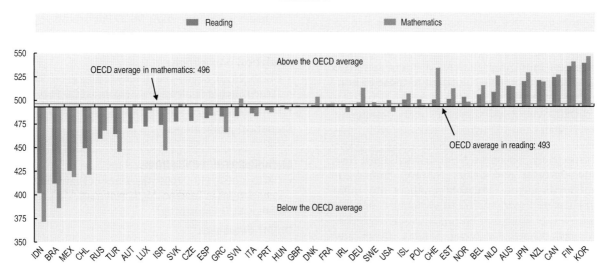

StatLink http://dx.doi.org/10.1787/888932709415

DISADVANTAGES IN SCHOOLS

The successful integration of immigrant students in schools is an important policy goal in many OECD countries. A country's success in integrating immigrant students is a key measure of its education system's quality and equity, and also sheds light on the efficacy of its broader social policies. The variance in performance gaps between immigrant and non-immigrant students across countries, even after adjusting for socio-economic background, suggests that policy has an important role to play in eliminating such gaps.

Definition

PISA distinguishes between three types of student immigrant status: i) students without an immigrant background, also referred to as *non-immigrant students*, are students who were born in the country where they were assessed by PISA or who had at least one parent born in the country; ii) *second-generation students* are students who were born in the country of assessment but whose parents are foreign-born; and iii) *first-generation students* are foreign-born students whose parents are also foreign-born. In this indicator, *immigrant students* include the students who are first- or second-generation immigrants.

Students are referred to as *students with low-educated mothers*, when their mothers have attained less than upper secondary education. The students whose mothers have a tertiary education are referred to as *students with highly educated mothers*.

Each sampled school in a country has been placed into a quartile defined according to the estimated (weighted) percentage of students in the school with low-educated mothers. The *disadvantaged schools* correspond to the 4th quartile, with the largest proportion of students with low-educated mothers. The *advantaged schools* are in the 1st quartile, with the smallest proportion of students with low-educated mothers.

Overview

Three different measures of concentration can be examined to see which one affects students outcomes in general, and those of the immigrant students in particular. These measures are different percentages of students in schools who are: i) immigrant students; ii) immigrant students speaking another language at home; and iii) students (whatever their origin) with low-educated mothers.

For immigrant students' performance in reading, the percentage of students with low-educated mothers in a school is more highly negatively correlated with individual reading performance for the immigrant students in all countries assessed (except Estonia) than the two other concentration measures. In many European countries, the association between immigrant outcomes and school disadvantage is especially high. The exceptions are the Nordic countries, Ireland and Spain, although, in general, outcomes for immigrant students in these countries are not always favourable compared to those of non-immigrant students.

Across OECD countries, there are more immigrant students than non-immigrant students with low-educated mothers in disadvantaged schools (56% and 50% respectively), except in Ireland, Israel, Italy, New Zealand, Portugal and Spain. However immigrant students with highly educated mothers are more strongly overrepresented in disadvantaged schools (26% on average) than non-immigrant students (14.5% on average), except for Brazil, Estonia, Israel and Norway. The disadvantaged quartile is characterised not by immigrant characteristics but, rather, by maternal educational disadvantaged.

Comparability

PISA covers students who are between 15 years 3 months and 16 years 2 months of age at the time of assessment, and who have completed at least 6 years of formal schooling, regardless of the type of institution in which they are enrolled and of whether they are in full-time or part-time education, whether they attend general or vocational programmes, and whether they attend public, private or foreign schools within the country.

Sources
- OECD (2012), *Untapped Skills: Realising the Potential of Immigrant Students*, PISA, OECD Publishing.

Further information

Analytical publications
- OECD (2012), *Equity and Quality in Education, Supporting Disadvantaged Students and Schools*, OECD Publishing.
- OECD (2010), *PISA 2009 Results*, OECD Publishing.

Statistical publications
- OECD (2010), *PISA 2009 at a Glance*, OECD Publishing.

Methodological publications
- OECD (2009), PISA 2009 Assessment Framework: Key Competencies in Reading, Mathematics and Science, PISA, OECD Publishing.

Online databases
- *OECD PISA Database*.

Websites
- Programme for International Student Assessment (PISA), *www.pisa.oecd.org*.

Students in disadvantaged schools and mean reading performance by mother's educational level

Results based on students' self-reports

	Students with low-educated mothers in disadvantaged schools, as a percentage of all students with low-educated mothers				Students with highly educated mothers in disadvantaged schools, as a percentage of all students with highly educated mothers				Mean performance on the reading scale of students			
	Immigrant students		Non-immigrant students		Immigrant students		Non-immigrant students		With low-educated mothers		With highly educated mothers	
	%	S.E.	%	S.E.	%	S.E.	%	S.E.	Mean score	S.E.	Mean score	S.E.
Australia	66.0	6.3	52.6	4.3	22.7	4.0	16.6	2.3	471	4.3	541	2.8
Austria	64.2	5.7	51.7	6.4	39.1	7.3	14.5	2.8	404	6.6	499	4.0
Belgium	76.5	3.7	47.0	4.3	30.6	4.5	16.0	2.2	465	3.9	535	2.5
Canada	66.4	6.3	58.3	4.4	23.8	3.9	18.6	2.0	491	4.7	537	1.7
Chile	..	..	46.7	5.2	..	..	7.3	1.4	416	3.4	487	3.6
Czech Republic	..	..	72.2	4.7	25.5	9.5	21.6	3.5	432	7.4	496	4.9
Denmark	68.3	5.0	44.4	5.1	36.4	4.6	18.6	3.0	451	3.7	512	2.5
Estonia	..	..	56.1	5.0	13.4	5.4	21.5	2.8	467	6.6	511	3.4
Finland	..	..	46.6	5.2	28.6	8.0	21.7	3.3	496	4.7	547	2.4
France	62.8	6.4	43.8	5.3	36.5	7.4	13.1	2.4	456	4.6	529	4.4
Germany	58.5	6.4	45.8	4.9	31.3	5.3	13.0	2.5	448	4.2	529	4.2
Greece	56.8	10.7	49.6	4.6	30.6	4.3	14.1	2.7	444	6.2	506	3.9
Hungary	..	..	60.8	4.6	..	..	9.1	1.3	421	6.0	534	4.6
Iceland	..	..	43.2	1.9	..	..	17.6	0.8	477	3.2	520	2.2
Ireland	26.2	8.8	47.2	5.6	28.6	6.0	15.6	3.2	461	4.0	519	3.3
Israel	47.2	7.1	80.6	2.7	7.3	3.0	12.3	1.6	401	6.3	516	3.8
Italy	40.1	5.4	43.7	2.1	18.7	4.2	11.0	1.0	459	2.6	503	2.4
Japan	..	..	66.0	4.4	..	..	14.9	1.6	483	7.3	542	3.6
Korea	..	..	54.7	5.0	..	..	14.7	2.8	504	7.2	555	4.9
Luxembourg	48.7	1.8	27.4	2.2	15.7	1.8	11.1	0.9	436	2.6	503	2.7
Mexico	52.5	5.9	35.7	2.2	25.8	7.3	7.5	0.7	408	1.9	455	2.4
Netherlands	71.4	6.0	40.6	5.2	41.7	9.1	15.3	2.7	479	5.8	526	5.5
New Zealand	40.1	6.0	47.3	4.7	18.0	3.0	17.3	2.7	493	4.0	551	3.2
Norway	57.8	8.0	53.6	5.6	18.1	4.8	21.4	3.0	465	6.0	516	2.8
Poland	..	..	55.3	5.3	..	..	14.9	3.1	444	5.1	553	3.9
Portugal	12.4	3.8	37.0	4.2	10.8	3.3	6.7	1.2	470	3.2	531	4.5
Slovak Republic	..	..	83.1	3.7	..	..	18.4	3.0	384	11.3	503	4.2
Slovenia	71.1	4.5	56.0	2.6	29.4	6.6	11.0	0.8	440	3.8	516	2.7
Spain	30.8	5.0	42.3	4.1	15.3	3.6	10.7	1.5	460	2.5	509	2.8
Sweden	59.7	8.1	45.0	5.1	37.5	6.7	19.6	2.8	447	6.1	513	3.2
Switzerland	49.3	4.3	39.7	4.5	25.1	3.9	14.2	2.2	463	3.9	522	3.5
Turkey	..	..	30.0	3.8	..	..	2.7	0.9	454	3.2	523	7.5
United Kingdom	79.8	8.1	57.1	4.6	42.5	7.0	17.7	2.3	454	5.4	516	2.7
United States	79.0	4.2	42.3	6.4	25.4	5.7	12.8	2.5	458	4.3	525	4.8
EU 27	..	..	..	..	..	..	..	..	..	..	..	..
OECD	55.9	1.3	50.1	0.8	26.1	1.1	14.5	0.4	453	0.9	520	0.6
Brazil	49.1	15.1	37.6	3.5	0.9	1.0	9.6	1.4	393	2.6	437	4.9
China	..	..	..	..	..	..	..	..	..	..	..	..
India	..	..	..	..	..	..	..	..	..	..	..	..
Indonesia	..	..	35.5	4.6	..	..	4.6	1.4	390	3.2	437	8.3
Russian Federation	..	..	75.9	6.1	23.0	5.6	21.9	3.6	397	12.3	468	3.2
South Africa	..	..	..	..	..	..	..	..	..	..	..	..

StatLink http://dx.doi.org/10.1787/888932709434

Correlations between reading outcomes of immigrant students and various measures of student concentration in schools

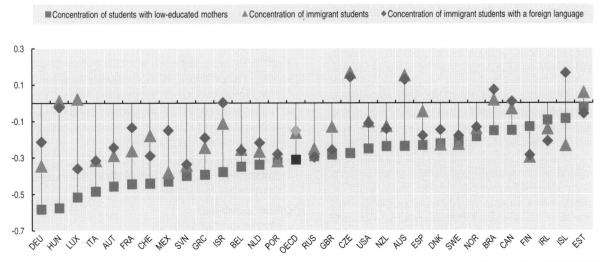

StatLink http://dx.doi.org/10.1787/888932709453

CAREER ASPIRATIONS OF 15-YEAR-OLDS

Education's impact on participating in labour markets, occupational mobility and the quality of life, has led policy makers and educators to focus in reducing educational differences between men and women. Significant progress has been achieved in weakening the gender gap in educational attainment, although in certain fields of study, such as mathematics and computer science, gender differences favouring men still exist.

Students' perceptions of what occupations lie ahead for them can affect their academic decisions and performance.

Definition

On the 2006 PISA assessment, 15-year-old students were asked what they expect to be doing in early adulthood, around the age of 30. Across countries many gender differences can be seen over the different career aspirations. This gender difference can be attributed to a number of factors. These include students' family characteristics and academic performance, but also the specific national labour market conditions and the features of national education systems that provide different options for 15 year-olds.

Comparability

The PISA target population is 15-year-old students. Operationally, these are students who were from 15 years and 3 (completed) months to 16 years and 2 (completed) months at the beginning of the testing period, and who were enrolled in an educational institution, regardless of the grade level or type of institution and of whether they participated in school full-time or part-time.

As far as occupational plans are concerned, student preferences tend to centre heavily on occupations that require at least some tertiary study. Using the nomenclature presented in the *International Standard Classification of Occupations* (ISCO), this preference by 15-year-olds boys and girls to expect high status careers refers mostly to categories 1 and 2 of the ISCO88 classification.

Overview

In almost all OECD countries, girls have more ambitious aspirations than boys. On average, girls are 11 percentage points more likely than boys to expect to work in high-status careers such as legislators, senior officials, managers and professionals. France, Germany and Japan were the only OECD countries where similar proportions of boys and girls aspired to these careers, while in Switzerland, boys generally had slightly more ambitious aspirations than girls. The gender gap in career expectations was particularly wide in Greece and Poland: in these two countries, the proportion of girls expecting to work as legislators, senior officials, managers and professionals was 20 percentage points higher than the proportion of boys expecting to work in those occupations.

In recent years, girls in many countries have caught up with or even surpassed boys in science proficiency. However, better performance in science or mathematics among girls, does not necessarily mean that girls want to pursue all types of science-related careers. In fact, careers in "engineering and computing" still attract relatively few girls. On average among OECD countries, fewer than 5% of girls, but 18% of boys, expected to be working in engineering and computing (including architects) as young adults. This fact may due to stereotypes with the representation of these fields as "masculine" and perceived to be more suited for men, whereas care-related fields, such as education or health, may be perceived as "feminine" and therefore more appropriate for women. Indeed, almost 20% of girls expected to be working in health and services, including nurses & midwifes, comparing to only 7% for boys.

Sources

- OECD (2012), *Education at a Glance*, OECD Publishing.
- OECD (2012), "What Kinds of Careers do Boys and Girls Expect for Themselves?", *PISA in Focus*, No. 14.

Further information

Analytical publications

- OECD (2012), *OECD Education Working Papers*, OECD Publishing.
- OECD (2012), *Post-Secondary Vocational Education and Training, Pathways and Partnerships*, Higher Education in Regional and City Development, OECD Publishing.
- OECD (2010), *Jobs for Youth*, OECD Publishing.
- OECD (2000), *From Initial Education to Working Life: Making Transitions Work*, OECD Publishing.
- Sikora, J. and A. Pokropek (2011), "Gendered Career Expectations of Students: Perspectives from PISA 2006", *OECD Education Working Papers*, No. 57.

Statistical publications

- OECD (2011), *Society at a Glance: OECD Social Indicators*, OECD Publishing.

Online databases

- *OECD Education Statistics*

Websites

- OECD Education at a Glance (supplementary material), *www.oecd.org/edu/eag2012*.

Career aspirations of 15-year-olds

	Percentage of 15-year-old students who are:											
	Planning to work in International Standard Classification of Occupations (ISCO) major occupational groups 1 and 2				Planning a career in engineering and computing, including architects				Expecting employment in health and services, including nurses and midwives			
	Boys		Girls		Boys		Girls		Boys		Girls	
	%	S.E.	%	S.E.	%	S.E.	%	S.E.	%	S.E.	%	S.E.
Australia	49.6	1.1	59.4	0.9	16.3	0.6	2.8	0.2	8.3	0.5	18.3	0.6
Austria	30.8	2.1	41.5	2.2	15.1	1.6	3.3	0.5	4.5	0.7	20.5	1.4
Belgium	50.2	1.6	65.9	1.3	18.7	0.9	5.1	0.4	6.2	0.5	17.2	0.7
Canada	51.2	0.9	66.6	0.7	18.8	0.7	3.2	0.3	11.8	0.6	30.1	0.7
Chile	67.2	2.1	73.2	1.3	25.9	1.4	5.9	0.5	14.2	0.8	30.6	1.8
Czech Republic	40.7	1.8	50.3	1.9	20.0	1.6	4.8	1.2	2.8	0.4	10.9	1.3
Denmark	39.3	1.2	43.6	1.5	13.0	0.8	3.3	0.5	5.4	0.5	20.2	1.0
Estonia	44.8	1.4	60.5	1.4	18.5	1.0	8.8	0.7	2.2	0.3	10.8	0.9
Finland	31.6	1.3	49.6	1.3	10.5	0.7	2.1	0.4	4.7	0.6	15.6	0.9
France	42.4	1.9	43.2	1.6	18.3	1.1	3.5	0.5	9.2	0.8	27.6	1.0
Germany	33.3	1.5	33.9	1.4	14.2	1.0	3.6	0.4	4.1	0.6	15.4	1.0
Greece	48.3	1.8	70.0	1.2	19.2	1.0	7.0	0.7	7.3	0.8	13.1	0.8
Hungary	40.9	2.1	50.7	2.0	19.1	1.6	4.1	0.5	3.9	0.6	12.1	1.1
Iceland	54.4	1.4	66.8	1.2	14.1	0.9	7.5	0.7	10.1	0.8	20.9	1.1
Ireland	53.8	1.5	65.1	1.4	18.1	1.0	3.4	0.5	9.5	0.9	23.7	0.8
Israel	65.3	2.4	79.9	1.3	15.6	1.5	6.8	0.8	14.3	1.4	26.7	1.4
Italy	52.7	1.3	65.6	1.0	21.4	1.3	4.9	0.5	8.6	1.0	16.4	0.8
Japan	42.5	1.3	43.0	1.7	15.1	1.2	3.2	0.4	6.4	0.7	16.4	2.0
Korea	59.5	1.2	63.3	1.2	12.4	0.8	2.6	0.4	5.2	0.4	9.6	0.8
Luxembourg	50.0	0.9	69.1	1.1	16.4	0.9	4.8	0.5	6.6	0.6	17.4	1.0
Mexico	77.7	1.0	82.5	0.7	27.3	0.9	7.8	0.5	12.4	0.8	20.4	0.8
Netherlands	43.2	1.4	47.8	1.5	7.8	0.7	2.4	0.4	6.0	0.6	25.2	1.1
New Zealand	46.3	1.3	62.0	1.0	12.2	0.9	3.7	0.4	9.4	0.8	21.7	1.0
Norway	44.4	1.3	58.4	1.4	19.4	1.1	7.4	0.7	4.7	0.5	21.8	1.1
Poland	43.6	1.3	65.6	1.4	32.6	1.2	7.2	0.6	5.7	0.5	16.5	0.8
Portugal	53.5	1.7	66.1	1.2	24.6	1.3	6.3	0.6	10.5	0.9	29.0	1.0
Slovak Republic	52.1	1.9	64.3	1.8	23.1	1.5	3.1	0.5	3.3	0.5	11.9	1.3
Slovenia	47.9	1.1	65.1	1.1	27.7	0.9	3.6	0.6	8.3	0.7	23.1	1.0
Spain	52.3	1.4	69.6	1.1	23.8	0.9	6.1	0.5	7.4	0.7	21.4	0.8
Sweden	34.1	1.1	44.9	1.3	15.3	0.9	4.4	0.5	4.6	0.6	15.8	0.9
Switzerland	35.2	0.9	31.6	1.2	14.8	0.6	3.1	0.4	2.8	0.3	18.2	0.9
Turkey	79.0	1.4	85.8	1.3	20.9	1.4	7.0	0.8	9.5	0.9	16.3	1.4
United Kingdom	46.5	1.1	56.9	1.1	12.6	0.6	2.1	0.2	7.9	0.6	17.8	0.7
United States	56.4	1.4	70.6	1.3	16.4	0.8	2.7	0.4	12.4	0.8	35.6	1.0
EU 27	..	..	..	..	..	..	..	..	..	..	..	..
OECD	48.8	0.3	59.8	0.2	18.2	0.2	4.6	0.1	7.4	0.1	19.7	0.2
Brazil	49.9	1.3	71.3	1.0	17.3	0.9	6.0	0.6	13.8	1.0	32.0	1.2
China	..	..	..	..	..	..	..	..	..	..	..	..
India	..	..	..	..	..	..	..	..	..	..	..	..
Indonesia	60.0	2.4	66.2	2.0	11.8	4.7	6.6	1.0	15.1	1.9	22.3	1.5
Russian Federation	54.7	2.0	73.5	1.0	20.9	1.6	5.3	0.6	3.6	0.4	14.4	1.0
South Africa	..	..	..	..	..	..	..	..	..	..	..	..

StatLink 🔗 http://dx.doi.org/10.1787/888932709472

Career aspirations of 15-year-olds

Percentage of 15-year old students

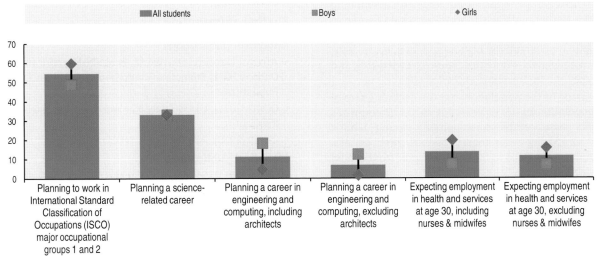

StatLink 🔗 http://dx.doi.org/10.1787/888932709491

YOUTH INACTIVITY

Young people who are neither in employment nor in education and training (the "NEET" population) are at risk of becoming socially excluded – individuals with income below the poverty-line and lacking the skills to improve their economic situation.

Definition

The indicator presents the share of young people who are neither in education and training nor in employment, as a percentage of the total number of young people in the corresponding age group. Young people in education include those attending part-time as well as full-time education, but exclude those in non-formal education and in educational activities of very short duration. Employment is defined according to the ILO Guidelines and covers all those who have been in paid work for at least one hour in the reference week of the survey or were temporarily absent from such work.

Overview

On average across OECD countries, 18.5% of the 20-24 year-olds and 8.1% of the 15-19 year-olds were neither in school nor at work in 2010.

For OECD countries as a whole, the proportion of the 20-24 year-olds who were neither in employment nor in education increased by 2.5 percentage points between 2008 and 2010, whereas it decreased by 1.6 percentage points between 2000 and 2008. The share of 15-19 year-olds who were not in employment nor in education also declined between 2000 and 2008 (by 1.5 percentage points), while between 2008 and 2010 it has remained broadly stable.

Differences across countries are large: in Luxembourg and the Netherlands less than 8% of young people in the age group 20-24 belonged to the NEET population. The ratio is substantially higher in Ireland, Israel, Italy, Mexico and Spain, where this figure exceeded 25%, and in Turkey, where the share exceeded 40%.

The ageing of the population and the declining size of the population of 15-19 year-olds in OECD countries should favour employment among young adults. However, during recessionary periods, high general unemployment rates make the transition from school to work substantially more difficult for the younger population, as those with more work experience are favoured over new entrants into the labour market. In addition, when labour market conditions are unfavourable, younger people often tend to stay in education longer, because high unemployment rates drive down the opportunity costs of education.

Comparability

In some countries, young people performing compulsory military service are considered as being NEETs. However, this would not result in a great change to the data shown here.

In Korea, the NEET population includes some people who are not classified as being in formal education, but who are training (in education) for employment or for tertiary entrance examinations.

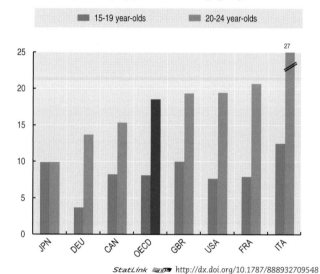

Youth who are not in education nor in employment in G7

As a percentage of persons in that age group, 2010

StatLink http://dx.doi.org/10.1787/888932709548

Sources

- OECD (2012), *Education at a Glance*, OECD Publishing.
- OECD (2012), *OECD Economic Outlook*, OECD Publishing.

Further information

Analytical publications

- African Development Bank, et al. (2012), *African Economic Outlook 2012, Promoting Youth Employment*, OECD Publishing.
- OECD (2012), *OECD Education Working Papers*, OECD Publishing.
- OECD (2010), *Jobs for Youth*, OECD Publishing.

Statistical publications

- OECD (2011), *Society at a Glance: OECD Social Indicators*, OECD Publishing.

Online databases

- *OECD Education Statistics*

Websites

- OECD Education at a Glance (supplementary material), *www.oecd.org/edu/eag2012.*

Youth who are not in education nor in employment

As a percentage of persons in that age group

	Youth aged between 15 and 19						Youth aged between 20 and 24					
	2000	2006	2007	2008	2009	2010	2000	2006	2007	2008	2009	2010
Australia	6.82	7.05	6.49	6.31	8.34	8.06	13.29	11.49	10.74	10.71	11.58	11.21
Austria	..	6.55	5.25	5.63	6.50	5.32	..	12.51	10.95	11.45	11.84	12.60
Belgium	6.52	7.11	5.21	5.47	5.67	5.95	16.04	16.87	15.41	14.14	16.10	18.02
Canada	8.20	7.34	7.27	7.26	8.15	8.23	15.73	13.04	13.70	13.02	15.17	15.32
Chile	..	..	..	..	..	..	..	..	..	..	..	..
Czech Republic	7.89	4.52	2.89	2.72	3.51	3.76	20.33	14.14	11.04	10.56	13.13	13.59
Denmark	2.72	4.42	4.10	4.01	5.03	5.54	6.61	5.87	7.99	8.16	10.13	12.12
Estonia	..	3.69	5.74	4.86	7.96	6.12	..	15.36	15.30	10.65	19.79	22.45
Finland	..	3.58	3.53	5.08	5.13	5.11	..	13.31	13.28	12.01	15.05	15.79
France	6.99	6.98	6.29	5.81	6.81	7.93	17.60	18.99	17.94	16.59	19.95	20.65
Germany	5.71	4.21	4.15	3.71	3.76	3.68	16.95	16.73	15.24	13.97	13.73	13.67
Greece	9.33	7.85	8.49	8.38	7.95	7.52	25.92	18.37	17.73	17.12	18.24	21.55
Hungary	8.63	6.02	5.00	5.70	5.63	4.64	21.99	18.51	16.91	18.39	20.90	21.51
Iceland	..	..	..	..	..	6.82	..	..	6.38	..	9.39	10.54
Ireland	4.38	5.01	5.10	8.49	11.00	10.45	9.65	11.76	12.12	14.57	20.83	26.44
Israel	..	24.27	25.75	22.24	24.68	22.48	..	40.58	39.65	37.51	37.45	36.94
Italy	13.13	11.79	10.17	9.59	11.22	12.47	27.47	22.82	22.58	22.02	24.76	27.10
Japan	8.76	9.08	7.63	7.37	8.46	9.87	8.76	9.08	7.63	7.37	8.46	9.87
Korea	..	..	..	7.04	6.95	8.47	..	..	..	22.20	23.01	23.51
Luxembourg	..	4.07	2.93	2.12	2.71	6.26	8.23	10.25	9.21	9.84	8.67	7.52
Mexico	18.31	17.82	17.55	17.75	18.42	18.60	27.14	26.64	26.52	26.50	27.59	26.62
Netherlands	3.71	3.04	3.62	2.06	3.57	3.77	8.23	7.29	5.24	5.63	7.91	7.79
New Zealand	..	8.97	9.66	8.50	12.38	10.44	..	13.66	14.24	15.27	18.32	18.43
Norway	..	3.43	3.67	3.98	4.18	3.49	8.03	9.08	8.76	7.05	9.40	9.03
Poland	4.52	3.79	2.46	2.38	3.63	3.59	30.76	20.67	18.34	15.56	16.44	17.66
Portugal	7.73	7.75	8.55	7.07	6.92	7.44	10.95	13.34	15.20	13.46	15.72	16.38
Slovak Republic	26.26	6.69	5.43	5.66	4.55	4.58	33.10	22.75	19.85	16.59	17.13	22.14
Slovenia	..	4.23	4.29	4.38	2.53	3.18	..	13.71	10.45	10.26	11.38	9.25
Spain	7.96	10.09	10.94	10.54	13.43	12.84	15.05	16.85	17.24	19.44	26.27	27.40
Sweden	3.63	5.30	5.45	4.40	5.54	5.39	10.69	15.20	13.11	12.92	16.50	14.32
Switzerland	7.90	7.57	8.16	9.38	7.95	4.77	5.92	10.79	10.36	9.14	10.73	11.06
Turkey	31.17	35.04	34.47	37.06	28.69	25.60	44.18	48.77	46.25	46.07	46.12	43.67
United Kingdom	8.04	10.92	10.70	9.77	9.60	9.99	15.37	18.24	18.07	18.33	19.14	19.34
United States	7.00	6.33	6.32	7.25	8.80	7.65	14.44	15.60	16.22	17.23	20.07	19.43
EU 27	7.95	6.08	5.73	5.61	6.32	6.45	17.35	15.41	14.52	13.89	16.36	17.49
OECD	9.39	8.18	7.99	7.89	8.42	8.13	17.65	17.11	16.06	16.01	17.89	18.53
Brazil	..	..	14.72	13.78	14.02	..	..	..	23.44	22.50	23.29	..
China	..	..	..	..	..	..	..	..	..	..	..	..
India	..	..	..	..	..	..	..	..	..	..	..	..
Indonesia	..	..	..	..	..	..	..	..	..	..	..	..
Russian Federation	..	..	..	..	..	..	..	..	..	..	..	..
South Africa	..	..	..	..	..	..	..	..	..	..	..	..

StatLink http://dx.doi.org/10.1787/888932709510

Youth aged between 20 and 24 who are not in education nor in employment

As a percentage of persons in that age group

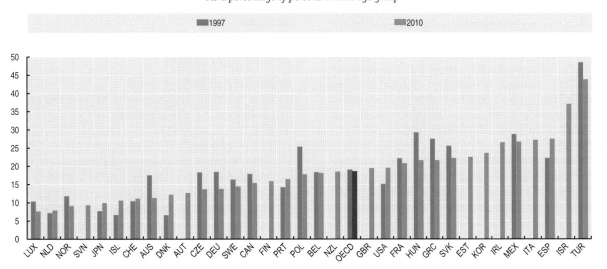

StatLink http://dx.doi.org/10.1787/888932709529

HOW MANY STUDENTS STUDY ABROAD?

As national economies become more interconnected, governments and individuals are looking to higher education to broaden students' horizons. It is through the pursuit of high level studies in countries other than their own that students may expand their knowledge of other cultures and languages, and to better equip themselves in an increasingly globalised labour market. Some countries, particularly in the European Union, have established policies and schemes that promote such mobility to foster intercultural contacts and help build social networks.

Definition

Students are classified as "international" if they left their country of origin only for the purpose of study. Students are classified as "foreign" when they are not citizens of the country where they are enrolled. This includes some students who are permanent residents, albeit not citizens, of the countries in which they are studying such as young people from immigrant families. Consequently, foreign graduation rates are not comparable with data on international graduation rates and are therefore presented separately.

Comparability

Data on international and foreign students refer to the academic year 2009/2010, based on data collected on education statistics, annually by the OECD. Additional data from the UNESCO Institute for Statistics are also included. Data on the impact of international students on tertiary graduation rates are based on a special survey conducted by the OECD in December 2011.

Overview

Over the past three decades, the number of students enrolled outside their country of citizenship has risen dramatically, from 0.8 million worldwide in 1975 to 4.1 million in 2010, more than a fivefold increase. Growth in the internationalisation of tertiary education has accelerated during the past several decades, reflecting the globalisation of economies and societies, and also the expansion of tertiary systems and institutions throughout the world.

Language as well as cultural considerations, quality of programmes, geographic proximity and similarity of education systems are determining factors driving student mobility. The destinations of international students highlight the attractiveness of specific education systems, whether because of their academic reputation or because of subsequent immigration opportunities.

Foreign students enrolled in G20 countries account for 83% of total foreign students, and students in the OECD area represent 77% of the total foreign students enrolled worldwide. European countries in the OECD were the destination for 40% of foreign students in 2010 followed by North American countries (21%). Despite the strong increase in absolute numbers, these proportions have remained stable during the last decade. In the OECD area, the number of foreign students in tertiary education is nearly three times as high as the number of national citizens enrolled abroad. In the 21 European countries who are OECD members there is a ratio of 2.7 foreign students per each citizen from an European country studying abroad.

More than 9 out of 10 OECD students enrol in another OECD country when pursuing tertiary studies outside their country of citizenship. Students from other G20 countries not in OECD also prefer to study in OECD countries, with 83% of them enrolled in an OECD country. European citizens from OECD countries are also mostly enrolled in another European country (76%), while in North America a large majority of students are citizens of a country from a different region.

Sources

- OECD (2012), *Education at a Glance*, OECD Publishing.

Further information

Analytical publications

- OECD (2012), *Higher Education in Regional and City Development*, OECD Publishing.
- OECD (2012), *Higher Education Management and Policy*, OECD Publishing.
- Keeley, B. (2009), *International Migration: The Human Face of Globalisation*, OECD Insights, OECD Publishing.
- OECD (2008), *Tertiary Education for the Knowledge Society*, OECD Review of Tertiary Education, OECD Publishing.
- OECD (2004), *Internationalisation and Trade in Higher Education: Opportunities and Challenges*, OECD Publishing.

Online databases

- *OECD Education Statistics*.

Websites

- OECD Education at a Glance, *www.oecd.org/edu/eag2012*

Evolution by destination in the number of students enrolled outside their country of citizenship

Thousand of persons

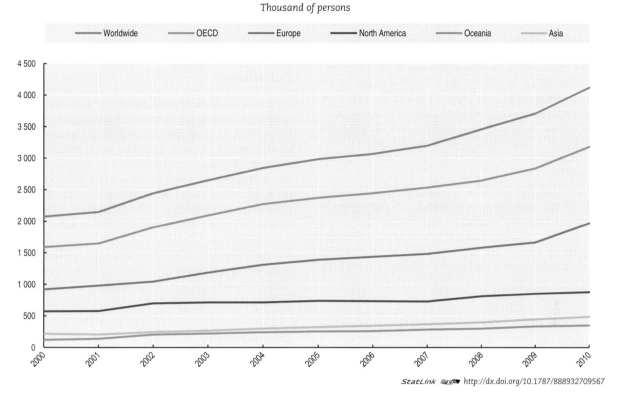

StatLink http://dx.doi.org/10.1787/888932709567

Impact of international/foreign students on graduation rate at tertiary-type A level

Percentage, 2010 or latest available year

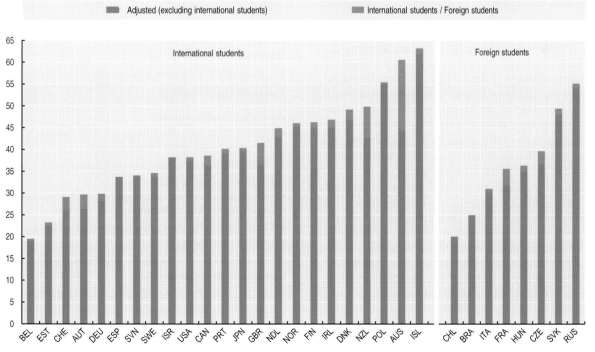

StatLink http://dx.doi.org/10.1787/888932709586

EDUCATIONAL ATTAINMENT

Educational attainment is a commonly used proxy for the stock of human capital – that is, the skills available in the population and the labour force. As globalisation and technology continue to re-shape the needs of the global labour market, the demand for individuals who possess a broader knowledge base, more specialised skills, advanced analytical capacities, and complex communication skills continues to rise. As a result, more individuals are pursuing higher levels of education than in previous generations, leading to significant shifts in attainment levels over time within countries.

At the same time, the rise of new economic powers – and sustained efforts by some countries to build and invest in their tertiary education systems – has shifted the global landscape of educational attainment as well. In recent years, countries with strong and long-held leads in attainment have seen their positions erode as individuals in other countries have increased their attainment at an extremely fast pace.

Definition

Educational attainment refers to the highest level of education completed by a person, shown as a percentage of all persons in that age group. Tertiary education includes both tertiary-type A programmes, which are largely theoretically-based and designed to provide qualifications for entry to advanced research programmes and professions with high skill requirements; and tertiary-type B programmes, which are generally not intended to lead to further university-level degrees, but rather directly to the labour market. Upper secondary education typically follows completion of lower secondary schooling. Lower secondary education completes provision of basic education, usually in a more subject-oriented way and with more specialised teachers.

Comparability

The *International Standard Classification of Education* (ISCED-97) is used to define the levels of education in a comparable way across countries. The *OECD Handbook for Internationally Comparative Education Statistics* describes ISCED-97 education programmes and attainment levels and their mappings for each country.

Overview

An indication of long-term trends in educational attainment can be obtained by comparing the current attainment levels of younger and older age cohorts. Tertiary attainment levels have increased considerably over the past 30 years. On average across OECD countries, 38% of 25-34 year-olds have a tertiary attainment, compared with 23% of 55-64 year-olds. Canada, Japan, Korea and the Russian Federation lead OECD and G20 countries in the proportion of young adults (25-34 year-olds) with a tertiary attainment, with 55% or more having reached this level of education. In France, Ireland, Japan, Korea and Poland, there is a difference of 25 percentage points or more between the proportion of young adults and older adults who have attained this level of education.

In 2010, over 30% of the population aged between 25 and 64 has attained tertiary level education in more than half of the OECD countries.

On average across OECD countries, 26% of adults now have only primary or lower secondary levels of education, 44% have upper secondary education and 31% have a tertiary qualification. Over the past decade most of the changes in educational attainment have occurred at the low and high ends of the attainment distribution. Between 2000 and 2010 the share of those who had not attained an upper secondary education decreased by 10 percentage points while the proportion with tertiary education increased by 9 percentage points across OECD countries. This largely reflects the fact that older workers with low levels of education have moved out of the labour force, and that many countries have expanded their focus on higher education in recent years.

Sources

• OECD (2012), *Education at a Glance*, OECD Publishing.

Further information

Analytical publications

• OECD (2012), *Let's Read Them a Story! The Parent Factor in Education*, PISA, OECD Publishing.
• OECD (2012), *OECD Reviews of Evaluation and Assessment in Education*, OECD Publishing.
• OECD (2012), *Higher Education in Regional and City Development*, OECD Publishing.
• OECD (2012), *Reviews of National Policies for Education*, OECD Publishing.
• OECD (2010), *Trends Shaping Education*, OECD Publishing.

Methodological publications

• OECD (2004), *OECD Handbook for Internationally Comparative Education Statistics: Concepts, Standards, Definitions and Classifications*, OECD Publishing.

Online databases

• *OECD Education Statistics*.

Websites

• OECD Centre for Educational Research and Innovation (CERI), *www.oecd.org/edu/ceri*.

Educational attainment

As a percentage of total population in that age group

| | Population with tertiary education 2010 or latest available year | | | | Population aged 25-64 | | | | | | | | |
| | 25-34 | 35-44 | 45-54 | 55-64 | Below upper secondary | | | Upper secondary and post-secondary non-tertiary | | | Tertiary education | | |
					2000	2005	2010	2000	2005	2010	2000	2005	2010
Australia	44.4	39.5	34.8	29.6	41.2	35.0	26.8	31.3	33.3	35.6	27.5	31.7	37.6
Austria	20.8	20.8	18.6	16.5	23.9	19.4	17.5	62.2	62.8	63.2	13.9	17.8	19.3
Belgium	43.8	39.4	30.9	25.6	41.5	33.9	29.5	31.4	35.1	35.5	27.1	31.0	35.0
Canada	56.5	56.8	46.8	42.2	19.3	14.8	11.6	40.6	39.2	37.8	40.1	45.9	50.6
Chile	38.5	27.5	21.5	18.9	..	..	28.6	..	..	44.6	..	..	26.8
Czech Republic	22.6	16.3	15.9	11.5	14.1	10.1	8.1	75.0	76.9	75.2	11.0	13.1	16.8
Denmark	37.6	36.8	31.2	27.9	21.5	19.0	24.3	52.4	47.5	42.4	26.2	33.5	33.3
Estonia	37.8	33.2	38.5	30.7	..	10.9	10.9	..	55.8	53.8	..	33.3	35.3
Finland	39.2	45.8	38.9	30.1	27.5	21.2	17.0	40.5	44.2	44.8	32.0	34.6	38.1
France	42.9	33.8	21.7	18.3	37.0	33.2	29.2	40.9	41.4	41.8	22.0	25.4	29.0
Germany	26.1	28.1	26.6	25.4	18.3	16.9	14.2	58.2	58.6	59.2	23.5	24.6	26.6
Greece	30.9	26.6	23.1	16.5	50.7	42.5	34.8	31.6	36.1	40.6	17.7	21.3	24.6
Hungary	26.0	19.1	18.3	16.5	30.8	23.6	18.7	55.2	59.3	61.2	14.0	17.1	20.1
Iceland	36.2	38.8	30.5	22.5	44.7	37.1	33.5	32.1	32.3	34.0	23.2	30.5	32.5
Ireland	48.2	42.3	29.8	21.5	54.0	35.5	26.5	27.5	35.4	36.2	18.5	29.1	37.3
Israel	44.2	48.8	44.4	44.6	..	20.8	17.9	..	33.4	36.5	..	45.8	45.6
Italy	20.7	15.8	12.0	10.7	57.9	49.9	44.8	32.7	37.9	40.4	9.4	12.2	14.8
Japan	56.7	49.6	45.8	29.0	17.1	..	..	49.2	60.1	55.2	33.6	39.9	44.8
Korea	65.0	46.9	26.7	12.8	31.7	24.5	19.6	44.4	43.9	40.7	23.9	31.6	39.7
Luxembourg	44.2	41.4	27.9	25.3	43.9	34.1	22.3	37.8	39.3	42.2	18.3	26.5	35.5
Mexico	21.8	16.2	16.3	12.0	70.9	68.4	63.8	14.5	16.6	18.8	14.6	15.0	17.4
Netherlands	40.8	33.5	30.2	26.0	35.1	28.2	27.0	41.5	41.7	40.6	23.4	30.1	32.4
New Zealand	46.4	42.5	39.1	33.8	36.8	31.6	27.0	34.3	29.4	32.4	28.9	39.0	40.7
Norway	47.3	41.0	33.4	27.3	14.8	22.8	19.4	56.8	44.5	43.3	28.4	32.7	37.3
Poland	37.4	23.4	15.1	12.9	20.1	14.9	11.3	68.5	68.2	65.8	11.4	16.9	22.9
Portugal	24.8	16.2	10.4	8.9	80.6	73.5	68.1	10.5	13.6	16.5	8.8	12.8	15.4
Slovak Republic	24.0	15.9	14.6	12.7	16.2	12.1	9.0	73.4	73.9	73.6	10.4	14.0	17.3
Slovenia	31.3	26.7	20.0	16.3	..	19.7	16.7	..	60.1	59.6	..	20.2	23.7
Spain	39.2	35.3	25.6	17.8	61.7	51.2	47.1	15.7	20.6	22.2	22.6	28.2	30.7
Sweden	42.2	37.2	30.0	27.5	20.8	17.1	13.5	54.4	53.9	52.4	24.8	29.0	34.2
Switzerland	40.5	38.2	33.3	27.7	16.1	14.8	13.9	59.7	56.5	51.0	24.2	28.8	35.2
Turkey	17.4	12.2	9.4	9.5	76.7	71.9	68.8	14.9	17.8	18.1	8.3	10.2	13.1
United Kingdom	46.0	40.6	35.2	30.0	37.4	33.2	24.9	36.9	37.1	36.9	25.7	29.7	38.2
United States	42.3	43.4	40.0	41.0	12.6	12.2	11.0	50.9	48.7	47.3	36.5	39.0	41.7
EU 27	..	..	..	..	..	..	..	..	..	..	..	..	..
OECD	37.8	33.2	27.5	22.9	35.8	29.8	26.0	42.5	44.1	44.1	21.7	27.0	30.7
Brazil	11.6	11.3	10.7	8.9	..	..	..	..	..	..	..	..	..
China	6.1	4.8	3.0	3.1	..	..	..	..	..	..	..	..	..
India	..	..	..	..	..	..	..	..	..	..	..	..	..
Indonesia	..	..	..	..	..	..	..	..	..	..	..	..	..
Russian Federation	55.5	58.1	54.3	44.5	..	..	..	..	..	..	..	..	..
South Africa	..	..	..	..	..	..	..	..	..	..	..	..	..

StatLink http://dx.doi.org/10.1787/888932709605

Population that has attained tertiary education

Percentage, 2010 or latest available year

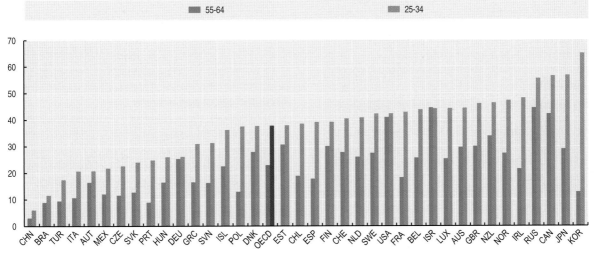

StatLink http://dx.doi.org/10.1787/888932709624

EDUCATIONAL EXPENDITURE PER STUDENT

Policy makers must balance the importance of improving the quality of educational services with the desirability of expanding access to educational opportunities, specifically at the tertiary level. In many OECD countries the expansion of enrolments, particularly in tertiary education, has not been paralleled by similar rises in educational expenditures. In primary, secondary and post-secondary non-tertiary education, enrolments are stable but expenditure has increased more than at the tertiary level.

Definition

The indicator shows change in expenditure on educational institutions in relation to the number of full-time equivalent students enrolled in these institutions. The indicator includes only those educational institutions, both public and private, and programmes for which both enrolment and expenditure data are available. Public subsidies for students' living expenses are excluded to ensure international comparability of the data.

Educational expenditure in national currency for 2009 is converted into equivalent USD by dividing the national currency figure by the purchasing power parity (PPP) index for GDP. PPP exchange rates are used because market exchange rates are affected by many factors that are unrelated to the purchasing power of currencies in different countries.

Comparability

The data on expenditures were obtained by a special survey conducted in 2011 which applied consistent methods and definitions. Expenditure data are based on the definitions and coverage of the UNESCO-OECD-Eurostat data collection programme on education. The use of a common survey and definitions ensures good comparability of results across countries.

In all cases, 2009 data is 2009 or latest year available.

Overview

In 2009, the average level of expenditure per tertiary student, across OECD countries, was USD 13 728. Spending per student at tertiary level ranged from USD 7 000 or less in Chile, Estonia, Indonesia, the Slovak Republic and South Africa to more than USD 20 000 in Canada, Switzerland and the United States. OECD countries in which most R&D is performed by tertiary educational institutions tend to report higher tertiary expenditure per student than countries in which a large part of research and development is performed in other public institutions or by industry.

The expenditure for tertiary education increased in real terms across OECD countries by an average of 46% between 2000 and 2009, when student enrolment at this level increased by an average of 28%. Spending per student at tertiary level increased by 15% on average. However, spending per student fell in Iceland, Israel and the United States, and public expenditure per student fell also in Brazil, Hungary and Switzerland (data on private expenditure are not available). In all of these countries the decline was mainly the result of a rapid increase (by 20% or more) in the number of tertiary students. Japan was the only country in which the number of tertiary students decreased between 2000 and 2009.

In 2009, the OECD average level of annual expenditure per student for primary, secondary and post-secondary non-tertiary education was USD 8 617. Between 2000 and 2009, a period of relatively stable student enrolment at these levels, spending per students increased in every country, rising by 36% on average. Over this period, expenditure per student increased by at least 16% in 24 of the 29 OECD and partner countries with available data. The rise exceeded 50% in Brazil, the Czech Republic, Estonia, Hungary, Ireland, Korea, Poland, the Slovak Republic and the United Kingdom.

Sources
- OECD (2012), *Education at a Glance*, OECD Publishing.

Further information

Analytical publications
- OECD (2013), *Trends Shaping Education*, OECD Publishing.
- OECD (2012), *Highlights from Education at a Glance*, OECD Publishing.
- OECD (2012), *Higher Education Management and Policy*, OECD Publishing.
- OECD (2012), *OECD Economic Surveys*, OECD Publishing.
- OECD (2012), *Reviews of National Policies for Education*, OECD Publishing.

Methodological publications
- OECD (2004), *OECD Handbook for Internationally Comparative Education Statistics: Concepts, Standards, Definitions and Classifications*, OECD Publishing.
- UNESCO Institute for Statistics (UIS), OECD and Eurostat (2011), *UOE Data Collection on Education Systems*, UIS, Montreal.

Online databases
- *OECD Education Statistics*.

Websites
- OECD Education at a Glance, *www.oecd.org/edu/eag2012*.

Expenditure on educational institutions per student and change in expenditure

	Primary, secondary and post-secondary non tertiary education						Tertiary education					
	Spending per student, USD, 2009, PPPs	Index of change, year 2005 = 100					Spending per student, USD, 2009, PPPs	Index of change, year 2005 = 100				
		Expenditure		Number of students	Expenditure per student			Expenditure		Number of students	Expenditure per student	
	2009	2000	2009	2009	2000	2009	2009	2000	2009	2009	2000	2009
Australia	9 139	82	127	100	89	127	16 074	83	124	117	..	106
Austria	11 681	97	109	97	95	112	14 257	75	117	133	73	87
Belgium	9 783	94	113	96	103	118	15 443	98	123	107	104	114
Canada	8 997	86	113	99	87	115	20 932	86	109	..	..	..
Chile	2 935	..	118	94	..	124	6 863	..	156	149	..	104
Czech Republic	5 615	76	111	91	71	123	8 237	65	141	127	90	111
Denmark	11 094	86	105	101	91	104	18 556	86	109	104	88	104
Estonia	6 149	80	117	86	66	137	6 373	92	150	99	108	151
Finland	8 314	81	108	100	85	108	16 569	86	112	97	91	115
France	8 861	100	103	100	98	104	14 642	93	116	99	98	116
Germany	8 534	100	105	94	97	112	15 711	94	119	109	101	109
Greece	..	78	..	..	77	..	..	42	..	..	63	..
Hungary	4 506	69	88	91	64	97	8 518	81	109	91	122	119
Iceland	9 309	72	101	102	77	100	9 939	69	110	112	103	98
Ireland	9 615	68	138	107	70	130	16 420	100	143	105	118	136
Israel	5 464	95	116	106	101	110	11 214	90	97	104	110	94
Italy	8 943	96	100	100	97	101	9 562	93	110	98	104	113
Japan	8 502	99	101	96	91	105	15 957	94	108	95	95	113
Korea	8 122	69	130	96	68	136	9 513	79	129	101	84	128
Luxembourg	18 018	..	108	105	..	103	..	..	..	..	..	..
Mexico	2 339	80	104	104	85	99	8 020	73	123	114	88	108
Netherlands	10 030	83	114	102	86	112	17 849	86	117	114	101	103
New Zealand	7 556	92	120	101	..	120	10 619	84	133	130	..	102
Norway	12 971	89	114	102	95	112	19 269	86	106	102	98	104
Poland	5 167	89	118	85	81	139	7 776	57	117	96	96	122
Portugal	7 288	98	109	103	90	106	10 481	70	105	103	78	103
Slovak Republic	4 781	73	129	87	68	148	6 758	67	125	125	94	99
Slovenia	8 670	..	104	91	..	113	9 311	..	110	107	..	102
Spain	8 818	93	120	104	87	116	13 614	88	123	109	82	113
Sweden	9 709	88	103	94	90	109	19 961	86	112	98	105	114
Switzerland	13 411	87	108	99	89	109	21 577	77	99	122	97	81
Turkey	..	..	..	..	..	..	..	..	..	..	..	..
United Kingdom	9 602	70	105	100	62	105	16 338	65	127	105	70	120
United States	11 831	92	116	100	95	116	29 201	85	95	114	96	83
EU 27	..	..	..	..	..	..	..	..	..	..	..	..
OECD	8 617	85	112	98	85	115	13 728	81	118	110	95	109
Brazil	2 304	66	156	94	67	166	11 741	79	128	117	112	109
China	..	..	..	..	..	..	..	..	..	..	..	..
India	..	..	..	..	..	..	..	..	..	..	..	..
Indonesia	418	..	..	..	..	..	972	..	..	..	..	..
Russian Federation	4 325	66	139	88	..	158	7 749	44	168	175	..	96
South Africa	1 697	..	..	..	..	..	3 616	..	..	..	..	..

StatLink http://dx.doi.org/10.1787/888932709643

Changes in expenditure on educational institutions in tertiary education by factor

Changes in 2000-09 or latest available period, 2000 = 100

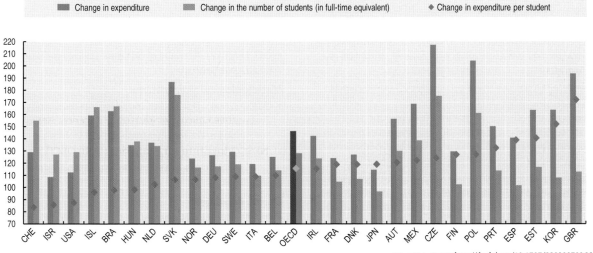

StatLink http://dx.doi.org/10.1787/888932709662

PRIVATE EXPENDITURE IN TERTIARY EDUCATION

Educational institutions in OECD countries are mainly publicly funded, although there are substantial and growing levels of private funding at the tertiary level. At this level, the contribution to the costs of education by individuals and other private entities is more and more considered an effective way to ensure funding is available to students regardless of their economic backgrounds.

Overview

In all countries, the proportion of private expenditure on education is far higher for tertiary education – an average of 30% of total expenditure at this level – than it is for primary, secondary and post-secondary non-tertiary education (9%).

The share of expenditure on tertiary institutions covered by individuals, businesses and other private sources, including subsidised private payments, ranges from less than 5% in Denmark, Finland and Norway, to more than 40% in Australia, Israel, Japan and the United States, to over 70% in Chile, Korea and the United Kingdom. Of these countries, in Korea and the United Kingdom, most students are enrolled in private institutions (around 80% in private universities in Korea; 100% in government-dependent private institutions in the United Kingdom), and most of the budget of educational institutions comes from tuition fees (more than 49% in Korea, and more than 58% in the United Kingdom).

On average across OECD countries, contribution from private entities other than households to financing educational institutions is higher for tertiary education than for other levels of education. In Australia, Canada, the Czech Republic, Israel, Japan, Korea, the Netherlands, the Slovak Republic, Sweden, the United Kingdom and the United States, 10% or more of expenditure on tertiary institutions is covered by private entities other than households. For example, in Sweden these contributions are largely directed to sponsoring research and development.

Between 2000 and 2009, 18 out of the 25 countries for which comparable data are available showed an increase in the share of private funding for tertiary education. The share increased by seven percentage points, on average, and by more than ten percentage points in Mexico, Portugal, the Slovak Republic and the United Kingdom (which saw a 38 percentage point increase). While the share of private funding for tertiary education rose substantially in some countries during the period, this was not the case for other levels of education.

Definition

This indicator covers private expenditure on schools, universities and other private institutions delivering or supporting educational services. Other private entities include private businesses and non-profit organisations, e.g. religious organisations, charitable organisations and business and labour associations. Expenditure by private companies on the work-based element of school- and work-based training of apprentices and students is also taken into account.

Private expenditure is recorded net of public subsidies to educational institutions; it also includes expenditures made outside educational institutions.

Comparability

The data on expenditure were obtained by a survey conducted in 2011 which applied consistent methods and definitions. Expenditure data are based on the definitions and coverage for the UNESCO-OECD-Eurostat data collection programme on education; they have been adjusted to 2009 prices using the GDP price deflator. The use of a common survey and definitions ensures good comparability of results across countries.

Sources

- OECD (2012), *Education at a Glance*, OECD Publishing.

Further information

Analytical publications

- OECD (2013), *Trends Shaping Education*, OECD Publishing.
- OECD (2012), *Highlights from Education at a Glance*, OECD Publishing.
- OECD (2012), *Higher Education Management and Policy*, OECD Publishing.
- OECD (2012), *Reviews of National Policies for Education*, OECD Publishing.

Methodological publications

- OECD (2004), *OECD Handbook for Internationally Comparative Education Statistics: Concepts, Standards, Definitions and Classifications*, OECD Publishing.
- UNESCO Institute for Statistics (UIS), OECD and Eurostat (2011), *UOE Data Collection on Education Systems*, UIS, Montreal.

Online databases

- *OECD Education Statistics*.

Websites

- OECD Education at a Glance, *www.oecd.org/edu/eag2012*.

Public and private expenditure on tertiary educational institutions

| | As a percentage of total expenditure | | | | | | | Index 2000=100 | |
| | Public sources | | Private sources | | | | | Public sources | Private sources |
	2000	2009 or latest available year	Total 2000	Household expenditure 2009 or latest available year	Other 2009 or latest available year	Total 2009 or latest available year	Of which: Subsidised 2009 or latest available year	2009 or latest available year	2009 or latest available year
Australia	49.9	45.4	50.1	39.1	15.4	54.6	0.5	135.0	161.4
Austria	96.3	87.7	3.7	2.9	9.4	12.3	8.8	142.2	517.7
Belgium	91.5	89.7	8.5	5.5	4.8	10.3	3.9	122.6	150.5
Canada	61.0	62.9	39.0	20.2	16.9	37.1	..	130.5	120.5
Chile	..	23.4	..	68.1	8.5	76.6	9.3	..	..
Czech Republic	85.4	79.9	14.6	8.8	11.3	20.1	..	202.4	298.3
Denmark	97.6	95.4	2.4	..	..	4.6	..	120.7	236.4
Estonia	..	80.2	..	18.2	1.6	19.8	..	163.3	..
Finland	97.2	95.8	2.8	..	..	4.2	..	127.3	198.0
France	84.4	83.1	15.6	9.7	7.3	16.9	..	121.7	134.3
Germany	88.2	84.4	11.8	..	..	15.6	..	119.9	166.1
Greece	99.7	..	0.3	..	..	..	..	..	..
Hungary	76.7	..	23.3	..	..	..	..	134.7	..
Iceland	91.8	92.0	8.2	7.4	0.6	8.0	..	159.4	154.5
Ireland	79.2	83.8	20.8	13.8	2.4	16.2	..	151.5	111.3
Israel	58.5	58.2	41.5	27.3	14.6	41.8	5.0	107.8	109.3
Italy	77.5	68.6	22.5	23.8	7.6	31.4	8.5	103.9	164.4
Japan	38.5	35.3	61.5	50.7	14.1	64.7	..	104.8	120.3
Korea	23.3	26.1	76.7	49.2	24.8	73.9	1.4	182.9	157.5
Luxembourg	..	..	..	..	..	..	..	..	..
Mexico	79.4	68.7	20.6	30.9	0.4	31.3	1.8	145.9	256.3
Netherlands	76.5	72.0	23.5	14.9	13.1	28.0	0.4	126.9	160.9
New Zealand	..	67.9	..	32.1	..	32.1	..	157.2	..
Norway	96.3	96.1	3.7	3.0	..	3.9	..	123.6	130.6
Poland	66.6	69.7	33.4	22.8	7.5	30.3	..	211.4	182.7
Portugal	92.5	70.9	7.5	22.3	6.8	29.1	..	109.0	548.4
Slovak Republic	91.2	70.0	8.8	11.7	18.3	30.0	2.0	138.9	619.6
Slovenia	..	85.1	..	10.8	4.2	14.9	..	..	..
Spain	74.4	79.1	25.6	16.8	4.1	20.9	1.7	149.3	114.8
Sweden	91.3	89.8	8.7	..	10.2	10.2	..	125.3	149.7
Switzerland	..	..	..	..	..	..	..	128.9	..
Turkey	95.4	..	4.6	..	..	..	..	..	..
United Kingdom	67.7	29.6	32.3	58.1	12.3	70.4	10.8	116.7	334.2
United States	31.1	38.1	68.9	45.3	16.6	61.9	..	137.5	100.9
EU 27	..	..	..	..	..	..	..	..	..
OECD	77.1	70.0	22.9	..	..	30.0	3.2	138.0	215.9
Brazil	..	..	..	..	..	..	..	162.5	..
China	..	..	..	..	..	..	..	..	..
India	..	..	..	..	..	..	..	..	..
Indonesia	..	..	..	..	..	..	..	..	..
Russian Federation	..	64.6	..	27.4	8.0	35.4	..	378.8	..
South Africa	..	..	..	..	..	..	..	..	..

 StatLink http://dx.doi.org/10.1787/888932709681

Share of private expenditure on tertiary educational institutions
Percentage

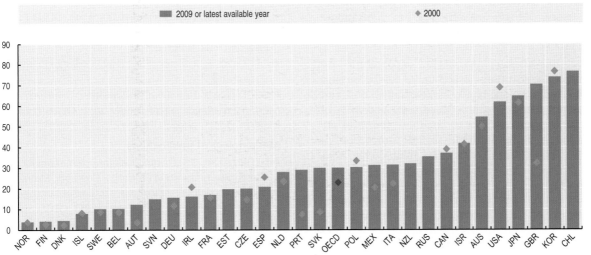

StatLink http://dx.doi.org/10.1787/888932709700

EDUCATION EXPENDITURE

Expenditure on education is an investment that can foster economic growth, enhance productivity, contribute to personal and social development and reduce social inequality. The proportion of total financial resources devoted to education is one of the key choices made by governments, enterprises, students and their families.

Definition

The indicator covers expenditure on schools, universities and other public and private institutions delivering or supporting educational services. Expenditure on institutions is not limited to expenditure on instruction services but includes public and private expenditure on ancillary services for students and their families, where these services are provided through educational institutions. At the tertiary level, spending on research and development can also be significant and is included in this indicator, to the extent that the research is performed by educational institutions.

In principle, public expenditure includes both direct expenditure on educational institutions and educational-related public subsidies to households administered by educational institutions. Private expenditure is recorded net of these public subsidies attributable to educational institutions; it also excludes expenditure made outside educational institutions (such as textbooks purchased by families, private tutoring for students and student living cost).

Comparability

The broad definition of educational institutions used here ensures coverage of expenditures on services by schools and universities (as it occurs in many OECD countries) or by agencies other than schools (as it happens in other countries).

The data on expenditure were obtained by a special survey conducted in 2011 which applied consistent methods and definitions. Expenditure data are based on the definitions and coverage for the UNESCO-OECD-Eurostat data collection programme on education; they have been adjusted to 2009 prices using the GDP price deflator. The use of a common survey and definitions ensures good comparability of results across countries.

No data for private expenditure are currently collected for countries ranked separately on the left-hand side of the chart.

Data for India, Indonesia and South Africa are based on UNESCO Institute for Statistics (World Education Indicators Programme).

Overview

In 2009, taking into account both public and private sources, OECD countries spent 6.2% of their GDP on educational institutions at the pre-primary, primary, secondary and tertiary levels. More than three-quarters of this amount came from public sources. The highest spending on educational institutions is in Denmark, Iceland, Israel, Korea, New Zealand and the Unites States, with at least 7% of GDP accounted for by public and private spending on educational institutions. Seven out of 37 countries with available data spent 5% or less of GDP on educational institutions; in India and Indonesia these shares are at or below 4%.

Nearly one-quarter of OECD expenditure on educational institutions is accounted for by tertiary education. On the one hand, Canada, Chile, Korea and the United States spend between 2.4% and 2.6% of their GDP on tertiary institutions; these countries are also among those with the highest proportion of private expenditure on tertiary education. On the other hand, in Belgium, Brazil, France, Iceland, Norway, Switzerland and the United Kingdom expenditure on tertiary institutions, as a portion of GDP, is below the OECD average; yet, these countries are among those with a share of GDP spent on primary, secondary and post-secondary non-tertiary education higher than the OECD average.

Sources

- OECD (2012), *Education at a Glance*, OECD Publishing.

Further information

Analytical publications

- OECD (2013), *Trends Shaping Education*, OECD Publishing.
- OECD (2012), *Quality Matters in Early Childhood Education and Care*, OECD Publishing.
- OECD (2012), *Reviews of National Policies for Education*, OECD Publishing.
- OECD (2011), *Designing for Education, Compendium of Exemplary Educational Facilities 2011*, OECD Publishing.
- OECD (2006), *Schooling for Tomorrow*, OECD Publishing.

Methodological publications

- OECD (2004), *OECD Handbook for Internationally Comparative Education Statistics: Concepts, Standards, Definitions and Classifications*, OECD Publishing.
- UNESCO Institute for Statistics (UIS), OECD and Eurostat (2012), *UOE Data Collection on Education Systems*, UIS, Montreal.

Websites

- OECD Education at a Glance, *www.oecd.org/edu/eag2012*.

Public and private expenditure on education

2009 or latest available year

	As a percentage of GDP						Index of change, 2000=100					
	Primary, secondary and post-secondary non-tertiary education		Tertiary education		All levels of education		Primary, secondary and post-secondary non-tertiary education		Tertiary education		All levels of education	
	Public	Private	Public	Private	Public	Private	Public	Private	Public	Private	Public	Private
Australia	3.6	0.6	0.7	0.9	4.5	1.5	155.0	150.4	135.0	161.4	150.8	157.9
Austria	3.8	0.1	1.4	0.1	5.7	0.2	112.4	114.6	142.2	517.7	118.2	175.5
Belgium	4.3	0.2	1.4	0.1	6.4	0.3	121.4	108.1	122.6	150.5	123.5	122.3
Canada	3.2	0.4	1.5	0.9	4.8	1.3	127.6	188.2	130.5	120.5	123.1	133.3
Chile	2.9	0.8	0.8	1.6	4.3	2.6	..	..	..	..	..	..
Czech Republic	2.6	0.3	1.0	0.2	4.2	0.6	144.9	159.4	202.4	298.3	158.1	193.5
Denmark	4.7	0.1	1.8	0.1	7.5	0.3	120.9	139.0	120.7	236.4	122.6	129.8
Estonia	4.1	0.1	1.3	0.3	5.9	0.4	146.8	..	163.3	..	150.0	..
Finland	4.1	..	1.8	0.1	6.3	0.1	132.7	160.3	127.3	198.0	131.8	157.4
France	3.8	0.2	1.3	0.2	5.8	0.5	103.4	109.5	121.7	134.3	108.1	120.8
Germany	2.9	0.4	1.1	0.2	4.5	0.8	106.2	101.9	119.9	166.1	112.6	123.1
Greece	..	..	..	..	..	..	..	..	..	..	..	..
Hungary	3.0	..	1.0	..	4.8	..	127.8	..	134.7	..	130.3	..
Iceland	5.0	0.2	1.2	0.1	7.3	0.7	139.4	141.8	159.4	154.5	148.4	134.9
Ireland	4.6	0.1	1.4	0.3	6.0	0.4	207.7	116.0	151.5	111.3	190.6	111.7
Israel	3.8	0.2	1.0	0.6	5.8	1.3	121.6	142.1	107.8	109.3	120.8	125.3
Italy	3.3	0.1	0.8	0.2	4.5	0.4	107.7	146.4	103.9	164.4	103.9	177.2
Japan	2.7	0.3	0.5	1.0	3.6	1.7	102.9	96.4	104.8	120.3	103.1	118.0
Korea	3.6	1.1	0.7	1.9	4.9	3.1	177.8	234.0	182.9	157.5	187.1	181.5
Luxembourg	3.2	0.1	..	..	..	..	..	..	..	..	..	..
Mexico	3.3	0.7	1.0	0.4	5.0	1.2	121.8	177.9	145.9	256.3	129.5	203.5
Netherlands	3.7	0.4	1.2	0.5	5.3	0.9	138.6	125.8	126.9	160.9	135.3	139.6
New Zealand	4.5	0.7	1.1	0.5	6.1	1.3	130.5	..	157.2	..	138.9	..
Norway	4.2	..	1.3	0.1	6.1	..	127.2	..	123.6	130.6	138.4	50.9
Poland	3.5	0.2	1.1	0.5	5.0	0.8	131.2	154.0	211.4	182.7	142.4	177.3
Portugal	4.0	..	1.0	0.4	5.5	0.4	111.7	85.0	109.0	548.4	112.5	534.0
Slovak Republic	2.7	0.3	0.7	0.3	4.1	0.6	149.8	881.5	138.9	619.6	146.8	751.1
Slovenia	3.6	0.3	1.1	0.2	5.3	0.7	..	..	..	..	..	..
Spain	3.1	0.2	1.1	0.3	4.9	0.7	128.5	129.4	149.3	114.8	142.3	147.5
Sweden	4.2	..	1.6	0.2	6.6	0.2	116.4	51.1	125.3	149.7	124.4	107.9
Switzerland	3.8	0.6	1.4	..	5.5	..	120.6	153.8	128.9	..	122.1	153.8
Turkey	..	..	..	..	..	..	..	..	..	..	..	..
United Kingdom	4.5	..	0.6	0.7	5.3	0.7	132.9	283.2	116.7	334.2	117.0	302.9
United States	3.9	0.3	1.0	1.6	5.3	2.1	126.5	118.1	137.5	100.9	129.1	103.1
EU 27	..	..	..	..	..	..	..	..	..	..	..	..
OECD	3.7	0.3	1.1	0.5	5.4	0.9	130.8	170.7	138.0	215.9	133.2	185.9
Brazil	4.3	..	0.8	..	5.5	..	237.3	..	162.5	..	215.4	..
China	..	..	..	..	..	..	..	..	..	..	..	..
India	2.2	..	1.3	..	3.5	..	..	..	..	..	..	..
Indonesia	2.0	0.4	0.5	0.2	3.0	0.6	..	..	..	..	..	..
Russian Federation	2.3	0.1	1.2	0.6	4.7	0.8	212.0	..	378.8	..	244.1	..
South Africa	3.9	..	0.6	..	4.8	..	..	..	..	..	..	..

StatLink http://dx.doi.org/10.1787/888932709719

Public and private expenditure on education for all levels of education

As a percentage of GDP, 2009 or latest available year

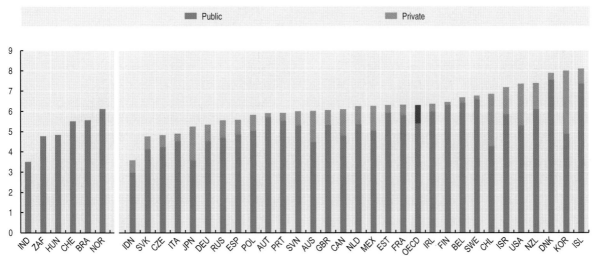

StatLink http://dx.doi.org/10.1787/888932709738

GOVERNMENT

GOVERNMENT EXPENDITURES, REVENUES AND DEFICITS

Net lending reflects the fiscal position of government after accounting for capital expenditures. Positive net-lending means that government is providing financial resources to other sectors and negative net-lending means that government requires financial resources from other economic sectors.

While general government and net lending is an important concept in the *System of National Accounts* (SNA) accounting framework and provides the basis for sound international comparisons, net lending is not necessarily the key fiscal measure targeted by governments. Some countries for example manage their budgets using broader notions that incorporate the positions of public corporations and others focus on more narrow concepts such as central government.

Definition

Total general government expenditures (GGE) include the following items: intermediate consumption, compensation of employees, subsidies, social benefits and social transfers in kind (via market producers), other current transfers, property income, capital transfers (payable), the adjustment for the net equity of households in pension funds reserves, gross capital formation and net acquisition of non-financial non-produced assets. It also includes taxes on income and wealth and other taxes on production that governments may be required to pay.

Revenues include taxes (on corporations and households, and those on income, wealth, production and imports),

social security contributions, property income and other income.

Comparability

The biggest issue affecting comparability across countries concerns the scope of the government sector. In many countries, hospitals, for example, are classified outside of the government sector and are instead recorded as public corporations on the grounds that they charge market prices for their services. EU countries have adopted a 50% rule, *i.e.* sales should cover at least 50% of the operating costs to qualify the relevant units as market producers outside government.

Another potential area where comparability may be affected relates to the determination of public ownership. The SNA requires that "control" be the determining factor for recording a non-market producer inside or outside government, and describes a number of criteria that can be used to assess this requirement. Recognising that this is non-trivial it includes a practical recommendation that a 50% rule relating to ownership should be adopted.

Generally however, the comparability of the figures presented here for countries is very high. For most general government expenditures there is little scope for ambiguity in treatment and the quality of underlying data is very good, so the level of comparability is generally good. Data for all countries are on a consolidated basis, except Canada (which consolidates only current transfers) and New Zealand.

Unlike previous years, all data for this indicator is now sourced from the *OECD Annual National Accounts* database.

Overview

Over the last four decades, the fiscal balance in the OECD as a whole has been typically in deficit, oscillating around 3% of GDP. This, however, masks diversified levels and trends among the OECD countries. Following the global recession of 2008-09, the OECD deficit increased to record levels in 2009 and 2010. In 2010, deficits larger than 10% of GDP were recorded for Ireland, the United States, Greece, the United Kingdom and Iceland. The large deficit in Ireland of 31.2% partly reflected one-off payments to support the financial system. In contrast, Norway had a surplus of 11.2%. In 2011, the fiscal balance in most OECD countries for which data are available, improved.

As with the fiscal balance, there is a big variation in the shares of expenditure and revenues in GDP across the OECD countries and over time. Looking at the revenues in 2010, the lowest government revenues as a percentage of GDP were reported for Mexico (21.9%) and the United States (31.8%). On the other hand, the Scandinavian countries all reported revenues over 50% of GDP.

Sources
• OECD (2012), *OECD Economic Outlook*, OECD Publishing.

Further information

Analytical publications
• OECD (2012), *OECD Economic Surveys*, OECD Publishing.

Statistical publications
• OECD (2012), *National Accounts of OECD Countries*, OECD Publishing.

Methodological publications
• OECD (2008), *OECD Glossary of Statistical Terms*, OECD Publishing.

Online databases
• *OECD National Accounts Statistics*.
• *OECD Economic Outlook: Statistics and Projections*.

Websites
• OECD Economic Outlook – Sources and Methods, *www.oecd.org/eco/sources-and-methods*.

General government revenues and expenditures
As a percentage of GDP

	Net lending				Revenues				Expenditures			
	2000	2005	2010	2011	2000	2005	2010	2011	2000	2005	2010	2011
Australia	-0.7	1.6	..	..	34.9	35.5	..	..	35.6	33.9	..	..
Austria	-1.8	-1.8	-4.5	-2.6	50.1	48.2	48.1	48.0	51.9	50.0	52.6	50.6
Belgium	-0.1	-2.6	-3.9	-3.9	49.0	49.3	48.6	49.4	49.1	51.9	52.5	53.3
Canada	2.9	1.5	-5.6	..	44.1	40.8	38.5	..	41.1	39.3	44.1	..
Chile	..	..	-0.3	..	..	..	..	..	..	..	..	..
Czech Republic	-3.6	-3.2	-4.8	-3.1	38.0	39.8	39.3	40.3	41.6	43.0	44.1	43.4
Denmark	2.2	5.0	-2.7	-1.9	55.8	57.8	55.1	56.1	53.7	52.8	57.8	58.0
Estonia	-0.2	1.6	0.3	1.0	35.9	35.2	40.8	39.3	36.1	33.6	40.6	38.2
Finland	7.0	2.7	-2.8	-0.9	55.4	53.0	53.0	53.9	48.3	50.3	55.8	54.8
France	-1.5	-3.0	-7.1	-5.2	50.2	50.6	49.5	50.8	51.7	53.6	56.6	56.0
Germany	1.1	-3.3	-4.2	-1.0	46.2	43.6	43.3	44.3	45.1	46.9	47.5	45.3
Greece	-3.8	-5.6	-10.5	-9.2	43.3	39.0	39.7	40.9	47.1	44.6	50.2	50.1
Hungary	-3.1	-7.9	-4.3	4.2	44.7	42.2	45.2	53.0	47.8	50.1	49.5	48.8
Iceland	1.7	4.9	-10.1	-4.4	43.6	47.1	41.5	41.7	41.9	42.2	51.6	46.1
Ireland	4.7	1.7	-31.2	-13.0	35.9	35.4	35.6	35.7	31.2	33.8	66.8	48.7
Israel	-3.9	-4.8	-4.6	..	47.4	44.6	40.4	..	51.3	49.4	45.0	..
Italy	-0.9	-4.5	-4.5	-3.8	45.0	43.4	46.0	46.1	45.9	47.9	50.5	49.9
Japan	..	-4.8	-8.4	..	..	31.6	32.4	..	..	36.4	40.8	..
Korea	5.4	3.4	1.3	..	27.9	30.0	31.4	..	22.4	26.6	30.1	..
Luxembourg	6.0	0.0	-0.9	-0.6	43.6	41.5	41.6	41.4	37.6	41.5	42.4	42.0
Mexico	..	0.4	-1.5	..	..	19.5	21.9	..	..	19.1	23.3	..
Netherlands	2.0	-0.3	-5.0	-4.4	46.1	44.5	46.1	45.4	44.2	44.8	51.2	49.8
New Zealand	1.7	4.6	..	..	39.5	42.4	..	..	37.8	37.8	..	..
Norway	15.4	15.0	11.2	13.7	57.7	56.8	56.7	58.2	42.3	41.8	45.5	44.5
Poland	-3.0	-4.1	-7.9	-5.1	38.1	39.4	37.5	38.5	41.1	43.4	45.4	43.6
Portugal	-3.3	-6.5	-9.8	-4.2	38.3	40.1	41.4	44.7	41.6	46.6	51.3	48.9
Slovak Republic	-12.3	-2.8	-7.7	-4.8	39.9	35.2	32.4	33.4	52.1	38.0	40.0	38.2
Slovenia	-3.7	-1.5	-6.0	-6.3	42.8	43.8	44.0	43.8	46.5	45.3	50.0	50.2
Spain	-1.0	1.3	-9.4	-8.6	38.2	39.7	36.4	35.5	39.2	38.4	45.7	44.1
Sweden	3.6	1.9	-0.1	0.1	58.7	55.8	52.4	51.5	55.1	53.9	52.5	51.3
Switzerland	-0.4	-1.1	0.3	..	35.2	34.1	34.0	..	35.6	35.2	33.8	..
Turkey	..	..	-2.6	..	..	..	36.4	..	..	..	39.0	..
United Kingdom	3.6	-3.4	-10.1	-8.2	40.4	40.4	40.1	40.5	36.8	43.8	50.3	48.7
United States	1.5	-3.2	-10.6	..	35.4	33.1	31.8	..	33.9	36.3	42.5	..
EU 27	..	..	..	..	..	..	..	..	..	..	..	..
OECD	..	..	..	..	..	..	..	..	..	..	..	..
Brazil	..	..	..	..	..	..	..	..	..	..	..	..
China	..	..	..	..	..	..	..	..	..	..	..	..
India	..	..	..	..	..	..	..	..	..	..	..	..
Indonesia	..	..	..	..	..	..	..	..	..	..	..	..
Russian Federation	..	6.0	..	..	..	40.2	..	..	..	34.2	..	..
South Africa	-3.3	-2.0	-6.0	..	..	..	..	..	..	..	..	..

StatLink http://dx.doi.org/10.1787/888932709757

General government net lending
As a percentage of GDP

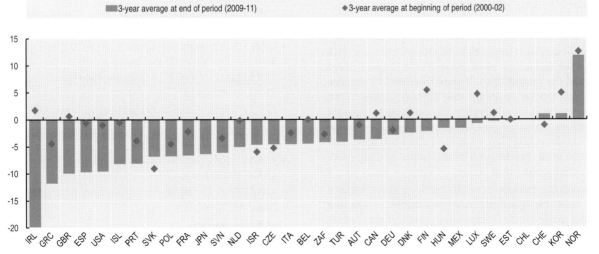

StatLink http://dx.doi.org/10.1787/888932709776

GOVERNMENT DEBT

The accumulation of government debt is a key factor for the sustainability of government finance. Apart from net acquisitions of financial assets, changes in government debt over time reflect the impact of government deficits.

The government debt-to-GDP ratio, calculated as the amount of total government debt of a country as a percentage of its Gross Domestic Product (GDP), is one of the indicators of the health of an economy.

Definition

Debt is commonly defined as a specific subset of liabilities identified according to the types of financial instruments included or excluded. Generally, debt is defined as all liabilities that require payment or payments of interest or principal by the debtor to the creditor at a date or dates in the future.

Consequently, all debt instruments are liabilities, but some liabilities such as shares, equity and financial derivatives are not debt. Debt is thus obtained as the sum of the following liability categories (according to the *1993 System of National Accounts*), whenever available/applicable in the financial balance sheet of the general government sector: currency and deposits; securities other than shares, except financial derivatives; loans; insurance technical reserves;

and other accounts payable. In line with the 1993 SNA, most debt instruments are valued at market prices.

Comparability

Across OECD countries, the comparability of data on general government debt can be affected through national differences in implementing the 1993 SNA definitions, especially in relation to the delineation of the government sector. See the indicator "Government expenditure, revenues and deficits" for more details.

The degree of consolidation within the government sector may also have an impact on the international comparability of data across OECD countries. The indicator is derived from consolidated data for all OECD countries, except: Chile, Japan, Korea and the United Kingdom. Consolidation means that general government debt does not include the debt issued by one government sub-sector and held by another. The result of any intra-governmental debt elimination is a lower general government debt.

Unlike previous years, all data for this indicator is now sourced from the *OECD Annual National Accounts* database.

Overview

In 2010, 17 OECD countries recorded debt-to-GDP ratios beyond 60% (the reference Maastricht value) compared to 12 countries in 2007. Japan recorded the highest debt ratio at 210%, followed by Italy (126%) and Greece (123%). The lowest debt-to-GDP ratios are found in Estonia (13%) and Chile (16%).

Ireland recorded the highest increase in its debt-to-GDP ratio between 2007 and 2010 (63 percentage points), reaching a level of 91.7%. Other countries with a considerable increase of more than 30 percentage points in the period 2007-10 were the United Kingdom (35.2 percentage points), the United States (31.6 percentage points) and Japan (30.2 percentage points). In contrast, Norway's government debt as a percentage of GDP declined by 7.2 percentage points between 2007 and 2010 with Sweden and Israel also recording small decreases for the same period.

The rapid rise in debt from 2007 reflects the effects of the crisis on governments worldwide, including reduced tax revenues, increases in government budget deficits and the cost of interventions to support the financial system. In Greece, however, government debt decreased by 23.5 percentage points in 2011, reflecting the fall in market prices of Greek government bonds.

Sources
- OECD (2012),"Financial Balance Sheets", *OECD National Accounts Statistics* (database).

Further information

Analytical publications
- OECD (2012), *OECD Economic Outlook*, OECD Publishing.
- OECD (2012), *OECD Economic Surveys*, OECD Publishing.

Statistical publications
- OECD (2012), *National Accounts of OECD Countries, Financial Accounts*, OECD Publishing.
- OECD (2012), *National Accounts of OECD Countries, Financial Balance Sheets*, OECD Publishing.
- OECD (2011), *Central Government Debt: Statistical Yearbook*, OECD Publishing.
- OECD (2011), *National Accounts at a Glance*, OECD Publishing.

Methodological publications
- OECD (2008), *OECD Glossary of Statistical Terms*, OECD Publishing.
- OECD et al. (2009), *System of National Accounts*, United Nations, New York.

Online databases
- *OECD National Accounts Statistics*.
- *OECD Economic Outlook: Statistics and Projections*.

Websites
- Financial statistics, *www.oecd.org/std/financialstatistics*.

General government debt
As a percentage of GDP

	1999	2000	2001	2002	2003	2004	2005	2006	2007	2008	2009	2010	2011
Australia	39.8	35.6	34.2	33.3	30.7	29.0	28.5	27.1	26.0	27.2	36.3	40.9	..
Austria	70.8	70.8	71.7	72.8	71.1	70.6	70.6	66.0	62.3	67.1	73.4	77.5	..
Belgium	119.4	113.6	111.9	108.2	103.3	98.2	95.9	91.6	87.9	92.8	99.8	100.0	102.4
Canada	116.3	105.6	105.5	103.9	98.7	92.2	91.2	89.2	83.9	89.1	102.9	104.2	106.3
Chile	..	..	..	..	..	..	17.4	14.1	12.2	12.4	13.4	15.6	18.1
Czech Republic	24.4	25.1	29.3	31.5	33.2	33.0	32.7	32.5	30.9	34.3	41.0	44.5	..
Denmark	..	..	..	..	56.6	53.6	45.4	41.0	34.3	41.4	51.2	54.8	61.8
Estonia	10.9	9.4	8.9	10.2	10.8	8.5	8.2	8.0	7.2	8.2	12.4	12.5	..
Finland	54.9	52.5	50.1	49.7	51.1	51.3	48.5	44.7	40.4	39.8	51.4	56.9	..
France	69.0	67.9	67.2	70.7	75.2	77.1	78.9	73.9	73.0	79.2	91.0	94.9	..
Germany	61.7	60.9	60.2	62.6	66.0	69.0	71.7	69.8	65.7	69.7	77.4	86.9	..
Greece	102.4	115.9	118.1	116.6	110.4	112.8	112.7	115.9	113.9	117.5	133.6	123.0	99.5
Hungary	67.5	61.7	59.7	60.8	61.8	65.1	68.4	71.8	72.8	76.3	85.8	86.3	..
Iceland	..	..	..	..	..	..	..	..	..	..	..	..	..
Ireland	51.5	40.2	37.4	35.0	33.8	32.5	32.4	28.6	28.7	49.6	71.2	91.7	..
Israel	..	..	96.8	101.5	106.8	104.8	102.1	90.2	87.7	86.6	89.5	86.5	..
Italy	125.5	121.0	120.1	118.8	116.4	116.7	119.4	116.8	112.1	114.6	127.7	126.3	..
Japan	131.1	141.5	151.4	161.8	172.3	178.8	180.2	180.0	180.0	184.2	207.3	210.2	..
Korea	..	..	..	19.2	19.7	23.3	25.5	28.6	28.7	29.9	33.3	34.2	36.0
Luxembourg	..	..	..	..	..	..	..	11.5	11.3	18.3	17.9	24.5	..
Mexico	33.6	31.1	31.2	33.2	32.7	31.0	31.2	28.9	28.2	30.1	37.7	..	..
Netherlands	71.6	63.9	59.4	60.3	61.4	61.9	60.7	54.5	51.5	64.8	67.9	71.7	75.9
New Zealand	..	..	..	..	..	..	..	..	..	..	..	..	..
Norway	29.1	32.7	31.8	39.0	48.4	50.9	47.8	59.0	56.8	54.3	48.9	49.6	33.8
Poland	46.6	45.4	43.8	55.0	55.9	53.3	54.1	54.2	51.0	55.7	58.4	62.7	..
Portugal	62.3	62.4	64.2	67.9	70.2	73.4	77.6	77.3	75.4	80.7	93.3	97.5	96.8
Slovak Republic	53.5	57.6	57.1	50.2	48.2	47.6	39.2	34.1	32.9	32.0	40.4	47.1	..
Slovenia	..	..	33.6	34.7	34.1	34.9	34.0	33.8	30.7	30.4	44.3	48.4	56.3
Spain	69.4	66.6	62.0	60.4	55.4	53.4	50.7	46.2	42.3	47.7	62.7	66.8	75.1
Sweden	73.0	64.0	62.0	59.8	58.8	59.5	60.2	53.6	48.8	47.5	51.1	48.0	..
Switzerland	47.7	48.9	48.5	54.9	54.5	55.1	53.0	47.1	43.9	40.2	38.7	..	..
Turkey	..	..	..	..	..	..	..	..	..	..	..	..	..
United Kingdom	54.6	54.5	49.3	48.8	48.6	50.7	53.4	53.0	53.5	63.9	79.5	88.8	104.9
United States	61.2	55.1	55.0	57.4	60.7	68.6	68.2	66.9	67.5	76.5	90.4	99.1	103.5
EU 27	..	..	..	..	..	..	..	..	..	..	..	..	..
OECD	..	..	..	..	..	..	..	..	..	..	..	..	..
Brazil	..	..	..	..	..	..	..	..	..	..	..	..	..
China	..	..	..	..	..	..	..	..	..	..	..	..	..
India	..	..	..	..	..	..	..	..	..	..	..	..	..
Indonesia	..	..	..	..	..	..	..	..	..	..	..	..	..
Russian Federation	..	..	..	..	..	..	..	..	..	..	..	..	..
South Africa	..	..	..	..	..	..	..	..	..	..	..	..	..

StatLink http://dx.doi.org/10.1787/888932709814

General government debt
As a percentage of GDP

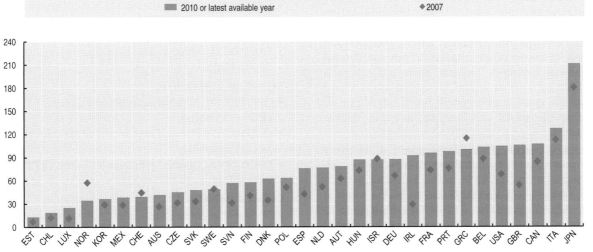

StatLink http://dx.doi.org/10.1787/888932709833

EXPENDITURES ACROSS LEVELS OF GOVERNMENT

The responsibility for the provision of public goods and services and redistribution of income is divided between different levels of government. In some countries, local and regional governments play a larger role in delivering services, such as providing public housing or running schools. Data on the distribution of government spending by both level and function can provide an indication of the extent to which key government activities are decentralised to sub-national governments.

Definition

Data are based on the 1993 *System of National Accounts* so that all countries are using a common set of definitions.

The general government sector consists of central, state and local governments and the social security funds controlled by these units. Data on the distribution of general government expenditures across levels of government exclude transfers between levels of government and thus provide a rough proxy of the overall responsibility for providing goods and services borne by each level of government. For the central level of government, data on expenditures are shown here according to the *Classification of the Functions of Government*. Data on central government expenditures by function include transfers between the different levels of government.

Comparability

Data for Australia, Turkey and Japan on the distribution of general government expenditures across levels of government include transfers between levels of government. The state government category is only applicable to the nine OECD member countries that are federal states: Australia, Austria, Belgium, Canada, Germany, Mexico, Spain (considered a de facto federal state here), Switzerland and the United States. Local government is included in state government for the United States.

Social security funds are included in central government in New Zealand, Norway, the United Kingdom and the United States. Australia does not operate government social insurance schemes; central government refers to commonwealth and multijurisdictional data. Data for Australia, Korea, New Zealand and the United States refer to 2009 rather than 2010. Data for Mexico are for 2003 rather than 2001. The OECD average does not include Chile, Japan and Turkey (and Australia and Mexico for central government expenditures by function). Data on central government expenditures by function for Canada and New Zealand refer to 2006 and 2005 respectively.

Overview

Across the OECD, in 2010, 46% of general government expenditures were undertaken by central government. Sub-central governments (state and local) covered 32% and social security funds accounted for the remaining share. However, the level of fiscal decentralisation varies considerably across countries. For example, in New Zealand (a unitary state), almost 90% of total spending is by central government. In contrast, central government accounts for less than 15% of total expenditures in Switzerland, a federal state where sub-central governments play a much larger role in financing the goods and services that they deliver themselves.

In general, central governments spend a relatively larger proportion of their budgets on social protection (*e.g.* pensions and unemployment benefits), general public services (*e.g.* executive and legislative organs, public debt transactions) and defence compared to sub-central governments. Expenditures on social protection represent the largest share of central government budgets for over half of OECD member countries. The central governments of Belgium and Spain allocate most of their budgets to general public services, accounting for over 60% of total expenditures.

Sources

• OECD (2011), *Government at a Glance*, OECD Publishing.

Further information

Analytical publications

• OECD (2011), *Making the Most of Public Investment in a Tight Fiscal Environment: Multi-level Governance Lessons from the Crisis*, OECD Publishing.

• OECD (2011), *Value for Money in Government*, OECD Publishing.

Statistical publications

• OECD (2012), *National Accounts at a Glance*, OECD Publishing.

• OECD (2012), *National Accounts of OECD Countries*, OECD Publishing.

• OECD (2012), *Quarterly National Accounts*, OECD Publishing.

Online databases

• "General Government Accounts: Government expenditure by function", *OECD National Accounts Statistics*.

• "National Accounts at a Glance", *OECD National Accounts Statistics*.

Websites

• Government at a Glance (supplementary material), *www.oecd.org/gov/indicators/govataglance*.

Structure of central government expenditures by function

Percentage, 2010

	General public services	Defence	Public order and safety	Economic affairs	Environmental protection	Housing and community amenities	Health	Recreation, culture and religion	Education	Social protection
Australia	..	..	..	..	..	..	..	..	..	..
Austria	17.0	2.7	4.9	12.8	0.6	0.7	4.5	1.2	13.4	42.2
Belgium	66.8	3.4	3.9	7.1	0.3	0.0	3.7	0.3	4.5	10.1
Canada	33.2	6.6	3.8	7.9	0.7	1.5	10.2	2.1	2.6	31.6
Chile	..	..	..	..	..	..	..	..	..	..
Czech Republic	12.3	3.3	6.1	13.9	0.4	2.0	5.5	1.3	11.7	43.5
Denmark	40.5	3.4	2.4	4.4	0.5	0.6	0.4	1.9	10.3	35.6
Estonia	14.8	5.8	7.3	11.3	-1.8	0.1	7.3	4.1	9.8	41.3
Finland	19.1	5.5	4.5	12.6	0.7	1.1	12.3	1.7	13.2	29.3
France	35.4	8.5	5.6	9.9	0.7	0.9	0.8	1.7	17.5	19.0
Germany	23.7	6.7	1.0	17.5	1.2	0.9	1.2	0.4	1.2	46.2
Greece	26.6	5.6	4.3	41.3	0.3	0.7	0.9	1.3	9.7	9.4
Hungary	26.9	3.8	5.5	15.2	0.6	0.2	10.3	3.3	10.8	23.6
Iceland	20.8	0.1	3.2	15.4	0.9	5.5	20.1	3.1	8.7	22.2
Ireland	7.3	0.8	3.0	41.3	0.8	0.6	14.5	0.6	10.0	21.2
Israel	18.5	17.2	4.2	6.0	0.3	0.8	13.5	2.5	16.5	20.5
Italy	29.5	4.9	6.1	8.9	0.5	1.3	14.2	1.4	12.6	20.5
Japan	..	..	..	..	..	..	..	..	..	..
Korea	13.6	16.0	5.1	40.0	1.1	1.8	11.3	1.4	6.6	3.1
Luxembourg	18.2	1.7	3.1	11.5	1.5	1.8	1.7	3.9	14.1	42.6
Mexico	..	..	..	..	..	..	..	..	..	..
Netherlands	26.9	4.5	6.0	13.0	0.7	0.6	9.0	1.2	15.7	22.4
New Zealand	12.0	2.8	5.4	8.3	1.1	1.1	18.5	1.6	20.8	28.4
Norway	19.5	4.2	2.3	8.7	0.3	0.2	15.2	1.4	5.6	42.6
Poland	21.2	5.2	6.7	12.8	0.5	0.4	3.8	1.3	16.2	31.8
Portugal	30.5	4.3	5.9	10.6	0.5	0.0	17.1	1.2	14.6	15.3
Slovak Republic	18.0	5.4	11.0	14.1	2.1	1.4	9.6	3.0	13.7	21.8
Slovenia	15.2	4.9	5.3	12.7	1.4	0.8	11.8	3.7	17.8	26.4
Spain	67.3	5.7	6.2	8.8	0.4	0.1	1.6	1.5	0.9	7.4
Sweden	26.1	5.2	3.9	10.7	0.5	0.4	4.5	1.2	6.5	41.1
Switzerland	25.2	7.2	1.7	22.9	2.4	0.0	0.4	0.7	8.3	31.2
Turkey	..	..	..	..	..	..	..	..	..	..
United Kingdom	13.3	5.8	4.2	5.2	1.1	5.0	17.8	1.3	12.1	34.4
United States	10.2	18.9	1.5	6.0	0.0	3.1	24.4	0.2	3.5	32.2
EU 27	..	..	..	..	..	..	..	..	..	..
OECD	24.5	5.9	4.6	14.2	0.7	1.2	9.2	1.7	10.6	27.5
Brazil	..	..	..	..	..	..	..	..	..	..
China	..	..	..	..	..	..	..	..	..	..
India	..	..	..	..	..	..	..	..	..	..
Indonesia	..	..	..	..	..	..	..	..	..	..
Russian Federation	..	..	..	..	..	..	..	..	..	..
South Africa	..	..	..	..	..	..	..	..	..	..

StatLink 🔗 http://dx.doi.org/10.1787/888932709852

Distribution of general government expenditures across levels of government

Percentage, 2001-2010

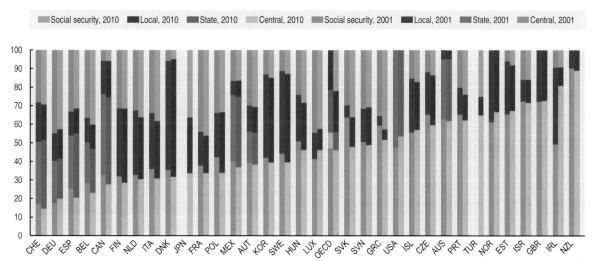

StatLink 🔗 http://dx.doi.org/10.1787/888932709871

GENERAL GOVERNMENT EXPENDITURES AND REVENUES PER CAPITA

Governments spend money to provide goods and services and redistribute income. To finance these activities governments raise money in the form of revenues (*e.g.* taxation) and/or borrowing. The amount of revenues collected or the expenditures spent per capita are two ways of comparing the size of government across countries. Variations across countries however can also reflect different approaches to the delivery of public services (*e.g.* such as the use of tax breaks rather than direct expenditures). Additionally, both revenues and expenditures are heavily influenced by economic fluctuations. The recent global and financial crisis had a strong negative impact on government revenues in many OECD countries.

Definition

The general government sector consists of central, state and local governments and the social security funds controlled by these units. Data are based on the *1993 System of National Accounts* or on the *1995 European System of Accounts* so that all countries are using a common set of definitions. The underlying population estimates are based on the *System of National Accounts* notion of residency. They include persons who are resident in a country for one year or more, regardless of their citizenship, and also include foreign diplomatic personnel, and defence personnel; together with their families and students studying and patients seeking treatment abroad, even if they stay abroad for more than one year. The "one year" rule means that usual residents who live abroad for less than one year are included in the population, while foreign visitors (for example, vacationers) who are in the country for less than one year are excluded.

Comparability

Differences in the amounts of government revenues and expenditures per capita in some countries can be related to the fact that individuals may feature as employees of one country (contributing to the GDP of that country via production), but residents of another (with their wages and salaries reflected in the Gross National Income of their resident country). Data for Australia, Chile, Korea, New Zealand and the Russian Federation refer to 2009 rather than 2010. The OECD average does not include Chile, Japan and Turkey in the time series data. Data for Mexico and the Russian Federation refer to 2003 and 2002 respectively rather than 2001. Data for Turkey are for 2006 rather than 2005.

Overview

On average in the OECD area, governments collected about USD 14 000 per capita in revenues in 2010, while spending nearly USD 16 000 per capita in the same year.

Luxembourg and Norway collected the most government revenues per capita in the OECD, topping more than USD 30 000 per capita, and reflecting the importance of cross-border workers and corporate taxes in Luxembourg and oil revenues in Norway. These two countries, and Ireland, also spent the most per citizen (above USD 25 000) in terms of government expenditures.

The governments of Turkey, Mexico and Chile collected the least revenues per capita; below USD 6 000 in 2010. Likewise, government expenditures in these countries were also much lower than average (close to or below USD 6 000 per capita). In general, central European countries also collect comparatively less revenues per capita, and also spend less than most OECD countries.

All countries except one (Israel) experienced increases in government revenues and expenditures per capita between 2001 and 2010. In real terms, over the period 2001-10 Ireland recorded an annual growth in government expenditures per capita of 9% followed by Estonia and Korea (both over 5%). During this same period, the latter two countries top also on real annual growth of revenues collected per person (about 5%).

Sources

• OECD (2012), *Government at a Glance*, OECD Publishing.

Further information

Analytical publications

• OECD (2011), *Making the Most of Public Investment in a Tight Fiscal Environment: Multi-level Governance Lessons from the Crisis*, OECD Publishing.

• OECD (2011), *Value for Money in Government*, OECD Publishing.

Statistical publications

• OECD (2012), *National Accounts at a Glance*, OECD Publishing.

• OECD (2012), *National Accounts of OECD Countries*, OECD Publishing.

Online databases

• "*General Government Accounts: Main aggregates*", OECD National Accounts Statistics.

• "*National Accounts at a Glance*", OECD National Accounts Statistics.

Websites

• Government at a Glance (supplementary material), *www.oecd.org/gov/indicators/govataglance*.

General government revenues and expenditures per capita

US dollars, current prices and PPPs

	General government revenues per capita				General government expenditures per capita			
	2001	2005	2007	2010	2001	2005	2007	2010
Australia	10 174	12 389	13 600	12 725	10 212	11 839	13 016	14 865
Austria	14 832	16 207	18 126	19 264	14 888	16 813	18 504	21 056
Belgium	14 110	15 861	17 172	18 413	14 010	16 705	17 206	19 895
Canada	12 508	14 340	15 632	15 051	12 315	13 797	15 092	17 221
Chile	..	..	3 711	3 003	..	..	3 231	3 479
Czech Republic	6 449	8 457	10 262	9 926	7 390	9 147	10 448	11 135
Denmark	16 297	19 190	20 976	22 140	15 949	17 524	19 165	23 226
Estonia	3 714	5 822	7 849	8 333	3 721	5 554	7 333	8 280
Finland	14 081	16 287	19 070	19 224	12 734	15 473	17 155	20 263
France	13 308	14 956	16 525	16 936	13 748	15 832	17 437	19 364
Germany	11 895	13 560	15 554	16 309	12 716	14 597	15 473	17 910
Greece	8 139	9 487	11 308	11 287	9 024	10 859	13 186	14 271
Hungary	5 853	7 159	8 627	9 283	6 407	8 505	9 598	10 163
Iceland	12 757	16 496	17 720	14 717	12 966	14 783	15 712	18 362
Ireland	10 454	13 778	16 656	14 412	10 163	13 130	16 628	27 020
Israel	11 095	10 364	11 455	10 723	12 563	11 486	11 775	11 933
Italy	12 144	12 280	14 759	14 682	13 014	13 551	15 269	16 110
Japan	..	12 646	14 350	14 951	..	14 111	15 047	17 775
Korea	5 130	6 828	8 721	8 678	4 342	6 058	7 501	8 988
Luxembourg	23 853	28 391	33 780	35 850	20 560	28 388	30 667	36 586
Mexico	2 087	2 425	2 893	3 323	2 080	2 377	2 963	3 545
Netherlands	13 883	15 628	18 507	19 483	13 961	15 727	18 441	21 591
New Zealand	8 496	10 696	12 360	11 622	8 170	9 528	11 107	12 364
Norway	21 297	27 077	32 208	32 445	16 358	19 913	22 539	26 043
Poland	4 219	5 427	6 755	7 470	4 796	5 989	7 070	9 032
Portugal	7 097	8 563	9 959	10 532	7 987	9 950	10 736	13 035
Slovak Republic	4 580	5 688	6 763	7 527	5 366	6 143	7 142	9 312
Slovenia	7 994	10 282	11 549	11 914	8 723	10 633	11 561	13 532
Spain	8 605	10 875	13 259	11 569	8 728	10 528	12 639	14 548
Sweden	15 837	18 247	20 984	20 616	15 390	17 611	19 606	20 637
Switzerland	11 122	12 261	14 537	16 207	11 164	12 512	13 817	15 931
Turkey	..	4 350	4 582	5 681	..	4 253	4 793	6 088
United Kingdom	11 207	13 313	14 703	14 323	11 073	14 432	15 675	17 934
United States	12 350	14 045	15 759	14 827	12 545	15 405	17 033	19 780
EU 27	..	..	..	..	..	..	..	..
OECD	10 825	12 786	14 775	14 835	10 744	12 735	14 242	16 578
Brazil	2 493	3 077	3 526	4 145	2 685	3 381	3 792	4 463
China	395	706	1 098	1 524	469	763	1 048	1 697
India	273	418	594	643	439	565	708	957
Indonesia	490	617	712	741	558	597	750	794
Russian Federation	3 333	4 751	6 832	7 090	3 387	4 039	5 898	7 897
South Africa	1 704	2 323	2 940	2 894	1 784	2 323	2 790	3 405

StatLink http://dx.doi.org/10.1787/888932709890

General government revenues and expenditures per capita

US dollars, current prices and PPPs, 2010

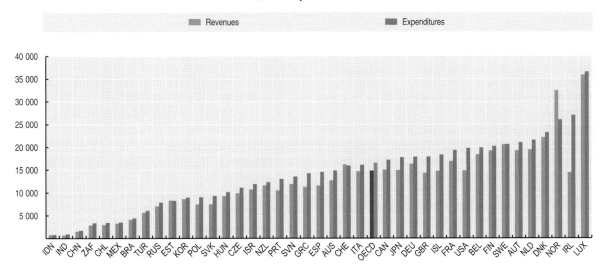

StatLink http://dx.doi.org/10.1787/888932709909

GENERAL GOVERNMENT PRODUCTION COSTS

Decisions on the amount and type of goods and services governments produce, as well as on how best to produce them, are often political in nature and based on a country's social and cultural context. While some governments choose to outsource a large portion of the production of goods and services to non-governmental or private entities, others decide to produce the goods and services themselves.

Definition

Governments use a mix of their own employees, capital and outside contractors (non-profit institutions or private sector entities) to produce goods and services. The latter is often referred to as "outsourcing".

This concept and methodology of production costs builds on the existing classification of public expenditures in the System of National Accounts (SNA). Specifically, government

production costs include: compensation costs of general government employees; costs of goods and services produced by non-government entities paid for by government (these include goods and services provided to both government and citizens); and, consumption of fixed capital (depreciation of capital).

The data include government employment and intermediate consumption for output produced by the government for its own use, such as roads and other capital investment projects built by government employees.

Comparability

Data are based on the 1993 System of National Accounts or on the 1995 European System of Accounts so that all countries are using a common set of definitions. However, cross-country differences in how employee pension schemes are funded can impair the comparison of compensation costs. In addition, some countries do not account separately for social transfers in kind via market producers.

Data for Australia, Chile, Korea, New Zealand and the Russian Federation are for 2009 rather than 2010. Data for Mexico are for 2003 rather than 2001. Data for the Russian Federation are for 2002 rather than 2001. The OECD average for production costs as percentage of GDP does not include Chile, Turkey and Japan.

Overview

In 2010, the production costs of government services and goods represented on average almost a quarter of GDP in the OECD, varying significantly countries. For example, production costs of government services and goods as a percentage of GDP in Denmark were roughly three times higher than in Mexico reflecting, in part, the different roles of government in these countries.

On average, production by governments' own employees is still somewhat more prevalent than outsourcing: compensation of employees accounts for 48% of the cost of producing goods and services, compared to 43% paid to non-governmental actors for intermediate goods and services or to deliver services directly to households. Consumption of fixed capital represents the remaining 9% of total government production costs. The Netherlands, Germany and Japan, where over 55% of the value of government goods and services is outsourced, rely comparatively more on corporations and private non-profit institutions to produce goods and services than other OECD member countries.

Total government production costs as a share of GDP increased in all but five OECD member countries (Israel, Poland, the Slovak Republic, Sweden, and Switzerland) between 2001 and 2010. This increase was primarily driven by increases in outsourcing (the costs of goods and services produced by non-government providers rose by 1.4 percentage points) and to a lesser extent by increases in compensation costs of government employees (0.5 percentage points). These increases could reflect that governments are providing more goods and services and/or that input costs have increased.

Sources
- OECD (2012), Government at a Glance, OECD Publishing.

Further information

Analytical publications
- OECD (2012), Corporate Governance, Value Creation and Growth, The Bridge between Finance and Enterprise, Corporate Governance, OECD Publishing.
- OECD (2008), The State of the Public Service, OECD Publishing.

Statistical publications
- OECD (2012), National Accounts at a Glance, OECD Publishing.
- OECD (2012), National Accounts of OECD Countries, OECD Publishing.

Online databases
- "General Government Accounts: Main aggregates", OECD National Accounts Statistics.

Websites
- Government at a Glance (supplementary material), www.oecd.org/gov/indicators/govataglance.

Production costs for general government

As a percentage of GDP

	Compensation of employees		Costs of goods and services used and financed by general government		Consumption of fixed capital		Total	
	2001	2010	2001	2010	2001	2010	2001	2010
Australia	9.4	10.1	6.7	7.4	2.3	2.1	18.4	19.6
Austria	9.8	9.7	9.3	10.2	1.4	1.3	20.5	21.2
Belgium	11.7	12.6	9.8	11.7	1.6	1.7	23.1	26.0
Canada	11.4	12.8	8.7	10.0	1.9	2.2	22.0	25.0
Chile	..	8.7	..	4.4	..	1.1	0.0	14.2
Czech Republic	7.1	7.6	11.5	12.1	4.6	4.3	23.2	24.0
Denmark	17.4	19.0	9.5	11.6	1.9	1.9	28.8	32.5
Estonia	10.2	11.9	9.3	9.4	1.6	2.1	21.1	23.4
Finland	13.0	14.4	9.8	14.1	2.1	2.2	24.9	30.7
France	13.3	13.4	10.1	11.9	2.2	2.7	25.6	28.0
Germany	8.2	7.9	11.5	13.0	1.7	1.7	21.4	22.6
Greece	10.5	12.2	6.3	6.0	2.0	2.4	18.8	20.6
Hungary	11.2	10.9	9.1	10.4	3.8	3.3	24.1	24.6
Iceland	14.7	14.8	10.3	12.2	1.9	2.2	26.9	29.2
Ireland	8.3	11.6	6.7	8.3	1.5	1.7	16.5	21.6
Israel	13.7	11.8	13.8	12.6	1.3	1.4	28.8	25.8
Italy	10.5	11.1	7.5	8.8	1.6	2.0	19.6	21.9
Japan	..	6.2	..	11.8	..	3.0	..	21.0
Korea	6.6	7.6	5.5	7.3	1.7	2.3	13.8	17.2
Luxembourg	7.9	8.0	7.9	8.5	1.7	1.9	17.5	18.4
Mexico	9.1	9.1	2.6	2.7	0.0	0.0	11.7	11.8
Netherlands	9.6	10.0	14.1	19.4	2.4	2.8	26.1	32.2
New Zealand	8.5	10.3	10.2	11.6	1.6	1.7	20.3	23.6
Norway	13.0	13.8	8.8	8.9	1.9	2.1	23.7	24.8
Poland	10.7	10.2	8.0	8.4	2.2	1.8	20.9	20.4
Portugal	13.9	12.2	6.4	10.0	1.9	2.2	22.2	24.4
Slovak Republic	8.9	7.7	9.4	10.2	3.8	2.7	22.1	20.6
Slovenia	11.7	12.7	8.7	9.1	1.5	2.0	21.9	23.8
Spain	10.1	11.9	6.7	8.7	1.5	1.9	18.3	22.5
Sweden	15.6	14.6	12.1	12.9	2.2	2.3	29.9	29.8
Switzerland	8.1	8.1	4.7	4.8	2.2	2.0	15.0	14.9
Turkey	..	8.6	..	9.4	..	0.2	..	18.2
United Kingdom	10.1	11.4	9.7	13.1	0.9	1.0	20.7	25.5
United States	9.8	11.0	7.3	9.2	1.4	1.6	18.5	21.8
EU 27	..	..	..	..	..	..	..	..
OECD	10.8	11.3	8.8	10.1	1.9	2.0	21.5	23.4
Brazil	..	..	..	..	..	..	..	..
China	..	..	..	..	..	..	..	..
India	..	..	..	..	..	..	..	..
Indonesia	..	..	..	..	..	..	..	..
Russian Federation	8.7	11.0	9.4	10.2	0.5	0.4	18.6	21.6
South Africa	..	..	..	..	..	..	..	..

StatLink http://dx.doi.org/10.1787/888932709928

Structure of general government production costs

Percentage, 2010

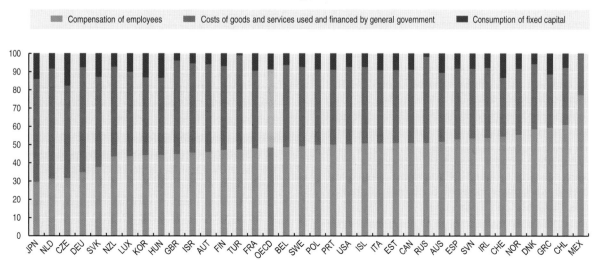

StatLink http://dx.doi.org/10.1787/888932709947

DISCLOSURE OF CONFLICT OF INTEREST

Ensuring that the integrity of decision-making is not compromised by conflict of interest is essential to maintaining trust in elected officials and government institutions. A conflict of interest arises when a public official's private interests could improperly influence the performance of official duties. If not adequately identified and managed, conflict-of-interest situations can lead to corruption. Disclosure of private interests by public officials is widely recognised as a principal tool to identify and prevent conflict of interest. Disclosures are usually mandated by law, but some officials or elected leaders provide them voluntarily. The public availability of disclosed information by top decision-makers is also important, allowing the public and civil society to monitor this information and hold government accountable.

Definition

Data refer to the percentage of private interests that are disclosed by ministers/cabinet members and legislators "of the lower house." Eight key types of information on private interests were analysed by the OECD, including: assets, liabilities, the amount and source(s) of any external income, any paid or non-paid outside positions, gifts received, and previous employment.

Assets refer to real estate and any moveable assets (such as cars, boats, stock and cash). Liabilities include loans and debts. Outside income (and its source) refers to any amount of income obtained other than from the compensation (salaries) received in the identified position. Outside employment includes both paid and non-paid (or volunteer) positions held outside of their position in government or Parliament. Disclosure of gifts received is recorded as per countries' own legislation or rules regarding thresholds for disclosure. Previous employment refers to the name(s) of entities where officials were employed prior to taking up their current post.

Comparability

All data were collected through the 2010 OECD Survey on Integrity. In some countries, certain types of private interests are prohibited (*e.g.* holding outside employment or receiving gifts). These are presented in the figures as the category "activity is prohibited." Thresholds for disclosure of gifts received vary by country. Data for Luxembourg are not available.

Overview

The disclosure of private interests by public officials and the public availability of such information is important to promote accountability and to reinforce trust in government. Furthermore, research has shown that economic development relies partly on citizens' trust in government. Yet, nearly all OECD member countries require only partial disclosure of private interests and make only some of this information public. Of the 8 interests analysed, for ministers and cabinet members, France and Switzerland disclose a small amount of information on private interests. Brazil, Slovenia and Turkey make most of the information disclosed available to the public.

Regarding lower house legislators, Finland and France request limited information on private interests to be disclosed. On the contrary, the Czech Republic and the United Kingdom require almost all information to be disclosed. In the United States and Korea all information on private interests for both positions is generally disclosed and made public.

Generally, paid and non-paid outside positions are the most regulated interests followed by gifts. These activities are prohibited in several (but not all) countries, although the threshold for having to report gifts varies.

Sources
- OECD (2011), *Government at a Glance*, OECD Publishing.

Further information

Analytical publications
- OECD (2012), *Lobbyists, Governments and Public Trust, Volume 2, Promoting Integrity through Self-regulation*, OECD Publishing.
- OECD (2011), *Corporate Governance of State-Owned Enterprises, Change and Reform in OECD Countries since 2005*, OECD Publishing.
- OECD (2010), *Post-Public Employment: Good Practices for Preventing Conflict of Interest*, OECD Publishing.
- OECD (2004), *Managing Conflict of Interest in the Public Service: OECD Guidelines and Country Experiences*, OECD Publishing.

Methodological publications
- OECD (2010), Accountability and Transparency: A Guide for State Ownership, *Corporate Governance*, OECD Publishing.
- OECD (2007), "Benchmarks for Integrity: Tracking Trends in Governance", *OECD Papers*, Vol. 7/7.
- OECD (2005), *Managing Conflict of Interest in the Public Sector: A Toolkit*, OECD Publishing.

Websites
- Managing Conflict of Interest in the Public Service, *www.oecd.org/gov/ethics/conflictofinterest*

Level of disclosure of private interests by ministers or cabinet members

Percentage of private interests analysed, 2010

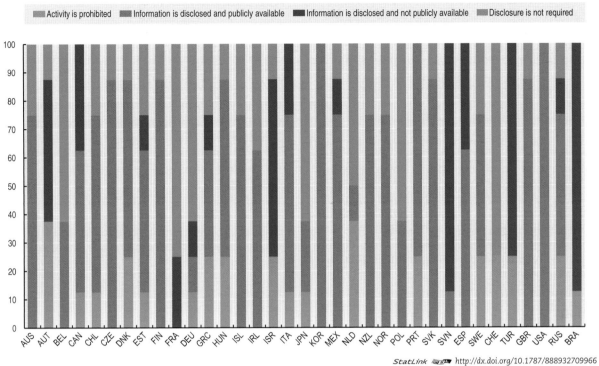

StatLink http://dx.doi.org/10.1787/888932709966

Level of disclosure of private interests by legislators in the lower house

Percentage of private interests analysed, 2010

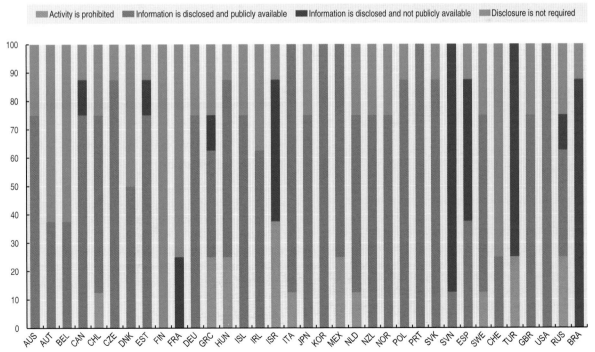

StatLink http://dx.doi.org/10.1787/888932709985

DEPTH OF CENTRAL GOVERNMENT FREEDOM OF INFORMATION LAWS

Freedom of information laws (FOI) – also referred to as access to information laws – are a fundamental pillar of open government. These laws contribute to strengthening transparency, enhancing government accountability and promoting informed participation in policy making. However, the strength and scope of these laws varies considerably across the OECD in terms of the institutions and types of information covered, reflecting different institutional and legal systems across countries.

In terms of institutional scope, for instance, the reach of FOI laws can potentially extend vertically to all levels of government (from central to local) and horizontally to all branches of central government (legislative, judicial and executive). In terms of coverage, FOI laws may contain lists of exemptions that may be applied to justify withholding certain information from disclosure. The *OECD 2010 Survey on Open Government* assessed both of these dimensions, looking at the breadth and scope of central/federal FOI laws in member countries.

Definition

Exemptions to FOI laws can include class tests and harm tests. Under class tests, any information that falls within a certain category (such as national security) can be denied. Under harm tests, the government can deny a request for information on the basis that disclosure would cause potential prejudice, for example, to an individual or harm to the defence of the state (the two most commonly used harm tests). Exemptions to FOI requests can be both mandatory (public entity is required to withhold the information) or discretionary (public entities can use their judgment to withhold or disclose information).

Comparability

Data were collected through the 2010 OECD Open Government Survey. Respondents to the survey were central government officials responsible for implementing open government initiatives. Data refer only to provisions in central/federal level FOI laws and exclude any additional FOI legislation which may exist at sub-national levels.

In some countries, public interest tests and/or ministerial discretion can override class or harms tests and lead to information disclosure if the public benefits from the information outweigh any harm that may be caused by disclosing it.

The survey was completed by 32 OECD countries, as well as by the Russian Federation. Data are not available for Germany, Greece and Luxembourg. The Italian FOI law applies only to administrative acts and does not refer to legislative acts.

Overview

In most OECD countries, the reach of FOI laws extends vertically to all levels of government. In the majority of countries, all bodies that form the executive branch of the central government (e.g. Ministries/Departments and executive agencies) are subject to FOI legislation. Legislative and judicial branches are less likely to be included. Private entities managing public funds, such as those contracted by the government to provide services to citizens, are subject to FOI laws in over half of member countries.

The class tests applied by the greatest number of OECD countries concern exemptions related to national security, international relations and personal data. The most common harm tests also relates to national security and international relations.

Sources
- OECD (2011), *Government at a Glance*, OECD Publishing.

Further information

Analytical publications
- OECD (2009), Focus on Citizens: Public Engagement for Better Policies and Services, *OECD Studies on Public Engagement*, OECD Publishing.
- OECD (2005), "Public Sector Modernisation: Open Government", *OECD Policy Brief*, OECD Publishing.
- OECD (2003), *Open Government: Fostering Dialogue with Civil Society*, OECD Publishing.

Methodological publications
- OECD (2010), Accountability and Transparency: A Guide for State Ownership, *Corporate Governance*, OECD Publishing.

Websites
- Government at a Glance (supplementary material), *www.oecd.org/gov/indicators/govataglance*.

Depth of central government freedom of information laws
2010

	Class test							Harm test				
	National security	International relations	Personal data	Commercial confidentiality	Law enforcement and public order information received in confidence	Internal discussions	Health and safety	Harm to persons	Harm to international relations, or to defence of state	Harm to commercial competitiveness	Harm to the economic interests of the state	Harm to law enforcement agencies
Australia	⊙	⊙	○	⊙	⊙	○	○	⊙	⊙	⊙	●	⊙
Austria	●	●	●	●	○	○	●	●	●	○	●	○
Belgium	●	○	○	○	○	○	○	●	●	●	●	○
Canada	⊙	⊙	●	●	⊙	⊙	○	⊙	⊙	●	⊙	⊙
Chile	⊙	⊙	⊙	⊙	⊙	⊙	⊙	⊙	⊙	⊙	⊙	⊙
Czech Republic	●	⊙	●	●	●	⊙	⊙	●	●	●	●	●
Denmark	⊙	⊙	⊙	⊙	⊙	⊙	⊙	⊙	⊙	⊙	⊙	⊙
Estonia	●	●	●	●	●	⊙	●	●	●	●	○	●
Finland	⊙	⊙	⊙	⊙	⊙	⊙	⊙	⊙	⊙	⊙	⊙	⊙
France	⊙	⊙	⊙	⊙	⊙	⊙	⊙	⊙	⊙	⊙	⊙	⊙
Germany												
Greece							.					
Hungary	●	●	●	○	●	○	○	●	○	●	○	○
Iceland	●	●	●	●	○	⊙	⊙	●	●	●	●	○
Ireland	●	●	●	⊙	⊙	⊙	●	●	●	⊙	⊙	●
Israel	●	●	●	⊙	⊙	⊙	○	●	●	⊙	○	⊙
Italy	●	●	⊙	⊙	●	⊙	●	⊙	●	⊙	●	●
Japan	⊙	⊙	⊙	⊙	⊙	⊙	⊙	●	●	●	●	●
Korea	⊙	⊙	⊙	⊙	⊙	⊙	.	⊙	⊙	⊙	⊙	⊙
Luxembourg												
Mexico	⊙	⊙	●	⊙	⊙	⊙	⊙	●	●	⊙	●	⊙
Netherlands	●	⊙	●	●	○	⊙	○	⊙	⊙	⊙	⊙	⊙
New Zealand	○	○	○	○	○	○	○	⊙	⊙	⊙	⊙	⊙
Norway	⊙	⊙	●	●	⊙	⊙	⊙	⊙	⊙	●	⊙	⊙
Poland	⊙	⊙	⊙	⊙	⊙	●	⊙	⊙	⊙	⊙	⊙	⊙
Portugal	●	●	●	●	●	●	○	●	●	●	○	○
Slovak Republic	●	●	⊙	●	⊙	⊙	⊙	⊙	⊙	⊙	⊙	⊙
Slovenia	⊙	⊙	⊙	⊙	⊙	⊙	⊙	⊙	⊙	⊙	⊙	⊙
Spain	●	○	⊙	●	●	○	⊙	○	○	○	○	○
Sweden	⊙	⊙	⊙	⊙	⊙	●	○	●	●	●	●	●
Switzerland	●	●	●	●	●	●	●	●	●	●	●	●
Turkey	●	⊙	●	●	●	⊙	○	●	●	●	●	○
United Kingdom	⊙	⊙	○	⊙	⊙	⊙	⊙	⊙	⊙	⊙	⊙	⊙
United States	⊙	⊙	⊙	⊙	⊙	⊙	⊙	⊙	⊙	⊙	○	⊙
EU27												
OECD							.					
● Mandatory	15	10	14	12	8	3	6	13	14	12	10	7
⊙ Discretionary	15	18	13	16	18	20	15	16	15	16	15	17
○ Not applicable	1	3	4	3	5	8	10	2	2	3	6	7
Brazil												
China												
India												
Indonesia												
Russian Federation	●	●	●	●	●	⊙	●	●	●	●	●	●
South Africa												

StatLink ᵍᵍᵍ http://dx.doi.org/10.1787/888932710004

Breadth of central government freedom of information laws
2010

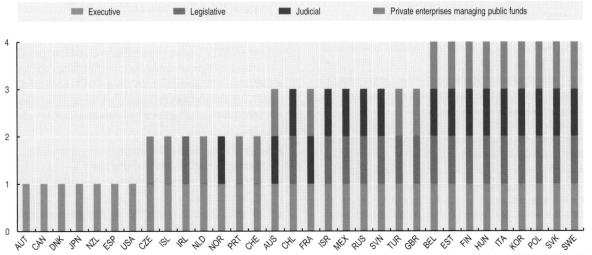

StatLink ᵍᵍᵍ http://dx.doi.org/10.1787/888932710023

SOCIAL EXPENDITURE

Social expenditures are a measure of the extent to which countries assume responsibility for supporting the standard of living of disadvantaged or vulnerable groups.

Definition

Social expenditure comprises cash benefits, direct in-kind provision of goods and services, and tax breaks with social purposes. Benefits may be targeted at low-income households, the elderly, disabled, sick, unemployed, or young persons. To be considered "social", programmes have to involve either redistribution of resources across households or compulsory participation. Social benefits are classified as public when general government (that is central, state, and local governments, including social security funds) controls the relevant financial flows. All social benefits not provided by general government are considered private. Private transfers between households are not considered as "social" and not included here. Net total social expenditure includes both public and private expenditure. It also accounts for the effect of the tax system by direct and indirect taxation and by tax breaks for social purposes.

Comparability

For cross-country comparisons, the most commonly used indicator of social support is gross (before tax) public social expenditure relative to GDP. Measurement problems do exist, particularly with regard to spending by lower tiers of government, which may be underestimated in some countries.

Data on private social spending are often of lesser quality than for public spending. Private data for Israel refer to private health insurance only.

No data on net expenditure are currently available for Greece, Hungary and Switzerland. Net data for France, Iceland, Luxembourg and Mexico have been estimated using data on direct tax rates of benefit income for 2007. In the absence of information on direct taxation of benefit income in Slovenia, net total social spending is overestimated for this country, and therefore it is not included in the OECD average.

For non-OECD countries, data are not strictly comparable with OECD countries.

Overview

Gross public social expenditure increased from about 16% in 1980 to 18% in 1990 and to 22% of GDP in 2009 across OECD countries. Spending was highest, at over 30% of GDP, in France and Denmark, and lowest, at below 10% of GDP, in Korea and Mexico. Keeping measurement-related differences in mind, non-OECD countries have lower levels of social protection than OECD countries, particularly in Indonesia and India. The three biggest categories of social transfers are pensions (on average 8% of GDP), health (7%) and income transfers to the working-age population (5%). Public spending on other social services exceeds 5% of GDP only in the Nordic countries, where the public role in providing services to the elderly, the disabled and families is the most extensive.

In 2009, gross private social spending was highest (at just over 10% of GDP) in the United States and lowest (at less than 1% of GDP) in the Czech Republic, Estonia, Hungary, Mexico, New Zealand, Poland, Spain and Turkey.

Moving from gross public to net total social expenditure not only leads to greater similarity in spending levels across countries it also changes the ranking among countries. Estonia, Denmark, Finland, Luxembourg and Poland drop 5 to 10 places in the rankings while Canada, Iceland, Japan, the Netherlands, the United Kingdom move up the rankings by 5 to 10 places. As private social spending is so much larger in the United States compared with other countries its inclusion moves the United States from 22rd to 2nd place when comparing net total social spending across countries.

Sources
- OECD (2012), *Social Expenditure Statistics* (database).
- For non OECD countries: OECD (2010), *Employment Outlook*, OECD Publishing.

Further information

Analytical publications
- Adema, W., P. Fron and M. Ladaique (2011), "Is the European Welfare State Really More Expensive?: Indicators on Social Spending, 1980-2012; and a Manual to the OECD Social Expenditure Database (SOCX)", *OECD Social, Employment and Migration Working Papers*, No. 124.
- OECD (2011), *Society at a Glance: OECD Social Indicators*, OECD Publishing.
- OECD (2011), *Doing Better for Families*, OECD Publishing.

Websites
- Social Expenditure (supplementary material), *www.oecd.org/els/social/expenditure*.
- OECD on-line Family database, *www.oecd.org/social/family/database*.
- Sickness, Disability and Work (supplementary material), *www.oecd.org/els/disability*.
- Statistics, Data and Indicators on Social and Welfare Issues, *www.oecd.org/social/statistics*.

Public, private and total net social expenditure

As a percentage of GDP

	Public expenditure								Private expenditure				Total net social expenditure
	1990	2000	2006	2007	2008	2009	2010	2011	1990	2000	2007	2009	2009
Australia	13.2	17.3	16.5	16.4	17.8	17.8	17.9	18.1	0.8	4.4	3.8	3.1	19.9
Austria	23.8	26.6	26.8	26.3	26.8	29.1	28.8	27.9	2.2	1.9	1.9	2.1	25.6
Belgium	24.9	25.3	26.0	26.0	27.3	29.7	29.5	29.6	1.6	1.7	2.2	2.3	28.1
Canada	18.1	16.5	16.9	16.8	17.6	19.2	18.6	18.3	3.3	5.0	5.3	5.1	22.9
Chile	..	12.8	9.3	9.4	10.4	12.0	12.4	12.1	0.6	1.2	2.7	3.0	13.8
Czech Republic	15.3	19.1	18.3	18.1	18.1	20.7	20.8	20.9	..	0.3	0.4	0.7	19.9
Denmark	25.1	26.4	27.1	26.5	26.8	30.2	30.1	30.0	2.1	2.4	2.6	2.9	25.3
Estonia	..	13.9	13.8	13.5	16.7	23.5	23.4	21.9	..	..	0.0	0.0	19.7
Finland	24.1	24.2	25.8	24.7	25.3	29.4	29.4	28.6	1.1	1.2	1.1	1.2	24.8
France	25.1	28.6	29.8	29.7	29.8	32.1	32.2	32.1	1.9	2.6	2.9	3.1	32.1
Germany	21.7	26.6	26.1	25.1	25.2	27.8	27.1	26.2	3.0	3.0	2.9	3.2	27.5
Greece	16.6	19.3	21.3	21.6	22.2	23.9	23.3	23.5	2.1	2.1	1.5	1.8	..
Hungary	..	20.7	22.8	23.0	23.1	23.9	22.6	21.8	..	0.0	0.2	0.2	..
Iceland	13.7	15.2	15.9	15.3	15.8	18.5	18.0	17.8	3.0	4.2	5.1	6.0	20.8
Ireland	17.3	13.4	16.1	16.7	19.7	23.6	23.7	23.4	1.4	1.3	1.5	2.2	23.3
Israel	..	17.2	15.8	15.5	15.5	16.0	16.5	16.3	..	0.3	0.5	0.6	14.9
Italy	19.9	23.1	25.0	24.7	25.8	27.8	27.8	27.6	3.9	2.2	2.2	2.3	25.5
Japan	11.1	16.3	18.4	18.7	19.9	22.4	..	..	0.3	3.9	3.6	4.0	25.3
Korea	2.8	4.8	7.4	7.6	8.3	9.4	9.2	9.2	0.4	2.9	2.7	2.7	12.4
Luxembourg	19.1	20.9	21.8	20.3	20.8	23.6	23.0	22.5	..	0.1	1.0	1.7	20.3
Mexico	3.3	5.3	7.0	7.1	7.5	7.7	7.8	8.1	0.1	0.1	0.2	0.3	8.8
Netherlands	25.6	19.8	21.7	21.1	20.9	23.2	23.5	23.7	6.1	7.3	6.9	6.7	25.3
New Zealand	21.5	19.0	18.9	18.6	19.8	21.2	21.5	21.8	0.2	0.5	0.4	0.5	19.3
Norway	22.3	21.3	20.3	20.5	19.8	23.3	23.0	22.6	1.9	2.0	2.0	2.3	20.7
Poland	14.9	20.5	20.8	19.7	20.3	21.5	21.8	20.7	..	..	0.0	0.0	18.3
Portugal	12.5	18.9	23.0	22.7	23.1	25.6	25.6	25.2	0.9	1.5	1.9	1.9	25.3
Slovak Republic	..	17.9	16.0	15.7	15.7	18.7	19.0	18.0	..	0.8	1.0	0.9	18.5
Slovenia	..	22.8	21.6	20.2	20.5	23.4	24.3	24.9	..	0.0	1.1	1.2	22.8
Spain	19.9	20.2	21.1	21.3	22.9	26.0	26.5	26.0	0.2	0.3	0.5	0.5	25.2
Sweden	30.2	28.4	28.4	27.3	27.5	29.8	28.3	27.6	1.2	2.6	2.9	3.2	26.1
Switzerland	13.5	17.8	19.2	18.5	18.4	20.1	20.0	20.2	5.3	8.3	8.3	8.0	..
Turkey	5.7	9.8	10.0	10.5	10.7	12.8	..	..	..	..	..	..	11.9
United Kingdom	16.7	18.6	20.3	20.4	21.8	24.1	23.7	23.9	5.1	7.7	5.4	6.3	27.7
United States	13.6	14.5	16.1	16.3	17.0	19.2	20.0	19.8	7.6	9.1	10.6	10.6	28.9
EU 27	..	..	..	..	..	..	..	..	..	..	..	..	..
OECD	17.7	18.9	19.6	19.3	20.0	22.3	22.2	21.9	1.8	2.4	2.5	2.7	21.9
Brazil	..	..	..	16.3	..	..	..	..	..	..	..	..	..
China	..	..	..	..	..	6.5	..	..	..	..	..	..	..
India	..	..	..	4.6	..	..	..	..	..	..	..	..	..
Indonesia	..	..	..	2.9	..	..	..	..	..	..	..	..	..
Russian Federation	..	..	..	15.5	..	..	..	..	..	..	..	..	..
South Africa	..	..	..	8.1	..	..	..	..	..	..	..	..	..

StatLink http://dx.doi.org/10.1787/888932710042

Public, private and total net social expenditure

As a percentage of GDP, 2009

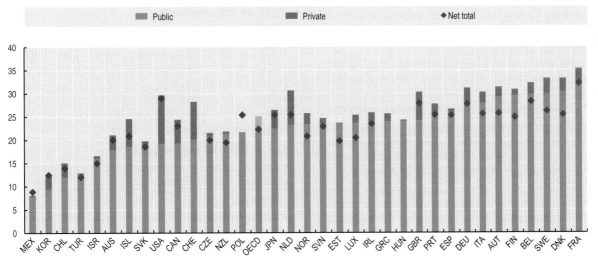

StatLink http://dx.doi.org/10.1787/888932710061

PENSION EXPENDITURE

Pension systems vary across countries and no single model fits all. Generally, there is a mix of public and private provision. Public pensions are statutory, most often financed on a pay-as-you-go (PAYG) basis – where current contributions pay for current benefits – and managed by public institutions. Private pensions are in some cases mandatory but more usually voluntary, funded, employment-based (occupational) pension plans or individual retirement savings plans (personal pensions).

Definition

Old-age pension benefits are treated as public when relevant financial flows are controlled by general government (*i.e.* central and local governments or social security funds). Pension benefits provided by governments to their own employees and paid directly out of the government's current budget are also considered to be public. Public pensions are generally financed on a PAYG basis, but also include some funded arrangements. All pension benefits not provided by general government are within the private domain.

Private expenditures on pensions include payments made to private pension plan members (or dependants) after retirement. All types of plans are included (occupational and personal, mandatory and voluntary, funded and book reserved), covering persons working in both the public and private sectors.

The data are shown for old-age and survivors cash benefits.

Comparability

Public pension expenditures come from the *OECD Social Expenditure* (SOCX) database while pension expenditures for private pension arrangements come from the *OECD Global Pension Statistics* (GPS) database. The GPS database provides information on funded pension arrangements, which includes both private and public pension plans that are funded.

Although the GPS database covers all types of private pension arrangements for most countries, for Austria, Canada, Germany, Luxembourg and the United States data only relate to autonomous pension funds. A break in series for Mexico reflects the inclusion of occupational pension plans registered by CONSAR since 2005. The large increase in private pension expenditures between 2008 and 2009 for Iceland reflects the increase in the number of people retiring due to the unemployment peak after the bank crisis and the passing of a special temporary Act allowing people to withdraw limited amounts of money from personal pension plans.

No data for private expenditure are currently collected for countries ranked separately on the left-hand side of the chart.

Overview

Public spending on old-age benefits averaged 7.8% of GDP in 2009, compared with private pension benefits of an average of 2.2% of GDP in the same year (in the countries for which data are available over the period 2004-10). Public spending on old-age pensions is highest – greater than 10% of GDP – in Austria, France, Germany, Greece, Italy, Japan, Poland, Portugal and Slovenia. By contrast, Australia, Iceland, Korea and Mexico spend 4% of GDP or less on public old-age pensions.

Private expenditure on old-age benefits is the highest in Australia, Denmark, Iceland, the Netherlands and Switzerland, where it exceeds 3.5% of GDP. However, private benefit spending remains negligible in around a third of OECD countries.

The share of private pensions in total expenditures on old-age benefits exceeds 50% only in Australia and Iceland. The average share of private pensions in the total is 22%.

Over time, public pension expenditures have grown a little faster than national income: from an average of 6.5% of GDP in 1990 to 7.8% in 2009.

Expenditure in private pensions has also grown between 2001 and 2010, from an average of 1.8% of GDP in 2001 to 2.1% in 2010.

Sources
- OECD (2012), *OECD Pensions Statistics* (database).
- OECD (2012), *OECD Social Expenditure Statistics* (database).

Further information

Analytical publications
- OECD (2012), *OECD Pensions Outlook*, OECD Publishing.
- OECD (2012), *Pensions at a Glance: Asia/Pacific*, OECD Publishing.
- OECD (2011), *OECD Pensions at a Glance*, OECD Publishing.
- OECD (2009), *OECD Private Pensions Outlook*, OECD Publishing.

Methodological publications
- OECD (2005), *Private Pensions: OECD Classification and Glossary*, OECD Publishing.

Websites
- OECD Pensions at a Glance (supplementary material), *www.oecd.org/els/social/pensions/PAG*.
- Pension Markets in Focus, *www.oecd.org/daf/pensions/pensionmarkets*.
- Social Expenditure Database (SOCX), *www.oecd.org/els/social/expenditure*.

Public and private expenditure on pensions

As a percentage of GDP

	Public expenditure						Private expenditure					
	2000	2005	2006	2007	2008	2009	2005	2006	2007	2008	2009	2010
Australia	3.8	3.3	3.3	3.4	3.6	3.5	3.7	3.9	3.4	5.5	4.6	4.5
Austria	12.2	12.4	12.3	12.2	12.4	13.5	0.2	0.2	0.3	0.2	0.2	0.2
Belgium	8.9	9.0	8.9	8.8	9.4	10.0	1.3	1.3	2.8	2.6	3.3	2.9
Canada	4.3	4.1	4.1	4.1	4.2	4.5	2.0	2.2	2.2	2.3	2.7	2.5
Chile	7.3	5.7	5.1	4.9	4.6	4.9	..	..	2.0	2.1	1.8	2.1
Czech Republic	7.2	7.0	6.9	7.1	7.4	8.3	..	..	0.3	0.3	0.4	0.5
Denmark	5.3	5.4	5.5	5.5	5.6	6.1	3.4	3.8	3.3	4.1	4.3	4.5
Estonia	6.0	5.3	5.3	5.1	6.2	7.9	..	..	..	..	0.0	0.0
Finland	7.6	8.4	8.5	8.3	8.4	9.9	..	0.5	0.5	0.5	0.7	0.6
France	11.8	12.4	12.4	12.5	12.9	13.7	..	..	..	..	0.4	0.4
Germany	11.1	11.4	11.0	10.6	10.5	11.3	0.1	0.1	0.1	0.1	0.3	0.2
Greece	10.8	11.8	11.8	12.1	12.4	13.0	..	..	0.0	0.0	0.0	0.0
Hungary	7.6	8.5	8.8	9.3	9.7	9.9	0.2	0.1	0.2	0.2	0.2	0.2
Iceland	2.2	2.0	1.8	1.9	1.8	1.7	3.4	3.5	3.7	3.8	6.4	5.5
Ireland	3.1	3.4	3.4	3.6	4.1	5.1	..	..	..	..	..	..
Israel	4.9	5.1	5.0	5.0	4.8	5.0	1.7	1.8	1.7	1.7	1.7	1.7
Italy	13.5	13.9	13.9	14.0	14.5	15.4	0.2	0.2	0.2	0.3	0.2	0.2
Japan	7.3	8.7	8.7	8.9	9.3	10.2	..	..	..	..	..	..
Korea	1.4	1.5	1.6	1.7	2.0	2.1	0.8	0.9	1.0	0.8	1.1	1.4
Luxembourg	7.5	7.2	6.8	6.5	6.6	7.7	0.1	0.1	0.1	0.1	0.1	0.1
Mexico	0.9	1.2	1.2	1.4	1.5	1.3	0.1	0.2	0.3	0.3	0.3	0.3
Netherlands	5.0	5.0	4.8	4.7	4.7	5.1	3.5	3.6	3.6	3.6	3.9	4.0
New Zealand	5.0	4.3	4.3	4.3	4.4	4.7	1.3	1.5	1.3	1.4	1.9	1.3
Norway	4.8	4.8	4.6	4.7	4.5	5.4	1.4	1.4	2.0	1.6	..	..
Poland	10.5	11.4	11.5	10.6	10.8	11.8	0.0	0.0	0.0	0.0	0.0	0.0
Portugal	7.9	10.3	10.6	10.7	11.3	12.3	0.9	1.0	1.0	1.4	1.0	0.7
Slovak Republic	6.3	6.2	6.0	5.9	5.7	7.0	..	..	..	..	..	..
Slovenia	10.5	9.9	10.0	9.6	9.5	10.9	..	..	0.0	0.0	0.0	0.0
Spain	8.6	8.1	8.0	8.1	8.4	9.3	0.5	0.6	0.5	0.6	0.6	0.6
Sweden	7.2	7.6	7.3	7.2	7.4	8.2	1.0	1.1	1.3	1.2	1.3	1.4
Switzerland	6.6	6.8	6.5	6.4	6.3	..	5.3	5.3	5.4	5.3	5.5	5.1
Turkey	..	5.9	5.8	6.1	5.5	6.8	0.0	0.0	0.0	0.1	0.1	0.1
United Kingdom	5.3	5.6	5.3	5.3	5.7	6.2	3.0	3.1	2.8	2.9	3.2	3.3
United States	5.9	6.0	5.9	6.0	6.2	6.8	2.9	3.1	3.3	3.0	2.9	
EU 27	..	..	..	..	..	..	..	..	..	..	..	..
OECD	6.9	7.0	7.0	7.0	7.1	7.8	1.7	1.8	1.9	2.0	2.2	2.1
Brazil	..	..	..	..	..	..	..	..	..	..	..	..
China	..	..	..	..	..	..	..	..	..	..	..	..
India	..	..	..	..	..	..	..	..	..	..	..	..
Indonesia	..	..	..	..	..	..	..	..	..	..	..	..
Russian Federation	..	..	..	..	..	..	..	..	..	..	..	..
South Africa	..	..	..	..	..	..	..	..	..	..	..	..

StatLink ᵐˢ˗ http://dx.doi.org/10.1787/888932710080

Public and private expenditure on pensions

As a percentage of GDP, 2009

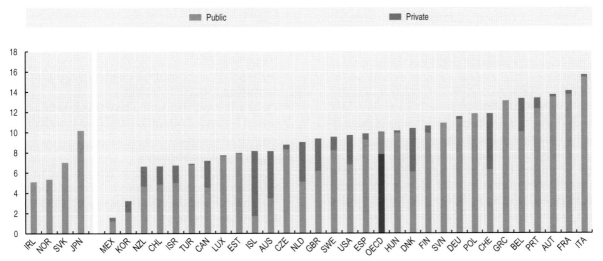

StatLink ᵐˢ˗ http://dx.doi.org/10.1787/888932710099

GOVERNMENT SUPPORT FOR AGRICULTURE

Governments provide support to agriculture through a variety of means, ranging from budgetary transfers financed by taxpayers to policies such as border protection and administered pricing that, by raising farm prices above the levels that would otherwise prevail, are equivalent to an implicit tax on consumers. While some of these measures may pursue commendable goals such as sustaining rural communities and encouraging more environmentally-friendly agricultural practices, they may also lead to production and trade distortions and environmental damage.

Definition

The OECD Producer Support Estimate (PSE) is an indicator of the annual monetary value of gross transfers from consumers and taxpayers to agricultural producers, measured at the farmgate level, arising from policy measures that support agriculture, regardless of their nature, objectives or impacts on farm production or income. PSE can be expressed as a total monetary amount, but is usually quoted as a percentage of gross farm receipts. This is the measure used here.

The measure is agreed by OECD member countries and is widely recognised as the only reliable indicator for comparing support across countries and over time. The European Union is treated as a single entity.

Comparability

Continuous efforts are made to ensure consistency in the treatment and completeness of coverage of policies in all OECD countries through the annual preparation of the *Monitoring and Evaluation* report. Each year, PSE provisional estimates are reviewed and approved by representatives of OECD's member countries, as are all methodological developments.

In the table, data are not shown for individual EU member countries. Austria, Finland and Sweden are included in the OECD total for all years and in the EU from 1995. The Czech Republic, Estonia, Hungary, Poland and the Slovak Republic are included in the OECD total for all years and in the EU from 2004. Slovenia is included in the OECD total from 1992 and in the EU from 2004. Chile and Israel are included in the OECD total from 1995. Agricultural producer support estimate by country: 2009-10 data instead of 2009-11 for Brazil, China, the Russian Federation and South Africa. The OECD total does not include the non-OECD EU member states.

Overview

There are large differences in the levels of agricultural support among OECD countries. Producer support estimates as a percentage of gross farm receipts currently range from almost zero to 60%. These differences reflect, among other things, variations in policy objectives, different historical uses of policy instruments, and the varying pace and degrees of progress in agricultural policy reform. Over the longer term, the level of producer support has fallen in most OECD countries. The average support as a share of gross farm receipt in 2009-11, at 20%, is lower than the 1986-88 average of 37% and has fallen in most countries. There has also been some change in the way support is delivered to the sector.

For the emerging economies covered here producer support estimates as a percentage of farm receipts have been lower than the OECD average for Brazil, China, Indonesia and South Africa, but higher for the Russian Federation, where it reached 22% and was above the OECD average in 2008-10. Trends in the level of producer support vary between economies. While in South Africa the level of producer support has fallen, in Brazil, China, Indonesia and the Russian Federation it has increased since the mid-1990s.

Sources

- OECD (2012), *Agricultural Policy Monitoring and Evaluation*, OECD Publishing.

Further information

Analytical publications

- Brooks, J. (ed.) (2012), *Agricultural Policies for Poverty Reduction*, OECD Publishing.
- OECD (2012), *OECD Review of Agricultural Policies*, OECD Publishing.
- OECD (2011), *Fostering Productivity and Competitiveness in Agriculture*, OECD Publishing.
- OECD and Food and Agriculture Organization of the United Nations (FAO) (2012), *OECD-FAO Agricultural Outlook*, OECD Publishing.

Methodological publications

- OECD (2010), "*Producer Support Estimate and Related Indicators of Agricultural Support: Concepts, Calculations, Interpretation and Use (The PSE Manual)*", OECD Trade and Agriculture Directorate.

Online databases

- *OECD Agriculture Statistics*.

Websites

- Producer and Consumer Support Estimates (supplementary material), *www.oecd.org/agriculture/pse*.

Agricultural producer support estimate by country
As a percentage of gross farm receipts

	1999	2000	2001	2002	2003	2004	2005	2006	2007	2008	2009	2010	2011
Australia	3.9	3.3	3.3	4.7	3.7	3.4	3.6	4.5	5.1	4.4	3.1	2.6	3.0
Canada	17.2	19.3	15.5	20.5	24.4	20.3	21.3	20.9	16.4	13.3	17.4	16.7	14.2
Chile	10.4	11.2	6.2	9.3	5.3	4.9	5.0	4.2	3.6	3.4	5.5	3.4	3.5
Iceland	72.5	69.6	62.6	66.4	65.0	65.9	66.9	64.5	55.5	52.4	51.3	47.1	43.7
Israel	20.1	22.7	20.5	16.1	11.8	10.3	10.6	7.9	1.8	15.4	11.7	12.6	14.0
Japan	59.9	59.7	56.3	57.2	57.5	56.0	53.8	51.6	46.7	48.3	48.9	53.3	51.6
Korea	65.3	66.1	57.7	59.7	56.7	61.3	59.7	58.6	57.4	45.5	50.9	44.8	53.3
Mexico	17.3	23.4	18.2	26.7	19.2	11.6	12.9	13.2	13.0	12.0	13.8	11.9	11.6
New Zealand	0.8	0.3	0.6	0.3	0.7	0.6	1.3	0.9	0.7	0.6	0.4	0.5	0.8
Norway	71.2	66.5	65.3	73.7	71.1	66.3	65.8	64.1	54.6	59.4	61.2	60.8	57.7
Switzerland	75.2	69.8	67.3	70.6	69.2	69.2	66.1	65.3	48.8	56.0	60.3	53.5	54.4
Turkey	34.2	30.5	14.3	26.1	31.2	31.5	33.2	33.4	26.2	26.3	28.4	25.5	20.2
United States	25.5	23.3	22.1	18.4	15.1	16.3	15.3	11.2	10.0	8.8	10.6	7.7	7.7
EU 27	38.2	32.7	30.2	33.8	33.6	32.6	30.4	29.0	23.5	22.0	23.3	19.8	17.5
OECD	35.1	32.2	28.8	30.5	29.2	30.1	28.5	26.4	22.0	21.0	22.7	19.9	18.8
Brazil	1.3	6.4	4.2	4.9	5.8	4.5	6.8	6.1	4.9	4.1	6.5	4.5	..
China	-2.6	3.0	4.7	8.4	10.1	7.5	8.5	12.3	10.1	3.3	13.2	17.4	..
India	..	..	..	..	..	..	..	..	..	..	..	..	..
Indonesia	-3.5	7.0	5.0	13.3	12.6	8.9	3.7	15.3	14.9	-10.5	5.8	21.0	..
Russian Federation	0.9	5.5	10.7	12.7	19.2	22.3	14.6	17.2	18.2	21.9	22.1	21.4	..
South Africa	8.0	5.8	3.7	10.1	7.1	7.9	6.2	9.2	4.2	3.1	4.3	2.2	..

StatLink http://dx.doi.org/10.1787/888932710118

Agricultural producer support estimate by country
As a percentage of gross farm receipts

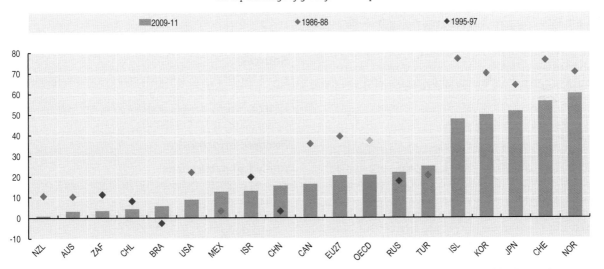

StatLink http://dx.doi.org/10.1787/888932710137

GOVERNMENT SUPPORT FOR FISHING

OECD governments provide financial support to the fishing industry, typically for the purposes of management, including surveillance and research. This financial support is important to ensure a sustainable and responsible fisheries sector.

Definition

The indicator on "Government financial transfers (GFTs)" provides a measure of the financial support provided by governments to the fisheries sector. GFT consists of direct revenue enhancing transfers (direct payments), *i.e.* transfers that reduce the operating costs and the costs of general services provided to the fishing industry. These general services consist mainly of fishery protection services and fisheries management; in some cases they also include the costs of local area weather forecasting and the costs of navigation and satellite surveillance systems designed to assist fishing fleets.

Comparability

The data are relatively comprehensive and consistent across the years. However, some year-to-year variations may reflect changes in national statistical systems. General services provided by governments may also include large and irregular capital investments. Some types of GFT (*e.g.* maritime surveillance) may be provided by another agency than fisheries agencies (*e.g.* in some countries maritime surveillance is carried out by the navy); some of these data

may not be available. Also, some figures, in particular for later years, are still preliminary.

GFT to fishing for selected countries
Million US dollars

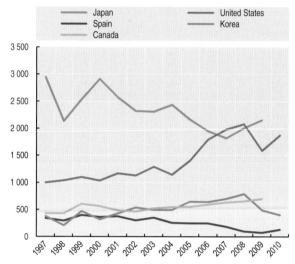

StatLink ⟨≡⟩ http://dx.doi.org/10.1787/888932710213

Sources
- OECD (2012), *OECD Review of Fisheries: Policies and Summary Statistics*, OECD Publishing.
- OECD (2007), *Review of Fisheries in OECD Countries: Country Statistics*, OECD Publishing.

Further information

Analytical publications
- Love, P. (2010), *Fisheries: While Stocks Last?*, OECD Insights, OECD Publishing.
- OECD (2012), *Rebuilding Fisheries, The Way Forward*, OECD Publishing.
- OECD (2009), *Reducing Fishing Capacity: Best Practices for Decommissioning Schemes*, OECD Publishing.
- OECD (2007), *Structural Change in Fisheries: Dealing with the Human Dimension*, OECD Publishing.
- OECD (2006), *Financial Support to Fisheries: Implications for Sustainable Development*, OECD Publishing.
- OECD (2006), *Subsidy Reform and Sustainable Development: Economic, Environmental and Social Aspects, OECD Sustainable Development Studies*, OECD Publishing.
- OECD (2005), *Environmentally Harmful Subsidies: Challenges for Reform*, OECD Publishing.
- OECD (2000), *Transition to Responsible Fisheries: Economic and Policy Implications*, OECD Publishing.

Websites
- OECD Fisheries, *www.oecd.org/tad/fisheries*.

Overview

Total government support for fishing amounted to USD 5 billion in 2008, the last year for which comprehensive data are available. Overall, transfers to the fishing industry in OECD countries have been fluctuating at around the USD 6 to 7 billion mark over the past decade. Around three-quarters of GFTs are categorised as general services and typically involve management, enforcement and research. Other types of general services included in the GFTs are harbour construction and maintenance, stock enhancement and habitat conservation.

Direct payments to fishers represent approximately 21% of the total GFT in 2008. In 2007, USD 287 million was dedicated to decommissioning schemes, while USD 25 million was used for programs related to vessel construction or modernisation. Other policies included in the direct payments category of the GFT are unemployment insurance (USD 244 million) and disaster relief (USD 266 million). The third category of GFTs, cost reducing transfers, accounted for 6% of the total GFTs.

Government financial transfers to fishing

Thousand US dollars

	1998	1999	2000	2001	2002	2003	2004	2005	2006	2007	2008	2009	2010
Australia	..	..	82 272	75 902	78 038	95 558	95 560	38 420	45 772	57 954	66 959	..	55 606
Austria	..	..	..	..	..	..	..	..	..	..	..	..	..
Belgium	..	4 473	6 849	2 830	1 607	1 668	6 328	8 613	7 132	3 288	1 268	9 132	..
Canada	..	606 443	564 497	483 982	464 257	522 581	547 923	553 193	595 220	634 525	657 050	699 537	..
Chile	..	..	..	..	..	..	..	..	..	39 351	48 247	64 555	88 139
Czech Republic	..	..	..	..	..	..	..	..	3 801	8 836	29 234	36 844	..
Denmark	90 507	27 765	16 316		68 769	37 659	28 505	58 108	89 991	63 717	83 224	80 138	102 975
Estonia	..	..	..	..	..	..	..	..	11 579	9 002	4 047	..	..
Finland	26 888	19 236	13 908	16 510	16 025	20 231	19 397	24 816	17 569	20 877	20 900	17 066	..
France	..	71 665	166 147	141 786	155 283	179 740	108 358	141 359	63 360	..	323 811	327 786	..
Germany	16 488	31 276	29 834	28 988	28 208	33 890	6 088	17 284	4 899	6 815	5 129	4 817	7 053
Greece	26 908	43 030	87 315	86 957	88 334	119 045	35 500	61 013	57 188	56 276	66 744	60 795	..
Hungary	..	..	..	..	..	..	..	..	..	..	..	..	..
Iceland	36 954	39 763	41 978	28 310	28 955	48 348	55 705	64 326	51 331	61 459	45 489	31 043	..
Ireland	111 675	118 143	87 636	71 421	60 811	62 326	21 231	21 926	65 000	200 181	245 913	212 712	..
Israel	..	..	..	..	..	..	..	..	..	..	..	..	..
Italy	..	200 470	217 679	231 680	159 630	149 270	170 055	74 524	194 696	123 276	56 855	..	91 119
Japan	2 135 946	2 537 536	2 913 149	2 574 086	2 323 601	2 310 744	2 437 934	2 165 198	1 952 853	1 821 144	2 008 992	2 153 732	..
Korea	211 927	471 556	320 449	428 313	538 695	495 280	495 280	649 387	644 000	702 990	793 569	490 126	403 345
Luxembourg	..	..	..	..	..	..	..	..	..	..	..	..	..
Mexico	..	..	..	..	..	177 000	114 000	84 973	88 760	85 267	..	..	..
Netherlands	..	..	1 389	12 779	12 443	6 569	5 218	13 685	18 501	5 635	42 726	3 206	12 405
New Zealand	29 412	29 630	27 273	15 126	18 981	38 325	29 973	37 147	37 926	40 545	41 805	38 795	43 723
Norway	153 046	180 962	104 564	99 465	156 340	139 200	142 315	149 521	188 488	237 347	261 244	253 826	..
Poland	..	..	..	..	..	..	..	97 327	34 264	28 326	..	..	..
Portugal	..	28 674	25 578	25 066	24 899	26 930	26 930	32 769	29 219	30 896	18 025	49 499	33 248
Slovak Republic	..	..	..	..	..	..	..	..	..	..	..	..	..
Slovenia	..	..	..	..	..	..	..	..	..	..	..	..	..
Spain	296 642	399 604	364 096	376 614	301 926	353 290	257 730	249 047	247 647	188 082	102 699	78 979	134 979
Sweden	26 960	31 053	25 186	22 505	24 753	30 650	51 129	49 780	50 057	89 310	92 766	66 789	77 963
Switzerland	..	..	..	..	..	..	..	..	..	..	..	..	..
Turkey	..	1 277	26 372	17 721	16 167	16 300	59 500	98 072	135 931	144 927	199 858	..	..
United Kingdom	90 833	75 968	81 394	73 738	64 743	81 997	87 863	90 579	103 347		30 092	10 680	14 248
United States	1 041 000	1 103 100	1 037 710	1 169 590	1 130 810	1 290 440	1 147 521	1 407 813	1 793 833	1 985 497	2 084 409	1 591 259	1 873 977
EU 27	..	..	..	..	..	..	..	..	..	..	..	..	..
OECD	4 183 511	6 046 665	6 153 955	5 949 321	5 734 867	6 307 763	6 080 611	6 173 933	6 456 480	6 671 916	4 919 816	..	..
Brazil	..	..	..	..	..	..	..	..	..	..	..	..	..
China	..	..	..	..	..	..	..	..	..	..	..	..	..
India	..	..	..	..	..	..	..	..	..	..	..	..	..
Indonesia	..	..	..	..	..	..	..	..	..	..	..	..	..
Russian Federation	..	..	..	..	..	..	..	..	..	..	..	..	..
South Africa	..	..	..	..	..	..	..	..	..	..	..	..	..

StatLink ᴍ͟ˢ͟ᴸ http://dx.doi.org/10.1787/888932710175

Government financial transfers to fishing

Average annual growth in percentage, 2000-2010 or latest available period

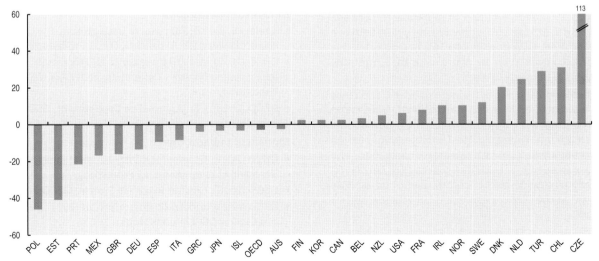

StatLink ᴍ͟ˢ͟ᴸ http://dx.doi.org/10.1787/888932710194

OFFICIAL DEVELOPMENT ASSISTANCE

Promoting economic and social development in non-member countries has been a principal objective of the OECD since its foundation. The share of national income devoted to Official Development Assistance (ODA) is a test of a country's commitment to international development. A long-standing United Nations target is that developed countries should devote 0.7% of their Gross National Income (GNI) to ODA.

Definition

ODA is defined as government aid designed to promote the economic development and welfare of developing countries. Loans and credits for military purposes are excluded. Aid may be provided bilaterally, from donor to recipient, or channelled through a multilateral development agency such as the United Nations or the World Bank. Aid includes grants, "soft" loans and the provision of technical assistance. Soft loans are those where the grant element is at least 25% of the total.

The OECD maintains a list of developing countries and territories; only aid to these countries counts as ODA. The list is periodically updated and currently contains over 150 countries or territories with per capita incomes below 12 276 USD in 2010. Data on ODA flows are provided by the 24 OECD members of the Development Assistance Committee (DAC).

Comparability

Statistics on ODA are compiled according to directives drawn up by the DAC. Each country's statistics are subject to regular peer reviews by other DAC members.

Net official development assistance
1960-2011

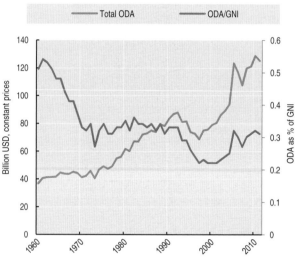

StatLink http://dx.doi.org/10.1787/888932710270

Overview

From 1960 to 1990, official development assistance flows from DAC countries to developing countries rose steadily. By contrast, total ODA as a percentage of DAC countries' combined gross national income (GNI) fell between 1960 and 1970, and then oscillated between 0.27% and 0.36% for a little over twenty years. Between 1993 and 1997, ODA flows fell by 16% in real terms due to fiscal consolidation in donor countries after the recession of the early 1990s.

Aid then started to rise in real terms in 1998 and since then a series of high-profile international conferences have boosted ODA flows. In 2002, the International Conference on Financing for Development, held in Monterrey, Mexico, set firm targets for each donor and marked an upturn of ODA after a decade of decline. In 2005, donors made further commitments to increase their aid at the Gleneagles G8 and UN Millennium + 5 summits.

Net ODA rose by 63% between 2000 and 2010, the year it reached its peak. In 2011, total net ODA from DAC members dropped to USD 133.5 billion representing a decrease of 2.7% in real terms compared to 2010. The weighted average of total ODA as a percentage of donor's combined GNI, was 0.31% in 2011.

Sources
• OECD (2011), OECD International Development Statistics, OECD Publishing.

Further information

Analytical publications
• Keeley, B. (2012), From Aid to Development, The Global Fight against Poverty, OECD Insights, OECD Publishing.
• OECD (2012), Aid Effectiveness 2011, Progress in Implementing the Paris Declaration, Better Aid, OECD Publishing.
• OECD (2010), OECD Journal on Development, OECD Publishing.

Statistical publications
• OECD (2011), Geographical Distribution of Financial Flows to Developing Countries, OECD Publishing.
• OECD (2010), Creditor Reporting System, OECD Publishing.
• OECD and World Trade Organization (2011), Aid for Trade at a Glance, OECD Publishing.

Online databases
• OECD International Development Statistics.

Websites
• Aid at a glance: by donor, recipient and region, www.oecd.org/dac/stats/aidcharts.
• OECD Aid Statistics, www.oecd.org/dac/stats.

OFFICIAL DEVELOPMENT ASSISTANCE

Net official development assistance

	As a percentage of gross national income						Millions of US dollars					
	2006	2007	2008	2009	2010	2011	2006	2007	2008	2009	2010	2011
Australia	0.30	0.32	0.32	0.29	0.32	0.35	2 123	2 669	2 954	2 762	3 826	4 799
Austria	0.47	0.50	0.43	0.30	0.32	0.27	1 498	1 808	1 714	1 142	1 208	1 107
Belgium	0.50	0.43	0.48	0.55	0.64	0.53	1 977	1 951	2 386	2 610	3 004	2 800
Canada	0.29	0.29	0.33	0.30	0.34	0.31	3 683	4 080	4 795	4 000	5 209	5 291
Denmark	0.80	0.81	0.82	0.88	0.91	0.86	2 236	2 562	2 803	2 810	2 871	2 981
Finland	0.40	0.39	0.44	0.54	0.55	0.52	834	981	1 166	1 290	1 333	1 409
France	0.47	0.38	0.39	0.47	0.50	0.46	10 601	9 884	10 908	12 602	12 915	12 994
Germany	0.36	0.37	0.38	0.35	0.39	0.40	10 435	12 291	13 981	12 079	12 985	14 533
Greece	0.17	0.16	0.21	0.19	0.17	0.11	424	501	703	607	508	331
Ireland	0.54	0.55	0.59	0.54	0.52	0.52	1 022	1 192	1 328	1 006	895	904
Italy	0.20	0.19	0.22	0.16	0.15	0.19	3 641	3 971	4 861	3 297	2 996	4 241
Japan	0.25	0.17	0.19	0.18	0.20	0.18	11 136	7 697	9 601	9 457	11 021	10 604
Korea	0.05	0.07	0.09	0.10	0.12	0.12	455	696	802	816	1 174	1 321
Luxembourg	0.89	0.92	0.97	1.04	1.05	0.99	291	376	415	415	403	413
Netherlands	0.81	0.81	0.80	0.82	0.81	0.75	5 452	6 224	6 993	6 426	6 357	6 324
New Zealand	0.27	0.27	0.30	0.28	0.26	0.28	259	320	348	309	342	429
Norway	0.89	0.95	0.89	1.06	1.10	1.00	2 945	3 735	4 006	4 081	4 580	4 936
Portugal	0.21	0.22	0.27	0.23	0.29	0.29	396	471	620	513	649	669
Spain	0.32	0.37	0.45	0.46	0.43	0.29	3 814	5 140	6 867	6 584	5 949	4 264
Sweden	1.02	0.93	0.98	1.12	0.97	1.02	3 955	4 339	4 732	4 548	4 533	5 606
Switzerland	0.39	0.38	0.44	0.45	0.40	0.46	1 646	1 685	2 038	2 310	2 300	3 086
United Kingdom	0.51	0.36	0.43	0.51	0.57	0.56	12 459	9 849	11 500	11 283	13 053	13 739
United States	0.18	0.16	0.18	0.21	0.21	0.20	23 532	21 787	26 437	28 831	30 353	30 745

StatLink ᵃᵉˢᵇ http://dx.doi.org/10.1787/888932710232

Distribution of net ODA from all sources by income group and by region

Million US dollars

	2006	2007	2008	2009	2010
By income group					
Least Developed Countries	28 931	34 034	39 162	40 334	44 805
Other low-income countries	19 203	10 969	10 647	16 042	14 552
Lower middle-income countries	28 893	29 288	32 570	26 357	25 176
Upper middle-income countries	6 274	6 405	8 536	7 554	7 374
Unallocated	24 014	27 914	37 002	36 681	39 201
More advanced developing countries and territories	24	-116	..	..	..
By region					
Sub-Saharan Africa	40 869	34 727	39 627	42 465	43 805
South and Central Asia	11 430	14 091	15 981	18 464	18 636
Other Asia and Oceania	8 646	9 585	9 858	10 886	10 628
Middle East and North Africa	17 058	17 891	24 138	13 370	12 086
Latin America and Carribean	7 340	6 987	9 288	9 022	10 718
Europe	5 082	4 337	5 377	5 731	5 856
Unspecified	16 913	20 876	23 647	27 028	29 378
Developing countries total	107 339	108 494	127 916	126 968	131 108

StatLink ᵃᵉˢᵇ http://dx.doi.org/10.1787/888932710289

Net official development assistance

2011

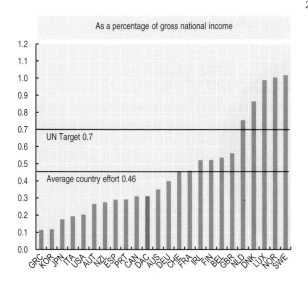

As a percentage of gross national income

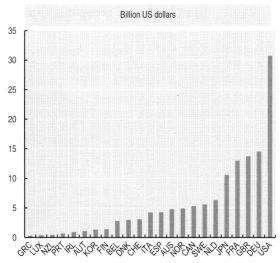

Billion US dollars

StatLink ᵃᵉˢᵇ http://dx.doi.org/10.1787/888932710251

Distribution of net ODA from all sources by region

Million US dollars

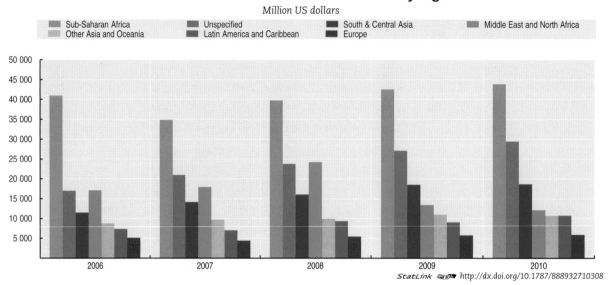

StatLink http://dx.doi.org/10.1787/888932710308

Distribution of net ODA from all sources by income group

Million US dollars

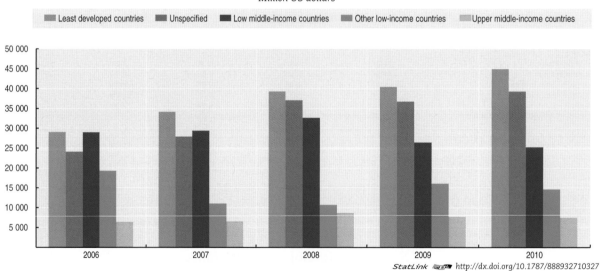

StatLink http://dx.doi.org/10.1787/888932710327

Distribution of gross bilateral ODA from DAC countries by income group

Million US dollars, 2009-10 average

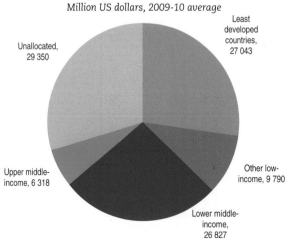

StatLink http://dx.doi.org/10.1787/888932710346

OFFICIAL DEVELOPMENT ASSISTANCE

Distribution of gross bilateral ODA from DAC countries by region

Million US dollars, 2009-10 average

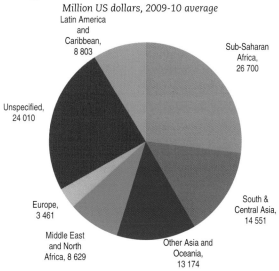

StatLink ᯔᯕᯱ http://dx.doi.org/10.1787/888932710365

Distribution of gross bilateral ODA from DAC countries by sector

As a percentage of total gross bilateral ODA, 2009-10 average

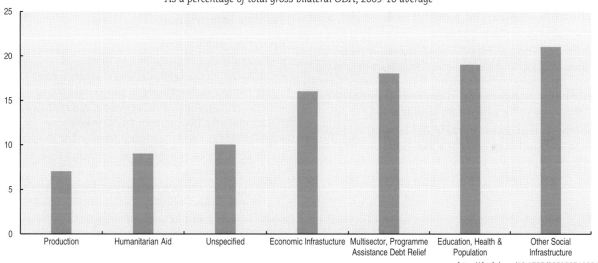

StatLink ᯔᯕᯱ http://dx.doi.org/10.1787/888932710384

Composition of aid from DAC countries

Million US dollars, 2010

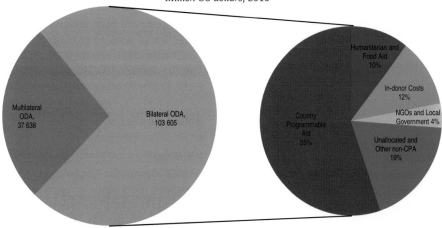

StatLink ᯔᯕᯱ http://dx.doi.org/10.1787/888932710403

TOTAL TAX REVENUE

Total tax revenue as a percentage of GDP indicates the share of a country's output that is collected by the government through taxes. It can be regarded as one measure of the degree to which the government controls the economy's resources.

Definition

Taxes are defined as compulsory, unrequited payments to general government. They are unrequited in the sense that benefits provided by government to taxpayers are not normally in proportion to their payments. The data on total tax revenue shown here refer to the revenues collected from taxes on income and profits, social security contributions, taxes levied on goods and services, payroll taxes, taxes on the ownership and transfer of property, and other taxes.

Taxes on incomes and profits cover taxes levied on the net income or profits (gross income minus allowable tax reliefs) of individuals and enterprises. They also cover taxes levied on the capital gains of individuals and enterprises, and gains from gambling.

Taxes on goods and services cover all taxes levied on the production, extraction, sale, transfer, leasing or delivery of goods, and the rendering of services, or on the use of goods or permission to use goods or to perform activities. They consist mainly of value added and sales taxes.

Note that the sum of taxes on goods and services and taxes on income and profits is less than the figure for total tax revenues.

Overview

In 2010, total tax revenues as a percentage of GDP rose in 17 OECD countries and fell in 13 compared to 2009. However in most cases, changes in the total tax to GDP ratio for countries were very small in percentage points. The slow upward trend in this ratio recorded in almost all OECD countries during the 1990s stopped in 2000. Since then, the total tax revenue as a percentage of GDP for all OECD countries has fallen by between 1 and 2 percentage points.

Revenue collected from taxes on income and profit accounted for 11.4% of GDP on average in 2009. This ratio showed an upward trend in the second half of the 1990s reaching a peak in 2000. After declining slightly in the following years, the average ratio in 2007 rose above the 2000 peak but has now fallen back again.

The OECD average for tax revenues on goods and services has declined by 0.5 percentage point since 2005 but at the same time has been remarkably stable since 1995 at a level of around 11% of GDP.

Comparability

The tax revenue data are collected in a way that makes them as internationally comparable as possible. Country representatives have agreed on the definitions of each type of tax and how they should be measured in all OECD countries, and they are then responsible for submitting data to the OECD that conform to these rules.

Sources
- OECD (2012), *Revenue Statistics*, OECD Publishing.

Further information

Analytical publications
- OECD (2012), *Consumption Tax Trends*, OECD Publishing.
- OECD (2012), *Global Forum on Transparency and Exchange of Information for Tax Purposes*, OECD Publishing.
- OECD (2012), *Tax and Development, Aid Modalities for Strengthening Tax Systems*, OECD Publishing.
- OECD (2011), *OECD Tax Policy Studies*, OECD Publishing.
- OECD (2010), *Tax Co-operation: Towards a Level Playing Field*, OECD Publishing.
- OECD (2006), *Encouraging Savings through Tax-Preferred Accounts*, OECD Tax Policy Studies, No. 15, OECD Publishing.
- OECD (2006), *Tax Administration in OECD and Selected Non-OECD Countries: Comparative Information Series (2006)*, OECD Publishing.
- OECD (2006), *The Political Economy of Environmentally Related Taxes*, OECD Publishing.

Statistical publications
- OECD (2012), *Taxing Wages*, OECD Publishing.

Methodological publications
- OECD and Council of Europe (France) (2011), *The Multilateral Convention on Mutual Administrative Assistance in Tax Matters*, OECD Publishing.
- OECD (2012), *Model Tax Convention on Income and on Capital 2010, Full Version*, OECD Publishing.

Online databases
- *OECD Tax Statistics.*

Websites
- OECD Centre for Tax Policy and Administration, *www.oecd.org/ctp*.
- Global Forum on Transparency and Exchange of Information for Tax Purposes, *www.oecd.org/tax/transparency*.

Total tax revenue
As a percentage of GDP

	1998	1999	2000	2001	2002	2003	2004	2005	2006	2007	2008	2009	2010
Australia	29.3	29.7	30.3	28.7	29.6	29.8	30.1	29.8	29.3	29.4	27.0	25.9	..
Austria	44.1	43.8	43.0	44.9	43.6	43.5	43.0	42.1	41.5	41.8	42.8	42.7	42.0
Belgium	45.1	45.0	44.7	44.7	44.8	44.3	44.5	44.6	44.2	43.6	44.1	43.2	43.8
Canada	36.7	36.4	35.6	34.8	33.7	33.7	33.6	33.4	33.3	33.0	32.2	32.0	31.0
Chile	19.3	18.6	19.4	19.7	19.7	19.3	19.8	21.6	23.2	24.0	22.5	18.4	20.9
Czech Republic	34.9	35.9	35.2	35.6	36.3	37.3	37.8	37.5	37.0	37.3	36.0	34.7	34.9
Denmark	49.3	50.1	49.4	48.5	47.9	48.0	49.0	50.8	49.6	48.9	48.1	48.1	48.2
Estonia	34.0	32.5	31.0	30.2	31.0	30.8	30.6	30.6	30.7	31.4	31.7	35.9	34.0
Finland	46.3	45.9	47.2	44.8	44.7	44.1	43.5	43.9	43.8	43.0	42.9	42.6	42.1
France	44.3	45.2	44.4	44.1	43.5	43.3	43.6	43.9	44.1	43.7	43.5	42.4	42.9
Germany	36.5	37.3	37.5	36.3	35.6	35.8	35.0	35.0	35.6	36.0	36.4	37.3	36.3
Greece	32.0	32.9	34.0	32.9	33.6	32.0	31.2	31.9	31.2	31.8	31.5	30.0	30.9
Hungary	38.1	38.9	39.3	38.4	38.0	37.9	37.7	37.3	37.3	40.3	40.1	39.9	37.6
Iceland	34.5	36.9	37.2	35.4	35.3	36.7	37.9	40.7	41.5	40.6	36.7	33.9	36.3
Ireland	31.3	31.5	31.2	29.0	27.8	28.3	29.8	30.3	31.7	31.0	29.1	27.8	28.0
Israel	36.0	36.0	36.8	36.8	36.3	35.5	35.5	35.6	36.0	36.3	33.8	31.4	32.4
Italy	41.7	42.5	42.2	41.9	41.3	41.7	41.0	40.8	42.3	43.4	43.3	43.4	43.0
Japan	26.8	26.3	27.0	27.3	26.2	25.7	26.3	27.4	28.0	28.3	28.3	26.9	..
Korea	20.3	20.7	22.6	23.0	23.2	24.0	23.3	24.0	25.0	26.5	26.5	25.5	25.1
Luxembourg	39.4	38.3	39.1	39.7	39.3	38.1	37.3	37.6	35.9	35.6	35.5	37.6	36.7
Mexico	15.1	15.8	16.9	17.1	16.5	17.4	17.1	18.1	18.2	17.7	20.9	17.4	18.1
Netherlands	39.0	40.1	39.6	38.1	37.4	36.9	37.2	38.4	39.1	38.7	39.1	38.2	..
New Zealand	32.9	32.9	33.1	32.6	33.9	33.7	34.7	36.7	36.0	34.9	33.6	31.5	31.3
Norway	42.4	42.7	42.6	42.9	43.1	42.3	43.3	43.5	43.9	43.6	42.9	42.9	42.8
Poland	35.6	35.1	32.8	32.6	33.1	32.6	31.7	33.0	34.0	34.8	34.2	31.8	..
Portugal	30.1	30.8	30.9	30.7	31.3	31.6	30.4	31.2	31.9	32.5	32.5	30.6	31.3
Slovak Republic	36.7	35.4	34.1	33.1	33.2	33.1	31.7	31.5	29.4	29.4	29.4	29.0	28.4
Slovenia	37.6	37.9	37.3	37.5	37.8	38.0	38.1	38.6	38.3	37.7	37.0	37.4	37.7
Spain	33.2	34.1	34.2	33.8	34.2	34.2	34.6	35.7	36.6	37.2	33.3	30.6	31.7
Sweden	50.7	51.1	51.4	49.4	47.5	47.8	48.1	48.9	48.3	47.4	46.4	46.7	45.8
Switzerland	28.5	28.7	30.0	29.5	29.9	29.2	28.8	29.2	29.1	28.9	29.1	29.7	29.8
Turkey	21.1	23.1	24.2	26.1	24.6	25.9	24.1	24.3	24.5	24.1	24.2	24.6	26.0
United Kingdom	35.5	35.8	36.3	36.1	34.6	34.3	34.8	35.7	36.4	36.0	35.7	34.3	35.0
United States	29.1	29.1	29.5	28.4	26.0	25.5	25.7	27.1	27.9	27.9	26.3	24.1	24.8
EU 27	..	..	..	..	..	..	..	..	..	..	..	..	..
OECD	34.9	35.2	35.3	34.8	34.5	34.5	34.4	35.0	35.1	35.2	34.6	33.8	
Brazil	27.3	28.6	30.0	30.9	31.5	31.1	31.9	32.9	32.8	33.4	33.6	32.6	..
China	..	..	..	..	..	..	..	..	..	..	..	..	..
India	..	..	..	..	..	..	..	..	..	..	..	..	..
Indonesia	..	..	..	..	..	..	..	..	..	..	..	..	..
Russian Federation	..	..	..	..	..	..	..	..	..	..	..	..	..
South Africa	..	..	..	..	..	..	..	..	..	..	..	..	..

StatLink http://dx.doi.org/10.1787/888932710422

Total tax revenue
As a percentage of GDP

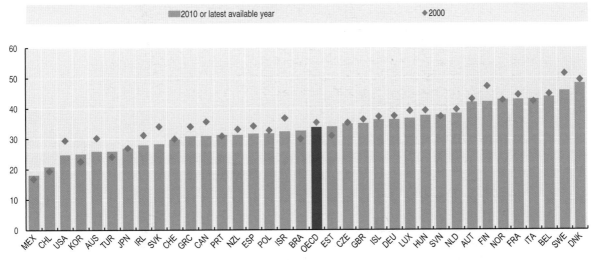

StatLink http://dx.doi.org/10.1787/888932710441

Taxes on income and profits
As a percentage of GDP

	1998	1999	2000	2001	2002	2003	2004	2005	2006	2007	2008	2009	2010
Australia	17.3	17.8	17.6	16.2	16.7	16.8	17.6	17.6	17.3	17.6	16.0	14.6	..
Austria	12.8	12.4	12.2	14.0	12.9	12.7	12.5	11.9	12.0	12.5	13.2	11.9	11.9
Belgium	17.5	17.1	17.2	17.5	17.3	16.8	16.9	16.3	15.9	15.7	16.0	14.6	15.0
Canada	17.7	18.1	17.8	16.7	15.4	15.4	15.7	15.8	16.2	16.2	15.9	15.2	14.5
Chile	4.2	3.7	4.5	4.6	4.8	4.9	5.9	7.8	10.5	11.0	8.4	5.7	8.0
Czech Republic	8.1	8.3	8.0	8.6	9.0	9.5	9.5	9.1	9.1	9.4	7.9	7.2	7.0
Denmark	29.4	29.6	29.8	28.8	28.6	28.8	29.7	31.2	29.9	29.3	29.1	29.4	29.6
Estonia	10.3	9.7	7.7	7.2	7.5	8.0	7.9	7.0	7.1	7.4	7.8	7.6	6.8
Finland	18.2	17.8	20.4	18.3	18.1	17.1	16.8	16.8	16.7	16.9	16.7	15.3	15.0
France	10.2	10.8	11.1	11.2	10.4	10.1	10.2	10.4	10.8	10.4	10.5	8.8	9.4
Germany	10.7	11.1	11.3	10.5	10.0	9.8	9.6	9.9	10.8	11.2	11.5	10.8	10.4
Greece	8.1	8.4	9.3	8.0	8.1	7.4	7.5	8.1	7.6	7.6	7.5	7.6	6.9
Hungary	8.5	9.1	9.5	9.8	10.0	9.4	8.9	8.8	9.2	10.2	10.4	9.8	8.0
Iceland	13.0	14.2	14.8	15.3	15.3	16.0	16.1	17.6	18.3	18.4	17.8	16.0	16.1
Ireland	12.9	13.2	13.2	12.2	11.1	11.3	11.8	11.7	12.5	12.2	10.9	10.1	10.1
Israel	12.9	12.7	14.6	14.5	12.8	12.0	11.7	12.1	13.3	13.2	11.1	9.4	9.4
Italy	13.6	14.4	14.0	14.3	13.4	12.9	12.9	12.9	13.9	14.6	14.9	14.2	14.1
Japan	9.0	8.4	9.4	9.1	8.0	7.9	8.4	9.3	9.9	10.3	9.5	8.0	8.0
Korea	6.2	5.1	6.5	6.1	5.9	6.7	6.5	7.0	7.4	8.4	8.2	7.3	7.1
Luxembourg	15.1	13.9	14.1	14.4	14.4	13.9	12.4	12.9	12.5	12.4	12.8	13.4	13.1
Mexico	4.3	4.6	4.6	4.8	4.8	4.6	4.2	4.4	4.6	4.9	5.2	5.0	5.2
Netherlands	10.3	10.2	10.0	10.1	10.2	9.4	9.2	10.7	10.6	10.9	10.6	10.8	..
New Zealand	19.1	19.1	19.9	19.3	20.2	20.1	21.2	23.1	22.4	22.0	20.3	17.9	16.8
Norway	15.7	16.0	19.2	19.3	18.8	18.5	20.1	21.4	22.0	20.9	21.7	19.7	19.8
Poland	10.3	7.4	6.8	6.4	6.3	6.0	5.9	6.4	7.0	8.0	8.1	6.9	..
Portugal	8.3	8.7	9.2	8.8	8.6	8.1	8.0	7.9	8.3	9.1	9.3	8.6	8.5
Slovak Republic	8.6	8.6	7.0	7.0	6.6	6.7	5.7	5.6	5.7	5.8	6.2	5.2	5.1
Slovenia	6.8	6.9	6.9	7.1	7.4	7.6	7.8	8.3	8.7	8.8	8.4	7.7	7.6
Spain	9.4	9.6	9.7	9.5	10.0	9.6	9.8	10.5	11.2	12.4	10.3	9.2	9.0
Sweden	19.8	20.6	21.0	18.7	17.0	17.6	18.3	19.1	19.1	18.4	16.8	16.5	16.3
Switzerland	12.5	12.0	13.2	12.4	12.9	12.5	12.5	13.0	13.2	13.3	13.8	14.0	14.2
Turkey	7.0	7.3	7.1	7.5	6.1	6.1	5.3	5.3	5.3	5.7	5.8	5.9	5.6
United Kingdom	13.8	13.8	14.2	14.3	13.2	12.6	12.8	13.7	14.5	14.2	14.3	13.2	13.1
United States	14.3	14.4	14.9	13.8	11.5	11.0	11.2	12.7	13.5	13.6	12.0	9.8	10.7
EU 27	..	..	..	..	..	..	..	..	..	..	..	..	..
OECD	12.2	12.2	12.6	12.2	11.9	11.7	11.8	12.2	12.5	12.7	12.3	11.4	..
Brazil	5.5	5.8	5.8	6.1	6.4	6.3	6.2	7.0	6.9	7.3	7.8	7.4	..
China	..	..	..	..	..	..	..	..	..	..	..	..	..
India	..	..	..	..	..	..	..	..	..	..	..	..	..
Indonesia	..	..	..	..	..	..	..	..	..	..	..	..	..
Russian Federation	..	..	..	..	..	..	..	..	..	..	..	..	..
South Africa	..	..	..	..	..	..	..	..	..	..	..	..	..

StatLink http://dx.doi.org/10.1787/888932710460

Taxes on income and profits
As a percentage of GDP

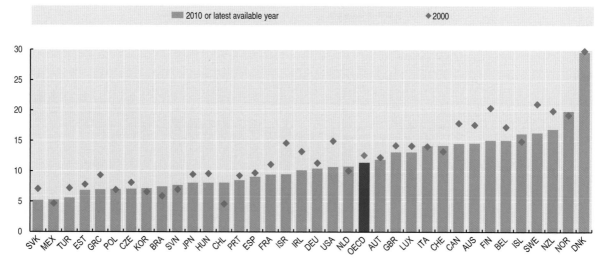

2010 or latest available year ♦ 2000

StatLink http://dx.doi.org/10.1787/888932710479

Taxes on goods and services

As a percentage of GDP

	1998	1999	2000	2001	2002	2003	2004	2005	2006	2007	2008	2009	2010
Australia	8.0	7.8	8.7	8.7	9.0	8.8	8.6	8.3	8.0	7.8	7.4	7.6	..
Austria	12.4	12.6	12.3	12.3	12.5	12.4	12.3	12.1	11.6	11.5	11.6	12.0	11.8
Belgium	11.1	11.5	11.4	10.9	11.0	10.9	11.2	11.3	11.3	11.0	10.8	10.9	11.1
Canada	9.1	8.8	8.6	8.8	8.9	8.9	8.7	8.5	8.1	7.9	7.6	7.6	7.5
Chile	12.5	12.1	12.4	12.2	12.2	11.7	11.2	11.1	10.0	10.5	11.4	10.3	10.7
Czech Republic	10.8	11.5	11.1	10.8	10.8	11.1	11.8	11.8	11.2	11.1	11.5	11.6	11.6
Denmark	16.4	16.5	15.9	15.9	16.0	15.8	16.0	16.3	16.4	16.3	15.6	15.4	15.3
Estonia	12.1	11.4	11.9	12.0	12.2	11.8	11.8	12.9	13.1	13.1	11.8	14.7	13.5
Finland	14.2	14.2	13.7	13.3	13.5	14.1	13.8	13.8	13.6	12.9	12.9	13.4	13.3
France	11.9	12.0	11.5	11.1	11.2	11.1	11.2	11.2	11.1	10.9	10.7	10.6	10.7
Germany	10.0	10.4	10.5	10.4	10.4	10.5	10.2	10.1	10.1	10.5	10.6	11.1	10.7
Greece	12.0	12.2	12.0	12.5	12.3	11.4	11.1	11.1	11.4	11.6	11.4	10.8	11.5
Hungary	14.8	15.7	15.9	14.9	14.3	14.9	15.4	14.8	14.3	15.2	14.9	15.9	16.1
Iceland	15.9	17.0	16.4	14.3	14.4	15.1	16.0	17.1	17.6	16.4	13.6	12.0	12.9
Ireland	12.3	12.2	11.7	10.5	10.8	10.6	11.2	11.4	11.4	11.2	10.8	10.1	10.3
Israel	12.8	13.0	12.3	12.2	13.0	12.9	13.0	12.8	12.4	12.7	12.6	12.3	12.9
Italy	11.5	11.7	11.8	11.2	11.2	10.7	10.8	10.8	11.1	11.0	10.6	10.6	11.1
Japan	5.3	5.4	5.2	5.3	5.3	5.2	5.3	5.3	5.2	5.1	5.1	5.1	5.1
Korea	7.7	8.3	8.7	9.1	9.0	8.9	8.4	8.2	8.1	8.3	8.4	8.2	8.5
Luxembourg	10.5	10.4	10.6	10.5	10.6	10.5	11.2	10.9	10.1	9.8	9.9	10.4	10.0
Mexico	7.5	7.9	8.9	8.8	8.1	9.1	9.5	10.2	10.3	9.4	12.3	8.7	9.8
Netherlands	11.3	11.7	11.5	11.8	11.6	11.7	11.9	12.2	12.1	12.0	11.9	11.8	..
New Zealand	11.9	11.9	11.5	11.6	11.9	11.9	11.8	11.8	11.8	11.1	11.3	11.5	12.3
Norway	15.8	15.6	13.5	13.3	13.3	12.9	12.7	12.1	12.0	12.4	11.1	11.9	12.0
Poland	12.3	12.8	11.8	11.4	12.1	12.2	11.9	12.7	13.3	13.0	13.0	11.7	..
Portugal	12.7	12.7	12.2	12.3	12.7	12.8	12.8	13.4	13.7	13.2	13.0	11.6	12.4
Slovak Republic	12.7	12.2	12.3	11.2	11.4	12.0	12.3	12.6	11.4	11.3	10.6	10.6	10.3
Slovenia	14.4	14.9	14.0	13.6	13.9	14.0	13.7	13.6	13.3	13.2	13.2	13.9	14.1
Spain	9.8	10.2	10.1	9.7	9.6	9.7	9.8	9.9	9.9	9.5	8.3	7.1	8.5
Sweden	12.7	12.5	12.7	12.6	12.7	12.7	12.6	12.8	12.6	12.6	12.9	13.5	13.5
Switzerland	6.2	6.6	6.7	6.8	6.8	6.8	6.8	6.9	6.8	6.6	6.4	6.4	6.5
Turkey	7.6	8.3	10.1	10.5	11.5	12.8	11.5	12.0	11.9	11.5	11.0	11.2	12.4
United Kingdom	11.7	11.8	11.6	11.3	11.2	11.2	11.1	10.8	10.6	10.5	10.3	9.9	10.8
United States	4.8	4.8	4.7	4.6	4.6	4.7	4.7	4.8	4.8	4.7	4.6	4.5	4.5
EU 27	..	..	..	..	..	..	..	..	..	..	..	..	..
OECD	11.3	11.4	11.3	11.1	11.2	11.2	11.2	11.3	11.2	11.1	10.9	10.7	..
Brazil	12.8	14.2	15.3	15.8	15.9	15.6	16.2	16.2	15.9	15.9	15.5	14.4	..
China	..	..	..	..	..	..	..	..	..	..	..	..	..
India	..	..	..	..	..	..	..	..	..	..	..	..	..
Indonesia	..	..	..	..	..	..	..	..	..	..	..	..	..
Russian Federation	..	..	..	..	..	..	..	..	..	..	..	..	..
South Africa	..	..	..	..	..	..	..	..	..	..	..	..	..

StatLink http://dx.doi.org/10.1787/888932710498

Taxes on goods and services

As a percentage of GDP

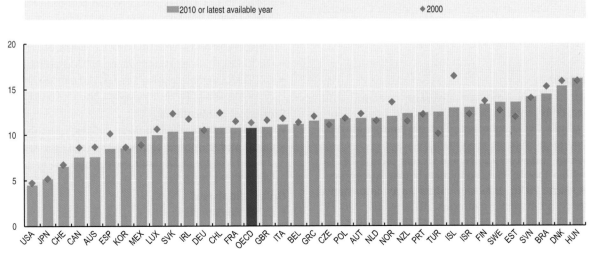

2010 or latest available year ◆ 2000

StatLink http://dx.doi.org/10.1787/888932710517

TAXES ON THE AVERAGE WORKER

Taxes on the average worker measures the ratio between the amount of taxes paid by an average single worker without children and the corresponding total labour cost for the employer. This tax wedge measures the extent to which the tax system on labour income discourages employment.

Definition

The taxes included in the measure are personal income taxes, employees' social security contributions and employers' social security contributions. For the few countries that have them, it also includes payroll taxes. The amount of these taxes paid in relation to the employment of one average worker is expressed as a percentage of their labour cost (gross wage plus employers' social security contributions and payroll tax).

An average worker is defined as somebody who earns the average income of full-time workers of the country concerned in Sectors B-N of the *International Standard Industrial Classification* (ISIC Rev. 4). The average worker is considered single, meaning that he or she does not receive any tax relief in respect of a spouse, unmarried partner or child.

Comparability

The types of taxes included in the measure are fully comparable across countries. They are based on common definitions agreed by all OECD countries.

While the income levels of workers in Sectors B-N differ across countries, they can be regarded as corresponding to comparable types of work in each country.

The information on the average worker's income level is supplied by the Ministries of Finance in all OECD countries and is based on national statistical surveys. The amount of

taxes paid by the single worker is calculated by applying the tax laws in each country. These tax wedge measures are therefore derived from a modelling exercise rather than from the direct observation of taxes actually paid by workers and their employers.

Taxes on the average worker
As a percentage of labour cost

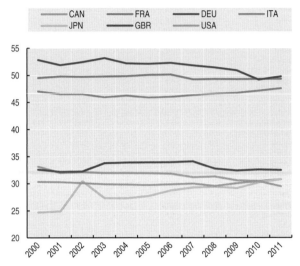

StatLink http://dx.doi.org/10.1787/888932710574

Sources
• OECD (2012), *Taxing Wages*, OECD Publishing.

Further information

Analytical publications
• Immervoll, H. (2004), "Average and Marginal Effective Tax Rates Facing Workers in the EU: A Micro-Level Analysis of Levels, Distributions and Driving Factors", *OECD Social Employment and Migration Working Papers*, No. 19.
• OECD (2007), *Benefits and Wages*, OECD Publishing.
• OECD (2006), *Encouraging Savings through Tax-Preferred Accounts*, *OECD Tax Policy Studies*, No. 15, OECD Publishing.

Statistical publications
• OECD (2012), *Revenue Statistics*, OECD Publishing.
• OECD and Economic Commission for Latin America and the Caribbean (2012), *Latin American Economic Outlook*, OECD Publishing.

Online databases
• *OECD Tax Statistics.*

Websites
• OECD Benefits and Wages: OECD Indicators, *www.oecd.org/els/social/workincentives.*
• OECD Centre for Tax Policy and Administration, *www.oecd.org/ctp.*
• OECD Tax Policy Analysis, *www.oecd.org/ctp/tpa.*

Overview

In 2011, taxes on an average worker, on average, represented around 35% of their total labour costs across OECD countries. This tax wedge ranged between 7% in Chile to 55% in Belgium.

On average, taxes on an average worker for the OECD as a whole have decreased by nearly two percentage points since 2000. However, there are important differences between countries. Of the 34 OECD member countries, 9 countries experienced an overall increase in the taxes on an average worker since 2000. The countries with the largest increases were Iceland and Japan. Of the 24 countries that have experienced an overall decline, the largest decreases were for Denmark, Finland, Hungary, Israel and Sweden.

Taxes on the average worker

As a percentage of labour cost

	2000	2001	2002	2003	2004	2005	2006	2007	2008	2009	2010	2011
Australia	31.0	27.6	28.0	28.2	28.2	28.5	28.3	27.7	26.9	26.7	26.8	26.7
Austria	47.3	46.9	47.1	47.4	48.3	48.1	48.5	48.8	49.0	47.9	48.2	48.4
Belgium	57.1	56.7	56.3	55.7	55.4	55.5	55.5	55.6	55.9	55.3	55.4	55.5
Canada	33.2	32.0	32.1	32.0	32.0	31.9	31.9	31.2	31.3	30.6	30.5	30.8
Chile	7.0	7.0	7.0	7.0	7.0	7.0	7.0	7.0	7.0	7.0	7.0	7.0
Czech Republic	42.6	42.6	43.0	43.2	43.5	43.7	42.5	42.9	43.4	42.0	42.1	42.5
Denmark	44.1	43.3	42.4	42.4	41.0	40.9	41.0	41.1	40.9	39.5	38.3	38.4
Estonia	41.3	41.0	42.1	42.3	41.5	39.9	39.0	39.0	38.4	39.2	40.1	40.1
Finland	47.8	46.4	45.9	45.0	44.5	44.6	44.0	43.9	43.8	42.5	42.5	42.7
France	49.6	49.8	49.8	49.8	49.9	50.1	50.2	49.3	49.3	49.3	49.3	49.4
Germany	52.9	51.9	52.5	53.2	52.2	52.1	52.3	51.9	51.5	50.9	49.2	49.8
Greece	35.2	34.7	35.1	35.2	35.8	35.2	35.8	37.0	37.0	38.2	38.2	..
Hungary	54.6	55.8	53.7	50.8	51.8	51.1	52.0	54.5	54.1	53.1	46.6	49.4
Iceland	28.8	29.3	30.9	31.5	31.9	32.1	31.8	30.5	30.9	30.5	33.4	34.0
Ireland	28.9	25.9	24.4	24.4	24.1	23.5	23.0	22.2	22.3	24.7	25.8	26.8
Israel	29.0	29.5	30.0	27.1	25.3	24.9	23.5	24.1	21.7	20.2	19.4	19.8
Italy	47.1	46.6	46.6	46.0	46.3	45.9	46.1	46.4	46.6	46.8	47.2	47.6
Japan	24.7	24.9	26.5	27.4	27.3	27.7	28.8	29.3	29.5	29.2	30.2	30.8
Korea	16.3	16.4	16.1	16.3	17.0	17.3	18.1	19.7	19.9	19.5	20.1	20.3
Luxembourg	37.1	35.7	32.9	33.5	33.9	34.7	35.3	36.3	34.7	33.9	34.3	36.0
Mexico	12.4	13.1	15.8	16.7	15.2	14.7	15.0	15.9	15.1	15.3	15.5	16.2
Netherlands	40.0	37.4	37.4	37.2	38.8	38.9	38.4	38.8	39.2	38.0	38.1	37.8
New Zealand	19.4	19.4	19.4	19.5	19.7	20.0	20.4	21.1	20.5	18.1	17.0	15.9
Norway	38.6	39.2	38.6	38.1	38.1	37.2	37.4	37.5	37.5	37.2	37.2	37.5
Poland	38.2	38.0	38.0	38.2	38.4	38.7	39.0	38.2	34.7	34.1	34.2	34.3
Portugal	37.3	36.4	37.6	37.4	37.4	36.8	37.1	37.7	37.6	37.5	37.6	39.0
Slovak Republic	41.9	42.5	42.1	42.5	42.2	38.0	38.3	38.4	38.8	37.7	37.9	38.9
Slovenia	46.3	46.2	46.1	46.2	46.3	45.6	45.3	43.3	42.9	42.2	42.5	42.6
Spain	38.6	38.9	39.1	38.6	38.8	39.0	39.1	39.0	38.0	38.3	39.7	39.9
Sweden	50.1	49.1	47.8	48.2	48.4	48.1	47.8	45.3	44.8	43.2	42.8	42.8
Switzerland	21.6	21.6	21.7	21.2	20.9	20.9	20.9	21.1	20.6	20.7	20.7	21.0
Turkey	40.4	43.6	42.5	42.2	42.8	42.8	42.7	42.7	39.9	37.4	37.9	37.7
United Kingdom	32.6	32.2	32.3	33.8	33.9	33.9	34.0	34.1	32.8	32.4	32.6	32.5
United States	30.4	30.3	30.1	29.9	29.8	29.8	29.9	30.0	29.6	30.1	30.4	29.5
EU 27	..	..	..	..	..	..	..	..	..	..	..	..
OECD	36.6	36.2	36.3	36.1	36.1	35.9	35.9	35.9	35.5	35.0	35.0	35.2
Brazil	..	..	..	..	..	..	..	..	..	..	..	..
China	..	..	..	..	..	..	..	..	..	..	..	..
India	..	..	..	..	..	..	..	..	..	..	..	..
Indonesia	..	..	..	..	..	..	..	..	..	..	..	..
Russian Federation	..	..	..	..	..	..	..	..	..	..	..	..
South Africa	..	..	..	..	..	..	..	..	..	..	..	..

StatLink ᴍᴤᴸ http://dx.doi.org/10.1787/888932710536

Trends in taxes on the average worker

As a percentage of labour cost

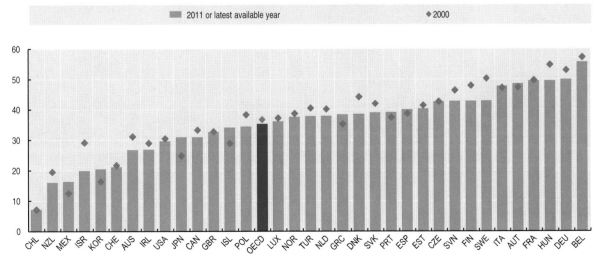

StatLink ᴍᴤᴸ http://dx.doi.org/10.1787/888932710555

HEALTH

LIFE EXPECTANCY

Life expectancy at birth is one of the most frequently used health status indicators. Gains in life expectancy at birth in OECD countries in recent decades can be attributed to a number of factors, including rising living standards, improved lifestyle and better education, as well as greater access to quality health services. Other factors, such as better nutrition, sanitation and housing also played a role, particularly in emerging economies.

Overview

On average across OECD countries, life expectancy at birth for the whole population reached 79.7 years in 2010, a gain of almost 10 years since 1970. Japan leads a large group (including almost two-thirds of OECD countries) in which the total life expectancy at birth is currently 80 years or more. A second group, including Portugal, the United States and a number of central European countries have a life expectancy of between 75 and 80 years. Life expectancy among OECD countries was lowest in Turkey and Hungary, followed by the Slovak Republic. However, while life expectancy in Hungary has increased only modestly since 1970, it has increased sharply in Turkey, so that it is quickly approaching the OECD average.

Nearly all OECD and emerging countries have experienced large gains in life expectancy over the past 40 years. Life expectancy at birth in Turkey, Korea and Mexico has increased by twenty years or more over the period 1970-2010. Among emerging countries, Indonesia, India and Brazil also show strong gains. Other countries such as the Russian Federation and South Africa are still characterised by high mortality rates and by a length of life well below the OECD average.

The gender gap in life expectancy stood at 5.6 years on average across OECD countries in 2010, with life expectancy reaching 76.9 years among men and 82.4 years among women. While the gender gap in life expectancy increased substantially in many countries during the 1960s and the 1970s, it narrowed during the past 30 years, reflecting higher gains in life expectancy among men than among women in most OECD countries. This can be attributed at least partly to the narrowing of differences in risk-increasing behaviours between men and women, such as smoking, accompanied by sharp reductions in mortality rates from cardiovascular diseases among men.

Higher national income (as measured by GDP per capita) is generally associated with higher life expectancy at birth, although the relationship is less pronounced at higher levels of national income.

Definition

Life expectancy at birth measures how long on average a newborn can expect to live, if current death rates do not change. However, the actual age-specific death rate of any particular birth cohort cannot be known in advance. If rates are falling (as has been the case over the past decades in OECD countries), actual life spans will be higher than life expectancy calculated using current death rates.

Comparability

The methodology used to calculate life expectancy can vary slightly between countries. These differences can affect the comparability of reported life expectancy estimates, as different methods can change a country's estimates by a fraction of a year. Life expectancy at birth for the total population is calculated by the OECD Secretariat for all countries, using the unweighted average of life expectancy of men and women.

Sources
- OECD (2012), *OECD Health Statistics*, OECD Publishing.

Further information

Analytical publications
- OECD (2010), *Health Care Systems: Efficiency and Policy Settings*, OECD Publishing.

Statistical publications
- OECD (2012), *Health at a Glance: Asia/Pacific 2012*, OECD Publishing.
- OECD (2012), *Health at a Glance: Europe 2012*, OECD Publishing.
- OECD (2011), *Health at a Glance: OECD Indicators*, OECD Publishing.

Online databases
- *OECD Health Statistics*.

Websites
- OECD Health Data, *www.oecd.org/health/healthdata*.
- OECD Health at a Glance (supplementary material), *www.oecd.org/health/healthataglance*.

Life expectancy at birth
Number of years

	Women				Men				Total			
	1970 or first available year	1990	2000	2010 or latest available year	1970 or first available year	1990	2000	2010 or latest available year	1970 or first available year	1990	2000	2010 or latest available year
Australia	74.2	80.1	82.0	84.0	67.4	73.9	76.6	79.5	70.8	77.0	79.3	81.8
Austria	73.5	79.0	81.2	83.5	66.5	72.3	75.2	77.9	70.0	75.6	78.2	80.7
Belgium	74.3	79.5	81.0	83.0	67.8	72.7	74.6	77.6	71.0	76.1	77.8	80.3
Canada	76.4	80.8	81.7	..	69.3	74.4	76.3	..	72.8	77.6	79.0	..
Chile	..	76.5	80.0	82.0	..	69.4	73.7	75.9	..	72.9	76.8	79.0
Czech Republic	73.1	75.5	78.5	80.9	66.1	67.6	71.7	74.5	69.6	71.5	75.1	77.7
Denmark	75.9	77.8	79.2	81.4	70.7	72.0	74.5	77.2	73.3	74.9	76.8	79.3
Estonia	74.0	74.7	76.0	80.5	65.4	64.5	65.1	70.6	69.7	69.6	70.6	75.6
Finland	75.0	79.0	81.2	83.5	66.5	71.0	74.2	76.9	70.8	75.0	77.7	80.2
France	75.9	80.9	82.8	84.7	68.4	72.8	75.3	78.0	72.2	76.8	79.0	81.3
Germany	73.6	78.5	81.2	83.0	67.5	72.0	75.1	78.0	70.5	75.3	78.2	80.5
Greece	76.0	79.5	80.6	82.8	71.6	74.7	75.5	78.4	73.8	77.1	78.0	80.6
Hungary	72.1	73.7	75.9	78.1	66.3	65.1	67.4	70.5	69.2	69.4	71.7	74.3
Iceland	77.3	80.5	81.8	83.5	71.2	75.4	78.4	79.5	74.3	78.0	80.1	81.5
Ireland	73.5	77.7	79.2	83.2	68.8	72.1	74.0	78.7	71.2	74.9	76.6	81.0
Israel	73.4	78.4	80.9	83.6	70.1	74.9	76.7	79.7	71.8	76.7	78.8	81.7
Italy	74.9	80.3	82.8	..	69.0	73.8	76.9	..	72.0	77.1	79.8	..
Japan	74.7	81.9	84.6	86.4	69.3	75.9	77.7	79.6	72.0	78.9	81.2	83.0
Korea	65.6	75.5	79.6	84.1	58.7	67.3	72.3	77.2	62.1	71.4	76.0	80.7
Luxembourg	73.0	78.7	81.3	83.5	66.2	72.4	74.6	77.9	69.7	75.5	78.0	80.7
Mexico	63.2	73.5	76.5	77.8	58.5	67.7	71.3	73.1	60.9	70.6	73.9	75.5
Netherlands	76.5	80.1	80.5	82.7	70.8	73.8	75.5	78.8	73.7	77.0	78.0	80.8
New Zealand	74.5	78.4	80.8	82.8	68.4	72.5	75.9	79.1	71.5	75.5	78.3	81.0
Norway	77.5	79.9	81.5	83.3	71.2	73.5	76.0	79.0	74.3	76.7	78.8	81.2
Poland	73.3	75.2	78.0	80.6	66.6	66.2	69.7	72.1	70.0	70.7	73.8	76.3
Portugal	69.7	77.5	80.2	82.8	63.6	70.6	73.2	76.7	66.7	74.1	76.7	79.8
Slovak Republic	72.9	75.4	77.4	78.8	66.7	66.6	69.1	71.6	69.8	71.0	73.3	75.2
Slovenia	..	77.2	79.1	82.7	..	69.4	71.9	76.3	..	73.3	75.5	79.5
Spain	74.8	80.6	82.9	85.3	69.2	73.4	75.8	79.1	72.0	77.0	79.4	82.2
Sweden	77.1	80.4	82.0	83.5	72.2	74.8	77.4	79.5	74.7	77.6	79.7	81.5
Switzerland	76.2	80.9	82.8	84.9	70.0	74.0	77.0	80.3	73.1	77.5	79.9	82.6
Turkey	56.3	69.5	73.1	76.8	52.0	65.4	69.0	71.8	54.1	67.5	71.0	74.3
United Kingdom	75.0	78.5	80.3	82.6	68.7	72.9	75.5	78.6	71.8	75.7	77.9	80.6
United States	74.7	78.8	79.3	81.1	67.1	71.8	74.1	76.2	70.9	75.3	76.7	78.7
EU 27	74.0	77.7	79.6	81.8	67.9	70.5	73.0	75.5	71.0	74.1	76.3	78.7
OECD	73.4	78.1	80.2	82.4	67.2	71.4	74.0	76.9	70.3	74.7	77.1	79.7
Brazil	60.7	70.2	74.1	76.7	56.5	62.7	66.4	69.7	58.6	66.5	70.3	73.2
China	63.6	71.1	72.9	75.0	62.2	67.9	69.6	71.6	62.9	69.5	71.3	73.3
India	48.5	58.7	62.6	66.7	49.8	58.1	60.6	63.6	49.1	58.4	61.6	65.2
Indonesia	53.5	63.8	67.3	70.6	50.3	60.5	64.1	67.3	51.9	62.1	65.7	69.0
Russian Federation	73.5	74.3	72.3	74.9	63.0	63.8	59.1	63.0	68.3	69.0	65.7	69.0
South Africa	55.6	65.3	57.3	52.8	50.3	57.9	52.3	51.4	53.0	61.6	54.8	52.1

StatLink http://dx.doi.org/10.1787/888932710593

Life expectancy at birth
Number of years

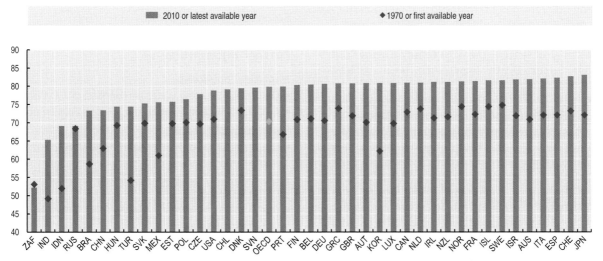

StatLink http://dx.doi.org/10.1787/888932710612

INFANT MORTALITY

Infant mortality reflects the effect of economic and social conditions of mothers and newborns, the social environment, individual lifestyles as well as the characteristics of health systems. Some countries have low levels of infant mortality and also low levels of health expenditure, suggesting that higher spending is not necessarily a precondition to improve outcomes in this area.

Overview

In most OECD countries, infant mortality is low and there is little difference in rates. A small group of OECD and emerging countries, however, have infant mortality rates above 10 deaths per 1 000 live births. In 2010, rates among OECD countries ranged from less than three deaths per 1 000 live births in Nordic countries (Iceland, Finland, Sweden, Norway), Japan, Portugal, Slovenia and the Czech Republic, up to a high of 10 and 14 in Turkey and Mexico respectively. Infant mortality rates were also relatively high (six or more deaths per 1 000 live births) in Chile and in the United States, although the rates in the United States (and Canada) may be higher than in other countries due to a more complete registration of very premature or low birth weight babies. The average across all OECD countries was 4.3 in 2010.

Around two-thirds of the deaths that occur during the first year of life are neonatal deaths (i.e. during the first four weeks). With an increasing number of women deferring childbearing and a rise in multiple births linked with fertility treatments, the number of pre-term births has tended to increase. In a number of higher-income countries, this has contributed to a levelling-off of the downward trend in infant mortality rates over the past few years. For deaths beyond a month (post neonatal mortality), there tends to be a greater range of causes – the most common being SIDS (Sudden Infant Death Syndrome), birth defects, infections and accidents.

All OECD countries have achieved remarkable progress in reducing infant mortality rates from the levels of 1970, when the average was approaching 30 deaths per 1 000 live births, to the current average of 4.3. This equates to a cumulative reduction of 85% since 1970. Portugal has seen its infant mortality rate reduced by over 7% per year on average since 1970, moving from the country with the highest rate in Europe to an infant mortality rate among the lowest in the OECD in 2010. Large reductions in infant mortality rates have also been observed in Korea and Turkey. On the other hand, the reduction in infant mortality rates has been slower in the Netherlands and the United States.

Definition

The infant mortality rate is the number of deaths of children under one year of age in a year, expressed per 1 000 live births. Neonatal mortality refers to the death of children during the first four weeks of life. Post neonatal mortality refers to deaths occurring between the second and the twelfth months of life.

Comparability

Some of the international variation in infant and neonatal mortality rates may be due to variations among countries in registering practices for premature infants. The United States and Canada, for example, are two countries which register a much higher proportion of babies weighing less than 500g. Most countries in principle have no gestational age or weight limits for mortality registration. Limits exist for Norway (where the gestational age required to be counted as a death following a live birth must exceed 12 weeks, a very low threshold) and in the Czech Republic, the Netherlands and Poland (which apply a minimum gestational age of 22 weeks and/or a weight threshold of 500g).

Sources
• OECD (2012), *OECD Health Statistics*, OECD Publishing.

Further information

Analytical publications
• OECD (2011), *Doing Better for Families*, OECD Publishing.
• OECD (2009), *Doing Better for Children*, OECD Publishing.

Statistical publications
• OECD (2012), *Health at a Glance: Asia/Pacific 2012*, OECD Publishing.
• OECD (2012), *Health at a Glance: Europe 2012*, OECD Publishing.
• OECD (2011), *Health at a Glance: OECD Indicators*, OECD Publishing.

Online databases
• *OECD Health Statistics*.

Websites
• OECD Health Data, *www.oecd.org/health/healthdata*.

Infant mortality rates

2010 and average annual rate of decline 1970-2010

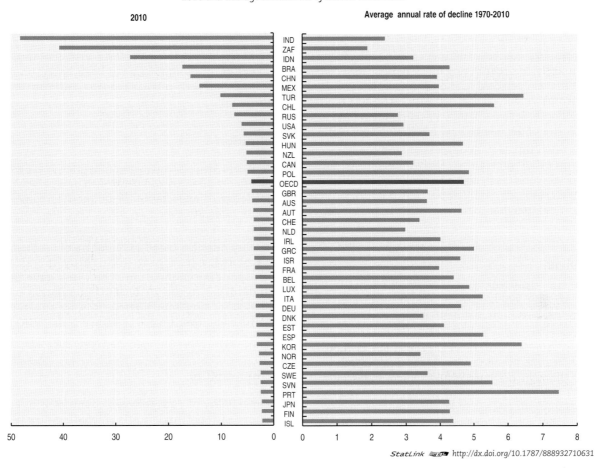

2010

Average annual rate of decline 1970-2010

StatLink http://dx.doi.org/10.1787/888932710631

Infant mortality in selected OECD countries

Deaths per 1 000 live births

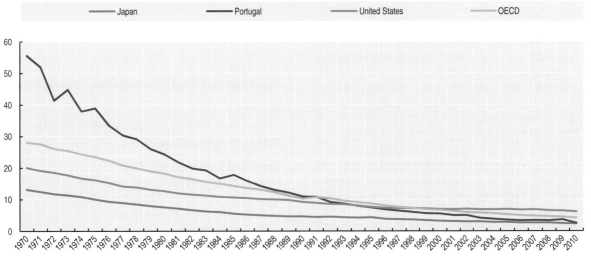

StatLink http://dx.doi.org/10.1787/888932710650

SUICIDES

The intentional killing of oneself can be evidence not only of personal breakdown, but also of a deterioration of the social context in which an individual lives. Suicide may be the end-point of a number of different contributing factors. It is more likely to occur during crisis periods associated with upheavals in personal relationships, alcohol and drug abuse, unemployment, clinical depression and other forms of mental illness. Because of this, suicide is often used as a proxy indicator of the mental health status of a population.

Suicide is often linked with depression and the abuse of alcohol and other substances. Early detection of these psycho-social problems in high-risk groups by families and health professionals is an important part of suicide prevention campaigns, together with the provision of effective support and treatment. Many countries are promoting mental health and developing national strategies for prevention, focussing on at-risk groups. In Germany, as well as Finland and Iceland, suicide prevention programmes have been based on efforts to promote strong multisectoral collaboration and networking.

Definition

The World Health Organisation defines suicide as an act deliberately initiated and performed by a person in the full knowledge or expectation of its fatal outcome. Data on suicide rates are based on official registers of causes of death.

Mortality rates are based on numbers of deaths registered in a country in a year divided by the size of the corresponding population. The rates have been age-standardised to the 2010 OECD population to remove variations arising from differences in age structures across countries and over time. The source is the WHO Mortality Database.

Comparability

Comparability of data between countries is affected by a number of reporting criteria, including how a person's intention of killing themselves is ascertained, who is responsible for completing the death certificate, whether a forensic investigation is carried out, and the provisions for confidentiality of the cause of death. The number of suicides in certain countries may be under-estimated because of the stigma that is associated with the act, or because of data issues associated with reporting criteria. Caution is required therefore in interpreting variations across countries.

Overview

Suicide is a significant cause of death in many OECD countries, with almost 150 000 such deaths in 2010. Rates were lowest in southern European countries (Greece, Italy and Spain) and in Mexico and Israel, at six or less deaths per 100 000 population. Suicides rates were highest in Korea, Hungary, the Russian Federation and Japan, at more than 20 deaths per 100 000 population.

In general, death rates from suicide are three-to-four times greater for men than for women across OECD countries, and this gender gap has been fairly stable over time. The exception is Korea, where women are much more likely to take their own lives than in other OECD countries. Suicide is also related to age, with young people aged under 25 and elderly people especially at risk. While suicide rates among the latter have generally declined over the past two decades, less progress has been observed among younger people.

Since 1990, suicide rates have decreased in many OECD countries, with declines of 40% or more in Denmark, Estonia, Hungary, Finland and Austria. On the other hand, suicide rates have increased in Korea, Chile, Mexico, the Russian Federation, Japan and Poland, although in Mexico rates remain at low levels. In Korea, rates have increased sharply and are well above the OECD average.

Male suicide rates in Korea more than doubled from 19 per 100 000 in 1995 to 50 in 2010, and rates among women are the highest in the OECD, at 21 per 100 000. Between 2006 and 2010, the number of persons treated for depression and bipolar disease in Korea rose sharply (increases of 17 and 29 per cent respectively), with those in low socioeconomic groups more likely to be affected. The economic downturn, weakening social integration and the erosion of the traditional family support base for the elderly have all been implicated in Korea's recent increase in suicide rates.

Sources
• OECD (2012), *OECD Health Statistics*, OECD Publishing.

Further information

Analytical publications
• OECD (2011), *Mental Health and Work: Evidence, Challenges and Policy Directions*, OECD Publishing.
• OECD (2011), *Health at a Glance: OECD Indicators*, OECD Publishing.
• OECD (2012), *Health at a Glance: Europe 2012*, OECD Publishing.
• OECD (2008), "Mental Health in OECD Countries", *OECD Policy Brief*, OECD Publishing.

Online databases
• *OECD Health Statistics*.

Suicide rates by gender

Age-standardised per 100 000 persons, 2010 or latest available year

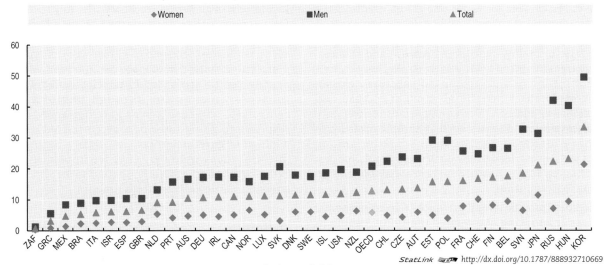

StatLink ⟨⟨⟨ http://dx.doi.org/10.1787/888932710669

Trends in suicide rates

Per 100 000 persons

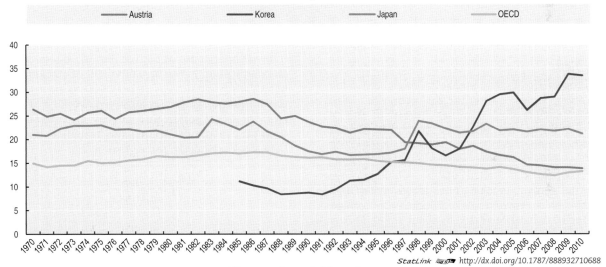

StatLink ⟨⟨⟨ http://dx.doi.org/10.1787/888932710688

Change in suicide rates

Percentage, 1990-2010 or latest available period

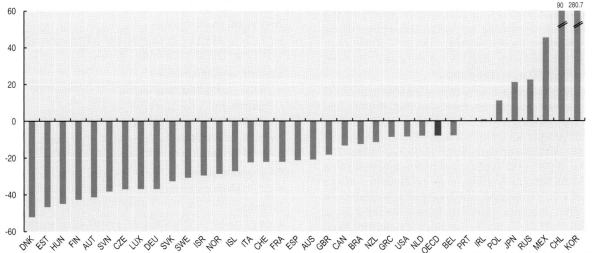

StatLink ⟨⟨⟨ http://dx.doi.org/10.1787/888932710707

SMOKING

Tobacco is responsible for about one-in-ten adult deaths worldwide, equating to about 5 million deaths each year. It is a major risk factor for at least two of the leading causes of premature mortality – circulatory disease and cancer – as it increases the risk of heart attack, stroke, lung cancer, cancers of the larynx and mouth, and pancreatic cancer. Smoking also causes peripheral vascular disease and hypertension. In addition, it is an important contributory factor for respiratory diseases such as chronic obstructive pulmonary disease (COPD), while smoking among pregnant women can lead to low birth weight and illnesses among infants. It remains the largest avoidable risk to health in OECD countries.

Several studies provide strong evidence of socio-economic differences in smoking and related mortality. People in lower social groups have a greater prevalence and intensity of smoking. The influence of smoking as a determinant of overall health inequalities is such that, in a non-smoking population, mortality differences between social groups would be halved.

Overview

The proportion of daily smokers among the adult population varies greatly across countries, even between neighbouring countries. Fifteen of the 34 OECD countries had less than 20% of the adult population smoking daily in 2010. Rates among OECD countries were lowest in Mexico, Sweden, Iceland, Australia and the United States. Although large disparities remain, smoking rates across most OECD countries have shown a marked decline. On average, smoking rates have decreased by about one-third over the past twenty years, with a higher decline for men than for women. Large declines occurred in Nordic countries, in Denmark (from 45% in 1990 to 20% in 2010), Iceland (from 30% to 14%), Sweden (from 26% to 14%), Norway (from 32% to 21%), and in the Netherlands (from 37% to 21%). Greece maintains the highest level of smoking among OECD countries, along with Chile and Ireland, with around 30% of the adult population smoking daily. Smoking rates are even higher in the Russian Federation.

Smoking prevalence among men is higher in all OECD countries except Sweden. Rates for men and women are equal or nearly equal in Denmark, Iceland, Norway and the United Kingdom. In 2010, the gender gap in smoking was particularly large in Japan, Korea and Turkey, as well as in the Russian Federation, Indonesia and China. Female smoking rates continue to decline in most OECD countries, and in several at a faster pace than rates for men. However, female smoking rates have shown little or no decline since 2000 in the Czech Republic, France and Italy.

In the post-war period, most OECD countries tended to follow a general pattern marked by very high smoking rates among men (50% or more) through to the 1960s and 1970s, while the 1980s and the 1990s were characterised by a marked downturn in tobacco consumption. Much of this decline can be attributed to policies aimed at reducing tobacco consumption through public awareness campaigns, advertising bans and increased taxation, in response to rising rates of tobacco-related diseases. In addition to government policies, actions by anti-smoking interest groups were very effective in reducing smoking rates by changing beliefs about the health effects of smoking, particularly in North America.

Definition

The proportion of daily smokers is defined as the percentage of the population aged 15 years and over reporting smoking every day.

Comparability

International comparability is limited due to the lack of standardisation in the measurement of smoking habits in health interview surveys across OECD countries. Variations remain in the age groups surveyed, wording of questions, response categories and survey methodologies. For example in a number of countries, respondents are asked if they smoke regularly, rather than daily.

Sources
- OECD (2012), *OECD Health Statistics*, OECD Publishing.

Further information

Analytical publications
- OECD (2010), *Health Care Systems: Efficiency and Policy Settings*, OECD Publishing.

Statistical publications
- OECD (2012), *Health at a Glance: Asia/Pacific 2012*, OECD Publishing.
- OECD (2012), *Health at a Glance: Europe 2012*, OECD Publishing.
- OECD (2011), *Health at a Glance*, OECD Publishing.

Online databases
- *OECD Health Statistics*.

Websites
- OECD Health Data, *www.oecd.org/health/healthdata*.
- Health at a Glance 2011, *www.oecd.org/health/healthataglance*.

Adult population smoking daily

As a percentage of adult population, 2010 or latest available year

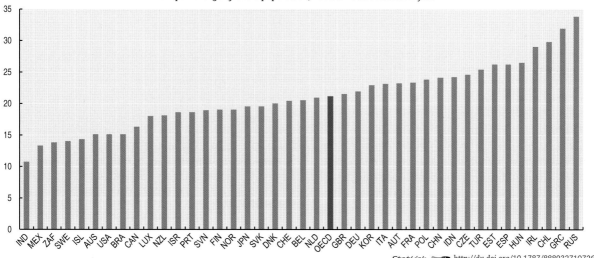

StatLink ᴍᴸ http://dx.doi.org/10.1787/888932710726

Change in smoking rates

Percentage change over the period 1990-2010 or latest available period

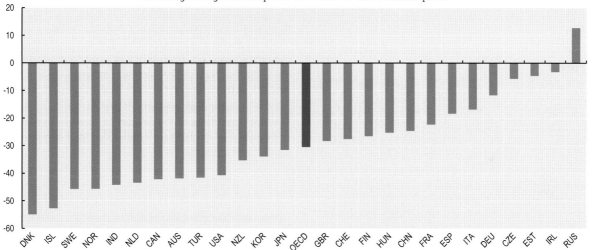

StatLink ᴍᴸ http://dx.doi.org/10.1787/888932710745

Adult population smoking daily by gender

Percentage, 2010 or latest available year

Women   Men

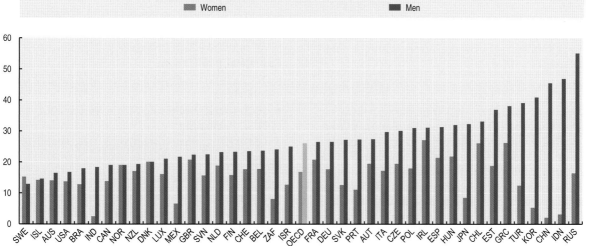

StatLink ᴍᴸ http://dx.doi.org/10.1787/888932710764

ALCOHOL CONSUMPTION

The health burden related to excessive alcohol consumption, both in terms of morbidity and mortality, is considerable. High alcohol intake is associated with numerous harmful health and social consequences, such as increased risk of heart, stroke and vascular diseases, as well as liver cirrhosis and certain cancers. Foetal exposure to alcohol increases the risk of birth defects and intellectual impairments. Alcohol also contributes to death and disability through accidents, injuries, assault, violence, homicide and suicide. It is, however, one of the major avoidable risk factors.

In 2010, the World Health Organization endorsed a global strategy to combat the harmful use of alcohol, through direct measures such as medical services for alcohol-related health problems, and indirect measures such as policy options for the availability and marketing of alcohol.

Overview

Alcohol consumption as measured by annual sales stands at 9.5 litres per adult on average across OECD countries, using the most recent data available. Leaving aside Luxembourg because national sales overestimate consumption, Austria, Korea and France reported the highest consumption of alcohol, with 12.0 litres or more per adult per year in 2010. Low alcohol consumption was recorded in Indonesia, India, Turkey and Israel where religious and cultural traditions restrict the use of alcohol among some population groups, as well as in China, South Africa, Mexico and some of the Nordic countries (Norway, Iceland and Sweden).

Although average alcohol consumption has gradually fallen in many OECD countries over the past three decades, it has risen in some others such as Korea, Iceland, Norway and Poland. There has been a degree of convergence in drinking habits across OECD countries, with wine consumption increasing in many traditional beer-drinking countries and *vice versa*. The traditional wine-producing countries of Italy, France and Spain, as well as Portugal, Greece, Switzerland have seen per capita consumption fall substantially since 1990. Alcohol consumption in the Russian Federation, as well as in Brazil and China has risen, although in the latter two countries per capita consumption is still low.

Variations in alcohol consumption across countries and over time reflect not only changing drinking habits but also the policy responses to control alcohol use. Curbs on advertising, sales restrictions and taxation have all proven to be effective measures to reduce alcohol consumption. Strict controls on sales and high taxation are mirrored by overall lower consumption in most Nordic countries.

Although adult alcohol consumption per capita gives useful evidence of long-term trends, it does not identify sub-populations at risk from harmful drinking patterns. Much of the burden of disease associated with alcohol consumption occurs among persons who have an alcohol dependence problem. The consumption of large quantities of alcohol at a single session, termed "binge drinking", is a particularly dangerous pattern of consumption, which is on the rise in some countries and social groups, especially among young males.

Definition

Alcohol consumption is defined as annual sales of pure alcohol in litres per person aged 15 years and over.

Comparability

The methodology to convert alcoholic drinks to pure alcohol may differ across countries. Official statistics do not include unrecorded alcohol consumption, such as home production. Italy reports consumption for the population 14 years and over, Sweden for 16 years and over, and for Japan 20 years and over. In some countries (*e.g.* Luxembourg), national sales do not accurately reflect actual consumption by residents, since purchases by non-residents may create a significant gap between national sales and consumption.

Sources
- OECD (2012), *OECD Health Statistics*, OECD Publishing.

Further information

Analytical publications
- Huerta, M. and F. Borgonovi (2010), "Education, Alcohol Use and Abuse among Young Adults in Britain", *OECD Education Working Papers*, No. 50.

Statistical publications
- OECD (2012), *Health at a Glance: Asia/Pacific 2012*, OECD Publishing.
- OECD (2012), *Health at a Glance: Europe 2012*, OECD Publishing.
- OECD (2011), *Health at a Glance*, OECD Publishing.

Online databases
- *OECD Health Statistics.*

Websites
- OECD Health Data, *www.oecd.org/health/healthdata.*
- Health at a Glance 2011,*www.oecd.org/health/ healthataglance.*

Alcohol consumption among population aged 15 and over

Litres per capita, 2010 or latest available year

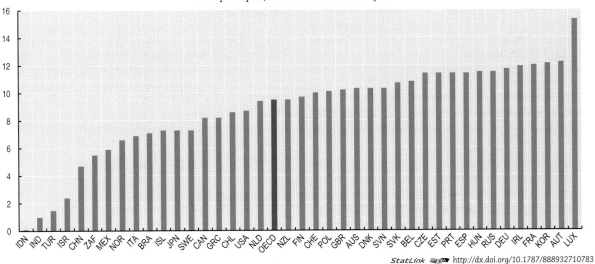

StatLink http://dx.doi.org/10.1787/888932710783

Change in alcohol consumption in litres per capita among population aged 15 and over

Percentage change in litres per capita over the period 1990-2010 or latest available period

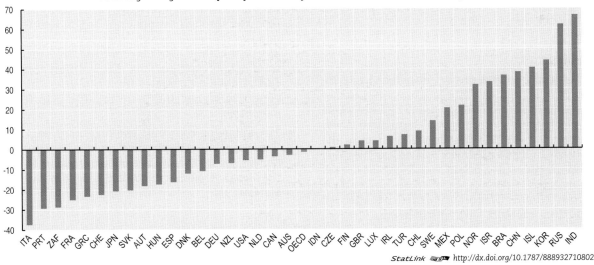

StatLink http://dx.doi.org/10.1787/888932710802

Trends in alcohol consumption among population aged 15 and over

Litres per capita

France — Hungary — United States — OECD

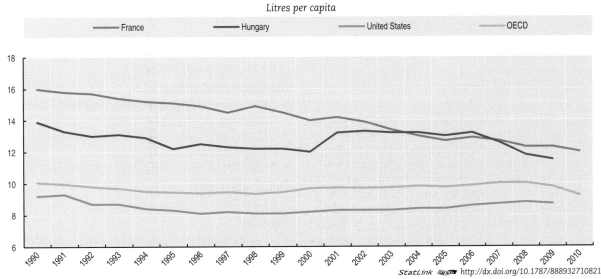

StatLink http://dx.doi.org/10.1787/888932710821

OVERWEIGHT AND OBESITY

The rise in overweight and obesity is a major public health concern. Obesity is a known risk factor for numerous health problems, including hypertension, high cholesterol, diabetes, cardiovascular diseases, respiratory problems (asthma), musculoskeletal diseases (arthritis) and some forms of cancer. A number of behavioural and environmental factors have contributed to the rise in overweight and obesity rates in industrialised countries, including falling real prices of food and more time being physically inactive.

Because obesity is associated with higher risks of chronic illnesses, it is linked to significant additional health care costs. There is a time lag between the onset of obesity and related health problems, suggesting that the rise in obesity over the past two decades will mean higher health care costs in the future. Mortality also increases sharply once the overweight threshold is crossed.

Overview

Based on latest available surveys, more than half (53%) of the adult population in the OECD report that they are overweight or obese. Among those countries where height and weight were measured, the proportion was even greater, at 57%. The prevalence of overweight and obesity among adults exceeds 50% in no less than 21 of 34 OECD countries. In contrast, overweight and obesity rates are much lower in Japan and Korea and in some European countries (France and Switzerland), although even in these countries rates are increasing.

The prevalence of obesity, which presents even greater health risks than overweight, varies almost tenfold among OECD countries, from a low of 4% in Japan and Korea, to 30% or more in the United States and Mexico. On average across OECD countries, 18% of the adult population are obese. Average obesity rates among men and women are similar, although there are disparities in some countries. In Chile, Turkey and Mexico, a greater proportion of women are obese, whereas in Iceland and Norway men are more likely to be obese.

Obesity prevalence has increased by more than 40% over the past 10 years in a number of countries, including Denmark, Sweden, Norway, France and the Czech Republic, with the OECD average rising from 13% in 2000 to 18% in 2010. The rapid rises occurred regardless of where levels stood a decade ago, with the prevalence of obesity increasing by half in both Norway and the Czech Republic, even though the current rate in Norway is around half that of the Czech Republic.

Definition

Overweight and obesity are defined as excessive weight presenting health risks because of the high proportion of body fat. The most frequently used measure is based on the body mass index (BMI), which is a single number that evaluates an individual's weight in relation to height (weight/height^2, with weight in kilograms and height in metres). Based on the WHO classification, adults with a BMI between 25 and 30 are defined as overweight, and those with a BMI over 30 as obese.

Comparability

The BMI classification may not be suitable for all ethnic groups, who may be exposed to different levels of health risk for the same level of BMI. The thresholds for adults are also not suitable to measure overweight and obesity among children.

For most countries, overweight and obesity rates are self-reported through estimates of height and weight from population-based health interview surveys. However, around one-third of OECD countries derive their estimates from health examinations. These differences limit data comparability. Estimates from health examinations are generally higher and more reliable than from health interviews.

The following countries use measured data: Australia, Canada, Chile, the Czech Republic, Finland, Hungary, Ireland, Japan, Korea, Luxembourg, Mexico, New Zealand, the Slovak Republic, the United Kingdom and the United States.

Sources
- OECD (2012), *OECD Health Statistics*, OECD Publishing.

Further information

Analytical publications
- Sassi, F. (2010), *Obesity and the Economics of Prevention: Fit not Fat*, OECD Publishing.

Statistical publications
- OECD (2012), *Health at a Glance: Asia/Pacific 2012*, OECD Publishing.
- OECD (2012), *Health at a Glance: Europe 2012*, OECD Publishing.
- OECD (2011), *Health at a Glance*, OECD Publishing.

Online databases
- *OECD Health Statistics.*

Websites
- OECD Economics of prevention project, *www.oecd.org/health/prevention*.
- OECD Health Data, *www.oecd.org/health/healthdata*.

Overweight and obesity population aged 15 and above

As a percentage of the population aged 15 and above, 2010 or latest available year

	Women			Men			Total		
	Overweight	Obese	Overweight and obese	Overweight	Obese	Overweight and obese	Overweight	Obese	Overweight and obese
Australia	31.0	23.6	54.7	42.2	25.5	67.7	36.7	24.6	61.2
Austria	29.9	12.7	42.6	44.9	12.0	56.9	35.3	12.4	47.7
Belgium	26.0	14.4	40.4	40.6	13.1	53.7	33.1	13.8	46.9
Canada	30.8	23.3	54.1	40.9	25.2	66.1	35.8	24.2	60.0
Chile	33.6	30.7	64.3	45.3	19.2	64.6	39.3	25.1	64.5
Czech Republic	28.0	21.0	49.0	40.0	21.0	61.0	34.0	21.0	55.0
Denmark	26.3	13.1	39.4	40.5	13.7	54.3	33.3	13.4	46.7
Estonia	28.4	16.8	45.2	36.6	17.0	53.6	31.7	16.9	48.6
Finland	31.3	21.1	52.4	46.6	19.3	65.9	39.0	20.2	59.2
France	23.3	13.4	36.7	37.6	12.4	49.9	29.9	12.9	42.9
Germany	29.1	13.8	42.9	44.4	15.7	60.1	36.7	14.7	51.4
Greece	31.7	17.3	49.0	45.6	17.3	62.9	38.5	17.3	55.7
Hungary	30.3	30.4	60.7	36.5	26.3	62.7	33.2	28.5	61.6
Iceland	31.1	19.3	50.4	44.0	22.7	66.7	37.5	21.0	58.5
Ireland	32.0	24.0	56.0	45.0	22.0	67.0	38.0	23.0	61.0
Israel	28.0	14.9	42.9	40.7	17.1	57.8	34.1	16.0	50.1
Italy	27.6	9.6	37.2	44.3	11.1	55.5	35.6	10.3	46.0
Japan	17.9	3.2	21.1	26.6	3.8	30.4	21.8	3.5	25.3
Korea	21.0	4.7	25.7	31.2	3.5	34.8	26.1	4.1	30.2
Luxembourg	29.2	21.0	50.2	42.6	23.6	66.2	36.7	22.5	59.1
Mexico	37.4	34.5	71.9	42.5	24.2	66.7	39.5	30.0	69.5
Netherlands	30.3	12.6	42.9	43.4	10.2	53.6	36.8	11.4	48.2
New Zealand	32.8	27.8	60.6	41.3	27.7	69.1	37.0	27.8	64.7
Norway	27.0	8.0	36.0	43.0	11.0	55.0	35.0	10.0	46.0
Poland	29.4	15.2	44.6	44.8	16.6	61.4	36.4	15.8	52.2
Portugal	31.4	16.1	47.5	41.4	14.6	56.0	36.2	15.4	51.6
Slovak Republic	31.0	16.7	47.7	40.7	17.1	57.8	34.6	16.9	51.5
Slovenia	29.6	15.8	45.4	47.9	17.0	64.9	38.7	16.4	55.1
Spain	29.9	14.7	44.6	45.5	17.3	62.8	37.6	16.0	53.6
Sweden	27.1	13.1	40.2	41.0	12.6	53.6	34.0	12.9	46.9
Switzerland	20.9	7.7	28.6	37.8	8.6	46.3	29.2	8.1	37.3
Turkey	28.4	21.0	49.3	37.3	13.2	50.4	33.0	16.9	49.9
United Kingdom	31.7	26.1	57.8	41.6	26.2	67.8	36.7	26.1	62.8
United States	28.2	36.3	64.5	38.6	35.5	74.1	33.3	35.9	69.2
EU 27	29.7	16.7	46.4	41.6	16.5	59.6	36.1	16.6	52.7
OECD	28.9	18.1	47.0	41.3	17.5	58.7	34.8	17.8	52.7
Brazil	28.8	15.5	44.3	37.7	14.4	52.1	33.1	15.0	48.1
China	15.4	3.4	18.8	16.7	2.4	19.1	16.0	2.9	18.9
India	9.8	2.8	12.6	8.0	1.3	9.3	8.9	2.0	10.9
Indonesia	14.2	3.6	17.8	4.8	1.1	8.4	11.0	2.4	13.4
Russian Federation	25.0	20.1	45.1	31.1	11.8	42.9	28.1	15.9	44.0
South Africa	27.5	27.4	54.9	21.0	8.8	29.8	24.3	18.1	42.4

StatLink http://dx.doi.org/10.1787/888932710840

Increasing obesity rates among the adult population

Percentage

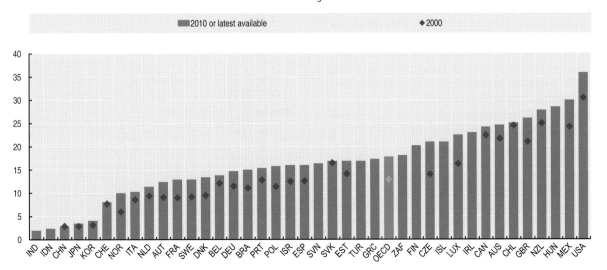

StatLink http://dx.doi.org/10.1787/888932710859

DOCTORS

Doctors play a central role in health systems, and there are concerns in many OECD countries about current or future shortages of doctors, and the problem this might create for access to care.

Definition

Practising physicians are defined as the number of doctors providing care to patients. Generalists include doctors assuming responsibility for the provision of continuing care to individuals and families, as well as other generalist/non-specialist practitioners. Specialists include paediatricians, obstetricians/gynaecologists, psychiatrists, medical specialists and surgical specialists. Medical doctors not further defined include interns/residents if they are not reported in the field in which they are training,

and doctors not elsewhere classified. The numbers are based on head counts.

Comparability

In several countries (Canada, Finland, France, Greece, Iceland, Ireland, the Netherlands, the Slovak Republic and Turkey), the data include not only physicians providing direct care to patients, but also those working in the health sector as managers, educators, researchers, etc. This can add another 5-10% of doctors. Data for Portugal refer to all physicians licensed to practice (resulting in a large overestimation). Data for Spain include dentists and stomatologists, while data for Belgium include stomatologists. Data for Chile are an under-estimation as they do not cover all practising doctors.

Not all countries are able to report all their practising physicians in the two broad categories of specialists and generalists because of missing information.

Overview

From 2000 to 2010, the number of doctors per 1 000 population has grown in all OECD countries, except in Estonia and Poland where it decreased slightly. On average across OECD countries, it increased from 2.7 doctors per 1 000 population in 2000 to 3.1 in 2010. The number increased particularly rapidly in countries which started with lower levels in 2000, such as Turkey, Korea and Mexico. But it also increased rapidly in Greece, although all of the growth took place between 2000 and 2008 and the number has stabilised since then.

In nearly all countries, the balance between generalist and specialist doctors has changed over the past few decades, with the number of specialists increasing much more rapidly. As a result, there are more specialists than generalists in most countries, except in Ireland, Norway and Portugal. This may be explained by reduced interest in the traditional mode of practice of "family medicine", given the workload and constraints attached to it. In addition, in many countries, there is a growing remuneration gap between generalists and specialists.

Virtually all OECD countries exercise some form of control over medical school intakes, often by limiting the number of available training places, for example in the form of a *numerus clausus*. In 2010, Austria, Ireland, Denmark, Greece and the Czech Republic had the highest number of medical graduates per 100 000 population. However, in countries such as Ireland and the Czech Republic, a large share of graduates is made up of foreign students who may return home upon graduation. Graduation rates were the lowest in Israel, Chile, Japan and France. The average across OECD countries was slightly over ten new medical graduates per 100 000 population in 2010, up from nine in 2000.

Sources

- OECD (2012), *OECD Health Statistics*, OECD Publishing.
- WHO-Europe for Russian Federation, and national sources for other non-OECD countries.

Further information

Analytical publications

- Fujisawa, R. and G. Lafortune (2008), "The Remuneration of General Practitioners and Specialists in 14 OECD Countries: What are the Factors Influencing Variations across Countries?", *OECD Health Working Papers*, No. 41.
- OECD (2008), *The Looming Crisis in the Health Workforce: How Can OECD Countries Respond?*, OECD Health Policy Studies, OECD Publishing.

Statistical publications

- OECD (2012), *Health at a Glance: Asia/Pacific 2012*, OECD Publishing.
- OECD (2012), *Health at a Glance: Europe 2012*, OECD Publishing.
- OECD (2011), *Health at a Glance*, OECD Publishing.

Online databases

- *OECD Health Statistics*.

Websites

- OECD Health Data (supplementary material), *www.oecd.org/health/healthdata*.
- OECD Health at a Glance (supplementary material), *www.oecd.org/health/healthataglance*.

Practising physicians

Per 1 000 inhabitants

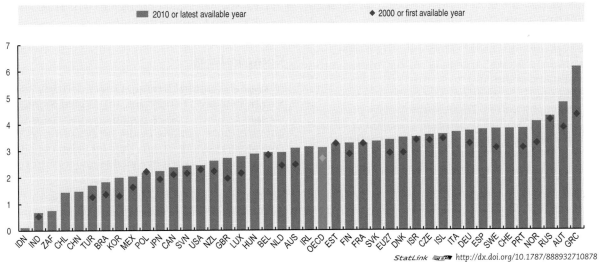

StatLink ᴍᴤ⌐ http://dx.doi.org/10.1787/888932710878

Categories of physicians

As a percentage of total physicians, 2010 or latest available year

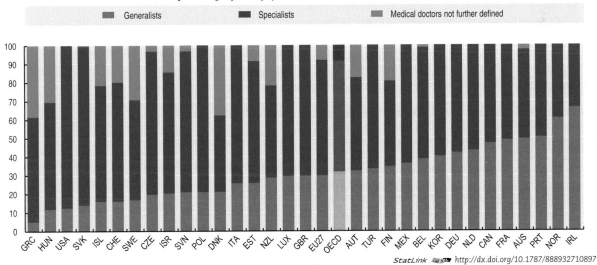

StatLink ᴍᴤ⌐ http://dx.doi.org/10.1787/888932710897

Medical graduates

Per 100 000 inhabitants

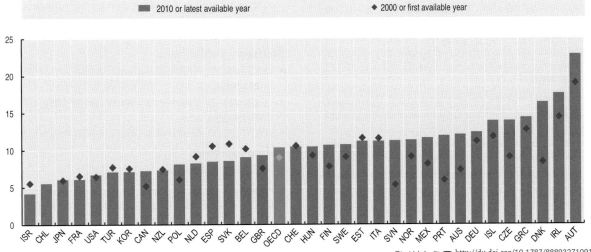

StatLink ᴍᴤ⌐ http://dx.doi.org/10.1787/888932710916

NURSES

Nurses are usually the most numerous health profession, outnumbering physicians on average across OECD countries by almost three to one. However, there are concerns in many countries about shortages of nurses, and these concerns may well intensify in the future as the demand for nurses continues to increase and the ageing of the "baby-boom" generation precipitates a wave of retirements among nurses. These concerns have prompted actions in many countries to increase the training of new nurses combined with efforts to increase the retention of nurses in the profession.

Definition

The number of nurses includes all those employed in public and private settings providing services to patients ("practising"), including the self-employed. In those countries where there are different levels of nurses, the data include both "professional nurses" who have a higher level of education and perform higher level tasks and "associate professional nurses" who have a lower level of education but are nonetheless recognised and registered as nurses. Midwives and nursing aids who are not recognised as nurses are normally excluded.

Comparability

In several countries (France, Greece, Ireland, Portugal, the Slovak Republic, Turkey and the United States), the data include not only nurses providing direct care to patients, but also those working in the health sector as managers, educators, researchers, etc. Data for Belgium and Italy refer to all nurses who are licensed to practice (resulting in a large overestimation).

Austria reports only nurses employed in hospitals, resulting in an under-estimation. Data for Germany do not include about 270 000 nurses (representing an additional 30% of nurses) who have three years of education and are providing services for the elderly.

Overview

On average across OECD countries, there were 8.6 nurses per 1 000 population in 2010. The number was highest in Switzerland and Denmark, with over 15 nurses per 1 000 population. It was also high in Belgium, although the data relate to all nurses licensed to practice, resulting in a large overestimation. The number of nurses per capita in OECD countries was lowest in Chile, Turkey, Mexico and Greece. It was also low compared with the OECD average in major emerging economies, such as Indonesia, India and Brazil, where there were fewer than 1 nurse per 1 000 population in 2010.

The number of nurses per capita increased in almost all OECD countries over the past decade, with the exception of Israel and the Slovak Republic. The increase was particularly rapid in Korea, Spain and Portugal, although the number of nurses per capita in these three countries remained well below the OECD average in 2010.

The number of nurses per doctor ranged from more than four in Japan, Denmark, Canada and the United States, to less than one in Greece and about one per doctor in Turkey, Chile and Italy. The average across OECD countries is just below three nurses per doctor, with most countries reporting between two to four nurses per doctor. In Greece and Italy, there is evidence of an over-supply of doctors and under-supply of nurses, resulting in an inefficient allocation of resources.

Sources

- OECD (2012), *OECD Health Statistics*, OECD Publishing.
- WHO-Europe for Russian Federation, and national sources for other non-OECD countries.

Further information

Analytical publications

- Buchan, J. and S. Black (2011), "The Impact of Pay Increases on Nurses' Labour Market: A Review of Evidence from Four OECD Countries", *OECD Health Working Papers*, No. 57.
- Colombo, F. *et al.* (2011), *Help Wanted?: Providing and Paying for Long-Term Care*, OECD Health Policy Studies, OECD Publishing.
- Delamaire, M. and G. Lafortune (2010), "Nurses in Advanced Roles: A Description and Evaluation of Experiences in 12 Developed Countries", *OECD Health Working Papers*, No. 54.

Statistical publications

- OECD (2012), *Health at a Glance: Asia/Pacific 2012*, OECD Publishing.
- OECD (2012), *Health at a Glance: Europe 2012*, OECD Publishing.
- OECD (2011), *Health at a Glance*, OECD Publishing.

Online databases

- *OECD Health Statistics*.

Websites

- OECD Health Data (supplementary material), *www.oecd.org/health/healthdata*.
- OECD Health at a Glance (supplementary material), *www.oecd.org/health/healthataglance*.

Practising nurses
Per 1 000 inhabitants

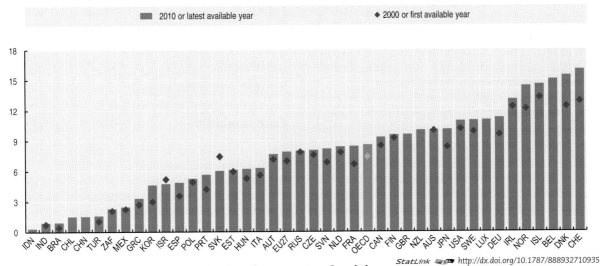

StatLink http://dx.doi.org/10.1787/888932710935

Ratio of nurses to physicians
2010 or latest available year

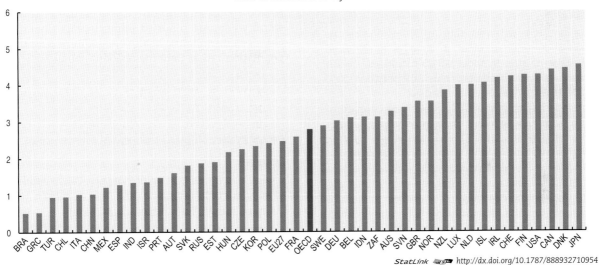

StatLink http://dx.doi.org/10.1787/888932710954

Nursing graduates
Per 100 000 inhabitants

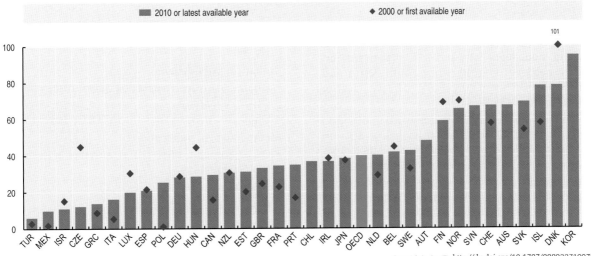

StatLink http://dx.doi.org/10.1787/888932710973

HEALTH EXPENDITURE

In most OECD countries, spending on health is a large and growing share of both public and private expenditure. Health spending as a share of GDP varies widely across countries, reflecting the relative priority assigned to health as well as the diverse financing and organisational structures of the health system in each country.

Definition

Total expenditure on health measures the final consumption of health goods and services plus capital investment in health care infrastructure. It includes spending by both public and private sources (including households) on medical goods and services, on public health and prevention programmes, and on administration.

Overview

Trends in the health spending to GDP ratio are the result of the combined effect of changes in GDP and health expenditure. In most OECD countries, health spending grew more quickly than GDP between 2000 and 2009. As a result, the average share of GDP allocated to health across OECD countries climbed to 9.6% up from 7.8% in 2000. This ratio dropped slightly to 9.5% of GDP in 2010. This decrease was mainly driven by slower or negative growth in public spending in the wake of the 2008 financial and economic crises. Many countries, including Ireland, Iceland, Estonia and Greece implemented a range of measures to reduce government health spending as part of broader efforts to reduce large budgetary deficits and public debt.

There remain large variations in how much OECD countries spend on health as a share of GDP. In 2010, the share of GDP allocated to health was the largest by far in the United States (17.6%), followed by the Netherlands (12.0%), France and Germany (11.6%). Estonia, Mexico and Turkey spent less than 6.5% of their GDP on health.

China and India spent 5.1% and 4.1% of their GDP on health respectively in 2010, while South Africa and Brazil allocated 8.9% and 9.0% of GDP to health, close to the OECD average (9.5%).

The share of public expenditure on health to GDP also varies among OECD countries from below 4.5% in Chile, Korea and Mexico to more than or equal to 8.5% in Denmark, France, Germany and the United States.

In 2010, public spending was the main source of financing of health expenditure in all OECD countries with the exception of Mexico, Chile and the United States. Private health spending was also the dominant financing source in India, South Africa and Brazil.

For a more comprehensive assessment of health spending, the health spending to GDP ratio should be considered together with per capita health spending. Countries having a relatively high health spending to GDP ratio might have relatively low health expenditure per capita, while the converse also holds.

Comparability

OECD countries are at varying stages of reporting health expenditure data according to the definitions proposed in the 2011 manual *A System of Health Accounts* (SHA). While the comparability of health expenditure data has improved recently, some limitations do remain, in particular on the measurement of long-term care expenditure.

In the Netherlands, it is not possible to clearly distinguish the public and private share for the part of health expenditure related to investments. In Belgium, total expenditure excludes investments. Estonia, Israel and Poland report expenditure financed from the rest of the world which are reported under private financing in the chart. In Luxembourg, health expenditure is for the insured population rather than the resident population.

Sources
- OECD (2012), *OECD Health Statistics*, OECD Publishing.
- For non-OECD member countries: World Health Organization (WHO) (2012), (database).

Further information

Analytical publications
- OECD (2010), *Value for Money in Health Spending*, OECD Health Policy Studies, OECD Publishing.
- Scherer, P. and M. Devaux (2010), "The Challenge of Financing Health Care in the Current Crisis: An Analysis Based on the OECD Data", *OECD Health Working Papers*, No. 49.

Statistical publications
- OECD (2011), *Government at a Glance 2011*, OECD Publishing.
- OECD (2011), *Health at a Glance*, OECD Publishing.

Methodological publications
- OECD, Eurostat, WHO (2011), *A System of Health Accounts*, OECD Publishing.

Online databases
- *OECD Health Statistics*.

Websites
- OECD Health Data (supplementary material), *www.oecd.org/health/healthdata*.

Public and private expenditure on health

As a percentage of GDP

	Public expenditure				Private expenditure				Total			
	1980	1990	2000	2010 or latest available year	1980	1990	2000	2010 or latest available year	1980	1990	2000	2010 or latest available year
Australia	3.8	4.5	5.4	6.2	2.3	2.3	2.7	2.9	6.1	6.7	8.0	9.1
Austria	5.1	6.1	7.6	8.4	2.3	2.3	2.4	2.6	7.4	8.4	10.0	11.0
Belgium	..	..	6.1	8.0	..	..	2.1	2.6	6.3	7.2	8.1	10.5
Canada	5.3	6.6	6.2	8.1	1.7	2.3	2.6	3.3	7.0	8.9	8.8	11.4
Chile	..	..	3.4	3.8	..	..	3.2	4.1	..	..	6.6	8.0
Czech Republic	..	4.4	5.7	6.3	..	0.1	0.6	1.2	..	4.5	6.3	7.5
Denmark	7.9	6.9	7.3	9.5	1.1	1.4	1.4	1.7	8.9	8.3	8.7	11.1
Estonia	..	..	4.1	5.0	..	..	1.2	1.3	..	..	5.3	6.3
Finland	5.0	6.3	5.1	6.6	1.3	1.5	2.1	2.3	6.3	7.7	7.2	8.9
France	5.6	6.4	8.0	9.0	1.4	2.0	2.1	2.7	7.0	8.4	10.1	11.6
Germany	6.6	6.3	8.3	8.9	1.8	2.0	2.1	2.7	8.4	8.3	10.4	11.6
Greece	3.3	3.6	4.8	6.1	2.6	3.1	3.2	4.2	5.9	6.7	8.0	10.2
Hungary	..	..	5.1	5.0	..	..	2.1	2.7	..	..	7.2	7.8
Iceland	5.5	6.8	7.7	7.5	0.7	1.0	1.8	1.8	6.3	7.8	9.5	9.3
Ireland	6.7	4.3	4.6	6.4	1.5	1.7	1.5	2.8	8.2	6.0	6.1	9.2
Israel	..	..	4.7	4.6	..	..	2.6	2.8	7.7	7.1	7.5	7.5
Italy	..	6.1	5.8	7.4	..	1.6	2.2	1.9	..	7.7	8.0	9.3
Japan	4.5	4.5	6.1	7.6	1.8	1.3	1.5	1.8	6.4	5.8	7.6	9.5
Korea	0.8	1.5	2.2	4.1	2.9	2.5	2.3	3.0	3.7	4.0	4.5	7.1
Luxembourg	4.8	5.0	6.4	6.6	0.4	0.4	1.1	1.3	5.2	5.4	7.5	7.9
Mexico	..	1.8	2.4	2.9	..	2.6	2.7	3.3	..	4.4	5.1	6.2
Netherlands	5.1	5.4	5.0	..	2.3	2.6	2.9	..	7.4	8.0	8.0	12.0
New Zealand	5.1	5.6	5.9	8.4	0.7	1.2	1.7	1.7	5.8	6.8	7.6	10.1
Norway	5.9	6.3	6.9	8.1	1.0	1.3	1.5	1.4	7.0	7.6	8.4	9.4
Poland	..	4.4	3.9	5.0	..	0.4	1.7	1.9	..	4.8	5.5	7.0
Portugal	3.3	3.7	6.2	7.1	1.8	2.0	3.1	3.7	5.1	5.7	9.3	10.7
Slovak Republic	..	..	4.9	5.8	..	..	0.6	3.2	..	..	5.5	9.0
Slovenia	..	..	6.1	6.6	..	..	2.1	2.5	..	..	8.3	9.0
Spain	4.2	5.1	5.2	7.1	1.1	1.4	2.0	2.5	5.3	6.5	7.2	9.6
Sweden	8.2	7.4	6.9	7.7	0.7	0.8	1.2	1.8	8.9	8.2	8.2	9.6
Switzerland	..	4.3	5.6	7.4	..	3.9	4.5	3.9	7.4	8.2	10.2	11.4
Turkey	0.7	1.6	3.1	4.4	1.8	1.1	1.8	1.6	2.4	2.7	4.9	6.1
United Kingdom	5.0	4.9	5.5	8.0	0.6	1.0	1.5	1.6	5.6	5.9	7.0	9.6
United States	3.7	4.9	5.9	8.5	5.3	7.5	7.8	9.1	9.0	12.4	13.7	17.6
EU 27	..	..	..	6.5	..	..	..	2.4	..	..	..	9.0
OECD	4.8	5.0	5.5	6.7	1.7	1.9	2.2	2.7	6.6	6.9	7.8	9.5
Brazil	..	..	2.9	4.2	..	..	4.3	4.8	..	..	7.2	9.0
China	..	..	1.8	2.7	..	..	2.9	2.4	..	..	4.6	5.1
India	..	..	1.1	1.2	..	..	3.3	2.9	..	..	4.4	4.1
Indonesia	..	..	0.7	1.3	..	..	1.2	1.3	..	..	2.0	2.6
Russian Federation	..	..	3.2	3.2	..	..	2.2	1.9	..	..	5.4	5.1
South Africa	..	..	3.4	3.9	..	..	5.0	5.0	..	..	8.5	8.9

StatLink ⟐ http://dx.doi.org/10.1787/888932710992

Public and private expenditure on health

As a percentage of GDP, 2010 or latest available year

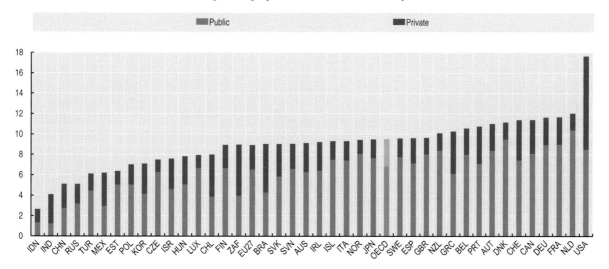

StatLink ⟐ http://dx.doi.org/10.1787/888932711011

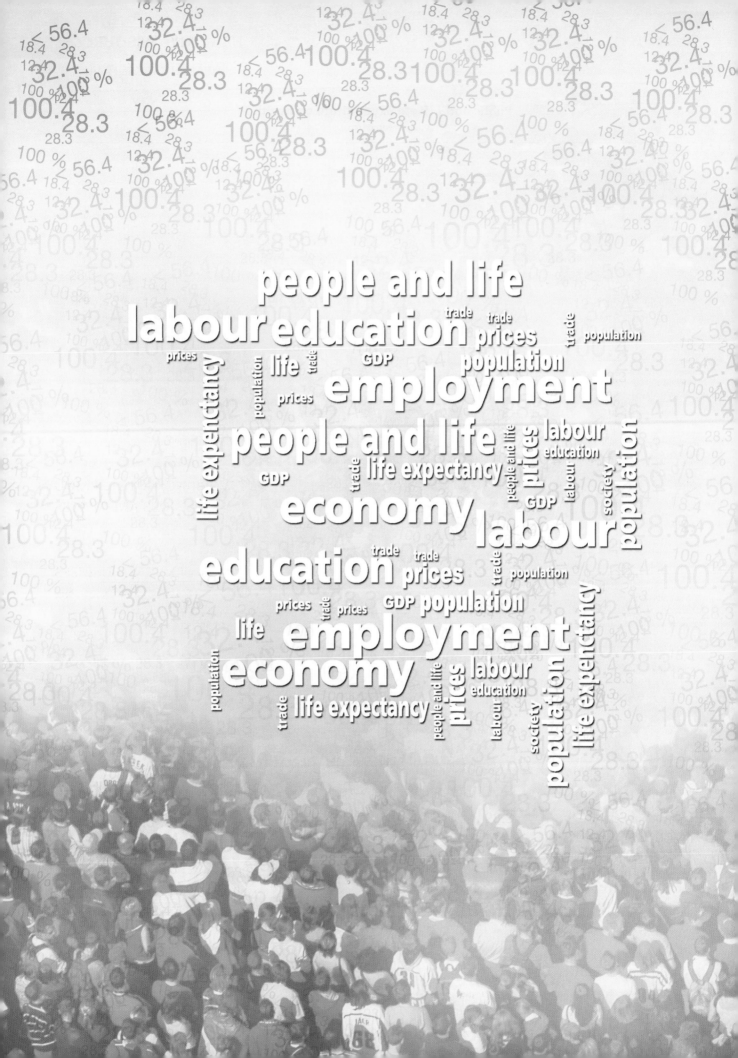

SPECIAL CHAPTER

GENDER EQUALITY

INTRODUCTION

The financial and economic crisis has underlined the importance of making the best use of all our resources – including people – if we are to achieve sustainable growth that benefits everyone in the years to come. Making the most of the talent pool means ensuring that men and women, boys and girls, have a fair chance to contribute both at home and in the workplace.

Things have changed considerably in OECD countries in the past 50 years – more girls now complete tertiary education than boys, and on average in OECD countries more than half of the women have a paid job. But women still earn less than men, do more unpaid work such as housework and childcare and are more likely to end their lives in poverty, partly as a result of economic inequality and because they live longer than men.

Education, skills and jobs

Years of effort by OECD countries to end disadvantage against girls in the education system has resulted in a situation where girls are more likely to complete secondary education than boys and more women than men graduate from college – and there are now concerns in some countries that something needs to be done to help the boys. Since the beginning of the OECD's PISA tests of 15-year olds' competencies, in 2000, girls have always scored higher in reading than boys – and by a substantial margin: the equivalent of one full year of formal schooling.

Even though more women are graduating, they are still less likely to study sciences and to take jobs in scientific fields. This is of particular concern given a shortage of science graduates in many countries to fill the jobs available. There are signs that things are changing at least in the health sector, where more women are becoming doctors – 43% of doctors on average across OECD countries are women, up from 29% in 1990.

Whatever career women choose, they are likely to end up earning less than their male counterparts. On average, women earn 15% less than men in OECD countries, and are far less likely to be in parliament or on a company board. They also undertake fewer hours of paid work – men average 41 hours a week and women 35 hours – but spend more time on unpaid tasks. On average men in OECD countries spend just over two hours per day doing unpaid work, while women spend more than four and a half hours cooking, cleaning or caring.

Some of these imbalances are due to cultural norms and longstanding habits, but policy also has a role to play. Even if a man wants to stay at home to care for children, for example, it may be simply unaffordable because he is the main breadwinner.

What can be done to help make it easier for people to find the work-life balance that works best for them and their family? Collecting and publishing gender data will raise public awareness of gender bias in the economy and society and ensure that the gender dimension is fully taken into account when crafting policies in every area, from pensions and employment to childcare and tax.

Note: The graphs show selected OECD countries. Additional countries are available in the Statlink.

Sources

- OECD (2012), *Highlights from Education at a Glance*, OECD Publishing.
- OECD (2012), *OECD Employment Outlook*, OECD Publishing.
- Miranda, V. (2011), "Cooking, Caring and Volunteering: Unpaid Work around the World", *OECD Social, Employment and Migration Working Papers*, No. 116, OECD Publishing.
- OECD (2012), *Closing the Gender Gap, Act Now*, OECD Publishing.

Further information

Analytical publications

- OECD (2011), *Doing Better for Families*, OECD Publishing.

Websites

- OECD Better Life Index, *www.oecdbetterlifeindex.org*.
- OECD Education, *www.oecd.org/education*.

Student performance in science
2009

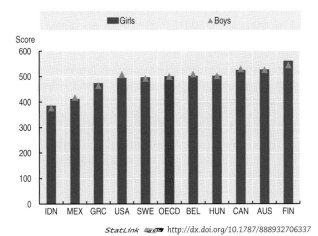

People with tertiary education, by gender
Percentage, 2010

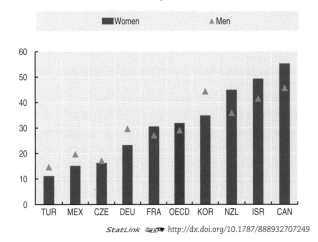

Part-time employment
2010, percentage of total employment

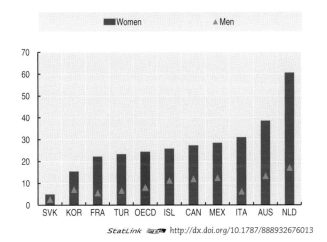

Gender gap in median earnings for full-time employees
Percentage, 2000 and 2010 (or nearest year)

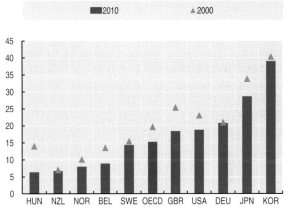

Share of women on boards
Percentage, 2009

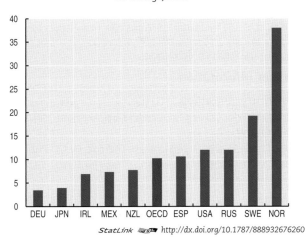

Share of women in parliament
Percentage, 1995 and 2011

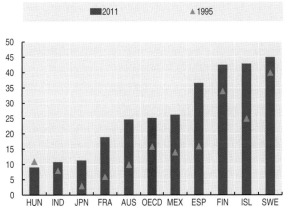

NOT WORKING, NOT LEARNING

Definition

Data on population and educational attainment come from OECD and Eurostat databases, which are compiled from National Labour Force Surveys. This request for data expands the request on labour force status by completed level of education and aims at describing the transition process of 15-29 year-olds from school to work.

The work status refers to the International Labour Organisation definition of employment, unemployment and not in the labour force. The type of employment refers to full-time or part-time employment based on a threshold definition of 30-usual-hours cut-off on the main job. Full-time workers are those who usually work 30 hours or more on their main job.

The school status is understood in terms of education and/ or training currently being received in the regular educational system.

Overview

Almost everyone in OECD countries has compulsory education to age 16. Having a good basic education is important, but what happens next sets the stage for adult working life. In many countries this varies considerably depending on whether you are a girl or a boy.

The average 15-year-old in an OECD country in 2010 could expect to spend the next 15 years as follows: seven years in education; five and a half years in a job, one year unemployed, and about a year and a half neither in education nor seeking work. But while girls will spend more time in education (7.2 years against 6.9 for a boy), they will spend less time at work, just 5.0 years compared with 5.9 for boys, and twice as long neither working nor learning, at 1.8 years compared with 0.9 for boys.

These figures, however, do not show how many young people are not working, learning or jobseeking at any given moment, or whether there are wide gender differences. In fact, some 18% of young women aged 15-29 in OECD countries were neither in education, employment or training (NEET) in 2010, compared with just under 14% of young men in the same age group. But situations vary widely from one country to another.

The NEET gender gap has narrowed over the years. In 1997, in the 22 OECD countries for which figures are available, there were twice as many women NEET as men, 21.7% against 10.5% for men. Before the crisis hit in 2008, in the 32 OECD countries for which figures are available, women (17.1%) were still far more likely than men (10.6%) to be in the NEET group. During the crisis, the rate for women has edged up (nearly 18% in 2010) while that for men has increased more sharply (to nearly 14%).

At a time of economic slowdown some young people may prefer to continue their education if they are unable to find work. The proportion of 15-29 year-olds in education has increased by around two percentage points for both men and women since 2007, to reach an average of 48% for women and 46% for men, but here again the situation varies widely between countries. In Turkey, for example, the proportion of women in education has risen from 21% to 28% since 2008, although women are still twice as likely as men to be NEET (52% compared with 21%). In Mexico, the gender gap is even wider: young women are three times more likely than young men to be NEET. These large disparities may be related to culture; it is likely that these young women have opted to start a family rather than pursue a career.

In other countries however, the crisis has seen fewer people continuing their education. In France, the number of 15-29 year old women in education has fallen from 46.4% in 2008 to 44.8% in 2010, while during the same period the number of men has fallen from 45.2% to 42.8%. In only a few OECD countries – Canada, Ireland, Israel and Spain, are young men more likely than young women to be NEET. The gender gap is narrow however.

Sources

- OECD (2012), "*Indicator C5 Transition from school to work: where are the 15-29 year-olds?*", *Education at a Glance: OECD Indicators*, OECD Publishing.

Further information

Analytical publications

- OECD (2012), *Closing the Gender Gap, Act Now*, OECD Publishing.
- OECD (2012), *OECD Employment Outlook*, OECD Publishing.
- OECD (2010), *Off to a Good Start? Jobs for Youth*, OECD Publishing.

Websites

- OECD Education, *www.oecd.org/education*.
- OECD Labour markets, human capital and inequality, *www.oecd.org/employment/ labourmarketshumancapitalandinequality*.

Percentage of 15-29-year-olds not in education, training or employment

2010 or latest available year

	Young men	Young women	Total
Australia	9.0	14.8	11.8
Austria	10.1	12.0	11.1
Belgium	12.3	16.1	14.2
Brazil	11.7	27.4	19.6
Canada	14.3	12.7	13.5
Czech Republic	8.6	18.2	13.2
Denmark	11.0	10.0	10.5
Estonia	18.1	20.2	19.1
Finland	12.4	12.9	12.6
France	15.2	18.1	16.7
Germany	10.2	13.8	12.0
Greece	13.4	23.3	18.3
Hungary	16.5	21.4	18.9
Iceland	12.2	8.2	10.3
Ireland	22.4	19.5	21.0
Israel	28.4	26.4	27.4
Italy	20.0	26.1	23.0
Japan	9.9	9.8	9.9
Korea	17.7	20.8	19.2
Luxembourg	7.3	7.0	7.1
Mexico	11.0	37.2	24.4
Netherlands	6.4	8.0	7.2
New Zealand	12.4	20.2	16.3
Norway	8.6	8.4	8.5
Poland	12.5	18.0	15.2
Portugal	12.2	14.8	13.5
Slovak Republic	16.0	21.8	18.8
Slovenia	8.3	9.3	8.8
Spain	24.7	22.8	23.7
Sweden	10.5	10.0	10.3
Switzerland	8.2	11.2	9.7
Turkey	21.3	52.1	36.6
United Kingdom	13.6	18.3	15.9
United States	14.3	18.0	16.1
OECD	13.7	17.9	15.8

StatLink ᘓᔖ☐ http://dx.doi.org/10.1787/888932663302

Percentage of 15-29-year-olds not in education, training or employment

2010 or latest available year

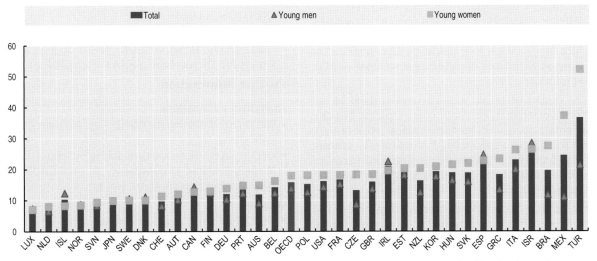

StatLink ᘓᔖ☐ http://dx.doi.org/10.1787/888932663378

JOBS AND WAGES

Definition

The gender wage gap is unadjusted and is calculated as the difference between median earnings of men and women relative to median earnings of men. Estimates of earnings used in the calculations refer to gross earnings of full-time wage and salary workers. Low pay is defined as less than two-thirds of gross median earnings of all full-time workers.

Overview

Girls are now doing as well as, if not better than, boys in most core subjects at school, but still earn 15% less on average in the OECD and are less likely to make it to the boardroom or senior management of companies.

The average gender gap in OECD countries has narrowed somewhat in recent years from 20% in 2000. And while the gender wage gap exists in all countries, its size varies considerably. The gap is narrowest in Hungary (6%) and Poland (10%) and broadest in Korea (39%) and Japan (29%).

Earnings tend to rise in line with people's level of education for both men and women. People with higher (tertiary) education can expect to earn 55% more on average in OECD countries than a person without tertiary education. Those who have not completed secondary education earn 23% less than those who have.

Nonetheless, across all countries and all levels of education, women earn less than men, and that gap actually increases with more education. A man with tertiary education can expect to generate a net return of USD 162 000 during his working life on the cost of his education, while the return for women is about a third less, at USD 110 000. The average net return on the cost of upper secondary education is close to USD 90 000 for men and USD 67 000 for women.

The gender gap runs right up the employment ladder – female top earners trail behind their male counterparts – but at the lower end of the pay scale it means that women are more likely to be in the low-paid bracket. About 18% of workers are low-paid on average in OECD countries for which figures are available, but the rate for women is 25%, while that for men is 14%.

Why is the gender wage gap so persistent? Girls at 15 are more ambitious than their male counterparts, but the reality of where men and woman actually work is very different from this aspiration. For example, among legislators, barely a quarter of parliamentarians in OECD countries are women, and no country has yet breached the 50% mark.

There is a similar gap between teenage aspiration and adult reality when it comes to managerial and professional positions. More girls may be aiming for jobs at this level at 15, but when they actually complete their tertiary studies almost twice as many men take up managerial posts, 9.7%

compared with 5.7% of women. In addition, on average in OECD countries less than one-third of managers are women.

Career stereotypes seem hard to shift; even when girls choose to study sciences, they are less likely to opt for a career in them – 71% of male graduates from the science field work as professionals in physics, mathematics and engineering, as opposed to 43% of female graduates.

One science area popular with women is the medical and health professions, where at least some ambitions are fulfilled. Certainly many more women are becoming doctors. In 2009, 43% of doctors on average across OECD countries were women, up from 29% in 1990.

Sources

- OECD (2012), *OECD Employment Outlook*, OECD Publishing.
- OECD (2012), "*Indicator A8 What are the earnings premiums from education?*", *Education at a Glance: OECD Indicators*, OECD Publishing.
- OECD (2012), *OECD labour market statistics*.
- OECD (2012), "What Kinds of Careers do Boys and Girls Expect for Themselves?", *PISA in Focus*, No. 14.

Further information

Analytical publications

- OECD (2012), *Closing the Gender Gap, Act Now*, OECD Publishing.
- OECD (2012), "How Are Girls Doing in School – and Women Doing in Employment – Around the World?", *Education Indicators in Focus*, No. 3.

Websites

- OECD Education, *www.oecd.org/education*.
- OECD Employment Outlook (supplementary material), *www.oecd.org/employment/outlook*.
- OECD Gender, *www.oecd.org/gender*.

Gender wage gap
Percentage, 2000 and 2010

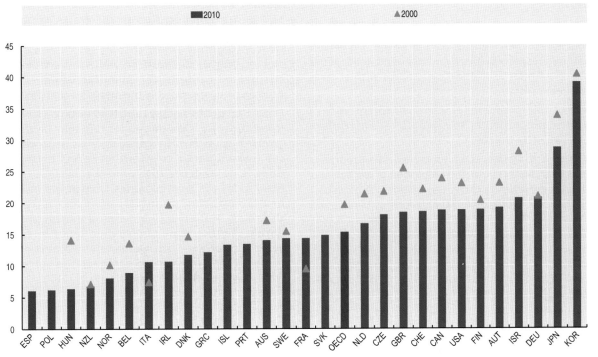

StatLink http://dx.doi.org/10.1787/888932652282

Incidence of low-paid workers by gender
Percentage, 2000 and 2010

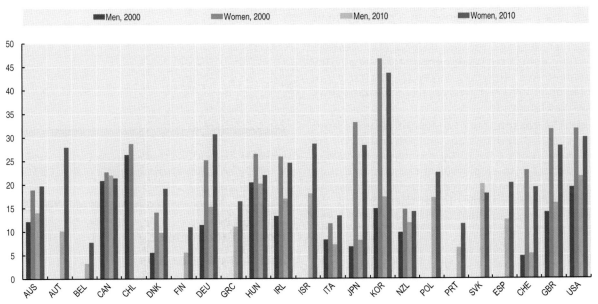

StatLink http://dx.doi.org/10.1787/888932707971

CREATING BUSINESS

Definition

Sole-proprietor enterprises are unincorporated enterprises with one single owner – female or male – who is a person with unlimited responsibilities over losses and debts of the enterprise. Data refer to sole proprietorships with at least one employee.

The share of sole-proprietor women-owned enterprises indicates the proportion of sole-proprietor enterprises which are owned by women.

The distribution of women and men-owned sole-proprietor enterprises by industry shows the proportion of women and men-owned enterprises in three aggregations of industrial activities. The first aggregation "Manufacturing, Mining and Utilities" includes NACE Rev. 2 (ISIC Rev. 4) sections B to E, the second aggregation "Trade, Transportation and Accommodation" includes NACE Rev. 2 (ISIC Rev. 4) sections G to I, the third aggregation "Professional and Support services" includes NACE Rev. 2 (ISIC Rev. 4) sections M and N.

Overview

Entrepreneurship has a key role to play in creating innovation, jobs and economic growth. Starting one's own business can be a way to realise a big idea, or to create one's own job when the labour market is tight. But this is a situation that seems to appeal more to men than women in OECD countries, where male entrepreneurs outnumber women and where women-owned enterprises on average show lower profits. Self-employed women work less and earn less than self-employed men. This may have something to do with why women start their own business – more women than men say they do it out of "necessity", because they do not see other options for entering the labour market. And often they choose to start their own business in order to have more flexibility and control over their work and family life.

Whatever the reason, only 20-40% of single-owner businesses (sole-proprietorships) in OECD countries are run by women. Across the 27 EU countries only 25% of business owners with employees are women and their share has only grown marginally over the last decade. This is also true of Canada and the United States, although the increase has been more marked in Chile, Korea and Mexico.

Indeed, Mexico and Korea now top the list in terms of sole-proprietorships owned by women, at around 40% – although they are both below the OECD average of 57% in terms of women in employment generally (53% for Korean women, 43% for Mexican women).

The women who do choose to start their own business opt for very different sectors than men – they are more likely to go into the wholesale and retail trade, transportation and accommodation, than manufacturing. In Korea and Mexico, women entrepreneurs follow this pattern, with 58% being concentrated in the trade, transport and accommodation sectors in Korea and 76% for Mexico. Italian women seem to pay less heed to gender stereotyping in this respect, with 11% of women-owned businesses being in the manufacturing, mining and utilities category, close to the men's level of 13%.

Female-owned businesses also tend to have a lower size and lower turnover. One reason for this may be that women have less experience in managing a business, which in turn can make it harder to attract loans and investment. But there is no evidence that women's businesses are more likely to fail – in most countries, women and men start-ups tend to have a similar survival performance three years after their birth. Performance in terms of employment creation during the first years of operation tends to vary greatly across countries, with women-owned new enterprises outperforming men-owned enterprises in some countries while lagging behind in others.

Sources
- OECD (2012), *Entrepreneurship at a Glance*, OECD Publishing.
- OECD (2012), *Closing the Gender Gap, Act Now*, OECD Publishing.

Further information

Analytical publications
- OECD (2012), *OECD Employment Outlook*, OECD Publishing.
- OECD (2012), *Financing SMEs and Entrepreneurs 2012: An OECD Scoreboard*, OECD Publishing.

Websites
- OECD Labour markets, human capital and inequality, *www.oecd.org/employment/ labourmarketshumancapitalandinequality*.

Share of women sole-proprietor enterprises

Percentage, 2009 or latest available year

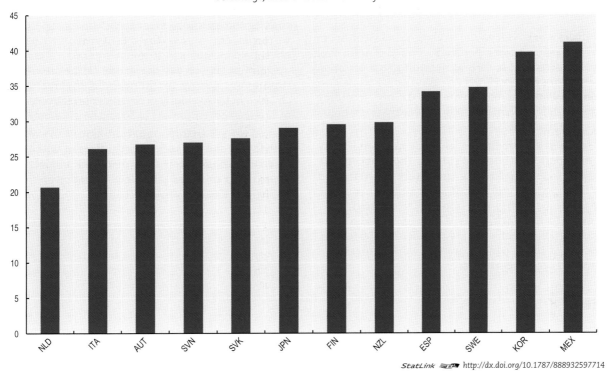

StatLink http://dx.doi.org/10.1787/888932597714

Distribution of sole-proprietor women-owned enterprises by industry

Percentage, 2009

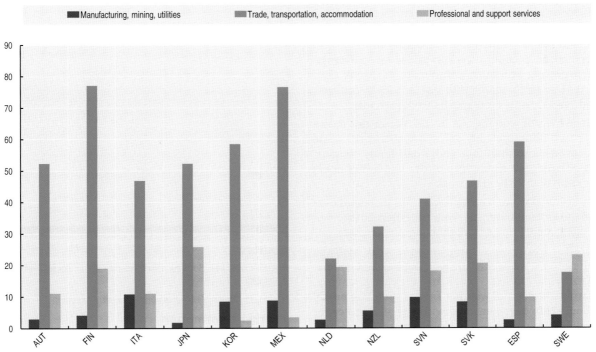

StatLink http://dx.doi.org/10.1787/888932597752

CARING AND SHARING

Definition

Hours in paid work refer to the average number of hours usually worked per week per person on the main job. Full-time employment is defined according to a common definition of more than 30-weekly-usual hours worked in the main job. Part-time employment is defined according to a common definition of less than 30-weekly-usual hours worked in the main job.

Unpaid work is the production of goods and services by family members that are not sold on the market. The boundary between unpaid work and leisure is determined by the "third-person" criterion. If a third person could be paid to do the activity (*e.g.* cooking, cleaning), it is considered to be work. Where this is not the case (*e.g.* watching a film), activities are considered to be leisure. The amount of time spent on unpaid work is measured using detailed time-use surveys.

Overview

Be it paid or unpaid, people spend about one-third of their time working. In most countries, people spend more time on paid work than on unpaid work such as cooking, cleaning, volunteering, home maintenance or childcare. On an average working day in OECD countries, people spend about eight hours per day in paid work. On an average day people spend nearly three and a half hours doing unpaid work.

But there are significant gender differences in who is doing the paid and unpaid work. People in OECD countries with jobs spend about 38 hours a week in paid work on average, with men putting in almost a day more per week than women at 41 hours compared with less than 35. By contrast, women do significantly more unpaid work than men.

On average men of working age in OECD countries spend just over two hours per day doing unpaid work, while women spend more than four and a half hours cooking, cleaning or caring – a gender gap of two and a half hours daily, or more than 17 hours a week.

The time spent by women on paid work has increased over time and the amount of unpaid work has fallen, but women are still doing more unpaid work than men everywhere.

In Korea, for example, women in paid work average 41.7 hours a week, while men are working 46.7. But when it comes to unpaid work – cooking, cleaning, caring, volunteering – women of working age are spending nearly three hours every day, compared with just 45 minutes for men. In the Netherlands, where women work 24.5 hours a week and men 35.7, the women are spending more than four hours a day in unpaid work, compared with about two hours (163 minutes) for men.

Even in Australia and Turkey, where people spend slightly more time on unpaid than on paid work, women are doing more unpaid work than men.

What is all this unpaid work time for? Most unpaid work is cooking and cleaning – on average 2 hours and 8 minutes of work per day across the OECD, followed by care for household members at 26 minutes per day. Shopping takes up 23 minutes per day across the OECD on average. The time spent caring for household members includes children but also elderly or dependent relatives. About 66% of carers between the age of 50 and 64 are women.

Unpaid work is an important contribution to well-being for individuals and for society, regardless of who is doing it. Measuring how much time men and women spend on unpaid work provides valuable information on the delivery of care services and work-life balance.

Sources

- OECD (2011), *Society at a Glance: OECD Social Indicators*, OECD Publishing.
- OECD (2012), *OECD labour market statistics*.

Further information

Analytical publications

- Miranda, V. (2011), "Cooking, Caring and Volunteering: Unpaid Work Around the World", *OECD Social, Employment and Migration Working Papers*, No. 116, OECD Publishing.
- OECD (2012), *Closing the Gender Gap, Act Now*, OECD Publishing.

Unpaid work by gender

Minutes per day, 1998-2009

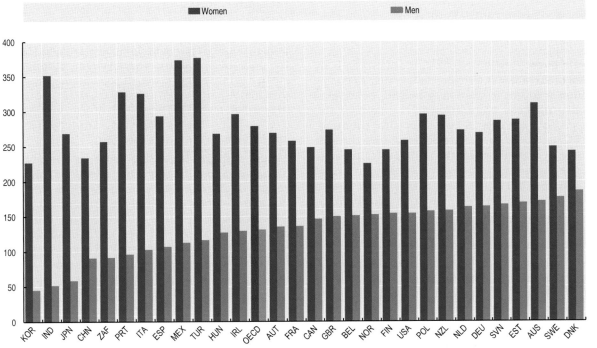

StatLink http://dx.doi.org/10.1787/888932381494

Paid work by gender

Weekly hours worked on main job, 2011

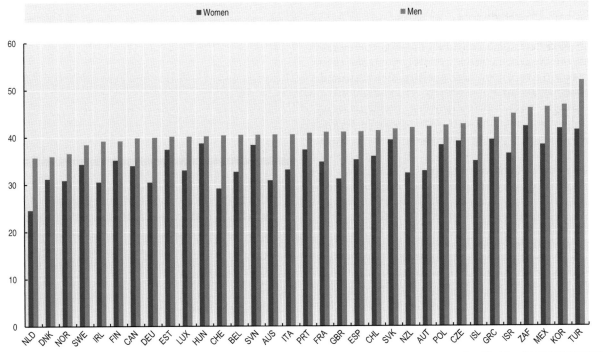

StatLink http://dx.doi.org/10.1787/888932708351

HEALTH

Definition

Overweight and obesity are defined as excessive weight presenting health risks because of the high proportion of body fat.

The most frequently used measure is based on the body mass index (BMI), which is a single number that evaluates an individual's weight in relation to height. For adults, overweight or obese population is the sum of the population with a BMI over 25 kg/m². For most countries, overweight and obesity rates are self-reported through estimates of height and weight from population-based health interview surveys. However, around one-third of OECD countries derive their estimates from health examinations. These differences limit data comparability. Estimates from health examinations are generaly higher and more reliable than from health interviews. For further details, see the indicator "Overweight and obesity".

Estimates of the prevalence of child overweight are made by the International Association for the Study of Obesity (IASO). The estimates are based on national surveys of measured height and weight among children.

Overview

Are people getting healthier? They are certainly living longer – since 1960, life expectancy has increased on average across OECD countries by more than 11 years, although there is a considerable gender gap. Women outlive men on average in OECD countries by nearly six years, at 83 years compared with 77 for men.

The factors that determine individual life expectancy are varied and complex, but lifestyle certainly contributes to whether people live a long and healthy life, men and women alike. Overweight and obesity for example are a factor in a whole range of potentially fatal problems from diabetes to heart disease – severely obese people die 8 to 10 years earlier than those of normal weight, a similar effect to smoking.

Until 1980, fewer than one in ten people in OECD countries were obese, but obesity rates have doubled or even tripled in many countries since then, with 59% of men recorded as being overweight or obese, compared with 47% of women. Furthermore, this is a problem that starts early in life. Overweight and obesity rates have soared among children during the past 30 years. Although rates are less than half the adult level and the gender gap is far narrower, boys are still more likely to be overweight or obese, with 23% of boys aged 5-17 in this category, compared with 21% of girls. Greece has the highest proportion of overweight and obese children, with 45% of boys and 37% of girls, while Turkey has the fewest overweight boys (11%) and Korea the fewest girls (10%).

In the United States, girls are marginally more likely than boys to be overweight or obese, at 36% compared to 35% for boys. This gap widens and reverses in adulthood, with the United States having the highest proportion of overweight and obese men among OECD countries (74%), while the rate for women is 65%. Mexico has the highest proportion of overweight and obese women (72%) and is the only OECD country where women outnumber men. Japan has the least overweight population, with just 30% of men and 21% of women. Outside the OECD, more than half of Brazilian men (52%) and South African women (55%) are overweight or obese, while in India and Indonesia less than one in ten men are in this category.

Gender and social standing matter in determining how likely adults, and their children, are to be overweight. In several OECD countries, women with little education are two to three times more likely to be overweight than more educated women (such differences are much smaller among men). These women are more likely to have overweight or obese children who themselves will have fewer chances of moving up the social ladder.

The most recent data suggest that obesity rates are levelling off, but gender disparities are still evident.

Sources
- OECD (2012), *OECD Health Statistics* (database).
- OECD (2012), "OECD Obesity Update 2012", *The Economics of Prevention*, Paris.OECD (2011), *Health at a Glance: OECD Indicators*, OECD Publishing.
- OECD (2010), *Obesity and the Economics of Prevention: Fit not Fat*, OECD Publishing.
- See also corresponding table in indicator Health: Overweight and obesity.

Further information

Websites
- Health, *www.oecd.org/health*.
- OECD Health Data (supplementary material), *www.oecd.org/health/healthdata*.

Overweight and obesity among children

Percent, children aged 5-17 years, overweight or obese, latest available estimates

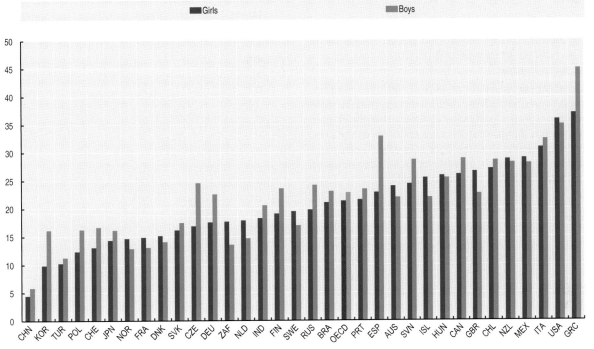

■Girls   ■Boys

StatLink http://dx.doi.org/10.1787/888932523994

Overweight and obesity among adults

Percent, 2010 or latest available year

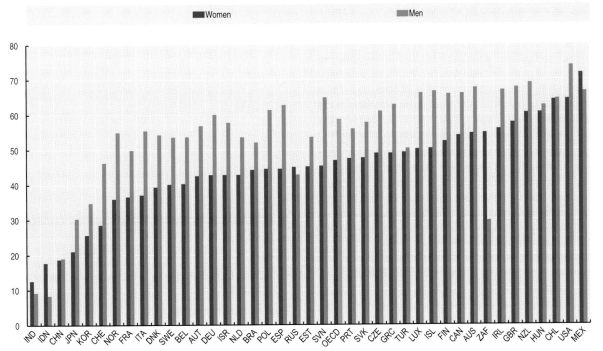

■Women   ■Men

StatLink http://dx.doi.org/10.1787/888932523956

GETTING OLDER, GETTING POORER

Definition

For international comparisons, the OECD treats poverty as a "relative" concept. The yardstick for poverty depends on the median household income in a particular country at a particular point in time.

The poverty threshold is set at 50% of national median, equivalised household disposable income. It should be noted that the use of a particular arbitrary threshold such as 50% of median income can be very sensitive to the level of minimum pensions in some countries (*e.g.* Australia or New Zealand), as a larger number of pensioners can be clustered around the 50% of median threshold.

Overview

In most OECD countries, older women outnumber men, making up 53% of 66-75 year-olds and 60% of those aged over 75. This reflects the fact that women on average, live five and a half years longer than men. However women also make up the bulk of poor pensioners; across the OECD some 15% of women over 65 are living in poverty, compared with 11% of men.

There are two main reasons for this: women build up fewer pension entitlements and they often end up living alone on a relatively small income.

Many pension benefits are earnings-related; since women spend less time in paid work than men, and earn less when they are working, they receive smaller earnings-related pensions. Today's older women generally spent less time in paid work and earned less than today's younger women. They also started a family earlier and had more children, often having long gaps without paid work or stopping work altogether. In a number of countries the official retirement age for women was below that of men (although this is now changing), so even if they worked all their lives, they worked fewer years, and thus built up lower pension entitlements.

Indeed, women in OECD countries aged 65 in 2008-09 had on average worked for 13 years less than men of the same age. This shorter working life also means that these women may not meet minimum contributory requirements for non-earnings-related pensions, and may have to rely on old-age safety nets or low-level non-contributory minimum pensions. In the United States, for example, women's income from public pensions was 40% lower than that of men at the end of the 2000s.

The higher poverty rate in old-age affects both married and single women. Since women live longer than men they are more likely to become widowed and possibly rely on a low survivor's benefit for income. Living alone is itself a poverty factor – elderly people living alone are 2.5 times more likely to be poor than elderly couples. But in most countries the poverty rate is higher for women living alone than for men living alone, and poverty risks are highest for women over 75.

Many OECD countries have specific mechanisms in place to compensate women who interrupt their careers to raise children, but while these help boost mothers' pension entitlements, they cannot bridge the gaps caused by career breaks.

Sources

- OECD (2011), *Pensions at a Glance*, OECD Publishing.
- OECD (2012), *Closing the Gender Gap, Act Now*, OECD Publishing.

Further information

Analytical publications

- OECD (2008), *Growing Unequal? Income Distribution and Poverty in OECD countries.*
- OECD (2011), *Divided We Stand, Why Inequality Keeps Rising*, OECD Publishing.
- OECD (2012), *OECD Pensions Outlook*, OECD Publishing.

Income poverty rates, by gender, mid 2000s

	All 65+	By age		By sex		By household type		Whole population (all ages)
		Older people (aged over 65)						
		66-75	75+	Men	Women	Single	Couple	
Australia	27	26.1	28.3	24.6	28.9	49.9	17.7	12.4
Austria	7.5	5.3	10.2	3.6	10.1	16.4	3.9	6.6
Belgium	12.8	10.5	16.0	12.7	12.9	16.7	10.0	8.8
Canada	5.9	5.2	6.8	3.1	8.1	16.2	3.9	12.0
Czech Republic	2.3	2.0	2.6	1.4	2.9	5.6	2.0	5.8
Denmark	10.0	6.9	13.7	8.0	11.5	17.5	3.8	5.3
Finland	12.7	8.2	19.5	6.5	16.9	28.0	3.9	7.3
France	8.8	7.2	10.6	6.6	10.4	16.2	4.1	7.1
Germany	8.4	6.5	11.1	5.1	10.8	15.0	4.7	11.0
Greece	22.7	19.2	27.8	20.4	24.5	34.2	17.6	12.6
Hungary	4.6	4.2	5.5	1.8	6.6	11.1	0.8	7.1
Iceland	5.0	5.0	5.0	5.8	4.3	9.8	2.3	7.1
Ireland	30.6	25.8	37.1	24.6	35.3	65.4	9.4	14.8
Italy	12.8	11.2	15.2	8.1	16.1	25.0	9.4	11.4
Japan	22.0	19.4	25.4	18.4	24.8	47.7	16.6	14.9
Korea	45.1	43.3	49.8	41.8	47.2	76.6	40.8	14.6
Luxembourg	3.1	3.4	2.6	4.0	2.4	3.6	2.9	8.1
Mexico	28.0	26.3	31.2	27.6	28.5	44.9	20.9	18.4
Netherlands	2.1	2.2	2.0	1.7	2.4	2.6	2.3	7.7
New Zealand	1.5	1.6	1.4	2.1	0.9	3.2	1.1	10.8
Norway	9.1	3.8	14.6	3.5	13.1	20.0	1.2	6.8
Poland	4.8	5.4	3.8	2.6	6.1	6.0	5.9	14.6
Portugal	16.6	14.4	19.9	16.0	17.0	35.0	15.7	12.9
Slovak Republic	5.9	3.2	10.6	2.0	8.4	10.4	2.9	8.1
Spain	22.8	20.0	26.4	20.1	24.7	38.6	24.2	14.1
Sweden	6.2	3.4	9.8	4.2	7.7	13.0	1.1	5.3
Turkey	15.1	14.9	15.6	14.6	15.6	37.8	17.3	17.5
United Kingdom	10.3	8.5	12.6	7.4	12.6	17.5	6.7	8.3
United States	22.4	20.0	27.4	18.5	26.8	41.3	17.3	17.1
OECD	**13.5**	**11.7**	**16.1**	**11.1**	**15.2**	**25.0**	**9.5**	**10.6**

StatLink ⫘ http://dx.doi.org/10.1787/888932371044

Income poverty rates, by gender, mid 2000s
65 years and over

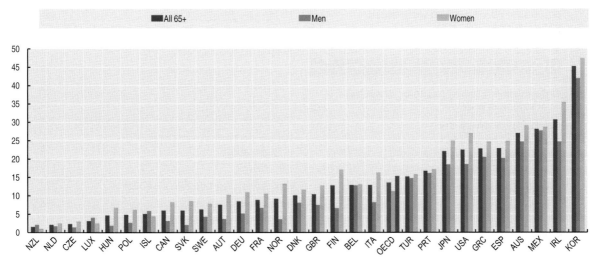

StatLink ⫘ http://dx.doi.org/10.1787/888932371044

Analytical index

U

V

W

Y

ORGANISATION FOR ECONOMIC CO-OPERATION AND DEVELOPMENT

The OECD is a unique forum where governments work together to address the economic, social and environmental challenges of globalisation. The OECD is also at the forefront of efforts to understand and to help governments respond to new developments and concerns, such as corporate governance, the information economy and the challenges of an ageing population. The Organisation provides a setting where governments can compare policy experiences, seek answers to common problems, identify good practice and work to co-ordinate domestic and international policies.

The OECD member countries are: Australia, Austria, Belgium, Canada, Chile, the Czech Republic, Denmark, Estonia, Finland, France, Germany, Greece, Hungary, Iceland, Ireland, Israel, Italy, Japan, Korea, Luxembourg, Mexico, the Netherlands, New Zealand, Norway, Poland, Portugal, the Slovak Republic, Slovenia, Spain, Sweden, Switzerland, Turkey, the United Kingdom and the United States. The European Union takes part in the work of the OECD.

OECD Publishing disseminates widely the results of the Organisation's statistics gathering and research on economic, social and environmental issues, as well as the conventions, guidelines and standards agreed by its members.

OECD PUBLISHING, 2, rue André-Pascal, 75775 PARIS CEDEX 16
(30 2012 02 1 P) ISBN 978-92-64-17706-2 – No. 60317 2013-08